Polity, Civil Society and Development

Modernization, Globalization and Social Transformation

Polity, Civil Society and Development

Essays in Honour of Professor Yogendra Singh

Edited by

Ishwar Modi

RAWAT PUBLICATIONS

Jaipur • New Delhi • Bangalore • Hyderabad • Guwahati • Kolkata

ISBN 978-81-316-0642-1

Published by
Prem Rawat for **Rawat Publications**
Satyam Apts, Sector 3, Jawahar Nagar, Jaipur 302 004 (India)
Phone: 0141 265 1748/7006; Fax: 0141 265 1748
E-mail: info@rawatbooks.com
Website: www.rawatbooks.com

New Delhi Office
4858/24, Ansari Road, Daryaganj, New Delhi 110 002
Phone: 011 2326 3290

Also at *Bangalore, Hyderabad, Guwahati* and *Kolkata*

Typeset by Mukesh Technologies Pvt. Ltd. Puducherry
Printed at Chaman Enterprises, New Delhi

Contents

Introduction

Ishwar Modi

I

The first of the four-volume set of the Festschrift for Professor Yogendra Singh outlined not only his academic journey and the worldview of his ideas on the relevance of Western scholars but also the major concerns and challenges before the sociologists in India, then as well as now, more so in the context of globalization. Besides this, several contributors also extensively and critically reflected on his academic contributions and personality. Taking into cognizance the thrust of the volume titled *Modernization, Globalization and Social Transformation*, almost all the contributors focused their papers not only on the conceptual dimensions of the concerned phenomena and their interlinkages but also examined in detail the relationship of these phenomena with other contemporary social and sociological concerns, such as marginalization, social movements, middle-class culture and consumer culture, technology, ethnicity, and even global society and risk society. Issues of modernity and postmodernity were also analysed in a wider context.

In continuation of the general title of the Festschrift – *Modernization, Globalization and Social Transformation* – the second volume came out under the title *Education, Religion and Creativity*, taking cognizance of the fact that a large number of papers by eminent scholars were contributed in the areas of their specialization broadly focusing on the themes of education, religion and creativity, including such aspects of creativity as art, music and literature, as well as such creative and recreational dimensions of creativity as television, leisure and tourism. As such, it was considered appropriate that these papers be put together in a volume having these themes.

In this third volume of the Festschrift titled *Polity, Civil Society and Development*, papers focusing on such aspects of polity and civil society as Indian democracy, dynamics of development, citizenship, Naxal movement, nativism, regionalism, nationalism, radical nationalism, freedom movement, civil resistance, Fiji Indian quest for power, socio-cultural transformation of Indians in the United States, and so on have been contributed by most eminent sociologists. Likewise, in the second section on development, such themes as sustainable development, Gandhi's development philosophy, social development and new economic policy, equitable development paradigm, communication as a development resource, technological advancements and its impact on youth, civilizational transformation of indigenous people, state, market economy and rural degeneration, dynamics of economic reforms in revamping rural India, sociology of health and health inequalities, agrarian social structure, suicides among cultivators, biotech crops, and so on have been discussed. Most of these themes have been examined in the context of globalization.

Although I am thankful to all the contributors of this third volume of the Festschrift, I pay my special gratitude and remembrance to late Professor Victor S. D'Souza. He was kind enough to have provided his paper for the Festschrift for Professor Yogendra Singh. Wish this Festschrift and particularly this volume could have been brought out in his presence. Alas, it could not become possible. However, I offer my special tribute to him.

II

In the very first paper 'What Ails Indian Democracy: The Enemy Within' under Part I 'Polity and Civil Society', Victor S. D'Souza points out that despite the compelling evidence to show that democracy is the only way possible so far for man to achieve the living to an optimal span of life, free of physical and psychological ailments and criminal threats, and with normal comforts of life, why is it so that India has not acquired the democratic character of freedom, equality and brotherhood – all of which are expected from its society. He further observes that this is not for want of trying by the Indian government. In fact, the removal of poverty and equalization of educational and job opportunities for all the sections of the society has been the major preoccupations of different governments. But, the result has not been commensurate with the efforts. Although India has successfully passed through its population transition and has shown a good trend of growth of life expectancy for its people, it presents a highly inconsistent picture when compared with other democratic countries of the world.

In terms of its economy, infrastructure, information and communication, agriculture and animal husbandry, industrial goods, minerals and films, India ranks among the world's ten fastest growing countries. On the contrary, in terms of the prevalence of diseases, malnutrition and poverty, it ranks in the bottom quartile among countries of the world. But worst of all, it is all the more galling for any dignified Indian to find one's country ranked as low as 119th in the UNDP's Human Development Index, 87th in the Corruption Perception Index and 134th in the Ease of Doing Business Index. D'Souza's paper delves into some of the deeper causes of the malady in the broader context of the collapse of the moral order of the Indian society that was hitherto based on the caste system that completely shattered the setting up of democracy in India. D'Souza concludes by observing that the real enemy of Indian democracy lies in the free but flawed conscience of the Indian individual who is symptomatic of both corruption and political misbehaviour. This calls for a modernization of Hinduism in tune with democracy.

It can hardly be overemphasized that democracy and civil society are closely intertwined. However, before this relationship is examined, it is equally important to know the history of civil society and to understand how civil society can be defined. Quoting J.P.S. Uberoi, Ananta Kumar Giri, in his paper 'Civil Society and the Calling of Self-Development', focuses our attention to the fact that

> If we divide the history of mankind into five periods, that is, the prehistoric, ancient, medieval, modern and post-modern, one can say that the history of civil society begins only when the institution of the sacred or the divine

> kingship begins to dissolve into two differentiated institutions at the dawn of the ancient, or at the very latest the medieval, period out of the past. [...] Even if this civil society was indeed the 'child of the modern world,' still it is the Christian society and its early modern reform that we may also have to consider, and not only the bourgeois society of modern capitalism. By this wider definition, the modern civil society was established or revived in Britain at any rate by the struggle of the Nonconformists, the new Christians, who together severed connection with the established Church of England when it accepted royal supremacy at the time of the Reformation [...] The new Christians wanted instead what we may call salvation through religion in society, with pluralist freedom of conscience and worship for all.

However, going beyond the history of civil society and its Christian notion, Giri suggests that we need a multidimensional understanding and realization of the sphere of civil society and its multiple activities. But for this, we need to overcome the dualism between tradition and modernity, right and good (cf. Habermas, 1990), civil society and good society (cf. Beteille, 2001) and institutionalization and mobilization. He suggests that the field of civil society consists of an autonomous space, but interpenetrated by overlapping and interpenetrative circles of society, religion, state, market, social movements/ voluntary organizations and self. Civil society is a space not only for 'mediating institutions' (cf. ibid.) but also for mobilization where the latter refers not only to socio-political mobilizations but also to socio-spiritual mobilizations, including reflective mobilization of self (cf. Giri, 2004a). In the same vein, state and civil societies are not to be conflated. State and civil society are not co-terminous – civil society refers to that conscious and mobilized aspect of society, which strives to create a space for critical self-reflections and public deliberations. Despite contentions and struggles, state and civil society are again related as per the logic of autonomy and interpenetration, and here social movements, different mediating institutions and voluntary organizations play a significant role. Civil society is also nourished by the support from market. Actors from market such as corporate leaders and other market leaders contribute to the resource base of civil society. Thus far as the relationship between religion and civil society is concerned, one great challenge here is to overcome the dualism of religion and secularism. Although for Beteille (2001), civil society is mainly a secular space, for Uberoi (1996) and Oommen (2001a), it is a space where religious associations and critical spiritual movements are also at work. Finally, civil society is also a space for work of self; in fact, self is an actor in all the intersecting and interpenetrating dimensions of civil society: society, state, market and religion. The quality of work of self and its mobilization in civil society and its above-mentioned intersecting dimensions determine the quality of civil society.

Pradip Kumar Bose in his paper 'Civil Society, Political Society and Citizenship in India' discusses the various conceptions of civil society and its association with citizenship in the broader context of democracy and development. He observes that there has been an argument that in India we can think of two different axes, *civil society–citizenship* and *political society–population*, when one deals with the question of democracy and development. It has been argued that in India, the colonial state produced only a civil society of subjects and not citizens so that the colonized can construct their national identities within a different narrative, that of community. In the post-independent India, the argument goes: the conditions for a proper civil society formation do not exist and community formation takes, rather, the form of *political society*; the difference being that in a civil society, people have active citizenship rights – lacking these, they negotiate with the state and its agencies for resources of livelihood and survival as a 'political' community. The paper discusses various conceptions of civil society in India and argues that the concept of civil society is inevitable if we are to understand the nature of citizenship and self-understanding of relevant actors in the post-colonial India. In associating civil society with citizenship question, the paper argues that civil society should be seen not only in a passive fashion, as a network of institutions but also actively as the context and product of self-constituting collective actors. It is also possible that social movements, empowerment and initiatives of citizens or proto-citizens through civil society are capable of influencing political culture without entry into the field of power politics.

Continuing the debate on democracy and democratization and its relationship with civil society, Anand Kumar in his paper 'Civil Society in India and the Dynamics of Democratization' observes that there is a relation of interdependence between the growth of civil society and deepening of democratic values, institutions and processes in the modern world system. As the concept of civil society is used by social scientist for identifying such a sphere of social life that is flanked by the domain of particularistic loyalties, on the one hand, and by the state, on the other hand, it is important to contextualize the understanding of civil society in India with reference to the Indian dynamics of democratization. According to Anand Kumar, civil society in India has been recognized as a necessary corrective measure for state in the colonial as well as the post-colonial phases. In the colonial phase, Gandhi represented the power of civil society. After independence, it has become the necessary corrective measure for the authority system based on representative democracy – particularly after the dark days of the Emergency era of 1975–77. Active citizenship, non-governmental voluntary associations, social movements and cultural identity-related formations are some of the major manifestations of the idea of civil society.

Anand Kumar's paper also provides a field view of the civil society in India by presenting two case studies. The issue of gender justice is the focus of activities of Centre for Social Research, New Delhi – from capacity building to petitioning, protest marches and parliamentary lobbying. It was established in 1981 by a group of young social scientists and social activists and has grown into one of the major organizations engaged in promoting women empowerment. The challenge of protecting economic and political freedom and sovereignty from multinational corporations and finance institutions was the key factor in the formation of Azadi Bachao Andolan in 1990. A collective of Gandhian, socialist and radical democratic activists and intellectuals came together to start a nationwide campaign against the government-initiated economic reforms identified with the paradigm of liberalization–privatization–globalization (LPG) and called structural adjustment programmes (SAPs). It has been in active existence for the past two decades and is now one of the key actors on the national scene with an all-India presence.

Whatsoever the strength of democracy and civil society, the existence of violent movements is a hard reality of Indian polity and society: Naxal movement is one such. Ashok Kaul and Anand Prasad Mishra in their paper 'Geographical and Social Dimensions of the Naxal Movement: A Micro-Level Observation' deal with the question of the Naxal violence. They argue that the Naxal violence emerged as a threat to democracy in the Indian state. These challenges have various dimensions in relation to geography and socio-cultural identity of the regions, and it attracted the policy makers and social scientists to study this problem in a detailed manner. The paper is an attempt by the authors to analyse various components of the Naxal movement, which prevail in the concerned regions. The paper also analyses the spatial pattern of poverty, human resource development (HRD), tribal economy, development-induced displacement and its relation to the Naxal movement. An attempt has also been made to incorporate a mechanism of the Naxal violence in a specific geographical terrain with a certain socio-cultural and political identity, in order to explain the present-day Naxal movement.

Although the Naxal movement and associated violence are well-established and recognized aspects of Indian polity, not much has been written, discussed and documented about the violence perpetuated and legitimized by Maharashtra Navnirman Sena (MNS) in Maharashtra, particularly Mumbai. Jasmine Y. Damle in her paper 'Nativism, Regionalism and the Legitimization of Violence: The MNS Way' documents the ideology and strategy of MNS in the context of nativism, regionalism and legitimization of violence to achieve its political agenda. Jasmine has attempted to examine not only the genesis and the development of MNS but also its ideology and the strategies. She points out that nativism is a form of assertion of local identity, which is often manifested through 'sons-of-the-soil' agitations. In fact, Myron Weiner (1977) had stated that 'In India, nativism is largely a middle-class sentiment. Nativism is a political response to conflicting forms of mobility–spatial mobility of the migrants and the aspiring mobility of a social class within the native population'. In her paper, Jasmine has tried to analyse the concept of 'nativism', or in other words the reassertion of ethnic, linguistic and geographic identity by making use of 'sons-of-the-soil' agitation in the context of the emergence of the MNS in Mumbai and in Maharashtra. She further points out that the very emergence of MNS is heavily steeped in regionalism. Regionalism in India has always been an important aspect of politics in India, especially since independence. But, in the late 1960s and early 1970s, regional claims verging on parochial demands for separation and autonomy grew so strong that they became a serious threat to the unity of India. Talking about the issues of identity, she opines that identity (*we* feeling) can foster hostility and hatred directed towards other communities and can brutally manipulate unrest and use of naked power/force over lives of 'suspected enemy'. Hence, in a nutshell, identity can be a source of richness and warmth as well as violence and terror. Conflict is manifested in the form of vigilantism that provokes violence and revenge initiating a dangerous cycle of vigilantism. By resorting to 'vigilantism', the MNS is trying to seek legitimacy for itself through 'legitimization of violence'.

Shifting attention from regional conflicts and violence to nationalism, C.N. Venugopal in his paper 'Nationalism in India: Culture, Ideology and Polity a Diachronic Perspective' insists that an alternative approach be taken up for exploring new sources of understanding India. He observes that during the past several decades, the Indian society has been studied with reference to its culture, its institutional networks (caste, community, etc.), religious behaviour, economic and political aspects and social change. Many outstanding contributions have been made by the scholars – Indian as well as foreign – in the fields of family and kinship, village, caste, urbanization, industrialization, religiosity, secularism and so forth. These studies have mainly used positivistic, structural–functional methodology to interpret the diversities of Indian society. The author has attempted to show that an alternative approach such as phenomenology is available for understanding Indian society.

Venugopal further observes that culture, ideology and policy need to be understood as existing on two levels: (i) there is an underlying primary level in which people's interactions are based on preformal, unwritten, apperceived ways and (ii) a secondary level in which there is an impressive layer of literary, canonical and political texts. In general, the first level deals with 'what is', whereas the second level deals with 'what ought to be'. So far as common people are concerned, the 'texts' with which they are familiar are not the written documents. The Hindu, Buddhist and Jain temples convey ideas through their architecture, sculptures, paintings and so forth, by drawing upon the epics, legends, historical events, war and peace. Besides, at the village level, the open air theatres, ballads and religious recital, are also engaged in a cultural transmission. Whole nights are spent in the villages, watching epic themes from Ramayana and Mahabharata that are enacted in the open air theatres. These 'texts' are pre-formal yet powerful influences that mould people's response. The fact that India is a thriving democracy despite widespread illiteracy is due to the onset of this pre-formal 'schooling'.

The alternative approach taken up in this paper provides scope for exploring new sources of understanding India. The topics of this paper may briefly refer to the cultural pluralism in Indian society. It has come due to a tolerant attitude that is in-built. Due to the pluralistic nature of Indian society, multiple political centres have prevented any formation of a unitary political culture. Different political systems have been working in Indian society with a bend towards the federal principle of governance. The *sattwa* becomes a moral force if people's energies are directed towards constructive nation-building. Venugopal holds that the polity in India was based on a representative character nurtured in self-governance.

Continuing the debate on nationalism and the 'nation-state', S.P. Gupta in his paper 'Globalization vs. Polarization: A Case of Emerging Concerns for "Nation-State" and "Radical Nationalism" in Indian Society' maintains that globalization is enhancing the tendency of 'radical nationalism' and weakening the concept of 'nation-state'. He holds that globalization as a process in India began its momentum with the process of liberation of economy as a consequence to the failure of welfare regime or socialist pattern of development. This process has sought for integration and homogenization of the societies of the world in 'One World Order'. However, this aspect of globalization has been found to be oriented towards establishment of the hegemony of dominant collectivities both from abroad and within the nation, polarizing the weak and minority collectivities to the periphery. It works not only against the secular principle of cultural diversities and pluralism in our society, but it has also strengthened the struggle for identity among various collectivities, consequently enhancing the tendency of 'radical nationalism' and weakening the concept of 'nation-state'. This altogether is becoming responsible for cumulative inequalities and oppression of a vast majority of population. Since no society can keep itself isolated from the process of globalization, whatever consequences may be arising out of it, what is needed is to adapt them with emerging circumstances. It has opened a debate for and against the establishment of civil society in India. Gupta's view is that civil society and modern nation-state can work with same ethos. What is of utmost significance is the protection and propagation of the concept of equal citizenship by maintaining the multiple cultural identities and harmonizing attitude between them. To a greater extent, these could be achieved through providing them equal access to economic and political rights along with eradicating existing disparities in social dimensions too.

Manjeet Chaturvedi in his paper 'Globalization and Rise of Civil Resistance to Indian Plutonomy' maintains that as globalization progressed, India crossed the stage of early capitalism and attained those economic conditions, particularly the emergence of super rich and vastness of economic inequalities, which made it a plutonomy. The rich has vigorously started the occupancy of the traditionally main resource of Indian economy – the land – which was eased by the new post-mixed economic Indian state. Surely, state and many of its agencies energized the Indian plutonomy during the process of globalization, but it was not without any opposition as is well known that India continues a predominantly agrarian society. The paper observes the process of the rise of civil resistance to Indian plutonomy and the consequences of India being a plutonomy for today and tomorrow. It concludes that the political economy and social and productive fabric of India are now offset by the consequences of its turning into a plutonomy avatar.

Paper by Shruti Tambe on 'City through the Prism of Movements: Aurangabad from 1915 to 1960' underlines the need to combine urban theory with development studies to gauge the socio-economic reality of medium-sized city like Aurangabad as reflected in and through movements. She states that in the past four decades, the city of Aurangabad has experienced conflicts and movements based on caste, ethnic issues, and religion as it passed through various stages of spatial and economic development. Diverging consciously from the ecological or functional classification and detailing in the study of a city, the focus here is on analyzing the city through the prism of different people's movements in the city over a period of time. This project tries to arrive at the ways in which a city is shaped by and shapes the forces of colonial capitalism to post-colonial developmentalism. At the global level, the trend in urban sociology is to study global or world cities to look into the recent economic restructuring and its impact on labour and working-class identities. At the Indian level, analysis of megalopolis and metropolis is undertaken either to review urban policies or issues related to governance from people's participation to surveillance of the State. The medium-sized cities that have grown tremendously in the past two decades are grossly neglected at present. These are the places that question the relevance of Western theories of urban development and pose fundamental questions about the adequacy of studies focusing on the new urban culture and identity politics. Unless the backdrop of developmental politics and resurgence of ethnic, caste and communal conflicts and movements are scrutinized, it is impossible to truly reach out the core of the existence of medium-sized towns and their problems. This paper reviews the prevalent approaches in the field of development studies and examines the relevance of these approaches to analyse conflicts in the medium-sized cities such as Aurangabad in the global South. Looking at the history of this multiethnic city, one is struck by the people with a diverse linguistic, caste and community background. The obvious question therefore is, why the city was suddenly enmeshed by different kinds of conflicts from 1920s? Does it have something to do with the emergence and evolution of the modern democratic capitalist state and the developmental strategies adopted by this State in its feudal (in the case of Hyderabad Princely State) and postcolonial era? To answer these questions, the public discourse on various conflicts and movements and the discourse on development have been analysed. Tambe highlights the need to consider not just social conflicts but also movements and collective actions as an index of people's aspirations and opinions. These collective actions structure the city and in turn are structured by the city. Unlike the West, this study suggests the importance of the impact of the region on the city rather than considering the city as an island.

Ethnographic analyses of two important moments in the history of Aurangabad – the joining of Republic of India in 1948 and the joining of Maharashtra in 1960 – probes into language-based ethnic movement in and around the city of Aurangabad. A comparison of *Hyderabad Mukti Sangram* with the *Samyukta Maharashtra Aandolan* is attempted to argue for the intertwining of national, regional and the local factors reformulating the city. She examines collective actions to ease out the texture of different conflicts and their relevance in terms of defining development, democracy and identity in different time periods. In short, this paper paves way for a new approach in urban studies by using the prism of social movements and collective action in the broader context of colonial and dependent capitalism and State-induced developmentalism in a democratic polity.

The hypothesis of the exercise in the paper 'India and the Fiji Indian Quest for Power' by I.S. Chauhan is that adversity necessitates search for security leading to enterprise in multiple areas of human endeavour. The story of Indians who went to Fiji 130 years ago amply proves this point. Land has been a non-marketable commodity in Fiji. The rural folks that migrated to that country had to look for other avenues for economic survival. They succeeded in business and professions. Their visible prosperity became the cause for envy among the natives who wished to halt this march so that it may not end up in usurpation of political power. It is a queer fact of history that India was called up on to play a crucial role in the political and diplomatic life of this country. Contrary to misgivings in several quarters, India played this role admirably well. Politics could not be played in isolation. It had to be in the arena where indigenous Fijians had a dominant voice. They abhorred the idea of an immigrant community that was welcomed as the guest was now making attempts to become the master of the house through a democratic system. Chauhan's paper focuses on the fascinating interplay of some of these forces.

Going beyond the political dimensions of the Indian diaspora, Surendra K. Gupta, in his paper 'Social and Cultural Transformation of Indians in the United States of America' draws our attention to the social and cultural aspects of the Indian diaspora in an altogether different parts of the world. Indians in the United States are the third largest group, after Chinese and Filipinos. Among Indians, the majority are Hindus and Sikhs. Among Hindus, Gujaratis have outnumbered others. In fact, Gujaratis and Sikhs account for nearly more than half of the Indian migrants. In this paper, an attempt has been made to analyse the social and cultural transformation of these two groups based on the available data. Indicators selected are settlement pattern, vocational activities, marriage and family, adoption of names, language, food habits, religious activities, social and cultural organizations, and contact with the parent culture. It has been found that the older generations try to adhere to their cultural norms; but although the younger generations appreciate the family values and closeness, they do not like the rigid religious activities and many other customs and traditions including the caste system.

Moving from the various dimensions of polity, civil society and movements to the issues of development in Part II, K.D. Gangrade in his paper 'Gandhi on Sustainable Development' maintains that balanced development is needed for sustainable development. It not only has to be maintained, but it must also continuously grow and improve. According to him, the factors that are required for such a unique process of development are (i) land reforms, land to the tiller of the soil; (ii) eradication of poverty, that is, everybody has food, clothing and shelter; (iii) equitable distribution of resources; (iv) policies, plans and programmes must be for people and not self-oriented; (v) implementation and execution must be corruption-free and time-bound; (vi) implementation policy must be to commence work by involving people bottom upwards and not to follow trickle-down theory; and (vii) all precautions and safeguards must be taken so that no individual, group/or country/ies through three powers – mind (knowledge), muscle (military) and money (financial) – are able to dominate and exploit others. Gangrade's paper has nine sections. The first deals with the problem of gigantic proportion of maldevelopment. The second describes critically the basic values of development, human dignity, availability and social justice. The third emphasizes that the process of development is aimed at overall personality enhancement. The fourth examines Gandhi's development philosophy that revolves around man, his society and nature and their respective and simultaneous development. The fifth evaluates government policies especially with reference to India. The sixth is concerned with the problem in the world today is not so much the development of recalled underdeveloped as it is of one of educating the educated. The seventh has focused on grassroots barriers and to develop strategy for their removal. Similar approach can be adopted from the lowest to the highest level. The eighth is crucial and soul of the paper. Unless land reforms are executed and land is transferred to the tiller of the soil, all attempts will be negative and unproductive. And, the ninth makes a plea to involve people in the decision-making process to have a stronger democratic society.

Any debate on development remains half-hearted and incomplete without taking cognizance of and highlighting the importance of social development. This is what Bhimasen Hantal in his paper 'Globalization and Social

Development in the Context of New Economic Policy in India' has attempted to do. The process of globalization has become a never-ending phenomenon. It had started embracing almost all aspects of socio-economic life of common people and opened the new vistas for promising entrepreneurs and thus for economic development. But whether the benefits of globalization reach the weaker sections of society is a matter of debate among the intelligentsia and politicians. The review of socio-economic development of common people in the context of new economic policy has put a big question mark over the nature of development itself! Whether we are moving towards greater division of society or establishing social equity are some of the contentious issues to be addressed. During pre-globalization stage, there was the policy of socialism for socio-economic development and equitable distribution that rather marred the social transformation and development of weaker sections primarily due to a lack of implementation/faulty implementation, resource crunch and prevalence of vested interest engulfed with familialism/orthodoxism/traditionalism; and now in the post-globalization era, there is a growing concern for inclusive development. But when we analyse the prevailing system of education, nature of employment or dimension of poverty, we find more of exclusive development systematized with massive corruption, greater cleavage of society, concentration of wealth and degradation of weaker sections coupled with neo-liberalism and capitalism. As the previous policy was also not conducive enough though at least theoretically its orientation was primarily for the concern of welfare of common people, it is not advisable to roll back the present policy of globalization, but its orientation for social transformation and development needs to be rekindled if at all the policy makers and other concerns are genuinely serious of making India a vibrant nation with the cherished principle of equality, liberty and fraternity; or else even after hundred years down the line, the subsequent generations will continue to live in two India or may be three or more India.

To continue the debate on development in its various aspects, Manish Kumar Verma in his paper 'Modernization of Indian Tradition: Introspecting Equitable Development Paradigm' examines the issues of equitable development and how it leads to modernization. It has been tried to be established by the development planners time and again that all the development projects essentially carry with it the seeds of development and modernization of the society as well as the nation as a whole. All the development projects, carried out by government, are based on the assumption of welfare of the society and visualize equality, equity, eradication of poverty, improvement of living standard of human beings and so forth. But, in reality, the spirit of welfare and modernization of the mass society does not find place in most of the development projects. The urban and industrial development model far from offering solutions is in fact the fundamental cause of many problems. It triggers the predicament of development-induced displacement of the host population, which in the long run enhances the poverty index and consequently hampers the much-acclaimed notion of modernization and welfare. The paper is an attempt to divulge into the details of development planning vide National Thermal Power Corporation (NTPC) projects situated in the Singrauli region, and to ascertain whether the equitable development agenda undertaken over there really modernized the society. It focuses on socio-cultural changes and assesses its consequent impact on ecology and environment and how far it helped in the modernization of the local people. For this purpose, the author has first of all delved into the details of modernization by focusing on its attributes and indicators.

To realize the goals of national development, R. Kannan in his paper 'Communication as a Development Resource' emphasizes the importance of need-based and tailored communication programmes. He opines that the need to bridge the information and interaction gap is more keenly felt today in order to realize the goals of national development. This task can be accomplished with an effective bottom-up communication. Hence, the planners and policy makers, who aim at development especially for the subalterns through media, may think of a shift in approach. The socio-economic profile of the audience and the tastes and preferences of the segment may be borne in mind while tailoring the programmes. This calls for a periodic audience research. Kannan suggests that featurized documentaries and docudrama would serve the purpose in the subaltern settlements, where the print and electronic media may not make any significant headway through their informative or instructive programmes. The development communicator is therefore urged to assess the psychographic and demographic profile of the receivers.

It can hardly be overemphasized that technology-led globalization has stimulated very complex and multiple processes of change especially in the socio-cultural sphere of activity. This is precisely what Rashmi Jain and Nidhi Bansal in their paper 'Globalization, Technological Advancements and Socio-cultural Impact on Youth' have tried to establish in the particular context of one of the most important segments of the Indian population, that is, youth. They assert that globalization is a process that has transformed the lives of people across the globe, cutting through the barriers of class, ethnicity, gender, age and so on. It denotes the process of interconnectedness altering the age-old concepts of time and space. Everyday, we witness the reality and existence of this change in our lives – through the people we meet, the products we buy, the gadgets we use, the information we get, the food we eat and the movies we watch. And further, technology has fuelled the pace and intensity of globalization. We witness the impact of this phenomenon in all arenas of our lives. The youth are generally at the forefront in using latest technologies and therefore the first to face its consequences as well. Technology-led globalization has stimulated very complex and multiple processes of change, especially in the socio-cultural sphere of activity. The paper attempts to analyse the socio-cultural impact of these changes on youth in India, bearing in mind the unique Indian scenario and concerns.

Although Jain and Bansal examined the impact of technological advancements on youth in the broader context of globalization, Ashish Saxena in his paper 'Dynamics of Economic Reforms and Revamping Rural India: Opportunities and Challenges' undertakes a similar exercise in the context of rural India. He observes that technological transformations, intertwined with globalization, are creating a new paradigm: the global network age. These transformations expand opportunities and increase the social and economic rewards of creating and using technology. Modern rural policy increasingly advocates empowerment of local communities to develop through deliberative processes their own strategies for the future, supported by appropriate multi-level governance structures and managerial technologies. Keeping in view the neo-liberal policies and the pace of globalization, there is an urgent need to re-look into the revamping rural India in order to identify the potentialities for future development. An optimistic approach towards such initiatives may help in bridging the rural–urban divide and make them spatially open arena for exposure, conflicts and modifications.

Satish K. Sharma in his paper 'State, Market Economy and Rural Degeneration: A Note on Pangs of Globalization' also examines the impacts and the consequences of globalization and that of the market economy on the rural masses. The Indian State, in the beginning of the 1990s, under tremendous pressure of world economic powers, resorted to socio-economic development following liberalization, privatization and globalization (LPG) mantra for bringing about social transformation. The move was highly opposed on the grounds that such a process will ultimately have its backlash on the economy that will severely affect the poor working class, marginal and poor farmers and the landless labourers in the villages. Over the past almost two decades, there has been tremendous change in the Indian society, quite visible in terms of glittering mega malls, infinite variety of brand consumer durables, emergence of a new class of highly paid corporate executives, world-class housing projects, multi-specialty hospitals, proliferation of automobile industry and so on. When one examines a fundamental question, for which class of people all the transformations take place, no wonder one invariably stops at the neo-rich class of urban people. Another question is, at whose cost? The answer, in a country of toiling millions living in the rural areas, stops at the rural people whose land, the only source of livelihood acquired in the name of SEZs, IT Parks and so on. The development strategies being pursued presently, apparently projected pro-poor, inwardly remain highly biased against the interests of the working class, the peasantry and the rural masses who suffer endlessly. The author tries to locate the reasons for such a state of affairs in the basic nature of the state and its pro-capitalist stance in pursuing the development goals.

While Satish Sharma discussed the impact of globalization and market economy on the rural people, P.S. Vivek in his paper 'Civilizational Transformation of Indigenous People: Globalization Effect and Sustainable Development' does the same in the context of the indigenous people who are hardly talked about in the mainstream sociological discourse. Vivek emphasizes that globalization comes down to local communities largely through the market. The market, of course, is not new to indigenous people. The market, with its associate privatization, does solve some existing problems in indigenous people's economies. New needs are created, along with cosmopolitan consumption and production systems, taking local products to the far corners of the world and bringing new goods into local consumption. He further asserts that the market is likely to destroy the traditional community. With a shift in production systems to maximize income, unlike with production for self-consumption, which is necessarily limited by the extent of local consumption, production for sale on the market is not locally limited. Mass production carries with it mass consumption and mass culture. Vivek's paper deals with changes in the social and economic system of indigenous people of India in the post-colonial era. It explores changes in the social and economic systems of indigenous people as a consequence of their integration into the global economy through market-driven processes. There are changes in the nature of the overall economic and social system, from one aiming at the stability of the social system to one based on accumulation, from production for self-consumption. The new system shifts to production for sale in the market. The way forward, the paper observes, is to create welfare systems based on taxes and new forms of community organization. New forms of community and continued non-market access to critical resources, such as land and forests, would allow for a greater spread of the benefits. The forms of collective functioning are also needed for maintaining critical natural resources, the paper concludes.

Taking up another dimension of development, Mohammad Akram and Sadaf Rafiq Beg in their paper 'Health Inequalities in India and the Challenges before Social Transformation' draw our attention to the state of inequality in the health sector of the country. They observe that health is a human right for every individual. Health contributes to a person's basic capability to function. Denial of health is not only denial of 'good life chance', but it is also denial of fairness and justice. The process of defining health and determining what counts as health and what as another type of social problems cannot be solved by the physicians and medical specialists alone but depends on other aspects of social institutions, and may change over time. The Alma Ata Declaration of 1978 and many other studies conducted by several global and national agencies in the past three decades exposed the widespread inequalities inherent in the health condition of the people. Health inequality does not mean any kind of health difference but the differences in health, which are potentially avoidable. Inequality in health can be explained as a particular type of difference in health in groups that could be potentially shaped by policies. Many important forms of inequalities can be identified in the field of health, which includes geographic disparities, gender disparity, disparity among socio-historically deprived groups and poverty disparity. India's public health system is affected by a large number of factors such as shortage of resources and budgetary allocations and organizational and managerial deficiencies. In addition to this, whatever resources are available are inequitably distributed towards the tertiary and urban-based health care services; thus the primary health care level suffers. An assessment of the health policies, developments and related programmes reflect our performance in achieving the goals of health for all is not satisfactory. We are unable to meet most of the health-related goals of the Millennium Development Goals (MDGs) and targets despite making tall claims. It is the need of the hour to identify the other invisible factors responsible for persisting and increasing health inequalities in India and suggest the remedies. Honouring Professor Yogendra Singh's interest in social inequalities and social transformation, the authors in their paper aim to look at the larger issues inherent in the processes. The paper is divided into six sections: (i) understanding health, (ii) concept of inequality in health, (iii) health indicators and ongoing disparities in India, (iv) health system in India, (v) health reforms and goals of social transformation and (vi) challenges before social transformation.

While Akram and Beg discussed the issue of health inequalities in India in a general and broader perspective, Madhu Nagla in her paper 'Sociology of Privatization of Health Care in India: Emerging Issues and Concerns' is concerned particularly with the questions of private health care and the role of market in this sector. Her paper attempts to collate literature from various sources, in an attempt to answer four pertinent questions related to private health care in India: first, emerging relationship between private health care and market; second, how the private health care sector is delivering health in terms of its quality; third, what is the structure and pattern of health care from the provider's perspective? Lastly, the paper tries to highlight some of the dehumanizing issues/aspects in private health care that are relevant for the consumers of health care.

Markets in the health care are also governed by the purchasing power of the individuals in society. They are not democratic institutions, and they result in the marginalization of the marginal. It is evident that the private health sectors attract and treat persons who can pay more, hence it is selective. Quality of health care in private sector is a myth as in private sector job insecurity and poor working conditions bound to affect the quality of care provided to the patients. Private health care professionals are essentially for the sale and use of goods produced by the health care industry. User charges, usage of high-tech diagnostic tools, irrational diagnosis and technology for money have become a culture of practice for the doctors. Professionals in health care defend unfair trade practices that sometimes lead to the unethical practices under the grab of professional independence.

Vidyut Joshi in his paper 'Socio-Economic Impact of Alang and Sosiya Ship-Breaking Yard' has taken up an altogether different aspect of development, more so of sustainable development, in the broader context of a ship-breaking yard in Gujarat also taking into cognizance its environmental impacts besides the social and cultural. Alang and Sosiya Ship-Breaking Yard (ASSBY), popularly known as Alang, was established in 1983. This was early and uninformed period of globalization that brought coastal area-based development in India. The Government of India started Department of Ocean Development. It also brought into effect the Coastal Zone Regulation Act, popularly known as CZRA. Ports and coastal areas need to be developed because it was projected that export–import on large scale will start from Indian ports. The Government of Gujarat declared privatization of 11 ports, and it also welcomed ship-breaking activities on Indian shore, as they were, now and not so preferred in developed countries. ASSBY was established as part of this policy. The activities started in 1983 and gradually grew as one of the biggest ship-breaking or ship-recycling yards in the world.

This paper is a part of larger multidisciplinary research project named 'Socio-Cultural, Economic and Environmental Impacts of ASSBY,' headed by the author of this paper. At different times, different methods were used for data collection. So far as villagers are concerned, out of 3,248 individuals, 485 households representing 3,053 individuals were selected. Apart from this, 350 workers were studied as part of the workers' study. The project proved to be challenging, not because of the socio-cultural, economic and environmental issues, but the real challenge was to involve diverse range of interests and stakeholders, who all share an economic interest in sustainable development of the yard. There were four stakeholders with different interests and abilities: (i) Gujarat Maritime Board (Government of Gujarat), (ii) ship-breakers (industrialists), (iii) the workers and (iv) the local community. The project tried a convergence of all the four stakeholders and tried to evolve a consensus for sustainable development. The paper is only a part of the larger project, as it deals with the impact of ASSBY on the workers and on the local community. Although the liberal industrial policy along with privatization and globalization was introduced at ASSBY, the corresponding rules and institutional structures to satisfy interests of all stakeholders were not introduced. It was only after a long process of opposition, litigation and consultation that corresponding institutional structures for sustainable development at ASSBY started emerging.

Indebtedness-led suicides among cultivators in several states of the country comparatively at a larger scale than before have attracted attention of both the academics and the policy planners. A. Satyanarayana and Sanjay in their paper 'Does Indebtedness Lead to Suicides among Cultivators? A Comparative Study of Suicide Victims, Normal Indebted Cultivators and Suicide Attempters in Sangrur District of Punjab' have drawn our attention to this comparatively new phenomenon in the particular context of a district of Punjab, namely, Sangrur, in a comprehensive manner. The authors have argued that suicides among cultivators of commercial crops, such as cotton, groundnut, chilli and soya, and cereals, such as wheat and paddy, became more tangible in Indian agriculture after the adoption of the Structural Adjustment Programme (SAP) and liberalization policies in 1990. Crop failure due to natural calamities, significant increase in the cost of production due to withdrawal of subsidies on agricultural inputs, and relative fall or slower increase in the agricultural produce prices as the developed countries provided subsidies to corporations for the export of agricultural produce and even developing countries adopting the same strategy, and consumption-related status enhancement have lead to indebtedness and its accumulation over time. These conditions are treated as the main cause of suicides among cultivators. The indebted cultivators in the colonial and post-green revolutionary periods have manifested their grievances through collective actions in the form of riots or burning the debt records and road blockades and filling the prisons. But scholars gave scant attention to understand the processes involved in the recovery of debt in villages where honour is highly valued. Second, they took only the households of suicide victims to assert that indebtedness is the main cause of suicide, but they refused to take evidence that rejects the conclusion as majority of the indebted cultivators are still able to cope with such status degrading and honour, lowering the mechanisms of debt recovery and are able to continue their normal life after its repayment. Thus, the paper makes an effort to realize the following questions: What mechanisms are adopted by the formal and informal lending agencies for the recovery of debt from the cultivators? What are the consequences of these mechanisms on the type of family, nature of mobility of the cultivators and fulfilment of expectations of the indebted cultivator by his siblings, kin and friends both in rural and urban economy at the time of crisis of repayment of debt? A study in the Sangrur district of Punjab with comparable sample of suicide victims and indebted normal cultivators was conducted, and data from the close members of the sample were collected through narratives about the observations they made at the time of receiving and repayment of loans by the household head. The study reveals that besides the above-mentioned causes of indebtedness, the market is dominated by the trader both as seller of agricultural inputs and purchaser of agricultural produce and as payer and receiver of payments. The payments to the cultivators are not only delayed inordinately without interest but also circulated as loan to the same cultivator with exorbitant rate of interest. Indebtedness may be a necessary condition, but the sufficient conditions are lesser integration of the indebted cultivator with the family; anomic conditions in terms of sudden downward mobility besides lowering of honour publicly, which is highly valued by the cultivators, seems to lead to suicides among cultivators of Sangrur. Finally, an effort is made to integrate the theory of Durkheim and psychoanalysis and its bearing on the empirical evidence are discussed.

In the concluding paper 'Biotech Crops of Bt Cotton and Bt Brinjal in India: Some Issues in the Wake of Globalization', R.B. Patil examines the issues involved with regard to biotech crops of Bt cotton and Bt brinjal in the wake of globalization, which until recently were heatedly debated and made headlines in the national news channels. It is common knowledge that India is a signatory to the World Trade Organization (WTO) and also has enacted the provisions of WTO in letters and spirit. The Indian Intellectual Property Rights (IPRs) laws have also been modified, which are consistent with the Trade-Related Intellectual Property Rights (TRIPS) of WTO. The provisions in the General Agreement on Tariffs and Trade (GATT) have created new issues of ownership of seeds. Biotechnology and genetic engineering pose a new threat to agricultural biodiversity originated from the new economic policies under the liberalization and globalization. The policies of WTO and GATT oblige member countries to open their markets to multinational companies, such as Cargill and Monsanto, who already control much of the world's grain and seed trade. The Union Environment Ministry's Genetic Engineering Approval Committee (GEAC) – the apex regulatory body for Germinated Modified Organisms (GMOs) – grants the final approval for crop tests, and subsequently the crop to be grown commercially. In 1994, the agro-chemical and pharmaceutical multinationals of the North used their governments to impose their own system of intellectual rights, the TRIPS agreement, within the framework of the WTO. Patil's paper deals with some issues in the wake of globalization with reference to Environmental Benefits Risks and of GMOs, global scenario of biotech crops 2009, pro- and anti-GMO studies and the situation of biotech crops of Bt cotton and Bt brinjal in India. The paper is based entirely on the secondary sources comprising articles in books, journals, magazines, newspapers, material from the Internet, etc.

On the whole, this third volume of the four-part Festschrift for Professor Yogendra Singh analyses the situation of democracy and civil society in India and also the various dimensions of development in the broader context of globalization. It has been pointed out and questioned that despite the compelling evidence to show that democracy is the only way known to man so far to achieve the living to an optimal span of life, free of physical and psychological ailments and criminal threats and with normal comforts of life, why it is so that India has not acquired the democratic character of freedom, equality and brotherhood, which is expected from its society. Relationship between democracy and civil society has also been discussed. Efforts have been made not only to trace the history and the beginnings of the concept of civil society, but it has also been suggested that the field of civil society consists of an autonomous space but interpenetrated by overlapping and interpenetrative circles of society, religion, state, market, social movements/voluntary organizations and self. Also that state and civil society are not to be conflated with each other and as such, society and civil society are not co-terminous – civil society refers to that conscious and mobilized aspect of society, which strives to create a space for critical self-reflections and public deliberations. The quality of work of self and its mobilization in civil society and its above intersecting dimensions determine the quality of civil society. The various conceptions of civil society and its association with citizenship in the broader context of democracy and development have also been discussed. It has also been argued that the concept of civil society is inevitable if we are to understand the nature of citizenship and self-understanding of relevant actors in the post-colonial India. It was observed that there is a relation of interdependence between the growth of civil society and deepening of democratic values, institutions and processes in the modern world system. Various components of the Naxal movement have also been analysed. Likewise, violence perpetuated and legitimized by MNS in Maharashtra has been discussed and documented comprehensively. One of the authors has advocated the use of alternative approaches for understanding Indian society. It has also been argued that globalization is enhancing the tendency of 'radical nationalism' and weakening the concept of 'nation-state'. Others maintain that as globalization progressed, India crossed the stage of early capitalism and attained those economic conditions, particularly the emergence of super rich and vastness of economic inequalities that made it a plutonomy. The need to combine urban theory with development studies to gauge the socio-economic reality of medium-sized cities as reflected in movements was also underlined. Adversity necessitates search for security leading to enterprise in multiple areas of human endeavour was examined in the context of Fiji Indians. Attention was also drawn to the socio-cultural aspects of the Indian diaspora in the United States.

Moving from the various dimensions of polity, civil society and movements, the second section of this volume focuses on the issues of development. Although some authors maintained that balanced development is needed for sustainable development and outlined the importance of Gandhi's development philosophy, others pleaded for social development more so in the context of new economic policy. Issues of equitable development in the context of modernization have also been examined. The importance of need-based and tailored communication programmes was outlined, and it was also emphasized that communication as a development resource be used mainly in case of the subalterns. How technology-led globalization has stimulated complex and multiple processes of change, especially in socio-cultural spheres of activity particularly among the youth, was also examined. A similar exercise has been undertaken in the context of rural India. Likewise, the impacts and the consequences of globalization and that of the market economy on the rural masses have been examined. Another paper does the same in the context of the indigenous people who are hardly talked about in the mainstream sociological discourse. Some other dimensions of development, such as health and health inequalities as well as health care, particularly in the context of private health care and the role of market in this sector, have been discussed. An altogether different aspect of development, more so of sustainable development, in the broader context of a ship-breaking yard in Gujarat, also taking into cognizance its environmental impacts besides the social and cultural, has also been taken up in a paper. Indebtedness-led suicides among cultivators as well as the impact and the interface between globalization and the rural society, particularly in the context of agrarian social structure, have been taken up. So also the issues involved with regard to biotech crops of Bt cotton and Bt brinjal in the wake of globalization have been discussed in this section.

Contributors

A. Satyanarayana, Professor and Head, Department of Sociology, University of Allahabad, Allahabad.

Anand Kumar, Professor of Sociology and Coordinator, Global Studies Programme, Centre for the Study of Social Systems, School of Social Sciences, Jawaharlal Nehru University, New Delhi. He is also the President of the Indian Sociological Society.

Anand Prasad Mishra, Associate Professor, Department of Geography, Banaras Hindu University, Varanasi.

Ananta Kumar Giri, Associate Professor, Madras Institute of Development Studies, Chennai.

Ashish Saxena, Associate Professor, Department of Sociology, University of Allahabad, Allahabad.

Ashok Kaul, Professor, Department of Sociology, Banaras Hindu University, Varanasi.

Bhimasen Hantal holds a Ph.D. from Jawaharlal Nehru University and belongs to Indian Ordinance Factories Service (IOFS). He is presently Deputy General Manager, Ordinance Factory Khamaria, Jabalpur.

C.N. Venugopal, former Professor of Sociology, Centre for the Study of Social Systems, School of Social Sciences, Jawaharlal Nehru University, New Delhi.

I.S. Chuhan, formerly Professor and Head, Department of Sociology and Vice-Chancellor, Barkatullah University, Bhopal. He is also a former High Commissioner of India in Fiji, Tonga, Tavalu and Cook Islands.

Jasmine Y. Damle, Associate Professor, Centre for Development Studies, School of Social Sciences, Tata Institute of Social Sciences, Mumbai.

K.D. Gangrade, Vice Chairman, Gandhi Smriti and Darshan Samiti, New Delhi, and former Pro Vice-Chancellor and Dean, Faculty of Social Sciences, and Head, Department of Social Work, University of Delhi, Delhi.

Madhu Nagla, Professor, Department of Sociology, Maharshi Dayanand University, Rohtak.

Manish Kumar Verma, Associate Professor, Babasaheb Bhimrao Ambedkar Central University, Lucknow.

Manjeet Chaturvedi, Professor and former Head, Department of Sociology, Banaras Hindu University, Varanasi.

Mohammad Akram, Associate Professor, Department of Sociology, Aligarh Muslim University, Aligarh.

Nidhi Bansal, ICSSR Post-Doctoral Fellow, Department of Sociology, University of Rajasthan, Jaipur.

P.S. Vivek, Professor, Department of Sociology, University of Mumbai, Mumbai.

Pradip Kumar Bose, Professor of Sociology, Centre for Studies in Social Sciences, Kolkata.

R.B. Patil, Professor and former Head, Department of Sociology, Shivaji University, Kolhapur.

R. Kannan, Senior Professor and Head, Department of Sociology and Chairperson School of Social Sciences, Madurai Kamaraj University, Madurai.

Rashmi Jain, Associate Professor, Department of Sociology and Director, Centre for Social Exclusion and Inclusive Policy, University of Rajasthan, Jaipur.

S.P. Gupta, Professor and Head, Department of Sociology, Jai Narain Vyas University, Jodhpur.

Sadaf Rafiq Beg, Lecturer, Government Boys Higher Secondary School, Anantnag, Jammu & Kashmir.

Sanjay holds a Ph.D. in psychology. He is presently Group Director and President, Sri Mangal Group of Institutions, Kanpur.

Satish K. Sharma, Professor of Sociology, Himachal Pradesh University, and presently a Fellow at the Indian Institute of Advanced Study, Shimla.

Shruti Tambe, Associate Professor, Department of Sociology, University of Pune, Pune.

Surendra K. Gupta, former Professor of Sociology, Punjabi University, Patiala, and Member-Secretary, Indian Association of Social Science Institutions, New Delhi.

Victor S. D'Souza, former Professor and Head, Department of Sociology, Punjab University, Chandigarh. He was also the President of the Indian Sociological Society (1986–87) and a recipient of its Lifetime Achievement Award (2005).

Vidyut Joshi, Emeritus Professor, Nirma University, Ahmedabad, and former Vice-Chancellor, Bhavnagar University, and Director, Centre for Social Studies, Surat.

Part I

Polity and Civil Society

1

What Ails Indian Democracy

The Enemy Within

Victor S. D'Souza

If living to an optimal span of life, free of physical and psychological ailments and criminal threats, and with normal comforts of life, is a universal value, then two British demographers have adduced in their path-breaking work *The Spirit Level (Why More Equal Societies Almost Always Do Better)*, compelling evidence to show that democracy is the only way (Wilkinson and Pickett, 2009) known to humans so far, to achieve that end. They do this by collating and comparing global evidence about rich and developed countries gathered by international agencies. In all, 23 rich and developed democratic countries for which comparable data were available are included in the above-mentioned study. In addition, within the United States for which more detailed data are available, a state-wise comparison of democratic adequacy is provided. In both settings, it has been found that the *desiderata* of good life are better achieved in the more democratic countries of the world or the relatively more democratic states within the United States.

What then is special about democracy? Democracy has three main features, namely freedom, equality and fraternity, a combination that gives society a unique spirit of sociability that enables members to regard each other with equal dignity, empathy and trust. Although all the features are important, equality seems to be the backbone of democracy. Equality creates the climate of mutual relations and empathy that ensures welfare of the whole society. If a democratic society with an egalitarian background relapses into a greater inequality, it loses its *desiderata* of good life. It practically loses the essence of democracy, displaying only its shell. This is essentially the fate of the United States as shown in the study referred to earlier, although at the time of Indian independence, the United States was the brightest star of democracy in the world. On the contrary, currently, Japan and the Scandinavian countries such as Sweden, Finland and Norway, which show a relatively more egalitarian trend, are also the ones that yield better standards of good life for their inhabitants.

The bare details of the above-mentioned study are given to draw attention to the type of democracy in India, a country that is on the way to becoming a rich and developed society, ready to be counted among the hitherto recognized more powerful countries of the world. India also adopted a democratic constitution almost six decades ago and embarked on the goal of development, which is indispensable for any country. It has made a serious attempt at introducing a democratic constitution and has restructured the form of the society in the democratic mould by treating every adult individual as a member and dividing the country into electoral precincts such as Village Councils (Gram Panchayats) in the rural areas and Wards in the cities as the smallest governing as well as balloting units in the rural and the urban areas, respectively. These are then grouped into larger units of states and the union legislatures and government. India is noted for scrupulously following its electoral proceedings. The new format of democracy in India has thoroughly disrupted the traditional form of society based on the caste structure.

Despite preserving its democratic form for over six decades and also attaining relatively high economic growth in recent times, India has not acquired the democratic character of freedom, equality and brotherhood, which is expected from its society. This is not for want of trying by the Indian Government. In fact, the removal of poverty and equalization of educational and job opportunities for all the sections of the society have been the major preoccupation of different governments. But the result has not been commensurate with the efforts. Although India has successfully passed through its population transition and has shown a good trend of growth of life expectancy for its people, it presents a highly inconsistent picture when compared with other democratic countries of the world. In terms of its economy, infrastructure, information and communication, agriculture and animal husbandry, industrial goods, minerals and films, India ranks among the world's 10 fastest growing countries. On the contrary, in terms of the prevalence of diseases, malnutrition and poverty, India ranks among countries of the world in the lower end of the scale. But worst of all, it is galling for any respectable Indian to find one's country ranked as low as 119th in the UNDP's Human Development Index, 87th in the Corruption Perception Index and 134th in the Ease of Doing Business Index. This paper is an attempt to delve into some of the deeper causes of the malady. An apparent symptom is the widespread and deep-seated corruption in the public domain, which the ruling governments even though they have the power to check, prevaricate in their duty to control, and some are even dependent on it for their very survival. An attempt is made here to pinpoint the nature of the malady.

At the outset, one may state that the Indian democracy is only a veneer and has not taken deeper roots. It is a form without its substance. One of the finest institutions in India is the Election Commission which ensures that elections are held at proper times and with right decorum. But it has no power to prevent persons with criminal records from contesting. That decision is left to the electorate, which is a heir to the narrow bonds of caste and kinship, language and region and various religious ideologies that prevail against democratic decisions. The democratic values of liberty, equality and brotherhood are of least consideration in their decision-making. It is a matter of great concern that Indian legislatures in both the country's Parliament and the State Assemblies are saddled with substantial number of members with tainted criminal records. At the drop of a hat, legislators are willing to change parties for a consideration. The ideals of democracy take a back seat.

Introducing democracy in the caste-ridden and male-dominated society of India has been a Herculean task. One of the major requirements of the Indian Government was to transform the inegalitarian caste system as well as equalize the unequal rights between men and women, which were peculiar to India before the introduction of the democratic constitution in 1950. The process could not but ruffle the feathers of the parties that were adversely affected, and it did bring about a churning of social relationships among religious and caste groups, which has shaped the political parties in the country.

It must be remembered that the leading lights of the freedom struggle against the British rule and also of the drafting of the democratic constitution of India were mostly the members of the upper castes. But the key ideologue who was the chairman of the drafting committee of the new Indian Constitution was Dr B.R. Ambedkar, the leader of the most downtrodden untouchable castes, who was ably supported by the enlightened champion of democracy Jawaharlal Nehru and the British bureaucrat Sir Maurice Gwyer. The last named was an ex-Chief Justice who was also the chief architect of the 1935 Act, which formed the model for the new democratic constitution. And the draft of the constitution that came out was really revolutionary, capable of demolishing the caste-based antidemocratic society of India. The members of the Constitution Assembly, having been exposed to Western ideas, and most of them having been freedom fighters themselves, had no objection to passing the Bill. It is the unfolding of the implementation of the Constitution that struck consternation in the minds of some of the leaders of the upper castes, because the new constitution implied the total negation of the former Hindu social order that gave prominence to the upper castes at the expense of the lower ones. It provided the best possible leeway for the former downtrodden untouchable castes and the tribal people tucked away from the mainstream society.

The most vexing of all the constitutional provisions were the dismantling of the structures of exploitation embedded in the former political and economic set-up. These included the integration of the former princely kingdoms, which were under the sovereignty of the British rulers now into the new Indian Union and the abolition of the property rights of the absentee feudal landlords and by restoring them to their tenant cultivators. These were also measures adopted for a more rational land distribution among cultivators who also adversely affected the upper castes. Laws were implemented for equalizing property rights and marital standards for men and women especially among the Hindus. And those too undermined the customs of the upper castes.

Most of the measures adopted as part of the implementation of the democratic constitution impacted the people of different castes in different ways: people of the higher castes mostly being adversely affected and the lower castes more favourably. Although all these measures were unquestionably contributory to the shaping of the society into the democratic mould, the people who were adversely affected by them were not amused. Obviously, there had been a shift between the objectives of the freedom struggle against the British and those of the set-up of the new constitution of free India. The freedom struggle was fought by and large by the middle class, mostly drawn from the upper castes, who naturally expected to occupy political and governmental leadership positions vacated by the British rulers. But as it turned out, the freedom struggle also stirred up ferment among the leaders of the lower castes and tribes about their own condition under the existing structure of the society. Although originally the freedom struggle was fought under the leadership of the Congress Party, it was meant to emancipate the country from foreign rule in which case all Indians were united, whether it be Hindu, Muslim or other religions. But once the freedom was in sight, the different groups seemed to have other visions suited to their own religious ideology and social condition. The Hindu–Muslim difference was conceded resulting in the partitioning of India.

After partition, Hindus formed over four-fifths of the total population of India. But the Hindus themselves were divided into two major groups in terms of their ideology of the future polity, bringing about radical changes in the society in the light of their exposure to Western social pattern. Roughly, the two different sections were represented by the socio-religious organizations, the Arya Samaj established by Dayananda Swami and the Brahmo Samaj set by Ram Mohan Roy; the former taking its cue from the Vedas proposed a reformed but revivalist Hinduism, introducing both traditional and modern educational institutions, whereas the latter following the modern values of reason and individuality from the Vedanta embarked on building up a reformed Indian society along Western lines. The latter view however prevailed in the end. Nonetheless, the prevalence of such a difference of opinion between the predominant sections of the society has given a peculiar twist to the Indian democracy.

India was fortunate in having a leader of the stature of Jawaharlal Nehru as its first Prime Minister, who set the standards for the inauguration of self-government and overseeing the proceedings of the making of the democratic constitution of India and its subsequent introduction. The passing of the Hindu Code Bill was the first major social reform of the Hindu society. But these first winds of change were not without their storm. There were strong protests from the Hindu Mahasabha and its activist wing, the Rashtriya Swayamsevak Sangh (RSS), which represented the interests of the upper castes. Nevertheless, because of the large support base of the Congress Party, the reforms were passed through. Eventually for wider appeal, the leader of the Hindu Mahasabha started a separate party with a new name, Bharatiya Janata Party or Indian People's Party (BJP), which is also linked with the RSS.

I have referred to a small fragment of the Indian political change, but it is a part that has crucial bearing on the functioning or non-functioning of Indian democracy. The BJP claims to represent the Hindu majority of the country. But it has failed to explicate its political ideology except maintaining it as *Hindutva*. What BJP proposes is to establish the rule by the Hindu majority, which would then give an opportunity for the pursuit of values and institutions of Hinduism.

It is difficult to fathom what are the exact values and institutions of Hindutva. If one can deduce these from the functioning of the BJP and its allies when they were in power at the Centre from 1998 to 2004, it becomes apparent that the party would like to introduce along with liberal economic developments also some traditional religious knowledge from the Vedas and Astrology. An attempt was also made to rewrite history as it would suit Hindu ideology.

On the contrary, the other main national party, namely the Congress has at least followed the trajectory of democracy. Along with economic development, it has also attempted measures to bring about a greater degree of egalitarianism. It has persistently distributed food to the very poor and has introduced many schemes for the welfare of the downtrodden, but to its chagrin has found that the major part of the aid is siphoned off by the officials charged with its distribution. Most of the efforts at building up a democratic pattern of society are thwarted by a corrupt network of politician–bureaucrat–contractor–businessmen. Democratic India has emerged as an openly corrupt society to the extent that a Chief Minister of a state was alleged with corruption, was caught saying that he was only copying his predecessors, which unhappily seems to be a fair statement.

This paper is an attempt to understand why corruption has become a major issue in Indian democracy. In brief, to test the following hypothesis, the setting up of democracy in India has completely shattered the caste system, which is the structural basis of the Hindu religion that also provided the moral order of the pre-democratic Indian society. The caste system also had impact on the minority religious communities of Indian Muslims and Christians despite the fact that their religions were opposed to it. This is because the caste system had a moral order, which integrated the whole society. When the caste system was pulled down by the inauguration of democracy, the moral order of Indian society collapsed. It is sad but true that no one has seriously questioned the issue of post-democratic moral order in India, except for saying that it is a secular one. What has happened is that the setting up of a democratic pattern of society has thoroughly battered the caste system, but its spirit still haunts the newly set up democratic society as a broken moral order, since the required new democratic moral order has not emerged. Whatever moral order has emerged since the introduction of democracy is being called Secularism.

It is true that the Western democracies regard their moral order as secular, but it is a moral order evolved from Christianity in which God has been replaced by reason. Secularization has not necessarily improved the Western democracies, but on the contrary has given rise to a type of idealization of personality termed 'narcissism', which is detrimental to democracy. In India, there has been a contradiction between the moral order of the caste system and the moral order of democracy. First, in the traditional caste/tribal society, the individual was tied to the local group and had no individual locus in society. The individual lacked the freedom of moral choice and was duty-bound to obey the mores of the group. Moreover, each caste had its own particularistic moral order, although there was a common moral order to deal with inter-caste issues, which was rather discriminatory to the lower castes.

Democracy, on the contrary, calls for a universal moral order, which is radically different from the moral practices followed before. Attention is focused here mainly on the Hindu moral order of Karma–Dharma (action and retribution), which is beautifully and powerfully expounded in the widely known *Bhagavad Gita* that is a part of the great Hindu epic, the Mahabharata. The *Gita* contains the moral advice given to Arjuna, the Pandava hero, by Lord Krishna in His guise as a charioteer when the former was driven by doubt about taking part in a war in which he would end up killing a vast number of relatives and friends. Nonetheless, the Lord advised Arjuna that fighting in a war is the bound duty of a warrior regardless of consequences. In his illuminating philosophical work on *The Idea of Justice*, the Nobel laureate Amartya Sen has rightly called attention to the fact that such a view only takes note of just a one-sided view of justice that, in fact, has two sides to it. The theory of justice, which emphasizes just doing one's duty, is termed 'deontology'. But there is the other side of justice that refers to the desired consequences, which is called consequentialism. In fact, any arrangement of just society should involve both these aspects.

However, the eminent author has not emphasized the fact that deontology is the only prescribed moral order of the traditional Indian society to the total neglect of consequentiality. There was no equity or fairness in the justice system of traditional India. Perhaps, such an assertion might have taken Sen farther away from his suave and magisterial philosophical analysis. But in the present discussion, which is focused on the society of India alone, it is necessary to pinpoint the fact that after the advent of democracy, the moral order in India has to imbibe both deontology and consequentiality. The traditional Indian society accepted the caste system as divinely ordained. In the *Bhagavad Gita*, Lord Krishna says that the fourfold caste (Brahmin, Kshatriya, Vysha and Shudhra) was created by Him.[1] He, who does action, resigning them to Brahman (Supreme God), is not soiled by evil, like unto a lotus leaf by water.[2] The sum and substance of several other verses referred to in the volume is that the members in each caste are born with capabilities suited to the occupations they are meant to fill because of their Karma (retribution of action) in their previous births. In other words, the division of people into a hierarchical caste system in India was due to their natural psycho-biological endowments of the members, thereby absolving the society of any blame for existence of the blatantly unjust social order.

The duties of the four *varnas*, which flow from the characteristics of their own nature, are also clearly specified in the *Bhagavad Gita*. The duties of Brahmins, born of their own nature, are the control of the mind and the senses, austerity, purity, forbearance and also uprightness, knowledge, realization and belief in a hereafter. The Kshatriyas should display prowess, boldness, dexterity and courage in battle, generosity and exercise sovereignty. The Vaishyas are to take care of agriculture, cattle-rearing and trade. The Shudras, on the contrary, should be the servants of the other three higher *varnas*.[3] Doing one's own task to the best of one's ability is not for the expectation of a better reward in this life but on the assumption of attaining a better position in the one after death. Each of these major castes in course of time was divided and subdivided so as to grow into innumerable castes in addition to many tribal groups living on the periphery and some castes doing unclean chores being regarded as the untouchables.

The philosophy of the *Bhagavad Gita* was developed in the bygone age of ancient and medieval times when the knowledge and understanding of human was at a much lower level. It was the time when the group determined the behaviour of the individual. It was as if the group had a collective identity and all members behaved alike in a given situation. What was good and right was determined by the mores of the group and not by individual judgements. This was so when the British invaded the country, which brought about not only a political disjunction but also a cultural one because the British by then had progressed from the traditional to the modern age where the individual had replaced the group as the unit in the society. There was a clash of world views between the British and the Indian opinion leaders about the nature of Indian society, which gradually tilted in the British way, leading to the acceptance of a democratic constitution for the liberated India.

The democracy that we attribute to India at present refers, by and large, to the form of the society and not to its spirit, to borrow the term from Max Weber. Because at the heart of the democratic society, there is a pattern of moral behaviour of individuals that has not acquired currency in the character of the Indian individuals in general. The democratic society in India, in the first instance, did not comprise people of democratic disposition, but of non-democratic people who were called upon to form the democracy. Today, we are faced with the question: Does the Indian population display a democratic character, namely a subjective disposition to work out the objectively constructed laws of the democratic constitution? Now that the Indian individual is free does s/he have the moral stamina to live with others in equality and with fraternal love? Freedom in a democratic society has a restricted meaning: free to do what is good and right. In the modern society, the individual has been liberated from the mores of the caste society and has been set free so that s/he can act freely according to one's conscience. In other words, the Indian individual under the democratic constitution has acquired individual power to act rightly or wrongly; whereas under the dispensation of the caste system, s/he could act only in the right way as dictated by the caste. The new freedom in democracy comes as a responsibility placed on the individual member as a matter of trust. And democracy can function properly only if the individual is able to act in the right manner.

For the democratic society to emerge, the individual has to do what is good and right as prescribed by the new constitution of the country. This has invested immense responsibility upon the individual. The democratizing process in the Indian society has imposed restrictions on some individuals and provided opportunities for others, and the mediating officials have been invested with the power of distribution of provision for the underprivileged. The concept of the neighbourhood has been completely changed. In the traditional society, one invariably lived in one's neighbourhood surrounded by one's kinsfolk and caste fellows. In a democracy, the neighbourhood assumes a complete transformation, transcending the restricted composition of the traditional neighbourhood. Amartya Sen has drawn pointed attention to this feature (Sen, 2009: 170–73). A cursory glance at the Indian society would reveal a serious inadequacy of democracy in this respect.

The main objective of this chapter is to pinpoint one of the possible lacunae in the Indian individual to face the challenges of democracy. It is that the Indian individual has not succeeded in acquiring the moral calibre, which is required of her by democracy. I am persuaded to make such a hypothesis because of the teachings of Max Weber who has made brilliant comparative studies of Occidental and Oriental societies including India. He is among the leading sociologists who have provided insights into the cultural aspects of voluntary actions and ethical decisions in the context of social change. Weber however was referring to the modern Western capitalism, which displayed a distinctly progressive character as compared with Oriental capitalism such as that of India of his times. His approach is particularly suitable for the study of social change in India brought about by the introduction of democracy, which is a Western social system transplanted in India. And moreover India too has adopted modern capitalism as a means of developing the society in support of democracy.

The spirit of Modern Capitalism that Weber had depicted is none other than that of modern democracy except that democracy specifically recommends the equalization of life-chances for all the members of the society. One of the most important requirements for either modern capitalism or democracy is the commitment of individual members to ethical maxims, which gives direction to practical conduct. For the functioning of democracy or modern capitalism, it is absolutely necessary that the members carry out their assignments as expected. It is the disposition of the individual to take the correct decision by one's own choice. This is a responsibility that is placed on a member who under the dispensation of the caste system had no choice. In general, religion provides the ethical fervour of its members. In India, we have yet to see any religious ferment following democracy to address the new need that has arisen. In the West, as pointed out by Weber, the districts of the highest development of the economy were also at the same time favourable for a revolution in the church (Weber, 1958: 36). It was a time when religious asceticism, which was confined within the walls of the monasteries, was prescribed to the ordinary layperson, which not merely elevated the status of the lowly occupation to that of a calling but also transformed the ethical conduct of the worker. Protestantism in which religious reforms were assiduously promoted marched economically ahead of the Roman Catholics who stuck to traditionalism.

Before the religious reforms, capitalism wherever it was acquired was pursued with absolute unscrupulousness and with selfish interests. Such a situation coexisted with religious traditionalism. On the contrary,

> Christian asceticism had a definitely rational character in the highest occidental forms even in antiquity. The great historical significance of Western monasticism, as contrasted with that of the Orient, is based on this fact, not in

> all cases, but in its general type. In the rules of St. Benedict, still more with the monks of Cluny, again with the Cistercians, and most strongly in the Jesuits, it has become emancipated from planless otherworldliness and irrational self-torture. It had developed a systematic method of rational conduct with the purpose of overcoming the *status naturae*, to free man from the power of irrational impulses and his dependence on the world and on nature. It attempted to subject man to the supremacy of a purposeful will, to bring his actions under constant self-control with a careful consideration of their ethical consequences. Thus it trained the monk, objectively, as a worker in the service of the kingdom of God, and thereby further subjectively, assured the salvation of his soul. This active self-control, which formed the end of the *exercitia* of St. Ignatius and of the rational monastic virtues everywhere, was also the most important practical ideal of Puritanism. (Weber, 1958: 118–19)

The Protestants especially of the Puritan sects who underwent the transformation described earlier became the trailblazers of the modern Western Capitalism. However, when Weber was writing his book, his conception had already begun to lose its moral fervour. He comments: 'In the field of its highest development, in the United States, the pursuit of wealth, stripped of its religious meaning, tends to become associated with purely mundane passions, which often actually give it the character of sport' (ibid.: 182). Since Weber's times, the United States has shown no greater improvements in its spirit of capitalism. Is it then any wonder that this great country is trailing behind all other developed countries in the *desiderata* of good life as pointed out above.

Drastic political reforms call for equally drastic religious reforms because the former calls for a radical change in the moral conduct, which is generally within the domain of the latter. As in the case of the Occidental societies so also in the Oriental ones including India, Max Weber has provided copious insights into the ways in which religion and morality of medieval societies could be transformed to suit modern societies. His classic study *The Religion of India* contains a mine of ideas, which can be harnessed for providing a religious design of a moral vision for the democratic society of India (Weber, 2000).

There have been, no doubt, demands for religious reforms in India. But they have been mostly addressed to the problems of lower castes not being allowed entrée into the temples dominated by higher castes. Problems such as these are being sorted out in terms of their political sagacity. Building bridges between people of higher and lower castes has become a matter of political expediency in the democratic regime. But the crux of the social reform needed lies at the core of the Hindu religion, namely its peculiar conception of society and its moral order. In other words, Hinduism has to change completely from traditionalism to modernization. Indians have already achieved a high level of modernization in terms of industrial development. This has been possible with their acquisition of modern science and technology based on rational methodology. Such knowledge is termed instrumental rationality. But for capitalism to become appropriate for the modern/democratic society, it should also acquire the quality of substantial rationality. The term *substantial rationality* refers to the appropriate moral attitude, which in this case is called the spirit of capitalism by Weber. The corruption that may appear in capitalism can be attributed to a deficiency in the character of the capitalist, which is a reflection of her religious upbringing. Hindu moral code is more concerned with the caste of the capitalist than with the mode of her functioning.

Max Weber has also pointed out why an 'inner-worldly', autonomous, life methodology of the occidental stamp was not possible in India because of the peculiar ethical conception here as compared with the West. In the West, the opposition between the sacred and the secular (between an ethical God and the power of 'sin' the radical evil, which can be overcome with active life conduct) historically conditioned the systematic unification of the life conduct that we call 'ethical personality' (ibid.: 336–37). But the opposition in India is not between an ethical God and the power of sin; for the radical evil, the sin is attributed to one's *karma*, which is the consequence of one's previous life. The problem in Hinduism lies in that it was not able to develop a religious mythology and cult in which the individual is left alone to take her moral stand.

In Hinduism, there are different paths to salvation that are available to the Individual, namely the path of knowledge *(jnana marga)*, the path of action *(karma marga)* and the path of devotion (*bhakti marga*). The *jnana marga* is based on the conviction that matter is evil and that emancipation comes through gnosis. By its very nature, such efforts are irrational. Likewise, the path of action is based on the belief that one is bound by the duties of the caste in which one is born is now rejected by the Indian constitution. Only the path of devotion provides a channel for asking God for forgiveness of sins and for developing a character of right conduct. But as Weber points out, the path of devotion or *bhakti marga* was made invariably conditional to the dependence of the disciple on the *guru* (spiritual guide). But none of these methods is aimed at personal rectitude or praying for the grace of God for the absolution of one's sins. Their main aim is to free oneself from the fate of rebirth (*sansara* and *karma*). Thus, Weber points out that notwithstanding the wide variety of changes Hinduism has gone through, it could not arrive at the simple belief that God dispenses his grace for correct behaviour. When it did come to such recognition as in the *bhakti marga*, it was made conditional to the dependence of the individual on the *guru*. Under any circumstances, the individual was not left free to make a choice on his own. According to Weber, the hagiolatry that is so widely prevalent in India has been a great block to the development of the right moral conduct. Thus, according to Weber the Hindu religious cult is full of irrational beliefs and practices. It is not immune to magic and sorcery and esoteric practices so that an ordinary believer is just lost in its elaborate ritual never pausing to ask what is its rational meaning to life (ibid.: 291–328). It is the same syndrome, which renders the corrupt Indian irresistant to its corruption.

Even the great political party such as BJP, which is wearing the mantle of Hindutva, does not appear to have come to terms with the contradiction between democratic values and the moral order of traditional Hinduism. Whereas democracy is based on the universal moral order, some of the political strategies of the party, such as the incitement of the minority religious categories for political gain, jeopardize the tenets of such a moral standard. On the contrary, without its reconciliation with all the sections of the population, the emergence of a universal moral order in India is not possible. This is not probable if the BJP is anchored on the ideology of *karma*. The real enemy of Indian democracy lies in the free but flawed conscience of the Indian individual, which is symptomatic of both corruption and political misbehaviour. This calls for a modernization of Hinduism in tune with democracy.

Acknowledgement

Thanks are due to Dr Rita S. Britto and Priya D'Souza for their helpful comments. The author alone is responsible for any shortcomings in the chapter.

Notes

1. See Srimad *Bhagavad Gita* translated by Swami Swarupananda, Calcutta, 996, Ch. IV, vs. 13: The fourfold caste is created by Me, by the differentiation of *Guna* and *Karma*. Though I am the author thereof, know Me to be the non-doer, and changeless.
2. See Ibid.: Ch. V, vs. 10: He who does actions forsaking attachment, resigning them to Brahman, is not soiled bye evil, like unto a lotus-leaf by water.
3. See Ibid.: Ch. XVIII, vs. 42–44 – Vs. 42: The control of the mind and the senses, austerity, purity, forbearance and also uprightness, knowledge, realization, belief in the hereafter – these are the duties of the Brahmanas, born of (their own) nature; Vs. 43: Prowess, boldness, fortitude, dexterity and also not flying from battle, generosity and sovereignty are the duties of the Ksatriyas, born of (their own) nature; Vs. 44: Agriculture, cattle-rearing and trade are the duties of the Vaishyas, born of (their own) nature; and action consisting of service is the duty of the Sudras, born of (their own) nature.

References

Sen, Amartya (2009). *The Idea of Justice*. London: Allen Lane, pp. 23–24.

Weber, Max (1958). *The Protestant Ethic and the Spirit of Capitalism* (translated by Talcott Parsons and R.H. Tawney). New York: Charles Scribner's Sons.

——— (2000). *The Religion of India: The Sociology of Hinduism and Buddhism* (translated and edited by Hans H. Gerth and Don Martindale (1958)). New Delhi: Munshiram Manoharlal Publishers Pvt Ltd.

Wilkinson, Richard and Kate Pickett (2009). *The Spirit Level: Why More Equal Societies Almost Always Do Better*. London: Allen Lane/Penguin Books.

2

Civil Society and the Calling of Self-Development*

Ananta Kumar Giri

If we divide the history of mankind into five periods, that is, the prehistoric, ancient, medieval, modern and post-modern, one can say that the history of civil society begins only when the institution of the sacred or the divine kingship begins to dissolve into two differentiated institutions at the dawn of the ancient, or at the very latest the medieval, period out of the past. [...]

Even if this civil society was indeed the 'child of the modern world,' still it is the Christian society and its early modern reform that we may also have to consider, and not only the bourgeois society of modern capitalism. By this wider definition, the modern civil society was established or revived in Britain at any rate by the struggle of the Nonconformists, the new Christians, who together severed connection with the established Church of England when it accepted royal supremacy at the time of the Reformation [...] The new Christians wanted instead what we may call salvation through religion in society, with pluralist freedom of conscience and worship for all.

J.P.S. Uberoi (2003: 115, 120).

There are groups as well as individuals all over the world who are increasingly conscious of their creative potentiality and wish to realise their aspirations. Contemporary history is about these multiple selves engaged in dynamic struggles. Some may be forward looking and emancipative while others may be regressive and irrational. But the overwhelming trend is likely to be one that demands respect for each self.

Manoranjan Mohanty (2002: 1).

---

*Most part of this was published in *Sociological Bulletin* and is included in my forthcoming book, *Knowledge and Human Liberation: Towards Planetary Realizations* (London: Anthem Press).

The Problem

It is Jurgen Habermas (1981) who quite some time ago had challenged us that now we need a new philosophy of science, which is not scientistic. It is worth asking Habermas and all of us sociologists for whom sociological engagement is nothing more than an elaboration of the agenda of modernity whether we need an understanding of and relationship with modernity, which is not modernistic. This enquiry is at the core of understanding paths of civil society and experiments with modernities not only in India but also in Europe, East Asia, Africa, Latin America and around the world. Both conceptions of civil society and modernity suffer from a profound modernistic bias and is part of the post-traditional telos of modernistic sociological theorizing[1], and here although the recent discourse of multiple modernities initiated by S.N. Eisenstadt (cf. Sachsenmaier and Reidel, 2002) has suggested some new possibilities, the approach of multiple modernities as that of universalistic modernity of Habermas suffers from a modernistic bias when it comes to understanding tradition.[2] Prefiguring my argument, I wish to submit that appreciating the significance of Indian modernities from Buddha to Gandhi challenges us to understand the relationship between modernity and tradition, state and society, and religion and secularism in a new way through a multi-valued logic of autonomy and interpenetration rather than through the dualistic logic of modernity. Such a dualistic logic has impoverished our understanding of civil society and modernity in the West itself what to speak of illuminating our historical paths and tryst with modernities in India.

The subject of Indian modernities is quite vast, and here I just wish to state that Indian modernities have emerged out of processes of criticism, creativity and struggles through history as in the revolt of Buddha, the rise of Upanishadic spirituality, Bhakti movements in medieval India, movement for a new renaissance in 19th century and the multi-dimensional anti-colonial and post-colonial struggles for freedom.[3] Tryst with modernities in India have involved a transformative dialogue between reason and tradition, tradition and modernity and rationality and spirituality, which has shaped their paths, contents and visions. These modernities have generated their own public spaces of coming together, dialogues and public deliberations that bear parallels to what we speak of civil society in the modern West. Civil society is not only an epistemic project, it is also an ontological project; in fact, it is a project of ontological epistemology of participation going beyond the modernistic privileging of epistemology and dualism between ontology and epistemology. Taking inspiration from Bkakti movements, Kabir, Nanak, Mira Bai, Sri Aurobindo and Gandhi, we can realize that the significance of Indian modernities lies in bringing to the fore strivings for multi-dimensional self-development where self-transformation contributes to world transformation and where an aesthetics and ethics of servanthood is an important mark of being modern rather than the will to power.

But such an open-ended approach to civil society and paths of Indian modernities seems to be missing from certain dominant sociological theorizing in India. For scholars such as Andre Beteille (2001) and Dipankar Gupta (1997), civil society is a modernist category of thought and practice guaranteed by state. Beteille writes:

> [...] I will not try to give a definition of civil society but instead sketch out the context in which it may be meaningfully described. While doing so, I would like to repeat that civil society is a feature of the modern world, and it will serve little purpose to look for alternative forms of it in the medieval or ancient world. (Beteille, 2001: 294)

For Dipankar Gupta, '[...] if tradition is allowed to gain the upper hand then it is not civil society and with it the concomitant growth of freedom that develops' (Gupta, 1997: 141). In discussing the potential for formation of civil society that the social mobilization of Bharatiya Kisan Union of Mahendra Singh Tikait of Uttar Pradesh, Gupta says: 'When it comes to the laudable objective of curbing liquor and drug addiction, here too methods are traditional and repressive. Even if someone gives some one the legitimate contract to vend liquor, the outlet should be forcibly closed' (ibid.: 145). But Gupta does not look into the repressive apparatus of the state itself in flooding villages with liquor. While talking about Mahendra Singh Tikait, Gupta writes the following, among others: '[...] many of his followers have told me that on several occasions the BKU chief leaves a meeting and goes to his prayer room where he is not to be disturbed' (ibid.: 60). But Gupta does not ask what significance prayer has in this movement leader's personal life as well as in his conduct in the public sphere. Such a derisive attitude is an instance of a modernistic bias and disdainful attitude towards tradition. Understanding civil society and paths of modernities in India challenges us to overcome this.

Towards a Multi-Dimensional and Multi-Valued Understanding of Civil Society

We need a multi-dimensional understanding and realization of the sphere of civil society and its multiple activities; but for this, we need to overcome the dualism between tradition and modernity, right and good (cf. Habermas, 1990), civil society and good society (cf. Beteille, 2001) and institutionalization and mobilization. I suggest that the field of civil society consists of an autonomous space but interpenetrated by overlapping and interpenetrative circles of society, religion, state, market, social movements/voluntary organizations and self. Civil society is a space not only of 'mediating institutions' (cf. ibid.) but also of mobilization where mobilization refers not only to socio-political mobilizations but also to socio-spiritual mobilizations including reflective mobilization of self (cf. Giri, 2004).[4] In the same vein, state and civil society are not to be conflated with each other. Society and civil society are not co-terminous – civil society refers to that conscious and mobilized aspect of society, which strives to create a space of critical self-reflections and public deliberations. Despite contentions and struggles, state and civil society are related again in a logic of autonomy and interpenetration, and here social movements, different mediating institutions and voluntary organizations play an important role. Civil society is also nourished by the support from market. Actors from market such as corporate leaders and other market leaders contribute to the resource base of civil society. In so far as the relationship between religion and civil society is concerned, one great challenge here is to overcome the dualism of religion and secularism. While for Beteille (2001), civil society is mainly a secular space, for Uberoi (1996) and Oommen (2001a), it is a space where religious associations and critical spiritual movements are also at work.[5] Finally, civil society is also a space for work of self; in fact, self is an actor in all the intersecting and interpenetrating dimensions of civil society – society, state, market and religion. The quality of work of self and its mobilization in civil society and its above intersecting dimensions determine the quality of civil society.

Critical spiritual movements such as Bhakti movements in Indian history have been important actors in articulating paths of Indian modernities and generating a space of autonomy, self-realization, social transformation and world transformation. Bhakti movements created a new social space of caste and to some extent gender equality, and they embodied inter-religious dialogue. For Chittaranjan Das (1997), the Sant tradition is a product of creative and transformative dialogue and encounter between Hinduism and Islam.[6] The participants of Sant tradition and Bhakti movements challenged people to go beyond accepted boundaries and generate a new space of togetherness.[7] The leaders of Bhakti movements wrote in people's language, not in Sanskrit. Their literature has been one of love, protest and affirmation; and for understanding paths of modernities in India, we need to understand the public sphere of creativity in language, religion and society that the Bhakti movements created. This is not possible as long as we are bounded to an *a priori* dualistic logic of modernity and civil society, which puts religion and civil society in two separate boxes.

Such an approach to civil society has a wider global significance, for example, understanding the relationship between Islam and civil society. As Nikamura Mitsuo writes urging us to take Gellner's views on the impossibility of civil society and Islam only with a pinch of salt:

> [...] for centuries Islamic civilizations have developed their own versions of civility and civil society which are different from the West. These have included the independence of Muslim communities (*ummah*) from the state under the spiritual leadership of the *ulama* (Islamic scholars), rule of law to protect personal life and property, religious and ethnic pluralism, consultative and consensus methods of decision-making. In short, there has been civility and public sphere in Islamic world in its own ways including mechanism to control the arbitrariness of state power and to guarantee the autonomy of diversified associational life. (Mitsuo, 2001: 5)

According to Madjid, '[...] the notion of civil society or civilized society coined in the constitution of Medina by Prophet Muhammed makes a genuine part of the common heritage of mankind' (ibid.). Giving the examples of voluntary organizations and political movements such as Nahdaltul Ulama and Muhamadiya, Mitsuo urges us to understand the religious resources for Muslim voluntarism in Indonesia. In his work on civil Islam in Indonesia, Robert Hefner (1998) also urges us to understand its role in democratization of politics and society in Indonesia. But Hefner makes a larger point that calls for consideration from those of us who are bonded to a 'post-traditional telos':

> Viewed from the ground of everyday practice rather than the dizzying height of official canons, the normative diversity of traditional societies is far greater than most sociological models imply. As in China, Romania, and Islamic Indonesia, there are always 'underdeveloped possibilities' – values and practices that hover closer to the social ground and carry unamplified possibilities. These low-lying precedents may not appear in high-flying discourse. Nevertheless, they are in some sense 'available' for engagement and reflection, even if they have long been overlooked in public formulations. Under conditions of cultural globalization or cross-regional transfer, some legal actors may seize on exogamous idioms to legitimate and elevate principles of social action (such as equality, participation etc.) already present in social life, if in an underdeveloped, subordinated, or politically bracketed manner. (ibid.: 20)

Here, Hefner may have to consider that there are underdeveloped possibilities not only in the so-called traditional societies but also in the so-called modern societies. As there is underdeveloped possibility for participatory politics in the so-called traditional societies, there are underdeveloped possibilities for reflective mobilization of self in contemporary modern and post-modern societies as well.

While civil society and reflective mobilizations of self have manifested themselves in varieties of societies, some of the unique features of their manifestation must not be lost sight of. This calls for a non-judgemental global comparative engagement with various manifestations of civil society, reflective mobilizations of self and spiritual movements in societies and histories. In India, socio-religious and socio-spiritual movements such as Bhakti movements generated new spaces of self and societal realization, but it did not offer a direct political confrontation of governing regimes. In India, public spheres and civil societies have not manifested themselves primarily in political terms though in the public sphere itself participants had access to political rulers.[8] For S.N. Eisenstadt (2005), this contrasts with the Islamic public sphere that was driven by a primacy of the political. In Islamic public spheres and civil societies, a notion of political community was quite at the centre, but this community though autonomous was still much more tightly controlled by the ruling political formation compared with the case of state and civil society in the modern West. But what is striking is that although in Islamic civil society political community and its autonomy was a key concern, in actual terms in India without sharing this key preoccupation with the political people had a 'relatively widespread access to the political arena' (ibid.: 21) which makes the situation 'very close to the ideal model of European civil society' (ibid.: 19).

But unlike both the modern European and the Islamic case, in Indian engagement with civil society politics was not at the core. For Eisenstadt, 'The political arena, the arena of rulership, did not constitute in "historical India" – as it did in monolithic civilizations or in Confucianism – a major arena of the implementation of the transcendental visions predominant in this civilization' (ibid.: 20). Such a conception of the political was closely related to the theory and practice of sovereignty that developed in India. It emphasized 'the multiple rights – usually defined in terms of various duties – of different groups and sectors of society rather than a unitary, quasi-ontological conception – real or ideal – of "the state" or of "society" – giving rise to what can be defined as fractured sovereignty' (ibid.: 21). In the pregnant phase of Eisenstadt, this was a condition of 'non-ontologization of the political arena' (ibid.: 22).

The non-ontologization of the political and work of fractured sovereignty in Indian engagement with civil societies challenges us to rethink the primacy of the political and cult of sovereignty in our dominant conceptions of state and civil society. Instead of looking at the Indian case as an aberration, this challenges us to make our conceptions of civil society a multiverse. It also challenges us to rethink our bondage to a cult of sovereignty that dominates European modernity. Transforming Eisesntadt's perspective of fractured sovereignty, it can be said that civil society is not only a place of fractured sovereignties but also a place of shared sovereignties and sacred 'non-sovereignty' (cf. Dallmayr, 2005; Giri, 2008b). In order that civil society can be helpful in being a space of self-development and social transformation, the cult of absolute sovereignty at the level of state, society and self has to be transformed to a condition of shared sovereignties where all the interacting parties are interested to learn from each other in a spirit of mutual listening, co-labouring experiments, mutual interrogations and transformations. In this space, the interacting parties do not want to dominate each other with a will to power and mastery; instead they wish to serve each other for mutual growth and transformation. This second aspiration and activity makes this space a space of 'sacred non-sovereignty' (cf. Dallmayr, 2005) animated by a will to serve, nurture, share and co-create rather than a will to dominate.

Towards a New Understanding of the Activities and Aspirations of Civil Society

If civil society is a multi-dimensional space of autonomy and interpenetration, what are some of its activities, works and aspirations? I suggest that these are love, labour, language and rules/law.[9] To begin with the work of love in the sphere of civil society, Uberoi (1996) urges us to realize how loving self-sacrifice of the martyrs is crucial to the work of civil society.[10] For Uberoi, it is the martyr, rather than either the heroes or the victims, who constitutes the universal foundation of civil society. Although Uberoi has not discussed the barbaric misuse of ideology of martyrdom for annihilating men and women in religious traditions such as Sikhism and Islam, his emphasis on 'loving self-sacrifice' is an important contribution to rethinking the modernist emasculation of civil society. For instance, one cannot understand the work of martyrs such as Shankar Singh Guha Niyogi of *Chhattisgarh Mukti Morcha*[11], without understanding the dimension of loving self-sacrifice in civil society not only as a space of association and mediation but also as a site of struggle. As Chandhoke writes about Chhattisgarh Mukti Morcha,

> Despite the fact that CMM used only non-violent means of protest, such as peaceful demonstrations, *dharnas*, strikes, *morchas* and petitions – all of which are permissible in civil society – their protests were savagely put down. During a conversation with one of the CMM's leaders, I wondered whether it was not legitimate to use violence in a society where the regime virtually used violence against its own people. His answer was an emphatic no; violence, he argued, would impoverish the movement and denude it of any spirit of commitment. (Chandhoke, 2003b: 206)

Here, the struggle is both a political struggle of democratization of state and society and the spiritual struggle of realizing 'power-free' existence (cf. Dallmayr, 2001), that is, not being a slave to the logic of power and using the instruments of power to oppress other people. This struggle is animated by a hope that the subaltern would embody a different subjectivity and intersubjectivity and would not try to imbibe the same logic of dominant hegemony (Chakrabarty, 2002). It is no wonder then that Chhattisgarh Mukti Morcha strives for a new meaning of 'what it means to be a Chhattisgarhi citizen. According to CMM, a Chhattisgarhi citizen is one who works in the region and who does not exploit either the resources or the people for his or her personal benefit' (Chandhoke, 2003b: 238).[12]

The relationship between the work of love and work of civil society becomes clearer in an interesting essay by Veena Das (2003) titled, 'The small community of love'. For Das,

> One cannot base the little community of love on an appeal to law – you cannot wait, as Cavell says, for the perfect larger community before you form the smaller communities of love. Thus the constitutional promise about life, liberty, and pursuit of happiness has the public face of what it is to claim this in law and the private face of what it is to ask that human society contain the room for these small communities to be built.

Elaborating this Das further writes:

> In a conference I attended recently, someone asked if a song like, *Tu Hindu banega na Musalman banega – Insaan ki aulad hai insaan banega* from *Dhul ka Phul* was still possible. I thought of Mr. Insaniyat [humanity] and how he learnt that the claims of building small communities of love was also a way of learning to be Indian.

In his article, 'Romantic Archives: Literature and the Politics of Identity in Bengal', Dipesh Chakrabarty (2004: 682) also writes: '[…] What politics can we reconstitute out of our romantic investment in language?' The politics I have in mind, however, is not programmatic. The making of a romantic literary legacy into a political archive is not something that we can call into being. Romantic thoughts no longer furnish our analytical frameworks, but the inheritance of romanticism is built into the Bengali language. Our everyday and unavoidable transactions with the poetry of language may thus be compared with the practice of vigilant waiting. This vigilant and active waiting can itself be political – listen to the romantic voice of a Bengali communist poet who captures its spirit:

[...] When the rains depart
We will put out in the sun
Everything that is wet
Woodchips and all
Put out in the sun
We shall
Even our hearts.

Continuing our exploration of the relationship between the work of love and work of civil society, from a philosophical and theological perspective, Giani Vattimo (1999) tells us that we are all in need of forgiveness not because we have fallen in love but because we have failed in love. Such a recognition of failure in love helps us to be repentant for our lack of inability to transform situations of conflicts and avert many social tragedies. Given the significance of the work of reconciliation and forgiveness in many societies such as South Africa or India after the violence of apartheid or communal conflicts, the work of love is quite central in civil society organizations working on post-conflict reconciliation.

From the aspiration and work of love in the sphere of civil society, let us come to the work of labour. Civil society is not only a sphere of public deliberations and discursive argumentations, but it is also a sphere of lab or where labouring bodies come together and build new spaces of habitations and hopes. Gandhi's conception of bread labour helps us in understanding this link between the work of labour and work of civil society so does Swadhyaya's (a socio-spiritual movement in contemporary India) vision and practice of *shramabhakti* – devotional labour (cf. Giri, 2008a). In Swadhyaya, participants come together and build foundations of collective well-being such as digging village wells through shared devotional labour. This is similar to the work of Habitat for Humanity, a Christian socio-religious movement in the United States that works in many countries around the world, where volunteers of Habitat build houses together with prospective homeowners (Giri, 2002a).

As civil society is also a sphere of institutions, rules and laws are quite central here though it is important to acknowledge that civil society as a space of mobilization may challenge many of rules and laws within which civil society institutions may function.

Now to come to theme of language in the work of civil society, in many ways it is quite central as has been attested by theorists of civil society and public sphere such as Habermas (1989). A Habermasian perspective on civil society helps us understand the key importance of communication, especially communicative action, in the work of civil society. In history of India, we find struggle for people's languages beyond the language of the elites and the *pundits*. Movements such as Bhakti as well as contemporary Dalit (cf. Pandian, 1998; Narayan, 2001) have played an important role in creating people's languages and literatures that contributed to a new self-awareness among people as well as new themes and spaces of discursive deliberations about self, society and polity. For example, in Orissa, Sarala Das wrote the epic Mahabharata in Oriya and the Panchasakshas or the five friends such as Achyutananda

Das and Jagannatha Das in 16th centuries not only translated epics such as Ramayana into Oriya but also created life-elevating literature. They also contributed to building study centres known as *Bhagabata Ghara* for studying these works in villages (see Das, 1997). These reading spaces, though limited by caste and gender inequality, contributed to the generation of new spaces of conviviality and conversations. But while understanding the relationship between language and civil society in these manifold ways, it is helpful at the same time to acknowledge the limits of language in the work of civil society. The language of civil society may be a heritage to a dominant language of class and culture, and here overcoming the limits of the dominant language calls for multi-dimensional cultural, political and social transformations.[13] Although civil society is a sphere of critical deliberations, this very work itself calls for listening on the part of participating actors, and this in turn calls for the ability to cultivate silence in discursive argumentations.

Civil Society and the Calling of Self-Development

Although modernist discourse of civil society has been imprisoned within a predominantly statist and political model, it is Hegel himself who urges us to understand the link between civil society and self-development when he urges us to understand the significance of inner conscience in overcoming one's egotism in civil society (Dallmayr, 1993; Giri, 2002b). Hegel was aware of the crucial need for taming the civil society. Hegel strives to tame civil society through 'pedagogy or *bildung*' as well as by designing a 'system of institutional mediations to consolidate incipient bonds between individuals in civil society' (Chandhoke, 2003c: 130). Before Hegel, the proponents of Scottish Enlightenment, Adam Smith and Adam Ferguson, also urged us to understand the link between civil society and self-development. In this tradition of Scottish Enlightenment, 'the idea of civil society came to rest on the notion of autonomous and moral individual as standing at the foundation of social order' (Seligman, 1995: 215). This individual in Smith, in the first instance, 'tempered by the instinct for approbation, sobered by the desire to be seen as praiseworthy'; she is also guided by 'another consideration altogether, the workings of what Smith calls the "impartial spectator" ' (Chandhoke, 2003c: 106). The impartial spectator needs not only to have sympathy for what it observes but also 'compassion': 'The compassion of the spectator must arise altogether from the consideration of what he himself would feel if he were reduced to the same unhappy or happy situation' (ibid.: 110). Recently, Amartya Sen (2002) has argued that Adam Smith's notion of impartial spectator suggests a different pathway of justice (where the individual takes responsibility for justice) than the Rawlsian one. The space of civil society also calls for development of the ability to be impartial spectators in and among the actors.

This capacity to be 'impartial spectators' can be accompanied by efforts to put oneself in the shoes of the others through 'sympathy' and compassion. This is also suggested in Edward Shils' plea for development of virtues of civility. As Beteille interprets:

> In his characterization of civil society, Shils assigns some importance to the virtues of civility. Civil society cannot prosper unless its members are able to put themselves, at least to some extent, in the position of their political opponents and their social inferiors. It is in this view of the subject [...] the idea of civil society comes closest to that of good society. (Beteille, 2001: 291)

Along with putting oneself into the shoes of one's opponents or inferiors, participation in the space of civil society also calls for the ability to listen rather than just talk and argue, demonstrate one's performative competence in discursive argumentation. Although Habermasian approach to civil society and public sphere is open to the rise of post-conventional moral sensibility in self and society, Habermas has not paid enough attention to the need for cultivation of capacity for listening or generating appropriate social and ontological condition for listening. The challenge here is a deeper one as it calls for a foundational border crossing going beyond a valorized linguistic pragmatics and acknowledges the constitutive as well as continued significance of silence in the work of discourse itself.

Such a border-crossing engagement calls for going beyond the modernist conception of rational self and to realize what William Connolly (2001) calls 'plurivocity of being'. Habermasian self as that of Bourdieu, and most of us modernists, is mainly a techno-practitioner (cf. Faubion, 1995), and here we need to realize that self has also a transcendental dimension, that is, that aspect of self which establishes friendship and solidarity across boundaries, for example between self and other. This is suggested in Spinoza's conception of transindividuality (cf. Gatens and Llyod, 1999) and Roy Bhaskar's (2002) recent discussion of transcendentally real self as an inalienable dimension in the work of our everyday life. Self-development refers to development of all the dimensions of self – sociological as well as transcendental. Considered from this point of view of challenge of self-development, much work needs to be done in theory and practice as even scholars who put the challenge of self at the core seem to take it for granted. Consider here the following reflections of Uberoi and Mohanty. For Uberoi (2003: 124), 'In Gandhi's civil society the self would always look at the other in the eye as its second self, and offer dialogue and non-violent conversation without fear of the possible consequences.' For Mohanty (2003), 'In the conception of creative self every entity grants other entities status for seeking creative fulfilment. In other words, *it is not placed as Self vs. Other. It is in a framework of Self and Self*' (emphases in the original). But how does one treat other as self and oneself as another? Does it call for ontological as well as social processes of self-development? Uberoi and Mohanty do not discuss the process of self-development and inclusion of the other. Put briefly in tune with the multi-valued perspective of civil society presented earlier, such a mode of relationship on the part of self calls for ongoing practices of self-development on the part of actors and institutions facilitated by participation in love, labour, language and rules/laws.

Civil Society and Self-Development: Some Further Issues of Theory and Practice

Civil society as a space of creativity, public deliberation, self-cultivation, socio-political and socio-spiritual struggles calls for continued self-development on the part of actors and institutions. As has already been suggested, some of the challenges of self-development in the sphere of civil society are development of the capacity of listening, overcoming the logic of power and domination, creating a condition for critical reflection and establishing relations of non-duality, non-domination and non-violence not only between self and other but also as a foundation of social order. It should be clear that these are as much challenges for individuals as for institutions. Beteille looks at civil society as mainly consisting of mediating institutions but does not explore the challenge of self-development and transformations such as realization of a reflective space of mutual learning and listening and dialogical democracy that institutions of civil society face so that these institutions contribute to multi-dimensional self-realization of actors rather than repress or suppress them.

Voluntary organizations and social movements are an important part of civil society. Often these organizations suffer from the problem of entrenched authoritarianism, and here self-development calls for realization of dialogical democracy on the part of leaders and institutions. Those who work with them many a time are treated as bonded labourers, and their need for self-development are not given sufficient attention (cf. Giri, 2004). In my study of one such NGO, I found that the funds allocated for staff development in this remained unutilized for years. This organization at the same time continues to provide support to tribal people in their struggle against multinational mining companies at great risk to itself and its workers. According to one of the leaders of this organization, voluntary action has both a constructive and confrontational side, and when it confronts state and market, its decision of confrontation cannot be solely an organizational decision. If there is not enough preparation in courage, self-sacrifice and integral moral responsibility towards suffering humanity, it is difficult to be on the side of the people when actors are confronted with dire consequences (cf. ibid.).

Such a challenge of self-development confronts not only voluntary organizations but also social movements. Many a time, social movements work as hegemonic entities suppressing creative unfoldment of its participants. In this context, what Mohanty (2003: 17) writes deserves our careful consideration: 'Self here is perceived as a creative self and not an obsessive self or exclusivist assertion of an identity. [...] We have also seen people's movements functioning as monolithic movements not allowing democratic dissent within or not allowing freedom to the sub-groups within the movement.'

In the era of globalization, the challenge of self-development has more facets than just doing yoga. It requires personal knowledge of the shifting trajectories of state, market and the global system.[14] First of all, voluntary organizations, movements and institutions in civil society can learn from each other. Voluntary organizations in countries such as India are not condemned only to receive funds from such donor agencies as HIVOS from the Netherlands and ACTIONAID from the United Kingdom and execute programmes among the poor in their localities; they should come and study condition of poverty in the United Kingdom and the Netherlands thus creating a condition for reciprocal learning. There has to be more people-to-people contact and learning; and when it happens as in the global village program of Habitat for Humanity (cf. Giri, 2002b) or in the mutual visit of each other's group in the slum dwellers' association of South Asia, it creates condition for critical and reflective learning. As Arjun Appadurai (2002) tells us, when leaders from slum improvement associations of Karachi visit their counterparts in Mumbai, they ask questions about funding and transparency, which one does not ask so innocently in one's home locations. Such questions create an opportunity for critical self-reflection on the part of the host organization.

By Way of Conclusion

Self-development has been a neglected theme in the discourse of civil society. This paper has explored links between civil society and self-development, that is, how civil society has to contribute to self-development of individuals and institutions and how self-development is crucial to a revitalization of civil society. But understanding this link challenges us for a multi-dimensional and multi-valued understanding of civil society going beyond many modernistic dualisms such as private and public, tradition and modernity, civil society and good society and religion and secularism. Such a multi-valued understanding helps not only in a new understanding of civil society but also paths of Indian modernities in particular and global modernities in general. It also provides a new aspiration namely of self-development and social transformation for self and civil society to live and strive towards.

Notes

1 For Giddens (1994), sociology is part of the post-traditional telos of modernity; and for Beteille (2002), sociology is a modern, neither a postmodern nor a traditional discipline.

2 For example, following Max Weber, S.N. Eisenstadt, a key proponent of the multiple modernities approach, defines the core of modernity as the deconstruction of a God-ordained worldview held by all axial civilizations. 'Since modern societies are no longer embedded in meaningful transcendental orders, they are in principle open to continuous transformation and adaptation' (Eisenstadt, 2002: 10).

3 For Uberoi,

> The struggle to define and establish civil society in India during the modern period runs parallel to the rise, development and recognition of the vernaculars and vernacularism everywhere in language, labour and culture; and it is the story of religion and politics proceeding from Kabir (1440–1518) to the martyrdom of Mahatma Gandhi. (Uberoi, 2003: 123)

Uberoi himself says that civil society is not only a modernistic category, and we can explore struggles for Indian modernities and civil societies from the strivings of Buddha and his social struggles to build new critical spaces.

4 For Neera Chandhoke, 'Civil society is not an institution; it is, rather, a process whereby the inhabitants of the sphere [i.e., civil society] constantly monitor both the state and monopoly of power within itself' (Chandhoke, 2003a: 57). Chadhoke approaches civil society from the vantage point of continued mobilization though she seems to be stressing more political mobilization and less on reflective mobilization of self. Similarly, Oommen (2001a) has a mobilizational approach to civil society, whereas Beteille (2001) has a predominantly institutional approach. This dualism between mobilization and institutionalization needs to be overcome for a fuller understanding of civil society.

5 Beteille asks: 'How far do religious movements and assemblies for moral, ethical and spiritual discourses contribute to the formation of civil society?' and answers:

> They may contribute a very great deal to the formation of the good society, depending, of course, on what one means by that phrase [...] I remain skeptical about what religious assemblies and movements can contribute directly to the formation of civil society, although there indirect contribution may be extremely valuable. (Beteille, 2001: 307)

But for Oommen, '[...] religious organizations were very much part of civil society in pre-independent India' (Oommen, 2001a: 229). It is interesting to note here that both Uberoi and Oommen are not following any universalizing conception of modernity. Oommen (2001b) follows a 'multiple modernities' perspective in his work while Uberoi (2002) is one of the few proponents of Indian modernity.

6 This is similar to Uberoi's (1996) argument about Sikhism that it is a product of dialogue between Hinduism and Islam.

7 As John S. Hawley writes of Bhakti poets:

> These poets' intimate involvement with their audiences – in their own life times, doubtless, but certainly down the generation as subsequent performers and their audiences – have taken up these roles – is the real democracy of *bhakti* (Hawley, 2005: 332).

8 In this context, what Eisenstadt writes about Bhakti movements is insightful:

> Many of the visions promulgated by those movements emphasized equality, but it was above all equality in the cultural or religious arena, with respect to access to worship, and only to some extent in the definition of membership in the political community (Eisenstadt, 2005: 23).

9 This four-dimensional conceptualization can be compared with four dimensions of civil society articulated by Cohen and Arato (1992) – publicity, plurality, legality and privacy. There are no references to love and labour in this framework though the theme of privacy may touch upon the theme of love to

some extent. But the theme of love in the present model also refers to socially transforming love.

10 In his reflections on civil society, Uberoi (1996) is not within the modernist trap. He neither considers civil society as a product of modernist transition in history (though he would not discount its significance in understanding the contour that civil society has taken in modern past and present) nor does he look at it through the dominant logic of power.

11 Chhattisgarh Mukti Morcha is a multi-dimensional social movement of tribals and workers in the Chhattisgarh region of India fighting for dignity and rights and its leader Shankar Singh Guha Niyogi was gunned down at the behest of the contractors and industrialists of the region.

12 The anonymous reader of this chapter for *Sociological Bulletin* has raised the question of how appropriate it is to use this notion of 'Chhattisgarhi citizen'. Chandoke uses the word, but the way I understand the significance of such words is that it challenges us to realize a multi-layered conception of citizenship. We are not only citizens of our nation states, but we are also citizens of our significant communities of belonging including citizens of the world. Today, the rise of transnational civic movements and emergent discourse and practice of cosmopolitanism challenges us to realize the limits of nation state centered discourse and practice of citizenship. This also challenges us to go beyond a purely *etic* use and understanding of categories such as citizenship and have an *emic* perspective that emerges from dialogues with people in conversations.

13 In her essay, 'Language, Translation and Domination', Neera Chandhoke (2003c) speaks about the condition of tribals and their languages in the discourse of civil society in modern India. For a tribal, a particular piece of land belongs to him because the bones of his ancestors are buried there. But this language is not easily comprehensible in the dominant language of property rights that dominate state and civil society in modern India. The agents of state and civil society may negotiate with these subaltern languages, but they do so from the perspective of the dominant language. For Chandhoke (2003c: 195),

> […] the more powerful language in civil society does not even have to practice savageness to bludgeon, club or hammer the less powerful language into insensibility, which is something that Habermas fears, and the he attempts to ward off through discourse ethics. The deliberative space of civil society has already been colonized, already saturated with power that privileges certain ideas of land proprietorship.

14 In this context, what Mohanty writes deserves our careful consideration:

> The current historical situation is characterized by an ever-intensifying contradiction between hegemony and self-realisation. It manifests at every level, global, national and local in spatial terms and class, caste, race, ethnic, gender and such other terms of social relations. The former reflects struggles over political power vertically and the latter involves contests horizontally while all of them intersect at numerous levels. Global capitalism is the principal force whose influence decisively permeates all the contradictions at present. (Mohanty, 2003: 15)

References

Appadurai, Arjun (2002). 'Deep Democracy: Urban Governmentality and the Horizon of Politics', *Public Culture*, 14(1): 21–47.

Beteille, Andre (2001). 'Civil Society and Good Society', *Sociological Bulletin*, 50(2): 286–307.

——— (2002). *Sociology: Essays on Approach and Method*. New Delhi: Oxford University Press.

Bhaskar, Roy (2002). *Reflections on Meta-Reality: Transcendence, Everyday Life and Emancipations*. New Delhi: Sage Publications.

Chakrabarty, Dipesh (2002). *Habitations of Modernity: Essays on the Wake of Subaltern Studies*. Chicago: University of Chicago Press.

——— (2004). 'Romantic Archives: Literature and the Politics of Identity in Bengal', *Critical Inquiry*, 30(3): 654–83.

Chandhoke, Neera (2003a). 'A Critique of Civil Society as the Third Sphere', in Rajesh Tandon and Ranjita Mohanty (eds), *Does Civil Society Matter? Governance in Contemporary India*. New Delhi: Sage Publications, pp. 27–58.

——— (2003b). 'When the Voiceless Speak: A Case Study of the Chhattisgarh Mukti Morcha', in Tandon and Mohanty (2003), op. cit., pp. 198–242.

——— (2003c). *The Conceits of Civil Society*. New Delhi: Sage Publications.

Cohen, Jean and Andrew Arato (1992). *Civil Society and Political Theory*. Cambridge, MA: The MIT Press.

Connolly, William E. (2001). *The Ethos of Pluralization*. Minneapolis, MN: University of Minnesota Press.

Dallmayr, Fred (1993). *G.W.F. Hegel: Modernity and Politics*. Newbury Park, CA: Sage Publications.

——— (2001). *Achieving Our World: Toward a Global and Plural Democracy*. Lanham, MD: Rowman & Littlefield.

——— (2005). *Small Wonder: Global Power and Its Discontents*. Lanham, MD: Rowman & Littlefield.

Das, Chittaranjan (1997 [1951]). *Achyutananda O Panchasakha Dharma* [*Achyutananda and the Religion of the Panchasakhas*]. Cuttack: S.B. Publications.

Das, Veena (2003). 'Small Community of Love'. http://www.india-seminar.com/2003/525/525%20veena%20das.htm.

Eisenstadt, S.N. (2005). 'Civil Society and Public Sphere in a Comparative Perspective', *Polish Sociological Review*, 27 October, 154: 143–66.

Faubion, James D. (ed.) (1995). *Rethinking the Subject: An Anthology of Contemporary European Social Theory*. Boulder, CO: Westview Press.

Gatens, Moira and Genevieve Lloyd (1999). *Collective Imaginings: Spinoza, Past and Present*. London: Routledge.

Giri, Ananta Kumar (2002a). *Building in the Margins of Shacks: The Vision and Projects of Habitat for Humanity*. New Delhi: Orient Longman.

——— (ed.) (2002b). 'Rethinking Civil Society', in *Conversations and Transformations: Towards a New Ethics of Self and Society*. Lanham, MD: Lexington Books, pp. 287–314.

——— (2004). *Reflections and Mobilizations: Dialogues with Movements and Voluntary Organizations*. New Delhi: Sage Publications.

——— (2008a). *Self-Development and Social Transformations? The Visions and Experiments of the Socio-Spiritual Mobilizations of Swadhyaya*. Lanham, MD: Lexington Books/Rawat Publications.

——— (ed.) (2008b). 'Introduction', in *The Modern Prince and the Modern Sage: Transforming Power and Freedom*. New Delhi: Sage Publications.

Gupta, Dipankar (1997). *Rivalry and Brotherhood: Politics in the Life of Farmers in Northern India*. New Delhi: Oxford University Press.

Habermas, Jurgen (1981). *Philosophical-Political Profiles*. Cambridge: Polity Press.

——— (1989). *The Structural Transformation of the Public Sphere*. Cambridge, MA: The MIT Press.

——— (1990). *Moral Consciousness and Communicative Action*. Cambridge: Polity Press.

Hawley, John Stratton (ed.) (2005). 'Bhakti, Democracy and the Study of Religion', in *Three Bhakti Voices: Mirabai, Sur Das, and Kabir in Their Times and Ours*. New Delhi: Oxford University Press.

Hefner, Robert W. (ed.) (1998). 'On the History and Cross-Cultural Possibility of a Democratic Political Ideal', in *Democratic Civility: The History and Cross-Cultural Possibility of a Modern Political Ideal*. New Brunswick, NJ: Transaction Books, pp. 3–49.

Mitsuo, Nakamura (2001). 'Introduction', in Nikamura Mitsuo, Sharon Siddique and Omar Faroul Bajunid (eds), *Islam and Civil Society in South East Asia*. Singapore: Institute of South East Asian Studies, pp. 1–30.

Mohanty, Manoranjan (2002). 'The Self as Center in the Emerging World of the Twenty-first Century: A Sino-Indian Perspective', *China Report*, 38(1): 1–10.

——— (2003). 'Creative Self and Its Enemies in the Emerging World', *Gandhian Perspectives*, X1(1&2): 15–21.

Narayan, Badri (2001). *Documenting Dissent: Contesting Fables, Contesting Memories and Dalit Political Discourse*. Shimla: Indian Institute of Advanced Studies.

Oommen, T.K. (2001a). 'Civil Society: Religion, Caste and Language in India', *Sociological Bulletin*, 50(2): 221–235.

——— (2001b). 'Multiple Modernities and the Rise of New Social Movements: The Case of India', *Indian Social Science Review*, 3(1): 1–16.

Pandian, M.S.S. (1998). 'Stepping Outside History? New Dalit Writings from Tamil Nadu', in Partha Chatterjee (ed.), *Wages of Freedom: Fifty Years of the Indian Nation-State*. New Delhi: Oxford University Press, pp. 292–309.

Sachsenmaier, Dominic and Jens Reidel with Shmuel Eisenstadt (eds) (2002). *Reflections on Multiple Modernities: European, Chinese and other Interpretations*. Leiden: Brill.

Seligman, Adam (1995). 'Animadversions Upon Civil Society and Civic Virtue in the Last Decade of the Twentieth Century', in John A. Hall (ed.), *Civil Society: Theory, History, Comparison*. Cambridge: Polity Press.

Sen, Amartya (2002). 'Justice Across Borders', in Pablo De Greiff and Ciaran Cronin (eds), *Global Justice and Transnational Politics: Essays on the Moral and Political Challenges of Globalization*. Cambridge, MA: The MIT Press, pp. 37–51.

Uberoi, J.P.S. (1996). *Religion, Civil Society and State: A Study of Sikhism*. New Delhi: Oxford University Press.

——— (2002). *The European Modernity: Truth, Science and Method*. New Delhi: Oxford University Press.

——— (2003). 'Civil Society', in Veena Das (ed.), *Oxford India Companion to Sociology and Social Anthropology*. New Delhi: Oxford University Press, pp. 114–33.

Vattimo, Giani (1999). *Belief*. Cambridge: Polity Press.

3

Civil Society, Political Society and Citizenship in India

Pradip Kumar Bose

Idea of Civil Society and Its Forms in India

The conventional understanding of civil society is to describe it as a sphere of human activity that is outside or apart from the structures of states and governments and in which free individuals form voluntary associations and establish pluralistic relations based on affinities and common interests rather than coercion. The distinction between state and civil society is an old one, but it can take very different and contradictory forms. Before coming to the question of recent resurgence of interest in civil society in India, let us recall that in routine discussions in liberal theory the coexistence between the civil society and the state was largely non-problematic. For the theorists of social contract in the West from Hobbes to Rousseau, the institution of civil society and the state puts an end to the war of every man against every man, which, as Hobbes said, characterizes the condition of nature. Lock in his classic description argued that men are born free, equal and independent, but they forego that natural freedom and put on 'the bonds of civil society' for harmonious living with one another. When individuals agree to enter civil society, they adopt the principle of majority rule; they are at liberty to leave civil society, but doing so means living in a state of nature that leaves them free but without any defence against others.

A rather different conception of civil society emerges from the Hegelian and Marxist tradition, which views it as something antithetical to the state, a popular view among Indian social and political scientists. For Hegel, civil society is a market society in which individuals enter into complex networks of production and exchange. German for civil society is *burgerliche Gesellschaft*, where the adjective *burgerliche* means 'civil', 'civic' and also 'middle-class bourgeois' and *Gesellschaft* (society) is any amicable association, whether temporary or enduring. Later, it has been used for the 'social order'. Tonnies later distinguished *Gesellschaft*, an organic community based on shared rules, affection, etc. (cf. Durkheim's distinction between 'mechanical' and 'organic' solidarity). For Hegel, civil society is a social formation intermediate between the family and the state. However, the danger is that the divergent interests at work in civil society will transform it into an indiscriminate multitude of individuals with conflicting and irreconcilable interests. The role of the state, defined as the embodiment of the principle of rationality, is to reconcile these divergent interests. According to Hegel, the ultimate destiny of civil society is its absorption into the rational state, which is 'actuality of ethical idea'. The state for Hegel is not an instrument of coercion (as Weber and Marx, saw it), but rather the epitome of ethical realization.

Marx both draws on and criticizes the Hegelian account of civil society. Defined by Marx as the site of crass materialism, modern property relations, the struggle of each against all, and egotism, civil society arose, he insists from the destruction of medieval society. Previously, individuals were part of various societies, such as guilds or estates, each of which had a political role, so that there was no separate civil realm. As these partial societies broke down, civil society with its property relations necessitates a type of politics that does not reflect this conflict but is abstracted and removed from it. The modern state is made necessary (and at the same time limited) by the characteristics of civil society. An important Marxist contribution to the theory of civil society is that made by Gramsci, who argues that state should be understood as meaning not only the apparatus of government but also 'private' sphere or the complex of structures in which the battle is waged for hegemony or for cultural and ideological domination.[1] The superstructures of civil society are the site for a war of positions between the conflicting classes brought into being by capitalism.

In India, the conceptions of civil society appear in different guises and have taken manifold forms. It has been associated with social movements, cultural associations and affirmative action; and consequently, the term has taken on a variety of meaning and connotation. However, instead of dismissing this proliferation of conceptions and interpretations as populist and superficial, it is profitable to view the contemporary debate around the concept in terms of the options now available to citizens of India. This can tell us a great deal about the sociology of our times as it allows us to reflect on the limits of liberalism in an age when there is a general disenchantment with the state. In India, sociologists have pointed out that interest civil society comes from the state's inability to deliver the fruits of development to the poor and marginal populations. Hence, civil society in India, according to some experts, resides among the poor and downtrodden.[2] One of the foremost exponents of this position, Rajni Kothari, argues that in India the government has stifled the initiatives of the poor and marginals by relying on a 'techno-managerial' structure, and it is with this section that impulses towards civil society lie.[3] In a similar vein, Ashis Nandy points out that with the hegemony of the Western educated elites in Indian state, people with indigenous cultural moorings are marginalized and often face hostility from the state.[4] Hence, civil society should protect the rich diversities among communities and oppose the state's grand homogenization project, which is carried out in the name of modernization. Civil society thus becomes identified with tradition and ascriptive bonds, a notion that is much different from the Western conception of civil society.

Andre Beteille and Gurpreet Mahajan, on the contrary, associate civil society with a set of institutions that are *open* and *secular*.[5] Beteille opts for a Tocquevillian notion of civil society and takes his cue from the Tocquevillian conception of intermediate institutions free of both church and state. In the Indian context, he argues that these institutions should be free from state control and traditional loyalties, both strong presences in the subcontinent. Hence for Beteille, civil society is made of institutions such as universities, hospitals, judicial courts, economic corporations and the like. For Beteille, these institutions function like buffers against the state that would amass excessive power. In his view, these institutions should not be cramped by the logic of state politics or sway by primordial loyalties but function according to their own rules. Unbiased functioning of such institutions can promote social development and justice, Beteille believes. Critics, however, point out that such institutions are part and parcel of a liberal polity, but liberal polity and ideology are not the only forces fashioning institutions of civil society. In other words, Beteille and Mahajan identify partial aspect of civil institutions as their entire aspect, and thereby produce a disjunction between the set of actually existing civil institutions and the civil society.[6]

It has been argued that even if the liberal conception of civil society is accepted, such a conception needs to be understood by confronting it to the actuality of civil institutions as they have developed historically in liberal societies. We have noted earlier the limitations of liberal idea of civil society as pointed out by Hegel, Marx and Gramsci. In India, liberal polity has been functional for about six decades now; however, liberalism here is severely constrained by a county's feudal past and colonial heritage. The idea of abstract citizenship remains weak and bereft of any unifying principle here. The vast majority of people, who do not enjoy even formal political rights, are outside the civil society of liberal polity. Hence, fight of people against the state takes the form of direct struggle unmediated by civil society and often expressed in the language of human rights. Now many call this arena of struggle itself as civil society.

Civil Society and Citizenship

In the 1970s, the political theorists announced the demise of the concept of citizenship, and some even stated confidently that 'the concept of citizenship has gone out of fashion among political thinkers.'[7] In more recent times, discussions on the impact of globalization on the citizenship question have tended to argue that globalization is eroding the capacity for meaningful democratic citizenship at the domestic level, as nation-states lose some of their historic sovereignty and become 'decision-takers' as much as 'decision-makers'. Meaningful citizenship in an era of globalization would require democratizing these transnational institutions that are increasingly responsible for important economic, environmental and security decisions.[8] The general argument is that globalization reduces the historic sovereignty of nation-states, and therefore undermines the meaningfulness of participation in domestic politics.

In the post-colonial nation states, the situation is further compounded by the fact that civil society is a fraught term in political debates. Suspicions have been raised about its applicability outside the liberal discourse and actual political context of Western democracies and also about its emancipatory potential. There is a belief that civil society is an underdeveloped or at least distinctively different phenomenon in post-colonial societies. Arguments have been made about the 'differences' of civil society in India as it emerges from colonial rule and the construction of communities. For instance, there is an argument that in post-independent India, communal movements, deploying cultural terms relating to language, ethnicity, caste and religion resemble and usurp the space of a civil society. The argument considers communalism today to be a feature of India's post-colonial public sphere – a domain of representation and contestation that lies between modern state and civil society.[9] Others argue that 'the colonial state produced only a civil society of subjects, not citizens so that the colonized can construct their national identities within a different narrative, that of community.'[10] The argument goes that in post-independent India, the conditions for a proper civil society formation do not exist, and community formation takes, rather, the form of *political society*, the difference being that in a civil society people have active citizenship rights – lacking these, they negotiate with the state and its agencies for resources of livelihood and survival as a 'political' community.[11] As Partha Chatterjee writes:

> For the majority of people in post-colonial societies, the normative status of the virtuous citizen will remain infinitely deferred until such time as they can be provided with the basic material and cultural prerequisites of membership of civil society. Until the arrival of that liberal millennium, however, they can deal with a governmental system with the resources they can muster in political society .... Community has a very tenuous place in the western liberal theory of civil society and state; in the new political societies of the East, communities are some of the most active agents of political practice.[12]

Others have also argued that the dispossessed in India who are engaged in 'direct struggles against the state' for their rights are not organized as a civil society or mediated by its institutions, and therefore must not be confused with normative civil society. Sanjay Kumar, for instance, writes that since the state routinely tramples upon the basic rights of the people, the struggle takes the form of human rights struggle and often labelled as the arena of civil society; but, he writes, this 'conception of civil society should clearly be distinguished from the civil society associated with liberal polity in which sections with social power participate.'[13]

Population, Political Society and Governmental Practices

The emergence of mass democracies in the West has produced a new distinction between the citizen and population; while the citizen connotes rights, political participation and ethics, the concept of population is descriptive and empirical; it is not a normative idea. Populations are amenable to statistical technique and available to the government as a target of its policies. Population is not conceived of as a collection of subjects of right, but it provides a hold for concerted intervention. Population appears as the end and instrument of government and signify a regime dominated not by structures of sovereignty but by techniques of government, which revolves around population. As Michel Foucault points out, one important characteristics of contemporary regime of power is a certain 'governmentalization of state'. In such a regime, the participating citizens are not really important for legitimacy, but an instrumentalist state using governmental technologies as a mode of development of population. Therefore, the first question is, how do we understand 'population' in India, and how is government of population related to the question of development? Historically, when population appeared as the final end of government, the end was understood as the ways to improve the condition of population to increase its wealth, its longevity and its health. Amongst other things, management of population required a health policy capable of reducing the infant mortality rate, preventing epidemics and lowering the rates of endemic diseases, intervening to modify and impose norms on living conditions (in a matter of diet, housing or town planning) and adequate medical facilities. The disciplines such as public hygiene and social medicine treated 'population' as a set of coexisting living beings with particular biological and pathological features, which needed to be understood in terms of specific forms of knowledge and technique. In other words, we see a series consisting of security, population and government. But as I have argued elsewhere, today the modern state by making security its sole concern has ultimately produced a regime where law and violence become indistinguishable.[14]

There has been an argument that in India, we can think of two different axes, *civil society–citizenship* and *political society–population*, when one deals with the question of democracy and development. It has been argued that in India, the colonial state produced only a civil society of subjects and not citizens so that the colonized can construct their national identities within a different narrative, that of community.[15] In the post-independent India, the argument goes, the conditions for a proper civil society formation do not exist, and community formation takes, rather, the form of *political society*, the difference being that in a civil society people have active citizenship rights – lacking these, they negotiate with the state and its agencies for resources of livelihood and survival as a 'political' community.[16] For instance, Chatterjee writes: 'Community has a very tenuous place in the Western liberal theory of civil society and state; in the new political societies of the East, communities are some of the most active agents of political practice.'[17] He describes the formation of a community of poor migrants in Calcutta who are illegal squatters on public land. Because of the uncertainty of habitation, survival needs and fear of eviction, the community was built, mainly, as defensive strategy. There are other networks built around the community, which are utilized in securing work or financial help. In fact, when the squatters were threatened with eviction, this was resisted by the concerted efforts of community as a whole; the demands for livelihood and habitation are made as collective right, which the migrants claim are need of the community.

This is an urban community that conducts its life not as citizens belonging to civil society, but as a political society negotiating claims and benefits with governmental agencies. The strategy of such urban communities, which do not have any citizenship rights, must exploit; 'on the one hand, the political obligations that governments have of looking after poor and underprivileged sections of the population; and on the other hand, the moral rhetoric of a community striving to build a decent social life under extreme harsh conditions.'[18] Thus, the imaginative power of traditional structure of community, its capacity to invent kinship relations, is integrated to modern idea of equality. In the post-colonial societies, people lacking substantive citizenship rights and active civil society participation, it is in the new political societies that communities have turned out to be some of the most active agents of political practice. Unlike in the West, the important feature of this strategic politics of the communities has been the issues of autonomy and representation, demanded not only for individuals but also for communities. This politics has been viewed by the communitarians as a desire for democratization, which is not carried out in the classical model of state and civil society, but in political societies of today.

In a study of identity politics and urban violence in Mumbai, it has also been shown that 'political society' had been the preferred domain of parties such as Shiv Sena.[19] For Shiv Sena, political society was the realm of mobilization, public protest and public violence, and it was the realm that enabled wider sections of Indian society to participate in politics. However, Hansen points out that political society has also promoted competing forms of sovereignty to grow and diversity in a manner that has challenged the sovereignty of the state.[20] In more general terms, political society in India acts itself out in an unruly, unpredictable manner; it is a theatre of ritualized violence and ritualized destruction of public property. As Hansen writes:

> political society in contemporary India is not about generating new rules; its primary drive is to contest existing rules in the broadest sense, to defy the law, and, most important, to make a community or cause as visible as possible in order to claim certain benefits, public services, or entitlements for that community or cause.[21]

As we have seen before, there has been an argument for making a distinction between *state–civil society–citizen*, on the one hand, and *community–political society–population*, on the other hand, where the state is governed by rationality and legality, and the other domain governed by forms of community and other local authorities. The study of Mumbai, however, shows that it is difficult to maintain a clear distinction between state and community or state and political society. Rather, it has been suggested that imperatives of political society force the state constantly to reinvent itself, and thus the process implies that the notion of Indian state as capable of resolving conflict, providing entitlements or stabilizing community identities through official recognition is no longer certain or stable.

A similar study of urban slum dwellers of Mumbai shows how poor communities are able to engage in partnerships with more powerful agencies that purport to be concerned with poverty and citizenship. Arjun Appadurai calls this phenomenon 'deep democracy', where in the era of globalization one can see an attempt to institute what we may call 'democracy without borders'.[22] The slum dwellers of Mumbai seek direct cross-national collaborations and exchanges among poor communities based on 'will to federate' and try to produce through this horizontal movement a series of stronger community-based partners for poverty reduction and development. The other interesting feature of the development of urban poor communities described by Appadurai is the adoption of self-enumeration and self-surveying technique. Generally, the state-sponsored slum policies have an abstract slum population as their target; at the same time since these populations are marginal in all sense of the term, they are uncounted and uncountable. By self-enumeration, they make visible to themselves. Since the social life of slums is in fact characterized by an almost complete lack of privacy, Appadurai writes, 'here, perpetual social visibility within the community (an invisibility in the eyes of the state) becomes an asset that enables the mechanisms of self-monitoring, self-enumerating, and self-regulation to operate at the nexus of family, land, and dwelling that is the central site of material negotiations in slum life'.[23] Appadurai calls this system as governmentality from below, although this may also be seen as a worrisome form of auto-governmentality, a combination of self-surveillance and self-enumeration.

How do we understand the series population – political society – government? Can we characterize the transaction and strategic politics of political society with its ambiguous terrain as politics of democratization? Or do we see in this a regime of power-making strategic conciliatory moves towards an excluded people?

Community and Civil Society

The thesis that language of community, in the post-colonial societies, articulating the demands of the majority of population and in effect restricting the arena of civil society, is somewhat problematic for several reasons. In the Western communitarian discourse, the community remains the repository of tradition, culture and values; it provides anchorage, meaning and identity to the individual's life – and the community is threatened by the state, market and economy. This is the classical sociological position elaborated by Tonnies. In India, critiques of modernity have focused on the failure of Indian state to recognize the centrality of community in everyday practices. However, they identify the colonial discourse and its discursive practices as the major source of modern community identities. The question remains as to how the identities continue to be politically constructed in the post-independent India. The general argument of the constructivist position highlights the rigidities of community identities produced by the colonial and the post-colonial state in India as the source of negotiation, demand and conflict. Since communities are constructed by the technologies of the government, the structure of modern government carries with it seeds of conflict. However, these identities in which people are forced into for negotiating with state are not real; they do not represent real communities. The real community lies submerged in the everyday practices, the fuzzyness of boundaries, whose authenticity has been denied and suppressed by the all-powerful state. It is in this sense that the constructivist perspective fall back on a variant of the age-old substantive concept of community.

Chatterjee argues that the concept of community is under-theorized in the East. Western theories posed an opposition between community as the relic of the pre-modern tradition and large, universalist and impersonal political identities as the hallmark of modernity. The nationalist project, borrowing the categories of opposition posed the difference as between Western materialism, individualism and Eastern spiritualism and community solidarity, and argued that the latter represented a more appropriate version of modernity for non-Western national states. In doing this, Chatterjee argues that nationalists played out the same argument that we witness in the liberal–communitarian debate. He argues that community in the East, thus theoretically remained narrow and impoverished. As he puts it, the task is to find 'an adequate conceptual language to describe ... the history of different modernities by practices and institutions that the universalist claims of western political theory have failed to encompass'.[24] The kind of collectivity in contemporary India that he illustrates with the example of squatters settlement do not conform to the standards of civil association or 'non-fuzzy' groups within the civil society but invoke 'imaginative power of a traditional structure of community, including its fuzziness and capacity to invent relations of kinship'.[25] However, it is possible to argue against the logic of labelling such a collectivity as a community and differentiating it from other kinds of political groups. More importantly, we can point out that in this formulation, the substantivist understanding of the community has been retained and the nature of this community remains uninterrogated. However, uninterrogated community in this literature continues to be regarded as the primary site of sociality and agent of political action. While the constructivist conception of community attempts to historicize the formation communities, social identities and their political constitution, the substantivist community continues to be an enduring element in this literature.

It is at this point that we can come back again to the question of civil society and citizenship. In the Western tradition, the origins of the modern citizen are necessarily associated with the idea of civil society. This civil society required the state as the institution that would historically regulate and control the tensions within civil society. Many scholars of citizenship have pointed out the issue of the cultural and historical specificity of civil society and citizenship in Western social and political theory. In other words, different social and political contexts would give rise to different types of civil society or arguments about civil society. The civil society here is associated with mediating institutions that are open and secular, which link individuals with state. Civil society here is an association of free citizens with rights, but here property ownership was a crucial criterion of freedom. Therefore, it is argued that liberalism has promoted the idea of civil society as bourgeois society in the sense used by Hegel and Marx. Marx objected to the notion that social membership and social participation could be defined merely in political or legal terms without a revolutionary transformation of the very basis of civil society.

There is, however, a more popular view of civil society in India, where civil society is defined in opposition to the state. Here civil society members and groups stand against the statist power and intervene to restrict the power of the state. Often general disenchantment with state forms the backdrop to the revival of interest in civil society. In this sense, civil society is linked to movements, protests and assertion of rights. As Dipankar Gupta has pointed out in India, interest in civil society comes from the state's inability to deliver the fruits of technology and modernization to the average citizen.[26] To recapitulate our argument, while some have argued that the task of the civil society is to protect diversities among communities against the state's homogenization project, some have even associated with tradition and ascriptive bonds. Others have argued that civil–social institutions be free from state control and traditional loyalties and should act against the state from acquiring excessive power. In this sense, the civil society is viewed not as integral to a democratic constitutional state; they are intermediate institutions, having their own rules.[27] These rules would promote rational efficiency; But such a view of civil society may be indifferent to considerations of citizenships, and thus the state may be let off the hook. Because if the intermediate institutions assume rational organizational forms and are internally efficient, they are fulfilling their purpose.

The other view considers that the state regularly violates the rights and liberties of the people, and it is within the arena of civil society that marginalized protest and struggle for their essential human and democratic rights. This view considers civil society as the domain for popular participation outside the formal institutional structure of the state. Participation in civil society activities thus prepares the way for empowering the common man and offers them the means for better citizenship rights. For instance, Rajni Kothari believes that civil society is a 'take-off point for human governance' and to restore the principles of citizenship and good life civil society operates through a variety of social movements. Here civil society incorporates a 'network of voluntary, self-governing institutions in all walks of life'.[28] For Kothari, these organizations provide the grass-roots model of mass politics in which people are more important than the state. In this model, civil society is viewed as a domain that allows people to participate directly, and it is associated with the people-centric institutions that stand outside the state and offer alternative political spaces.

In other words, the concept of civil society is inevitable if we are to understand the nature of citizenship and self-understanding of relevant actors in the post-colonial societies. One might argue that civil society itself has emerged as a new kind of utopia that includes a range of complementary forms of democracy and a complex set of civil, social, and political rights that must be compatible with modern differentiation of society. But this tendency also reveals that sympathetic theorists are still oriented by the utopian ideals of modernity. In associating civil society with citizenship question, we argue that civil society should be seen not only in a passive fashion as a network of institutions but also actively as the context and product of self-constituting collective actors. It is also possible that social movements, empowerment and initiatives of citizens or proto-citizens through civil society are capable of influencing political culture without entry into the field of power politics.

Notes

1. Antonio Gramsci, *Selections from the Prison Notebooks of Antonio Gramsci* (translated and edited by Quintin Hoare and Geoffrey Nowell-Smith). London: Lawarence and Wishart, 1971.
2. Dipankar Gupta, 'Civil Society in Indian Context: Letting the State Off the Hook', *Contemporary Sociology*, Vol. 26, No. 3, 1997, p. 305.
3. Rajni Kothari, *State against Democracy: In Search of Human Governance*. New Delhi: Ajanta, 1988.
4. Ashis Nandy, *The Romance of the State and the Fate of Dissent in the Tropics*. New Delhi: Oxford University Press, 2002.
5. Andre Beteille, 'The Idea of Civil Society', *Biblio*, February 1996, pp. 21–22; *Civil Society and Its Institutions*. Calcutta: USEFI (The First Fullbright Memorial Lecture), 1996; 'The Conflict of Norms and Values in Contemporary Indian Society', in Peter L. Berger (ed.), *The Limits of Social Cohesion*. Boulder, CO: Westview Press, 1998, pp. 265–92; 'Citizenship, State and Civil Society', *Economic and Political Weekly*, 4 September 1999, pp. 2588–91; Gurpreet Mahajan, 'Civil Society and Its Avtars: What Happened to Freedom and Democracy'? *Economic and Political Weekly*, 15 May 1999, pp. 1188–99; 'Civil Society, State and Democracy', *Economic and Political Weekly*, 4 December 1999, pp. 3471–72.
6. Sanjay Kumar, 'Civil Society in Society', *Economic and Political Weekly*, 29 July 2000, pp. 2776–79.
7. Herman van Gunstern, 'Notes on a Theory of Citizenship', in Pierre Birnbaum, Jack Lively and Geraint Parry (eds), *Democracy, Consensus and Social Contract*. London: Sage Publications, 1978, p. 9.
8. David Held, *Democracy and the Global Order: From the Modern State to Cosmopolitan Governance*. London: Polity Press, 1995.
9. Sandra B. Freitag, 'Contesting in Public: Colonial Legacies and Contemporary Communalism', in David Ludden (ed.), *Making India Hindu: Religion, Community and the Politics of Democracy in India*. New Delhi: Oxford University Press, 1996.
10. Partha Chatterjee, *The Nation and Its Fragments: Colonial and Post-Colonial Histories*. New Delhi: Oxford University Press, 1994, p. 236.
11. Partha Chatterjee, 'Community in the East', *Economic and Political Weekly*, 7 February 1998, pp. 277–82.
12. Ibid., p. 282.
13. Kumar, 'Civil Society in Society', p. 2779.

14. Pradip Kumar Bose, 'Security and the Democratic Paradox', in Samir Kumar Das and Rada Ivekovic (eds.), *Terror, Terrorism, States and Societies: A Historical and Philosophical Perspective*. New Delhi: Women Unlimited, 2010.
15. Chatterjee, *Nation and Its Fragments*, p. 236.
16. Chatterjee, 'Community in the East'.
17. Ibid., p. 282.
18. Ibid., p. 281.
19. Thomas Blom Hansen, *Urban Violence in India: Identity Politics, 'Mumbai' and the Postcoloniality*. New Delhi: Permanent Black, 2001.
20. Ibid., p. 229.
21. Ibid., p. 230.
22. Arjun Appadurai, 'Deep Democracy: Urban Governmentality and Horizon of Politics', *Public Culture*, Vol. 14, No. 1, 2002, pp. 21–47.
23. Ibid., p. 36.
24. Chatterjee, 'Community in the East', p. 279.
25. Ibid., p. 281.
26. Gupta, 'Civil Society in Indian Context'.
27. Beteille, 'Citizenship, State and Civil Society', pp. 2588–91.
28. Kothari, *State against Democracy*, p. 202.

4

Civil Society in India and the Dynamics of Democratization

Anand Kumar

In the social sciences, there is no consensus as to the theoretical and empirical separation of political, economic and social elations. The shifting meaning of the concept of 'civil society' indicates changing theoretical attitudes towards the relationship between economy, society, and state.

Dictionary of Sociology (2006)[1]

Civilization is that mode of conduct which points to man the path of duty. Performance of duty and observance of morality are convertible terms. To observe morality is to attain mastery over our mind and our passions. So doing, we observe ourselves. The Gujarati equivalent for civilization means 'good conduct'.

Gandhi in *Hind Swaraj* (1909)[2]

Civil society flourishes not under totalitarian regimes but under liberal, pluralist and secular regimes, and it is a defining feature of the latter that they accommodate diverse conceptions of the good society. A theocratic regime accommodates only believers, whereas a secular regime accommodates unbelievers as well as believers, and believers of different religions. A totalitarian regime accommodates partisans only of a particular political cause; a liberal regime accommodates partisans of different political causes. The framework within which I seek to understand civil society has three basic components. These are: (a) the state, (b) citizenship, and (c) mediating institutions.

Andre Beteille (2000)[3]

Introduction

The expression 'civil society' is commonly used to describe a sphere of human activity that is outside or apart from the structures of states and governments and in which free individuals form voluntary associations and establish pluralistic relations based on affinities and common interests rather than coercion. There has been duality in the relationship between the state and the civil society in the history of modern Europe. There are two strong traditions in the patterning of linkages between the state and the civil society in recent European history. In the context of the theories of social contract, the evolution of civil society is closely linked with the formation of modern state. They together have contributed in 'putting an end to the war of all against all' and transformed the human beings from the state of natural freedom to the 'bonds of civil society'. The classics of Hobbes, Rousseau and Alexis de Tocqueville provide an intimate view of this process associated with the European renaissance. On the contrary, there has been a different approach about the emergence of civil society in the traditions of Hegel–Marx–Gramsci. There is an assumption of a dialectical relationship between the state and the civil society around conflict of interests among the classes of individuals. In the post-colonial and post-communist world order, some of the social scientists have come forward to argue beyond these two major traditions and suggest that civil society is an essential imperative of liberal democracy, which is based on the citizen's need for keeping a check on the state and is also protected by the state for promoting active citizenship as a guarantee against religious fundamentalist group and authoritarian political forces.[4]

In historical terms, the roots of civil society traditions in India go back to Kabir and the other Bhakti Movement poet-philosophers and social reformers between the 14th and 19th centuries. They spread awareness about the need to stay away from the state power and the religious establishment as both have coercive approach towards people and society. Therefore, it is important to stay away from both in order to experience the life of peace, dignity and happiness through the promotion of love and kindness among fellow human beings. Gandhi represented this trend in the Indian culture during the modern era. The disenchantment with the role of religious community organizations during the partition of India (1946–47) and the post-colonial communal conflicts, and the shocking confrontation with the authoritarian tendencies inherent in the modern state system during the emergency years (1975–77), have been the two major phases in the 20th century, which have contributed towards the enlargement of civil society-related processes, formations and networks in contemporary India.

The Indian version of the concept of civil society has the following distinct features (as reflected in the quotation of Gandhi in the beginning of this chapter): (i) it assumes that the human beings are equipped with the capacity of moral evolution and goodness; (ii) society is a system in existence due to love force and not fear of the king or priests; (iii) religion should be approached as a source of good conduct rather than a body of rigid customs, rituals and identities; and (iv) the Western civilization, as represented by the British in India, is a non-sustainable God-less way of life around greed for power and other material things. There has been a demystification of the limits of the state-centric models of 'good governance' and market-oriented approach of machine-based 'material progress'. Therefore, there is very limited 'genetic' or historical affinity between the Indian approach to civil society and the Hobbsian or Hegelian orientation about the idea of civil society. But it has shared (i) the historical context of the making of modern state system, the citizenship and the interlinking secular structures and (ii) the intellectual agenda of the European thinkers associated with it as it was an engagement to find the possibility of a social order beyond the family and the state and also without the princes and the priests.

The J.P.-Led Protest Movement and the Emergency Era as the Turning Point

There has been a phenomenal growth of civil society initiatives and organizations in India since the 1970s, which coincided with nationwide people's unrests, particularly the J.P.-led movement for Total Revolution between 1973 and 1979. It had a great appeal among youth and students and social activists of Gujarat and Bihar in the first phase. The people's mistrust of the state became an all-India phenomenon due to the imposition of Emergency (suspension of democratic freedoms in the name of national security) from June 1975 till the change of the government through people's vote in 1977.

The formation of a national network of citizen's bodies for protection of civil liberties represented by Peoples Union for Civil Liberties and Peoples' Union for Democratic Rights may be identified as the first major step in the direction of civil society-based citizen's activism. The watchdog role of these organizations made a great impact on the citizen–state relations, which needed decolonization and democratization.

It was soon complemented by the effective coming together of women activists for resistance to violence against women. It took a constructive turn by demanding the change of the laws to end the atrocities related with dowry system and sexual violence. Many of the demands of the Indian women movement were accepted during the prime ministership of Rajiv Gandhi (1984–89). It included new laws to protect women from sexual and marital violence in the light of the judgements of the Supreme Court of India and 33 per cent reservation for women in the grass-roots governance at the local levels in villages and cities.

India also experienced the spread of environmental activism around the problems of deforestation, large-scale displacements in the name of development and water and air pollution. From Chipko Movement in the hills of the Himalayas to Narmada Bachao Andolan in the Narmada Valley of central India and Silent Valley Movement in the deep South, there was a nationwide people's mobilization, which did not depend on either political elite or classical interest group organizations such as the trade unions and the Kisan Sabha: the two basic channels of political intervention so far. This was mobilization with a difference. In the colonial period, such protest activities were in conjunction with the political parties, particularly the Indian National Congress, and active consultation with the national leaders such as Tilak, Gokhale, Gandhi, Subhash Chandra Bose, Swami Sahajanand, Periyar, Nehru, Patel, Ambedkar and others. But the citizen's protest of the 1970s and after years was an expression of alienation from the mainstream political process and an act of distancing from the political leaders and political parties by several sections of the society.

The Era of Liberalization–Privatization–Globalization or the Growth of Four Deficits

There has been a significant change in the nature, reach and impact of civil society organizations in India since the 1990s. Why? Because this has been a period of paradigm shift in the context of the Indian nation-state, which has created a new framework of polity–economy–society relationship with increasing role of market forces, transnational capital and foreign companies in the national economic life. It has been called the era of liberalization coupled with privatization and globalization (LPG approach). There has been a rolling back of the state from the spheres of political economy of India since 1992. The state became involved in 'disinvestment' and encouraging 'foreign direct investment'. The new paradigm has produced paradoxical results from the perspective of civil society–state relationship. On the contrary, there has been a sharp increase in the rate of growth from 4 per cent to 8–9 per cent per annum during the decade of the 1990s. But there has been a decline in employment generation (jobless growth). The service sector experienced an unprecedented boom coupled with negative growth in the agricultural sector. The declining significance of the state in the affairs of the society made an adverse impact on the relationship between the people and the political elite, the political parties and the political processes including the elections and protest movements. The new paradigm has been insisting on creating more space for the civil society bodies, particularly the non-governmental organizations (NGOs) to make up for the receding role of the state in the field of welfare activities including health, education, livelihood and environmental protection. There has also been increasing interrelationship between the local, national and global NGOs.

But, in the final analysis, there is a growing divide between the gainers and losers of liberalization. There has been a growth in the middle classes without any substantial decrease in the numbers of people trapped in chronic poverty. There has been no substantial increase in the purchasing power of the working millions in the unorganized sector, which contains at least 77 per cent of the total working population of India. According to a national commission report about the condition of the minorities, particularly the Muslims, there is an overall condition of downward mobility. The cumulative result of the LPG paradigm among the marginal sections and marginal regions is reflected in the rise of anti-democratic influences and anti-constitutional activities. It can be argued that India, after two decades of engaging with the LPG paradigm, is confronting four major deficits in the context of state and civil society interaction:

(i) Development deficit (as reflected in the high levels of chronic poverty and increasing inequality between various regions)
(ii) Democratic deficit (no effective decentralization of power and inclusion of the marginal groups including the women and the most backward sections of the society)
(iii) Legitimacy deficit (related with increasing gap between the expectations of the people and performance of the people's representatives, pollution of the political processes due to influence of money power in elections and criminalization of politics)
(iv) Citizenship deficit (declining frequency and efficacy of collective action for common cause; increasing tendency of identity politics on caste, ethnic, regional and communal lines; ignoring social evils such as female foeticide and dowry deaths)

Drive for Deepening of Democracy and the Civil Society Activism

These deficits have created a major crisis for the process of democratic nation-building as well as good governance. There has been a difference of approach about these deficits between the political elite and the civil society groups. The political elite have been exploring new electoral alliances and new equations of reservations and quotas to attract the voters within the existing framework of the LPG paradigm. But, the civil society groups and networks have been asking for qualitative changes in terms of relations between the people and the state, the voter and the representatives, and the community and the bureaucracy. As a result, there has been an increasing emphasis on systemic changes to address the root causes of these deficits. This has been called by various names such as 'development with human face', 'need of inclusive growth', 'participatory development', 'transparency and accountability' and 'promoting good governance'. It has also resulted in a set of civil society-oriented reforms in the past few years. A brief overview of four of the major reform initiatives may provide some idea about the new terms of engagement between the state and the civil society in the LPG era in India.

First, the Right to Information (RTI) can be underlined as the foremost reform for promoting citizen empowerment and civil society engagement in the affairs of the state. It has created a new role for the vigilant citizens and a new responsibility for the people in authority as the RTI empowers every citizen to be watchful about the functioning of the public system. It is a complementary right with reference to the right to vote, which has the power to make the people's representatives and public servants accountable. It is empowerment of the citizens for controlling the governance apparatus through democratic ways.

Second, there has been a radical intervention by the state going beyond the norms of the LPG approach in the sector of employment guarantee for the rural poor. The incremental introduction of Rural Employment Guarantee Scheme in the past few years and its culmination into Mahatma Gandhi National Rural Employment Guarantee Act is a phenomenal action in favour of the economically excluded. By giving a guarantee of 100 days of employment to the rural jobless masses, the state ensures that there is provision of a basic minimum of economic citizenship for the marginalized millions of landless illiterate working men and women in rural India. It has become a reality due to sustained work by many civil society groups in conjunction with the trade unions, political parties, media and academic experts about the need to address negative fallouts of the rolling back of the state from the economic sphere and declining investment in rural India.

Similarly, there has been introduction of Right to Education (RTE) as a response to civil society mobilizations of the past several decades. A large number of citizen groups have been campaigning for eradication of mass illiteracy and non-availability of avenues of education for the children of the poorer sections. Whereas these two national problems had become marginal in the manifestos of the major political parties. Therefore, inclusion of RTE is a great change in favour of the weaker sections and excluded millions of the Indian voter community.

Increasing the reservation for women from 30 per cent to 50 per cent in local self-government bodies or the Panchayati Raj Institutions (PRIs) is a radical step to address the perennial issue of gender deficit in the Indian democracy. It began from Bihar and has become an all-India phenomenon in a period of just few years. By increasing feminization of the instruments of the governmental decision-making through 50 per cent reservation for women in general, and proportionate reservation for women of different layers of society in particular, Indian democracy has taken a big leap towards better participation and more meaningful engagement of the women citizens of India.

Conclusions

India has a rich tradition of civil society institutions and activism since the pre-colonial times. It has its own unique features, which separate it from the Western tradition in some ways. It got legitimized and popularized during the national struggle for freedom from foreign rule. The Gandhian approach to civilization and freedom made it more relevant during the final phase of anti-colonial mobilizations. The increasing engagement of civil society in the affairs of the Indian nation-state and increasing interaction between the civil society and the state has been a significant feature of democratic India since the 1970s, particularly the emergency years of 1975–77.

The introduction of liberalization, centrality of market forces and consequential rolling back of the state from the day-to-day affairs of common citizens has been the new context of enlargement of civil society networks and activities. After going through a phase of low-level impact during the 1990s, the civil society organizations have acquired a significant voice and role in underlining the major deficits of the present Indian state and society. It is also taking a lead role in identifying and promoting systemic changes for checking the deficiencies of Indian project of democracy as evident in the context of RTI, right to employment, RTE and increase of reservation for women from 30 per cent to 50 per cent in the PRIs. Thus, there has been an increasing interrelationship between growth of civil society and deepening of democracy during the new century in India.

Notes

1. Abercombie, N. (2006). *Dictionary of Sociology*. London: Penguin Books, p. 54.
2. M.K. Gandhi wrote *Hind Swaraj* in 1909 as a critique of the Western civilization's colonial approach towards India and the world. It has been most systematically edited, introduced and analysed by Anthony J. Parel in *Hind Swaraj and Other Writings*. New Delhi: Cambridge University Press India, 2001, p. 63.
3. Beteille, Andre (2000). *Civil Society and the Good Society*. New Delhi: Zakir Hussain College, pp. 1–2, 8.
4. See David Macey (2001). *The Penguin Dictionary of Critical Theory*. London: Penguin Books, pp. 62–63.

5

Geographical and Social Dimensions of the Naxal Movement

A Micro-Level Observation

Ashok Kaul and Anand Prasad Mishra

Theoretical Contentions

India achieved freedom as an old society and new state. The rationalities of the old society and the logic of the new state have at times been put to contradictory mode of unfolding by the process of modernization. The initial thrust taken from the modernization theory that the development should be linear, and with the passage of time the melting pot thesis would bring equilibrium in the society. Those who believed in Marxian ideology would stress on economic development by rejecting primordial mode of production to produce poverty. The whole poverty debate would revolve round the linear mode of development. It only invited more exclusive interventions from the state, resulting in the dilution of tribal population and land grabbing from outside. The inherent assumption that the change would be holistic and the new society would stand contrast to the previous one proved wrong. Hence, modernization of tribes not only failed but also gave rise to the manufactured social insecurities. The tribe as a category of resourceless peasantry proved to be a flawed theoretical category (see Desai, 1979; Oommen, 1990). The decades from the 1950s to 1980s created uneven distribution, whereas the state had stressed on growth and taken distribution for granted. There was a shift from modernization plank to internal colonization. These studies essentially would describe peripheral border states in their content of analysis rather than dealing with the simmering discontentment within the core states. And with the advent of the new century, the internal colonization theory has been replaced by the corporate colonization of market rationale.

The post-1989 debates of developmental decentring thesis were blurred with the processes of globalization and privatization. The new capital accumulation process does not need industry and the owner to work from the same venue. They hold lands without obligations. It has given rise to the '*benami* land holdings'. The new economic zones and corporate capitalism have not only brought the rupture in the tribal mode of existence but deprived it with the inclusive life world that had sustained it over centuries. This has brought dismal halt to social movements of people's oriented projects in the absence of the direct confrontation. The new social movements transcend the borders and are laid with moral contents rather than consents of bread, land, ideology and death, the previous parameters of old social movements. It has marginalized the movements of resistance within the nation-states. Resulting in asymmetrical mode of protest, it has created pockets of violence. Its actors presume classes in pure abstraction.

Naxalism of late has posed serious threat to the internal security of India. About 160 districts are affected by Naxal influence. Of the 13 affected states, the movement is intense in parts of Chhattisgarh, Madhya Pradesh, Andhra Pradesh and Maharashtra, whereas it is growing in Uttar Pradesh, Bihar, Odisha, Karnataka, Tamil Nadu and West Bengal. Our policy makers do not consider this problem to be a mere law and order problem, and it needs to be studied in a framework of socio-economic dimension. Identification of people's problems, cause of poverty and effective implementation of pro-poor development programmes are the key issues to counter socio-economic causes of Naxal unrest. The Naxal movement has its origin in deep-rooted structural crisis of land holding, livelihood, displacement and overall state ignorance to poverty-stricken region and its people. In 1946, the Telangana movement and, in 1967, the Naxalbari movement both emerged through peasant uprisings. In socio-economic terms, this is the area that the Indian state needs to pay attention to. Basically, the issue is mostly related with the question of land and development in agrarian economy. Ajay K. Mehra (2007) observed that 'there are instances from the very out set that when ever the land and development question has been attended, the support to Maoism has also declined.' The main architect of this Naxal movement, Charu Mazumdar, realized that 'wherever there, have been movements on vested land, the peasant who gets the possession of the vested land and the license to occupy it, does not remain active any longer in peasant movement.'

During the periods of globalization, a large amount of capital investment and its impact on production systems are another sector, where attention will be required by policy-initiated makers to look into the matter. In fact, a large part of the Indian people are tied to land and forests and mostly depend on it for their livelihood, and now this is under constraints due to liberal policy by government. On the basis of emerging conflict in underdeveloped area, our land and agrarian policies need fresh attention from the section of policy makers and social scientists to search out an alternative to the problem. Naxal movement, in its spatial pattern, follows some geographical features, that is, peasant/rural economy, rough terrain with forest, tribal culture, predominated by agricultural labourer and mostly in poverty-stricken regions. D. Bandyopadhyay (2007) observed that,

> ... fifty eight per cent of Indian labour force is still engaged in agriculture and allied occupations. Tribals are being pushed up the hills because of illegal incursion of outsiders in their traditional domain. Dalits continue to swell the ranks of agricultural proletariat, which is increasing in an alarming way. Poverty ratio among the SCs and STs continue to be much higher at 35 per cent and 44.2 per cent, respectively, as against the national average of little over 26 per cent. Neoliberal development process totally bypassed them.... This has a depressing effect on rural wages and has aggravated casualization of labour on terms grossly unfavourable to them.

These prevailing phenomena have close linkages to the origins and pattern of Naxal movement.

Most of the discussions on Naxal movement have paid attention in terms of either new political alternative path or as law and order problems. But these two streams have failed to explain the Naxal movement. It requires another socio-economic initiative to search out the causes of this problem and its solution by alternative policy framework. The present paper is an attempt by authors to examine the various aspects of Naxal movement, especially its association with poverty and geography of the regions. The nationally debated socio-economic components have been also analysed at the micro level.

Trajectories

Naxal movement has attracted the people of both right and left ideologies. The state and its machinery consider these issues as most challenging threats for the stability of law and order in the country. Government machinery mostly considers these issues as a problem that could be solved by police. But this deep-rooted crisis requires in-depth analysis in a comprehensive way. Only a teamwork of social scientists, state operators, policy makers and social and political activists could be reached at some point, where solution might be arrived. Generally, Naxal movement follows the spatial pattern of geographical variation, combination of cultural isolation, underdeveloped productive system and mostly the problems generated by development-induced displacement of people from rich resource regions. This socio-cultural and geographical identity and its antagonistic relation with emerging economic development have initiated a new political movement, which seek an alternative path of development. The emerging issues of Naxal movement now require to be studied as a research problem for social scientists. Most of the Naxal-affected areas in their socio-economic terms are the areas that need attention. The Naxal-affected area is mostly covered by forest and tribal population. Recently, forest resources in the country too have been commercialized alienating the *adivasis/girijans* from forest produce. Industrialization, mining and the construction of big developmental projects have also initiated massive displacement of the tribes without proper resettlement policies. The tribal and dalit development programmes over the years have created new elite structures in the community, leaving patches of acute poverty and causing distress migration from there (Mehra, 2007).

The above-mentioned aspects have significant value in any discussion, for understanding the Naxal movements and its further in-depth analysis. Most of the Naxal groups have mostly raised the question related to land and livelihood. The editorial team of *Yojana* (2007) have identified the recommendation for Naxal problems. These measures are

> land reforms should be taken on priority and surplus land allotment to landless people. The state should focus greater attention on the affected area to accelerate people-centric development activities and try to create employment opportunities in Naxal-affected areas with special focus on the creation of physical infrastructure in terms of roads, communication, power and also social infrastructure such as schools, hospitals, etc. (ibid.: 7).

On the basis of the above emerging discussion, it is observed that the issues that have been addressed by the Naxal group mostly are an agenda and the need of a civil society. The feudal and undemocratic nexus for exploitation create space for growth to Naxal upsurgence.

Considering the various aspects of Indian development process and alienation of common people from the fruits of development originated the problem of development versus discontent. Most of the Naxal-affected areas of Jharkhand, Chhattisgarh, Odisha, Bihar, Madhya Pradesh and Uttar Pradesh are dominated by the exploitative nexus of contractors, bureaucrats and politicians, which disturbed the harmony between the people, nature and resources of the regions. Moreover, the Naxal movement tried to express the issues of civil society, which have been ignored by feudal forces of the resource-rich regions. The movement can be conceptualized as 'the naxalite try to address the emerging issues of agrarian transformation, tribal people's rights, nationality movement, people's aspiration against imperialism and discontent of globalization and adding up to as solution of these challenges what they conceptualize as people's democratic resolution to change the power structure of Indian state' (ibid.).

A Case Study

The Vindhyan and Kaimur Plateau regions of Uttar Pradesh, Bihar, Chhattisgarh and Jharkhand are severely hit by Naxal attacks. The identified areas of Naugarh Block of District Chandauli, Babhani, Dudhi Block of District Sonbhadra and some hilly regions of Mirzapur district of Uttar Pradesh have recently experienced Naxal attacks and attracted the attention of different sections of society. The occurrence of Hinaut and Bhavanipur village Naxal violence in these regions reveal some ground facts about Naxal movements. The predominance of Naxal groups in Babhani Block needs socio-cultural, political and economic enquiry prior to framing a policy for Naxal problems. The present paper is an attempt to examine the various emerging dynamics and prevailing socio-cultural elements related to Naxal problems. The basic hypothesis of this paper regarding Naxal problems is associated with the conflict between the aspiration for civil society versus feudal-capitalist exploitation. These issues have been analysed in a detailed manner at the micro level. The study of ten sample villages of Babhani Block of District Sonbhadra, Uttar Pradesh, has taken into account to explain the problem.

The study area, Babhani block (see Figure 5.1), is a tribal-dominated region comprising most backward economy and poverty-stricken block of newly constituted district Sonbhadra of Uttar Pradesh. The study area is expanding in 6,788 sq km. It has 1,078 sq km dense forest and 1,369 sq km open forest. The forest covers 36.05 per cent of the total geographical area. During the periods of 1981–91 and 1991–2001, high decadal population growth was registered, and it was 38.18 per cent and 36.13 per cent, respectively. This population growth is high in comparison to the state, and it happened through migration from outside towards the industrial parts of the regions. The local resource bases of forest, stone, tinker, minerals, etc., also attracted the commercial individuals and groups to settle their economic activity over the resource base of a region.

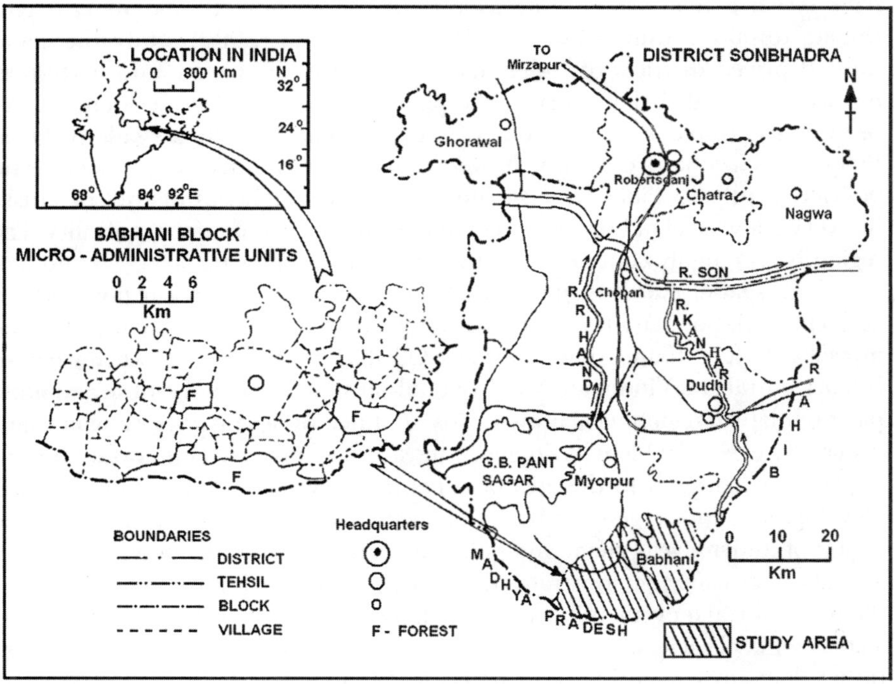

Figure 5.1 *Location of Babhani block*

On the basis of the trajectories of the movement and the depth analysis of the case study, the Naxal movement could be analysed on the following assumptions.

Geographical Dimension

The Naxal-affected regions have revealed a close relation between the geography of area and magnitude of movement. The Planning Commission (2007) has classified Naxal movements into four tiers based on its intensity and magnitude. These are the first severely affected districts (51); second, moderately affected districts (18); third, marginally affected districts (62); and fourth, targeted districts (34).

The spatial pattern of this movement shows that mostly the affected areas have been confined in central Southern, eastern part of the Indian subcontinent; geographically, these regions reveal a specific physiographic, soil, contour, drainage pattern, forest covers, demography, culture and overall level of development. The combination of geography, dynamics of development, spatial conflict and problem of displacement have added quite new socio-political phenomenon in the concerned area. It also generated new dynamics in the context of resource, development and poverty, which needs a fresh orientation and theorization in social science researches. The Naxal movement has a very close relationship with geography and nature of poverty with primitive mode of agrarian production.

In the Indian context, the prevalence of poverty and its spatial pattern have revealed many interesting aspects of Indian poverty and its emerging threats towards future growth. Dutta and Sharma (2000) study the seven most deprived districts of India. Table 5.1 shows the nature and pattern of poverty. It revealed that most of the poverty regions and its severeness have been concentrated in the regions of Odisha, Bihar, Madhya Pradesh, Uttar Pradesh, Rajasthan, etc., which were also severely affected by social and political conflicts. Table 5.1 also shows that the Kalahandi district of Orissa has very a low level of literacy and extremely high level of infant mortality. The region is also highly confined with the severeness of poverty.

The spatial patterns of Naxal-affected area and poverty regions have a very close relation, and it reflects that poverty has become the engine of Naxal movement. It is found that Southern Odisha, Northern and other parts of Bihar, Central and Vindhyan, Madhya Pradesh, eastern Uttar Pradesh and some parts of plateau region have been mostly confined by severe poverty, which also generated Naxal problems. Moreover, most of the poverty and Naxal-affected regions concentrated in the area of tribal predominance, low level of Human Development Index, geographical and socio-cultural isolation and overall the region of underdevelopment and political alienation from the power structure. This ground reality demonstrates the dynamics of Naxal movement. The facts related to Naxal movement have also explained about the problems and put it as a crisis for civil society, and it is a people's resistance against feudal exploitation rather than any classical Marxist movement in nature.

Figure 5.2 depicts the geographical dimension of Naxal-affected regions. Mishra et al. (2009) observed,

> the pattern of development, existing nature of poverty and resource distribution have explained the emerging conflicts between the axis of east and west in India. There is tremendous pressure on the unity of east and west geographical regions and its continuing social and cultural phenomenon. It also explains a tragic story of resource rich regions where the lack of human resource development has deprived the people of the concerned area to their native resources during the process of modernisation and industrialization.

The study also observed, 'the eastern parts of India reveal its severe condition of human poverty, social conflict and underdevelopment and have posed a challenge for sustainability of modern development' (ibid.). The emerging socio-economic and political dynamics have relation with Naxal movement.

Table 5.1 *Most deprived and poverty-stricken region of India*

State	Region	Districts	% of rural poverty population	% of severely poor population	% of urban poverty population	% of severally poverty urban population
Orissa	Southern	Kalahandi	69.02	34.08	45.64	33.53
Bihar	Northern	Kishanganj	58.68	27.62	49.37	21.68
MP	Central	Damoti	50.13	21.78	53.68	32.96
MP	Vindhya	Shandol	36.71	13.80	50.45	24.32
UP	Eastern	Bahraich	48.60	23.20	38.60	18.48
UP	Western	Badaun	29.59	10.24	31.03	14.37
Rajasthan	Western	Barmer	25.48	5.84	23.68	7.43

Source: Dutta and Sharma, 2000.

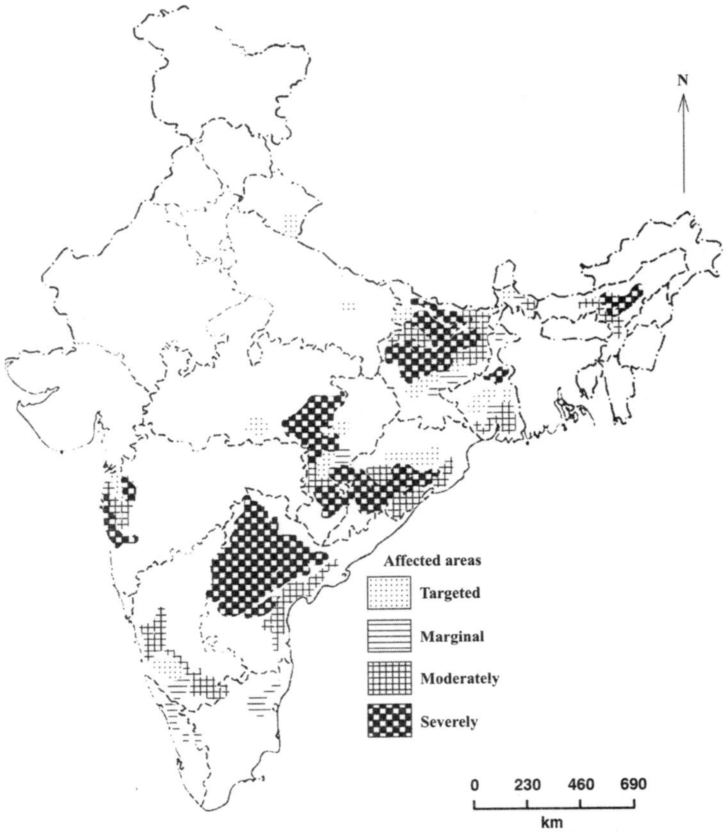

Figure 5.2 *Naxal-affected areas in India, 2007*

Another dimension of Naxal movement is related with the pattern of land holding and isolation of tribal culture and its people from modern developments. Most of the Naxal-affected areas reflect a very poor success rate in land reforms expansion of education and lackness in the implementation of several government-sponsored schemes through effective democratic systems. All these emerging issues create constraints for proper functioning of civil society, which leads towards conflict in social systems. The districts of Kishanganj, Plamau, Purnia, Sitamari, Bastar, Betul, East Mimas, Guna, Jhabuas, Manella, Panns, Sarguja, Tikamgarh, Ganjam, Kalahandi, Koraput, etc., reveal the severity of human poverty, lackness of land reforms and components for modernization (NIRD, 1995; Planning Commission of India, 2007). Sumit Roy (1996) conceptualized these emerging problems of agrarian economy and its relation to conflict in development process. They observed, 'The sustainable development at the national level, demands investigating, within a global – national frame, key aspects of transformation of developing countries from an agricultural-rural to an industrial society.'

Worldwide expanding patterns of terrorism have a similarity with Naxal movement. United Nations General Assembly studied this problem in a holistic way. According to the study, 'poverty, prolonged unresolved conflicts, dehumanization of victims of terrorism, lack of rule of law and violation of human rights, ethnic, national and religious discrimination, political exclusion, socio-economic marginalization and lack of good governance', are the basic causes for conflict and terrorism. In a more comprehensive way, it further observed, 'to pursue and reinforce development and social inclusion agenda at every level....especially on youth unemployment, reduce marginalization and the subsequent sense of victimization that propels extremism and terrorism' (UNO, 2006).

On the basis of the above discussion, the Naxal movement could be analysed as a problem of poverty, deprivation, social exclusion, lack of people participation in economic as well as political process and overall related to the question of civil society. In context to this reality, this chapter is an attempt to examine the various segments of the Naxal-related problems at a micro level. The emerging dynamics of Naxal movement has linkages to the geography, culture, economics and politics of the regions, which needs a theoretical and empirical explanation from researchers and policy makers. To meet these challenges, at a micro level, the study of Sonbhadra District of Uttar Pradesh is being made and some of major findings are as follows.

Economic Predicament

The study area reveals a very severe condition of poverty and deprived socio-economic condition of primitive, underdeveloped and isolated tribal society. About 88.30 per cent people have lost their livelihood and employment, which creates constraints in social ecology of the area. The level of illiteracy (89.90 per cent), low level of agricultural productivity, higher dependency ratio (1:8), predominance of uneconomic primary occupation (90.24 per cent), non-availability of full-time employment, etc., are some of the important features that create the problems of deprivation, poverty and social conflict. The prevalence of illiteracy, bad health care facilities, unhygienic condition, accumulated cultural poverty from generation to generation and nutritional deficiency has developed a fatalistic attitude towards life and society. This emerging socio-economic dimension turns into a process of alienation and leads to violence; this needs in-depth study by social scientists.

In this context, Tables 5.2 and 5.3 reflect some important aspects of poverty on the basis of a sample survey on a tribal-dominated village. It presents the consumption–expenditure pattern and nature of poverty. It observed that the level of poverty varied from a minimum of 56.90 per cent in Babhani village to a maximum of 78.50 per cent in Hathiyar village Moreover, the average proportion of population below poverty line is very high in the study area, Babhani blocks (73.32 per cent), compared with that of state of Uttar Pradesh (51.00 per cent) and India (46.00 per cent). Through micro analysis of poverty, the extent and magnitude of the problems show the severity of deprivation into four tiers (Table 5.3). These are as follows.

Table 5.2 *Poverty structure of Babhani*

Name of sample villages	% of family under different categories				
	Severe destitute ₹ 40–45	Destitute ₹ 45–55	Poor ₹ 55–59	Just below the poverty line	
				₹ 59–105	% of family living below the poverty line
Ranadah	18.25	40.50	6.00	8.00	72.75
Hathiyar	16.50	45.00	8.00	9.00	78.50
Chapki	15.00	35.00	17.00	10.00	77.00
Jiganhawa	17.00	39.00	8.50	10.00	74.50
Duba	13.50	50.00	7.25	6.35	77.10
Babhani	2.25	35.00	10.65	9.00	56.90
Pokhara	7.00	50.00	10.00	10.00	77.00
Chauna	5.00	35.00	20.00	10.50	70.50
Machbandhawa	15.00	35.00	25.00	2.00	77.00
Asandih	17.00	20.00	10.00	25.00	72.00
Average	12.65	38.45	12.24	9.48	73.32

Source: Mishra, 2005.

Table 5.3 *Poverty structure of the sample villages in Babhani block (2000)*

S. No.	Poverty structure	% of total population
1.	Severe destitute	12.65
2.	Destitute	38.45
3.	Poor	12.24
4.	Just below the poverty line	9.98
5.	Total below the poverty line	73.72

Source: Based on field survey conducted by investigator, 2000.

1. The first acute poverty level may be defined as, 'severe destitute' in Babhani block, the proportion of severe destitute varies from a minimum of 2.25 per cent in the village of Babhani to a maximum of 18.25 per cent in the village of Ranadah. This category of people suffers from severe malnutrition and complete absence of modern facilities.
2. The second level of poverty is classified as destitute. Although these categories are a little better than first severe destitute, they are still short of meeting even the basic needs of survival. The proportion of this poverty level in the study area ranged from a minimum of 20 per cent in village Asandih to a maximum of 50 per cent in Pokhara and Duba. This segment of poor population suffers a little less malnutrition compared with the first categories of severe poverty.

3. This category is designated as poor and its configuration varies from a minimum of 6 per cent in Ranadah to a maximum of 25 per cent in village Machbandhawa.
4. The fourth categories of poor population are considered as just below poverty line, and it ranges from 2 per cent in the village of Machbandhawa to 25 per cent in Asandih.

The above-mentioned four tiers of acuteness have explained about the extent and magnitude of the prevailing problems of poverty. These facts about the tribal-dominated regions associated with the level of employment, emerging spatial organization and its conflict, and the problems of development induced displacement. It requires fresh enquiry and scientific analysis to understand about the socio-political dimension of the regions and its pattern of conflict.

Flawed Distribution and Primitive Employment

In the study area, a large chunk of the population is engaged in primary occupation, that is, agriculture and primitive employment related to forest and hill. This prevailing employment is highly primitive in nature, yielding very low per capita productivity. Employment of agricultural labourers and other tribal occupational working days are highly seasonal with low earnings. During the summer months (March through May), gathering of 'Mahuas' fruits and other minor agricultural produce are the only local source of income for poor people. Both employment and wage get their highest score in summer (March through May) due to Ravi harvesting and forest fruits. But it becomes non-existent during the rains (July through September). This emerging phenomenon explained the stagnant character of tribal economy with periodic poverty status. Moreover, the spatial dynamics of poverty and its components, that is, illiteracy, malnutrition, unemployment, etc., show equality among poor in context to their mass deprivation. However, the observed condition of poverty may be classified as ultra poor as defined by the developed nation poverty criterion (Lipton, 1983). The level of employment is directly associated with the severity of poverty. The predominance of tribal productive system in the economy has low diversification in its development pattern, which limits the employment opportunities to the people. Local people find gainful working days only at the time of sowing and harvesting of crops. Table 5.4 shows that employment patterns in tribal society are highly seasonal in character and primitive in nature.

In the study area, most of the tribal people are highly dependent on forest, hill and other primitive modes of agrarian production. These emerging phenomena have shaped the nutritional condition and its periodic nature among the masses. Table 5.5 explains the prevailing characteristics of nutritional calendar of the area.

Spatial Dynamics

Through various observations on the issues of tribal poverty and its relation to social and spatial conflict, many dimensions into the circle of social scientist and policy makers have been highlighted. In fact, the problems of

Table 5.4 *Number of working days month wise (1991)*

S. No.	Village	Months (from January to December)											
		J	**F**	**M**	**A**	**M**	**J**	**Ju**	**A**	**S**	**O**	**N**	**D**
1.	Ranah	10	9	15	20	25	20	8	5	7	10	11	10
2.	Hathiyar	8	7	15	21	19	25	5	7	6	9	12	13
3.	Chapki	10	7	14	24	26	14	7	6	5	10	11	15
4.	Jiganhawa	6	10	11	15	17	7	3	8	5	11	15	11
5.	Duba	10	17	11	14	10	4	7	2	4	9	7	7
6.	Babhani	12	15	25	17	18	9	6	3	5	10	12	11
7.	Pokhara	10	18	19	20	17	8	9	4	5	7	10	11
8.	Chauna	9	13	19	20	17	8	9	4	5	7	10	11
9.	Machbandhawa	9	14	16	15	18	8	5	3	6	8	15	10
10.	Asandih	7	10	17	16	13	5	5	6	5	15	16	10

Source: Based on personal field survey, 1991.

Table 5.5 *Nutritional calendar of Babhani block (1991)*

S. No.	Village	Months (from January to December)											
		J	F	M	A	M	J	Ju	A	S	O	N	D
1.	Ranah	2	2	1	1	1	2	3	3	3	2	1	1
2.	Hathiyar	2	2	1	1	1	2	3	3	3	2	1	1
3.	Chapki	2	2	1	1	1	1	3	3	3	2	1	2
4.	Jiganhawa	3	2	1	1	1	1	3	3	3	2	1	1
5.	Duba	2	1	1	1	1	3	2	3	3	1	1	2
6.	Babhani	2	1	1	1	1	2	3	3	3	2	1	1
7.	Pokhara	2	1	1	1	1	2	3	3	3	2	2	2
8.	Chauna	2	2	1	1	1	2	3	3	3	2	1	1
9.	Machbandhawa	2	1	1	1	1	2	3	3	3	2	1	1
10.	Asandih	2	1	1	1	1	2	3	3	3	1	1	1

Notes: 1. Represents normal calorie status and represented by 2,400 calories.
2. Represents destitute calorie status represented by 1,500–2,000 calories intake.
3. Represents severe destitute conditions of calories status and represented by below 1,500 calories intake.

Source: Based on personal field observation, 1991.

tribal poverty are generated by the prevailing dominance of primitive social base without any progress in human resource development and penetration of state-sponsored capitalism. These emerging socio-economic trends have the following consequences on tribal society and regions:

1. The local resources have been exploited by the new traders, officials, agencies and influential people. Most of the tribal people get their livelihood through local forest, hill and land resources. However, their rights in the contemporary process of industrialization have gone under great constraints, and it posed a problem for survival to common people.
2. The emerging development patterns have many consequential impacts on region, society and economy. This region is the power capital of India. Most of the mega power projects were established by the National Thermal Power Project Corporation of India in the area. It covered large land resources of the area, and also major chunk of local population were displaced through these mega projects. The process of displacement creates the problems of deprivation and most of the masses alienate from ongoing mainstream development process, that is, political, social and economic.
3. The area is characterized by inadequate irrigation facilities and stagnancy in agricultural productivity and economy. This prevailing phenomenon helped to perpetuate poverty among the common masses. These emerging patterns of agrarian dynamics have originated the issues of conflict between developments versus poverty with discontent.
4. The traditional rights of tribal people over the local resources, that is, forest, land and water have been destroyed due to modern projects and other developmental activities, without any new alternative.

These changes in the socio-economic spheres of life have posed threats towards the old livelihood security pattern of tribal people and also compelled the dependent people to move out of their past set-up and try to enter into a new one. But this process creates many constraints for unskilled local population. This socially deprived population lose their command in decision-making process and also develop deep antagonism and dissatisfaction towards ongoing state-sponsored capitalist development.

The above-mentioned local dynamics through its cumulative impact alienated tribal people from decision-making process, and in turn the tribal people had a discontented attitude to the whole political process. It also generated anger and violence against deprivation and exploitation among the masses, which gives space for ultra left organization. On the basis of ground investigation in the study area, the dynamics and mechanism of Naxal movement is explained in Figure 5.3.

Conclusions

Recently, Naxal violence became the challenging issues in both political and academic discourse. Most of the Naxal movements confined in the areas of geographical regions where inadequate administrative and political institutions

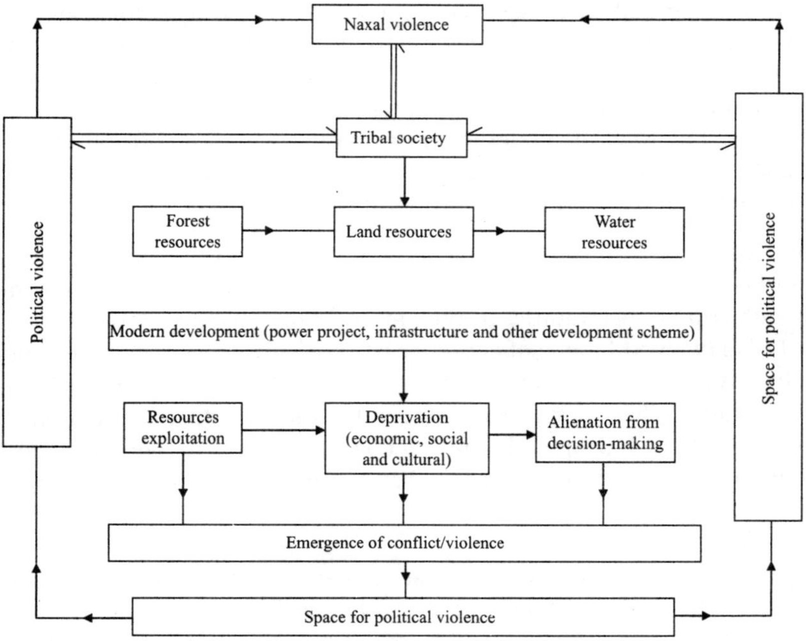

Figure 5.3 *Mechanism of Naxal violence*

are in practice. These inadequacies promote the exploitative nexus in Naxal-affected areas, which give space for exploited segments of population to consider Naxal ideology as an alternative system for development. It also promises all kinds of emancipation to these deprived masses and for this ideal condition the use of a gun is necessary. Actually, most of the affected areas (about 460 police stations in 11 states in 2005) are predominated by tribal people with agrarian economy and geographically hilly terrain with forest covers, which reveals a unique geographical social-cultural and political identity. During the periods of different planned development, the people and regions of Naxal movement have lost their command over the natural resources and other benefits of modernization. Under this condition, Naxal violence gets legitimacy for concerned people. However, the emergence of violence in Naxal-affected areas is very much associated with the demand of civil society, that is, liberty, justice, self-respect and participation in all kinds of development processes. The Naxal movement/violence can be explained as follows:

- Most of the Naxal-affected areas formed a rough terrain physiographic, which is completely isolated from road, communication, education, health and other modern facilities. This geographical isolation has close association with the emergence of Naxal movement.
- Most of the tribal communities and culture have deep organic link to the forest and its environments. Recently, ongoing development schemes have displaced tribal people from their natural environment and livelihood, and under these circumstances the livelihood of the tribes and

their cultural identity face many constraints and threats for their survivals. This process compelled people to participate in Naxal movement.

- Overall, Naxal movement has linkages with issues of land reform, low level of human resources development, bureaucratic–contractor exploitation, low level of modern infrastructural facilities, cultural crisis and optimum participation in democratic process. These entire questions are related with the democracy and norms of civil society.

Despite legal restrictions over acquisition of property of non-tribals, the state has not been averse to new economic zone policy that has been a major cause for manufactured uncertainties in the life world of tribal populations of India. Its inclusive life world mode of existence has not only experienced the rupture, but it has also led to the emergence of anarcho-militarism of these poor deprived people of India. Therefore, it is recommended that the democratic desire and needs of concerned people should be taken into policy framework in the participatory form of development so that Naxal violence could be minimized.

References

Bandyopadhyay, D. (2007). 'Rural Unrest', *Yojana*, February, New Delhi, p. 11.

Desai, A.R. (1979). *Peasant Struggles in India*. Bombay: Oxford University Press.

Dutta, K.L. and Sarita Sharma (2000). *Level of Living in India*. New Delhi: Planning Commission.

Lipton, M. (1983). 'Poverty, Under Nutrition and Hunger'. World Bank Staff Working Paper No. 597, Washington, DC: World Bank.

Mehra, Ajay Kumar (2007). 'India's Gordian Knot', *Yojana*, February, New Delhi, pp. 38, 37–40.

Mishra, A.P. (2001). 'Nature of Mass Poverty in Tribal Regions: A Case Study of Babhani Block of Sonbhadra District of U.P', in P. Nag, C.S. Kumar and S. Sengupta (eds), *Population, Environment, and Development*. New Delhi: Concept, pp. 80–91.

——— (2005). 'Impact of Poverty on Social Environment and HRD Management in Under Developed Agrarian Economy', *National Geographical Journal of India*, 6(1–2): 45–56.

Mishra, A.P. et al. (2009). 'Poverty as a Threats for the Sustainability of Earth', in H.N. Mishra (ed.), *Planet Earth: A Blueprint for Sustainability*. New Delhi: Prentice Hall.

National Institute of Rural Development (NIRD) (1995). *Report on Rural Development*. Hyderabad.

Oommen, T.K. (1990). *Protest and Change: Studies in Social Movements*. New Delhi: Sage Publications.

Planning Commission of India (2007). *Report on Naxal Movement*. New Delhi.

Roy, Sumit (1996). 'Development, Environment and Poverty Some Issues for Discussion', *Economic and Political Weekly*, 27 January, 31(4): 29–41.

United Nations General Assembly (2008). United Nations General Assembly Resolution, 60/288, A/RES/60/288, 8 September, New York.

Yojana (2007). Naxalism: Development and Discontent. February, New Delhi.

6

Nativism, Regionalism and the Legitimization of Violence

The MNS Way

Jasmine Y. Damle

Introduction

The recent Municipal Elections held in February 2012, in Pune, Mumbai and Nasik have brought about interesting political development in urban Maharashtra. The steady rise to prominence of the Maharashtra Navnirman Sena (MNS) party has raised eyebrows, which was earlier considered to be just a splinter group of Shiv Sena (breakaway group of Shiv Sena Party). One can notice the rising graph in the number of seats won by MNS since 2009. It had won seven seats in Mumbai, which has now gone up to 28; in Pune, it had eight seats that shot up to 29 in 2012, and in Nashik in 2009 it had 12 seats that has now shot up to 40 seats and has now made MNS party a force to reckon with. In this paper, I examine the genesis of the MNS, its development, its ideology and its strategies.

The Genesis of the MNS

The MNS is a Maharashtra-based regional political party operating on the motto of 'sons of the soil' ideology (*Bhoomiputra* ideology) (Weiner, 1978). The MNS was founded on 9 March 2006 in Mumbai by Mr Raj Thackeray (nephew of the Shiv Sena (SS henceforth) party Chief Mr Bal Thackeray). Mr Raj Thackeray left the SS due to ideological differences with his cousin Mr Uddhav Thackeray as well as the differences of opinion over the distribution of the election tickets. Mr Raj also believed that the SS had lost its previous glory and was at present run by petty clerks and because of which the SS had lost its past glory. Thus, the MNS is a breakaway party from the SS; the party's ideology rests on the cardinal principle of 'sons of the soil' or *Bhoomiputra* ideology' (ibid.). MNS is also a right wing-based party, working and striving towards the development of the state of Maharashtra, Marathi nationalism (read Militant/ Reactionary type). It is a regional (parochial) party. The motto of the party is 'I am for Maharashtra and a Marathi-speaking local, hence Maharashtra is my bhoomi/land.' The MNS is committed to restoring the 'lost Marathi glory, its pride, upliftment of the Marathi people, language and culture'. The literal meaning of Maharashtra Navnirman Sena is Maharashtra's new beginning Army Reconstruction. The MNS during the parliamentary elections held in April 2009 as well as for the State Assembly elections had declared a nine-point agenda.

According to the manifesto of the MNS party (Wikipedia, 2009-Navnirman Sena http://enwikipedia.org/wiki):

1. The MNS will guard the interest of Maharashtra in the parliament/ legislature. Anybody insulting the state by action or words will have to face the wrath of the MPs/MLAs of Maharashtra.
2. All precautions will be taken to ensure that the Marathi *Manoos* (Individual/ person) gets top priority in the recruitment in all state and central establishments. Priority will be given for the locals in all enterprises of the state, and preventive measures will be taken to stop the state from becoming a dumping ground of migrants. MNS will ensure that all relevant laws be implemented in letter and spirit.
3. I (Raj Thackeray) will hold myself personally responsible and accountable for the acts and deeds of my MPs and MLAs. I will see that they act as the state's trustees in Delhi.
4. All political parties have been fooling many farmers by making hollow promises. My party will promote farming amongst the youth, by protecting the interests of the farmers in food grain production chain.
5. MNS will ensure that the state receives central funds in proportion to its contribution to the government's kitty.
6. We will also keep a tab on the state's utilization of the central funds. This is to ensure that it meets its intended targets.
7. We are used to seeing important infrastructure projects overshooting their time period; we will ensure that such projects are duly completed on time.
8. MNS will act as a watchdog to save open spaces.
9. For the past 60 years, Maharashtra has been given a secondary treatment by the central government; hence, MNS will act as a pressure group for the speedy and timely implementation of all the projects. All hurdles in their implementation such as red-tapism corruption will be dealt with firmly in the true MNS style.

The MNS is a regional political party and has been surrounded by many controversies ranging from the attacks on North Indian taxiwalas, shopkeepers, vendors to attacking Bihari/UPian candidates who appeared for the All India Railways Recruitment Examination (western region) at Kalyan near Mumbai, at 13 different centres in Mumbai. The issue raised by the MNS was that the 'outsiders' were called for job interviews and the local Marathi *Manoos* was thus deprived of job opportunities. A 'sons of the soil agitation' thus broke out followed by a spate of unruly incidents such as MNS protests at Pune MIT College, where the MNS party workers had checked the admission list and had again arrived at the same conclusion that the local Marathi students had been left out and that the bulk of the selected candidates were from Uttar Pradesh and Bihar proverbially labelled by the MNS as being 'outsiders' or at times perceived to be 'infiltrators/job predators'. The MNS workers thus broke furniture and glass windows to vent their anger and also threatened the administration of the college of dire consequences if they did not heed to the demands of admitting Marathi students as it was the legitimate right of the local students to get admission at the college. The sporadic attacks on Bihari construction workers at Pune as well as at Nasik bear ample testimony to the strong at times rabid convictions of the party as has been manifested in the party's vehement opposition to the performance of the 'Chhat Pooja' in Mumbai by an ex-minister from Bihar, which had culminated into street violence, stone pelting, burning of tyres, riots, etc. The MNS ideology rests on the principle of the development of the state, rekindling of Marathi nationalism, right-wing ideology. The use of 'violence' as a weapon often to generate fear or as a retaliatory mechanism can be seen in the unruly incidents such as riots, bandhs, stone pelting, beating people and hurting them, overindulgence in acts of hooliganism, burning of buses (destruction of government property) *Dadagiri* or *Sirf todd-phod* or *Halla-boll* mechanism, vandalism at times vigilantism, thereby instilling fear in the minds of the non-Marathi immigrants (especially people from Uttar Pradesh and Bihar). Thus, the sojourn of 'legitimization of violence' (Apter, 1997) began, which appears to be extremely xenophobic, ethnocentric, fascist and 'sons of the soil' movement.

Ideology of the MNS

Nativism an Assertion of Identity

Nativism is a form of assertion of local identity, which is often manifested through 'sons of the soil' agitations. In this chapter, I have tried to analyse the concept of 'nativism' or in other words the reassertion of ethnic, linguistic and geographic identity by making use of 'sons of the soil agitation' in the context of the emergence of the MNS in Mumbai and in Maharashtra.

In multiethnic societies, migrations often kindle nativist sentiment. Often, nativism gets politicized and finds an expression in demonstrations and riots and gives rise to nativist political parties such as the SS and currently the MNS. Nativism is manifested mostly in urban areas, cities and centres. Mumbai as a case in point is an industrial, commercial and financial capital of India. Mumbai has attracted a lot of migrants from distant culturally diverse regions of India. The heterogeneous population forms the seedbed of nativist politics. The main grudge of the local/natives has been securing more government jobs for the local people. At present, the Government of Maharashtra (2009) has promised that 80 per cent of the jobs shall be reserved for the local people.

The crux of the issue lies in the loss of jobs for the local people and that the jobs are being snatched by non-Marathi migrants in the city of Mumbai who are often termed as 'outsiders' or *pariahs*. The entire philosophy underlying the 'sons of the soil' movement has been so far to espouse feelings of nativism, ethnocentrism and at times xenophobism. The bone of contention being that the state government documents have officially defined local people to mean anyone residing in a locality for more than 10–15 years. However, in practical terms, a local person is often considered one whose mother tongue is Marathi (local language).

As pointed out by Dipankar Gupta (1977),

> The economic contributions in the social milieu determine both the causes behind the rise of a movement (in this case SS and now MNS) and also its outcome and limitations. It is basically socio-economic disparity, loss of jobs-employment for the locals-'sons of the soil' (bhoomiputras) that triggers extreme parochialism, xenophobism which sets in motion agitations, bandhs, rioting, etc.

Myron Weiner (1978) in 'sons of the soil' has argued that anti-migrant movements in India have always been linked to the phenomenon of nativism; they represent the response of the emerging nationalities.

Myron Weiner (1978) had stated that nativistic movements convert cultural differences into cultural conflicts; however, cultural conflicts should be viewed as effects and not the determinants of nativism. Methodologically speaking, it is an exercise to locate the 'if' and 'then' conditions. Hans Zetterberg (1954) had propounded the concept of 'axiomatic ordering'. For a social phenomenon to exist for nativism, certain conditions become necessary and at the same time must be sufficient. Thus, for nativism to exist, Myron Weiner (1978) stated that the first condition is that

1. Each area with a nativist population should have migrants from outside the cultural region that is sufficient/necessary condition such that the number of migrants and their descendants are greater than the local population. In Mumbai, in 1961, the Marathi-speaking population was only 42.8 per cent compared with the people from other states of India. However, in 1971, the number of migrants to Mumbai city was about 8.7 lakhs, whereas in 1960–61, when Mumbai experienced 'sons of the soil' agitations, the out-of-state migrants in Mumbai was over 36 per cent. In 1970–71, it was 39.5 per cent migrants; and in 1961, it was 49.5 per cent migrants in Mumbai city. However, 1980–81 saw a low contribution of net migrants; it was only 17 per cent compared with 39 per cent in 1991–2001. However, according to the 2001 census, it was 43 per cent compared with 64.2 per cent in 1961 when there was a growth in regional parties and 'sons of the soil' agitations. Thus, migration to Mumbai has always been dominated by migrants from other states in 1981–91; it was 16.77 per cent migrants to Mumbai (Singh, 2007, 2009). In 2001, the picture changed dramatically and the percentage of migrants such as those from the state of Uttar Pradesh was 24.3 per cent compared with 12 per cent and from Bihar it was 3.5 per cent compared with 0.2 per cent earlier; thus, we find a steady increase

in the percentage of migrants from both Uttar Pradesh and Bihar as well as during the last 50 years or so (Singh, 2007). Thus, this sharp rise in the percentages of migrants from both Uttar Pradesh and Bihar has added fuel to fire in terms of the presence of new regional political parties such as the MNS. Today, the percentage of Marathi-speaking population in Mumbai is 42 per cent, which is indeed a worrisome figure as there has been a steady decline of the Marathi population from 76.5 per cent in 1971 to 68.8 per cent in 2001, whereas in sharp contrast the percentage of Hindi speakers rose from 55 per cent to 11 per cent and Uttar Pradesh has 4.23 lakh migrants and from Bihar it is 0.51 lakh migrants. Maharashtra Economic Survey (2008–09) thus found that the 'sons of the soil' campaign has returned to the centre stage of the state politics during the past few years and is likely to linger longer and has thus paved the way for the emergence of the MNS.

2. The second condition for nativism to flourish or for 'sons of the soil' agitation to grow is when there is some perceived cultural difference between the migrants and the local community, no matter how small it may be. These differences can take any form such as language, religion, preference about food, dress and belief systems. The recent attacks on Samajwadi Party MLA Mr Abu Azmi for taking oath in Hindi, instead of in Marathi, which is the official language of the state. The MNS party MLAs had manhandled as well as slapped him as it was an insult of the native community to its Marathi *Asmita* (identity) as well as had hurt the *Manasikta* (psyche) of the Marathi *Manoos* (individual) who have a distinct cultural honour and pride (better known as the Marathi *Banna*), which no Maharashtrian would allow to trample upon. The Marathi *Manoos* would rather break than bend or succumb to any outside pressures. *Modenn pann vakanar nahin*! The staunch opposition to the shop name, name plates written in Hindi or in English first by the SS and now by the MNS. The stopping of screening of Amitabh Bachchan films by the MNS in Mumbai because his wife, noted actress and Samajwadi party MP Jaya Bachchan had commented that '*Hum UP ke log hain toh Hindi mein hee baat karenge*!' The hue and cry over the performance of 'Chaat Pooja' in Mumbai by an Ex-central railways minister. Anything that seems to be anti-Marathi or Maharashtra is viewed as an encroachment into the Marathi land, may it be the playing of Bhojpuri film songs during a college cultural event at Nasik or the burning of non-Marathi sign boards. Mr Raj Thackeray, the president of the MNS, coined a term '*hut Pooja*', that is, asking the non-Marathi migrants especially from the BIMARU states of Uttar Pradesh and Bihar to get out of Mumbai and Maharashtra.

3. The third condition of nativism is that in areas with a nativist movement, the local population is likely to be immobile compared with the other groups in the population. According to Myron Weiner (1978), in the mid-1970s, the percentage of Marathi population living outside Mumbai/Maharashtra was only 2.2 per cent compared with in 2001–09, when the highest number of migrants (37.4 per cent) reported place of birth within

the state of Maharashtra. The maximum number of migrants originated from Ratnagiri (Konkan) and Sindhudurg (Konkan); 60 per cent are from Ratanagiri, Satara, Pune and Raigad. However, during 1961–2001, the percentage of immigrants from Ratnagiri declined from 44.5 per cent to 31.5 per cent; one of the main reasons attributed is the closure of the textile mills in Mumbai strike during 1981–83, whereas the population from Marathwada region such as Latur, Nanded, Parbhani, Jalna, Osmanabad and Beed have a high percentage of migrants to Mumbai, one of the main reasons being lack of infrastructural and industrial backwardness. These are the push factors that propel inter-district migration (Singh, 2007, 2009). Out-migration from Maharashtra is at present seen in the software sector, IT sector and quest for higher education (both within and outside India). Hence, it is more of skilled labour that migrates out of the state of Maharashtra; today, we find many highly trained Marathi people working in Bangalore and Hyderabad. Thus, it is the pull factor that attracts them both within India and abroad.

4. The fourth condition for the rise of nativism is that the quantity of out-migration is a surrogate for variable that is the ability of the people to compete in the labour market: the rate and pattern of employment. In Mumbai, in the 1960s, the emergence and rise of the SS was due to the high level of unemployment among the indigenous middle class in education/employment but not in employment and income, where a substantial proportion of the middle class (clerical and administrative posts) were held by culturally alien migrants; thus, a nativist political movement had occurred. In Mumbai, in the 1960s and 1970s, most of the clerical, typist and stenographer jobs were held by the South Indians, who knew English and had good typing and shorthand speed. Thus, Mr Bal Thackeray, the party leader of SS, had told the locals to improve as well as learn typing and shorthand so as to compete with the alien migrants for such jobs and finally oust them out. Thus, Bal Thackeray wrote an article in SS mouthpiece 'Marmick' (subtle/satire in Marathi) that 'where ever there is a vacancy there is a Madarasi for the job!!' Today, MNS is also urging Marathi youth to take up dairy milk production as an occupation to challenge the monopoly of the migrants from UP-dhoodhwalas by selling cow's milk at the rate ₹ 30/litre and buffalo's milk at ₹ 40/litre under 'Mumbai milk: Swaad (flavour) Maharashtracha'.

However, today, with the emergence of MNS and its strong anti-Uttar Pradesh and Bihar migrants stand, most of the professional, technical and clerical administrative jobs are dominated by the non-migrants. Service jobs are held by both the migrants and the locals. However, the low-paid manufacturing sector jobs are dominated by the migrants who work at cheap rate. According to D.P. Singh (BMC Report on Human Development 2009: article on migration in Mumbai), the allegations that the migrants have taken away the jobs from the locals is not true. Singh states that the migrants have provided job opportunities to the locals.

A large chunk of the migrants who come from remote villages of North India provide support to essential services in the city of Mumbai such as dhobis, milk supply, construction workers, carpenters, taxi service, security guards. These jobs are on the platter for everyone, hence there is no question of job snatching from the locals. Migration is the root cause of all cultural and economic progress. Thus, the crux of the issue lies in whether the local people are willing to take up these jobs, which are often low paid, and instead raise issue of jobs for the 'sons of the soil', that is, 80 per cent of the jobs should be reserved for the local population.

5. The fifth condition is that the areas with the nativist movements have experienced a rapid growth of educational opportunities for the lower middle class. Myron Weiner (1978) had stated that although Maharashtra is a literate, and progressive, state, the Marathi people lagged behind the Parsees, Gujaratis and Sindhis; he too has reaffirmed on the basis of the D.T. Lakadavala study (1963) by stating that a Marathi person earned 4.9 per cent, that is, a little more than ₹ 500/month compared with a South Indian who earned 10.1 per cent, and in sharp contrast, a Gujarati earned 17.3 per cent. Mary Katzenstein (1973) stated that most of the SS party workers belonged to the lower middle class and held jobs such as clerks, salesmen in bookshops, towing operators and inspectors in BMC. However, today the MNS has its party workers ranging from lawyers (Mr Archit Jaykar is the party vice-president as well as their legal advisor), ex-bureaucrats, along with these middle as well as the lower middle class, especially children of Mumbai textile workers (grown-up sons and daughters). The MNS also has a strong Dalit following (blue colour/flag), and the party also aspires to work for the Marathi Muslims of the state. The party is also constituted mostly by rebels from the SS party, who had also left the parent party, mostly young workers who supported Mr Raj Thackeray. Thus, the crux of the issue lies in as to who has access to the 'capital'? (both economic and social and of course political). Unfortunately, even today, we find that nothing much has changed, that is, the Gujaratis, Parsees, Marwaris and Sindhis control business, *Le Capital*, in Mumbai (financial capital of India) and thereby start educational, charitable trust-run schools, colleges and institutions of higher learning. Today, we find the Marathi *Manoos* who start educational empires or are fondly known as the '*Shikshan Samarats*' or '*Maharshis*'; many of the state ministers often are in the field of education thus often transforming into an 'academic market place', charging hefty fees, thus paving the way for the entry of non-Marathi students, which also triggers nativism and the assertion and emergence of regional political parties such as the MNS. Thus, nativism, according to Myron Weiner (1978), is associated with a blockage to social mobility for the native population by a culturally distinguishable migrant population and is largely a middle class sentiment and a rising middle class in terms of both their ambitions and aspirations as well as their size. Thus, nativism is a political response to conflicting forms of mobility, the spatial mobility of the migrants and the aspiring social mobility of a social class within the native population.

Regionalism

The very emergence of MNS is heavily steeped in regionalism as well as nativism and thus forms a pivotal aspect of the chapter. Regionalism in India has always been an important aspect of politics in India, especially since independence period. But in the late 1960s and early 1970s, regional claims verging on parochial demands for separation and autonomy grew so strong that they became a serious threat to the unity of India.

> The term 'regionalism' (S.K. Khanna, 1999) has two connotations: negative and positive. In the negative sense, it implies excessive attachment to one's region in preference to the country or the state. However in the positive sense, it is a political attribute associated with people's love for their region, culture, language with a view to maintain their independent identity. Positive regionalism is welcomed in so far as it encourages people to develop a sense of brotherhood and commonness on the basis of common language, religion or historical background, whereas the negative regionalism is a great threat to the unity and integrity of our country.

In the Indian context, the term 'regionalism' has often been used in the negative sense and is used to indicate an agglomeration of all those factors that are generally considered to be centrifugal to secession and nationalism. In this chapter, I have tried to look into the negative sense of the term 'regionalism' and its subsequent consequences that are often manifested through violent agitations, beating, assaulting, burning houses, public property and of course through vigilantism as a type of violence that can be both spontaneous and premeditated. The MNS attacks on Uttar Pradesh and Bihar migrants into Mumbai has often been expressed by extreme xenophobic and ethnocentrism right from the days of the SS party, and the mantle has been carried forward now by the MNS. Thus,

> regionalism is a process subsidiary of political integration in India. Manifestation of these residual elements which do not find expression in the national polity and national culture and on being excluded from the centrality of the new polity, express themselves in the political discontent and political exclusionism. It could include forces that the gravitational or centripetal forces of a society may thus fail to absorb, assimilate and internalize. The feeling of regionalism may arise either due to continued neglect of their region by some governmental authorities. (S.K. Khanna, 1999)

To give an illustration from the sub-region of 'Vidarbha' in Maharashtra, the people of this sub-region often feel that they should get a separate state of 'Vidarbha' due to a feeling of constant neglect of their region by the ruling state government. Thus, as stated earlier, regionalism in the negative sense (fissiparous tendencies) is often manifested in India... Thus, regionalism may spring up as a result of a particular area/region by increasing political awareness of the backward people that they have been discriminated against. Quite often, unscrupulous political leaders encourage the feeling of regionalism and maintain their hold over the issue, a particular area or a group of people; for example, the MNS had stirred the issue about uncontrolled flow of migrants, especially from Uttar Pradesh and Bihar resulting in loss of jobs for the 'Marathi' local people (sons of the soil). It is indeed a classic case of 'self-fulfilling prophecy' (Merton, 1957). Also, the same point is harped upon again and again so much so that ultimately the people start believing in it. Thus, regionalism in India is a multidimensional composite phenomenon, which is considered to be detrimental to India's unity, especially due to secessionist and fissiparous tendencies exhibited by the people of certain regions/states, which if left unattended can surely lead to balkanization of India. Thus, the phenomenon of regionalism may emerge out of the culmination of variations pertaining to the socio-cultural, economic and political spheres. Regionalism comprises two determinants: (i) subjective and (ii) objective.

(i) The subjective components of regionalism are the way of life, customs, traditions, forms of art, language, literature, social heritage, beliefs and values related to the group, whereas (ii) the objective components are territorial and regional and a complex environment within which the regional group lives. Taken together, the subjective and the objective components constitute the determinants of regionalism. Regionalism is not a new phenomenon in the Indian political system; right from the days of the British, regionalism had encouraged people to think in terms of their region rather than as a nation to maintain their hold over India. The infamous British policy of 'divide and rule' was by itself trying to kindle and rekindle regionalism. However, after independence, our national leaders tried to foster the feeling that all people belong to one nation – India. In fact, our pledge and national anthem as well as our constitution point out to it. However, due to the vastness of our country, its different regions, languages, cultures, etc., regionalism makes its presence predominantly felt. Many European scholars felt that India was a subcontinent just like Europe.

Thus, violence has indeed become a global phenomenon and needs to be explored, and thus, the last part of the chapter deals with the concept of 'legitimization of violence' or strategies adopted by the MNS. As a prelude to understanding the concept of legitimization of violence, a basic understanding of the concepts of nation, regionalism and parochialism is essential as these often contribute to rekindling of regional identities, thereby inciting violence.

The Strategies Adopted by the MNS

Legitimization of Violence

This concept was brought into vogue by the noted political scientist David Apter (1997). To understand the concept of legitimization of violence, I use the concept of 'hate crime', which is closely associated with Max Scheller's concept of 'ressentiment' (1913) inspired from Nietsze. I find both these concepts extremely useful, in order to understand and analyse the rationale and ideology behind the attacks (brutal) by the MNS activists against Bihari and UPian migrant workers, job seekers and taxi drivers in Mumbai, who are often labelled as 'outsiders' by the MNS. The concept of 'hate crime' is very closely associated with the concept of 'ressentiment'. 'Hate crime' is a type of crime that is directed against persons of a particular race, religion, ethnic orientation or sexual orientation. Well-known examples are those such as the Boston strangler, Jack the Ripper, in India the 1992 Mumbai bomb blasts after the demolition of the 'Babri Masjid' and the communal riots of March 1993, which had devastated the city of Mumbai. The 1984 anti-Sikh riots in Delhi after the assassination of India's PM Smt Indira Gandhi by her two Sikh bodyguards, Godhra killings in Gujarat and the 26/11 November attacks in Mumbai; the list unfortunately seems to be endless!!

Max Weber (1947) in his classification of types of authority has given us the concept of charismatic type of authority. The way the people especially the youth are swayed/enamoured and attracted to certain political leaders is that these youth are literally mesmerized by the charisma of such leaders. For example, the youth icon Raj Thackeray's fiery/inflammatory speeches before the state/centre elections that made many of them forget their multiple identities; for example, a Maharashtrian is first and foremost an Indian citizen, but nowadays, we find that the very notion of 'Marathi *Manoos*' (person), *Asmita* (identity) and *Manasikta* (psyche) is being constantly hammered on the minds of the Marathi youth by such 'so-called charismatic young dynamic leaders' by their fiery and provocative actions, riots, agitations, *bandhs* and inflammatory speeches. Sociologically speaking, the Mertonian R.K. Merton (1957) concept of 'self-fulfilling prophecy is extremely apt here. The method of constantly bombarding young minds with distinct ideas about' Marathi identity (*Asmita*), injustice inflicted on them by other migrant communities, deprivations, etc., it so happens that the youth are completely mesmerized into believing every word of it to be true and nothing but the truth!!

Sociologically speaking, it is nothing but 'in-group and out-group'. The in-group in this case is the 'insider'-Marathi *Manoos*, and the out-group is the 'outsider'-migrants in Mumbai especially from Uttar Pradesh and Bihar. The adversity of exclusion can be made to go hand in hand with cultivated violence associated with identity conflicts.

Conflict is manifested in the form of vigilantism, which provokes violence and revenge initiating a dangerous cycle of vigilantism. Often, institutions are burnt, targeted. Long-standing tensions between the local people and the trans-migrants are compounded and exacerbated by the inequitable economic conditions and conflict. The outcome is a society in which insecurity, danger and fear are all pervasive. Vigilantism is a type of conflict (violence) whereby the practice of an individual/group is to take justice into his/their own hands; for example, the MNS's motto is to teach migrants from Uttar Pradesh and Bihar a lesson. Vigilantism can be pre-meditated as well as sporadic.

Vigilantism is basically of two types: (i) spontaneous level: it occurs when a person or a group of people are caught in the act of doing it. It is at this moment that the community emotions/anger are at a peak; for example, MNS activists torching buses, damaging shops or after an accident on the road, the angry, unruly mob turning violent and burning tyres, beating the bus driver for killing innocent lives, blocking the traffic, etc. The second type of vigilantism is the (ii) the pre-meditated type: it occurs when an individual is suspected to be a thief or culprit, for which the punishment could be death. However, in both types of vigilantism, the aggrieved person takes the law in his own hands and indulges in killing the accused; for example, after the assassination of India's PM Smt Indira Gandhi in 1984 in Delhi, the angry mob targeted the houses of Sikhs and torched them. The culture of vigilantism is often widely accepted by the members/party workers/supporters of the MNS and is often termed as *Halla-bol/Sirf todd-phod* or retaliation the MNS way – *Dadagiri*/hooliganism. Very often, vigilantism takes an ugly turn and many innocent deaths may occur. Often, vigilantism is guided by revenge (vendetta) to teach the others a lesson and is the most effective way to settle scores. Refer to http://www.preventiveconflictorg/portalmain in research violence: conflict in Lampung (PDF file), Indonesia.

Vigilantism on a wider scale is extremely dangerous, which can generate a cycle of violence. Thus, vigilantism can be compared with a forest fire (uncontrolled and wild), which is termed as '*Vanava*' in Marathi. A close factor associated with violence is votes inciting violence; vigilantism is a common feature before elections. Very often, political parties promote ethnic violence, which includes religious, racial and linguistic, as stated by S. Wilkinson (2004) in his major work *Votes and Violence: Electoral Competition and Ethnic Riots in India*. A classic example of religious violence is at first the demolition of the Babri Masjid in December 1992 and then the subsequent Hindu–Muslim riots that followed, the bomb blasts in Mumbai in January 1993 and also in March 1993. The BJP and the SS came to power in 1995 at both the central level and the state level. Thus, the BJP with the complete support of the RSS, Bajrang Dal and VHP had pulled down the Babri Masjid located near the disputed land where in olden times Ram Temple existed (Ram Janmabhoomi, Ayodhya, birthplace of Lord Rama). Thus, these saffron parties had in fact unfurled the sacred Hindu saffron flag, claimed it to be a Hindu site, by using evidence from the Archeological Survey of India by showing that there were old bricks with Lord Rama's name embossed on them, and that there also existed a kitchen of his wife 'Sitamayya'. Thus, such riots and acts of violence and vigilantism are always used keeping in mind the forthcoming elections. The case in point, the MNS has very intelligently made use of linguistic and 'sons of the soil' agitation during parliamentary as well as the state elections. The sojourn from beating taxi drivers, construction workers, attacking shops owned by UPians and Biharis. Thus, violence begets violence; for example, attacking non-Marathi candidates appearing for Central Railways Recruitment Examinations, which resulted in attacks on Marathi families settled in Jamshedpur (Tata Steel company employees). According to S. Wilkinson (2004):

> Riots are used by political parties not only when elections are coming up, but also when the margin in the previous election was close. Thus when the group that starts the violence at the behest of a prominent political party (MNS in this case) and they realize that the police are not going to stop violence, they might loot the other group's stuff e.g. shops/stalls/taxis owned by the Bihari and UPian migrants. Thus violence begets violence. People think about how the other group has responded in the past, thus a history of violence makes violence more likely.

The various types of attacks on the migrants in Mumbai by the MNS triggered a young boy named 'Raj', a student hailing from Patna (Bihar), to come to Mumbai to kill Mr Raj Thackeray; but instead, he nearly killed a bus passenger on an Andheri-bound BEST bus and had to be finally killed by the police as he had literally taken law into to his own hands by threatening the passengers and firing few rounds in the bus. The infamous slapping incident led to the suspension of the four MNS MLAs, as well as a warning issued by the Samajwadi Party MPs that they would not allow any MP from Maharashtra to step into Delhi or try to go inside Maharashtra Sadan. Thus, fascism often begets violence and retaliation also begets violence. Thus, the crux of the issue lies in as to whether one can attribute ethnic conflict primarily to political incentives? MNS by its hate speeches or religiosity, cultural and historical often ethnocentric or xenophobic, fascist explanations are equally responsible for tension, conflict and violence and thereby vigilantism, thus unleashing the politics of fear, terror or fear psychosis.

Psychosociologically speaking, the MNS assertion of identity Marathi *bhoomiputra*, 'sons of the soil', ideology rests on the basic belief of 'group identity'. Refer to S. Kakkar (1996):

> The notion of group identity constitutes in a person's feelings and attitudes towards self and as a member of an ethnic/religious/cultural community or collectivity. This particular self-image is transmitted from one generation to another through the group's mythology, history, ideals, values and shared cultural symbols. Group identity is an extended part of individual's self experience, although the intensity of this experience may vary across individuals and with time. It can range from feelings of nominal affiliation with the group to a deep identification or even to the feelings 'honor' are reacted to a strongly as damage to one's own self. Psycho-social forces in a particular period of history bring out latent group identities and turn them violent ends.

S. Kakkar's concept (1996) of 'out group', 'them' and 'others' often motivates and rationalizes arson, looting, killing or resorting to vigilantism, which can be both sporadic and pre-meditated. Sociologically, it is a case of 'in-group' feelings of affinity and loyalty towards the group that one belongs to (ethnocentrism). Whereas 'out group' feelings towards other communities may be that of envy, hatred, animosity and, revenge, which can be traced back to a bloody history between the two in the past, and may be due to past experiences or the traditional religious identification – communalism. S. Kakkar (1996) explained as to how territory and passion play a vital role in shaping one's identity, mindset or psyche (old traumatic experiences often shape the degree and intensity of violence that can be inflicted on the other group, an old vendetta rooted in history). S. Kakkar (1996) analysed the genesis of Hindu–Muslim animosity, riots, carnage, etc. Another crucial element is 'territory', a sense of belonging. In this case, the SS has constantly tried to espouse the cause of the 'mother land – *Matrubhoomi*' by citing examples of as to how Shivaji Maharaj fought against the Mughals against all odds to set up his kingdom in Maharashtra. S. Kakkar in his masterpiece *Colors of Violence* has explained as to how violence becomes morally acceptable when communally and religiously sanctioned. Thus, religious intolerance and hatred against a specific community are often experienced during riots. In this chapter, the issue of legitimization of violence the MNS way, that is, the *Halla-bol/Sirf todd-phod* way has in fact tried to explore into the main issues such as those of identity (ethnicity, linguistic, cultural and social). In India, Mumbai (Maharashtra) as a case in point, there are certain cleavages of language, ethnicity and religion that have figured predominantly in the literature on migration and ethnic conflict.

Myron Weiner (1978) in his cardinal work *Sons of the Soil: Migration and Ethnic Conflict in India* has examined movements demanding preferential hiring policies for members of the indigenous ethnic groups or 'sons of the soil' (*Bhoomiputra* ideology). Mumbai (Maharashtra) has witnessed the emergence of the SS, which bears testimony to the growth of regionalism and parochialism based on locals versus outsiders along linguistic lines, and in recent years, the genesis of the MNS, which has been often perceived as 'an overdose of regionalism'. The MNS has a strong anti-migrant stand, especially migrants from Uttar Pradesh and Bihar. The bone of contention lies in the loss of jobs for the locals and that jobs should be reserved only for the local (Marathi people only) 'sons of the soil' movement.

Due to the uncontrolled/unchecked flow of migrants into Mumbai city, especially from Uttar Pradesh and Bihar, it has added to violent clashes, beating of taxi drivers, construction workers and street vendors, attacking Bihari candidates appearing for Central Railways examinations and committing atrocities on construction workers forcing almost 10,000 workers to flee from Pune, Nasik and Mumbai. Thus, the MNS has tried to legitimize violence by adopting vigilantism both of the sporadic and the pre-meditated type against the 'outsiders' (UPian and Bihari migrants).

Lewis Coser (1966) stated while explaining some functions of violence that violence serves as an achievement. Very often, individuals seize upon the manipulation of violence; it has a cathartic effect – the pent up emotions such as anger, frustrations are expressed through the channel of violence. Today, we find that attributes such as linguistic and ethnicity are extremely crucial and often differences in socioeconomic position, linguistic and ethnic differences often add fuel to incite violence. Very often, anti-migrant regional movements make use of these differences to settle old scores by legitimizing violence between the locals/natives and the migrants (outsiders). Thus, the MNS resorted to register protest by often initiating violence and vigilantism, their constant reiteration of the MNS style (*Halla-bol*/hooliganism). The main objective of the MNS has been to bring about a change, that is, restoration of the past glory to Mumbai and Maharashtra and full employment to the locals. Thus, the name 'Navnirman Sena' itself reflects the ideology that is the rebirth of a new Maharashtra state. Thus, by indulging and inciting acts of violence, the MNS has tried to seek assertion of its identity and thereby legitimacy. If one were to compare MNS with revolutionary violence, the MNS workers by participating and indulging in acts of violence offer an opportunity to affirm/reaffirm its identity, participate in violence, thereby symbolizing their commitment to the 'revolutionary cause' and loyalty/affinity to the party. Thus, MNS activists/workers/supporters use violence as a danger signal to warn and threaten the migrants from Uttar Pradesh and Bihar to leave Mumbai/Maharashtra and go back to their own states or bear the consequences, that is, getting beaten up, manhandled or even killed.

Sudhir Kakkar (1996) in his major work *Colors of Violence* has emphasized this point while explaining about Hindu–Muslim riots; the subjective experiential aspects of conflict, hatred, prejudice are deeply etched in the minds of the people. Old memories are painful and thus have a long-lasting impact on the minds of the people. A similar situation would arise if MNS continues to go on its rampage – generating fear psychosis and thereby anxiety neurosis in the minds of the UPian and Bihari migrants. Thus, to put it sarcastically, pride (Marathi *Asmita* (identity), *Manasikta* (psyche) along with *Bhoomiputra*/'sons of the soil' ideology exists side by side with prejudice (hatred towards the UPian and Bihari migrants).

Violence also acts as a catalyst whereby using violence as a means the MNS has tried to produce and arouse the moral sentiment of the public. The use of violence to settle old scores, by trying to legitimize violence, is the current modus-operandi of the MNS, which is trying to legitimize its use of violence by often indulging in issuing threats to organizations that if they do not hire locals, MNS would teach them a cruel lesson by using the MNS style – *Sirf todd-phod*/*Halla-bol*/acts of *goondagiri*/hooliganism; for example, the threats given to the State Bank of India to give jobs only to the locals (Mumbai branch). Thus, for the MNS, resorting to violence serves as an achievement and danger signal as well as acts as a catalyst. The MNS party founder and president Mr Raj Thackeray has in fact literally cut his teeth (as a youth leader of his uncle's SS Party) where he had observed and learnt and often masterminded the use of violence to settle old scores, instil fear, terrorize people and try to assert and reassert identity of the party, thus had learnt the use of hooliganism, which is indeed one of the major 'isms' of the modern political world! Thus, the MNS is indeed a case of search for legitimacy/recognition and asserts its identity by trying to legitimize violence.

Conclusion

This chapter thus has tried to examine MNS issue by tracing its genesis and thereby its ideology nature and its role in trying to establish and the strategies, assert and reassert its identity by constantly harping on the issue of loss of jobs for the local due to the unchecked and uncontrolled and unabated flow (influx) of migrants especially from the Northern states of Uttar Pradesh and Bihar. The need for the reassertion of 'Marathi identity', 'Marathi *manoos*', *Asmita* (identity), the espousal of ethnocentric, parochial, cultural and linguistic (ethno-regional) identity evokes territorialism and the notion of 'insider' versus 'outsider', and the use of violence by the MNS in order to achieve their goals.

Thus, by resorting to 'vigilantism', the MNS is trying to seek legitimacy for itself through 'legitimization of violence' (Apter, 1997). The issue of regionalism is in fact nothing but an 'overdose of regionalism' or a very bloody (violent) form of 'parochialism'. The *Todd-Phod*, *Halla-bol* (hooliganism) method and the mentality of the MNS are to assert their 'identity' by often resorting to 'violence'. The issues of 'nativism' and 'regionalism' have been viewed in the context of 'anti-migrant movements'. If these acts of violence go uncontrolled, I am sure that in no time, it will be a case of 'legitimation crisis' for the MNS! Last, the MNS in Marathi language translates into *Manna se*; whereas in Hindi, it would mean 'Act according to your mind'; thus, the impulsive actions, especially by using violence/vigilantism both spontaneous and pre-meditated, commonly used by *Manna se* bears testimony to the literal translation of the MNS in Hindi.

References

Apter, David (1997). *The Legitimization of Violence*. Basingstoke: Macmillan Publication.

Coser, Lewis (1966). 'Some Social Functions of Violence', *The Annals American Academy of Political and Social Sciences*, March, 304(1): 8–18.

Guha, Ramchandra (2007). 'India Together - Feeling Left Out-Regionalism in India', 23 January. http://www.indiatogether.org/2007/janrgh.regions.html.

Gupta, Dipankar (1977). 'The Causes and Constraints of an Urban Social Movement', *Contributions to Indian Sociology*, 11(1): 69–90.

Kakkar, Sudhir (1996). *The Colors of Violence: Cultural Identities, Religion and Conflict*. Chicago: University of Chicago Press.

Katzenstein, Mary Fainsod (1973). 'Origins of Nativism: The Emergence of the Shiv Sena in Bombay', *Asian Survey*, April, 13(4): 386–99.

Khanna, S.K. (1999). *Contemporary Indian Politics*. New Delhi: Discovery Publishing House.

Lakdawala, D.T. (1963). 'Work, Wages and Well-Being in an Indian Metropolis' Bombay: Bombay University publication, p. 281, cited by Mary Fainsod Katzenstein 'Political Nativism: Shiv Sena in Bombay'. PhD dissertation, MIT, 1974.

Merton, Robert King (1957). *Social Theory and Social Structure*. New York: Free Press.

——— 'Hate Crimes: Race, Prejudice and Discrimination', in *Inter Group Relations-Social-Psychological Factors*. New Delhi: Sage Publications India Pvt. Ltd.

Singh, D.P. (2007). 'Migration in Mumbai: Trends in Fifty Years', *Demography India*, July-December, 36(2): 315–27.

——— (2009). 'Population Trend: Numbers Could Have Been Worse, but Implications Could Worsen', *Mumbai Human Development Report 2009*. Mumbai: UNDP and BMC-Municipal Corporation of Greater Mumbai.

'Vigilantism'. http://www.preventiveconflict.org/portalmainresearchviolence: Conflict in Lampung Indonesia Report.

Weber, Max (1947). 'The Nature of Charismatic Authority and Its Routinization', in *The Theory of Social and Economic Organization* (translated by A.M. Henderson and Talcott Parsons). New York: Oxford University Press.

Weiner, Myron (1978). *Sons of the Soil: Migration and Ethnic Conflict in India*. New Delhi: Oxford University Press.

Wikipedia (2009). 'Maharashtra Nav Nirman Sena'. http://enwikipedia.org/wiki.

Wilkinson, Steven I. (2004). *Votes and Violence: Electoral Competition and Ethnic Violence in India*. Cambridge: Cambridge University Press.

Zetterberg, Hans (1954). *On Theory and Verification in Sociology*. New York: Almqvist and Wiksell/Tressler Press.

7

Nationalism in India

Culture, Ideology and Polity – A Diachronic Perspective

C.N. Venugopal

Introduction

During the past several decades, Indian society has been studied with reference to its culture, its institutional networks (caste, community, etc.), religious behaviour, economic and political aspects and social change. Many outstanding contributions have been made by the scholars – Indian as well as foreign – in the fields of family and kingship, village, caste, urbanization, industrialization, religiosity, secularism, etc. These studies have mainly used positivistic, structural-functional methodology to interpret the diversities of Indian society. In this paper, I intend to show that an alternative approach such as phenomenology is available for understanding the Indian society.

The social sciences, which mainly developed under the aegis of the positivistic approach, have been challenged by new approaches such as phenomenology, hermeneutics and ethnomethodology. Since positivism was modelled in the 19th and 20th centuries on physical sciences, it relied heavily on sense-based data such as formal interviews, observation, etc. Even within the physical sciences, reality is no longer confined to what is known objectively. The physical universe is not confined to what is observed through the instruments of quantitative measurement. Early in the 20th century, notions about time and space were modified by the relativity theory of Einstein; later, his associates developed what is called 'quantum science'. Here, consciousness was treated as an integral part of the enquiry. In other words, the physical world does not exist outside the human consciousness. Further, there are subatomic structures, such as protons, electrons, particles, etc. These infinitely small units are usually invisible and can be inferred only through the quanta or mathematically divided probabilities.

Similarly, in sociology, there are some dimensions of behaviour that cannot be quantified. It was Edmund Husserl[1] who stressed the role of subjectivity.

According to him, the *ideas* about mathematics, physics and chemistry originated in human mind. Therefore, the models, which guided the scientist's exploration of the physical world, were constituted in the human consciousness. In addition, intentionality guided the individual's social activity. Actions are not merely the result of values and norms, which are objectively located in society, but they are modified by the human intentionality; yet, an individual can transcend his or her subjectivity through reflection (*eidos*). If intentionality is disregarded, the human actions cannot be properly understood, for example, when a widow pledges her wedding ring at a pawnbroker's shop, two very diverse reactions can be noticed with reference to this object. The widow recalls the memories (sweet and bitter) associated with the ring, whereas the pawnbroker merely treats it as an item, which serves as security for the loan given.

In social sciences, the questionnaire or schedule-based interview has failed to notice many *subtle* signs, gestures, etc. In domestic settings, married couples, siblings, etc., carry on their activity by verbal message as well as non-verbal gestures. Further, in close circles, the sentences used for exchanging information are elliptically formed (i.e., incompletely structured). There is also the fact that structured interviews cannot accommodate the responses of interviewees without 'glossing' over. What is recorded does not necessarily include the nuances; it is just an approximation of the verbal responses given by the interviewer. Cicourer[2] has referred to these lacunae in the positivistic approach.

Alfred Schutz[3] treated the social sciences as second-order constructs. The 'common sense world' was one where men, women and children interacted with each other in a pre-reflective or pre-formal way. In the daily encounters between people in a market place, foreground of the church or a neighbourhood, they are appresented to each other, that is, they are brought into contact without any previous design or plan. These primary encounters are apperceived. Each is intuitively aware of the other person. During these encounters, the previous prejudices usually melt away, and there is a human bond that is forged without any intermediation. He called this the 'umwelt' interaction, wherein person-to-person meetings are the crucial element. For Schutz, the primary world is the paramount reality, whereas the social sciences are the finite province of meaning. The dominance of positivistic models has led to the neglect of the fact that the society we are studying is part of ourselves. The scientific objectivity is in no way affected by the recognition of subjectivity. In the group interaction, individuals modify each other's subjectivity in such a way that they are likely to reach 'intersubjectivity', that is, they share their objectivity.

The above references help us to look at the Indian society in a different way. Culture, ideology and policy need to be understood as existing on two levels: (i) there is an underlying primary level in which people's interactions are based on pre-formal, unwritten, apperceived ways; and (ii) there is an impressive layer of literary, canonical and political texts. In general, the first level deals with 'what is', whereas the second level deals with 'what ought to be'. So far as the common people are concerned, the 'texts' with which they are familiar are not the written documents. The Hindu, Buddhist and Jain temples convey ideas through their architecture, sculpture, paintings, etc., by drawing upon the epics, legends, historical events, war and peace. Besides, at the village level, the open air theatre, ballad and religious recital are also engaged in a cultural transmission. The whole nights are spent by the villagers in watching epic themes from Ramayana and Mahabharata, which are enacted in the open air theatre. These 'texts' are pre-formal but powerful influences that mould people's response. The fact that India is a thriving democracy despite widespread illiteracy is due to this pre-formal 'schooling'.

It is not right to think that only the religious ideas are conveyed through such 'texts'. The ballad, drama and religious recital referred to above are memorized through the hereditary training, but they are receptive to contemporary events. The characters who stride across the dais in a village setting often make snide comments on secular politics of the day. Similarly, veiled references are made to the corruption or political inefficiency. Thus, religious imagery enters the secular life through various forms of entertainment.

Inclusiveness is the outstanding aspect of Indian culture: folk, tribe and caste have been drawn together in religious behaviour such as pilgrim circuits, temple building and in the craft work. The terms 'aristocratic' and 'folk' are not translated as 'marga' and 'deshi' in so far as India is concerned. In other words, all those who are engaged in work – be it preaching god's name, sculpture, architecture or craft work – are *margis* whether they are from caste, folk or tribe. Their background is not relevant; it is their engagement that serves as the index. By contrast, all those who are engaged in profane or philistine work are *deshis*. The extraordinarily rich miniature paintings, murals, etc., which we find in Rajasthan, Gujarat, Kangra valley etc., are of the *marga* type. The portraiture of individuals with a view to glorification is an example of 'deshi' art. Both Ananda Coomaraswamy[4] and Radhakamal Mukerjee[5] have pointed that the Indian art and culture are the composite products of all the diverse groups, namely, caste, folk and tribe. The two main features of the *marga* art are that it is anonymous and the physical features of gods, men, women and children are impersonal, that is, they do not represent anyone in particular.

Even in the field of epic literature, Valmiki who composed Ramayana and Vyasa who wrote Mahabharata were not drawn from a high-caste background. In the Bhakti period (6th–17th century AD), many men and women composed songs, hymns to the deities in regional languages; they did not belong to elitist or literary circles and get their works (i.e., collections of their compositions) are vibrantly alive to this day. Mention may be made of Kabir and Guru Nanak in North India, Tukaram in Maharashtra and Purandaradasa in Karnataka and many others.

The alternative approach taken up in this paper provides scope for exploring new sources of understanding India. The two contemporary figures – Sri Ramakrishna and Sri Ramana Maharshi – were not learned. They were entirely foreign to religious pomp, privilege and coterie of admirers. Yet, their simplicity drew thousands to them. Ramakrishna referred to the gross desires – search for wealth, sensual pleasure – as the obstacles to the attainment of spirituality. Ramana Maharshi taught that *ego* (the 'I' ness) was the stumbling block indeed; we are all 'self-realized' people, but the ego has thrown an opaque veil on the face of realization. Earlier, a reference was made to the primary and secondary constructs. In Indological or historical studies much emphasis has been placed on the canons known as *dharmashastras*. But the writ of *dharmashastras* did not run across the entire country. In the courts of kings or urban centres, they were preeminent. But, in India, right from the pre-Mauryan times, there were republican states in which customs were the guides to action. In South India, the panchayats or local councils functioned effectively even during the dynastic rule. Both in the past and in the contemporary times, folk and tribal communities have existed in Indian hinterland where the literacy and learning are not preeminent. The *dharmashastra* tradition, which is a secondary nstruction, has its own importance, but it is not an exclusive source of normative behaviour. Even where the *dharmashastras* reigned, the *rishis* and *gurus* have modified some injunctions by using their moral authority. In fact, many *dharmic* injunctions were drawn from the diverse customs of the people, which were mostly in an unwritten form.

The topics of this paper may be briefly referred to. The cultural pluralism in Indian society has come about due to a tolerant attitude that is inbuilt. Despite ethnic or linguistic diversity, sectarian clashes, ideological rivalries, and political or historical exigencies, the underlying harmony has been reinforced by temple towns located in diverse parts of India, pilgrim circuits and social religious movements. A notable aspect of Indian culture is that its arts and crafts, religion and philosophy migrated to countries outside India, such as Sri Lanka, Cambodia, Thailand, Indo-China and Tibet without any political sponsorship. The people in these countries willingly accepted ideas and techniques from India and incorporated them into their local cultures. The cultural exchange between India and these countries was volitional. Even today, in the Indonesian Bali Island, the Ramayana is enacted by local troupes with much enthusiasm. This paper looks into cultural migration, arts and crafts and the role of guilds.

Force and non-violence can be viewed as interrelated dimensions of Indian society: while the political control of society has been dependant on the deployment force by rulers to curb disorder, non-violence has been favoured by some groups as a national objective. The Buddhist and Jain doctrines were based on a non-violent approach to life. Vegetarianism, abstinence from destruction of flora and fauna and simple ethical living were the most significant tenets of these doctrines.

Dharma and *rita* are interrelated. *Dharma* may be defined as a formal system based on socio-religious injunctions. *Rita* has been derived from the Veda, which was predicated on man's relationship with nature.

Due to the pluralistic nature of Indian society, multiple political centres have prevented any formation of a unitary political culture. Not only the king or ruler but also the caste, guild, folk and tribal councils have exercised autonomy in the governance of common people. Although these groups aimed at keeping their autonomy intact, the king alone had the authority to command an army, which was necessary to preserve the national identity.

To sum up, the alternative approach referred to earlier has been used innovatively in some of the studies. An outstanding example is the phenomenological approach in Sir Evans Prichard's study of Azande witchcraft. In ethnomethodology, Garfinkel and Cicourel have conducted valuable studies.

Earlier, Hegel's work on phenomenology and Jung's work on collective unconscious had opened up new frontiers of enquiry, but the studies mentioned above are more subjectivistic in their orientation.

Cultural Pluralism

Diversities of various types – linguistic, ethnic, political, economic and social – are the permanent features of Indian society. Epics such as Ramayana and Mahabharata have referred to a variety of castes and tribes, some of which can be identified even today. No region in India is monolithic in the sense that only one ethnic type fills in the social space. For example, in Jammu and Kashmir state in the northern region, Muslims, Hindus, Tibetan Buddhists and Baltis (a North European tribe) have lived adjacently. In the coastal region of Gujarat and Maharashtra, an African tribe known as Sidhi has been living since the 17th century, and many of its old customs are still intact. The pre-Gupta art of the Mathura region in Uttar Pradesh came under Greek and Iranian cultural influence during the rule of Kushans (1st–5th century AD). These foreign influences were absorbed into the Indian style, and a distinctive art (related to sculpture, etc.,) began to flourish there. Tamil Nadu, Puducherry and Karnataka had extensive trade links with the early Europe. Greek and Roman colonies were established near ports in the southern region. The ethnic adjacency has not been confined to economic exchange; there has been, in most cases, a cultural exchange. There were strifes and clashes amongst these diverse groups, but the dynamics of give and take was also there. An absence of 'ethnic cleansing' has been India's cultural hallmark. N.K. Bose writes:

> It is often overlooked that caste was a way of organizing production. The system fostered a much more fine-grained texture of communities, each identified with an occupation and maintained by intra-marriage, competition was deliberately discouraged. The caste communities were often distinguishable by differences in customs and cultures but they were traditionally bound by mutual ties of exchange of goods and services. Such differences were not suppressed but were even encouraged to exist in their own right.[6]

In fact, during the medieval period (around 6th–17th century AD), castes, trade guilds and temples were interconnected. The trade guilds were federations of working families engaged in the pursuit of particular trades such as silk weaving, carpentry, sculpture, building work and production of religious objects (such as idols, vessels used in rituals, etc.). Besides, the guilds were also engaged in weapon-making, production of household utilities, storage and distribution of grains and banking; they also standardized products, provided raw materials to the workers and received protection from the local rulers. Apart from purchasing their products, the temples and monasteries provided them warehousing facilities. The local rulers not only protected the hereditary rights but also provided safe passage to the traders in moving their goods within their realm.

At this juncture, a point related to the Indian culture may be highlighted. Indian society has been mostly referred to as a caste oppressed society. This has not deterred Indians from cultivating a voluntaristic attitude. A few examples may be provided: the three well-known languages of India – Sanskrit, Persian and English – were dominant at one time or the other. Political, social or economic need made people learn Persian or English to earn their livelihood, but many people across caste and class learnt these languages on their own. For example, in Kerala, a number of Christian and Muslim teachers in Sanskrit are found, despite the differences in religion. In the West, linguistic felicity is mostly found among the literati. Here, even common people learn different languages in spoken form.

Similarly, taking up the role of a soldier or becoming an ascetic or craftsman or a tradeer has not been confined to particular caste groups, but the individuals have/had a free choice. As Vivekananda noted in one of his lectures abroad, India is the only country in the world where there is a total religious freedom. One may choose a personal deity of one's choice or follow a thought pattern, which is different from that of his caste members. For example, a Hindu may be a Buddhist or Jain in terms of *mental attitude*, while remaining in the caste on an *existential basis*.

Although Max Weber recognized the significance of the guilds in Indian economy, his remark that guilds suffered a setback due to caste rivalry, is not sustainable. It was the decline of political patronage and the disintegration of religious networks after the 10th century AD, which gradually weakened the hold of guilds. In Europe too, the guilds were the mainstay of the feudal economy. Even in the industrial era in Germany and Japan, up to the end of the 19th century guilds were controlling production, finance and banking. In contrast to the factory work, the guilds functioned in a non-competitive manner. Within the guilds, the clash between managers and workers did not gain upper hand because the ties between people were multiple and derived from hereditary rights and obligations.

Despite factory-based production in India at present, selected crafts have not lost their appeal or uniqueness. Therefore, the silk-weaving done in Banaras or Kanchipuram, textiles from Kutch region of Gujarat, Chanderi in Madhya Pradesh, Sambalpur in Orissa, Lucknow in Uttar Pradesh, and handloom products from Erode in Tamil Nadu have a distinctive craft-based texture. These crafts in design, weave, etc., have a strong ritualistic association. Marriages, religious ceremonies and festive occasions call for their use in homes, temples and social gatherings.

The transmission of Indian philosophies and religion was accomplished on two levels. History records the visits of Fahien and Huen-Tsang who came to India to study Buddhism, studied manuscripts and carried some of them with them. These were subsequently translated into the Chinese language. The Buddhist universities such as Nalanda and Takshashila disseminated not only knowledge of religion or ethics but also of Ayurveda. The Chinese medical system, which is highly advanced, was based to a considerable extent on the Ayurvedic texts drawn from India. Since many students from outside India had come to these universities, the cultural transmission reached many foreign locations.

The non-literary transmission was attained through the migration of craft techniques from India. The great monuments such as Angkor Wat (Cambodia) and Borobudur (Java) bear strong Indian influences in sculpture and architecture. Coomaraswamy[7] noted that a Chola king in the 8th century AD sent many craft families from Tamil Nadu to Sri Lanka, in response to a request from the Sinhalese Buddhist king. These artisans were engaged in raising Buddhist monuments. Thus, in cultural transmission, the Indian crafts have played an important role.

Previously, a reference was made to the guild-based productions. The crafts, which were placed under the aegis of these guilds, were fostered in families, in which men, women and children participated in the work. The members of the family learnt craft by not attending schools, but by day-to-day engagement in carpet-weaving, silk-weaving and working on textile design. Here, it would be necessary to show that the usual distinction made in sociology between 'ascribed' and 'achieved' statuses does not hold good, where the crafts are concerned. To learn a craft or master, the technique requires several years of dedicated work. It is not something that is just passed on in a family. For, although the craft is inherited within the ambit of the family, painstaking commitment to work is the only way through which a novice can become skilled. When one visits a handloom centre for textiles or workshop where carpentry or metal work is done, one can observe the dedication of the workers.

So far as crafts are concerned, three types of chieftainship may be noticed. Earlier, the temples had large resources to buy craft-produced goods. Then, the guilds and individual craftsmen often presented their work to the local chiefs, rulers and important individuals. Here, the gifts were given to these people as articles of presentation. Actually, both the temples and palaces became veritable storehouses of art and craft. Further source is the pilgrimage. Pilgrims who move across India on religious circuit carry craftwork in memory of their visit to a holy place. An example would be the sealed metallic pots containing Ganga water. These are purchased in thousands by pilgrims at Banaras, Hardwar and Prayag and are carried to many parts of India.[8] The relationship between crafts and clients is not based on monetary considerations alone. The wares purchased from craft centres are usually passed on from one generation to another as family heirlooms. A monetary consideration cannot explain fully the symbolic value of the object. In this regard, Coomaraswamy wrote:

> Instances could be multiplied, but it will suffice to say that the arts have been universally referred to a divine source, that the practice of an art was as much a life as a trade. And that the artefact itself had a double value, that of the tool on the one hand and that of the symbol on the other hand.[9]

In passing, it may be noted that despite secularization of Indian society in the recent decades, the textiles, jewellery, etc., still carry the symbols seen as elephant, temple or peacock. In the folk or tribal craft of Kutch or Rajasthan, the ritualized designs are still used. The Madhubani and Tanjore paintings are mostly based on religious themes. These arts and crafts are an unceasing source and wonderment. Despite large-scale industrialization, household-based production is still thriving in many regions in India by household members working on woollen and cotton goods, by making dolls and decorative items, readymade dress, carpets, etc. Here, there in an extensive participation by women members too. Across India, in many town centres, displaced persons from Tibet (mostly women) carry on a thriving trade in readymade woollen and leather goods. Household production is exceptionally strong in Kashmir Valley, Gujarat, Rajasthan, Odisha, Haryana and Tamil Nadu. In other states too, craftwork is being carried out. There is a good deal of hardship in craft production: in the freezing winter of Kashmir Valley or hot climate of Kutch, households engage themselves in craftwork. All that they do is part of 'learning'. Ivan Illich's 'de-schooling'[10] has a relevance to craftwork.

In the post-independent India, much public money has been spent under the various educational programmes to spread literacy. Many of these projects have floundered. Where simple farming or craftwork is concerned, the literacy is redundant and it has a limited value. Even if peasants or artisans become literate, they still do not operate bank account or with a few exceptions read literary works. Ivan Illich says that those who have escaped 'schooling' are fortunate because they are learning the game of life in the courtyard of the house.

While summing up this section on cultural pluralism, a few specific features of craft and art may be mentioned. The following are the underlying unities in the culturally pluralist society of India: (i) anonymity, (ii) collective orientation and (iii) impersonality.

The artist does not claim that he has produced his work. The great temples that are found in South India, Khajuraho in Madhya Pradesh, Konarka in Odisha, Mount Abu in Rajasthan and Palitana in Gujarat mostly do not carry 'signatures' of sculptors or painters or architects. The work of art is not focused on 'aesthetic pleasure' (which is reserved for the philistine elements), but on gaining collective recognition for itself. Further, the crafts do not represent any individuals but ethnic types. Thus, gods and goddesses or kings and queens whose images we find in temples and palaces are not the replicas of particular individuals. It is in this sense that the Indian art (also medieval European art) is not *realistic*. Once the underlying *symbolism* is understood, then, the many-armed goddesses or many-hooded cobras do not appear grotesque. Viewed from the above perspective, the modern Indian art, which has fascinated the present-day elitist sections from an urban background, is rather disoriented.

Force and Non-Violence: The Two Facets of National Life

As stated earlier, the Vedic ceremonies led by the Yajamana (ruler) and the Purohit (Brahmin ritualist) centred around animal sacrifice. Both Jainism and Buddhism protested against such animal sacrifices. The vegetarian habits that are widespread in India have been the offshoots of these two belief systems. India is the only country in the world where there are a large number of vegetarians. Although Jainism has been consistently vegetarian, Buddhism outside India has no such commitment to it. Among the three upper castes of India – Brahmin, Kshatriya and Vaishya – only the last mentioned group is firmly rooted in the vegetarian habit. Brahmins in eastern India and up country north (parts of Uttar Pradesh and Kashmir) consume meat. Most Hindus, Buddhists and Jains would uphold vegetarianism as an *ideal type of habit*, although in practice some groups consume meat. The religious advocacy of vegetarianism is based on a few points, which are linked to man's relationship with nature.

Joseph Campbell,[11] a noted American commentator on India, gave some insights into this practice. According to him, plants, trees, creepers, grass, etc., which go under the common rubric 'vegetation' are continuous in their life span. The grass is grazed by livestock everywhere, yet the grass grows back again; the trees, shrubs and creepers are pruned by those who are engaged in agriculture, horticulture or gardening. These plants are actually stimulated by pruning, and they grow back with renewed vigour. A tree may be felled by a storm or by an axe; yet if its roots are intact, it recovers its lost portions. By contrast, the fauna, which comprise animals, birds and reptiles are discontinuous. The living beings die if their limbs are cut off. For example, the wheat seeds found in a pyramid germinate in the soil, whereas the egg of a reptile cannot hatch after a lapse of time. The religious attitude, therefore, discouraged the killing of animals by human beings. However, in practice, some groups within Hinduism allowed ritual consumption of meat.

Secondly, the plants, etc., have a low threshold of pain, and this is why they are able to withstand grazing or pruning. Most animals react strongly to pain. The crustaceans (crabs, etc.) have a low threshold of pain just like plants, but they do not have the regenerative capacity; if they are injured, they will die. Hence, it was declared to be less painful, if vegetarianism was cultivated. Modern researches in medicine have supported the view that a vegetarian habit is more conducive to human health.

In this regard, a few clarifications may be given. The term 'tamasik' does not by itself mean consumption of meat. This term refers to consumption of food that is 'oily, spicy and heavy'. Even the *rishis* ate ritually prepared meat. Indeed, a vegetarian who consumes a large quantity of food is as much a *tamasik* as a heavy meat eater. When Charaka, the ancient Ayurvedic practitioner, was asked by a person to give advice on food, he said: 'eat a limited quantity of food; eat according to its suitability; and eat according to season'. It is common observation that many people in India at present times have grossly set aside Charaka's advice. Material prosperity has ushered in an era of overconsumption. In urban centres, gorging on food and lack of physical exercise have had a harmful effect on human health.

For the ascetics in India, the ideal food habit has been the pursuit of *shiloncha vritti* (the gathering of seeds and berries, which have fallen on the forest floor). Alternatively, living on the leaves of trees or shrubs is followed. Swami Vivekananda stayed for some time with a reclusive *sadhu* in the Himalayan region. For months, this *sadhu* (who was a Rama devotee) lived on a handful of lemon tree leaves that he consumed every day. The local people called him *pavhari baba* (one who lived on air). Some of the *sadhus* who dwell in this region have lived far beyond the ordinary life span. Perhaps, a more interesting point is that the *sadhus* live in Himalayan, submontane and forest locations, without any fear from wild animals. Swami Rama,[12] in his autobiography, has affirmed that no *sadhu* has been killed by a wild animal in the Himalayan region. He lived as a young man in this region for some years; later, he came down to the plains of India. He meditated on the sands of the Narmada river in Madhya Pradesh for some six months. Around him lay crocodiles, which came to rest on the sand. These animals did not interrupt his meditation!

The above digression was made to highlight the simple truth that if we are non-violent in mind, even the wild animals do not harm us. In fact, no wild animal attacks human being without provocation. Perhaps, the crocodile and the hippopotamus are the only two animals, which attack human beings without being provoked. This phenomenon reveals that there is an *invisible* or *intangible* bond between human being and animals or other living entities of nature. In fact, parrot, pigeon, deer, peacock, dolphin, etc., seek human company through their friendly gestures.

In Indian philosophy, there are four states of consciousness, which are described as follows:

1. *Turiya* (supra conscious stage) usually attained by yogis or rishis in the *samadhi*.
2. *Sathwika* (a pious or non-violent state).
3. *Rajasika* (a state of passion).
4. *Tamasika* (a state of inertia or grossness).

These are only the analytical types. The Samkhya school of Indian philosophy has made a detailed reference to the second, third and fourth types. All the major religions of India have incorporated the Samkhya philosophy in their doctrines. Besides, it may be mentioned that Samkhya, Nyaya and Vaisheshika are the three systems of Indian philosophy that are highly ratiocinative.

In fact, in most periods of Indian history, *rajas* and *sattwa* have worked together in order to keep *tamas* at bay. Aurobindo[13] wrote as follows:

> Sattwa can never be the cause of downfall; indeed, a nation which is predominantly sattwik cannot remain bound in slavery. The spiritual power of the true Brahmin is the chief result of the sattwa; the prowess of the Kshatriya is the foundation of spiritual power. Spiritual power cannot survive when there is no Kshatriya prowess ... the cause of the downfall of the country is not an excess of sattwa but want of rajas and preponderance of tamas. Owing to the lack of rajas, the sattwa inherent in us becomes weak and concealed in tamas.

Aurobindo pointed out that it was absolutely essential for *rajas* to be guided by *sattwa*. Otherwise, the *tamas* would predominate and destroy the very goal, which the *rajas* wanted to attain. He cited the example of the French Revolution.[14] The early revolutionary fervour in France (in favour of the oppressed) later degenerated into mindless killings of people by the deployment of guillotine; this event was a clear manifestation of *tamas*. The colonial period of India's history was dominated by the *tamas* of people who were subjected to inertia or mental slavery. The tragedy was that all ranks of people (elites, folks, town dwellers and villagers) fell into a stupor.

In this context, it may be mentioned that both Vivekananda and Aurobindo were critical of the Buddhists. Vivekananda[15] stated that Buddhism (in the 8th or 9th century AD) became tainted with tantrik beliefs and practices. Aurobindo[16] stated that large groups of Kshatriyas laid down their arms under a misguided motion of pacifism. It was nothing short of a national calamity; the country becomes vulnerable to hordes of foreign invaders. In contrast to

India, Buddhism in other countries existed within the ambit of warlike political systems. In Sri Lanka, Burma, Cambodia, Thailand, etc., the rulers deployed military strength to quell rebellion within the realm and to prevent invaders from coming in. In the 17th century, the Tibetan army marched over to the mainland China and controlled a strategic portion of that country for some years. In recent years, the Dalai Lama's pacific approach has been questioned by some of his followers.

According to Aurobindo,[17] the Gandhian approach was not Indian. It was modelled on Tolstoy's philosophy and Quaker's pacifism. In some of the Buddhist centres outside India, the martial arts (such as Kung-Fu Karate, etc.) were cultivated with great dedication. It was Bodhidharma, the monk from India, who launched this activity in the Shaolin temple (China) in 5th century AD subsequently. These arts have reached spectacular heights. These marital techniques are in consonance with Buddhism; in their *pristine* form, these arts do not involve bloodshed but only disablement of the opponent and prevention of aggression.

Non-Violence as a National Ideology

The Gandhian ideology of non-violence has justly gained international recognition. The civil rights movement in North America, the anti-Apartheid protest in South Africa and in many other international movements, the Gandhian ideology has illuminated the path of struggle. In India, pre-independence struggle was mainly guided by Gandhian ideology. It mobilized a large number of volunteers for the struggle, revived interest in rural development and set a personal example in implementing his projects. His ascetic habits and practices inspired many others in India, and people conferred upon him the saint's status; however, his followers were not always up to the mark in terms of purity or change of heart.

During his lifetime, Gandhi fasted on several occasions (as for example during the textile agitation in Ahmedabad and protest against the British legislation, etc.). In a sense, the employer or the ruling authority was morally coerced by the fasting *satyagrahi*. Besides, in the post-independence period, the *satyagraha* technique has been used mainly for parochial or limited ends. The blockage of road and rail traffic and stoppage of work in offices and factories have adversely affected the national interest. In such protests, the pursuit of truth has become less important than securing benefits and privileges. Thus, the *satyagrahi*'s idealism has often floundered on short gains.

By hindsight, it is now clear that the end of British rule in India did not come about only through the Gandhian struggle. During the Quit India Movement of 1942, millions of people protested against the British rule. The British government had become tired due to the prolonged Second World War, and it was becoming a burden to keep India under its political authority. The world opinion was also impinging on its colonial policy. But there were two additional factors, which made Britain act decisively with regard to the settlement of India's demand for full freedom. Towards the later phase of the Second World War, Subhas Chandra Bose organized the Indian National Army which, with the help of Japanese army, reached the northeastern frontier of India. In 1944, there was a widespread mutiny in the Bombay docks by the Indian Royal Navy. The British authorities militarily crushed the revolt; hundreds of Indians sailors were killed in the struggle. The Gandhian movement and the two above events made the British rulers apprehensive about the future of their control over India; and in 1947, they conceded full freedom to it. Thus, at the national level, both force and non-violence have had an impact on political issue.

Dharma and Rita

These two terms are related, but they imply different meanings. The *dharma* is a relativistic term: it varies from society to society on account of differences in history and culture; social norms such as right and wrong and reward and punishment are modified by economic, political and social exigencies. In India, *dharma* is known as *smriti* (literally meaning recollected text). The *rishis* heard the text from a divine source and composed the Vedic hymns (CE 5000). The term *rita* is closer to the Veda, and it has a universal quality. It stands for a harmonious relationship with nature. It may be mentioned there that the Veda propitiates Surya, Agni, Varuna, Marut, Ushas, Aditi and other deities who are a personification of nature. In Japanese religion (Shintoism) too, the nature's forces, collectively known as 'Kamikaze' (storm gods), are propitiated. Also both in India and Japan, some locations have assured a significance. Just as Mount Kailas or Mansarovar is invested in India with a sacrality, for Japanese Mount Fuji (a volcano) is a sacred mountain.

While the *dharma* is mainly concerned with the regulation of social and religious behaviour, the *rita* is a way of life in which common people seek to live in harmony with nature so that their households, kith and kin live in peace. In the academic works on Indian society, much emphasis has been placed by the scholars on the religio-judicial texts and the *varna* and *ashrama*. It would be helpful to see the complementary role of *rita* by making a detailed reference in this paper. A.K. Sen, an indologist, writes: 'There is another conception in the Vedas which is intimately connected with the concept of *dharma*. This is *rita*, meaning the order and harmony in the universe and in human society.'[18]

An early sociologist W.G. Sumner used the terms 'crescive' and 'enacted'. The first term refers to something that is inherited from a timeless past, i.e., a custom. The second term refers to man-made provisions in law. The *rita* is allied to the first term, whereas *dharma* is related to the second term. The customs are derived from the experience of early human societies, which lived in close proximity to nature, following some natural rhythms in hunting, seafaring and growing crops. They observed seasonal variations that are part of the nature's rhythm (to pursue hunting, seafaring or agriculture). The Biblical statement that there is a time to sow and a time to reap is suggestive of this practice. The early religious experience is based on a *reciprocal relationship* with nature. In particular, this entailed a self-imposed control on hunting, fishing, etc. If too much was extracted from nature, the balance was upset, for example, hunting should not lead to extinction of herds or fishing should not be done during spawning period. In most human habitats around the world, reciprocity (not wantonness) has been the rule.

It is for this reason that fertility cults, harvest festivals, collective worship of deities who are the guardians of nature have been nearly universal. The Greeks- and Romans-sponsored public cults derived from these elements. The Eastern and Far Eastern countries, such as India, China and Japan, derived a number of rituals from the folk practices. In Europe, although Christianity treated some of these practices as Pagan, it could not completely eliminate them. Just as Vedas, which had a poetic component and a philosophical component, the *rita* has some abstruse implications. Kirit Joshi (a follower of Aurobindo) writes:

> The *rita* (right) is founded in the truth of reality and of the universe (*satyam*). Its field of action is the totality which is the infinite vast (*brihat*). The *rita*, therefore, cannot be prescribed or circumscribed by any legislation or human-made law *rita* issued from the vast consciousness, and it is thus superior to any human standards of action or any laws of the individual and collective life. It is this idea of *rita* that lay behind the governing ideas that determined the various aspects of life in India.[19]

Joseph's term 'vast consciousness' is implied in the term 'supra consciousness' in Indian philosophy. Coomaraswamy used the term 'unknown referent'. The poet Robert Browning wrote: 'petty done and undone vast'. In this field, we have known little (petty done), and there remains a vast unknown field (undone vast). Carl Jung's theory of the collective unconscious refers to this hidden reservoir in human psyche.[20] Husserl's term 'sedimented consciousness' implies that every individual has a submerged mental layer.

Vedas and Upanishads have underlined the reciprocal relationship between human and nature. In other words, human is not at the mercy of nature; he can modify it and derive from it not only physical sustenance but also peace and security. The Vedic fire sacrifices made an effort to propitiate Varuna, Agni, etc., in order to secure their benevolence. If the ruler performed these sacrifices in proper order, his realm would be free from famine and pestilence, but this relationship was not founded on fear as it was wrongly interpreted by Max Muller. The heavenly deities were also dependent on the earthly ruler. The non-performance of fire sacrifice unsettled the heavens. Viswamithra, unlike other rishis, did not perform fire sacrifice. He pursued *tapasya* which happened to upset the heavenly order. Hence, Indra, the divine ruler, sent an Apsara to distract him. The implication of the above passage is that *without human intervention*, nature itself would be unsettled. The recurrence of floods, forest fires, tidal waves and large-scale destruction of bio-diversity areas have clearly indicated that human management of the nature has gone wrong, as man's attitude to nature at present is characterized by wantonness. Those who can afford eat too much, or spend too much energy for keeping themselves in comfort or mindlessly destroy nature's verdant fields through industrialization or urbanization.

It was mentioned earlier that *dharma* was a secondary construct. The primary source was the *rita*. In India, Jainism and Buddhism protested against Vedic ritualism, especially the fire sacrifices involving the animal slaughter. Although the Vedic hymns suggest the reciprocity between human beings and nature, obsessive concern with Vedic ceremonies was taking people towards a materialistic path. For example, the participants prayed for victory in battle, progeny or wealth. Thus, many of the Vedic hymns were misinterpreted. As Aurobindo mentioned in his work on the Vedas, these hymns were directed towards the inner self or awakening. The words such as 'herds of cattle' were metaphors for *intuitive* ideas that enabled one to reach the higher goal.[21] Neither Buddha nor Mahaveera disputed the Vedanta which was a metaphysics of the Veda. Vedanta, Jainism and Buddhism share some common notions on *karma* and *moksha* (nirvana) and ethics. Hence, the protest of these sects corrected the Vedic diversion into the sacrificial cults.

In the post-Vedic stages, the *dharmashastras* that broadly included writings of Manu, Yajnyavalka and Kamandaka among others and enjoined upon the people to adhere to the prescribed duties, loyalty to *varna* and correct observance of rituals or rites of passage. In course of time, numerous commentaries on *dharma* appeared. These texts were necessary at the time, because without regulation of the society, anarchy would thrive. The *dharmashastras* generally flourished within the ambit of empires, where large-scale populations were brought under a centralized rule. Unto Tahtinen, an Indologist, writes:

> According to law givers the king should discharge his functions without anger and greed (*lobha*) following the sacred in association with and seeking advice from learned Brahmins. The king who is well-versed in *dharma* is expected to give his ruling after properly considering the *dharma* of sub-castes, country, noble people, family and his own *dharma*.[22]

There are two implications that can be derived from the above quotation: first, the king is mentally non-violent while using force to subdue evil-doers. Second, the king does not dictate terms to his subjects. He protects the rights and privileges of the individuals and groups that have come to them through their heredity.[23] It is for this reason that in India the 'divine right theory' did not exist in absolute terms. The kingship was respected, but it could not assume arbitrary powers of reward and punishment. At the most, the king presided over a federation of diverse groups and people looked up to him as a guardian of their rights. The king stepped in only when there was an infringement of the *dharma*. Tahtinen further notes:

> Ancient legal writers were fully conscious of the deterrent effects of punishment. Yet they emphasized that the most efficient deterrences were provided by the fear of the necessary metaphysical consequences of all actions. Effect of *karma* works without failure and everyone has to enjoy the fruits of his action – good or bad. Basically deterrence was felt to be efficient due to the metaphysical consequences of action.[24]

Although the *dharmashastras* become the great religio-juridical documents, the violations of these provisions often took place. Not all the rulers were wise and unselfish. Further, the people who committed wrongs did not always come forward to receive punishment. In large-scale societies, moral evasions are not infrequent. In small-scale societies, which are less impersonal, such evasion is difficult. This is the reason for different types of ethical behaviour within the same society. The elites are more resourceful and can collude with each other to conceal wrong doing, while maintaining a good image in the society. To give an example from contemporary times, in India, a number of educated people in the modern type of employment indulge in white-collar crimes (financial manipulation, falsification of records, etc.). The less privileged people, usually the poverty-stricken masses, are less prone to crime of the urban type, especially breach of trust. In rural households, a strong sense of morality prevails; and if a few individuals do the wrong act, the whole family loes reputation. In the villages where the residents know each other well, concealment is not possible beyond a point.

The Bhakti movements[25] usually mitigated the harshness of provisions made by the *dharmashastras* and motivated them to look inward. Since people came from a variety of backgrounds, the *satsang* enabled the participants to pray together, eat the same food and share the same lodging. Besides, gurus often modified the *dharmic* rules. Since some of these gurus came from non-literary backgrounds, their moral guidance was based on intuition and communion with nature. What is described as *samadhi* is an attempt to delve into the submerged consciousness. To sum up, revitalization of the *dharma*[26] is effected through our periodic return to the primary level (the *rita*). The recognition of *dharma* and *rita*, as interrelated phenomena, is helpful in getting a clear picture of Indian society.

Political Dimension

Different political systems have been working in Indian society with a bend towards the federal principle of governance. In the pre-Mauryan times, small republican states existed over the north. They usually had an elective type of kingship and a popular assembly; the erring ruler was often replaced by the assembly and a new one was elected. These small, autonomous states existed alongside each other. There were rivalries and skirmishes among them, but there was no centralization of polity or scope for a militarily dominant dynasty. The Buddhist Jataka tales, which were composed in both Pali and Sanskrit, provide information about them. During the ascendancy of the Mauryan state (CE 300), many of these states were demolished by subterfuge or conspiracy, which was initiated by the agents of the empire. Kautilya's *Arthashastra* has listed the devious steps, which the emperor had to adopt to keep the republican trend under check.

The second major type of political structure was the universally present panchayats that governed the villages in India. These panchayats were autonomous and supported a democratic framework within the village. As controllers of land, these panchayats occupied a position of privilege in the agrarian society. These panchayats and other local councils were powerful in Tamil Nadu, where the successive kings nurtured their autonomy. Although the panchayats in North Indian declined in importance after the 10th century AD, in the South they continued for a longer time. The third type of political control was exercised by temples, guilds, caste, folk and tribal councils. The rulers, who provided security for their legitimate work, assured their autonomy too.

The three noted political treaties, which are representative of the Indian traditional thought, are Kautilya's *Arthashastra*, Shukra's *Nitisara* and Bhishma's *Shantiparva* address.[27] In these documents, all of which were originally composed in Sanskrit, some guidelines were laid down for the governance of people by the rulers. All the Hindu, Buddhist and Jain rulers followed broadly the same texts. First, the ruler had to live a disciplined life; and in order to command respect of his subjects, he should desist from arbitrary acts. Second, in order to protect the *dharma*, *varna* and *ashrama*, he had to follow the *dandaniti* (i.e., a system of rewards and punishment). It was his moral duty to punish the offender; wielding the sword to quell internal rebellion and prevent invasion from outside were his most important missions. If the king became lax in this regard, he not only incurred sin but also lost the people's trust that was reposed in him.

Third, the king had to use some strategies to consolidate his political gains and expand his military control over his territory. The deployment of espionage, creating divisiveness within the rival ruler's camp, raising an efficient army, etc., were also commended in the texts. Buddhism and Jainism had no doubt shown a new spiritual path because the Vedic truths were submerged in many rituals. But anarchic trends were gaining the upper hand, due to the warring republics. Hence, these texts sought to revive a Brahminical order resting on *varna* and *ashrama*. A.K. Sen writes:

> *Manusmriti* was a kind of Hindu reaction against Buddhist domination. Same was true of Kautilya's *Arthashastra*. Kautilya mobilized the people of Magadha by raising the prospect of Greek invaders coming to India. In creating a high status for the emperor he revised the Brahminical order and curtailed the Buddhist influence. Even the *Nitisara* of Shukra and Bhishma's *Shantiparva* discourse on polity contributed to a Brahminical order.[28]

Despite their democratic nature, the republican states were becoming unstable. There were intrigues and murders within these republics; their internal defenses were weak and rivals raided each other's territory through open warfare or covert operation. The Buddhist story of Amrapali, a court dancer who later became a disciple of Buddha, recounts the political turbulence of times. Many of the Jataka tales record the intrigues. However, the king never attempted to abrogate traditional authority within his realm. He was conscious of his role as a defender and protected. A.K. Sen writes:

> In general, the Hindu king did not create rights and duties. The individual was free to pursue his swadharma. Only if the rights of other were tampered with, then the king stepped in. This autonomy or freedom was evident throughout the society but the king was greatly needed to maintain the social order. The swadharma was by itself a compex term inclusive of Jati, Kula and Vritti Dharmas.[29]

As noted earlier, Buddhism came to be associated with 'otherworldliness'. The pacifistic outlook, which developed among the ruling classes, endangered the unity of India. The martial spirit of the people did not disappear, but it became dispersed. Prithviraj Chauhan was the last of the great Hindu rulers of North India (10th century AD) who fought against invaders. Otherwise, the diffused martial spirit is still evident in Indian society. There has never been any conscription, and numerous people have enlisted for military service without any hesitation. In the Mauryan army, there were soldiers from the Mysore region (Karnataka). During medieval times, both Hindu and Muslim soldiers enlisted in the provincial armies irrespective of religious consideration. There were Hindu soldiers in the Sultan's army, whereas Rana Pratap, Shivaji and Rani Laxmi Bai used the services of Muslims. During the first two world wars, the Indian soldiers were employed by the colonial rulers. What Aurobindo regretted was the abandonment of the legitimate role by the Kshatriya groups, at the opportune moments of Indian history.

Karma and Political Destiny

Belief in *karma* (or reincarnation) is nearly universal. It is the belief that a human life is not a chance occurrence, but there is a past to it and a future too. Ancient Egyptians, the Kabalist sect of Judaism, early Christians and Sufis among Muslims believed implicitly in the hands of destiny, which guided people through many lives – past, present and future. The Hindu, Buddhist and Jain religious creeds explicitly recognized the *karma* doctrine. *Karma* can exist on both individual and collective levels. In either case, the *karma* theory does not propagate fatalism; on the contrary, it supports the efforts to overcome the existing hurdles and move forward.

John Mumford, a Westerner, who has become a Hindu monk of Advaitic path, has stated that *karma* is not associated with the Judeo-Christian notions of sin and punishment; here, a god sits in judgement over the deeds of mortals. *Karma* is always a self-directed process; but to some extent; its grip can be modified by the ritualistic activity. What this means is that a ritual or ceremony can enable individuals to look at their lives in an altered perspective or a positive outlook. *Karma*, according to him, is a *process* in which the reactions to human action operate in subtle ways; this process is different from a *mechanism*, which is bound by the dimension of time and space. He writes, 'Altering *karma* is often the primary function of ritual in all religions and all system of inner growth. The secondary function of ceremony is to alter your state of consciousness in a shift from the gross to the subtle.'[30]

All religions make an effort to come to terms with the *karma* or destiny of individuals. This religious enterprise cannot be described as fatalism, which is a kind of non-action. The 'otherworldliness' of Roman Catholics, Buddhism, Jainism and Hinduism was extensively discussed by Max Weber in his sociology of region. This stance was not generally shared, but it was mostly confined to the ascetics and monks. John Mumford further writes:

> There is actually no retribution involved in *karma*. *Karma* is a universal law of action and reaction... Justice is a human concept, variable from culture to culture. *Karma*, from the Eastern view, is not a human concept, but a transcultural fact that belongs to the large inherent cosmic order.[31]

As referred to earlier, *dharma* and *rita* are different in the sense that the former implies a system of justice, whereas the latter refers to a universal process. Mumford has noted that the word 'ritual' is derived from the Sanskrit prefix 'ri' (which is a cognate of *rita*). He has also noted that the word 'ceremony' is derived from *kri*, which is a cognate of *karma*.

Although *karma* – good or bad – operates on all levels, its relationship with polity needs special attention. Although individuals and groups are engaged in negotiating with their *karma*, a whole nation can reach a higher level through the deeds of a great leader. Emperor Ashoka was such an individual. In his realm, trees were planted, roads were laid, shelters for human beings and animals were provided and medical care reached the common people. These were the simple, pious acts of national consciousness. All sentient beings become parts of the society. He used the term *dharma* in his rock edicts in a purely non-sectarian sense.

On the reverse side, a nation may be led by a tyrant or a dictator, who eliminates his opponents without trial, set up labour or concentration camps for political dissidents and through propaganda projects himself as the saviour. Joseph Stalin, Adolph Hitler and Francisco Franco were the prime symbols of oppression on the European continent.

The subtle workings of *karma* are such that both types of leadership – the benovalent and the tyrannical – are due to the conscious or subconscious actions of people. When Jesus said, 'as you sow, so shall you reap', he implied that we deserve the kind of political development. For example, we have seen that in the post-independentce India, political leadership at several levels is tainted with corruption. This has not occurred by chance. Most Indians tend to be tolerant towards corruption. In public, it is denounced by educated people, but in primary groups (household, kith and kin, etc.), there is a latitude. The official or businessman who has made money on the side is not usually censured by those who are close to him; but on the contrary, he is admired. It is only when the level of corruption becomes very high that a drastic opinion may be formed against him. Likewise, postponement of work, laxity of rules and indifferent altitude towards the outcome of work are also the national traits.

Paradoxically, early writers such as Max Mueller and Sir Henry Maine had lavished praise on the truthfulness of Indians. It is likely that they were looking at a different social level. In general, common people in India have been more stringent in their attitude towards the outcome of social behaviour; centuries of religious teachings, the exemplary lives of *rishis*, *munis* and ideal rulers have influenced their dealings. Until recently, in most parts of India, mutual trust was the basis of many agricultural and commercial dealings in villages or towns.

By contrast, the departure from rules has become more widespread among the educated groups. Documentation and computerization facilities that are available in urban centres have often been grossly misused in banking, real estate and business enterprise. Mass communication has indeed subverted the 'ideal speech pattern' held up by Habermas as the true form of communication. Toynbee in his study of Greeks used the term 'collective karma'. In India's political destiny, whatever has happened previously can still be used as lesson from the past, and future can be altered. If due to our collective *karma* we have endured political oppression and social inertia, then we can still alter it through our future actions.

For instance, in the early years of India's post-independence, the foreign periodicals, newspapers and even academic publications harped upon Indians' imminent disintegration due to caste, rural backwardness, etc. The progress achieved in agriculture, industry and business enterprises has over the years considerably altered the doom predicted for India. But it is of utmost importance to define our political destiny on our own terms. Aurobindo regretted the rapid Westernization of Japan, whose cultural refinements are well known. As an aside, we may note that Japan, despite high advances in technology, has suffered from economic recession during the past decade. The early industrialists led by Sir Jamshedsji Tata firmly laid the path of India's development through mostly indigenous resources. As a case in point, the excessive reliance of Indian Information Technology on foreign clientship is the opposite of what Jamshedji had stood for. The national rebuilding finds sanction in the scriptural tradition of India. The Bhagavad Gita has been interpreted from diverse standpoints. But its underlying message is that only action can help us overcome the challenges of life. This message is retained in nearly all such interpretations. Aurobindo wrote:

> I do not regard the ascetic way of life as indispensable to spiritual perfection or as identical with it. There is the way of spiritual self-mastery and the way of spiritual self-giving and surrender to divine, abandoning ego even in the midst of action or any kind of work or all kinds of work demanded by the divine ... the Indian scriptures and the Indian tradition, in Mahabharata and elsewhere, make room for the spirituality of the renunciation of life and for the spiritual life of action [32]

Conclusion

In the introductory chapter, a mention was made of the need for an alternative approach to study human society. The positivists and structural functionalists, who dominated the social science research till the mid-20th century, based their models, hypotheses, etc. on the physical science models. The 'objectivity' was thought of as existing outside the observers and researchers. However, in truth, both physical science and social science models have originated in human mind, as pointed out by Husserl. Therefore, the role of subjectivity cannot be ruled out even within the framework of these models.

Schutz noted that positivism became the basis of numerous studies on different dimensions of society: these studies were constructs of the second degree. They drew their observations from the commonsense world but recorded their findings in a logical, formal manner. At the primary level, the commonsense world was a pre-logical, pre-reflective world. The commonsense encounters were appresented and apperceived, that is, they were without premeditation. Garfinkel noted that even the engagement in scientific work is a kind of folk behaviour. Just like the common man on the street or at the neighbourhood, the scientist too has faltered in his steps, corrected himself and arrived at some destination.

A seasoned sociologist such as R.K. Merton seemed to think that the achievements of science in the recent times (17th–20th century AD) were the summit of human achievement. It may be noted here that technology as contrasted with science has been coextensive with human society. The present-day scientists are still discovering the technical wonders of ancient China, Egypt,

India, Mayan civilization in Mexico, etc. On hindsight, it seems that science is a kind of *post factum* exercise. P.K. Feyerabend, the Cambridge scientist, noted that the Western science has been based on a unilinear approach; by contrast, a pluralistic approach would recognize that non-Western cultures too had their own contributions to make *cite an example*. Alburini (10th century AD), who was well versed in many fields of knowledge, referred to the gravitation principle discovered by Brahma Gupta (an Indian astronomer), but only Newton's work on these topics is known around the world.

The quantum science that has developed fast in the post-Einstenian era has come far away from the older science. Nature is no longer viewed as "something out" there. The role of human consciousness (subjectivity) is clearly recognized in the new approach. Here, the observation of nature is no longer confined to the sense data. There are many invisible forces and fields around us and they are also intangible. There are protons, electrons, radio waves, etc., whose behaviour is mathematically expressed. Mani Bhaumik, a scientist, has written:

> Some prominent contemporary physicists indeed believe that the mysteries of consciousness and quantum physics are linked. Most quantum systems have properties that are complementary and inseparable. From this perspective the primary realities of unified field and consciousness may be viewed as inseparable aspects of the same underlying process, permeating all space and time.[33]

Bhaumik also referred to the subtle nature of the subatomic universe.[34] He also stressed that quantum science and Vedanta share a common understanding of the reality of the universe. Two additional points may be mentioned. Ernest Schrodinger, a leader in this field, has noted that the discovery in science is similar to the discovery of the self. A recent research[35] has confirmed that the super atom discovered by Bose–Einstein (water in a state of absolute non-agritation) is akin to the *samadhi* described in Indian religions. Since phenomenology recognizes the significance of subjectivity, the intangible elements in the Indian culture can only be grasped apperceptively.

The second part of this paper has referred to India's cultural pluralism, which has been manifested through its ethnic diversity, pilgrim circuits and arts and crafts; crafts and arts have provided a visible dimension to Indian society. A great achievement in Indian culture was the evolution of Gupta art that reached a high point in the 6th century AD. Subsequently, it influenced many provincial art styles, irrespective of religious divide. The Ajanta paintings of Buddhist caves in Maharashtra, the numerous Hindu and Jain temples that display the stone sculptures in the northern, central and southern regions derive from the basic motifs from the Gupta art. Their visibility was a significant vehicle for educating many generations of Indians about their heritage. Hence, the scholarly and elitist sections of India have not been the sole respositories of cultural values.

Force and Non-Violence

Paradoxically, these two elements have played a complementary role. The crafts and arts of India have gained an enduring fame. The numerous temples that we find in different parts of India were raised in large number during the medieval period. This was also the period in which internal rebellion and aggression from outside took place. It was the sword-wielding ruler who provided safety and security to the thousands of craftsmen, such as sculptors, architects, painters of murals, etc. The Ganga, Chandela, Chalukya, Hoysala and Vijayanagar dynasties were engaged either in quelling internal disorder or meeting threat from Islamic aggression. These temples have a variety of sculptures, wall panels, murals depicting mythological scenes of war (such as gods and goddesses vanquishing evil force), which make a veiled reference to the then existing turbulent times. These depictions, according to Radhakamal Mukerjee,[36] are the heralds of national awakening for freedom. Besides, the Hindu temples have gods and goddesses in weapon-bearing posture, for example, Chamundi, Bhairava, Hanuman and Kartikeya. Even some of the Jain temples whose focus is on the *tirthankaras* have wall panels depicting mythological warfare, drawn from a Hindu background. Paradoxically, while wars were raging near the borders, the artisans worked in temple yards in peace and security.

Dharma and Rita

These two juridical aspects are interrelated in Indian society. As mentioned earlier, the literary and textual background of *dharmashastras* secured for them an elevated position in royal courts, temples and monasteries, where the elite gathered for discourse. During the monsoonal addresses to the audiences (*Chaturmasya*), the gurus and monatic heads often referred to the injunctions drawn from the Hindu *dharmashastras*. But, the elitist discourses were limited to the few centres mentioned earlier. Among the tribes, folks and self-governing communities, such as castes, usually the unwritten customs and mores exerted their authority, especially in a panchayat setting, wherein elders enforced their authority through recourse to expiatory rites, fines, etc. Mumford, to whom a reference was made earlier, tells us that the word 'ritual' means to flow with, that is, the moving forward with the rhythm of nature. In sum, the rituals were not created by the canons; instead, the already existing rituals were incorporated into Sanskrit. Caste ranking, priestly privileges and unequal punishment awarded to the offenders were distortions, which crept into the textual dispensation of justice. A deconstruction of the texts will reveal the underlying truth that deeds (and not the rank) call for juridical action.

Polity

As noted earlier, the ruler who punished the offenders was a non-violent person. He had no personal motive because he only defended the *dharma* of his realm. Exercise of force for the good of realm is an expression of the ruler's *rajas*. Force becomes *tamasik* only when there is hatred or ill-will. Although M.K. Gandhi mobilized a vast number of people, it was difficult to say whether those who joined his movement had a change of heart. Especially in the post-independence era, protests that start peacefully later become turbulent. The protesters often prevent the *non-protesters* from attending to their work or perform their assigned duty. This is a blatant misuse of the *satyagraha* strategy. The *sattwa* becomes a moral force if people's energies are directed towards constructive nation-building.

Notes

1. For reference to Edmund Husserl, *Macmillan Student Encyclopaedia of Sociology*, London: Macmillan Press, 1985, pp. 286–87.
2. For reference to Cicourel, see David Walsh, 'Sociology and the Social World', in Peter Worsley (ed.), *Modern Sociology*, 2nd ed., London: Penguin, 1972, pp. 79–91.
3. For reference to Alfred Schutz, *Macmillan Student Encyclopaedia of Sociology*, London: Macmillan Press, 1985.
4. A.K. Coomaraswamy, *The Dance of Shiva*. New Delhi: Munshiram Manoharlal Pvt. Ltd. (Indian edition), 1971.
5. Radhakamal Mukerjee, *Flowering of Indian Art*. Bombay: Asia Publishing House, 1964.
6. N.K. Bose, 'Calcutta in the 1960s: A Premature Metropolis', in Peter Worsley (ed.), *Modern Sociology*, op. cit., p. 493.
7. A.K. Coomaraswamy, *History of Indian and Indonesian Art*, New Delhi: Munshiram Manoharlal, 1972, p. 164.
8. The Ganga water kept in a sealed vessel retains its freshness for years. In most Hindu households (cutting across difference of caste and tribe), the Ganga water is administered to dying person, after breaking open the seal. The sealed pot is quite small in size for which only a small sum is paid as price. However, silver pots are also available at a higher price.
9. A.K. Coomaraswamy, *Christian and Oriental Philosophy of Art*, 2nd ed. New Delhi: Munishiram Manoharlal Pvt. Ltd., 1972, p. 80.
10. Ivan Illich, 'Phenomenology of School', in Peter Worsley (ed.), *Modern Sociology*, op. cit., pp. 300–06.
11. Jainism in India has given many insights regarding the flora and fauna in human society.
12. Swami Rama, *Living with the Himalayan Masters* (translated into Kannada) Pennsylvania: Institute of Yogic Sciences (Indian edition), Bangalore, 1991, pp. 163, 200.
13. Sri Aurobindo, *The Chariot of Jagannatha*, III ed., Puducherry: Sri Aurobindo Ashram, 1995, p. 8.
14. Ibid., p. 9.
15. Vivekananda, *Colombo to Almora*, Calcutta: Advaita Ashrama (reprint), 1978, p. 173.
16. Sri Aurobindo, *India's Rebirth*. Faridabad: Thomson Press, 1993, p. 106.
17. Ibid., p. 174.
18. A.K. Sen, *Hindu Political Thought*, New Delhi: Gian Publishing House (Indian reprint), 1986, p. 99.
19. Kireet Joshi, *The Veda and Indian Culture*, New Delhi: Motilal Banarasidas (II reprint), 1994, p. 47.
20. Aurobindo regarded the superconscient (supra-consciousness) as a better source of inner knowledge than inconscient (unconsciousness). He wrote: 'The significance of the lotus is not to be found by analyzing the secrets of the mud from which it grows here: Its secret is to be found in the

heavenly archetype of the lotus that blooms for ever in the light above'. See Aurobindo, *India's Rebirth*, op. cit., p. 196.

21. See Joshi, *The Veda and Indian Culture*, op. cit., pp. 13–15.
22. Unto Tahtinen, *Non-Violent Theories of Punishment*, New Delhi: Motilal Banarasidas (Indian edition), 1983, p. 21.
23. L. Hearn, a Western writer who spent many years in Japan wrote: 'Under all the outward aspects of individual activity that modern Japan presents to the visitor's gaze, the ancient conditions really persist... I do not refer to any written law, but only to the old unwritten religious law, with its host of obligations deriving from ancestor worship'. Japan, Charles Tuttle and Company, Singapore, 1st ed., 1977, p. 250.
24. Tahtinen, *Non-Violent Theories*, op. cit., p. 32.
25. Aurobindo wrote:

    The people of India, even the 'Ignorant Masses' are by centuries of training nearer to the inner realities ... where else could the lofty, Austere and difficult teachings of a Buddha seize so rapidly the popular mind? where else could the songs of Tukaram, A. Ramprasad, A. Kabir, the Sikh Gurus and the Tamil saints with their fervid devotion... Have found so speedy an echo and formed a popular religious teaching, p. 146.

26. Rituals in a sense are linked to the submerged conscious participation in ritual activity, which opens the door of perception to *rita*. In cross-cultural context *rita* is manifested in various forms. The oracles of ancient Greece, the *shamans* of some American Indian tribes, the Bhagat or Ojha of north India, the Turkish Sufis who perform a whirling dance (sema) are some examples of individual who enter a communion with unseen spirits or enter into a trance state to attain a divine experience. The *samadhi* of Indian yogis is another example.
27. Sen, *Political Thought*, op. cit., pp. 16–48.
28. Ibid.
29. Ibid.
30. John Mumford, *Karma Manual B*, New Delhi: Jain Publishers, 2001, p. 20.
31. Ibid.
32. Aurobindo, *India's Rebirth*, op. cit.
33. Mani Bhaumik, 'Physics and Vedanta: So Much in Common', *The Best of Speaking Tree*, vol. 2, New Delhi: Times of India Publication, pp. 85–86.
34. Mani Bhaumik writes even the most sophisticated instrument does not allow a glimpse of the natural realm of subatomic particles: we can only analyse it mathematically *speaking tree*. Ibid., p. 29.
35. Deepak Ranade, 'A Neuro Surgeon', *Times of India*, 30 December 2008, p. 6.
36. Radhakamal Mukerjee, *Flowering of Indian Art*, op. cit.

Suggested Readings

Chopra, Deepak (2008). *The Third Jesus*. UK: Rider.

Geertz, Clifford (1960). *The Religion of Java*. Glencoe, Il: The Free Press.

Krishnamurthy, U.G. (1982). *The Mystique of Enlightenment*, 1st ed. Goa: Dinesh Vaghela.

Sharma, Arvind (1995). *The Philosophy of Religion*. New Delhi: Oxford University Press.

Unnithan, T.K.N., Indra Deva and Yogendra Singh (eds.) (1965). *Towards a Sociology of Culture*. New Delhi: Prentice-Hall.

Venugopal, C.N. (1998). *Religion and Indian Society*. New Delhi: Gian Publishers.

Yogananda, Paramahansa (1998). *Autobiography of a Yogi*. Mumbai: Jaico Publishing House.

8

Globalization vs. Polarization

A Case of Emerging Concerns for 'Nation-State' and 'Radical Nationalism' in Indian Society

S.P. Gupta

> Globalizing influences do not work exclusively towards integration. Although there are some fundamental respects in which a planetary social order has been created. Globalization also divides, marginalizes and excludes...
>
> Giddens (1992: 2)

I

Since the past two decades, the world as a whole and the Indian society in particular have been marked by a rapid process of globalization. It is a fact, that this process is as old as the process of Westernization, with increasing emphasis on technology, communication and spread of Western and modem values. In other words, this process has facilitated interaction between different sociocultural collectivities all over the world. It is a process that emphasizes the creation of 'one world order', linking cross-national boundaries and states along with worldwide flow of capital, communication, commodities and culture from region to region. Not only this, these days even the process of militarization all over the world is linked with the process of globalization too. The global structural transformation has led the process of restructuring of economies in terms of liberalization and free market along with accountability of authority and state, expansion of democracy to create a common international forum to fight against global terrorism. When we talk of integration of societies and homogenization aspect of globalization, one finds that it includes the components of both Westernization and modernization.

Similarly, there has been growing consensus that the process of globalization is not only providing answers to the economic issues but also to the sociopolitical processes. The world seems to develop a system of governance, which may gain strength from extreme interventions of other nations in the form of proposed 'new world order'. Today, it is the utmost need of the world laying more and more emphasis on a single unified and managed world that can better serve for international security and peace as well as the settlement of disputes and conflicts both between different nations and between various groups and classes within the nations.

When we think of India, there has been the acceptance and the rapid pace of the process of globalization because of growing emphasis on market principle as the consequence of the failure of the socialist pattern of development and the breakdown of the communist block during 1980s at the global level. Even prior to these events, global capitalism had already produced a whole new technology of communication, cheaper and efficient means of transportation, satellite television, etc., which made India possible for a virtual leap in the field of communication and exchange. Thus, the global flows of information, money, people and culture made India to enter into the process of globalization during which 'welfare regime' paradigm was severely put to question. Since the 'welfare regime' in India witnessed various shortcomings as it failed to deliver the benefits of development and could not fulfil the aspirations of masses in terms of providing jobs, technological innovation, education, health and sociopolitical empowerment. Consequently, liberalization of trade and investment along with globalization were initiated only as a viable alternative of development in the Indian society. India had to resort to the path of such policies looking into the unsatisfactory economic record of previously closed economies such as East Germany, China, Poland and U.S.S.R. On the contrary, the open economies such as Hong Kong, Singapore, Taiwan and South Korea had progressed well, thereby justifying the process of liberalization through globalization.

We should not forget here that the globalization though understood in economic terms covers all other facets of life such as political, social and cultural. It is generally feared too that the government would completely abandon all forms of control and place the entire economy at the mercy of the multinationals; and likewise, it will give up its concern for equality. But the officials and government say it is not so because the important thrust of globalization in India is to remove certain imbalances and restrictions that hamper the free flow of trade. It aims at improving the economic performance of the nation. The government's policy is designed to generate culture of competition and to promote high efficiency in production, technology transfer, mutual sharing of benefits of research and development.

Kim and Park (1989) had established that globalization would result in better capacity utilization and economies of scale. Similarly, there have been efforts to support the hypothesis that there is positive association between the degree of openness and efficiency gains. Krueger (1978) had tried to show that countries more open to global trade and competition have higher gross national product (GNP) growth rate. The social aspect of globalization is that it provides an opportunity for rapid increase in knowledge as it creates an atmosphere for new potentials for developing countries to grow faster by means of global interaction and competition. It is assumed that if countries such as India are attracted by Western and modem life styles, then such countries will adopt other features too such as dignity of labour, responsibility for neighbourhood or community welfare, respect for law and order and respect for knowledge and character – there would be positive advantages in terms of social change.

Thus, the process of globalization has its sociocultural and political implications besides the economic one. It aims at the integration of the Indian society with the rest of the societies of the world, aspiring for homogenization that may lead to well-being of the masses.

II

Here in this paper, our objective is to analyse the changing concept of nation state and emerging processes of fragmentation in the Indian society due to globalization as it is witnessed these days that there are certain negative repercussions of this process. Having given a proper thought to the process of globalization that aims at the integration and homogenization of various nations into 'one world order', our concern here is to examine yet a very crucial aspect of this process that can be visualized in the form of cut-throat competition, which is to a greater extent responsible for weakening the political, social and economic independence of the developing countries. Although, there is a growing emphasis on defining the world as a global village, on the contrary, we can see increasing strength of ethnicities and pluralities of culture consciousness that are dividing nations instead of uniting them. The increasing dominance of superpowers of the world over rest of the world and tensions and conflicts within the nation as well as rise of fundamentalism may be considered as best examples. These experiences make us believe that globalization has created various forms of polarization at a global level. Hence, our concern as social scientists should be to probe these questions.

Let us examine first of all the polarization emerging in the context of nation state. There is growing consensus these days more particularly in the developing societies that globalization has created an atmosphere for the marginalization of the state by growing disempowerment of the state and of the national elites, both in its power to enforce national priorities and their control over subordinates. It is because they are being dictated either from foreign agencies or their own governments that work at the behest of foreign corporations such as the International Monetary Fund (IMF), World Bank, World Trade Organization (WTO) and other such institutions in the United States and Western Europe. Not only this, these nations and trade institutions have been associated in one way or the other in manufacture and trade of arms to which countries such as India are made hostage both due to perceived threats from abroad and pressures and demands from within emanating from our own people belonging to lower classes, the minorities, the revolting regions and nationalities (Kothari, 1995a: 1593). Not only this, the disempowerment and marginalization of the nation-state may be attributed to the growing evidence of individual alienation and social anomie because of the failure of the nation to provide them opportunities for their socio-economic and political empowerment. There is growing disenchantment with the state because a post-colonial bourgeois state has steadily lost its legitimacy largely because it followed a path of development that gave neither equality nor justice to the common man (Mahajan, 1999a: 1193–94). Consequently, the masses have begun to realize that the state is no longer available to them because the prime marker of welfare socialist regime is on decline on the part of the state. As a result, the normative structure of society and polity is becoming weak, and many institutions related to them are becoming dysfunctional. In such a situation, the masses (mostly underprivileged) have to find out some other alternatives in terms of resources, means and institutions for their empowerment and well-being. Then, why should they give weightage to the 'nation-state'? Thus, it is assumed that the processes of globalization and liberalization have put the state in a situation of crisis. As the transformation initiated by these twin processes in the social structure motivate the masses not to accept the authority of such a state that is changing its priorities just to suit the multinationals and developed societies (Kothari, 1991: 11–12; 1994b). It is uprooting the masses from the social structure. The present state of disorders and maldistribution of resources at a global level have initiated duality both at international and intra-national level. On the one hand, the nations of the globe are being divided into the privileged and the underprivileged. Intra-nationally, a similar form of duality can be visualized in most of the countries where a small privileged group at a centre is surrounded by a large mass of underprivileged on the periphery. It again puts a question mark at the functioning of the nation-state.

Another attribute concerning nation-state in India is the relationship between these two. We know that India as a nation consists of different identities, and affiliations such as social, regional, linguistic and cultural give a key role to the state through which the 'composite integrated nation' can be maintained. It is possible only through decentralized planning with a greater degree of participation of masses in various institutions of the state. Thus, the major dilemma in this context is intra-national centralization of governance and decentralized democratic planning. Our view is that to overcome such dilemma and to save the nation-state from crisis is to maintain a proper balance between these two even in this fast track of globalization.

However, in reality the balance between these two is getting disturbed, and the concept of nation-state is in turmoil as it is ceased to be the central mechanism of the nation because the nation is moving towards a state of acute fragmentation, multiple polarization and likely disintegration. Obviously, centrifugal forces inherent in the form of primordial collectivities such as ethnicity, religion, culture and language are eroding the nation and retarding the state. In this process, the state is being hijacked by the global order and market (centripetal forces), and the nation is facing serious challenges from within, from the large number of peripheries as well as different regions and nationalities (Kothari, 1995a: 1594). Thus, we see that along with the process of globalization, its antithesis too has emerged in the form of increasing regional chauvinism and ultra-nationalism based on primordial collectivities; more important among these is religious fundamentalism, which seeks to suppress various pluralities. Similarly, increasing challenges to the authority and legitimacy of state by various regional movements aimed either at autonomy or separatism have weakened the state too.

The Indian state that had been making efforts for its self-reliance and autonomy since its independence has gone to the periphery as it is being threatened and challenged by the so-called super powers of the world with the help of the Group of 77 (G-77), International Labour Organisation (ILO), World Bank, IMF and WTO and other such agencies on economic fronts. Likewise, on the social fronts too, such polarization can be witnessed within the country with reference to providing job opportunities to the minorities, the economically backward classes, tribal communities, women and children, health, education and housing. Such dualities have been intensified with the process of democratic processes, as these have been able to create rise in mass consciousness among the vast majority of society, and they feel themselves neglected and marginalized to the periphery of the society. Galtung (1971: 81) regards the centre–periphery polarization as the essence of neo-imperialism in the form of globalization that splits up collectivities. Similarly, nearly all independent scholars, such as Paul Baran, Immanuel Wallerstein, Andre Gunder Frank and Samir Amin too, conceptualize the capitalist world economy as a 'core–periphery division of labour', linked via 'external exchange relations'. They viewed core–periphery relations as one of the unequal exchange. They all agree that new form of capitalism emerging due to globalization has failed to spread economic development and socio-economic justice. The world system constitutes core and periphery. The periphery is conditioned by the core due to its relations of dependence; and in this relationship while the core develops, the periphery underdevelops. There is the development of underdevelopment – a dialectical relation between the two. Frank (1969) says these days, neo-colonialism perpetuates through trade and not by the state or army, etc., therefore, ever-growing capitalist development will lead to ever-growing capitalist underdevelopment.

All these tendencies are examples that show erosion and retreat of the nation-state at three levels: (i) technology, (ii) homogenizing mission and (iii) new ideology (Kothari, 1995b: 2515). According to him, technology seems to be replacing politics and socio-economic factors in the functioning of the society. It may be homogenizing diverse cultures and social sectors, but marginalizing the political process and weakening the nation-state. It is also true that the whole world is confronted with the situations of tension and violence due to increasing consumerism, which has tried to increase assertion of cultures, ethnicity, religion, language, nationalities and pluralism. The state is ceasing to be a protector of the minorities, the poor, the weak and the oppressed. The third challenge comes from the emergence of a new ideology or mindset. It is merely a utopia that holds of a new integration of human enterprise, of joining diverse cultures and civilizations into a single market place. In real practice, it is not an integration but a tantamount polarization with the old idea of survival of the fittest in which the poor and the dispossessed sections of population cannot be fit and dispensed with (Kothari, 1987).

Globalization that was sought for the process of social development along with the openness of economy has left the Indian society with the increasing incidence of inequality, growing injustices and inhumanities; crimes and corruption, particularly to the violations of basic human rights of the masses. It leaves us with no option but to believe that in this globalizing world, fragmentation serves as the basis of integration and homogenization.

The question here is that how can one think of preserving the concept of 'nation-state' in such a situation? The answer to this question is not so simple. It is suggested that in this dispersed and decentralized world order, it is necessary to preserve the integrity and uniqueness of each by creating a multicultured and plural state on federal lines so that their goals of autonomy and self-determination can better be realized instead of undermining the legitimacy and authority of the state that will contribute towards further dominance of developed nations. Therefore, it is in the interest of the nation as well as to the people not to raise issues of legitimacy and authority of the state. But the nation-state as well as oppressed social strata, ethnic and regional groups must work towards a common goal, which will enable them to withstand the challenge from both transnational and global powers (Kothari, 1988). Our objective should be to create an atmosphere among the minds of oppressed and marginalized groups that the state is impartial and final arbiter. Their interests and well-being is safe and secure in the proper functioning of the nation-state. Because ours is a heterogeneous, hierarchical and plural society where there is disjuncture between citizenship and nationality; the latter being defined in terms of membership in different racial, religious and language groups, which is often the source of inequality. Therefore, the primordial groups of our society often pursue the goal of shared sovereignty and decentralization of authority. Here, the concern of the nation-state should be to emphasize the issues of removal of poverty and social, economic and political disparities rather than economic and technological forces to determine the scene to acquire autonomy of its own. Similar view is expressed elsewhere too (Oommen, 1997).

III

In what has gone before, we have seen the challenges posed by the globalization towards the weakening of the 'nation-state'. The concept of fragmentation evolved with the process of unification and integration has brought the Indian society where it has been stimulated by anti-modern and fundamentalist reactions. Here, we thought it appropriate to discuss another very important aspect of globalization in the context of emerging fundamentalism in our society. Pandey (1990) suggests that globalization ultimately contributes to the growth of radical cultural nationalism, which is neither global nor universal nor modern, but it serves as a metaphor for subordination of the West.

Along with the process of globalization, there have been the phenomena of increasing radical Hindu nationalism in India and Islamic radical nationalism throughout the world. During past decades, there has been an emergence of increasing Islamic revival in Iran, Pakistan and the Middle East. This revival embarked a new generation of Indian Muslims to open a discourse and strategy among the Muslim youths from the large and very poor Muslim community around distinctively religious issues and symbols. For example, the construction and renovation of large number of mosques and dargahs in western India using funds generated by Indian Muslim workers in the Gulf countries (Hansen, 1996: 608). Consequently, because of a growing feeling of dislocation of the Indian nation and the national identification, the Hindu nationalist movement in India grew steadily during the same period due to a highly successful strategy of cultural mobilization of Hindus against the steps taken by Muslims. These two processes are still in their crucial phases with the process of globalization.

Somewhat similar views have been expressed by Robinson (2001: 236–37) too, explaining that religion rather than caste or language alone is the main marker of Indian identities. This phenomenon has gathered momentum due to managed fears of modernity resulting from globalization and the revival and recovery of spiritualism in the Indian society. The rise of Hinduism is only partly linked to the suppression of it by the 'modern secular nation-state' while it must also be linked historically to the rise of identities in the colonial period when already Hinduism, Islam and Christianity were pitched against each other in the battle for soul (ibid.: 242). Saberwal (2001: 201) carries somewhat similar views when he highlights that segmentation in terms of caste and religious categories in India though has facilitated the spread of democratic process as these carry social bonds on which to build political support; but it also carries animosities and antagonism, which can work for strengthening hostile feelings towards each other. He quotes the example of acute ethnic conflicts such as the anti-Sikh riots of 1984, deployment of Kashmiri pandits from Kashmir during the 1990s, the demolition of Babri Mosque and more recently the Gujarat incident. This is all because that in this globalizing world, the search of identity is the prime factor; and when it is caught in antagonistic realities, it may lead to the phenomena of *Jehad* and *Hindutva* in our society in terms of power and all that flows from power (ibid.).

On the similar line, the ideology of *Hindutva* as being propagated by BJP argued that true secularism is possible only through true equality, which must start from the premise that Hindus constitute the majority population; hence, true secularism meant rule by the Hindu majority. Not only this, the Indian Muslims are also seen as blocking element in the process of modernity and modernization due to their cultural backwardness and excessive population growth. They also block the full realization of democracy due to their block voting. In nutshell, one can infer that according to radical Hindu nationalist, the Indian Muslims are the major source of the dislocation of the Indian nation in the contemporary world. Hence, it is feared that the process of globalization will strengthen the quest for recognition for cultural purification and cultural difference in order to enter the globalized modernity as equal partners (Hansen, 1996: 614). The real problem thus is not that the nation-state is in turmoil, but it is Hinduization of the Indian nation. Chandhoke (1995: 241–45) too is critical of the way the fundamentalist exclusivist ideology of *Hindutva* (i.e. redefining nation as the Hindu state) has been raked up by the Hindu majoritarian BJP and how such ideology would eliminate any scope for contestations and dialogue. The same Indian society, which is pulled between tradition and modernity, has left Dalits, women, minorities and tribals in vacuum. Therefore, the real crux of problem is that of a tussle of value system with each other, and it is not an easy task to create harmony between them (Robinson, 2001: 249). We should note that to the extent cultural pluralism is perceived to be an obstacle to the realization of the political integration and economic development, our society will be in a situation of national crisis. Therefore, for the Indian society, if it is to be modern, open, secular and civil must synthesize the value system of all the communities without any bias.

IV

From the preceding discussions, it is evident that these days the Indian society faces two major problems as a consequence of globalization, that is, the weakening of the nation-state and radical cultural nationalism. It is consequently responsible for creating cumulative disparities between various strata and groups of the society dividing them between the privileged and the deprived. Similarly, the nation-state faces threats and challenges when its sociocultural identity if linked with the ideology of *Hindutva*. It works against the belief that India's sociocultural identity is not a single faceted as projected by the ideology of *Hindutva* but by its form as a plural society (Khan, 1992: 6). Sharma (1996: 317–18) too asserts that India's spiritual–cultural identity or sociocultural identity faces no danger of minority ethnicism; instead, its current political incarnation in terms of *Hindutva* seem to be formidable threat to ethnic minorities as well as sociocultural identity of the Indian society. He feels that the Indian society, in its drive to promote modern nationalism, has attempted to suppress ethnic identities, which consequently has generated a sense of ethnic insecurity that further results in ethnic reactivity. Hence, it is not the ethnic pride but the modem nation-state that constitutes a threat to ethnic diversities and pluralist identity of the Indian society (ibid.: 318). He further reveals that 90 per cent of the nations of the world are multiethnic rather than uniethnic. Therefore, ethnic unity and cultural plurality may serve as an enviable basis of nation-building, and these can be achieved by maintaining pluralistic nature of the society, which is based on cultural rights, decentralized democracy and egalitarian development (ibid.: 319). Somewhat similar view has been expressed by Oommen (1996: 156) that homogenization part of globalization is often oriented to establish the hegemony of the dominant collectivity, annihilation of the weak and minority collectivities that endanger the principles of maintaining diversity and developing pluralism. Not only this, most of the societies are constantly exposed to alien influences and hence characterized by frayed edges and loose textures. Our society is not an exception. Therefore, in such a situation, the only viable option is to accommodate diversity, foster pluralism and nurture inter-group equality. According to him, individual-based equality is conceptually inadequate and praxeologically untenable in heterogeneous, hierarchical and plural societies. Hence, unless and until the inter-group equality is established, some of the groups would remain subjected to cumulative inequality and oppression. Therefore, inter-group equality should be our premise to establish pluralism as a value for effective functioning of society like ours (ibid.).

Foregoing analysis of the Indian society in the present context of globalization, changing facets of the nation-state and emergence of modern radical nationalism, makes us think about the future course of action for our society. Some believe that to overcome the challenges of various forms, it is better to evolve the concept of civil society, which is possible in a society that is liberal, pluralist and secular. They view that the core of civil society consists of the open and secular institutions that mediate between the citizens of the state in modem democratic societies (Beteille, 2001: 287). Various institutions of civil society are able to protect individual autonomy and freedom in a non-discriminatory manner and are controlled neither by the state nor by the religion. Civil society is necessary for India as autonomy of individual, protection of individual right to equal citizenship and access to decision-making apparatus, and participatory democratic process can best be attained where still Hindu caste society observes strict norms and practice of hierarchy and *Hindutva*, radical nationalism is in operation too (Dhanagare, 2001: 188).

Contrary to these views, Sharma holds the view that 'modern nation-state' laying emphasis on the supremacy of civil culture will render ethnic cultural diversities insignificant, promoting culture of modem nationalism; that is, individuals will outgrow their narrow ethnic loyalties than individuate into citizens. According to him, neither modernism nor nationalism has succeeded in solving ethnic identities; instead, these have helped in crystallization of ethnic identities (Sharma, 1996: 319).

Besides these two views, there is another view that holds synthesis of the two emphasizing that modem nation-state and civil society are not contradictory to each other. In fact, in a society like ours, democracy, state and civil society act together with the same ethos. The state formulates laws that objectively embody conditions necessary for enhancing equal citizenship. Civil society operates in accordance with the established system of laws and rights so that individuals can pursue their particular ends while simultaneously respecting claims for equal citizenships (Mahajan, 1999b). Thus, civil society and citizenship are closely associated. But citizenship rights can be protected and promoted only when opportunities and privileges are more or less equally distributed. The ethos of equal citizenship requires that socially valuable assets are not the monopoly of any group or community in society (Gupta, 1998: 509–23). This could be done by deleting and overthrowing ascribed identities as the basis of distributing resources or opportunities to attain the goal of equal citizenship. In country such as India which is still in a soft state, rules and laws are easily played in the hands of personal, community and other vested interests. Therefore, what is important is to emphasize the primacy of rational rules and impersonal laws for cherishing the real goal of our society, that is, to maintain the rights of all individuals as equal citizens and to strengthen such institutions that protect the rights of individuals against any sort of eventuality. We know ours is a plural society, hence the rights of minorities, weaker sections, oppressed and marginalized could be protected by providing them autonomy at two lines, that is, cultural and political instead of interference and suppression attitude by the society or the state. Unless we are cautious on these grounds, it is likely that our society may fall prey to the process of neo-colonialism in the form of globalization. It is also necessary for us to adhere to democratic decentralized planning for a self-sustained development of the society. At the same time, the principle of secularism must be followed not in its current usages as envisaged by radical national fundamentalists, but by following the principle of plurality and coexistence. It is the strength of plural society that can protect the Indian society from the war of globalization with the help of cultural rights, decentralized democracy and egalitarian development. The long-cherished values of our society have to be inculcated, which are in the process of erosion by globalization. It is by process of maintaining plural society that we can synthesize tradition and modernity. Different societies have territorial dimensions; despite globalization and emergence of 'one world', they are located in different regions. Thus, with ecological and environmental pluralism, there are differences in economy, values and institutions too. Therefore, the society that seeks to maintain its identity and specificity should pursue the path of pluralization instead of jumping on to the bandwagon of globalization (Oommen, 1996: 158). Thus, our society should not give up its concern for equality, democratic participation and egalitarian development. Hence, there shouid be a proper balance between the state and the market as well as between the social responsibility and private enterprise. Similarly, by maintaining cultural plurality and their coexistence, we can take our society to real secularism instead of being guided by radical modern nationalism, which may prove fatal to nation-state as well as destroying the long-cherished cultural identity of our society in this globalizing world.

References

Beteille, A. (2001). 'Civil Society and the Good Society', *Sociological Bulletin*, 50(2): 286–307.

Chandhoke, Neera (1995). *State and Civil Society: Explorations in Political Theory*. New Delhi: Sage Publications.

Dhanagare, D.N. (2001). 'Civil Society, State and Democracy: Conceptualizing a Discourse', *Sociological Bulletin*, 50(2): 167–91.

Frank, Andre Gunder (1969). *Capitalism and Underdevelopment in Latin America: Historical Studies of Chile and Brazil*. New York: Monthly Review Press.

Galtung, John (1971). 'A Structural Theory of Imperialism', *Journal of Peace Research*, 8: 81.

Giddens, Anthony (ed.) (1992). *Human Societies: An Introductory Reader in Sociology*. Cambridge: Polity Press.

Gupta, Dipankar (1998). 'Recasting Reservations in the Language of Rights', in Gurpreet Mahajan (ed.), *Democracy, Difference and Social Justice*. New Delhi: Oxford University Press, pp. 509–23.

Hansen, Thomas Blom (1996). 'Globalization and Nationalist Imaginations: Hindutva Promise of Equality through Difference', *Economic and Political Weekly*, 9 March, pp. 603–16.

Khan, Rasheeduddin (1992). 'Political Integration in Federal India', *The Times of India*, 19 November, p. 6.

Kim, K.S. and J.K. Park (1989). 'The Utilization of Capital and Growth of Output in a Developing Economy', *Journal of Economic Development*.

Kothari, Rajni (1987). 'Of Human Governance', *Alternatives*, p. 12.

——— (1988). *State against Democracy: In Search of Human Governance*. New Delhi: Ajanta.

——— (1991). 'State and Statelessness in Our Time', *Economic and Political Weekly*, 26(11–12): 553–58.

——— (1994a). 'Rise of the Dalits and the Renewed Debate on Caste', *Economic and Political Weekly*, 25 June.

——— (1994b). 'The Crisis of Representation', *Hindu*, 31 August.

——— (1995a). 'Under Globalization: Will Nation-State Hold?' *Economic and Political Weekly*, 1 July, pp. 1593–603.

——— (1995b). 'Globalization and "New World Order": What Future for the United Nations?' *Economic and Political Weekly*, 7 October.

Krueger, A.O. (1978). *Liberalization: Attempts and Consequences*. Cambridge, MA: Ballinger.

Mahajan, Gurpreet (1999a). 'Civil Society and Its Avatars: What Happened to Freedom and Democracy', *Economic and Political Weekly*, 34(20): 1188–96.

——— (1999b). 'Civil Society, State and Democracy', *Economic and Political Weekly*, 4 December, pp. 3471–72.

Oommen, T.K. (1996). 'Reconciling Equality and Pluralism: A New Agenda for the Developed Societies', *Sociological Bulletin*, 45(2): 143–60.

——— (1997). *Citizenship, Nationality and Ethnicity: Reconciling Competing Identities*. Cambridge: Polity Press.

Pandey, Gyanendra (1990). *The Construction of Communalism in Colonial North India*. New Delhi: Oxford University Press.

Robinson, Rowena (2001). 'Religion on the Net: An Analysis of the Global Reach of Hindu Fundamentalism and Its Implications for India', *Sociological Bulletin*, 50(2): 236–51.

Saberwal, Satish (2001). 'Democracy and Civil Society in India: Integral or Accidental', *Sociological Bulletin*, 50(2): 192–205.

Sharma, S.L. (1996). 'Ethnic Challenge to Indian Society: Rethinking Culture-Polity Interface', in N.K. Singhi (ed.), *Theory and Ideology in Indian Sociology*. Jaipur: Rawat Publications, pp. 309–324.

9

Globalization and Rise of Civil Resistance to Indian Plutonomy

Manjeet Chaturvedi

Towards Liberalization and Globalization of Indian Economy or from Intermediate Regime to Plutonomy

Before opening up to the world, for a long time, the Indian economy was a big size mixed economy dominated by public enterprise and the state-owned banking capital. Walls built by the bureaucratic statism protected the welfare system. As the economic rationality was governed by democratic state's policies, blended with popular or populist decisions, aberrations appeared. After the phases of the land reforms and the green revolution – rural development and the state-backed industrial-urban middle-class formation, the steam began exhausting with the heat gone from the state-owned growth engines; policies continued to take a lot of money from under the control of state with not enough coming along the way of solving India's problems of overall development, poverty and unemployment. Then, the liberalization of India in early 1990s with a word of advice to corporate sector 'either to swim or sink' without state protection and subsidies was responded by the corporate industry now unbound and acting smart. Looking less and less local and more and more global in outlook, the private enterprise in India contributed to a large extent in overcoming the financial crisis this time not towing the old-fashioned domesticated industrial development kind of line but venturing, using modern technologies, identifying new areas in software, diversifying, raising lots of money and demanding a new deal. The state was freed to take care of infrastructural and social sectors in a multi-sectored highly divided society. It had, under a mixed economy, built mega structures and had taken important affirmative actions that laid the corner stone for the unprecedented economic boom. India's postcolonial state-controlled economy during the era of bipolar world, which denoted one of the examples of the 'intermediate regime' (Kaleki, 1972) and which built modern India, finally ended; but before the end came, out of this process grew a confident and techno-potent industry that quickly constructed products for and offered solutions to the knowledge economy of the world. The ground in the Indian political economy was prepared by the intermediate classes composed of small farmers, self-employed, profit-making traders and agriculturists (Mitra, 1977) and small industrialists in order to bring forth the present generation of the Indian plutonomy.

Indian Plutonomy and the Civil Resistance

The Indian plutonomy is evident by the size and speed with which the wealthy Indians buy properties from London to Indian countryside, acquiring companies and making themselves heard at internationally noted meets. Some fought, in family or outside, and fell apart, but an increasing number of wealthy Indians may go on with combining each other to attain 'monopoly plutonomy' and also individually or collectively attempt to form international federation, if they can, to become globally bigger plutonomy.

The plutonomy is different from its own earlier version of corporate sector and other present corporations. The making of the super rich on the wave of economic opportunity is also reflected in celebrating flamboyancy in person and as a group. Some are showing off and are visibly assertive in life-styles. By big way, conspicuous consumption and displaying lavish living – larger-than-life image – of the new array of the rich resembles the Western cine stars if not Moghuls. The way in which the glamour is added in business through organizing events of sports, fashion shows, wedding receptions, car races, social responsibility and property is resounding and unprecedented.

A lot of preparations and pains are taken to demonstrate the 'blinding glow of money', creating an environment, an aura and an effect. Effect on audience is dramatic and surrealistic. For more benefits or to create respect and fear among peers and to claim the epitome in otherwise democratic societies with their routine middle classes and toiling intermediate classes, the richer among the rich would thus go on to form a class of their own. The public enjoys the presence of their affluence but tolerate to the extent that businesses are not turned against their life chances.

The way in which the Indian economy is now hyper-driven by the ultra-rich is also important as the role contributing to the success of the globalization at large – a process in which India is maintaining a very high rate of growth. Domestic stellar growth has become privy to a global wealth creation. Internationalization by the India Incorporated is executed by mergers and acquisitions of foreign companies, a strategy that has the liberal support of the central bank. It is a deal exporter plutonomy now (KPMG Study, 2008a). Coupled with its hunger for tax sops (PricewaterhouseCoopers Report, 2008), which it receives mainly in the sectors of software and communications technology, special economic zones (SEZs), backward area benefits and the legalized land grab, the Indian plutonomy with its policy of 'development pockets' is walking on a tight rope. Besides this, the government first acquires rural lands from the numerous small landholders, compensates them on less than market rate and transfers the chunk to the company or helps the company to buy on less than market rate directly from the holders. It is not much different from its global bite (acquiring foreign companies) as long as plutonomy expansion by acquisition is concerned. A question that is being asked in intellectual circles is, will the socially distinct and extremely large categories in economy made of land-based occupations in rural areas prosper with these growth engines?

Meanwhile, there is however an amazing response in the form of civil resistance to the plutonomy in India. Rural communities, peasants, landholders, cultivators, farm labour and tribal are organizing movements to protect their livelihood means, mainly lands, from being bought by the rich. Peoples' action is turning violent at times inviting police intervention. These movements in some cases are mentored by political groupings. Civil response and the Indian plutonomy in combat seem to have disturbed not only peace but also the conventional tools and skills using which the state has progressed. It has also seemingly created confusion in the ranks and file of political parties. Quite a few political parties are not always adhering to their sworn ideologies; they side with the industry.

The greater expansion of the Indian corporate as a calculated risk-taking exercise adopted from conservative-to-aggressive growth path in the inner circles of the Indian political economy and in fact has attracted civil resistance recently. It is quite obvious that the mainstream of this resistance is offered by the landowners in the countryside who were dispossessed (most recent movements include Nandi Gram, Singur in West Bengal, Kalinganagar in Odisha, against SEZs in Goa and Dadri and Bhatta Parsaul in Uttar Pradesh) and not by the urban groups who are directly not under any threat. In the urban fringe when the city balloons, the victims of the 'land-use change' (land owners/cultivators/settlers) start protest against low-cost package. Urban groups of small traders and manufactures, however, demonstrate against the entry of big business in retail, particularly in small and medium towns. Thus, what is most striking in today's Indian political economy relates to civil collective action by the 'intermediate classes' resistant to plutonomy whose economic role in pre-globalization era was helpful in achieving that stage in economic development, which became the launching pad for plutonomy. And whose political choice was for such groups of ruling classes that proved conducive to the globalization of India.

The civil resistance is gaining a lot of media attention in news, features and heated TV discussions as it is seen as deciding:

(a) the growth of plutonomy internally,
(b) the choice of sectors left to the plutonomy expansion,
(c) the employment, economy, money (EEM) factor as some entrepreneurs like to put the creation of jobs for the sons of soil (and others), the economic development of the geo-people area and the sector (larger economy is the main context), and the profit to the company,
(d) the message to the India Incorporated and the World Incorporated.

Academics, media, polity, evicted community, civil society, leaders of plutonomy sit around the same table and debate the issue, and all voice one concern – a prosperous Indian economy but how to structure it along with the plutonomy leaving the land-based people intact! The bone of contention is 'land'. The war is between the corporations and the landowners, and it is fought to mutate the normal political economy of India into a plutonomy.

Indian urban set-up and collective mind are not particularly hesitant towards India's plutonomy. The perception of the people who are directly affected by the turning of economy into plutonomy is a mixed response. In many sectors such as manufacturing, aviation, ultra mega power (Chaturvedi, 2010), information and communications technology including entertainment and telecommunications, the spread has been very fast and welcome. It is a different story when the plutonomy engulfs the means of subsistence of the affected people who realize that they are losers to the rich and that their loss is inadequately compensated.

The Agrarian Question

The question that looms large as to what would happen to the peasants and agriculturists, the rural labour and the artisans who will hardly survive as a free life category? After bulldozing the conventions of agrarian past, where would the 'debris' be dumped and what if the real populations refuse to come out?

The super rich in India is driving away that part of economy also, which mainly holds the peasantry on their lands. Fast and furious, the Indian plutonomy is hardly a sphere for sustaining popular life. The rich, in partnership with the political powers that be, without such alternatives would not merely be served by rhetoric of corporate social responsibility, or an innovative marketing strategy to sell their 'plutonomy', or only offer some sort of employment rehabilitation programmes for the dismantled people as the numbers are in millions and the majority disfavours their uprooting from the soil. This is happening so fast that in the past few years, quite a good number of special economic zones were set up and most have been resisted by the local community; even a proposal of this kind would meet civil resistance for they express fear of losing their reliable subsistence. This is evident by the fact that although many SEZs have been approved, the people's resistance from the peasantry classes has come up not exactly for better land price or job negotiations but for keeping their land intact for cultivation. The Naxal menace, an extreme and violent form of movement, has already spread its wings in 17 provinces of India, which could also prove a deterrent to the super rich policy of capital accumulation by encroachment of rural land in these regions.

The layout is, however, not so simple and raises more questions. Even if the poor peasantry is left on its own, in the wake of today's closeness between the state and the plutonomy, the whole Indian economy as it is booming for some time now the reproduction of poverty for these people could just be one form of destiny as far as one could see. They do not have sufficient agriculture to progress on the path of quality life and its good deal of chances as they perceive their future. That is obvious in the cases of the indebted farmers committing suicide in the past few years.

The Subprime Crisis and High and Low of Indian Plutonomy

The Indian rich was hit by one of the worst crises of its life by subprime crisis, sending simmers all over the world that has opted for globalization. Assets of Indian super rich have been downsized from 47 per cent to 23 per cent by the flight of finance capital from the stock market. Interestingly, many major banks in India are state owned; the subprime has not touched banking sector significantly. It was expected that the subprime crisis would decelerate the consumer market. In India, the major hit has been taken by the textile, jewellery and IT industries. The industrial labour in manufacturing of textiles and gems has been retrenched, whereas the falling dollar took its toll by de-escalating the growth of BPOs in India and bringing the pay packets of top management down for a short time. The luxuries were, however, still afforded because the super rich were ready to show their guts in critical periods of testing times. It is like creating more effect, an aura and an environment of power and force. Despite some hiccups, the strength of the Indian plutonomy was in that the central government raised the wages of its employees by implementing pay commission recommendations, and the rich went on with land acquisition spree among other things during meltdown (KPMG Study, 2008b).

Centring of plutonomy depends on the factors of growth and prosperity; traditionally, the centre has been thought to keep its hegemony throughout the modern world by creating and controlling peripheral economies, but there are more than one centres now of a different order. Its redesigning is more like flag pins spread in many parts of the world, including Asia, Russia, Latin America and some parts of Africa. India is a new entrant in the world of plutonomy with consumption levels going up and behavioural expressions changing. With recession weakening as it appears, however, India brand is asking for its larger share in regional and global economic treaties to gain more in international terms of trade. The projection of Chindia (China and India) looking for top slots in the later course of globalization and BRICS (Brazil, Russia, India, China and South Africa) being the most successful developing countries are kind of things so much favoured for enduring Indian plutonomy.

Plutonomy under Threat

The Slowdown

Wealth creation in the plutonomy stage is thought to be easy when the take-off starts, but it is easier to understand that wealth would accumulate in the hands of the ultra rich. Percolation is yet to be seen here in order to justify the march of the plutonomy against the civil resistance despite what the government communicates.

The sociological point in plutonomy, other than economic, is just not limited to reminding either a corporate of its social responsibility or the state of its welfares, but it is beyond that – millions of rural people residing in thousands of homes, but reproducing poverty for several generations, are turning into spontaneous settlers in urban areas. From grounded people to the people living on the edge is not a passage of distribution of wealth (Chaturvedi et al., 2007).

Everything would have gone right for the plutonomy if the state was less eager to recline from its social responsibility by taking steps for an extra mile to provide on its own or put pressure on the corporations to arrange sufficient life support system for the uprooted. State in India is capitalistic in nature and pro-globalization is its compelling choice to develop and grow as a world economic power. The dividing line between the major political parties is intrinsic in their genesis and is drawn on their respective actions towards the minorities, but their response to the plutonomic issues is built upon the side of power they happen to be; but generally, these all are facilitators. Some small-scale regional political groups are opposed to the uprooting of their constituency of the peoples and build up solid resistance to expansion. They are very often joined by civil society groups, individual celebrities and local leaders. The Indian regime is now a conglomeration of the classes of the people far removed from each other on the development scale – recent growth of civil society organizations, major political parties often getting less sure of themselves, break away or new political groups mostly rallying around individual politicians who want a share of pie – the plutonomic powerhouse is most evident in changing the urban built environment and the rural landscape.

Conclusions

In this analysis, the following observations would prove useful:

A hard look on the Indian political economy returns serious facts by the way the modern state is positioned, and thus handling the implications of plutonomic machine, which is expanding its business by encroaching on agricultural/rural land – the only one resource traditionally available in abundance to the vast majority of Indians' economic activity for subsistence. Indications are that the state in India is complex in deliberations, slow and even evasive in some cases.

The result of peoples' response in plutonomy era's wake is consequent upon the domestic industrialization of the kind that the plutonomy is affecting or imposing. Growth in this democratically complex situation may have to take a detour; the industrial areas may become over-industrialized while under industrialization, or no industrialization continues to be the fate of many parts of India. Though there are unevenness and deformities in certain sectors, the modern state formation in India is interesting today and will be so tomorrow. It is, however, in no way a question that an intermediate regime kind of statism would return. New avatar of Indian corporate has no other option except for marching on the path of plutonomy. A point in Indian history is reached where the state could regain its strength as an autonomous polity on the indecisive battle between the plutonomy and the basic social classes for a short time, but the real strength of this kind of classic state would be tested by the unknown complexities of global phenomena in the long run.

Points to Ponder for Further Study of Indian Plutonomy

Indians are inheritors – possessive of property. They have a deep sense of belongingness to their possessions that are meagre in value for the majority. The wealthy microscopic minority is showing dynamism and enterprise to take risks and venture upon sensitive areas that return super profit. They create further wealth; rags-to-riches is not common, but when it happens it is miraculous. Part of the corporate establishment (the established corporate, the family-run business, the colonial time's national bourgeoisie, the green revolutionaries and the cash-rich mega corporates) is familiar with the ways of state bureaucracy, the people's reactions, etc., and know how to deal with them with their managerial battery. It becomes risky when the media are adverse and political parties and local groups convert it into an arena when the Indian rich try to expand into rural areas – the land – vast land to exploit and create wealth at a lower investment rate. The participation by state in the liberalization and globalization process is okay and wins the support of the middle classes, but the state support to plutonomy activity is resented when the victims give voice to their suffering by protests and demonstrations. Public opinion goes against the government, the supporters of the plutonomy and the plutonomy itself, and begins to seek more concessions to those affected.

1. Plutonomy is a destabilizer to the balance made of state, economy and the predictability of people's action.
2. It follows a tried-and-tested way (along with the entrepreneur behaviour of global standards in business) of expansion to encroach and engulf rural lands.
3. The state nod and the legal support to do so, the de facto property situation at the location.
4. Its most disturbing consequence is that the revival of the civil resistance by farmers on the verge of getting uprooted is taking place wherever the super rich acquire their land.
5. The Indian rich are working on the back of 'global imbalances'.
6. State is not playing the role of a conflict-resolving institution, nor is it capable of doing so because it has been lately accepting the presence of super rich.
7. India's super wealthy (high net worth individuals) are easy to locate by their king-sized lifestyle, a highly flamboyant beyond 'leisure class', 'conspicuous consumers' rather a 'showcase stage'.
8. They are driving the economy, or a good part of it, towards one set goal – wealth creation.
9. They create hedge funds, rent (not buy) property, buy paintings and other collector's items, own expensive cars in the West; the Indian rich are copying their Western counterparts in many ways and showing off guts in expensive events and glamorous occasions; but in India, they build mansions, mansion-like flats, buy rural property, farm lands and expand into rural areas – on its lands by establishing SEZ, etc. and are trying entry into microfinance, insurance in a big way, but less in labour-intensive manufacturing, so much needed for India's march to social and economic prosperity.
10. They also hold control over capital market to a great extent, but their inclination is to save taxes.
11. The reasons of civil resistance to Indian plutonomy include a sustaining agrarian mode of production, contemporary to industrial-urban society, wherein unskilled/semi-skilled labour force abounds and technology is insufficient and to a great extent old fashioned; the domination of financial form of capital, a government eagerly looking to solve problems through the driving force of plutonomy.

12. Largely, the movements have been non-violent barring incidental clashes in some places, but a notable fact is that these organized or unorganized resistances have been totally different from the Naxal. Another interesting fact is that the civil resistance to Indian plutonomy has begun achieving public attention through media reports and political participation, and judicial intervention has come around for the good of the affected people. This is because of the legacy of judicial activism, equipped with still some intact pro-people laws and political–electoral compulsions in a democracy. In part, success of these movements can be assigned to their distance from violence (Chenoweth and Stephan, 2011). However, the answer to the question as to why the state first let the plutonomy grow (which of course is not strange in a fast-globalizing country) on the cost of people and their means of subsistence and now how come the agencies are attempting SOS has to be searched into the core functioning of a democracy and in what ways it is trying to reassert itself in trying to recreate a genuine and vibrant civil society on broadest base in the era of plutonomy.

    But other questions relevant to Indian plutonomy shall also be raised:
13. What is their internal bickering?
    Are they homogenous?
    Have they collected themselves for better leverage?
14. Do the crises that eventually augmented facilitation of plutonomy in India still have scope to return? Is it that a new political economy has to be written to analyse plutonomy?
15. Does the theory of globalization require readjustments or rationalization beyond the United States and Western Europe in the wake of the Indian plutonomy?

Even though the tiny number of super rich is characteristically a divided house, they function as one for (i) making and stabilizing India as a plutonomy, (ii) changing the nature of the traditional rural property, its proportion in country's general political economy and causing landlessness, (iii) influencing the set of scale of relative deprivation in society by raising it to new heights, (iv) poking holes in the consumer's pockets (v) creating new icons as if the society wished to enter into 'new medieval era'. No doubt that this stage of Indian plutonomy is receiving great attention, great investments, restructuring the rural classes in strange way (for example, a dependent landless class who could have cash in hand 'for a while' by selling out their subsistence resource but hardly left with a productive enterprise; even the cash in hand would fly away either in basic or in non-basic consumption or repayments). The story of 'I sold on cash' Hukka smoking crorepatis was an eye opener that if that was the case, the Indian society was all set to watch a new array of class doing not much. A sort of dependent people holding on leftovers. India as plutonomy may seem so attractive to the state, to the numerous members of urban middle class and that may be projected as the road map of expanding the existing middle classes, which may be a buffer zone for the state and its allies. The Indian rich in some cases divided the people into pro- and anti- for its own end, used legal recourses, threats and relocations, influenced power corridors, although the super rich did not come out always clean. No doubt India became another plutonomy outside of the North in a race of Asian economies going global.

But when everything was a prized business plan, why did the people indulge into civil resistance?

Notes

1. For original concept of plutonomy, see Robert Frank's blog 'The Wealth Report' in *The Wall Street Journal*, 8 January 2007, 8:15 AM ET, Frank writes 'Ajay Kapur, global strategist at Citigroup, and his research team came up with the term "plutonomy" in 2005 to describe a country that is defined by massive income and wealth inequality.
2. An earlier version of this paper was presented and discussed in the Session on Responses to the Emerging Global Plutonomy of RC 02: Economy and Society, First ISA Forum of Sociology, Barcelona, Spain, September 2008. In its present form, however, it has been greatly revised and updated 3, including current references.

References

Chaturvedi, Manjeet (2010). *Afterlife for the Uprooted: Giving Them Another Chance*. Germany: VDM.

Chaturvedi, Manjeet et al. (2007). People Living on Edge: Effects of Encroachment on Rural Lands, Presented Paper in RC 21: Social Problems and Marginalized Groups; 33rd All India Sociological Conference, November 2007, Dharwad.

Chenoweth, Erica and Maria J. Stephan (2011). *Why Civil Resistance Works: The Strategic Logic of Nonviolent Conflict*. Columbia: Columbia University Press.

Kaleki, Michael (1972). *Essays on the Economic Growth of the Socialist and the Mixed Economy*. London: Unwin.

KPMG Study (2008a). The EMIAT figures for the first half of 2008 revealed 90 emerging-to-developed (E2D) deals compared to 161 developed-to-emerging (D2E) deals. Indian buyers accounted for a huge 50 out of the 90 E2D deals, and have contributed significantly in helping the emerging countries bridge the gap with the developed countries.

——— (2008b). Ian Gomes, Chairman, KPMG's New and Emerging Markets practice in the UK, said, 'This is testament to the growing power of the Indian corporate base. At a time when everyone is talking about the credit crunch and Sovereign Wealth funds, Indian trade buyers have simply continued doing what they have been doing for several years now'.

Mitra, Ashok (1977). *Terms of Trade and Class Relations: An Essay in Political Economy*. London: Frank Cass.

PricewaterhouseCoopers Report (2008). See www.noidascoop.com/story/2008/8/26/23363/8821.

10

City through the Prism of Movements

Aurangabad from 1915 to 1960

Shruti Tambe

Introduction

Although the rate of urbanization in India is growing in an unprecedented way, the urban scene in India is full of complexities. With a few global cities and a number of metropolitan cities, the rest of urban India is made up of medium cities and small cities. These cities are growing very fast and are affected by regional, state-level, national, industrial and trade and commerce-related policies. These in turn shape the sociocultural–political texture of contemporary Indian life. Most of the writings on urban phenomena either take a microscopic view focusing on urban history in isolation or are looking at the emergent 'new urban' India, blurring the dynamics at the city level. This paper aims at undertaking a comprehensive analysis of one such city in order to illustrate that a city can be analysed in a more comprehensive way by not focusing on the physical form, demographic composition or conflicts. A city seen through the prism of movements can give us a view from within and from the perspective of the residents.

In this paper, I analyse the case of one of these numerous cities – Aurangabad in Western India. It expanded in an extensive way. According to the 2011 census, the population of Aurangabad was 11,71,330. At the same time, the city has experienced conflicts based on caste, ethnic issues and religion as it passed through various stages of spatial and economic development. Diverging consciously from the ecological or functional classification and analysis of functional zones in the study of a city, this book aims at pointing out the ways in which a city is shaped by and shapes the forces of colonial capitalism in the pre-1948 period to developmentalism in the post-independence period.

This exercise is based on the scrutiny of a number of collective actions including agitations as well as campaigns turning into movements in the city of Aurangabad and around it from 1930 to 1960 in order to understand the underlying ideologies of democracy, modernization and developmentalism. These ideologies were articulated through collective actions related mainly to self-determination and linguistic identity. Who were the actors in these movements, and what were they reformulating collectively? To answer these questions, the public discourse on various conflicts, two social movements and the discourse on development were analysed. For this, ethnography and unstructured personal interviews were supplemented by secondary source of analysis.

At the global level, the research trend in urban sociology is to study global or world cities to look into the recent economic restructuring and its impact on labour and working-class identities (Freidman, 1986; Sassen, 1991; 2001; Gugler, 1997). Analyses of megalopolis and metropolis are undertaken either to review urban policies or issues related to governance ranging from people's participation to surveillance of the State. In such studies, the impact of a new kind of 'developmentalism' – giving importance to improvements in housing, participation of people, infrastructural development and service delivery – is observed (Pugh, 1995; Gugler, 1997). But the medium-sized cities that have grown tremendously in the past two decades worldwide are grossly neglected in the recently undertaken research projects (Shatkin, 1998; Robinson, 2002).

Voluminous works on social movements (Shah, 1977; 2002; 2004; Oommen, 1990; 2004; 2010) in India are published from time to time. Parallel to these volumes is the growing literature on urban phenomena in India, especially focusing on the global and metrocities in contemporary India in terms of infrastructure, governance and services. However, the proliferation of numerous 'middle-sized cities' or 'medium-sized cities' in different parts of India hardly gets a mention. In fact, the socio-political reality in these small and medium cities questions the relevance of currently popular Western theories in the field of urban studies and sociology of social movements. Research questions regarding what constitutes the 'urban'; what is 'urban development', on the one hand; and what we mean by social movements, on the other hand, should not be answered in a mechanical way as the situation in these cities suggest. Research questions that are drawn on the basis of Western paradigms are proven to be inadequate as those questions focus either on changes in the urban phenomena as a result of policy changes or on movements taking place in these locales. In other words, the city is looked at only as a site, where development or movements take place.

Alternatively, if we look at these cities as sites and factors in the process of capitalist growth and its socio-political ramifications, many new insights can come to the fore. Seen this way, analysis of developmental politics at the global and national levels combined with interrogation into local processes enables to grasp situation in small cities. To interpret the resurgence of ethnic, caste and communal conflicts in India alongside capitalist developments, small cities are the best sites.

Following the works by scholars on peripheral capitalism and dependent urbanization in the South (Castells, 1983; Safa, 1982; McGee, 1967; Walton, 2000; Robinson, 2002), this paper underlines the need to combine urban theory with new insights in the field of developmental studies and movement studies to gauge various types of social movements in small- and medium-sized cities in India, such as Aurangabad in Western India. In doing so, I argue that analysis of social movements could be the best tool to unravel the trajectories of 'development' and 'identity-based movements' that these middle-sized cities follow.

Interpreting Cities through the Paradigm of Development

This section reviews the most dominant approaches in the field of development studies and examines the relevance of these approaches to analyse conflicts and collective action in the medium-sized third-world cities such as Aurangabad. This exercise is needed especially as current debates on urban issues focus mostly on global cities or world cities. But medium-sized cities – not megalopolis or metropolitan cities – are kept outside the purview of these studies. Western theories and theorists regard global cities or world cities as a matrix to understand urbanization in the world. Aurangabad and other such similar cities remain outside the frameworks of these studies. In order to bring in the focus on these cities, an attempt has been made in this book to synthesize diverse approaches and theoretical insights.

Approaches in Development Studies

Until very recently, development was mostly defined in terms of economic growth, and it was measured with economic criteria. Starting from mercantilism, approaches to development have been for the most part dominated by economic notions of growth and in recent times by its related indices such as per capita income, gross national product and the like.

The modernization paradigm that was highly popular in the post-1940 period assumed the universal applicability of the Western developmental experience across the world. In the newly emerging nation-states that were impoverished and exploited during colonial period, the economic model of Western capitalist industrial mode of production was prescribed as the 'ideal' one. This 'modernization' paradigm was very influential in the field of social theory from 1940s to 1970s. This approach considered the industrial city as the center of the modern world. Traditional societies with agrarian social relations were conceived as the opposite of modern industrial urban social relations. When this approach is analysed for its relevance and applicability for the so-called third-world cities, it is clear that the 'Western city' is taken as 'the norm' by this approach, ignoring the variation and structural inequalities in the urban scene throughout the world (Robinson, 2002). Again a linear notion of city development was assumed to be the solution to follow the Western pattern.

Modernization paradigm dominated the academic and policy scene roughly from 1940s to 1970s. Coming from the 'developed' Western capitalist countries, this perspective privileged the Western experience of capital-intensive model of industrial development as ideal. Indicators based on the experience of Advanced Capitalist countries in the West were considered as the basic yardstick on which newly independent countries in Asia, Africa and Latin America could be classified into developed, developing or underdeveloped. A number of scholars including Lerner, Rostow, Levy and McClelland defined development in terms of industrial employment, use of electricity, expansion of services such as communication through radio, 'achievement' orientation of actors and stages in growth. On the basis of these and related indices, a number of eminent scholars including Lerner, Rostow, Levy, McClell and analysing the situation in Africa, Latin America and Asia put different countries and their developmental experiences in different pre-defined slots and labeled them as developing or underdeveloped and traditional or modern (Preston, 2001; Pandey, 1988, Webster, 1990). Most of these analyses completely neglected the differences in the histories of colonialism and socio-political peculiarities, thereby undermining the differences in their trajectories after decolonization.

As Jan Nederveen Pieterse pertinently states, modernization theory 'evolved from a marriage of evolutionism and functionalism, with modernization conceptualized either as a critical variable or a dichotomous theory' (Pieterse, 2001: 20). This paradigm was also based on and prescribed a bipolar or dichotomous conception of values and behaviour patterns associated with modernity. 'Modern' societies were supposed to possess certain values and the exact opposite of it was believed to be associated with 'traditional' societies.

Application of this approach to understand the urban reality at the global level means positing a scale in mapping the urban culture. Impact of traditional values, traditional occupations, ascriptive categories vis-à-vis achievement orientation, 'modern' occupations, more use of electricity, increased newspaper circulation, etc., were taken as the criteria and panaceas to 'modernize' these cities and regions by scholars such as Lerner and McClelland.

Dependency Theories

The neo-Marxists put forth theoretical explanations based on the experiences of countries from Asia, Africa and Latin America having the common history of colonial exploitation. Paul Baran (1973), Samir Amin (1974; 1976) and Andre Gunder Frank (1967; 1975) were some of the forerunners of this perspective. According to these scholars, underdevelopment in the developing countries is due to external factors such as extraction of surplus by more powerful countries. Relations of domination and subordination then become significant in deciding the flow of surplus extraction. Thus, the world was conceived in dichotomous categories such as the centre and the periphery or the metropolis and the satellite and so on. This theoretical perspective facilitated the analysis of play of global- and national-level factors determining the nature of economy in peripheral societies affecting the nature and form of urban centres as well as the nature of activities therein especially in the 'third-world' countries. Scholars such as Castells (1983) have shown how it portrays the cities in the periphery as a dependent entity. It obscures the understanding of internal hierarchies and divisions in these societies, which contribute to the unevenness of development.

Developmentalism

This approach assumes that social change goes on in a pre-established way. Developmentalism has different versions – liberal and radical, secular and religious. It also became a neo-colonial discourse around the 1960s. For the newly formed governments in the decolonized world, institutionalization of democracy was a challenge. New definitions of nation, citizenship, state, civil society and representative government were articulated on the Western lines arguing as if those are universal (meaning as per the Western norm). As modernization paradigm lost its popularity by the late 1960s, 'development' emerged as the new mantra. This transition meant that from a 'broad sociological ethnocentric concept of modernization the discourse shifted to a narrow economic ethnocentric concept' (Pieterse, 2001: 23–4). According to Pieterse, it was underwritten by the international community and was encoded in the UN development decade policy documents. The State was assigned with the role of executing the development goals. Development meant economic development measurable in PCI, GDP, NI compared and monitored internationally by institutions such as the International Monetary Fund, World Bank, various development banks and so on. In a way, this approach also privileged the Western experiences as central and was therefore linear and ethnocentric. There was enormous optimism about the applicability of this approach, especially in the newly independent countries. By the late 1980s, of course there was disenchantment all over and especially in the third world about the effectiveness of this mantra.

The application of this paradigm meant that cities are privileged over villages as centres of development with industries, banks, offices of developmental bureaucracies and higher educational institutions established in cities including that of technical education. In case of urban situation in the newly independent countries with new developmental model based on capital-intensive industrial sector, a number of changes in the vision and policy were witnessed. Spatial growth of cities resulting in shifting of growth centres and functional differentiation and establishment of industrial estates were some of the major visible signs of hegemonic developmentalism in countries such as India.

Social Movements in Cities

Social conflicts and movements are omnipresent in the urban scenario. Indian cities are no exception to this. Challenging the authority of the state was staged in cities in and through collective actions of various kinds. The Indian freedom struggle of 1857 was played in cantonment towns established by the British. During the nationalist freedom struggle in the early 20th century, cities emerged often as centres of political protest. In other words, these movements were not about urban issues per se; yet, they were played out in urban centres.

In the phase of developmentalism throughout the 1970s and 1980s, the masses expressed grievances against the state in cities through collective action. Here, I argue in support of using social conflicts and movements as an index of people's aspirations and opinions. After independence, language-related collective action evolved around 1955 as reorganization of states under the structure of the republic was debated (Subramanian, 1999). All over India, the 1960s and 1970s witnessed campaigns and agitations for development (Shah, 1977; Tambe, 2004). Aurangabad was no exception to this. In the city of Aurangabad, the recurrence of conflicts based on language, caste and religion was observed as the city expanded from the 1940s to the 1990s. These conflicts structured the city and in turn are structured by the city. In this particular case, the conflicts were not always about urban social issues. The structure and social composition of the region and the power dynamics related to it framed the collective actions in cities including Aurangabad. Unlike Western studies and theories of and about cities, this study suggests the importance of the impact of the region on the city rather than considering the city as an autonomous socio-economic island.

Theoretical Approaches to Social Movements

According to Outhwaite and Bottomore (1993: 597–600), there are six main theoretical paradigms to the study of social movements. In the 1920s, symbolic interactionism of the Chicago school initiated interactionist approach. It focused on collective behaviour including social movements as a process of interaction. As per this approach, individuals and groups act on the basis of shared understandings and common goals and expectations. Social movements arise when these shared meanings and goals are lacking, or are broken down or need redefinition. The popularity of this approach lies in its acknowledgement of psychological factors such as emotions, communication, expression of solidarity and expressive behaviour. Marxist and neo-Marxist approach highlight the conflictual nature of social relations. In industrial society, social movements and revolutions emerge due to the basic contradiction between capital and labour. Antagonistic social classes defined by this systemic contradiction are also considered as historical actors. As per this approach, analysis of objective conditions and accounting for a more subjective process through which social movements arise is considered important.

Structural-functional paradigm in the study of social movements had a number of variants, which analysed social movements as arising out of challenges to social organization and harmony. Mass society theories maintain that rapid social change, urbanization and loss of traditional bonds, isolation from normative reference groups uproot and atomize individuals who are then likely to join social movements. Relative deprivation theories, which are quite popular even today in mainstream sociological analyses of movements, see the genesis of social movements in terms of subjective feelings of conditions of structural discrepancies. Maheu rightly argues that this model fails to explain the broader functioning of a social system and to interrogate into the patterns of domination and exploitation experienced in everyday life. According to Maheu (1995: 4), resource mobilization theory offers a broad analytical framework within which to 'site' collective rational choice issues. The label 'new social movements' was coined to describe different kinds of movements that erupted through the West in the 1970s and early 1980s. These contestations in the form of issue-oriented campaigns and loose organizations or movements laid claims for alternative lifestyles, values and norms to create new social and cultural spaces. Sociology of action perspective integrated various theoretical approaches and defined social life as conflictual self-production. Touraine, the chief proponent of this approach, argued that permanent struggle over the use of new technologies and the social control of society's own transforming capacities is at the very centre of social life. According to the premises of this approach, there is a constant conflict over social control of the main cultural patterns namely knowledge, investment and ethics. Social movements are the social actors involved in these conflicts (Outhwaite and Bottomore, 1993: 600). The conflict field comprises I (identity), O (opponent) and T (totality). It is suggested that social conflict must not be separated from the cultural orientations. According to Touraine, different kinds of social movements should be analysed on different levels of analysis.

In Maheu's analysis, only two schools of thought on social movement remain polarized today. Resource mobilization theory offers a broad analytical framework within which to 'site' collective rational choice issues. It suggests that important focal point in the study of social movements is the form a social movement takes and what politico-institutional mechanisms are used to inscribe it. New social movement approaches according to Maheu, in contrast to resource mobilization theories, take the 'why' behind collective action as opposed to the 'how' of it. Here, the emphasis is placed on collective and conflicting worldviews that subjectivize and filter social factors into forms of collective action.

Some recent collections claim to attempt theoretical or conceptual synthesis at various such efforts to link and assimilate two or more approaches. But he calls it 'conceptual poaching' (Buechler, 2000: 53) and gives an alternative approach to the analysis of social movements. Buechler's structural approach to social movements, as he names it, rests in a particular kind of conception of society as consisting of multiple, overlapping, and intersecting levels of social reality that may be designated as global, national, regional and local structures.

Cities are usually portrayed as 'theatres of collective action' in various studies. This paper argues that cities are not only the sites where collective action occurs, but they also contribute to the factors that shape collective actions.

Contested City: Insights from Urban Collective Action

For the present project, the insights from works on social movements in Latin America and the approach by Manuel Castells is found more relevant than mainstream theories of development and/or mainstream theories of social movements. In an important collection on social movements in Latin America, edited by David Slater (1985), different scholars have come out with innovative insights for the analysis of social movement in the post-1960 period in the non-European, non-North-American parts of the world. Using Althusser, these scholars have attempted to understand the predominance and sometimes resurgence of what Western theorists call 'primordial identities' in Latin American social movements.

Manuel Castells in his famous work *The City and the Grassroots* (1983) put forth a theory of understanding urban social movements in different cross-cultural settings. According to him, 'urban social movements are collective actions consciously aimed at the transformations of the social interests and values embedded in the forms and functions of a historically given city' (ibid.: XVI). Stating that collective action is a reaction to urban crisis, he insists that if the process of production of cities by societies is most evident in the case of social revolt and spatial innovation, it is not limited to such exceptional events. Everybody in every context, people acting individually or collectively, produce or reproduce the rules of their society, and translate them into their spatial expression and their institutional management (ibid.).

Observing that urban structures will always be the expression of some institutionalized domination and urban crisis will be the result of a challenge that comes from new actors in history and society, Castells privileges the study of urban social movements to analyse urban crisis. In the post-independent Indian context, these theoretical indices put forth by Castells can be helpful in understanding the contradictions unfolding in democratic setup and in the developmental aspirations of the population. Analysing Indian cities with this approach can enable a deeper analysis of urban phenomena in terms of the interplay of ethnic, linguistic collective identities in the context of democratic politics.

Castells argues that the city is a social product, resulting from conflicting social interests and values. Although he acknowledges the role of grassroots mobilization in the process of defining what a city is, he also reminds that the dominant interests also affect it through democratic institutions. Finally, according to Castells although class relationships and class struggle are fundamental in understanding urban conflict, they are not, by any means, the only primary source of urban social change. The autonomous role of the state, the gender relationships, the ethnic and national movements, the movements that define themselves as citizen are among other alternative sources of social change (ibid.: 291). As most of the analyses that Castells put forth is based on experiences in the Western context, his definitions of urban social movements are different than what we experience in Indian cities.

A closer scrutiny of socio-spatial dynamics in cities of the global South including India and that too in non-metropolitan cities reveals their peculiarities setting them apart from 'the normative Western city'. These cities are not necessarily industrial centres driven by one particular kind of industry. Most Indian cities that expanded in the post-independent period are in fact administrative and bureaucratic centres with only a few that can qualify as 'industrial centres'. In fact, under the influential developmentalist paradigm national-and state-level governments established 'industrial estates' and district industrial centres in the 1970s under the central government initiated Five-Year Plans. Yet, the industries that were started with governmental schemes and subsidies were subsequently closed down in non-metropolitan cities such as Aurangabad. In other words, these cities did not adhere to the Western ideal type of an industrial city.

The ways in which industrial capitalism originated and expanded in Europe and other parts of Western world is fundamentally different from the trajectory it took in India, where it was introduced by the colonial powers. It was therefore dependent and peripheral capitalism based on the surpluses of agriculture, and the land-owning classes were strengthened and their powers were reinforced by the British. Hence, the process of class formation was totally different in India (Chakrabarty, 1989; Chandavarkar, 2009). Even today, the makeup of medium-sized cities bears testimony to this historical trajectory. Deb (2006) and Parthsarathy (1997) have commented on this issue in the context of Indian cities.

Buechler (2000) argues that social movements are important actors in any society, especially in the contemporary period. Since movements represent the dominant and alternative interests, analysis of movements can throw light on the social conflicts constructing the social relations in cities. Hence, study of a city through the prism of movements over a period of time can be beneficial in explaining nature of the city and the negotiations and contestations over power in cities. In non-metropolitan cities, as Parthsarathy (1997) shows, the regional elite and the regional socio-political dynamics play a vital role in defining the orientation and fabric of collective action. Tilly explains how urban history constructed through event catalogues can facilitate better understanding of important developments in a campaign or agitation. Chandavarkar illustrates the reorganization of spatial geography and expansion of capital in Mumbai in an intertwined way. Taking cues from Castells, Robinson and Tilly, this paper argues that the analysis of interplay between economic development of a region represented in a city, unfolding of democratic political processes and changing urban spatial patterns through expansion and reorganization enables the study of a non-metropolitan city. It helps to tease out the criss-cross between local, regional, national and global factors in making and unmaking of a city.

City and the Region: Collective Action in Non-Metro Cities

By looking at two important moments in the history of Aurangabad city – the joining of Republic of India in 1948 and joining of Maharashtra in 1960 – this section probes into language-based ethnic movement in and around the city of Aurangabad to bring out the underlying texture of different conflicts in the city and their relevance in terms of defining development, democracy and identity in different time periods. It also examines how the spatial dimension was reorganized as an effect of this movement.

For the past four centuries, Aurangabad city attracted various rulers in the Deccan. The city of Aurangabad was established by Malik Ambar – the Prime Minister of the Adilshahi Dynasty in 1610 at the site of village Khirki. He made it as a capital city and also stationed his army there. Within a decade, it became an imposing city. This city had water distribution system set up by Malik Ambar through aqua ducts and terracotta pipelines. After 1633, it came under Mughal rule; and in 1653 when Aurangzeb was appointed as the viceroy of the Deccan, he made it his capital and called it Aurangabad. Later, it became one of the important centres of Mughal power in the Deccan. As an administrative and military centre from the beginning, it attracted various linguistic, religious and ethnic communities right from the early 17th century. Arabs, Rohilas, Mughals and Rajputs were among the administrative and military officials in the Subhedari here. New traders from Rajasthan, Marwar and Gujarat settled in this town. Sikhs also settled in Aurangabad. Since the Hindus, Jains, Sikhs and the Muslims populated this city under Adilashahi rule and the Mughal rule, the culture of this city is different than other cities in Maharashtra. For a long time, there is a history of sporadic Hindu–Muslim confrontations. This town was walled during the Mughal period and had segregated ethnic neighbourhoods.

In 1720, Nizam of Asaf Jah (who was a Moghal general) made Aurangabad his capital. Later after the year 1724, he shifted capital to Hyderabad. The British established a military camp near Aurangabad. As an administrative centre and a garrison centre, it expanded even further with the cantonment area.

Although Hyderabad was the capital city and hence attracted people from Marathwada region for higher education and administrative matters, Aurangabad was well established as the regional social, cultural, administrative and political centre. After Police Action in Hyderabad State , Aurangabad became the sub-regional headquarter.

In the first half of the 20th century as anti-colonial struggles gathered momentum in British India, Marathwada in Hyderabad State was also influenced by the aspirations for self-determination and freedom. The city of Aurangabad with divisional headquarters of the Nizamshahi government was a theatre of protests. Marathwada sub-region of contemporary Maharshtra State was then a neglected part of the Hyderabad Princely State ruled by the Nizam belonging to Asafiaya dynasty. Located at the centre of India, the British considered it strategically important to control this State through a treaty signed by the Nizam and the British.[1]

Hence, the Hyderabad State showed a peculiar combination of a premodern feudal political order with infiltration of capitalist market through trade and commerce treaties with the British. The ruler, on the insistence of British in this region, encouraged cotton and oilseeds production. The agrarian structure had two patterns of land holding – Khalsa and Jagirs. Jagirs had two kinds of tenures: Sarf-e-Khas and other jagirs. Sarf-e-Khas land was used for Nizam's private use and for the maintenance of some army. Sarf-e-Khas land holdings were so large that the revenue fetched was as high as 20 million rupees. Other jagir lands were given to nobility created by the Nizam. For these jagir plots, the nobility had absolute powers of revenue collection. The oppression of cultivators on Jagir lands was absolute, as the control of judiciary was absent there. Jagir lands were very important, as they constituted one-third of the entire land at disposal. The middlemen of the Jagirdar levied many kinds of illegal taxes adding the burden on cultivators.

Khalsa land, on the other hand, was given to individual peasant proprietors for cultivation. They were called *pattedars*, and they had to pay revenue to traditional revenue collectors such as Deshmukhs and Deshpandes.[2]

This pattern of agrarian ownership resulted not only in economic oppression and inequalities, but it also helped to ensure complete political subordination and adherence to feudal value structure. Values of servitude, complete loyalty without questioning, importance of duties rather than demanding rights and complete allegiance to hierarchical social relations were some of the aspects of this value structure that influences the social ethos to some extent even today. In Marathwada region, most of the land was under Sarf-e-Khas and the rest was under Jagirs. This meant that culture of servitude and patronage was widely accepted, and the rulers were absolute authorities as far as Marathwada region was concerned.

The Nizam banned education in languages other than Urdu. As a feudal state, there were restrictions on social gatherings except those permitted by the Nizam. The Nizam had established an intermediate college in Aurangabad and Osmania University in Hyderabad. Up until the 1960s, there were no colleges with private initiative. In the early 20th century, a number of schools and libraries were established in Aurangabad City, which became centres of discussions on socio-cultural and political issues.

Hyderabad Mukti Sangram

Post-colonial societies with peripheral states in most of the global south show certain common trends and problems. Late entry into markets, very high rates of urbanization and social movements of varied kinds are symptomatic and at the same time resultant of inherent contradictions in these ex-colonial societies.

India became independent in 1947 in the global context of uneven capitalist development. As such, the whole of India was not part of direct colonialism. There were provinces carved out by the British for administrative and revenue purposes named as British India, and the rest were kingdoms led by British approved kings, queens, Nawabs and Nizams – the hereditary monarchs termed 'princely states'.

The notions of democracy, citizenship and nationhood were therefore differentially understood, defined and articulated in these two different kinds of regions within what we refer to as 'India' in a homogenized way. The incorporation of these regions into capitalist economy and modern democratic setup also did not take place in a homogenous and similar way. The form and content of their merger into the Indian Republic, their access to financial resources for infrastructural developments including irrigation facilities and participation in newly established democratic institutions and decision-making processes were differentially structured as per the British policy and stage of joining capitalist modernity.

The ideologies of democracy, ideas of liberty, equality and citizenship as against subject position in the Nizam dominion percolated in the Hyderabad State through the organs of civil society in neighbouring British India. Hyderabad Mukti Sangram (hereafter referred to as HMS) was a long struggle that the people of Hyderabad State were engaged in to throw the Nizam's feudal rule. From the beginning of the 20th century, the demand for merger in Indian Union made on the basis of the principle of self-determination of the majority and democratic political principles was pushed through the HMS in the milieu of nationalist struggle in British India.

The HMS was based on two kinds of ideological positions. One was joining of Indian Republic through right to self-determination. Dream of economic development was the other ideology behind this movement. There were multiple actors associated with the HMS. The Arya Samaj, Hindu Mahasabha, Indian National Congress were the main forces behind it. The actors involved in HMS were students, teachers, journalists, lawyers, literati and intellectuals. Most of them were Hindus. Collective actions associated directly or indirectly with HMS were eclectic in nature. Schools and colleges imparting education in the region through regional language – Marathi – as against Urdu – the official language of the Nizam's State – were involved in collective action around self-determination. These institutions in Aurangabad facilitated setting up of support networks for HMS. Symbolic protest through singing of *Vande Mataram* as a prayer was one of the forms of protests. The press publishing in regional language highlighted aspirations for self-determination. The gymnasiums disseminated ideas of self-rule. All these locations in the city were linked in the various activities related to HMS, including constitutional means and strategies, publishing, disseminating and discussions.

Although the rest of India got independence from British colonial rule in August 1947, Hyderabad State merged in Indian Federation only in 1948 when the Indian Army cooperated with the HMS volunteers to defeat the Nizam. The HMS thus successfully dismantled the feudal, undemocratic rule of the Nizam and joined the Indian Republic as a part of the Hyderabad State in September 1948.

Samyukta Maharashtra Andolan

The merger of Hyderabad State in Indian Republic in September 1948 was jubilantly welcomed and celebrated with the hope that the era of political oppression was over and that the democratic aspirations of the masses could be realized. As the restrictions on the press, education in regional language as against in Urdu – the language of administration and of the ruling class – establishment of different associations and organizations were removed; the possibilities of the expansion of modern civil society were seen round the corner.

The decade of the 1950s was the period of democratic restructuring of the post-colonial India. Different presidencies established by the British and the merged princely states had to be re-organized in states under the Indian Union. This process was called 'reorganization of states'. This process was obviously full of contestations throughout Indian Union, given the linguistic, religious, regional, sub-regional variation and heterogeneity. This process was complete by 1960. The new states were by and large organized on the basis of linguistic continuity of regions, thereby mixing the erstwhile princely states and British India provinces.[3]

This in turn shaped and was shaped by the course of capitalist development and market penetration in different states of the Indian Union after independence. The Indian National Congress was the major contender of political power in the nationalist movement. Given the heterogeneity based on linguistic, religious, caste and class background of the masses, the Indian National Congress emerged as an 'umbrella' organization during freedom struggle and in the post-colonial period balancing and negotiating between elite and mass interests in a way that facilitated expansion of ruling class.

From 1948, when Hyderabad State merged in the Indian Union, Marathwada sub-region was one of the three parts of newly carved Hyderabad State. This sub-region pleaded for merger in the Maharashtra State based on Marathi language in 1956. Aurangabad City, the largest town in Marathwada sub-region emerged as the Administrative centre in 1956 in the then Bombay State.

During these decades of Hyderabad Mukti Sangram, Aurangabad City experienced establishment of modern institutions including Government College in the Navkhanda Palace outside the Bharkal Gate on the Northern side of the city. In 1891, the first industrial school and in 1894 the first agricultural school was established by the Nizam. In *Madarse Fokaniya* – that is, Government High School, classes in English medium were started in 1892. Janata Shikshan Parishad, Social Conference, Humanitarian League and Adi Hindu League were some of the organizations established during the first quarter of the 20th century. The *Vande Mataram* campaign articulating aspirations for joining the freedom struggle in British India was initiated in this campus of the Intermediate College at Aurangabad. Shree Saraswati Bhuvan Shikshan Sanstha established in 1914, Balwant Vachanalay (1920) – library named after famous nationalist leader and journalist Bal Gangadhar Tilak in 1920, the Ganesh and Samarth Vyayamshala of Aurangabad can be termed as an important factor in the growth of the city and also a result of its increasing significance in the region. The actors in this movement were the lawyers, teachers, students of the Government College and additionally members of the landed classes from the Marathwada region.

The HMS was successful in dismantling the feudal rule of the Nizam of Hyderabad and marked the entry of Marathwada sub-region with Aurangabad city as its capital officially in the democratic Republic of India. HMS was also based on the ideology of developmentalism, and therefore demands for capitalist development through extended irrigation facilities and educational facilities, and schemes for rural development were constantly voiced in newspapers, magazines and through political representations to the Nizam.

Ironically, the contradictions in a democratic society and within the process of development in an unequal social setting were awaiting the citizens of Aurangabad City and Marathwada as was illustrated through the Samyukta Maharashtra Aandolan after 1948.

The first prime minister of India, Pandit Jawaharlal Nehru, was advocate of the 'Unity in Diversity' discourse, and hence opposed language as the basis of reorganizing territories across India. As Subramanian (1999) shows eloquently, popular sentiment was on the side of language-based reorganization of States. The Government of India appointed an official commission to examine the demands for inclusion or exclusion in States across India.

From 1948 to 1956, Marathi-speaking Marathwada sub-region continued to be a part of Hyderabad State with Andhra region, Telangana and Kannda-speaking sub-region. During this period, Marathwada strongly demanded its inclusion in Maharashtra State based on the principle of linguistic identity. The national leaders of Congress Party contested this claim as they epitomized Hyderabad State to be the symbol of the rhetoric of 'unity in diversity' and Hindu–Muslim composite culture. According to them, the old princely state had three major linguistic groups and two important religious communities living together for centuries. Hyderabad State was seen in a way as a 'celebrated case' to show that the two-nation theory based on religious identity making the birth of Pakistan possible was grounded on erroneous assumptions regarding 'nationhood'.[4] As Bhalerao (1987) suggests, the leaders in Marathwada region were convinced that the policies of the Nizam had kept the region and city underdeveloped, and hence continuously asked for 'development' of this 'backward area'. Hence, demands for increased plan outlays for the region were demanded to the Hyderabad State Assembly.

Since the movement for the establishment of Andhra composing of Telugu-speaking population gathered momentum and the prime minister had to concede to that demand in 1953, the leaders in Marathwada joined the elites in Western Maharashtra for establishing Samyukta Maharashtra Aandolan. This demand was based on the principle of linguistic contiguity of Marathi-speaking people. As a result, from 1956 to 1960, Marathwada was a part of the bilingual Bombay State with Gujarati- and Marathi-speaking population. The movement for the unilingual State of Maharashtra took momentum from 1956 and went on till the establishment of Maharashtra and Gujarat states separately in 1960.

During this period, the representatives of the landowning classes and castes from the region of Marathwada emerged as strong political leaders. The old leadership comprising of the intellectuals and literati, which had emerged in the HMS was in a sense replaced by these sections. The erstwhile urban elite leadership was sidelined in the process. The new actors were swinging from one lobby in the Congress party to the other to fulfill their democratic aspirations. Politics of patronage and populism characteristic of democratic politics in the post-independent period echoed itself in Marathwada region and Aurangabad City represented it. Aurangabad City, being the divisional headquarters, was the stage for this power play.

On the national level, the emerging post-colonial Central State followed a peculiar nation-building agenda till the early 1960s. With Jawaharlal Nehru as the first prime minister of the country, the period from 1947 to 1960 is termed the 'Nehruvian era', wherein commitment to social justice and socialism was combined with modernization on the lines of Western capitalist countries. This combination triggered 'internal colonialisms', which intensified erstwhile inequalities on different geographical scales resulting into stark socio-economic inequalities within and between regions and old and new hierarchies in access to resources and decision-making powers in different geographical locales. As a result, some states, some regions and sub-regions and some cities were labeled 'backward' in comparison with other parts of Republic of India.

There was so much optimism at the time independence that the citizens, both in British India and princely states, saw the post-colonial state as both the liberator from socio-economic oppression and as an agent of modernization. By the end of 1960s, however, it was clear that the alliance between feudal-bourgeoisie elements controlled the state (Bose and Jalal, 1997; Chatterjee, 1997). Aspirations of those who were pushed near the margins of the development process from before independence could not be fulfilled even after independence.

Aurangabad City expanded spatially during this period as it became the new administrative, educational and industrial centre in the period between 1948 and 1960.

Why Use Prism of Movements?

Our reference point is Hyderabad Princely State from 1920 to 1960. The ideologies of self-determination and developmentalism combined with linguistic, religious and regional identities were played out through HMS and SMA. In other words, 'modern' ideologies of Western democracy and development along with 'primordial' parochial identities based on language and regional identity conflated in an interesting way to demand dismantling of feudal Nizam State and territorial reorganization of parts of erstwhile Bombay State and Hyderabad State to carve out a new State in Western India.

Analysis of these collective actions leads me to pose the following questions: Is there any significance of the fact that a medium-sized city such as Aurangabad is found bustling with social movements for more than four decades? Was the city at the centre of these movements?

While answering these questions, I argue that social movements are themselves important actors in any society, especially in the contemporary period. Since movements represent the negotiations and contestations between the dominant and alternative interests in a society at a given point, analysis of movements can throw light on the conflicting interests in a city and the resultant construction of a city. In the case of metropolitan and global cities, the dynamics are more influenced by global capital flows. On the other hand, to understand the socio-economic dynamics of a non-metropolitan city, the use of prism of movements through the years would prove to be beneficial. It unfolds the changing relationships between various groups and communities and their interests in shaping the city. Both local cultural milieu and ethos and national, state-level economic and political factors combine in unexpected ways that create collective actions. The locales in the city – ethnic neighbourhoods, linguistic identities, places of recreation such as gymnasia (called *taleem* in Marathi) and educational institutions are spaces where the ideologies behind collective action are defined and constructed, and also those spaces in turn reformulate repertoires of collective action.

Finally, I argue that in a medium-sized city such as Aurangabad where industrial capitalism does not develop the way it does in advanced capitalist countries or like it develops in Indian metropolitan cities, movements around class and class consciousness is not seen evolving. Neither 'urban' issues of infrastructure, services and affordable housing seem to trigger collective action on a large scale. The region and the sub-region construct the collective action in terms of ideologies and repertoires. The actors are not always the industrial workers or the urban ruling classes as expected by social movement theorists. Instead, the sub-regional elite with feudal, semi-feudal vested interests in land ownership believing in feudal values control the political and economic processes. The movements in such a city are therefore expressions of sub-regional interests than a direct reaction to urban crisis or collective consumption in the city as such.

Thus, the analysis of major instances of collective action and conflicts over self-determination and development, and language-based identity in Aurangabad City has proven to be more a study of concerns of the sub-region (joining Maharashtra State); and in some cases, even national concerns (self-determination) than the concerns of the City. At the same time, one should not forget that these conflicts and forms of collective action are not entirely divorced from the city or these are not imposed artificially by the sub-regional elite on the city. In other words, these conflicts represent the changing economic relations and its impact on the changing political equations in the city and the region.

The State–Civil Society Relationship

For a democracy to function effectively, the existence of a strong civil society is a necessity as it is supposed to be the protective shield of citizens against exigencies of the State machinery. But in most of the societies with the history of colonialism and therefore dependent capitalism, development of civil society is thwarted. Whether civil society in India is matured enough to restrain the State from controlling and oppressing the citizens has been a polemical issue among scholars. Some feel that civil society is adequately developed to be able to protect the interests of the masses and to create a ground for reasonable dialogue. Other scholars felt that the Indian state faced a crisis of legitimacy in the post-1970 period. And in such a situation, civil society alone could not control the monopolizing, exploitative and oppressive aspects of Indian polity.[5]

Since Aurangabad City was a part of Hyderabad State under the rule of the autocratic monarch – the Seventh Nizam, the development of civil society was purposely restricted. The ruler was considered as the ultimate authority in all respects. The last Nizam in fact issued a government order banning participation in civil society and restricted civil rights considerably. Therefore, civil and democratic rights were almost non-existent to subjects in the pre-1948 period.

Throughout the sub-region of Marathwada, access to secular education was almost completely denied and religious education was compulsory. Subjects were not allowed to form associations without prior permission, and publication of many newspapers, magazines, pamphlets and books was banned as these authors and publishers were suspected to have anti-Nizam opinions. In other words, all the major expressions of Western capitalist modernity otherwise introduced by the British in British India were not allowed to unfold in the Hyderabad State till 1948.

To conclude, the Aurangabad City with its deities, temples, mosques and schools; old palaces and religious processions, a few select newspapers and magazines bustled with collective action was limited mostly to the walled city areas till 1960s. The Walled City was in fact a metaphor for the ethos of this non-metropolitan city struggling to enter the 'modern' era. After the 1960s, the city actually expanded much beyond the Walled City areas and engaged with dynamics of modernity. Of course, that is another story.

Acknowledgements

This is a much revised version of some parts of the unpublished essay submitted to Sarai-CSDS studentship programme in 2003. I thank Ravi Sundaram and Ravi Kant for many conversations. I am especially grateful to Sujata Patel for many meaningful and invigorating discussions for fleshing out the ideas beyond my doctoral work through the years. Some of the arguments that appear here have been presented at ISA Methodology Lab in 1999 at Onati, Spain. I particularly benefitted from discussions with Bert Klandermans in 1999 and in 2003 and with Ron Aminzade in 2009. I thank all the commentators for pushing the discussions ahead. Thanks are also due to Sumati Unkule and Prashant Apte for research assistance and discussions.

Notes

1. Sir Berton William has quoted in *White Paper on Hyderabad*. New Delhi: Government of India, 1948.
2. See Dhanagare (1983) for a detailed analysis of the feudal structure in the Hyderabad State.
3. Narendra Subramanian (1999) and Robert King (1997) have discussed the language politics in India.
4. The local newspapers and leaflets of associations constantly defy this claim as they saw linguistic affinity as more important denominator of their merger in democratic process than anything else. See, for example, Bhalerao (1987) and the issues of the local Newspaper 'Marathwada' in this period.
5. *Sociological Bulletin*, Vol. 50, No. 2, 2001, Indian Sociological Society, Delhi.

References

Amin, Samir (1976). *Unequal Development*. Sussex: Harvester Press.

Aurangabad District Gazeteer (1977). Government of Maharashtra. Bombay.

Baran, P. (1973). *The Political Economy of Growth*. Harmondsworth: Penguin.

Bhalerao, Anantrao (1987). *Hyderabadcha Swatantrysangram aani Marathwada*. Aurangabad: Swami Ramanad Teerth Samshodhan Sanstha.

Bose, S. and Jalal, A. (eds) (1997). *Nationalism, Democracy and Development: State and Politics in India*. New Delhi: Oxford University Press.

Buechler, Steven M. (2000). *Social Movements in Advanced Capitalism: The Political Economy and Cultural Construction of Social Activism*. New York: Oxford University Press.

Castells, Manuel (1977). *The Urban Question: A Marxist Approach*. London: Edward Arnold.

——— (1983). *The City and the Grassroots*. Berkeley and Los Angeles: University of California Press.

Chakrabarty, D. 1989, *Rethinking Working-Class History*, New Delhi: Oxford University Press.

Chandavarkar, Rajnarayan (2009). *History, Culture and the Indian City*. New Delhi: Cambridge University Press.

Chatterjee, Parth (1986). *Nationalist Thought and the Colonial World: A Derivative Discourse?* New Delhi: Oxford University Press.

——— (1993). *The Nation and Its Fragments: Colonial and Post-Colonial Histories*. Princeton: Princeton University Press.

Desai, A.R. (ed.) (1985). *Caste and Communal Violence in Independent India*. Bombay: C.G. Shah Memorial Trust Publication.

Deshpande, Jayant (2001). 'Pune: Past, Present and Future', *The Hindu*, 12 August, Chennai.

Devalle, Susana B. (1992). *Discourses of Ethnicity: Culture and Protest in Jharkhand*. New Delhi: Sage Publications.

Dhanagare, D.N. (1983). *Peasant Movements in India*. New Delhi: Oxford University Press.

Dupont, V., E. Tarlo and D. Vital (eds) (2000). *Delhi: Urban Space and Human Destinies*. New Delhi: Manohar.

Eder, Klaus (1995). 'Does Social Class Matter in the Study of Social Movements? A Theory of Middle Class Radicalism', in Louis Maheu (ed.), *Social Movements and Social Classes: The Future of Collective Action*. London: Sage Publications and International Sociological Association, pp. 21–54.

Engineer, Asghar Ali (1984). *Communal Riots in Post-Independence India*. Hyderabad: Sangam Books.

Frank, A.G. (1966). *The Development of Underdevelopment*. Boston, MA: New England Free Press.

Frank, A. G. (1967). *Capitalism and Underdevelopment in Latin America*. New York: Monthly Review Press.

Frank, A. G. (1975). *On Capitalist Underdevelopment*. Oxford University Press.

Frankel, Francine R. and M.S.A. Rao (eds) (1989). *Dominance and State Power in Modern India Decline of a Social Order*, Vol. I. New Delhi: Oxford University Press.

Freitag, Sandria B. (1990). *Collective Action and Community: Public Arenas and the Emergence of Communalism in North India*. New Delhi: Oxford University Press.

Government of India (1948). *White Paper on Hyderabad*. New Delhi: Government of India Press.

Gugler, Josef (ed.) (1988). *The Urbanization of the Third World*. Oxford: Oxford University Press.

Gugler, Josef (ed.) (1997). *Cities in the Developing World: Issues, Theory, and Policy*. New York: Oxford University Press.

——— (1996). *The Urban Transformation of the Developing World*. New Delhi: Oxford University Press.

Guibernau, Montserrat and John Rex (eds) (1997). *The Ethnicity Reader*. Malden, MA and Cambridge, UK: Polity Press.

Hall, Tim (1998). *Urban Geography*. London and New York: Routledge.

Karna, M.N. (1999). 'Language, Region and National Identity', *Sociological Bulletin*, March-September, 48(1&2), pp. 75–96.

Khilnani, Sunil (1998). *The Idea of India*. New Delhi: Penguin Books.

King, Robert D., 1997, *Nehru and the Language Politics of India*, New Delhi: Oxford University Press.

Klandermans, Bert (1997). *The Social Psychology of Protest*. Oxford: Wiley-Blackwell.

Kosambi, Meera (1994). *Urbanisation and Urban Development in India*. New Delhi: ICSSR.

Lebas, Elizabeth (1982). *Urban and Regional Sociology in Advanced Industrial Societies: A Decade of Marxist and Critical Perspectives*. London: Sage Publications.

Lele, Jayant (1981). *Elite Pluralism and Class Rule: Political Development in Maharashtra*. Bombay: Popular Prakashan.

——— (1990). 'Caste, Class and Dominance: Political Mobilization in Maharashtra', in Francine K. Frankel and M.S.A. Rao (eds), *Dominance and State Power in Modern India*, Vol. II. New Delhi: Oxford University Press.

Lustiger-Thaler, H. and Louis Maheu (1995). 'Social Movements and the Challenge of Urban Politics', in Louis Maheu (ed.), *Social Movements and Social Classes*. London: Sage Studies in International Sociology/ISA.

McGee, T.G. (1967). *The Southeast Asian City: A Social Geography of the Primate Cities of Southeast Asia*. New York: Praeger.

Mohan, Rakesh (1996). 'Urbanization in India: Patterns and Emerging Policy Issues', in Josef Gugler (ed.), *The Urban Transformation of the Developing World*. Oxford: Oxford University Press.

Oommen, T.K. (1977). 'Sociological Issues in the Analysis of Social Movements in Independent India', *Sociological Bulletin*, March, 26(1): 14–37.

——— (1990). *Protest and Change: Studies in Social Movements*. New Delhi: Sage Publications.

——— (1999). 'Conceptualising Nation and Nationality in South Asia', *Sociological Bulletin*, March-September, 48(1&2), pp. 1–18.

——— (2004). *Nation, Civil Society and Social Movements: Essays in Political Sociology*. New Delhi: Sage Publications.

——— (ed.) (2010). *Social Movements I: Issues of Identity*. New Delhi: Oxford University Press.

Outhwaite, William and Tom Bottomore (1993). *The Blackwell Dictionary of Twentieth Century Social Thought*. London: Blackwell Publication.

Pandey, R. (1988). *Modernization and Social Change*. New Delhi: Criterion Publications.

Parthsarathy, D. (1997). *Collective Violence in a Provincial City*. New Delhi: Oxford University Press.

Patel, Sujata (2006). 'Introduction', in Sujata Patel and Kushal Deb (eds), *Urban Studies*. New Delhi: Oxford University Press.

Patel, Sujata and Kushal Deb (eds) (2006). *Urban Studies*. New Delhi: Oxford University Press.

Paul, Baran (1974). *The Political Economy of Growth*. Harmondsworth: Penguin.

Pieterse, J. N. (ed.) (1992). *Emancipations: Modern and Post-modern*. New Delhi: Sage Publications.

——— (1996). 'Varieties of Ethnic Politics and Ethnicity Discourse', in Edwin N. Wilmsen (ed.), *The Politics of Difference*. Chicago and London: The University of Chicago Press.

Pieterse, J. N. (2001). *Development Theory*. Nottingham: Sage Publications.

Preston, P.W. (2001). *Development Theory: An Introduction*. Oxford: Blackwell Publishers.

Pugh, C. (1990). *Housing and Urbanization*. New Delhi: Sage Publication.

Punalekar, S.P. (1989). *Aspects of Class and Caste in Social Tensions: A Study of Marathwada Riots*. Surat: Centre for Social Studies.

Reddy, G. Ram (1989). 'The Politics of Accommodation', in Francine R. Frankel and M.S.A. Rao (eds), *Dominance and State Power in Modern India Decline of a Social Order*, Vol. I. New Delhi: Oxford University Press, pp. 367–415.

Robinson, Jennifer (2002). 'Global and World Cities: A View from off the Map', *International Journal of Urban and Regional Research*, 26(3): 531–54.

——— (2003). 'Postcolonizing Geographies: Tactics and Pitfalls', *Singapore Journal of Tropical Geography*, 24(3): 273–89.

Saberwal, Satish (2001). 'Democracy and Civil Society in India: Integral or Accidental?', *Sociological Bulletin*, 50(2): 192–205.

Safa, Helen (ed.) (1982). *Towards a Political Economy of Urbanization in Third World Countries*. New Delhi: Oxford University Press.

Sassen, Saskia (1991). *The Global City*. Princeton: Princeton University Press.

Sassen, Saskia (2001). *The Global City*. USA: Princeton University Press, Princeton.

Savage, Mike and Alan Warde (1993). *Urban Sociology: Capitalism and Modernity*. London: Macmillan Press.

Shah, Ghanshyam (1977). *Protest Movements in Two Indian States*. New Delhi: Ajanta Publishers.

——— (1990). *Social Movements in India*. New Delhi: Sage Publications.

——— (2002). *Social Movements and the State*. New Delhi: Sage Publications.

——— (2004). *A Review of Social Movements in India*. New Delhi: Sage Publications.

Shatkin, G. "'Fourth World' Cities in the Global Economy: The Case of Phnom Penh, Cambodia," *International Journal of Urban and Regional Research*, 22(3): 378–393.

Silva, Kalinga Tudor (1999). 'Caste, Ethnicity and Problems of National Identity in Sri Lanka', *Sociological Bulletin*, March-September, 48(1&2): 201–16.

Singh, Rajendra (2001). *Social Movements, Old and New a Post-Modernist Critique*. New Delhi: Sage Publications.

Slater, David (1985). "The Peruvian State and Regional Crises: The Development of Regional Movements, 1968-1980" in Slater, David (ed), *New Social Movements in Latin America*, CEDLA, Amsterdam.

Smith, David A. (1996). *Third World Cities in Global Perspective*. Boulder, CO: Westview Press.

Soja, Edward W. (2000). *Postmetropolis, Critical Studies of Cities and Regions*. Oxford: Blackwell Publishers.
Subramanian, Narendra (1999). *Ethnicity and Populist Mobilisation, Political Parties, Citizens and Democracy in South India*. New Delhi: Oxford University Press.
Tambe, Shruti (2004). 'Collective Subjectivity, Domination and Democracy: The Case of MJVA, Marathwada, India', *Current Sociology*, 52(4): 671–93.
Walton, John (2000). 'Urban Sociology', in Stella R. Quah and Arnaud Sales (eds), *International Handbook of Sociology*. London: Sage Publications, pp. 299–317.
Webster, A. (1990). *Introduction to the Sociology of Development*. Hong Kong: Macmillan Education.
Zukin, Sharon (1980a). 'A Decade of the New Urban Sociology', *Theory and Society*, 9: 539–74.
——— (1980b). 'The Cutting Edge: A Decade of the New Urban Sociology', *Theory and Society*, 9: 575–601.

11

India and the Fiji Indian Quest for Power

I.S. Chauhan

Fiji is a small nation. Despite its territorial size, it is the most important country in the South Pacific. In the past two decades, Fiji has gone through enormous social, economic and political upheavals. Two coups took place in 1987: the third in 2000 and the fourth in December 2006. These have damaged the delicate fabric of this multiethnic society.

The roots of Fiji's problem can be traced back to its own history. During the pre-colonial period, the country was not what it is today. There were several Polynesian and Melanesian tribes fighting amongst themselves to acquire territories and supremacy. A few sailors who had abandoned their ships and settled in the area introduced guns and complicated the situation by pushing new ideas about warfare and governance. They persuaded the warring chiefs to surrender the sovereignty to Great Britain. Such an offer was refused once and finally accepted in 1875.

To make the new colony an economically viable nation, the first Governor General decided to emulate the Mauritian model and introduced sugar industry with the help of Indian indentured labourers. Nearly 60,000 Indian indentured labourers who came between 1879 and 1915 stayed back to settle down in the country. Their population grew rapidly and in the next 50 years, they began to outnumber the natives. They were not able to purchase land as most of it was not a marketable commodity. They farmed on leased land and searched for economic security and prosperity in professions, in trade and in almost every other areas of life. Their success in some measure becomes the cause of envy and suspicion against them.

During the colonial period, the British continued their divide-and-rule policy, but they did not allow the differences between the two major races to flare up. However, on the eve of independence, they displayed a concern for the protection of the rights of both the communities by providing a constitution that would prevent conflict in future. In reality, they were aware that the indigenous psyche could not accept the idea of an immigrant community outnumbering them and gradually outsmarting them in acquiring economic and political power. The British also anticipated that the anger of the indigenous people could erupt in the form of violence against the Indo-Fijians. They felt that a slight tilt in the constitution of independent Fiji in favour of the indigenous community could remove their suspicions and prevent violence against the Indo-Fijians. They were, however, not able to convince the local Indo-Fijian leadership on this issue, which led to the breakdown of the pre-independence tripartite negotiations.

Subsequently, the colonial power sought India's help in resolving this dilemma. Two senior diplomats, T.N. Kaul and Jaipal Rikhi, were sent to Fiji to assess the situation. Their report, which concurred with the British point of view, was accepted by the Government of India, and a Minister, Jaisukh Lal Hathi, was sent to convince A.D. Patel, who was the most prominent Indo-Fijian leader. He was fighting to obtain political equality between the two communities through the adoption of common electoral rolls. Patel finally relented but blamed India for abandoning the cause of the Indo-Fijians.

Indian acceptance of the British proposal was realistic. At that time, the Indo-Fijians outnumbered the indigenous people and were in control of the economy. Consequently, India's approach averted a civil unrest and helped to protect the lives and property of the Indo-Fijians.

The Indian approach was based on the realistic appreciation of the peculiar conditions prevailing in this country. Indigenous people owned most of the land and mineral and marine resources, which could not be bought or sold. They were predominant in the disciplined forces and had the capacity to flex their muscles or turn a blind eye if they did not wish to intervene in a given situation. With India's tacit backing, the 1970 constitution containing a slight tilt in favour of the indigenous people was finally adopted. It had a provision for a subsequent review to accommodate future changes in circumstances after a mutual dialogue between the various stakeholders.

As a cornerstone of its own policy, India commenced direct interaction with both the indigenous and the Indo-Fijian leadership. In an attempt to engage him, Ratu Mara was invited to visit India even before he became PM. He subsequently paid several visits to India, which helped to enhance India's image in Fiji. He also hosted India's Prime Minister in Fiji in 1981. This amicable relationship continued until the 1987 coup.

During the pre-coup period, India not only interacted with the leadership of the two major communities but also promoted an approach involving a healthy dialogue between them in Fiji. However, after the coup in 1987, the communication between India and the indigenous community broke down.

Let us now discuss about the diversions, flash points and conflicts facing the country. After independence in 1970, an era of quicker economic growth, industrialization and urbanization commenced. This was followed by a rapid transformation of the social, economic and political landscape of the country. These processes resulted in further fragmentation of both the major communities. Each of them now is so heterogeneous that it may not be entirely correct to talk about the 'Indian' or the 'Fijian' point of view, although the bulk of each community at times hold perceptions that are wide apart from each other.

In the past 38 years (except for a year), indigenous dominated governments have held political power. The pattern of governance always took into consideration the claims and counter-claims of various provinces and confederacies (of provinces). Ignoring the traditional protocols and aspirations would have landed the rulers into difficulties.

During the past 38 years of independence, a ruling elite has developed in the country. In fact, the British who had obtained power from the chiefs wanted to hand it back to them. Hence, they trained some traditional high chiefs and handed over the country to them at the time of independence. These chiefs and their descendents became the powerful pillars of the ruling elite, the ranks of which were later opened up for well-educated commoners as well.

The ruling elite has developed vested interests and would like to remain in power at any cost. Thus, for example, even the People's Coalition Government that was ousted by the 2000 coup had more indigenous ministers than the Indians. But these Fijian ministers were not the members of the ruling elite, hence they were ousted in a coup, which was as much against them as it was against Mahendra Chaudhry.

The situation in Fiji is very complicated. There is conflict between races and on several issues within each ethnic group. Ethnic, confederacy, province, religious, cultural and class loyalties criss cross the community. Political management in a situation like this would be a tricky business.

It is against this background that I would like to consider the presentation of the Promotion of Reconciliation and Tolerance Bill in Fiji's parliament.

The results of the 2001 elections in which both the main contenders fell short of majority gave rise to the need for coalition formation. The group that had staged and/or backed the coup in 2000 formed a political party, the Conservative Alliance Matanivanua (CAMV), and won nearly 10 per cent (7 of 71) of all seats in the parliament.

The election was bitterly fought. It was free for all where even hitting below the belt happened. SDL and FLP floated policies that were opposite to each other. Qarase announced that it will be a violation of the mandate given to him mainly by his ethnic Fijian electorate to share power with Mahendra Chaudhry under the multiparty cabinet provision of the constitution. He carried the legal battle through several stages to the Supreme Court and obtained a vague verdict that allowed him to achieve what he wanted.

Meanwhile, Qarase's SDL party and the CAMV aligned to form a coalition government. There was pressure all along on Qarase to find ways and means to be soft on the coup plotters, some of whom were either in jail or facing prosecution. Fijian society places great value on forgiveness. If sought through proper traditional protocol, even a murder can be forgiven. This psyche was pitted against international pressure for allowing the rule of law to take its own course.

In fact, in the past five years, a major part the political management of the nation consisted of the PM's struggle to delay, resist or accommodate the demands of the CAMV. It was a tightrope walk and juggling around with pressures from his coalition partners, the army, the opposition in the parliament and the international community. In the last year, before the elections due in August/September 2006, some measure akin to the PRTU bill was really inevitable.

I am sure that the government was aware of the heat likely to be generated. In an attempt to obtain legitimacy, the bill was sent to the provincial councils. Consideration on the bill was then postponed till the last session of the parliament in 2005. The success of this bill was a political necessity of Qarase.

The PRTU bill faced stiff resistance from the opposition in the parliament led by Mahendra Chaudhry and the Army Commander Bainimarama. I was witness to the degree of humiliation they had to suffer at the hands of George Spate and his cronies. No wonder, Bainimarama was not finding it easy to forgive and forget. He had been warning Qarase not to go soft on the coup plotters through the PRTU bill.

When Qarase was facing rough weather on this issue, Australia reportedly advised him to go in for early elections. Even after the elections in May 2006, the situation did not change much. This time, the former CAMV members or the coup supporters were part of his own party in the government together with labour legislators who had joined the cabinet under the constitutional multiparty system of governance.

After emerging victorious in the general election, Qarase once again tried to push the PRTU bill and another controversial legislation relating to indigenous land rights. In the Qoliqoli bill, he wanted the parliament to transfer from the state to indigenous landowners, rights over the continental shelves next to the coastal land. This was considered a very regressive move and the entire hotel and tourism lobby as opposed to it for fear of interference by landowners in the water bodies next to their hotels.

In August 2006, when I called on Qarase, he appeared to be confidant and firmly in control. Once he had even tried to dislodge the Army Commander who had gone overseas, but he did not succeed. Eventually, after several warnings Army Commander Bainimarama staged a coup in early December apparently to prevent Qarase going through the two controversial legislations.

The situation in Fiji, as we all know, is very complex. The conflict there is always interpreted as between the indigenous and the Indo-Fijians. As we have seen, all this is not entirely true and the coups have not all been anti-Indo-Fijian.

Chaudhry supported the December 2006 overthrow of the Qarase government, which he very convincingly argued was not elected democratically but came to power through rigging of the elections. He joined the post-coup Bainimarama government claiming that for the first time the history of Fiji has presented an opportunity to reform the electoral system and make it ethnicity free and truly democratic by eliminating communal/ethnic constituencies. He thus hopes to establish within a couple of years one-vote-one-value system, which will encourage inter-ethnic dependence and cooperation.

Although the demolition of democracy must be denounced, one has to go into the causes behind it to analyse its full implications. I personally know all the major power players in Fiji. I always got them all together to share the same forum, while dealing with India. I am confident that their wisdom will prevail and even without external pressure, they will work out satisfactory solutions to their problems and restore democracy sooner than expected.

12

Social and Cultural Transformation of Indians in the United States of America

Surendra K. Gupta

Indians are the third largest group, besides Chinese and Filipinos, among the Asians residing in the United States. Between 1990 and 2000, the growth of Indians in the United States was around 106 per cent. The US Immigration and Naturalization Service Report for the year 2001 specified that Indians were the second highest migrants between 1 October 2000 and 6 September 2001. Of the total 1,064,318 permanent migrants during that period, 70,290 were from India. In 1965, only 4,000 persons were recorded under the Alien Address Programme; the number increased to 109,000 by 1977 of whom 88 per cent were permanent residents; and another 1,300 took American citizenship. Indian immigrants in America during 1965–77 registered an increase of 3,000 per cent (Leonard-Spark and Saran, 1980). By 1980, the number of Indians residing in the United States increased to 387,223; and in 1990, it reached 815,447 (Rangaswamy, 2000). According to rough estimates, now the number of Indians in the United States is around two million.

People from almost all the states of India have migrated to the United States. But the Punjabis and Gujaratis have outnumbered all others. Among the Punjabis, it is the Sikh community that has migrated in large numbers. The number of Gujaratis is highest among the Hindus living in the United States. Gopa Kumar's (2003) estimate for the first decade of this century suggests that there were 400,000 Gujaratis in the United States. Together, these two groups account for nearly half of the migrant Indian population.

I

Conceptual Framework

Attempt has been made in this paper to answer the following queries:

1. How the Indians with different socio-cultural background have transformed and adjusted themselves in an alien society?
2. To what extent their cultural, contextual and situational conditions have affected their transformation and adjustment?

Sandwich culture model proposed by Yogesh Atal (1989) has been used to answer the above queries. The concept of sandwich culture is applicable to those people who have settled at a place whose culture is different from the culture of the migrants. The concept is applicable at various levels, national and international. For survival in an alien society, it is essential that all migrants adopt some aspects of cultural traits of the host society such as language that might be a necessity. Acculturation in fact has been accepted as the first step in integration and assimilation by scholars such as Eisenstadt (1954) and Gordon (1959).

Atal[1] has used two sets of factors that operate to facilitate or hinder the process of formation of sandwich culture. The following indicators from sandwich culture model have been adopted to discuss the socio-cultural transformation. The selected indicators are settlement pattern, vocational activities, family and marriage, adoption of names of the host society, retention of cultural diacritical, language, formation of voluntary organizations, religious activities and contact with the parent culture.

The socio-cultural transformation will also be affected by the cultural, contextual and situational factors. These three factors refer to the conditions at the native place of migrants, the conditions they encounter at the place of migration and the situational conditions that may not be the same for all migrants.

The material for the article has been scanned from the various studies available on Indians in the United States. Although Indians belonging to various religious groups are residing in the United States, in this paper we have mainly concentrated on Sikhs and Hindus (mainly Gujaratis).

The history and pattern of migration of Indians to the United States has been described in the next section. Socio-cultural transformation on selected indicators has been presented in the third section. The last section has been devoted to major findings.

II

History and Pattern of Migration

Immigration of Indians to the United States began in 1901 when about 7,000 Sikhs of Malwa and Doaba regions of Punjab migrated to Canada to work on the Canadian Pacific Railways. The drought and famine conditions, as also changes in the land tenure system in Punjab, forced some of them to migrate to the United States to work in the lumber mills of Bellingham and Everett in the Washington State. Some of them decided to move to California. Before that, some Indian merchants occasionally visited New York and San Francisco. In 1907, there was a revolt against Indian migrants who were working in the lumber mills of the United States Pacific Northwest because local labourers perceived these Indians as a threat to them as they were working on less wages compared to them. It was considered an invasion by Hindus and Sikhs on the American Labour market.

Although the number of Indian migrants, most of whom were Sikhs, was not more than 6,000 between 1904 and 1923, their distinctive turbans, beards, language and dress made them noticeable. The US government also issued exclusion order from the United States against Asians, including Indians.

In 1904, majority of the Indian immigrants were Sikhs, although there were few Hindus and Muslims also. During summer months, they worked on the farms in the Sacramento, San Joaquin and Imperial Valley and shifted to Yuba City, Stockton and El Centro California in winter.

There were a few educated Indians who came for higher education. There were some political refugees who migrated to escape British repression. These early migrants had to face many hurdles including discriminatory laws that forced some of these people to leave. In 1946, the Luce–Celler Bill was passed, which gave Asian Indians the right to become American citizens, own property and bring relatives to America. This also enabled the families to migrate to America and reunite with their husbands.

Post-independence there was a surge in Indian migration. The government of the United States also helped the process by granting scholarships and travel grants to Indian students. They also sent their researchers and policy makers to assist India in its drive to hasten the process of development.

American Immigration Act of 1965, however, changed the pattern of Indian migration. It imposed restrictions on the migration of unskilled, uneducated and self-employed people and gave precedence to professionally oriented and technically trained personnel. The new Act encouraged the professionals not only from India but also from other Asian countries to migrate to the United States. The new Act also helped the migration of relatives of those already settled in the United States.

La Brack (1983) divided the history of Indian immigration to the United States into the following five periods:

1. The first period includes Sikh migrants who came to the West Coast of the United States from Canada between 1904 and 1923. About 10,000 were admitted, but at any time their number did not exceed more than 6,000.
2. The second period includes illegal migrants who came from Mexico between 1923 to early 1930. Their number was around 3,000.
3. The third period, between 1930 and 1946, can be called as a lull period when the migration was negligible.
4. The fourth period, between 1946 and 1964, has been called as Quota period of restricted immigration.
5. The fifth period is the period of Open Migration, which began in 1965 with the changes in the immigration policy. Those who came after 1965 can be further classified into the following three categories:
    (i) The first category includes those who were sponsored by the early settlers in the United States (mainly Sikhs in California). As the new immigration law gave highest priority to the reunification of families, about two-third of the visas were granted to relatives of American citizens and permanent residents.
    (ii) The second category includes all those who migrated as professionals and technical persons.
    (iii) Another group of Indians who came to the United States were those who migrated from East Africa due to political upheavals especially in Kenya and Uganda in the 1970s.

Since the cultural, contextual and situational conditions of these migrants varied significantly from the earlier migrants, the transformation process of these new migrants differed substantially from the earlier settlers. The overwhelming majority of Sikhs who came to California for settlement were farmers, poorly literate and belonging to Jat caste. Migrants who were sponsored by the early settlers came from rural Punjab and belonged to the same region of Doaba. They came with the intention to settle permanently. Majority of them brought their families. They came as they were promised all help including financial from the early settlers. Very few could speak English and had no technical training except farming. They came as they believed that America is a land of opportunities and it would be good for them as well as for their children. Thus, the cultural conditions of new migrants were similar to the earlier settlers, but the contextual and situational conditions differed significantly. They not only belonged to the same region but also shared religious and caste affiliation.

The migrants, who came to the United States after the changes in immigration law in 1965, included those who came as students but later on changed to permanent resident status. There were few who came to settle permanently. Among those who came on student visa, some came with their spouses and children; a few brought their spouses and children after a stay of one or two years. Some of those who were unmarried went back to India to get married and returned with their spouses. There were a few others who married Indians in America. There are very few cases, where Indian students have married either an American or somebody other than American or Indian. Among those who came on permanent immigrant visa, some came with their families, or brought their families after a stay of one year.

Indians who migrated to the United States after 1965 had an edge over earlier migrants, and over the migrants sponsored by them. A majority of these new migrants were professionals possessing specialized skills that were in great demand at that time. They were also fluent in English. They originated from different states of the Indian Union. In a survey conducted in the New York Metropolitan Area in 1977–78 by Leonard-Spark and Saran, it was found that about one-third of the immigrants were from the State of Gujarat and about 20 per cent were from the Hindi-speaking regions including Delhi. The pattern of migration after 1965 shifted 'From the North toward the Middle and South of India, that is away from the areas that were historically under the greatest English colonial influence toward those with different language and cultural patterns and less direct influence by the British Raj. The shifts also suggest that within the Indian community there is increasingly greater diversity in the ethnic-regional backgrounds of the Indians who comprise it' (Leonard-Spark and Saran, 1980: 143).

III

In this section, the socio-cultural transformation of Indians on selected indicators has been discussed.

Settlement Pattern

Punjabi Jat Sikhs who migrated from Vancouver in Canada settled in different parts of California, but their main concentration was in the Imperial, Sacramento and San Joaquin valley areas. They were uneducated farmers who were in their mid-50s. All of them hailed from the Doaba region of Eastern Punjab and belonged to the same religion and caste. Thus, they shared common values and attitudes. Some of these Sikhs were *Amritdharis* (baptized members of the Khalsa), who pledged to maintain the traditional Sikh values and customs as well as five K's.[2] There were others known as *Sahajdharis* who were not bound to keep the outward symbols of their faith. They cut their hair short and did not grow beard.

Prejudice and discrimination against the immigrant groups by the members of the host society was imminent, because the immigrant group was doing better economically than the local members of the host society. The Sikhs who settled in California did not react to such behaviour on the part of the locals and maintained limited interactions with the Americans. Most of the Sikhs lived outside the town on their large ranches. Working on the farms, they did not have much direct contact with the Valleyside Americans. The Valleysiders came in contact with them in either shops or banks. Most of the Valleysiders did not regard Sikhs as part of them, as they were different in dress, language and religion, and were farmers. The attitude of Valleysiders towards Sikhs became more negative with the increase in the number of immigrants over the years. The attitude of Sikhs towards Valleyside Americans was mixed. Although the Sikhs had unpleasant experience in interactions with the whites of their neighbourhood, they regarded them as isolated incidents, and learnt to live with them. Most of them tried to play down the negative and prejudiced behaviour of the Valleysiders. They also held white teenagers responsible for such acts rather than adults. Sikhs did not harbour negative attitude towards Americans, as a group.

Regarding the settlement pattern of Indians who migrated after 1965 Rangaswamy writes that

> Indians seemed to prefer to live close to work or in neighbourhoods where property values held up rather than to cluster together in a single area. The general tendency was toward dispersal in the white suburbs. Sometime the development of a strong commercial complex in a specific area may have encouraged residential concentration in the same area, as in the case of Devon Avenue in Chicago, but the more affluent they became, the more Indians tended to get away from such concentrations. (Rangaswamy, 2000: 54)

By and large, Indians move safely in the United States except in some areas where they are living amongst lower income groups who feel threatened by the prosperity of the newcomers as happened to Sikhs in California. It happened in Jersey City when some working class white youth calling themselves 'dotbusters' (dot refers to the *bindi* used by Indian women on their forehead) assaulted and even killed Indians on the street. This had its repercussions on the settlement pattern of Indians in the United States.

Vocational Activities

Early migrants from India worked as farm labourers. Since family members were not allowed to migrate most migrants lived as singletons. In fact, their employments as well as their living arrangements were temporary. As majority of them hailed from the same region, they joined hands to form 'labour gangs'

(La Brack, 1983). In the process, they also revived their kinship relationship based on subcaste, lineage and village affiliation. Besides sharing residence, they also shared the expenses and hired a cook to prepare Punjabi meals. Working as farm labourers, they gained experience and knowledge about land, working conditions, irrigation methods, machinery, as well as about transportation and processing systems, which came handy once they became land owners. As the Alien Land Laws of 1913 and 1922 prevented them to own land they

> put the title in an American citizen's name, which could be an American – born or naturalized wife, wife's relative, or even a trusted American friend. In the 1930s and 1940s they used another method to place the title in the names of American-born children from marriages which took place between Sikhs and European or Mexican women. (ibid.: 219)

The locals did not like the idea of Sikhs owning land and agitated against it in many parts of the country. The Sikhs, however, managed to survive with the help and support of well-wishers and friends. Gradually, they purchased more land and became prosperous.

The Sikh migrants of later years who were sponsored by the early settlers also settled in California along with their relatives and friends. They also took to farming, as this was the only option available to them. They were encouraged and helped by their well-wishers. They enjoyed the rural atmosphere similar to back home in Punjab. As farm labourers, they earned much more than what they did in India. Despite living in the United States for many years, there was not much change in their way of life. Financially, they were better-off in the United States compared with India. Life in the United States was comfortable compared with Punjab due to availability of all sorts of food including readymade clothes, washing machines, televisions and air-conditioned houses.

The attitude of Sikhs towards their womenfolk changed noticeably after living in the United States. In India, women never worked in the field; but after living in America for many years, they changed their lifestyle and started working outside home for money. It was in the 1970s that the first Sikh woman broke the tradition. She became the object of teasing in the beginning, but gradually her new role was accepted by others. Now, Sikh women contribute substantially to the family income. They also found that women who were unable to find steady work became eligible to get unemployment compensation during the months they were laid off. The attitude of Sikhs towards their daughters also changed. They allowed their daughters to have sufficient education, which enabled them to obtain a 'clean' and secure job in banks, schools and offices. Thus, the Sikhs have transformed themselves to the new conditions to further their economic interests.

There was another group of Indians who migrated under the preferential categories of professionals and technical persons and also the relatives of dependents of those who either lived as resident aliens or took US citizenship. It included people of both the sexes. All of them were highly educated and technically skilled professionals who made their mark in a relatively short time period. They were, in fact, welcomed in the United States because of their professional skills or potential technical contributions. They migrated to settle permanently but at the same time maintained their relations with the people back home. Some of those who migrated as professionals and technical persons later on shifted to other types of occupations that were financially more remunerative. With the increase in Indian population, some enterprising entrepreneurs especially Gujaratis started the business of supplying Indian groceries and other items to Indians. Some opened restaurants and retail stores and some others started insurance and travel agencies. One consequence of all these developments was that the Indian community not only became stable but also self-sufficient. There were some Gujaratis who, besides working as professionals, were running business with the help of their wives, children and other family members. Few left the job to concentrate full-time in business. Indians with professional degrees also faced the same problem when their degrees were not recognized, and they were required to get an American degree. As a consequence, some abandoned their professional career and started business (Fisher, 1980).

By 1990, the '...Indian population was a multi-layered community, with affluent professionals and business persons at the top and an increasing number of middle- and working-class immigrants in lower strata' (Khandelwal, 2002: 6). In fact, 'most post-1965 immigrants to the United States fitted broadly into a white collar, middle-class continuum. But a growing number of those arriving in the 1980s and 1990s did not fare as well, and a sizable number among them were even clearly downwardly mobile' (ibid.). According to the 1990 Census of the United States, 30 per cent of Indian workers were in professional occupations; majority of them were in health profession. Some of them were working as engineers and scientists. Indians are also working as private practitioners in various professions such as medicine, law, engineering, accounting and business. Few Indians, mainly Sikhs, are working as taxi drivers and owners in large metropolitan centres. Majority of Gujaratis are in hotel business and running other small business (Gopa Kumar, 2003).

The shifts in the American economy in the 1980s made things difficult for immigrants especially for those who came after 1975. The fiscal crisis in 1975 and stock market crash in 1987 affected the employment conditions. As a consequence, '...number of immigrants moved into the underground economy of cash transactions, tax avoidance, and subminimum wages. Global economic change since the late 1980s, particularly the upsurge of Asian economies ... have created shifts in Asian immigration flows to the United States' (Khandelwal, 2002: 95). As a result, some of the Indian professionals in the United States began to relocate to India. Some of the immigrants who came after 1980 faced difficulty in securing a job and had a tough time to survive. Some of the Indian businessmen employed new immigrants from India, but the conflict between employer and employee created more tension than ethnic solidarity.

Family and Marriage

As the early settlers were not allowed to bring brides from India, some of them decided to remain single, whereas there were others who married non-Indian women. Sikhs who were engaged in farming married Mexican women and those in teaching profession and students married American-born or foreign-born women of European descent. 'By 1930s a pattern of intermarriage was established between rural Sikh men and Spanish-speaking women, facilitated by ... compatible cultural views of food, male-female roles and family life' (La Brack, 1983: 222). By marrying Mexican and other European-American women, the social life of the Sikhs became a mix of Punjabi, Spanish and Euro-American traits. The social life of the Sikhs changed. They became members of Mexican-American society and participated in their family functions. The names of the children born to such union were given mixed names such as Jesus Singh and Esmeralda. There was a steady decline in Punjabi customs. Even visits to Gurdwara were restricted to three or four times a year, mainly on certain occasions such as Guru Nanak's birthday. Children were raised as Catholics – the religious faith of their wives – and they could not learn anything about the Sikh religion. They did not learn Punjabi language and did not know the social system of their father's parent culture. The relatives of wives became frequent visitors and in few cases lived in the same house. As a consequence, the social foundation of Sikhs based on religion, caste and joint family became superfluous (ibid.).

Under the Immigration Act of 1946, Indians became legalized immigrants in the United States, which allowed them to become naturalized citizens. This also gave married men a choice to reunite with their wives and children in India and for bachelors to select brides from India and also to sponsor other relatives. But this Act allowed only a quota of 100 Indians per year. The change in immigration policy, however, in 1965 allowed more migrants from Punjab. The new migrants who settled in California received all kinds of support from the early settlers. Besides providing accommodation, the early birds also supported them financially. The new migrants sponsored by the early settlers brought with them cultural tidbits and thus helped revive their culture and customs in an alien land. It also affected the family life in several ways. For example, those who had married Mexican women began divorcing them so as to marry Jat Sikh brides from amongst the later migrants.

The period between 1947 and 1967 has been called as the revival period when 'Questions of Sikh identity became increasingly associated with strict, orthodox Punjabi behavioural norms and *Khalsa* religious practices' (ibid.: 227). This brought significant changes in the life of Sikhs in California. Joint family system was restored and with that family functions were revived. Endogamous marriages became the norm and the number of spouses imported from India increased substantially. Sikhs started growing beard and wearing turbans. Women also started using traditional dress of *salwar kameez* and *saree* (ibid.).

Indians who came after 1965, irrespective of the fact that whether they came on student visa or as permanent immigrants, preferred to select an Indian spouse. Their first preference was to select a spouse from India, failing which they preferred to marry an Indian already living in America. Those who came to India for marriage married a person selected by their family members who belonged to the same religion and caste. But those who selected a spouse among Indians in America, in majority of the cases, the region and caste factors were ignored. For instance, a Maharashtrian Brahmin may select a Kayastha spouse from Uttar Pradesh or vice versa. There are a few cases of inter-religious marriages where some Indians have married white Americans. In some cases, they married even when the relationship was not approved by either one of the parents or the parents of both sides.

To maintain continuity and stability in the family, the old timers, by and large, preferred to marry a person of the same caste. Even for those who married a person of different caste or region, the approval of the family played a significant role. But parents are put in a dilemma when their American-born grown-up children want to select their own life partner. Most of the first-generation migrants are against love marriages as they believe that such marriages are short-lived, whereas arranged and endogamous marriages are likely to be more stable. Social compatibility in marriage is considered necessary, but it has also been realized by parents that they have to broaden the search. Marriage with a person of different religion is not acceptable to most of the parents. Different yardsticks are adopted for sons and daughters. People are more liberal with their sons compared with their daughters as they fear that the reputation of their daughter may affect the marriage prospect of other sisters. Some parents are against the marriage of their sons with US-reared Indian women as they are seen as Americanized and thus difficult to adjust. Such parents return to India to choose a bride, and they are assisted by the relatives in the process. In some cases, a young man who wanted to immigrate to the United States through marriage may accept the proposal (Khandelwal, 2002).

One of the major concerns of the first-generation immigrants regarding their grown-up sons and daughters is the problem of dating and marriage. Since most of the first-generation migrants are not familiar with the concept of dating, they do not approve of their children going out on dating. They are stricter with girls. Despite the restrictions, quite a large number of younger generation people do date but do not tell their parents about it although they would prefer to have Indian spouse (Agarwal, 1991; Sheth, 2001). For most of the Indian immigrants settled in America, dating is related to premarital sexual relations. Parents allow their wards to go out in groups, where children of both the sexes participate. In fact, the parents prefer that their son and daughter bring their friends over to their house for the weekends. By and large, Indians want their children, both boys and girls, to marry the one selected by the parents. That is one of the reasons that most of the parents do not favour their daughters to go to college education. Although selecting a mate for their ward, Sikhs give preference to region, religion and caste. Earlier, Sikhs in the United States used to select a mate for their ward from among the Indians, but now marriages among Sikhs have really become transnational as the marriage partners are selected from all over the globe. As the matrimonial advertisements are available not only in newspapers but also on the Internet, which makes it easy to negotiate (Gopa Kumar, 2003).

On the grounds of 'compatibility', interracial marriages are not approved. Parents allow their wards to marry an Indian spouse of their choice, rather than opting for the traditional, arranged marriage. Quite a large number of the second-generation people prefer to marry other ABCD (American-Born Confused Desi) rather than marrying a person selected by their parents (Agarwal, 1991: 51). Younger generation women are more 'averse' to importing a spouse from India compared with men.

Family in America becomes the main institution of socialization for Indians, as in school they are exposed to the American way of life. At home, children are taught the traditional patterns of language, diet, dress, religion and other customs, necessary to maintain their identity as Indian. Most of the Indians in America are in constant touch with the family members back in India either through visits to India or through the visits of the relatives to the United States. The visits of elderly persons from India not only provide domestic and household aid but also serve as a traditional role model for their children in America.

Serious problems are faced by the parents when they want to inculcate Indian values among their children. Children who are exposed to the American way of life in school as well as through media develop an ambivalent attitude towards their parent culture. A rift is created between parents and children. Children very often ask many questions when their parents pressurize them not to follow American values and customs. To solve these problems, some parents send their children to India for schooling, and there are few cases where parents have decided to return to India. But all parents make serious efforts to expose their children to Indian values, customs and way of life.

Americanization of Indian Names

Indians found that Americans are unable to pronounce their names. To make convenient for Americans to pronounce, some of the Indians have shortened their names such as Bhupinder became Bob, Jagmohan Jack, Ravindra Romi, Priyanka Pinky, Sandhya Sandy, etc. (Fisher, 1980; Sheth, 2001). But as the migrants grow old, most of them feel more comfortable with their Indian names; as a result, 'many drop the Americanized version of their names in favour of their given names. For example, Roger reverts to Raj and Michael metamorphosizes into Munjal' (Agarwal, 1991: 37–8).

But the problem becomes serious with the names of South Indians. The naming system in South India is different from other parts of India. Even in South India, there are variations from state to state. For instance, a Brahmin from Karnataka is given four names. The first is the name of the village or place of origin, the second name is that of the father, the third is the name given to an individual and the fourth (if at all) is the caste name. First, two names are abbreviated by their initials. Few South Indians drop their caste name and in that case those who are not familiar with the system assume that the third name, which is the given name of a person, is the surname. The problem becomes acute when a South Indian migrates to America. Since surname is required to get US visa and also for the enrolment of children in schools, the given name of the person becomes his surname and all his children use it as a surname. 'As a result of this phenomenon, a South Indian wife addresses her husband by the name which the family simultaneously uses as its new surname' (Fisher, 1980: 50). Some of the South Indians have divided their given name into two parts, and the second part becomes a new surname. For example, the name Harimohan may become Mr Hari Mohan and later on Hari may become Harry.

Retention of Cultural Diacritical

Sikhs, among Indians, stand out for turban, beard and steel bangle on their wrist. Even those Sikhs who have cut their hair short keep beard and use steel bangles on their wrist. Because of their physical appearance, Sikhs are easily identifiable in any group. In the early stages of their settlement, they faced many problems as Americans could not distinguish between Hindus and Sikhs. Some of them changed their physical appearance; but with the arrival of new migrants, they reverted to their original appearance.

Other Indian men generally wear Western dress when they go out, and one cannot distinguish them on the basis of dress. But at home, all of them might not be using the similar outfit. For instance, the traditional dress of most of the South Indian men is white long cloth called *dhoti* that is worn below the navel and touches the ankle; when working, they fold it half way to cover the portion up to the knee. South Indians use traditional dress on two occasions: (i) when they visit temple or (ii) when a religious ceremony is performed at home (ibid.).

Under the influence of American culture, most of the Sikhs have started cutting their hair and also shaving their beards; this is more so among the younger ones. Often, one can find that in one family the eldest son may keep long hair and beard, but the younger sons are allowed freedom to choose whether to keep beard or remain clean shaved.

Generally, Indian women wear *sari*, though use of *salwar kameez* has also gained popularity. In fact, women of all the South Asian countries wear identical dresses although each country, India, Pakistan, Bangladesh and Sri Lanka, has made slight changes in wearing them to make subtle differences to foster separate identities. It is now more common for Indian women to wear Western dress (not frocks, but jeans and *kapris* and female T-shirts and *kurtis*). On the basis of the traditional dresses of Indian women, the region to which they belong can be discerned. South Indian women generally prefer dark coloured silk *saris*, whereas women from North India wear pastel colour *saris*. South Indian women also like brocaded borders of gold on the edge and bottom. Even the style of wearing *sari* can distinguish women from one region to other (Fisher, 1980; Khandelwal, 2002). Other diacritical marks used by Indian women are *bindi* on their forehead. For Hindu women, use of *bindi* is a sign of marriage, although nowadays some young girls also use this. In 1980, in New Jersey, some young Americans started teasing them as 'the dotbusters'. The married females from South India as well as from Gujarat and Maharashtra use *mangal sutra* (a black and golden beaded necklace) (ibid.).

Language

Increasingly, Indians are becoming particular about their children learning the mother tongue besides English. Therefore, most Indian families use their regional language at home. To expose their kids to regional language, parents take their children to temples and Gurdwaras where most of the ceremonies are held in regional languages. Another way to expose their children to regional language is to show them Indian movies, and play Bollywood music at home.

Sometimes, regular classes are also organized by various groups to expose their children to regional language. Although most of the Indians become bilingual, the majority in interpersonal communication use their regional language. The regional languages are also promoted by various associations of Indians. The other ways of promoting the regional languages are the publication of newspapers in these languages (Khandelwal, 2002).

The use of native language is, however, declining among children who are born and brought up in the United States. Most of these children may understand the language but are not able to speak. In fact, those parents who are not fluent in English encourage their children to learn and speak English as was done by the Sikhs in California. The intergenerational communication has also been affected due to language gap between immigrants and US-born children. Parents complain that their children speak English in American accent, whereas children feel embarrassed by their parents' English (ibid.).

Food

Food is essential for the survival of all living beings, but what has to be eaten, how it has to be cooked and how it has to be eaten is basically determined by culture. It does not only affect the diet and food practices of a society, but food habits and diets also considerably influence the culture of the group. Food habits are determined not only by the availability of the items but also by the preferences that are culturally transmitted. For instance, in America, beef is readily available, but it is religiously taboo to Hindus; similarly, pork is taboo to Muslims. One area in which Indians settled in America are not ready to compromise is their food and eating habits. There might be few exceptions, but majority do not change their food habits, particularly when they cook at home. In addition, it may be mentioned that in recent years, there has been a mushroom growth of Indian restaurants and eateries. Practically, all major cities and towns have such joints, and these are frequented not only by the Indians, but also by people of other nationalities, including Americans. Thus, some Indian dishes are becoming popular amongst all Americans – Tandoori Chicken and Dosa are good examples. Also, people savour curries.

However, a distinct change can be seen amongst Indians in America. Many vegetarian migrants took to non-vegetarian food after settling down in the state, perhaps as part of their effort to own the values of the host culture. Of course, such a shift is partial; while turning to non-vegetarian food, many Hindus still avoid eating beef; and Muslims avoid eating non-*halal*[3] meat as well as pork. Amongst the younger people, even this fine line of distinction seems to be disappearing. Even some parents eat McDonald's Hamburgers and Kentucky Fried Chicken for the sake of children, without verifying whether the meat is *Halal* or *Jhatka* (Nandan and Eames, 1980). By and large, Indians retain their tastes for traditional food of chapatti, spices and vegetables and rice prepared in Indian style. Italian pizza has become quite popular as it is seen as a different version of a Tandoori roti. However, there might be some differences between families with children and those without children. Families with children have a more flexible attitude and at least for convenience's sake may cook American-style meals as well. However, a majority of the Indian immigrants resist any change in their food and eating habits, although they have become more conscious about the nutritional value of food. Women avoid items that are fattening and often go on restricted diets.

Indians also prefer to invite friends for lunch or dinner at home or some time visit them but avoid eating out in restaurants. Indians not only invite friends for cocktails like Americans but also serve food. In a majority of the Indian families, food is cooked in traditional pattern; only in few cases, the American style is preferred (Angelo, 1997). While cooking food, Indians use flavoured aromatic spices that are commonly used in India (Nandan and Eames, 1980). In all the functions organized by various Indian organizations, only Indian food is served, which may be a mixture of items from various states of India.

Social and Cultural Organizations

In the beginning, when the number of Indian migrants was not large, there was only one organization of all Indians. But with the increase in number of Indians, various organizations based on religion, region and language and even caste have been formed. The first pan-Indian organization was formed in 1960 when professional Indian immigrants joined hands. The main objective was to protect the interest of immigrants ignoring their cultural and religious differences. It was done to retain their separate identity as Indians. Three major pan-Indian associations, namely, the Association of Indians in America (AIA), the Federation of Indians in America (FIA) and the National Federation of Indians in America (NFIA) were formed between 1967 and 1980. They represented Indians in multicultural and multiethnic activities in America. The AIA and NFIA formed local chapters all over the United States. The leaders of these associations were upper-middle-class professionals who were the early immigrants in the country. The AIA succeeded to get 'Asian Indian' category in the US Census under the 'Asian and Pacific Islanders' and minority status to the immigrants of South Asian Americans for civil rights purposes. Later on, it represented the interests of foreign medical graduates within the American Medical Association. It also conducted voter registration drives and youth projects and ran 'Project India', which through 1991 had channelled 'more than Fifteen Million dollars worth of funds and equipment to projects and relief works in India' (Khandelwal, 2002: 162).

The Federation of Indian Associations was the principal umbrella group for the growing number of Indian organizations. It mainly concentrated on celebrating certain functions such as Indian Independence Day, Republic Day, Gandhi Jayanti and US Independence Day (Leonard-Spark and Saran, 1980; Khandelwal, 2002). In 1989, the First Global Convention of People of Indian origin was organized in New York City. It was attended by Indians from all over the world and discussed the issues of ethnic image and representations but could not reach any decision. Later, they formed another association called Global Organization of the People of Indian Origin (GOPI).

Various programmes are organized by these organizations varying from presentation of dramas, showing of a film, musical performances and even talks from visitors from the home state. These associations also sponsor celebrations of religious festivals. Annual picnics are also arranged by these associations. One important feature of these organizations is that in all such gatherings, the food served is typically indigenous of that particular state. Such occasions also provide an opportunity to members to renew their relationships. Thus, such associations play a significant role in maintaining ethnic identity, and the children get exposed to the culture of the home state. Irrespective of their educational and occupational background, people participate in large numbers in the activities of these organizations.

Besides these associations, there are 'India Clubs' in many university campuses. 'India Clubs' are university-affiliated organizations, which encourage interaction between students of Indian origin. The activities of these clubs are both social and cultural. They also organize dance programmes and parties and invite dignitaries to deliver lectures on India. The needs of Indian students in the United States, especially of those newly arrived, are also met in these clubs. In fact, there are separate organizations for those Indian students who directly come from India. The main reason for their increased affinity with Indian background is due to the fact that 'others' identify them as Indians, regardless of the way they perceive themselves. In other words, it can be said that they have been forced to do so by 'others'. Thus, a distinction is made between 'we' and 'they'.

Religious Activities

The foundation of Hinduism in America was laid in 1890 with the establishment of Ramakrishna Mission by Swami Vivekananda. It was further strengthened by the formation of the *International Society for Krishna Consciousness* (ISKCON) and building temple complexes all over America. The number of religious organizations mushroomed with the increase in the number of Indians.

In the beginning, Hindus used to invite well-known and revered religious leaders from India to visit various cities and deliver speeches and preach the religion. Out of such activities emerged Hindu temple societies. These societies took initiative in building temples. They built big temples in New York and Pittsburgh, and several others in places that were a little far-off from the cities. It was from the mid-1980s that Indians started buying land for the construction of temples. Sculptors were either called from India for making idols of gods and goddesses or they got them made in India and imported to the United States. Besides constructing a sanctum sanctorum where the idols of gods and goddesses were placed for worship, these temple buildings also have eating places and small libraries and reading rooms. Ram Mandir near Chicago, Shiv temple near Los Angeles and Swaminarayan temple in New York are quite famous. First, a single temple of Lord Muruga was opened in Washington DC in May 1999. Most of the temples in America have idols of various Hindu gods and goddesses.

Sikh religious organizations are the most highly organized. They have established Gurdwaras where services are held at least once a week, and on all major festivals. They also emphasize maintaining the sanctity of the Sikh religion through observable symbolic representations of their religion, which includes wearing the turban and steel bangles and keeping the beard. For congregational worship generally three steps are followed by Sikhs. After settling down at the new place, they look for other Sikh families in the vicinity. Once a group is formed congregational worship begins and each family invites the group by turn. At the end of the worship, meal cooked in Punjabi style is served to all those present. As the number of families increases, they look for a place where a Gurdwara may be built. Donations are collected for building. All Sikh families also keep religious book called *Granth Sahib* at home, which is a collection of sacred hymns that are recited regularly (Nandan and Eames, 1980).

The attitude of Indian immigrants towards religion has become more favourable since emigration. To socialize the child in their traditional way of life and also to inculcate traditional values and attitudes, some parents suitably modify their own behaviour and attitudes. In fact, some of the parents participate in religious functions and visit temples and Gurdwaras as they want to reinforce religious values of their parent culture among their children. The participation in religious activities of immigrants enhances when they have teenagers at home. Since most of the parents of the subcontinent are afraid of peer group pressures on their children regarding dating, marriage, drugs, alcohol and familial relations, they accelerate their participation in the activities of religious organizations in order to expose their children to their own culture. It has been observed by many scholars that Indians settled in America have become more religious compared with Indians living in India.

Sometimes, the religious functions are combined with social occasions to reinforce their primordial identity. On their visits to India, most of the Indians buy religious storybooks to bring back to the United States; these contain stories about various deities such as Shiva, Ganesh, Ram and Krishna; *Panchatantra* stories are other favourites amongst the NRIs. Most of the Indians, especially Hindus, Jains and Sikhs, keep a special place for worship in their homes. Some of them have made replicas of temples in their homes to keep images and idols of deities. They have also formed their social and religious organizations and set-up temple trusts. The building of *Akshardham* temples in several cities in the United States is a case in point.

Contacts with Parent Culture

Even after settling abroad, Indians remain in contact with their relatives and friends in India; of course, the frequency and intensity of such contacts varies from family to family. Their decision to apply for American citizenship also depends on family considerations. By adopting American citizenship, it is easier for them to help their kith and kin to migrate to the United States. The new arrivals from India did not feel as strangers in a new country because of the presence of their relatives already settled there. The family networks are extensive and it is quite common to have all of their primary relatives and, in some cases, even secondary relatives in the United States. This networking also plays a significant role in the adjustment of new arrivals in the new environment. Their visits to India are generally confined to the villages, city or region of origin. The adaptation of the traits of the host culture would depend on the consistency and frequency with which contact and communication with family in India are maintained (Angelo, 1997).

Before the revolution in information technology, communications with relatives and friends were maintained through letters and occasionally through telephones. But the IT revolution has altered the entire scenario. Now, communications through letters are increasingly becoming obsolete. Letters are replaced by telephone calls and the Internet. Chatting through the Internet with your friends and relatives in any part of the world has become a common affair. By installing webcam in the computer, one can also watch live action of the other party. These developments have abridged the gaps and have strengthened the family ties and somewhat weakened the chances of integration into the host society.

Through social networking, Indians settled in the United States have maintained their relations with their kith and kin all around the world including India. Through this network, they not only send remittances but are also involved in many national and international organizations. Sikhs have developed two levels of social network: one with the relatives back home and the other with the Punjabis all over the globe. Sikhs help their family members in improving their financial status by sending money, which is used to buy land and establishing business such as transport companies. They also contribute in development work such as building schools and hospitals. Kinship ties are also kept alive by either visiting Indian or inviting family members to the United States, although the frequency of visits varies from case to case. Regarding their return to India, the situation now is in a flux. There are some who see advantage in reverse migration, whereas others think otherwise. In fact, reverse migration is more prominent among technical and professional people as they see greater opportunities in the growing economy and in the corporate sector.

Gujarati Hindus have also developed transnational networks through which they remain in touch with their relatives in India and with other Gujaratis in the United States and in other countries. Gujarati Hindus' network also operates at two levels. The personalized and informal linkages are maintained through telephones, the Internet and personal visits. Through this, they are able to remain in touch with fellow Gujaratis in India and in other countries. These links are maintained in the form of marital relations, kinship network, remittances and religious activities (Gopa Kumar, 2003). Then, there are linkages between Gujarati diaspora and the mother country and among the diaspora community in other countries. Besides maintaining contact with the Government of India and the Government of Gujarat for developmental activities, they have also established international associations and organizations. Through these associations and organizations, Gujaratis interact with Gujaratis all over the world (ibid.). Gujaratis have also developed websites, and also created global directories of individuals, community associations and business organizations owned by the Gujarati diaspora community.

Indian remix music and dance is the most popular subculture visible and audible among Indian American youth. Hindi film music and *Bhangra* have been remixed with American rap, techno, jungle and reggae, and this has become part of the broader popular culture. This remix first emerged in the mid-1980s among British-born South Asian youth and since then has travelled to New York, Delhi, Bombay, Toronto, Port of Spain, etc. One significant feature of this remix is that though it emerged among urban areas, its expressions are shaped by local context (Maira, 2002: 29–30). The parties where this remix music is played are attended even by those youth who had not been to college.

Thus, continuous interactions with friends and relatives back in India and exposure to Indian culture through movies have curtailed the chances of integration and assimilation in the host society.

IV

Summing Up

The early migrants from India to the United States maintained their separate identity and resisted absorption into the mainstream. Except for a short period when they were marrying Mexican women, they maintained separate identity and a shared sense of peoplehood. They were particular in adhering to their cultural norms, putting pressure on their young children to uphold Punjabi Sikh values and customs; and at the same time, they were receptive to change and ready to learn new ways from other groups. Their strategy of accommodation without assimilation helped them maintain their separate identity.

Most of the Indian parents show real concern for their children. Parents like some of the characteristics of American culture, but they do not appreciate when children start questioning them for everything. In fact, a derogatory term *American-Born Confused Desi* or 'ABCD' has been used for Indian youth as they face identity crisis. Some of the young people call themselves as 'coconuts – brown on the outside, white on the inside' (Agarwal, 1991: 34). This situation arises as the parents of young people would like their children to have two identities, both as Indians and Americans. While comparing Indian youth with other Asian groups, Agarwal points out that 'The Indian culture maintains a more severe taboo on openness in pre-marital, male-female relationships. Dating is not an institution in India, as marriages are traditionally arranged by one's family' (ibid.: 36). One complaint most of the youth make against their parents is that they use the same standards with which they themselves grew up in India over 25 years ago without realizing that conditions have changed even in India.

The younger generation people appreciate the family values of Indians, and the closeness is considered as the essence of Indianness. They also like religion as well as many customs and traditions of India. But a majority did not approve the caste system or social stratification. Some of the other characteristics of Indians, which are criticized by the second generation, include rigid food habits and attitude towards women and so many rituals. According to them, it is their social attitude and religious beliefs that did not allow them to integrate in mainstream America (Agarwal, 1991; Sheth, 2001).

Although the first-generation people were more inclined to associate with individuals from the same region due to language and customs, the younger generation people do not have such preference. A majority of them prefer to have friends of mixed international background. Since the second-generation people are more exposed to non-Indians either in school or at the place of work, they have better chances of assimilation into mainstream American society. These people also do not like the perpetuation of regionalism and sectionalism. They would prefer to have pan-Indian identity rather than promoting regionalism. On the whole, the younger generation people born and brought up in the United States would prefer to have 'dual culture', what Atal has called 'Sandwich Culture'. It was felt by most of them that 'they need to be given the sense that they are both Indian and American, not Indian guests in a foreign land' (Agarwal, 1991: 60). They want to absorb positive culture of both the societies. 'The young Indian is determined, studious, focused, and family oriented, while the young American is self-confident, independent and well-rounded' (ibid.). Some of the teenagers remarked that they were born in the United States as their parents chose to migrate. As they had no choice, they have every right to be a part of the mainstream American society.

Acknowledgements

This paper is part of a projected book on the Indian Diaspora in various parts of the world. I am grateful to Professor Yogesh Atal for his comments and suggestions on the earlier draft of this paper.

It would be worthwhile to examine the socio-cultural transformation of Indians settled in the United States. In this paper, an attempt has been made on the basis of available data to discuss the socio-cultural transformation of Indians.

Notes

1. Two sets of factors that operate to facilitate or hinder the process of formation of sandwich culture given by Yogesh Atal are aperture opening and insulator mechanism. Aperture openings include intermarriages, adoption of language of the host culture, religious conversion, promotion of inter-commensality, adoption of food habits and developing a taste for the host cuisine and adoption of names of the host society. Insulatory mechanisms include retention of mother tongue, concentration of living quarters to promote greater interaction with the members of the group, provision of separate educational facilities for the children, practice of endogamy, concentration in certain occupations, formation of voluntary organizations, pursuit of parental religion, continuation of food habits and taboos associated with eating, retention of cultural diacriticals, particularly in the manner of dressing, racial features and keeping apertures open to the parent culture in the form of frequent visits, schooling of children either in parent society or using the textbooks and reading material in separate schools, affinal relations, exposure to media, books, music, films and postal and telecommunication.
2. It is called Kakas; five items all named with the initial letter 'Ka' are prescribed for Sikh males. A Sikh is supposed to wear Kanga (comb), Kesh (hair – no haircut and shave), Katar (dagger), Kada (bracelet) and Kachchh (underwear). These are his dress diacriticals.
3. There are two ways of killing an animal for food. One is called *Jhatka,* meaning a single-stroke killing; this is used by the Hindu non-vegetarians. The other is called *Halal* religiously sanctioned for the Muslims; this involves slow killing of the animal through a knife as in surgery; Muslims

eat only *Halal* meat. That is why restaurants serving food boldly announce the kind of meat served by them. The Muslims are very particular about it compared to the Hindus.

References

Agarwal, Priya (1991). *Passage from India: Past 1965 Indian Immigrants and their Children Conflicts, Concerns and Solutions*. Palos Verdes, CA: Yuvati Publication.

Angelo, Michael (1997). *The Sikh Diaspora Tradition and Change in an Immigrant Community*. New York: Garland Publications, Inc.

Atal, Yogesh (1989). 'Outsiders versus Insiders: The Phenomenon of Sandwich Culture', *Sociological Bulletin*, 38(1): 23–41.

Eisenstadt, S.N. (1954). *The Absorption of Immigrants*. London: Routledge and Kegan Paul.

Fisher, Maxine P. (1980). *Indians of New York City: A Study of Immigrants from Indians*. New Delhi: Heritage Publisher.

Gibson, Margaret A. (1988). *Accommodation without Assimilation: Sikh Immigrants in an American High School*. Ithaca: Cornell University Press.

Gopa Kumar, R. (ed.) (2003). *Indian Diaspora and Living Pattern of Indian Americans in USA*. New Delhi: Charities Aid Foundation India.

Gordon, M.M. (1964). *Assimilation in American Life: The Role of Race, Religion and National Origin*. New York: Oxford University Press.

Khandelwal, Madulika (2002). *Becoming American Being India: An Immigrant Community in New Delhi*. Ithaca: Cornell University Press.

La Brack, Bruce (1983). 'The Reconstitution of Sikh Society in Rural California', in George Kurian and Ram P. Srivastava (eds), *Overseas Indians: A Study in Adaptation*. New Delhi: Vikas, pp. 215–40.

Leonard-Spark, P.J. and P. Saran (1980). 'Indian Immigrant in America: A Demographic Profile', in Parmatma Saran and Edwin Eames (eds), *The New Ethnics: Asian Indians in the United States*. New York: Praeger Publication, pp. 136–62.

Maira, Sunaina M. (2002). *Desis in the House: Indian American Youth Culture in New York City*. Philadelphia: Temple University Press.

Nandan, Y. and Edwin Eames (1980). 'Typology and Analysis of the Asian Indian Family', in Saran and Eames (1980), op. cit.

Rangaswamy, Padma (2000). *Namaste America: Indian Migrants in an American Metropolis Pennsylvania*. University Park: The Pennsylvania State University Press.

Sheth, Pravin (2001). *Indians in America: One Stream, Two Waves, Three Generations*. Jaipur: Rawat Publications.

Part II
Development

13

Gandhi on Sustainable Development

K.D. Gangrade

Problem of Gigantic Proportion

Maldevelopment, peacelessness and violence are stalking the globe today. Although by the year 2100, about 13 per cent of the world population will be consuming 90 per cent of its resources, a craze for 'development', which is the other name for the acquisition of wealth by a few at the cost of the others, is expanding the areas of absolute poverty everywhere both in the rich as also in the poor nations. The present-day technologies, institutions, professions and practices borrowed from the rich society create such problems and project the phantoms of violence. At the inaugural session of the three-day 44th annual meeting of the World Bank of the IMF attended by finance ministers and officials from 152 member nations, the WB President Barber B. Conable and IMF Managing Director Michel Camdessus highlighted the criminal diversion of $200 billion annually towards their defence projects by the developing countries. They gave a clarion call to every nation in the world to be realistic now and be cautious about the 'human consequences of these (military) choices'. WHO Director General Hiroshi Nakajima said that for $50 million or the cost of a modest commercial building in New York City, we could cut deaths from diarrhoeal diseases by two million per year. He further called the health problem a 'preventable tragedy' because the developed world has the resources and technology to end common diseases worldwide. Twenty per cent of the world's population or one billion people have disease, have poor health or are malnourished. The greatest health problems are in sub-Saharan Africa where 160 million are ill and undernourished. Forty per cent of the population in South and East Asia – India, Bangladesh, Indonesia, Nepal and Sri Lanka – were characterized as having 'serious health problems'.

Challenges of Development

The Third World comprises 141 nations and has a large population living in villages, numbering about three billion. That is, 60 per cent of the world population is living in villages, and out of this 85 per cent or 2.5 billion live in Asia and Africa. The living standard of villages is far behind that of the cities as the national income of these countries is much less than that of the affluent countries. UN data show that in these countries the urban population consists of 35–65 per cent of rural migrants.

The affluent nations being basically urban and the poor nations rural, rural development is a critical factor to be tackled, which would bring about a less exploitative and more satisfying system of all-round development. Gandhi in the context of India aptly said:

> If India is not to perish, we have to begin with the lower rung of ladder. If that was rotten, all work done at the top or at the intermediate rungs is bound to ultimately fall. (*Harijan*, 13 April 1935: 68)

Gandhi in his writings further dramatized the problems of city–village:

> The blood of the villages is the cement with which the edifice of the city is built. I want this blood that is today inflating the arteries of the cities to run once again in the blood vessels of the villages. (*Harijan*, 23 April 1946: 198)

Gandhi did not talk simply in terms of city-village dichotomy. In addition to referring to the village exploitation and role of the city, he spoke of alienation of city dwellers. He referred to village as a 'community', rather than a socially and culturally structured unit.

The purpose of the paper is to rescue Social Sciences from this plight and to help to investigate the causes that create these problems. Naturally, our main task will be to evolve a theory of social change that may lead to a no-poverty, a no affluence and a non-violent society. It will also draw heavily from the experience of both the cultures of poverty and of affluence of the North and the South world. The purpose is to find global solutions of the problems of human settlements that function at the level of the small community and vice versa.

It would thus discuss a quest for the logical fruition and some of the ideas and processes that lie germane in history and have found repeated expressions in the contributions of many a leader of thought and action. The latter include, among others, Ruskin, Tolstoy, Gandhi, Martin Luther King, Schumacher, Jawaharlal Nehru and Jayaprakash Narayan. Some of their thoughts had once helped, and could help again, in rediscovering the community that lies at the root of our culture and seems to be withering away. The paper shall not search for alternatives to the existing distortions of cultures that the world of the megalomaniac megalopolises, dreaded multinationals and super-technologies have now introduced in a bid to react to them; it would indeed look beyond that movement of alternatives to the logical conclusion of a heritage that might yet survive, despite all efforts at its mutilation. The purpose is to analyse the macro and the micro social environs of both the cultures of affluence and poverty, the objective being to provide an integrated overview of the struggles, aspirations and experiments that are being conducted the world over in the field of community building and constructive work that arise logically out of the culture in which the humankind has grown.

In my opinion, our ultimate aim should be to have no poverty in society. Man exploiting man should cease, to have peace in the world. The process of planning and development should be to raise the standard of living and quality of life of masses. It should not lead to inequitable distribution of resources, creation of inequalities and uprooting them from their present environment without providing for their adequate rehabilitation.

The main philosophy of modern development, especially of economic development, has been one of maximization of current or future consumption. Given the limited production capacities and iniquitous distribution of purchasing power, development activities have tended to create avenues for excessive consumerism of some, as against the continued deprivation of many others. Gandhiji, in his early writings, had clearly advocated the restrictions of wants voluntarily. In fact, he had said that there is enough in this world to meet the needs of everybody, but there is not enough to meet even a single man's greed.

The market economy is based on the principle of maximizing profit and relegates the issue of inter-human relations and human welfare to the background. Taking care of the needs as defined by the people involved in the economy should override the principle of maximizing profits. Profits are not to be used to build a hierarchical business in which there are masters and servants.

The distinction between growth and development has to be specifically remembered. Growth is no longer a guarantor of trickle-down effect. It is now being increasingly recognized in the developing world that there is need for special attention to that group of population, which has been left behind in the process of growth. The basic needs approach, enunciated by the planning process in India, needs to be adopted as a major plank of development strategies. Improvement in facilities for education, health and infrastructure welfare should receive priority attention in the development process. To sum up 'Economic Development' minus 'Social Development' is 'No Development'.

Unfortunately, since the beginning of the process of industrialization in Europe towards the end of the 18th and early 19th centuries, development is defined in terms of shifting from agriculture towards industry and later towards service activities. Developing countries have followed blindly this model of development. This has created two types of problems. Often, the labour share in agriculture may not fall to the same extent as share of agriculture in GDP. This means labour dependent on agriculture continues to be substantial, whereas the share of agriculture in GDP accruing to the labour force dependent on it, falls more sharply.

This leads to uneven distribution of development in two segments of population. The second problem arises out of the nature of linkages between agriculture and industry, due to both production linkages of backward and forward kinds of income-induced linkages of demand for each other's goods.

Many developing countries have permitted weakening of these linkages in their over-enthusiasm for rapid industrialization in a highly diversified structure. With the majority of the population still dependent on agriculture and still also with a highly rural bias in the culture of population, weakening of these linkages is a serious matter of concern.

The present-day social scene at the level of either individual nations or in the global context is beyond doubt one of crisis and disarray. The situation has become complex, partly because of the simultaneous operation of a multitude of factors and partly because received theories and analytical tools have lost their relevance. Development can no longer be identified as a process of shifting surplus labour from agriculture to the industrial sector.

In the present stage of world economy, no country can remain delinked from the rest of the world. There are different approaches for getting a nation integrated with the rest of the world. Integration with the international environment should not necessarily mean total opening of the economies. It is a twin process of learning from external development and at the same time strengthening the internal capabilities for endogenizing the process of development. This requires strengthening of the human resource element and institutional basis of the developing countries.

Concept of Development

The word 'development', like the phrase Third World, is an Anglo-Saxon concept. Few ideas in our time have been invested with as much respectability or historic significance as the concept of development: How to make poor people rich and undeveloped countries advanced? By and large, the philosophy of development has restricted its concerns to the poor of the Third World: development schemes are formulated by experts, planners and voluntary agencies to deprive 'these people' of their poverty and to wrench them above the poverty line. Gunnar Myrdal defines development as follows:

> By development I mean the movement upward of the entire social system, and I believe this is the only logically tenable definition. The social system endorses besides the so-called economic factors, all non-economic factors, including all sorts of consumption by various groups of people, consumptions provided collectively; educational and health facilities at all levels; the distribution of power in society; and more generally economic, social and political stratification; broadly speaking institutions and attitudes to which we must add and exogenous set of factors, induced policy measures applied in order to change one or several of these endogenous factors.

Fundamentally, development implies the replacement of general competence and abundant subsistence activities by the use and consumption of commodities. Development implies the monopoly of wage labour over all other work. It implies the redefinition of needs in terms of goals and services, produced on a mass basis according to expert design. Ivan Illich says that the development paradigm is more easily repudiated by those of us who are adults on 10 January 1949. That day, most of us came to know the term 'development' in its present meaning for the first time when President Truman announced his Four-Point Programme. Until then we used the term development to refer to species, real estate and moves in chess – only thereafter to people, countries and economic strategies. Since then, there has been a deluge of development theories. Wherein one comes across concepts such as growth, catching up, modernization, dualism, dependency, basic needs, transfer of technology, world system and industrialization.

Common Factors of Development

Development is neither a static nor a uniform concept. As a historical fact, the classical model remained the only model in the West until 1913. After the First World War and particularly after the Russian Revolution and the Great Depression, the classical model declined and alternative forms emerged. After the Second World War, the world entered another new stage of development. Development must be defined in each of these stages. Further, development always varies widely in different countries. Yet, there are important features of development common to all phases and to all types of modernization. The most important common feature is that of growth: to develop a means to advance, to further, to evolve or to expand by a process of growth. A modern society is one that is growing, expanding or advancing.

Development is a process of societal transformation from a traditional society to a modern society, and such a transformation is also known as modernization. A modern society is also a rational society. Although all societies have rational and irrational elements, modern society is rational in the sense that it is not dominated by supernatural factors by tradition and that it assigns high value to making decisions on the basis of reason and performing tasks in accordance with rational methods and procedures. Another common feature is the building of nation-state as the unit of development. This is why modern development is often known as national development. Development involves institutional changes. Institution is a significant element in the life of a culture, which is persistent and enduring, which regulates pattern of behaviour, and which is widely tolerated, sanctioned or legitimized by the society.

Development is considered to be a process of improving the capability of a nation's institutions and value system to meet increasing and different demands social, political and economic. Development has also been defined as economic growth plus social change as bread plus dignity, as a technical solution to under development, as institutional building, human development, a more equitable spread of distribution and development resources. However, in the First UN Development Decade that began in 1961, development was almost always equated with economic growth. During this decade, the world's total Gross National Product increased by $1,000 billion. About 80 per cent of this increase went to countries with per capita income of $1,000 with 25 per cent of the world population. Only 6 per cent of the increase went to countries where per capita yearly income average is $200 or less and areas comprise 60 per cent of the world population.

The Second UN Development Decade, therefore, stated that development for the developing countries is not simply an increase in productive capacity but a major transformation in their social and economic structures. Economic growth and social progress are not only mutually interdependent but are also organically related parts of a simple process of development.

In developing countries, poor, disadvantaged, economically weak and less privileged are often used interchangeably. The basic underlying characteristics of these groups are the miserably low levels of income and the palpably small productive resources at their command. In terms of caste structure, most of the members of the scheduled castes, scheduled tribes, service castes and other backward castes generally would fall under the category of weaker sections. Further, the term 'weaker sections' cover those who live below the poverty line (BPL), which is defined in terms of minimum level of consumption (Anirudh Prasad, Editor's Note, *Jharkhand Journal of Development and Management Studies*, XISS, Ranchi, Vol. 1, No. 2, March 2003, pp. ix–xvi).

About development decades, Jules Feiffer, the cartoonist, had a famous cartoon in which a poor voter declared. I used to think I was *poor* – I was *needy*. Then, they said needy was an expression that is self-defeating. I was actually *deprived*. Then again, they said deprived created a bad image. I was actually *underprivileged*. Now, they say underprivileged is inaccurate. I am actually *disadvantaged*. I still do not have a dime. But I surely have a rich vocabulary (cited by Anirudh Prasad, ibid.).

Gandhi's Doctrine of Trusteeship, which is in fact foundation of all theories of corporate governance and governance by governments, played a vital role in shaping of the contours of modern corporate ethics – science of morals, and which do not preclude profitability. He further pleads the same model of behaviour (mutual trusteeship) on the part of the corporate, or the business houses, or government, capital and labour and supplement and help each other; what things to produce should not be determined by personal whim or greed. This order still has tremendous potential for reshaping the policies, programmes and strategies of modern corporate and governments. This order has also proved to be the best in discharging the social responsibility towards the society.

There is a beautiful story with moral overtones titled how much land does a man require? by Leo Tolstoy: a poor Russidre saves the life of the Tsar. In return, the Tsar granted him the right to take all the land he could encircle on foot between sunrise and sunset. The peasant woke up at dawn and began running round the neighbouring fields. He refused to rest, eat or drink water at all; it was just for one day, and he would be able to take land, which would help him and his descendants to prosper. Hence, he ran on and on till the evening. A few minutes before the sun was about to set, he saw a particularly best piece of agricultural land. Hence, he put all the stamina that remained in him to encircle this as well. Utterly exhausted, he got back to the spot where he had started. Then he collapsed and died. He was buried in a six-foot long grave. That was all the land he acquired (Anirudh Prasad, Editor's Note, *Jharkhand Journal of Development and Management Studies*, XISS, Ranchi, Vol. 1, No. 5, December 2003, pp. vii–x).

The moral of the story is that we should not fall into the trap of greed.

Value Base

The basic values of development are human dignity, equality and social justice. These three concepts are not separate and distinct but interrelated and dependent on each other. Another principle implied in social development is the emphasis on cooperation as against competition. It lays emphasis on collectivity as against rugged individualism. It does not deny the right of full development expression of the individual and his/her role in decision-making that affects their lives. It lays greater emphasis on the well-being of the total society and all its individuals.

Development based on the principles of human dignity, equality and social justice can be defined as a goal and process that aims to achieve an integrated, balanced and unified (social and economic) development of society. It is international in scope and has a holistic, interdisciplinary, inter-sectoral and inter-regional approach to societal issues and problems. It focuses on 'qualitative' development as measured by (i) the participation of people in matters affecting their lives, (ii) the nature of social and interpersonal relations and (iii) the relationship of people to their environment. Quantitatively, social development aims at structural and institutional reforms to bring about changes in the distribution of income, wealth and services.

In fact, social development means something more than merely economic, political, social and environmental. It is not merely an effort to provide ad hoc growth targets in each of the sectors of planning. Social development planning requires the perception and delineation of the nature of interrelationship between the different sectors. Social development is an integrative concept and this integration depends on the clear enunciation of the values and the type of society towards which planning is to be undertaken.

Briefly stated, the word development has its origin in an Italian word 'Velupara' of the 12th or 13th century. It means to unwrap, to disentangle, to rid of something. The opposite of 'develop' is 'envelop', which means to hide, to cover up, to put up constraints – that we do when we envelop something. When we develop something, we do the reverse – we remove these constraints whatever they may be. The word 'development' is a positive term meaning progress, and when applied to man, indicates a comprehensive growth that enables an individual to feel that he is as much a part of mankind as anybody else.

Development Philosophy and Objectives

Our view of development is a process by which one's overall personality is enhanced. This is so for society as well as for an individual. For society, the identity is collective. Thus, development for society means development of the collective personality of society. Development of collective personality requires physical, material and economic development, but it is above all the development and application of consciousness and faculties. A child may grow physically, whereas his personality does not develop. Therefore, it is with society. Thus, 'economic development', while it is vitally necessary, cannot be treated as an independent variable divorced from its social bearings. Development of a society is social development, a process in which 'economic' and 'non-economic' elements interact organically with each other. Attempts to isolate the economic elements and fit them into hypothetical model of 'economic development' are therefore unscientific. Development thus defined is a multivariate quantitative and qualitative change. It would be futile to attempt to measure any country's social development quantitatively and expect consensus about it. The world's richest society may be considered to be its sickest, and hence not developed at all. Such positions can be understood but cannot be refuted, and yet scientific judgements may be given on such a basis. Although scientific judgements about social development need to be reasoned, cardinal quantification has often served as a fetish that has detracted from, rather than helped evaluate the more essential qualitative attributes.

The Individual and the Collective

The individual and the collective might be thought to have conflicting interests. Our concept of the collective rules this out. The collective exists to the extent that individuals acquiesce in its sovereignty, and develops as individuals acquire more of this collective spirit. Thus, a nation of 'self-seekers' may be a collective only in the sense that its members have agreed to hold a common passport; if there is no more of the 'collective spirit', it would be a very weak collective indeed. The 'collective spirit' is not necessarily an abnegation of individual interest in favour of a mystified concept of 'society'. We view the collective as a method of serving individual interests while at the same time raising individual consciousness, so that one progressively aspires to fulfilment of higher orders including fulfilment in developing together.

Aspirations Frontier

Within the framework of the above philosophy, development has to have its operational objectives. One of these is growth of the collective spirit. Stimulating the spirit of cooperation is another, by means of which the collective consciousness may be promoted and the quantity of social good to be produced may be raised. Creativity and innovativeness, and a problem-solving approach to life, are essential attributes of a dynamic personality and have to be cultivated. Improvement of knowledge is a basic requirement. A will to develop and faith in the collective creative potential of man are fundamental prerequisites with which society must be equipped.

Somewhat more complex is the question of attaining an 'aspirations frontier'. At any point of time, individuals in a society have certain natural aspirations, such as minimum of nourishment, clothing and shelter, some leisure and opportunity for cultural-scientific pursuits. For India, this may have to be set as a long-term objective, beyond the material possibilities in the short run. This leaves the problem of sustaining morale in the short run. The solution lies in the direction of creating values that gives a sense of fulfilment in the very austerity that is necessary in the short run. Such fulfilment is possible only if the austerity is shared in a framework of collective effort for progress.

Self-Reliance

Of all the new values to be created, self-reliance is the single most important. India has depended too long on external masters. This is much more true of rural India, which has depended too long on external masters. Rural India has depended too long on the city. The rural poor subservient too long to the rural rich and to the 'officer' sent from the city, a subservience that has been forced upon them; in the process, their own initiative and vitality have been sapped. The result is a history of exploitation of the 'dependant' by the 'master'. The dependant, appearing to have no self-respect, commands no respect from others. He is laughed at by the world and despised at the same time as he is squeezed.

India cannot develop unless it rejects the soft option and resolves to be self-reliant. This means building up a combination of materials and mental reserves that enable one to choose one's own course of evolution, uninhibited by what others desire. It requires maximum mobilization of domestic resources for poor societies; but above all, it requires psychological and institutional staying power to meet crisis situations when the supply of essential materials is too short. This staying power is best attained collectively. Individually, a hungry man feels isolated and his mental reserve wanes; collectively, this reserve is reinforced for each and collective resolve gives individuals strength to fight a calamity with their heads high.

Self-reliance does not necessarily mean self-sufficiency. With psychological staying power, a self-reliant society can open up and negotiate from a position of strength. But some measure of self-sufficiency in strategic areas that are easily prone to manipulation by exploitative interests, is desirable. Such vulnerable areas are staple food production, technology and spare parts, and military resistance power.

All these make the development of appropriate technology indispensable. Although development of a modern sector is imperative, the technological revolution has to be primarily internally achieved.

Participatory Democracy

The collective as we conceive it functions through the active participation of the people. Without this the individual would not belong organically to the collective and the collective itself would not be to that extent be a reality. Hence, the collective and participatory democracy are inseparable concepts. Participatory democracy is not the formal voting of leaders into power once every five years and passive obedience in between; it is not merely government of the people but also, and more fundamentally, 'by the people'. Participatory democracy rules out the dominance of any minority group over the broad masses of people. In the Indian context, it precludes, therefore, dictatorship of the 'elite' over the masses, of the city over the countryside and of the modern sector over the traditional, and new forms of external control, which would dilute the processes of democracy. Moreover, there is no room in this participatory system for power-wielding, though intelligent leadership, which is alien to the broad masses of the people and tends to strengthen its own position at the expense of the latter; nor is there a place for the unaccountable and unresponsive bureaucrat who considers it beneath his dignity to have any interaction with the masses.

Consciousness Gap

The problem of a 'consciousness gap' between the leaders of a society and the masses of the people remains. In concrete historical conditions, in any society, some persons may be ahead of others in perceptions of the need for social change, in their ability to systematize ideas whose origins are in the masses themselves, in seeing through complex relationships and in relevant technical expertise. Such men are natural leaders of society, whom the masses of the people tend to follow without coercion. Participatory democracy in such situations would not yet be complete, nor would the leaders be fully accountable to the people in a real sense. Such a relationship may be formally 'democratic', but in the depth of the situation lies the seed of leadership ego, which may grow and gradually alienate the leader from his people, so that finally he leads them to a vision that is more his than theirs. This would, in turn, alienate the people and inhibit the growth of their collective personality. The leadership and masses must, therefore, move in a mutually interacting process that systematically reduces the consciousness gap. Democracy in this sense is not a system to be implanted, but an objective to be realized through a process.

De-Alienation

Many of the above objectives imply a regeneration and development of values that man has lost or nearly lost through ages of subordination to exploitation, maladministration and misdirection. Regressive social relations and cultural taboos have paved the way for such alienation from man's original and inherent potentials. In essence, the development philosophy and objectives that we have enunciated centre around the following five core concepts that stand inseparably together:

1. Man as the end of development, which is, therefore, to be judged by what it does to him.
2. De-alienation of man, in the sense that he feels at home with the process of development in which he becomes the subject as well as the object.
3. Development of collective personality of man in which he finds his fullest expression.
4. Participation as the true form of democracy.
5. Self-reliance as the expression of man's faith in his own abilities.

In India, whose situation we are reviewing, rural development is the key to its overall social development.

The personality of India cannot be enhanced without raising the personality of rural India. This leads us to a strategy of development that points that the countryside should be the centre of activity for contemporary India. The inner-directed strategy that we are seeking encompasses the city, but the focus and driving spirit is the village where the new Indian drama will inevitably have to be played.

Gandhian Philosophy, Concept and Programme of Development

Philosophy

Gandhi's development philosophy revolves around man, his society and nature and their respective and simultaneous development. He had a philosophy of work, health and happiness of man in line with the religious and ethical philosophies of the East as well as the West. His philosophy was governed by two fundamental and interrelated principles: truth and non-violence (*ahimsa*). In recent years, his vision of life, society and civilization has been increasingly shared and practised in various parts of the country and the world with reference to several basic and contingent problems such as poverty, violence, discrimination based on caste and religion, ecology, centralization of wealth and power. This has created a tremendous interest in the people to know and understand his philosophy of development: As already stated in general terms the word development in brief can be explained in the following ways:

1. Development is a term that is applicable to man only. Both society and nature are merely regarded as factors facilitating the development of man. The term, when used with a prefix or a suffix, refers to a superstructure or to an infrastructure, necessary for the development of man.
2. Human development has three complimentary aspects: physical, mental and spiritual development (not coterminous with religious development).
3. A comprehensive development programme is a combination of all the three aspects of development.

Physical development depends basically on proper nutrition, treatment of ailments, healthy living surroundings and enough clothing to protect the body from the ravages of nature. As long as a minimum quantity of these are not made available to the individual, he remains much too preoccupied with the problems of survival. A person dependent on others for primary necessities of life can hardly declare that all men are equal and he is a part of a society of equals. The word 'development', because of this emphasis on economic condition in the developing region particularly, has thus been regarded mainly as an economic concept concerned with the increased production and distribution of goods and services in a more or less integrated system controlled by various agencies as partners in the exercise of state power. It still means affluence and is growth-oriented. Its maturation logically aspires after affluence. This development is planned mostly by state, which, with the help of bureaucracy and technology, carries out development tasks and projects.

Concept

Affluence as a goal of development was not in Gandhi's mind. He believed that it is sufficient to meet the needs of people, but not their greed. He, therefore, refused to accept any move towards affluence as the goal of Indian society. He believed that the type of development that had been achieved in Europe was the result of a systematic colonization and exploitation of both people and nature. He, therefore, rejected not only the supportive mechanism of development such as bureaucracy, technology and elitist education but also the whole idea of development as conceived by the builders of the industrial society. His opposition to this approach should be understood in relation to his philosophy of development, which is closely linked with his life philosophy. As a great unifier not only of persons but of ideas: his social, economic and political ideas are all interrelated and interdependent.

Gandhi had a holistic view of life. Accordingly, his development philosophy revolved around man, his society and environment (nature) and their respective and simultaneous development. He believed that, instead of man exploiting the society and both exploiting nature, there is a symbiotic way of life which is in harmony with each other. In his frame of reference for development, man is the centre of attention. The objective is the moral and spiritual development of man. Man is primarily his consciousness, his capacity to be self-conscious and his built-in potential to judge between good and evil, between what will help him in his evolution to higher levels of being and what will obstruct his path. This gives him a leverage, not only to aspire after higher levels but to endeavour to attain the same. Gandhi believed in this self-effort, and the path he outlined lay through ethical, moral and spiritual disciplines. The key note of his ethics is love, which means near identity of interest with every sentiment. This love has to be expressed in the form of service and sacrifice. His ethics in relation to material things and property consisted in his concept of trusteeship. Every human being is a trustee not only of his faculties and attainments but also of everything he comes by, and trusteeship consists not only in using his powers and goods properly but also in using them selflessly and for the well-being of all others. The concepts popularized by Gandhi during his socio-political *yojana* in India's freedom and prosperity are as follows:

Truth
Ahimsa
Prohibition
Self-control
Worship
Eradication of untouchability
Women's emancipation
National integration
Village uplift
Khaddar
Swadeshi
Manual labour

Programmes

Purity of ends and of means formed an important aspect of his thinking. He believed that means must justify the ends and refused to accept the maxim that ends should justify the means. He stressed on means because he felt that it is within the individual's control and not the ends. It should, however, be remembered that there is no rigid dichotomy between the two; sometimes, end is changed into means to another end. Ends and means are interrelated and interdependent – means is the end in making, the 'end in embryo'. It is determined and conditioned by the end. As a man of action, Gandhi, therefore, tried to work out the means to achieve his desired ends – Sarvodaya and Swaraj – the new society of his thinking. Gandhi was not only a man of ideas. He could not rest by merely enunciating his idea on development. He tried to practise it. Based on his own experiments, he worked out the details regarding a wide variety of things that he named as 'Constructive Programme' and that he considered as vital for building a new society.

Government Policies

The poverty in India was linked to the British exploitation of Indian resources through trade and transfer described as the Drain Theory. The British refused to permit the growth of industries, the British policy of land settlement in India and even the British educational system that was alleged to be meant to produce clerks for the Raj rather than to train people to solve the country's problems. In independent India, a systematic approach to poverty seems to be that growth is for the rich and distributive justice for the poor.

In terms of the distribution of resources, the vast majority of people in our economic system can at best expect to survive while a small minority almost automatically have a surplus and can get this surplus to grow. The natural propensity of the system, therefore, is to respond to the requirements of those who own and control resources, and in that process make those who have little resources even more dispossessed. This is the paradox. It is, therefore, necessary that a substantial reduction in the existing concentration of the ownership of resources, especially land, takes place to effectively solve the problem of poverty. In this sense, the eradication of poverty is a political task, and the prospects for the future will depend on the extent to which the political processes are geared to the purposive mobilization of social power to achieve a major transformation in the socio-economic order. Is it possible to expect such a human act from our politicians? They are spending over $1 trillion in armaments. Winston Churchill said:

> If the human race wishes to have a prolonged and indefinite period of material prosperity, they have only got to behave in a peaceful and helpful way towards one another and science will do for them all they wish and more than they can dream.

Role of Leadership

The type of leadership required at the grass-roots to organize people to help themselves is of two types: leadership from outside and leadership from within. The outside leaders are bearers of new ideas and specialized skills. In my own work, I found that the skill most called for is that of working with communities. This is hard to acquire and harder to practise. In my case study of a 'school is built' (see my book *Community Organization in India*, Popular Prakashan, Bombay, 1971), this view has been in the text. I have highlighted the need for patience, idealism, resourcefulness and above all a skill in relationship on the part of a community organizer. Here, I had to begin with an apathetic, if not hostile, community. I had to find out a project that will appeal to all, induce the need for it, organize the material and human resources of the community and patiently pursue my objective of bringing together the various groups in the community despite many reverses. In a large countrywide programme, the factors of time and skill both tend to be sacrificed in the interests of coverage and the urgency of target achievement. We substitute short-term 'trained' workers for adequately qualified personnel and use a 'multipurpose' functionary in place of a team of development professionals. The type of training input needed and the kind of workers or officials required to eradicate poverty has to receive proper attention. I feel that training, research and extension must become an integral part of any system of work with people. It is wrong to artificially separate them from one another. There is possibility of degree of variances depending on the interest of an individual or a set of workers.

Educating the Educated

The central problem in the world today is not so much the development of the so-called *underdeveloped*, as it is one of educating the educated. The task is verily one of educating or developing the so-called *developed* and the educated. To use a new coinage, one that has, by now, become almost a new-classical expression in the field of social change, we need to de-school or de-educate the leaders, the vanguard or the elite of the global society first. If the poor and the deprived, the sick and those awaiting self-determination, have to be helped, the task needs to be redefined.

What is called for is not to help those who apparently stand in need on a priority basis, but to offer succour to all those who think that they are qualified enough to meet the needs of the afflicted.

It is the doctor who needs to heal himself. For, it is the projection of the values of the systems, most of whom are still the products of a colonial, imperialist past, which continues to haunt the process of give and take that is involved in any helping process. Unless the helper is healed, the persons or cultures at the receiving end cannot be helped at all. The following extracts from a recent news item will make our contention clear. It will make it evident how much of help the so-called *giver* needs.

> A vaccine against primary liver cancer caused by hepatitis B virus was developed by Australian scientists of the whole world, including that of the do-gooders of the Third World that plans such exercises. Example? While a number of 'Wasp' radicals are agitating in both Australia and the United States for the banning of the Deprovora injection, it is the elite of one of the countries of South Asia who are demanding that the injection should be administered on their poorer compatriots. Why? Because the latter by virtue of their birth itself pose a threat to the consumption basket of the elite of these countries? Here too, the elite are busy saving their own species. For the question is, are the elite prepared to try the injections on their own anatomy first? Or is it that the elite do not believe, any further, in the dictum that charity begins at home?
>
> Charity has to begin at home. The helpers and the educators must be de-educated. They must learn certain basic facts about human anatomy, society and culture, which constitute the A, B, C and D of human civilization. They must know that what is true of the poor is also true of the rich elite of any society.
>
> Unless the elite learn this basic grammar of civilization they cannot help anyone. Not even themselves. All that they can do in the eventuality of failing to learn this grammar is to move away from the poor and block their sun. This is the advice that one of the starving sages had given to Alexander the Great. When the latter had introduced himself, as the emperor of the world, to the former, he generously asked the sage 'what can I do to help your situation? You have only to ask for it'.

'Don't block my sun', came the quick reply, 'Please stand aside. That is the only help that you can offer'.

Possible Strategies

In many societies, the majority of the people were still confined within the remnants of a feudal past. Feudalism could often mean that the control of society was vested in a few powerful individuals who regulated it, maintained the status quo, with the majority of the people remaining BPL and being denied basic human rights.

The purpose here is to identify the barriers and to develop a strategy for their removal. Mentioned in this connection are certain possible strategies that would help the situation. Some of them could be stated as follows:

1. Identification of a target group: a whole village or some specific community in the village?
2. Target in terms of women: a special desire to reach women as a target group?
3. Priorities and objectives: what is more important? To work with a village to acquire greater share of the resources of the country or the internal process of redistributing the internal resources and power within the village?
4. What is the point of entry?
5. What is the attitude towards confrontation? Is confrontation central and desirable or harmful?
6. Is there an attempt in one's work to integrate the villages/communities into the government system, for example, in the areas of health, education, agriculture or to develop a parallel system, more effective than the governmental one?
7. What is the value of foreign aid as an alterative to helping communities to take a greater share of the existing government schemes? Which is favoured?

Regarding strategy number 7, that is the one relating to foreign aid; one feels that a judicious investment of foreign aid by a conscientious and powerful non-governmental organization can save a nation from the de-liberating and destabilizing forces of colonial rule more effectively than what indigenous governments that are mostly flooded with foreign funds can do.

Land Reforms Commission Urgently Needed

Ownership pattern of land has remained skewed: the top 20 per cent hold more than 60 per cent of the land, whereas the lower 20 per cent has less than 5 per cent. The government got an angry wake-up call: 25,000 people marched from Bhopal to New Delhi to share their stories of dispossession. Their stories were near-similar: land illegally taken over by landlords or the land mafia, displacement due to industrial projects, urbanization and policies denying them access to traditional sources of livelihood, such as forest produce or fishing rights. Janadesh (2007), as the march was called, demanded framing and implementation of policies on resolution of land and livelihood issues as a means of alleviation of poverty, reducing forced migration and preventing starvation in rural areas – all key to inclusive growth promised by United Progressive Alliance.

The Planning Commission says the government has had limited success in changing the ownership pattern of cultivable land. Another report of the Eleventh Five-Year Plan says that economic liberalization has pushed land reform off the government agenda. It also points out that there is a strong lobby working to enhance or give up land ceilings. The anger against the disparities has been visible in West Bengal portrayed by the Left as an example of successful land reforms: second-generation reorganization has not happened. Singur was the face of that discontent. In July 2007, police in Andhra Pradesh had to open fire on protestors demanding land reform and redistribution. Recently, the Supreme Court has made a distinction between lands acquired for public purposes and land acquired for a private enterprise, stating that a land acquisition notification cannot state both reasons simultaneously.

There is no doubt that the government has what is known as the 'permanent sovereignty' over 'natural resources', which empowers the state to take property for public use without the owner's consent. But the state cannot make this as an absolute right, especially when its idea of compensation leaves much to be desired. Since ownership of land will always remain the central point, the government would do well to establish a National Land Commission to formulate land policies, provide direction to states and monitor progress on land distribution. With industrialization on at a frenetic space, it will be worth-while to set up a time-bound mechanism to settle conflicts involving land rehabilitation and related compensation ('Ground to a Halt', *Hindustan Times*, New Delhi, 29 October 2007, p. 12).

Janadesh Rally – The rally organized by Ekta Parishad reached Delhi on Sunday (28 October 2007). P.V. Rajgopal of Ekta Parishad said, 'After 60 years of independence we want the government to give us food and honour to live. If they don't listen to us, we will not go back empty-handed' (Dipash Kumar Dash and Dwalpayan Ghosh, 'March Roll Into Capital', *The Times of India*, 29 October 2007, New Delhi, p. 7).

I feel land reforms are central, crucial and soul of the poor man. This needs immediate attention of the government to constitute a Land Reforms Commission to address all the problems concerning land and suggest appropriate remedies to get the land to the tiller of the soil.

The other six factors are an integral part of land reforms; and unless they are fully activated, most of the suggestions and recommendations will remain on paper. I am not dealing with each of these factors separately as they are self-explanatory.

Sustainable development is a continuous process. The river is beautiful because it is flowing continuously. It is, therefore, essential that land must belong to the tiller of the land who works on it and passes it from generation to generation. The government and politicians should take immediate steps to make it possible. The farmer should be given all aids in terms of seed, fertilizer and loan to grow crops and give a better price for his produce. This will prevent farmers from committing suicide as is the case in India today. The leaders need to be reminded of Lenin's words: 'It is not intentions that lead us anywhere. It is the result of our actions that eventually count.'

Conclusion

The planning and development process and land reforms may not yield any result unless it goes the whole hog to build a 'no poverty society', else poverty will remain a shibboleth. This would mean nothing short of the leopard changing his spots. But can we? This can be done if we have political will backed by a plan of action. Failing which, the development plans will remain like the famous sunstone kept surrounded by a bundle of cotton wool. The stone by itself cannot reduce the cotton but when the sunrays are focused on it, as to fall on the wool, by virtue of the heat that generates on the focal point the latter is turned to ash. So too, a 'plan of action' properly drawn and put into action may help us to reach our cherished goal of 'no poverty society' by having active participation of people.

Development deals with a subject fraught with political sensitivity. It touches the lives of common people whose well-being determines the prospects of political stability, particularly in countries that are characterized by a wide disparity in incomes, high levels of unemployment and a paucity or lack of capital stock relative to the unemployed force. Such countries for want of a better term are referred to as developing countries.

A democratic polity derives its legitimacy and more important than that its real strength from the people. The greater their involvement and participation in the decision-making processes, the stronger the fabric of a democratic society to build the nation a key to sustainable development.

We tend to punish those individuals who are responsible for such exploitation and disorders to serve as a deterrent to further aggravation. Punishment, however, can produce only temporary results. To transform violence to harmony, jealousy to praise, greed to generosity and impurities to purity, we must not rely on negative and reactive punishments.

We must promote in a proactive manner, mutual understanding and respect, compassion, collaboration and honest transactions among all people. The principles of mutual understanding via continuing dialogues, practice of concession and resources, state and national redistribution and aid systems need to be applied in the arena of state and national politics and economics.

This will help reduce conflict among different landless poor and landowners and ensure sustainable development.

Today, at the pinnacle of the world's industrial and material glory, we see that there is neither an end in sight to poverty nor any contentment in those who have been part of this growth. In fact, the new society, based on the ideology of wealth, and ever widening gap between the rich and poor, is one of the causes of war and terrorism that are plaguing us. The liberal policy of land being made available for special economic zone has further shattered sustainable development and people have been alienated from each other. Immanuel Kant said that to treat another person or persons as means is an immoral act.

Societies are shaped by the collective rules that man agrees to live by. The India we inherited, the India in which we all have right to life, liberty, livelihood, expression and religion, is not for a self-perpetuating magic state. It is a state that was articulated by the heroic imagination of our founding fathers: a state we will have to struggle and fight to retain. If we do nothing, we will turn a dangerous corner as a nation. Our certitude will slip away from us. We will become morally rudderless and sustainable development will remain a distant dream.

References

'*Anasakti Darshan' International Journal of Non-Violence in Action* (2007), January-June, 3(1): 128.

Ekka, Beni Alphonse (2005). *Land Reforms Administration in India: An Unfinished Task*. Ranchi: Xavier Institute of Social Service (XISS), p. 282.

Gandhi Marg: Quarterly Journal of the Gandhi Peace Foundation (2007), April-June, 24(1): 132.

Gangrade, K.D. (2001). *Working with Communities at the Grassroot Level Strategies and Programmes*. New Delhi: Radha Publications, p. 441.

——— (2005). *Gandhian Approach to Development and Social Work*. New Delhi: Concept Publication Company, p. 267.

Indian Association of Social Sciences Institutions (IASSI) (2006a). 'Approach to Ending Poverty and Deprivation', *IASSI Quarterly*, Special Issue in Memory of the Late Shri Tarlok Singh – I, January-March, 24(3): 162.

——— (2006b). 'Dimensions of Poverty Concern', *IASSI Quarterly*, Special Issue in Memory of the Late Shri Tarlok Singh – II, April-June, 24(4): 156.

'*Management in Government' Journal of Administrative Reforms* (2007), January–March, 38(4): 120.

Misra, R.P. (2007). *Rediscovering Gandhi, Hind Swaraj – Gandhi's Challenge to Modern Civilization*. New Delhi: Concept Publishing Company, p. 428.

Varma, Ravindra (2006). *The Spiritual Reflections of Mahatma Gandhi*. New Delhi: Rupa & Co., p. 209.

Appendix I

This is a case study of Ralegan – a shining example of sustainable development on Gandhian principles.

From an obscure, barren and water scarcity-hit village to a green belt, Ralegan Siddhi in Ahmednagar district, about 110 km from Pune, serves as a shining example for sustainable development on Gandhian principles. Unwittingly, the village has become a part of the newly found anti-corruption movement spearheaded by its son, Anna Hazare.

Nearly four decades ago, the village of 2,500 people was like most others, mired in poverty with 33 liquor dens boosting the illicit trade. Water scarcity meant little farming and with no other source of livelihood, the per capita income was just ₹ 271.

Hazare, a soldier who took voluntary retirement, returned to the village and began to transform it. The village's Yadavbaba temple became the focal point of his agitations. He donated ₹ 3,000 for its renovation. He made the fellow villagers take an oath. They swore to his five commandments: prohibition, family planning, voluntary labour and a ban on open grazing and on felling trees. Voluntary labour was necessary to ensure minimum dependence on the government for dole. As expected, Hazare ran into opposition, especially when he insisted on prohibition.

A village youth Datta Awari (27) said the liquor den owners threatened him with dire consequences. Anna stood up to them. 'Today we are reaping the benefit of listening to Anna. For us, he is nothing short of God,' he said.

He targeted open grazing next by imposing a complete ban and insisted on stall-feeding of cattle. The village opted out of cultivating water-intensive crops such as sugar cane and instead sowed pulses, oilseeds and cash crops, which needed less water.

'Jowar and onions grown in our village are now sold outside. Anna started a water recycling project last year. Water is lifted from the check dam in the village, treated and recycled,' Awari said.

The village now has a bank run by women where every villager donates one sack of grain every year. 'The grain is stored properly and auctioned to raise funds whenever the village needs money for any development work. Those who have left the village and settled elsewhere, send money every year for development,' Awari said.

The village dairy has a milk bank that operates like the grain bank. When well water became available for irrigation, the villagers formed cooperative societies that brought more land under cultivation. It spiralled into developments such as double cropping, change of farming system, vegetable cultivation and dairy farming. All this brought about political change too. All elections to local bodies are now held through consensus.

There were other spillover effects. A new system of sharing of labour grew and people volunteered to work on others' land. This way, the landless labourers gained employment. Today, Ralegan Siddhi's residents plan to buy land from adjoining villages.

(Source: *The Times of India*, 10 April 2011, New Delhi, p. 14.)

14

Globalization and Social Development in the Context of New Economic Policy in India

Bhimasen Hantal

Today, the world economy is marching towards very different path, by encompassing almost all the nations of the world into its fold and through the process of uniform policies for all nations. This new path popularly known as the path of globalization is indeed different from earlier economy, the international economy, which was restricted to economic activities between few nations, mostly through bilateral approach and in some cases through multilateral approach, and the concerned governments were playing active role in designing their economic policies in relation to international economy. On the contrary, in globalization, the policies of economic activities are designed by the world body, which claims to represent all member nations and asks all nations to comply with such uniform policies through structural adjustment process of their respective domestic economies.

'Globalization, according to Hamdani, is "triggering a process of systemic convergence in which all governments face pressures to pursue more or less similar policies to enhance their national (or regional) competitiveness, vis-à-vis other countries, as location for international production", *marketing and other competitive economic activities*' (Hamdani, 1997: 3). The text in italic are not quoted but added by the author of this paper.

The recent economic developments in the world in the form of stimulation to liberalization and privatization of economy and other activities related to it or even otherwise are regarded as globalization. Various scholars have defined globalization in different ways. More systematic definition may be that of Lewis's. According to him,

> Globalization refers to the multiplicity of linkages and interconnections between the states and societies which make up the present world system. It describes the process by which events, decisions and activities of one

part of the world come to have significant consequences for individuals and communities in quite distant parts of the globe.

Globalization has two distinct phenomena: scope (or stretching) and intensity (or deepening). On the one hand, it defines a set of processes which embrace most of the globe or which operate worldwide; the concept, therefore, has a spatial connotation... On the other hand, it also implies an intensification of the levels of interaction, inter-connectedness (or inter-dependence) between the states and societies which constitute the world community; accordingly, alongside the stretching goes a deepening of global processes (McGrew, 1992: 23).

Similarly,

> Economic globalization is a process towards the widening of the extent and form of cross-border transactions, and of the deepening of the economic inter-dependence between the actions of globalizing entities – be they private or public institutions or governments – located in one country, and those of related or independent entities located in other countries (Dunning, 1997: 13).

Dunning also distinguished between the two forms of globalization: *shallowest* and *deepest*. The shallowest form of globalization is where an economic entity in one country engages in arm's length trade in a single product with another economic entity in other country. By contrast, the deepest form of globalization, most easily distinguished from other forms of internationalization, is where an economic entity transacts with a large number of other economic entities throughout the world; where it does so across a network of value-added chains; where these exchanges are highly coordinated to serve the worldwide interests of globalizing entity; and where they consist of a myriad of different kinds or forms of transactions.

The structure of world economy is very different today than it was even a generation ago. Dunning emphasizes, in particular, three features: (i) the significance (and scope) of all kinds of cross-border transactions has greatly increased; (ii) the value of the foreign production of firms, that is production financed by foreign direct investment (FDI) and that arising from cross-border strategies alliances – both of which are deeper forms of internationalization than that of arm's length trade, now considerably exceeds that of trade; and (iii) there are a variety of signs that the major institutional players are changing their ways of thinking and mode of operation, and are adopting a more systematic approach to their behaviours and activities (ibid.: 14).

The pace and pattern of globalization has been very uneven among firms, sectors and countries. Moreover, although some markets, for example, financial markets, are largely globalized, others, for example, those for technology and most kinds of labour, still remain national or regional. Some scholars have agreed that the term 'regionalization' better describes the current stage of development. Certainly, intra-regional production and transition of all kinds in Europe, America and Asia have risen faster than inter-regional transactions. Certain parts of the world, notably Sub-Saharan Africa, have been relatively unaffected. But like ripples in a pond, regionalization may spread outwards. Indeed with growth rates in advanced countries slipping, inter-national transactions involving developing countries have risen faster in recent years than those internal to the Triad countries (ibid.: 14–15).

Another aspect that needs mention is that most of the authors confined their scope of the globalization to economic areas leaving other interrelated areas such as global politics, diplomacy, culture, information and communications technology, scientific collaborations, environmental treaties, issues of human rights, etc.. Though these aspects have been the areas of concern and discussion of the intellectuals and the statesmen since the end of the Second World War so as the international trade in the backdrop of the General Agreement on Tariffs and Trade (GATT), recently these issues have been affecting the globe much more prominently like that of recent form of economic than ever before. Whether the nuclear issues of Iran or Korean terrorism, the recent terror strikes at the World Trade Centre or Mumbai, global warming, AIDS and malnutrition of Africa and South Asia, sport or cultural event, etc. concern more to the people of every part of the Globe like that of Global recession, American slowdown, rise/fall of oil prices, inflations, etc. than ever before. Hence, the process of globalization has embraced all other interrelated aspects under its belt despite confining itself to pure economic aspect alone. Professor Singh's narration of identity and culture in this context needs, therefore, special reference in which he has beautifully crafted the relationship between individual identity, national culture and globalization and their influences on each other (Singh, 2000). One should give serious thought to the ongoing sociological fact that although influentials of East are emulating the West, there is also reverse process inform of adhering to eastern values and culture by the West is occurring. It is more pronounced in recent times. Can't we say, therefore, that this is due globalization?

Issues of Poverty, Education and Employment

People of the world are divided with respect to various lifestyles and life chances. It is usually the people of the Third World whose life chances are not satisfactory, hence their life styles too. Among the important determinants of life chances are the poverty, education, health and employment. These factors are interlinked to each other and cause the cumulative addition of their misery.

In early international economic order, the social issues such as poverty were not highlighted much by the world leaders because they mainly emphasized on the economic relationship between the so-called North and South. But in the 1980s, it started touching the heart of intellectuals/leaders. For example, Ian Fronk says:

> Fifteen years ago I considered the aim of poverty reduction quite independently from the issue of a New International Economic Order, because I considered poverty as much more related to domestic power structures than to change in international economic power relations. During the 1980s we experienced that the link between international structures and domestic poverty is quite close. There is close indirect relation, because domestic poverty is related to the economic fate of a nation which itself partly depends on the international environment. There is also a close direct relation between national poverty and international structures, because the character and direction of national

> adjustment to changing exogenous developments is affecting the poor much more than other social classes. This is true both when adjustment is imposed by external institutions, and when the path of adjustment is deliberately chosen because there is no alternative. (Fronk, 1994: 230)

At the beginning of the 1990s, the analysis can carry even further. The changing character of today's world is considered not only with merely technological and economic globalization reasons but also with political and other sociopolitical reasons, especially after various events such as Gulf War, and therefore 'poverty' can be well discussed only with reference to the global order issues. Poverty and conflict are very much related, and there is no development conflict without international dimensions. One of the basic agenda of the new world order started in 1990s in form of globalization was human resources development especially providing food, shelter, education, health, good environment to the people all over the world. The purpose of the present work is mainly to evaluate the globalization of economy pertaining to the social justice.

The United Nations Development Programme (UNDP) released its Poverty Report 2000 on April 2000. According to it, attempts to wipe out poverty around the world are often 'hot and miss' on the part of the donor and then badly handled, planned or organized by the government using the funds. Moreover, foreign assistance is channelled into specific prospects at the whim of donors rather than having governments integrate such programmes into a larger strategy. Despite criticizing rich nations for releasing decreasing amounts of the aid, the report puts much of the blame on inept, corrupt or indifferent isolated programmes on the part of the receiving governments. Aid is isolated into one ministry at the national level and often not coordinated at all with local groups. The report was equally critical to undemocratic and authorizations political regime on the one hand and to the unresponsive central bureaucracy on the other hand.

According to report, 'Until countries set targets to measure progress it is difficult to believe that they are mounting a concerted campaign to address poverty.'

The Word Bank released its World Development Report, 2000–01: Attacking Poverty, in September 2003. The central message of the report is that poverty is multidimensional and not merely an expression of inadequate earnings as earlier understood. Poverty can mean not only low incomes and low consumptions but also lack of education and poor health and nutrition. Further, the report expands the definition of poverty to include powerlessness, voicelessness, vulnerability and fear. Giving statistics on world poverty, the report says that at a time of unprecedented wealth for many countries, 2.8 billion people – almost half the world population – live in less than $2 a day. According to the report of these people, 1.2 billion live on the very margins of life, on less than $1 a day – a poverty line adopted by the World Bank. In high-income countries, fewer than one child in 100 die before reaching five years of age. On the other hand, in the poorest countries, the number is five times higher. In well-off countries, fewer than 5 per cent of children under the age of five are malnourished, whereas in poorer countries as many as 50 per cent of the children suffer from eating too little food. According to the report, this destination persists even though human conditions have improved more in the past century than in the rest of the century. Global wealth, global connections and technological capabilities have never been greater. But the distribution of these gains is extraordinarily unequal. The average income in the richest 20 countries is 37 times the average in the poorest 20 – a gap that has doubled in the past 40 years.

Progress in poverty reduction has varied widely across the region. In East-Asia, the number of people living on less than $1 a day fell from around 420 million in 1987 to around 280 million in 1998. But in Sub-Saharan Africa, South Asia and Latin America, the number of poor people have been rising steadily. In the countries of Eastern and Central Asia in transition to market economies, the number of people living in poverty has been 20 fold. Within countries too, poverty rates vary enormously. In some African countries, infant mortality rates are much lower among politically power ethnic groups. In Latin America, indigenous groups have far less schooling than non-indigenous groups. In South Asia, women have only about half as many years of education as men, and middle-school enrolment rates for girls are only two-third that of boys.

According to the report, major reductions in poverty are possible, but achieving these will require a more comprehensive approach that directly addresses the needs of poor people in three important areas:

(i) *Opportunity*: expanding economic opportunities for poor people by stimulating economic growth, making market works better for poor people and working for their inclusion, particularly by building up their assets such as land and education.
(ii) *Empowerment*: strengthening the ability of poor people to shape decisions that affect their lives and removing discrimination based on gender, race, ethnicity and social status.
(iii) *Security*: reducing poor people's vulnerability to sickness, economic shocks, crop failure, unemployment, natural disasters and violence, and helping them cope when such misfortune occur.

The report says that action at national and local levels will often not be enough for rapid poverty reduction. There are many areas that require international action – especially by high-income countries – to improve the prospects for poor countries and their people. An increased focus on debt relief and making development aid more effective are part of the story. Equally important are actions in other areas such as expanding the areas to developed country markets, promoting the public goods that benefit poor people such as vaccines for tropical diseases and agricultural research, combating HIV/AIDS, enhancing global financial stability, closing of the digital and knowledge divide, enabling the participation of poor countries in international discussions and fostering global peace, the report says:

> It has also been observed that the global economy especially after 1990s is not contributing towards growth of employment rather helping growing unemployment worldwide. Though the problem of unemployment has been

major issues for the last 100 years (approximately) all over the world, it was attracted the attention of various governments and forums after 1950s (Commonwealth Secretariat, 1990). The issue of unemployment first figured in a substantive manner at the 1981 meeting of Heads of Government in Melbourne. Their decision at that meeting that Commonwealth Ministers of employment/labour should have regular meetings reflected the fact that tackling unemployment had by then become a preoccupation of governments. Concern over persistent high unemployment was voiced at all meetings of Ministers of Employment/Labour from their inception, and it was on their recommendation that Heads of Government in 1985 decided that an expert group should study youth unemployment. (ibid.: 212–27)

The experts considered that the significantly higher unemployment rates for the youth could be explained partly in terms of the advantages of accumulated knowledge and experience which those who had held jobs over those joining the labour market. The disadvantage of the new comer was considerably increasing where the work was skilled and experience counted. In the developed countries, especially, the skill levels demanded of young people were rising as employment was growing largely in the service sector, particularly in countries making intensive use of information technology, considerable investment in education or vocational training were required. In developing countries, the failure of wage and non-labour costs to adjust sufficiently to reflect the relative disadvantages – actual or perceived, of employing youth was seen as a further contributing factor. In the developing countries, the impact of high population growth was seen as a crucial problem. The very high number entering the labour market each year were likely to exceed the increase in jobs generated in these condition. In addition, expansion in the number of young people being educated led to rising aspirations as well as to mismatch, both between skills and work opportunities and between the location of those possessing the skills and the most favoured employment opportunities (ibid.: 217).

Recently, after the policy of liberalization, the debate has been restarted pertaining to its impact on employment. Increased trade linkage, mobile capital and technological changes are raising new questions over the attainment of old employment objectives. Debates in such countries on insecurity of work and unemployment of unskilled workers find strong echoes in recent evidence from some developing and transition countries (Diwan and Walton, 1997: 1–15). The impact of liberalization on skilled–unskilled wage differential and other related problems are highlighted by various scholars (Pissarides, 1997: 16–32; Wood, 1997: 33–58).

According to the report titled 'Income Security and Social Production in a Changing World' on 20 June 2000 in Geneva (ILO, 2000), 75 per cent of the 150 million unemployed people around the world lack any insurance protection, whereas the vast majority of the populations in many developing countries including the informal sector wage earners and self-employed persons have no social protection whatever. The International Labour Organisation (ILO) insists that the major focus must be on the extension of coverage to these workers because societies that do not pay enough attention to security, particularly of their weaker members, eventually suffer destructive black cash.

It also points out that even the world's richest member in Europe and North America has reduced protection provided by unemployment insurance in the 1990s. However, of all ILO member countries, the report identifies Austria, Belgium, Denmark, Finland, Germany, Ireland, Luxembourg, the Netherlands, Norway, Portugal, Spain, Sweden and Switzerland as providers of the 'most generous unemployment protection system'.

According to the report, millions of people in the informal sector earn very low incomes and have an extremely lowered capacity to contribute to social protection schemes. The report highlights the situation of rural and urban informal workers in developing countries – including 750–900 million underemployed workers – for whom hardly any unemployment protection exists. The ILO also makes various proposals to extend social protection that now covers less than half of the world population. The three main options towards meeting the global include (i) extension of existing programmes, (ii) creation of new programmes that target informal sector workers and (iii) the development of tax-financed social benefit systems.

Another ILO global report titled 'Your Voice at Work', released in May 2000, highlighted the crucial role of freedom of association and the effective right to collective bargaining in achieving decent work for all in today's world. According to the report, the increasing globalization has led to significant representation gap in the world of work, which is not acceptable because 'achieving the ILO's goal of decent work for all women and men in condition of freedom, equity, security and human dignity is possible only if they have a say in what this means for them'.

The Commission on Nutrition Challenge of the 21st Century, a panel of international experts set up by the United Nations Organisation (UNO), released a report on 20 March 2000, warning that 1 billion children will be permanently handicapped over the next 20 years if the world does not adopt a new approach to tackle malnutrition. The report titled *Ending Malnutrition by 2020* said, in a world of plenty, malnutrition was 'immoral'. Malnutrition is most acute in North Africa, Sub-Saharan Africa and South Asia. Over half of the children in Bangladesh and South India are growing inadequately because of malnutrition.

The United Nations Children's Fund (UNICEF)'s annual global publication – *Progress of Nations* (PoNs) was released in July 2000, which highlighted that India held the 'highest number of polio cases, HIV/AIDS cases, malnourished children and child labours in the world'.

The Human Development Report (HDR) 2000 released by the United Nations Development Programme (UNDP) in mid-2000 focused on the theme *human right and human development for freedom and solidarity*. The report says that there are new threats to human freedoms in the 21st century-conflicts within national boarders, economic and political transitions, global inequalities and marginalization of poor countries and poor people, etc., and calls for bold new approaches to tackle the threats. Similarly, the World Bank released the World Development Indicators 2000 (WDI), an annual statistical portrait of people and the state of their world on April 2000, and according to the report, a sixth of the world's population, primarily the people of North America, Europe and

Japan, received nearly 80 per cent of the world income, an average of $70 per day, in 1998. At the same time, 57 per cent of the world's population in 63 poorest countries received only 6 per cent of the world income, an average of less than $2 per day. The Bank defines extreme poverty as an income not exceeding $1 a day. It estimates that 1.2 billion people, about 20 per cent of the total world population, fit into that group.

As stated earlier, the world economic order did not give much importance to human face until recently. And the recent trend of global competition on economic activities also put a question mark on social development. However, it has become a concern of international leaders. The United Nation's Department for Policy Coordination and Social Development, mandated by the UN General Assembly, organized first ever World summit for Social Development on March 1995 at Copenhagen (Denmark). The summit aimed at making social development a major priority for the international community by means of global cooperation to eradicate poverty, generate employment and promote social integration. Negotiations among the participating countries resulted in a two-part agreement that was adapted by consensus by over 180 countries. The two parts of the agreement were the Copenhagen Declaration and the Programme for Action.

The non-binding Copenhagen Declaration contained a list of 10 specific commitments that the governments agreed to. The highlights of the declaration are as follows: (i) Rich nations of the world are urged to spend 0.7 per cent of their gross national product (GNP) on foreign aid. Incidentally, only four countries, Norway, Sweden, Denmark and Holland fulfil this target at the time. (ii) A '20–20' 'compact' was approved under which the donor nations agreed to channelize 20 per cent of their foreign aid towards basic social programmes and recipient nations agreed to earmark 20 per cent of their nationals budgets for such programmes. The 'compact' aims at mobilizing the additional spending 30–40 billion dollars needed to achieve the basic needs of every human being. The 'compact' was to be a bilateral option and not an international requirement. The '20–20' idea was evolved by Mahbul-ul-Haq, the brain behind the HDR. (iii) Rich nations were asked to cancel the debts of poor countries. (iv) Improvement in health care, sanitation, food production and literacy especially among women was urged so as to lower the rate of birth.

The word summit also adopted a five-chapter programmes of action, for achieving social development objectives. The recommendation included measures to eradicate poverty, social integration and reduce unemployment. However, the recommendation did not envisage any clear plan. The solution to the problems needed greater initiative on the part of developed nation, which was lacking. Thus, the summit was not much successful.

A large number of people are illiterate and uneducated in the world. The worst picture is seen in Asia (especially South Asia) and Africa. The more severe is the problem of marginalized sections such as women, tribe and other of lower stratum. Hence, international leaders also gave attention on this issue. The World Conference on Education for All, held in 1990 in Jomtien, Thailand, marked a joint commitment by 155 nations and the UNO to universalize basic education and eradicate illiteracy. The Jomtien Framework for Action articulated an expanded vision of basic education to include the following six dimensions: (i) expansion of early childhood care and developmental activities, especially for poor, disadvantaged and disabled children; (ii) universal access to and completion of primary education by the year 2000; (iii) improvement of learning achievements; (iv) reduction of the adult illiteracy rate by one of its 1990 level by the year 2000, with sufficient emphasis on female literacy; (v) expansion of basic education and training in other essential skills required by youth and adults; and (vi) increased acquisition by individuals and families of the knowledge, skill and values required for better living and sound and sustainable developments, made available through all education channels including the mass media, other forms of modern and traditional communications and social action.

The largest education conference of the past decade – the World Education Forum – was held at Dakar in Senegal from 26 to 28 April 2000. The conference reviewed the extent to which the national commitments made at the 1990 world conference education for all, held in Jomtien, Thailand, in report of *provision of education for all* (EPA), by the year 2000, have been fulfilled, and discussed strategies for the future.

The Dakar Framework of Action was adopted by all the 182 of the world's 193 countries that attended the forum. It recognizes the right to education as fundamental human right. It reaffirms the commitment to the expanded vision of education as articulated at Jomtien Conference. It calls for renewed action to ensure that every child, youth and adult should receive education by 2015. Apart from general commitment, in the face of the wider change in the past decade – the political, economic and social shifts in Eastern and Central Europe, the rapid development of information technology and the Internet, the growth of poverty and increasing debt, the growth of inequalities with the swift advance of economic and cultural globalization – some thrust areas have been identified.

The Dakar Framework focuses attention on the excluded and marginal groups, countries and regions. South Asia, Sub-Saharan Africa and countries in conflict have been mentioned as priority areas. UNO Secretary-General Kofi Annan formally launched a 10-year Girls' Initiative – on *educational intervention for girls* – to be coordinated by UNICEF. In his opening speech, he listed the excluded groups, the poor, minority, and ethnic groups, the disabled, refugees, street and working children, to name a few and called for careful targeting to ensure access to these groups.

The Director-General of UNESCO, Koichiro Matsuura, made a resounding appeal in favour of education that is authentic, accessible to all without exclusion or discrimination, modern and universally affordable. He identified some major failures and pointed out that in at least six respects, we have stayed from the original objectives: (i) Formal schooling has been the main preoccupation, which entailed neglect of non-formal avenues of learning; (ii) many countries have been slow in redefining their educational needs; (iii) inequalities within educational systems have been increasing, and this resulted in the marginalization of the poor, minority groups and people with special learning needs; (iv) early childhood education has not made much progress and tilts in favour of the better-off urban population; (v) the digital divide has marginalized the poorest social sectors even further; and (vi) basic education is chronically underfinanced by the government and the donor community.

The commitment to free and compulsory primary education of good quality emerged as the second major thrust area in Dakar. A major gain of Dakar was the commitment that no country with a noble plan for education would be allowed to fail for want of resources. Education in the past decade was under-financed by most countries and the donor community. One of the reasons why education did not get the necessary status in the past decade was the lack of structures and mechanism to achieve the EFA goals post-Jomtien. At Dakar, the focus of EFA structures shifted from the international to the national level. National EFA plan are to be prepared by countries latest by 2002. Addressing all six EFA goals, these would be developed by national government in consultation with broad-based alliance of civil society groups. In fact, a major gain of Dakar was the emergence of groups–trade union and non-governmental organizations (NGOs) at national and international levels under the banner of the Global Campaign for Education. However, what is important is the implementation of action programmes in letter and spirit. In other words, past trend put a question mark about its probability of education for all by 2015.

In sum, it is good that the global leaders started action in various problems such as poverty, unemployment and illiteracy, but how far the social sectors would withstand the acute competition posed by the globalization of economy is yet to be seen.

The New Economic Policy and Social Justice in India: Critical Evaluations

In this section, evaluation of the new economic policy and social justice in India is being done under various sub-headings as follows.

Poverty

Perhaps, it cannot be incorrect to define India as the land of poverty, illiteracy and inequality as millions of people are without access to basic necessities of life. It is pathetic to note that despite poverty line being measured only on the basis of calorie requirement, such a huge numbers are under the clutch of below poverty line (BPL). The calorie requirements are fixed at 2,400 kcal per capita for urban India and 2,100 kcal per capita for urban India, respectively.

The poverty lines for the year 1993–94 are ₹ 229 and ₹ 264 per capita per month for rural and urban areas, respectively. However, ₹ 228.9 and ₹ 264.1 in 1993–94 no longer correspond to the expenditure norms corresponding to 2,400 kcal and 2,100 kcal as per the definition of poverty line. The price of consumption has been changed significantly. In food items, its cost is much higher than that of non-food items. Second, due to penetration of urban businessman or outsiders into the poor locals, the price of basic essential items has been increased greatly. Third, because of the crises of availability of money, the rural poor either sell themselves partly or fully to their respective dominant persons or sell their livelihood to them and migrate to other parts, especially into urban belts for the sake of employment as labours. Fourth, the relative prices of the basic goods have been increased more than proportionately. For instance, the conditions of housing and transport in urban areas have been deteriorated to the extent of forcing people to live away from their places of work and to spend on transport; similarly, the rural labour force has to migrate away from their village in order to get work.

In India, poverty is measured only in term of the calories intake for survival. It does not include other 'essential expenditures' of human being, that is, cloth, shelter, health and medicine. It does not go to see other 'necessary expenditures' of human being, that is, education, housing, healthy food, etc. It does not include expenditures on 'necessary of efficiency of life', that is, recreational, sports and other miscellaneous expenditure for growing children.

Marx was perhaps right when he said that in capitalist world, the human being would be equated with machine (Marx, 1844). He would be provided with wages for survival as if the fuel was provided to machine for its survival.

Marx contention may not be fully true in democratic – industrial nations where the quality of opportunity is granted and where there is much concern about relative deprivation rather than the absolute deprivation; but in India where there is mass poverty and inequality, Max viewpoint cannot be ignored. Here, in India a man is not even provided with 'basic necessities of life' for his survival. He cannot think of 'necessary expenditures' as his capability is sufficient even to the extent of filling up 'essential expenditures' for survival. It is pathetic to note that even though the 'essential expenditures' of the existence is not fully covered while measuring the poverty line by the government, millions of people in India are under the clutches of poverty line.

According to the Planning Commission, people under the BPL were reduced from 25.49 per cent in 1987 to 18.96 per cent in 1993–94 (Economic Survey, 1995–96: 169). However, as per modified expert group methodology, the Planning Commission in its Ninth Five-Year Plan states the figure of BPL as 38.9 per cent for 1987–88 and 36 per cent for 1993–94 (Ninth Five Year Plan: 29). Hence, in contrast to its previous claim of reduction poverty to 19 per cent in 1993–94, the Planning Commission agreed that the figure was in fact double the previous that is 36 per cent in 1993–94.

The data indicate that despite non-inclusion of the all 'essential', 'necessary' and 'efficiency' expenditures, more than 36 crores Indian are under the BPL. Therefore, if such expenditures were included, perhaps more than 75 crores Indian would have been trapped under the poverty line. This is primarily due to the growing inequalities of wealth and income and concentration of such in the hand of few elites. For example, top 10 per cent of rural Indian owned 51 per cent of assets, whereas bottom 10 per cent population of it owned only 0.1 per cent in 1971 (Sixth Five-Year Plan: 8). The figures of such inequality are still persistent in country.

Thus, most of the wealth is being owned by a few sections of society, making the rest empty stomach. The worst of the worse sufferers in India are the people who belong to the SCs, STs and MBCs of OBCs. They constitute in the lower ladder not only in terms of caste system but also in terms of class.

Table 14.1 *Comparative study showing the BPL in percentage*

Year	Total population	SCs	STs
1977–78	45.2	64.6	72.4
1983–84	40.4	55.1	58.4
1987–88	33.4	44.7	52.6

Source: Eighth Five-Year Plan, Planning Commission, Government of India, pp. 419–20.

In other words, the position of caste also in most cases signifies the position of class. Hence, the wide gap between these lower ranked people in comparison with others is evident from Table 14.1.

The poverty line of the total population also includes the SCs and STs; and therefore when the SCs and STs are excluded from such, the poverty line becomes around 22 per cent. This figure also does include other backward classes who as per government report comprise around 52 per cent of the total population. Thus, the poverty line ratio of SCs, STs and OBCs is deducted from the general poverty line ratio; it will significantly become thinner. In other words, it can be stated that the BPL comprises mostly the SCs, STs and OBCs, but some cases existing at individual levels among other sections of society cannot be ruled out. The new economic policy that has adversely affected the poorer has been reported form various studies (Gupta, 1994; Tendulkar and Jain, 1995; Sen, 1996).

As per the compilation of data by S.P. Gupta and Abhijit Sen and C.P. Chandrashekhar from 1987–88 to 1990–91 the year before the reform, the poverty ratio declined from 39.3 per cent to 35.5 per cent. But in the post-reform era, the poverty estimate rose considerably to 40.69 per cent in 1992 (Gupta, 1994; Chandrashekhar and Sen, 1996). By analysing two alternative poverty ratios given by Tendulkar and Jain (1995), Dev called the 'lower end of poverty ratio as the ratio for ultra-poor or ultra-poverty'. According to Dev, the ultra-poverty to total poverty was declining at faster pace till the new economic reform, but the ratio increased again during the 18 months of the reform period (Dev, 1995).

It is known that the total consumption of a person or household consists of both private and social consumption. Tendulkar and Jain's concern in their paper was mainly on private consumption (Tendulkar and Jain, 1995). It is difficult to get information of social consumption at the household level. However, many studies have shown that social sector expenditure declined considerably during the first few years of reform period (Tulsidhar, 1993; Prabhu, 1994; Guhan, 1995; Gupta, 1995). These studies have shown that expenditure on health and education and other sectors have declined, and it would affect the human development indicators. Decline in expenditure on important sectors such as preventive health care was also noticed.

According to Sen, the structural adjustment acts adversely on the poor because of the policy-induced rise in the relative price of food and contractionary stabilization policies to reduce inflation will lead to contracting non-agricultural employment and falling wages in the organized sector (Sen, 1996; 1997). Unni has also described the impact of structural adjustment on poor through review of literatures in his article (Unni, 1998). Martin Ravallion concludes 'that policy reforms which entail a sustained increase in food prices are a threat to India's poor in the longer term' (Ravallion, 1998: 34). In another article, Ravallion and Datt have studied that though the output growth in the primary sectors reduced poverty in both rural and urban areas, the secondary sector growth did not reduce poverty in either (Ravallion and Datt, 1996).

Jay Mehta has criticized Sukhatme's assertion that in India, daily calorie intake be reduced to 1,800 kcal and lamented on the data released by 48th round of the National Service Scheme or NSS (NSS 48th Round 1994) that only 97.3 per cent in urban and 92.3 per cent were getting two-square meals a day in the year 1992 (Mehta, 1982; 1995). Mehta has narrated the poverty-related death and other miseries from various corners of India such as Maharashtra, Odisha, etc., although the reform was in a full swing (Mehta, 1995).

The recent poverty-related death in various parts of Odisha especially from Kashipur – where to satisfy hunger the poor had to eat poisonous mango kernel, should be an eye opener to those who profess that the economic growth through new economic policy only would alleviate poverty. Until and unless the institutional structure prevailing in the social order is re-corrected through rigorous socio-legal reform, mere growth of the economy is not going to do justice to the poor. Because of the rigidity of structure and divergence inequality existed in the country, the new economic policy would rather make the poor more poorer and the rich more richer and consequently widen the rich–poor gap.

The global economic order, as per the data spelled out by various studies notably by the World Bank, does not bridge the gap between the rich and poor countries rather than widening it.

> The average per capita income of the poorest and middle thirds of all countries has lost ground steadily over the last several decades compared with the average income of the richest third. Average per capita GDP of the middle third has dropped from 12.5 to 11.4 percent of the richest third and that of the poorer third form 3.1 to 1.9 percent. In fact, rich countries have been growing faster than poor countries since Industrial Revolution in the mid 19th century. A recent estimate suggests that the ratio of per capita income between the richest and the poorest countries increased six fold between 1870 and 1985. (World Development Report, 1999/2000: 14)

According to World Development Indicators 1998, the number of poor people has risen worldwide; and in some regions, the proportion of poor has also increased (World Development Indicators, 1998). By citing the data of World Development Indicators 1998, the World Development Report 1999/2000 brought out figures of people under poverty line – that is, those living on less that $1 per day (World Development Report, 1999/2000: 24–26).

According to such report, poor people have slightly declined from 464 million to 446 million from 1987 to 1993 in East Asia and pacific region. But during such period, the poor has risen in other parts of the world: from 2 million to 15 million in Europe and Central Asia; from 91 million to 110 million in Latin America and the Caribbean; from 10 million to 11 million in middle East and North Africa; from 480 million to 515 million in south Asia; and from 180 million to 219 million in sub-Saharan Africa.

Percentagewise, it declined marginally from 28.8 per cent to 26 per cent in East Asia and Pacific; from 4.7 per cent to 4.1 per cent in Middle East and North Africa; and from 45.4 per cent to 43.1 per cent in South Asia. However, poverty increased from 0.6 per cent to 3.5 per cent in Europe and central Asia; from 22 per cent to 23.5 per cent in Latin America and the Caribbean and from 38.5 per cent to 39.1 per cent in 846 Saharan Africa. Similarly, the document also reported the decline of life expectancy from some countries such as Russian federation, Kazakhstan, Zimbabwe, Uganda, Rwanda and Zambia from 1980 to 1997 (ibid.: 26).

The widening of economic disparities and climate change are two serious factors impending progress towards the UN Millennium Development Goals, as has been noted by the UN Millennium Development Goals Report 2007, released on 2 July 2007 at New Delhi. According to it, almost 30 per cent of population of South Asia lead life with a dollar per day. There are disparities within the countries – rural–urban, women and children and various groups. There is low progress in child nutrition, and highest number of maternal deaths occurs in South Asia and Sub-Sahara Africa. The World Development Indicators of the World Bank released in April 2007 states that excluding China, there has not been any improvement as the total people under poverty rose from 855 million in 1981 to 857 million in 2004. However, if China is included, people in extreme poverty have fallen from 1.489 billion in 1981 to 986 million in 2004. In Latin America and Sub-Saharan Africa, the people under extreme poverty at present are more than at the start of the 1980s. In fact, the extreme poverty has risen by 60 million in Sub-Saharan Africa.

According to World Institute for Development Economic Research of the United Nations, richest 1 per cent of the globe owns 40 per cent of the global wealth, and they belong to United States, Europe and Japan. China is in the middle and bottom third occupied by India, Africa and low-income Asian countries. Richest 10 per cent of adults own 85 per cent of the global asset, whereas 50 per cent of global adult own only 1 per cent of global wealth. The UK-based Legatum Institute of Global Development in its report – Global Prosperity Index released in 2007 ranks India 46th in a list of 50 countries. In other words, India fairs very poorly. In various World Social Forums such as the recent one held on 23 January 2007, in Nairobi, Kenya, voiced about the crippling conditions of the poor countries and the widening disparities among the nations on socio-economic fronts. The Food and Agriculture Organisation (FAO) in its review of the state of food and agriculture in November 2006 reiterated that hunger and poverty continue to be daunting problems in the world. According to it, around 854 million people of the world are chronically under-nourished out of which 820 millions are in under-developing countries. India accounts for the largest number of 212 millions followed by Sub-Saharan Africa with 206 millions and the China at distance of 150 millions.

The Annual Trends in Unemployment, report of International Labour Organisation (ILO), released in January 2007 states that there are all-time high of 195.2 millions number of unemployed in the world. In 2006, global unemployment rate stood at 6.3 per cent, a slight drop of 0.1 per cent over the previous year. In another report of ILO titled Labour and Social Trend in Asia and the Pacific 2006: Towards Decent Work, brought out in August 2006, it has warned that the economic growth had failed in employment generation and better wages. Young adult, both man and woman of age between 15 and 24 years are bearing brunt with 11.3 per cent. The unemployment rate is more among the female than the male counterparts. The UNICEF Report on Lack of Basic Sanitation and Drinking Water released on 28 September 2006 has stated that approximately 2.6 billion people of the world especially Africa and Asia lack access to basic sanitation, increase the risk of diarrhoea and other disease that are fatal to children. Various other reports of the UNO on health, education, gender, children, etc., have highlighted that there are substantially large number of people of the world without access to education, under-deteriorated health conditions, other socio-economic discriminations, sociocultural exploitation, child abuse, gender discrimination, disparities, etc.

Two conclusions can be drawn from the prevailing inequality and poverty in the world: First, the increasing gap between rich and poor countries indicates that the global policy designed is to protect mainly the vested interest of rich countries. To strengthen and maintain their economic and political supremacy, the rich countries have adhered to unequal, unfair and discriminatory policy. The poor countries despite knowing such political hypocrisy are integrated into global policy forum as they do not have other choice to survive. Moreover, there are some elite sections in poor countries too whom the present global policy suits for their own survival.

Second, the elite sections too have designed their domestic policy to protect, maintain and strengthen their own vested interests. Because of which they too adhere to the unequal, unfair and discriminatory policy, thereby never allowing the gap between the rich and the poor to be bridged. However, they enunciate various social package to poor like developed nations offer to poor nations, but they never implement such in letter and spirit or implement such through their self-style such as wrong identification and corruption, so that they achieve twin objectives: they retain the confidence of poor, on the one hand, and maintain the prevailing inequality of social system on the other hand.

One glaring example of implementation of development programme through wrong identification bought out by the Government of India itself is stated in Table 14.2. As per Table 14.2, only 1.14 per cent destitute group, 4.27 per cent very very poor, 12.95 per cent very poor and 24.68 per cent poor were benefited out of Jawahar Rojgar Yojana (JRY) in the year 1993. However, 56.96 per cent of people above the poverty line were the beneficiaries of such programme.

Table 14.2 *Percentage distribution of JRY workers by annual income: All India conument evaluation*

Group by annual income	Percentage
Destitute group (up to ₹ 2,265)	1.14
Very very poor (₹ 2,266–3,500)	4.27
Very poor (₹ 3,501–4,800)	12.95
Poor (₹ 4,801–6,400)	24.68
Above poverty (₹ 6,401 and above)	56.96

Source: Concument Evaluation of JRY (January through December 1993) a Report, Ministry of Rural Development, July 1993.

The poor implementation of programmes, politicization and interference of vested interests, corruption and prevalence of social rigidities are the main hurdles of socio-economic mobility of poor. According to the World Bank, social factors found to be associated with persistent poverty include very low-caste status, dependency relationship, vulnerability and risk adversity (A World Free of Poverty, 1998). Various scholars have also lamented the poor or wrong implementation of programme by the Government of India (Sethi, 1984; Jain, 1985; Nayak, 1995; Hantal, 1996; Samal, 1998).

On the period of reform, the World Bank's household surveys in India suggested that poverty reduction was particularly sluggish over the 1990s in India's rural areas, which contain more than 70 per cent of the poor. The picture is one of wide disparity in poverty across and within Indian states and of uneven poverty reduction. The report also found that the large poor states in the north and east, containing 40 per cent of India's population, have lagged in reducing poverty since the late 1970s. According to Sanjay Kathuria, a senior economist in the World Bank's New Delhi Office,

> Broadly speaking the reforms would be most effective to the extent they reduce the risk of macro economic instability, increase the access of the poor to human development, improve governance and reduce distortions and improve the demand for poor. Poorer states in particular will need to enact these reforms to overcome the initial lags and to accelerate development.

The World Bank's senior economic policy advisor James Hanson says if such reforms take root, then growth would accelerate to the 7.5 per cent and higher levels of mid-1990s. India would then have a real opportunity to reduce poverty substantially in the new millennium (A World Free of Poverty, 1998).

However, growth alone is not sufficient to reduce poverty; in fact, there are some countries whose growth is substantially below than India's, but have achieved higher social development. Hence, growth would automatically reduce the poverty as mere illusion as history has taught such lesson to us. The war against poverty should be started very vigorously and seriously rather than sitting in arm chair in anticipation of growth to reduce poverty. Impact of growth on poor has been vengefully stated by various scholars among other by Anand Teltumbde in his article 'Impact of new Economic reforms on dalits in India' (Teltumbde, 1996). The Government of India has recently defined the BPL with 13 new parameters such as landholding, type of dwelling, clothing, food security, hygiene, capacity for buying commodities, literacy, minimum wages earned by the household, means of livelihood, education of children, debt, migration and priority for assistance. According to the Government of India, the matter that was stayed by the Supreme Court has been vacated in early 2006. If the new parameters are to be taken into account, more number of people would be under the clutch of poverty.

More discussion on impact of new economic policy on poor would follow in subsequent pages. Below, the impact of new policy on education and literacy is highlighted.

Literacy and Education

Education is one of the vital sectors of human development. The need of modern education was felt not merely by the Britishers to rule India more conveniently but also by other then social reformers. The educated Indians headed by Mahatmaji led India's freedom struggle to attain freedom from foreign yokes.

Therefore, the importance of education to all of its people was felt after India got independence. Several provisions were laid down in the Constitution of India for educational development of people, the notable of which are articles 45 and 46. Article 45 states about free and compulsory education to all children till they attain the age of 14 years. According to Article 46, the educational and economic interests of SCs and STs would be protected by the state. Recently through 86th Constitutional Amendment, elementary education has been made fundamental right. As per the guidelines of the constitution, several programmes and schemes were formulated for educational progress in the country. Various schools, colleges, universities, technological and professional institution were set up.

Despite this, however, the educational development in the country was not satisfactory. As per 2001 census, only 65.38 per cent of India's total population were literate, and women's literacy rate was just 54.16 per cent; therefore, more than 37 crore Indians were still counted as illiterate. The case is very pathetic among population belonging to SCs and STs, particularly amongst the girls belonging to these community.

The educational development that has taken place in India so far has benefited few well-off sections, and left large sections of the poor mass illiterate. Thus, the large poor sections are still being alienated from the mainstream of educational system. The mass education in India was felt even during colonial era, that is, Woods Despatch 1854, Hunter Commission 1882, Sadler's Commission 1917, Religh Commission 1929, Sergent Plan 1942, etc. In post-independent India, the Kothari Commission Report of 1966–67 was regarded as landmark for mass education. But like colonial India, independent India too could not spread its education to the poor mass. Thus, social justice becomes only chant or slogan in India. In the ongoing battle of the various elite groups to retain their supremacy, the poor masses have always been sidelined from mainstream whether it is in the field of education, economy, polity and so on. Kiran Bhatty, in her articles, has accused poor quality of schooling and education, prevailing poverty, child labour, lack of parental motivation and lack of strong government policy for prevalence of ugly picture of illiteracy and un-educational development in the country (Bhatty, 1998).

However, before the new economic policy, their (poor sections) problems were to some extent taken into consideration by government at least at policy level. But in post-liberalization era, the exploitation is more, severe and dangerous. Now they are in the verge of complete alienation. The new policy of the government is trying for more and more privatization, and education is not escaped from such harsh policy. This is borne out of the fact that wherever the developmental expenditure by the states was 12.01 per cent in 1990–91, it fell sharply to 11.33 per cent in 1992–93. The growing impact can be seen in the higher education: its share shrinking from 11.47 to 6.7 per cent in the VIII plan with the consequence that Vice-Chancellors of university are being repeatedly told to look for the funds from industry and business (Raina, 1995: 83; Hantal, 1996: 126–27). Hence, education in India is in state of crises, and it is not wrong to state that it is in grave danger. This is because the poor sections cannot afford to have quality education.

The inequalities that characterize Indian society in general and the educational system in particular are getting further reinforced due to the post-1990 economic changes. Market forces are being allowed an enhanced role leading to the private sector taking on greater role in education. Using the experience of Asian countries, it may be stated that there is an inverse relationship exists between the deterioration in educational system and the policies of structural adjustments, except in those countries that have undergone vary rapid economic growth. It is anticipated, therefore, that primary school enrolments in India may be adversely affected as was the case in Pakistan and Bangladesh. Market forces are not pro-welfare and given a free hand, the educational institutions run by the private sector are more likely to the governed by the profit motive than by public or social good. This phenomenon is also taking place in China and is reminiscent of the development in our own country. The poor sections are more alienated from professional colleges of engineering and medical education (Shukla and Kaul, 1998).

Shotton argues that the period of structural changes in economy under the aegis of the International Monetary Fund (IMF) and the World Bank and the much publicized liberalization have only compounded difficulties for the ruling class in social services and education sector. He affirms that the thrust of the new stabilization and structural adjustment programme implies a combination of budget containment measures for the public education system, limited access to post primary public education and higher user fees for education at the secondary and tertiary levels; there is a fall in the government spending on buildings and resources at the primary levels from 15 per cent of pre-liberalization era to 2 per cent after it. The government seems to have little option but to follow the policy prescription of the IMF and the World Bank, which indicate the social costs of adjustment programme. Expenditure on the social service, poverty alleviation and rural development programme has been badly hit, resulting in a sharp rise in the cost of living (Shotton, 1998).

Various scholars have expressed their dissatisfaction over the new economic policy pertaining to education in general and children's development in particular. In a recent article, Paromita Shastri has shown the grim reality Indian children are facing. As part of evaluation of recent union budget with regard to child, she states: (i) Out of every ₹ 100 spent by the centre in the 1990s, only 60 paise has gone to children's education, 40 on their development and 20 on their health. The 2002–03 budget is much kinder; it hopes to spend about ₹ 1 on education, 34 paise on health and 45 paise on child development; (ii) every sixth girl dies due to gender bias; yet Balika Samridhi Yojana, the first scheme to incentivise her birth, died after three years; and (iii) about 75 million children are under-nourished. India's biggest aided child care plan, Integrated Child Development Service (ICDS) reaches only 20 million, at a mere 19 paise per child per day. The actual cost of reasonable child care is minimum of ₹ 15 per day per child or ₹ 200 crore per year. Over half of child health budget comes from foreign loans, which the government often fails to spend. We spend 1.5 per cent of GDP on education. Still, about half of the children are out of school. They are all potential child labour (Shastri, 2002: 54–55).

Despite the fact that the Kothari commission recommended 6 per cent of GDP for educational sector, it has never been implemented; about half of the recommended percentage, 3.6 per cent, is spent on education. Moreover, out of the total amount allotted for education, about 95 per cent goes into teachers' salaries and very little left for sensitive aspects of quality development, content and process.

Although education is in concurrent list, the union government's share in the total revenue expenditure by the union and the state was only 8 per cent. The plan outlay for education in 1995–96 increased by about 16 per cent (in current price) as compared to 1994–95. The fact was highlighted by the finance minister in his budget speech. He did not mention that the allocation under the non-plan category was reduced by 4.4 per cent, pushing down the overall increase to only about 8 per cent. Taking into account the 10 per cent inflation rate in 1994–95 and expecting low significant deviation in the trend in 1995–96, the increase in allocation in real term is very modest. The non-plan and the total allocation in 1995–96 are in fact much lower than the 1994–95. This makes 1995–96 the second consecutive year having registered a decline in total budget allocation for education. Similarly, 85 per cent of the total allocation for elementary education is accounted for by the three major programmes, that is, blackboard, non-formal education and teachers training. Most of the remaining 15 per cent of the allocation for elementary education relates to foreign-aided projects. A large part of the expenditure (about 80–100 per cent) of their projects is fully reimbursed by external aid organizations; the remaining part is mostly met by the state; this led many caution that the growth in public expenditure on elementary education is largely borrowed growth (Tilak, 1995).

In the case of secondary education, two-third of the total allocation in 1995–96 budget is captured by elite Novodaya and Kendriya Vidyalayas – 37 per cent and 29 per cent, respectively. The vocational education programme has not progressed satisfactorily at all – the allocation for vocational education has been reduced from ₹ 88.5 crores in 1994–95 to ₹ 82 crores in 1995–96 (ibid.).

The impact of reform on education is felt primarily on its initial stage and put a question mark on government's policy on national educational development in the country. It is evident from the fact that its expenditure to total expenditure was 1.44 in 1990–91, 1.44 in 1991–92, 1.33 in 1992–93, 1.38 in 1993–94 and again 1.38 in 1994–95. Thus, data prove that union's share in education has been too less. It is because of one of these reasons of government's discriminatory attitude for the mass education that the country continues to possess the dubious distinction of having the largest number of out of school children – 22 per cent of global total and adult illiterates – 30 per cent of the world's population (Observer, 1995).

India's allocation to education is much lesser not only in comparison with the developed countries but also in comparison with other developing and poor nations – South Korea and a poor nation such as Thailand allocated seven times, Srilanka six times and Malaysia ten times more to education than India (Raina, 1995: 83).

The most important problem the people of India face today is that the education is gradually being privatized. Now the huge quantity of private schools is growing up as their growth has been activated and encouraged by the new economic policy. These schools are known as elite schools where not only the fees are very high to be paid by the students, but also the other school-related expenses are too very high, which ordinary Indians cannot afford, and as already discussed in preceding section, huge population of India are under the clutches of poverty and therefore, practically the policy is a bigger step to alienate the poor mass from educational system, and negligence of government in existing government schools only compound the crises of mass education. The problem is more acute in higher and professional education.

In addition, most universities are now opening up vocational course that target the small but lucrative sectors and are charging very very high fees for the same. As a result, basic subjects are being neglected both by universities and by students as they keen to chase the dream of lucrative career opportunities (Shukla, 1996: 110). Now in higher educational and professional careers, due to privatization policy mostly, the rich students are only enrolling. The poor students are being alienated. Hence, through the changing scenario of environment, the policy of state is also being changed in favour of elite sections who have been enjoying all the benefits since long past.

Thus, the deprived are always deprived; if one method of deprivation is over, another method is adopted to stab from back. The deprived sections are always kept few steps backward so that they can never reach to the level of those who determine the state their deprivation. And knowing the importance of the present educational system, the dominant sections are again now through the new policy of deprivation deceiving and estranging the deprived so that the deprived remain the deprived forever.

Now again, the question arises as who are the deprived, who are the real sufferer of the present hegemony of elitism of privatization of education. To deal with these questions again, the caste and class factors come into forefront. If proper investigation is made, one will see that the deprived sections especially the SCs, STs, and Backward Classes or, in sum, the Dalits who have been deprived of their due since time immemorial are also today's deprived and exploited group.

Although due to some programme and policies, some improvements are seen among few sections of Dalit communities, the gap between them and other is increasing. The illiteracy gap between the SCs, STs and rest of the population is increasing as it was 17.59 per cent in 1961, 19.13 per cent in 1971 and 19.84 per cent in 1981 among the SCs and the rest of population. In case of the STs, the figures are 19.33 per cent, 22.50 per cent and 24.87 per cent, respectively, for 1961, 1971 and 1981 (Eighth Five-Year Plan: 420). The wide gap of dropout rate between the SCs, STs and the rest of the population is not unknown to the government of India as it also prepares the report on such (Agenda No. 18, 1990).

> In the overall context of inadequate public resources for schooling, greater privatisation of quality education for the elite and search for non-formal alternatives for the educational backward, it is likely that socially and economically disadvantaged groups will suffer greater neglect. Unless the present state of formal education is brought centre stage and the issue of equity in education is regularly addressed, we will continue to witness the abdication by the state of its social responsibility in education. (Nambissian, 1996: 1002)

Therefore, it can be concluded that the present policy of the government is sidelining the down-trodden or Dalits from the educational institutions (roughly like that of ancient India under religious doctrine), which they were slowly but steadily getting since independence. Now, due to privatization, the Dalit cannot have access to these institutions; now they cannot be employed as physical labour too. Because due to easy technology transfer under the new policy, the workers are likely to be replaced and neglected. Thus, they unlike in the past are now neglected physically as well as mentally. Therefore, they are now in the verge of worst stage of their life. Even the universal education through Sarva Siksha Abhiyan (SSA) or mere elementary compulsory education are not proper solution but are definitely big steps by the government though lately these have been taken in new millennium. Because through these, a poor may gain literacy or elementary education but can neither get employment nor become self-entrepreneur. Besides, the quality of education is poor. Hence, he will be matchless to other affluent who have achieved professional or technical education. That does not mean the poor is debarred from such technical and private education, but the inherent poverty would create barrier against him/her especially for attaining education through private bodies. Nonetheless, optimistically, it can be said that many such types of education are offered through distance education system of government such as by IGNOU where entry as well as course fees are not too high; moreover, there is provision of reimbursement of fees to the people of the weaker sections. Another thing should be borne in mind by the people especially weaker sections that unless they themselves are ready and struggle for such higher education government or for that anybody cannot help. In fact, they should take inspiration from the scholars such as Ambedkar.

Labour and Employment

One of the most important social sectors is labour and employment. As India is one of the most populated countries in the world (second position), it needs an employment-oriented growth; not only will wealth be concentrated on a very few individuals if only technology is being used, but millions will also be unemployed and starving. Hence, one of the prime motives of the new economic policy was to provide full employment by the end of 2000 AD. Let us analyse the impact of this policy on labour and employment.

According to the Planning Commission, the additional employment increased from 3 million in 1991–92 to 7.18 million in 1994–95 (Economic Survey, 1995–96: 181). However, according to critics, the liberalization policy adversely affected employment in the country. According to Ruddar Datt, during the first two year of the Eighth Five-Year Plan, the employment growth rate in the organization sector that constitutes about 9 per cent of total employment in 1992 was only 0.36 per cent. Second, the Planning Commission's proclamation of 2.03 per cent average growth of employment is also much lesser than the target of 2.6 per cent per annum set up by the planners for employment generation. In absolute terms, this indicates a shortfall of over 6 million jobs between1992–93 and 1994–95 (Datt, 1996: 10).

Practically, the employment growth rate under reform period is very slow. The growth rate generation during 1992–93 to 1994–95 at 2.03 per cent per annum (average of which is claimed to be higher than the average annual rate of employment growth of 1.78 per cent during the preceding seven years, 1985–92) is much lesser than the growth rate generated during 1972–73 to 1977–78, which was 2.82 per cent, also it is lesser than the growth rate generated during the 1977–78 to 1983 which was 2.22 per cent. Despite the lower growth rate during the period 1983 to 1987–88, which was 1.55, the employment growth rate form 1972–73 to 1987–88 which is 2.21 is quite higher than the economic reform growth rate of 2.03 per cent (Datt, 1995: 106).

The Planning Commission's comparison of current reform period's growth with the period 1983–87 is not even justifiable as during the 1983–87, the process of new economic policy was already started by Rajeev Gandhi Government. The comparison of current reform growth rate of employment with that of the period before 1983 indicates a decline in the rate of growth in current reform period.

Another study by Gangopadhyay and Wadhwa concludes that employment growth has slowed down between 1973–83 and 1984–93 for all industries except for textiles, leather, metal products and other manufacturing. Rate of growth of wage earnings has also been falling in all industries except the four listed earlier. However, capital intensity as measured by capital per workers has been going up (Gangopadhyay and Wadhwa, 1998: L40–49). According to other case studies of Ahmedabad, the new policy has led to displacement of workers and also has an adverse effect on the employment situation and the lives of workers (Roy, 1996; Noronha and Sharma, 1999: 1454–60). Biplab Dasgupta, in his article 'SAP: Issues and Conditionalities' highlights that structural adjustment leads to a freeze in public employment and the private sector employment also seldom grows because of low level of private investment (Dasgupta, 1997: 1100–101).

Chandrashekhar and Abhijit Sen have also criticized the new economic policy on the ground of its negative impact on employment. They looked at the industrial distribution of workforce for the years 1989–90 and 1992 based on NSS data. Since daily status details were not available, they looked only on usual status employment. Their finding says that the growth of employment is not declined in case of agricultural employment; whereas in non-agricultural employment unit, it declined significantly between pre- and post-reform periods.

Similarly, the actual share for the period 1977–78 to 1992 shows that the share of primary sector increased in the post-reform period as compared to pre-reform period for both males and females. This can be interpreted that the now economic policy could not absorb the workers in secondary and tertiary sectors, thereby compelling the workers to return to agricultural fields (Chandrashekhar and Sen, 1995).

Parthasarathy and Reddy, attacking the new policy said 'one of the disturbing features of the present reforms regime is the uninhibited false propaganda. For the past three years, there has been frantic effort to propagate the idea that the economic reform policies have been according the highest priority to labour intensive growth...'. The claims on employment growth are based on the planning commission's projection of employment. There is hardly any information available either on the method or on the composition of these estimates. A closer examination of reforms shows that there is nothing in the changes that can be claimed as inducing a labour-intensive pattern of growth. If we look at the trends in the organization, which comprises of public sector and private corporate establishments employing more than 10 persons, a distinct declaration in terms of employment since 1989–90 is discernible. The annual addition to employment in 1989–90 in the organized sector was 4.5 lakhs, and during the period 1992–93 to 1994–95, the public sector shows a decline compared with 1989–90. In fact, the private corporate sector's addition to employment in 1992–93 was negative, and the later recovery is marginal, 0.19 per cent (Parthasarathy and Reddy, 1996: 28).

Through special employment and poverty alleviation programmes, substantial portion of job have been generated as reported by the Economic Survey 1995–96. According to its estimates, these special programmes generated 2.65 million jobs in 1992–93, 3.6 million in 1993–94 and 4.14 million in 1994–95. It shows that, on an average, more than half the estimated employment generation has been through the special employment and poverty alleviation programmes, and these have absolutely no relation to the economic growth of the country. It is well known that the primary focus of these special programmes is employment and not growth or asset creation. Hence, this may be characterized as 'growthless job'. Although not necessarily questioning the validity of these programme to project the poor by way of 'safely net', it would be a gross distortion of facts to include these jobs as arising out of growth (ibid.: 29–30).

Further, as calculated by Partharsarthy and Reddy, if employment generated through special programme is included, the residual jobs in the entire productive sector, which are the focus of the new reforms, have been an average accounting for about 45 per cent of the jobs. If one talks about agriculture, the rest of the economy accounts for hardly 15 per cent of the estimated jobs. Out of this, 15 per cent of the estimated additional employment, the large number of jobs are in the unorganized sector – most of which are in the form of casual employment. A very small proportion of employment has been generated in the organized industry, which is the focus of the reforms and growth and is also shown as a proof of sources of reforms (ibid.).

On referring the figures pointed out by B.B. Bhattacharya and Arup Mitra (Bhattacharya and Mitra, 1993: 1989–95), Ruddar Datt stated that in contrast to Government claims of growth of employment, the new economic policy had been the instrument of growth of unemployment in the country – 11 million unemployment in 1990–91, 17 million in 1991–92, 19 million in 1992–93, and further it increased to 21 million in 1993–94 (Datt, 1995: 106).

After analysing the labour and employment under structural adjustment, Jayati Ghosh says that the rate of growth of organized sector employment decelerated significantly at 1.5 per cent per annum and would be below the rate of population growth. Within this, the main impetus of employment generation was provided by state government and some quasi-government organizations such as the nationalized banks. The private organization was the most sluggish with the employment at only 0.2 per cent per annum over the decade and even employment in central government and industrial undertaking grew very slowly. Moreover, over this decade, there was a sharp drop in labour absorption by the organized sectors. She further laid that over this decade, there was a sharp drop in labour absorption by the agricultural sector and as a result agricultural employment grew not only slower than population growth but also less than it had been growing in earlier decades (Ghosh, 1995: 572).

Ghosh is also of the view that pattern of structural adjustment and government economic strategy since 1991 has been one that has involved further reductions in employment generation in organised sector, both public and private. It has also affected adversely rural non-agricultural employment because it has involved the reduction of expenditure in rural areas in several ways (ibid.: 573).

Sudha Deshpande and Lalit Deshpande, however, by analysing the 50th survey round on employment and unemployment in India have concluded that the liberalization has increased the demand for casual worker particularly the women though not of regular workers (Deshpande and Deshpande, 1998: L31–39). However, such casual type of employment may have short-run social safety net, but in true sense not the solution of unemployment problem in India. In fact, it could be regarded in Parthasarathy and Reddy's term as growthless employment, and hence not the real growth of structural employment in the country.

Commenting upon the liberalization policy in India, Professor Prabhat Patnaik says

> It is the workers who are the main victims of such policy package. Unemployment, apart from affecting the living conditions of a section of them directly, has effect of slapping their bargaining strength and decimating their organization, the trade clinics. What is more unemployment which can be caused in this particular case by a reduction specifically is welfare expenditure and transfer payments to the workers, which again affect both their living conditions directly as well as their bargaining strength. The worker thus face a double attack either of which alone would affect their lives and their strength adversely, but both of which together constitute a severe blow. (Patnaik, 1997)

He further writes that it is a retreat from the commitment to the welfare state and high and near full employment. Instead of a seemingly non-partisan state standing above classes and acting in the interests of society, are now witnessing a transition in the capitalist world to a bluntly partisan state (ibid.: 200).

It can be safely concluded that liberalization policy has not been really employment friendly so far. Although, through special programmes some social safety is tried to build up, yet it is not the employment in true sense.

The new policy is employment unfriendly presently for two reasons. First, after evolution of such policy in India, the government has been cutting fresh employment in government sectors, public sectors, autonomous bodies, etc., thereby compelling millions of youths either to go for underemployment or to survive without it. Moreover, government has been evolving the voluntary retirement scheme to retrench the employees. It has been cutting employment to boost the growth. However, such growth in India's inequality system would rather increase the gap between the rich and the poor. The employees under privatized PSUs/autonomous bodies/government sectors are more likely to suffer especially in the long run. Second, the private bodies are not interested in social service such as providing employment as their primary motive is to earn profit and boost growth of their enterprises. The incentive providing for privatization to boost export or growth may achieve export or growth, but the fruits of such growth would be appropriated by influential few. If any so-called social safety net are provided, as is seen, those are rather just like providing food to survive in misery and reproduce other miseries of subsequent generations so that the disparity between the rich and the poor is maintained, preserved and perpetuated from generation to generation. Rampant corruption and other sociocultural maladies would rather strive to maintain such disparity. The weaker sections especially the Dalits are more likely to be depressed through such policy.

In the above essay, the fate of weaker sections in the context of ongoing globalization has been elaborated. The elaboration has been quite critical to the globalization process. But all of us should be practical enough to understand that reversing the process of globalization also is not going to yield the desired outcomes. Since, after more than 40 years of the nationalistic pattern of development had not been successful in alleviating socio-economic problems of the weaker sections, we should not look back to such type of the system to reoccur again. Similarly, the blind privatization or liberalization is not conducive. Hence, the process of social transformation and development should incorporate the equilibrium forces generated through nationalization versus globalization and economic development versus social development. For that to occur, strong sociopolitical and intellectual revolution from not only India but also from various parts of the globe is necessary. But start of it can be done from anywhere, and the media should play crucial role in spreading the message and for arousing consciousness to the people, on the one hand, and for re-structuring the national and global polices to the statesman and intellectuals, on the other hand; else, in the long run, the sociopolitical revolutions, riots, crimes, terrorism, etc., might increase their base and strengthen their forces by tapping and nurturing the poor by the vested interest. Moreover, these socio-economic problems should not be viewed as isolated one. Approximately, 20 crore Indians not belonging to special category of SC, ST and OBC are also under the clutch of poverty, illiteracy, ill-health and in poor socio-economic conditions. The social justice and other social welfare programmes should not be haphazardly dispensed with till the process of social transformation and development gain strength and becomes self-sustenance and perpetual through the system of integrated governance.

Bibliography

Agnihotri, Indu (1996). 'Gender and Women: Need for a More Engender Alternative Development Plan', in Alternative Survey Group (eds), *Alternative Economic Survey 1995–96*. New Delhi: Delhi Science Forum.

Ambedkar, Babasaheb (1987). *Writing and Speeches*, Vol. 1. Bombay: Maharashtra Government Education Department.

——— (1994). *Writing and Speeches*, Vol. 13. Bombay: Maharashtra Government Education Department.

Bhatt, Anil (1987). 'Social and Political Dimensions of Administering Development', in John Ickis, Edilberto de Jesus and Rushikesh Maru (eds), *Beyond Bureaucracy*. West Hartford, CT: Kumarian Press.

Bhattacharya, B.B. and Arup Mitra (1993). 'Employment and Structural Adjustment: A Look at 1991 Census Data', *Economic and Political Weekly*, 28(38).

Bhattacharya, Dipankar (1999). 'Political Economy of Reforms in India', *Economic and Political Economy*, 5 June.

Bhatty, Kiran (1998). 'Educational Deprivation in India: A Survey of Field Investigation', *Economic and Political Weekly*, 4–10 July, 33(27): 1731–40 and 11–17 July, 33(28): 1858–69.

Chandrashekhar, C.P. and Abhijit Sen (1995). 'Labour Scene in Perspective', *Business Line*. July.

——— (1996). 'Statistical Truth: Economic Reform and Poverty', *Frontline*. Chennai, 23 February.

Commonwealth Secretariat (1990). *International Economics Issues: Contributions by the Commonwealth 1975–1990*. London: Marlborough House.

Dasgupta, Biplab (1997). 'SAP Issues and Conditionalities, a Global Review', *Economic and Political Weekly*, 17–24 May 1997, pp. 1091–104.

Datt, Ruddar (1995). 'New Economic Reforms: Need for Some Rethinking', *The Indian Economic Journal*, January-March, 42(3).

——— (1996). 'Myth and Reality about Economic Reforms', *Mainstream*, July, 34(31).

Deshpande, Sudha and Lalit Deshpande (1998). 'Impact of Liberalization on Labour Market in India: What do facts from NSSO's 50th Round Show?', *Economic and Political Weekly*, 30 May – 5 June, 33(22).

Dev, S.M. (1995). 'Economic Reforms and Rural Poor', *Economic and Political Weekly*, 19 August, 30(33).

Diwan, I. and M. Walton (1997). 'How International Exchange Technology and Institutions Affect Workers: An Introduction', *The World Bank Economic Review*, 11.

Dunning, John H. (1997). 'Advent of Alliance Capatalisation', in John H. Dunning and Khalid A. Hamdani (eds), *The New Globalisation and Developing Countries*. Tokyo: United Nations University Press.

Fronk, Jan (1994). 'Patting People First: Whose New World Order', in Jan Willem Gunning, H. Kox, W. Tims and E. de Wit (eds), *Trade, Aid and Development: Essay in Honour of Hems Linnemann*. Amsterdam: St. Martin's Press.

Gandhi, J.S. (1982). *Lawyer and Touts: A Study in the Sociology of Legal Profession*. New Delhi: Hindustan Publishing Corporation.

Gangopadhyay, Shubhashis and Wilima Wadhwa (1998). 'Economic Reforms and Labour', *Economic and Political Weekly*, 30 May, 33(22).

Ghosh, Jayati (1995). 'Employment and Labour under Structural Adjustment in India Since 1991', *The Indian Journal of Labour Economics*, October-December, 38(4).

Government of India (1980). *Sixth Five Year Plan (1980–85)*. New Delhi: Planning Commission.

——— (1985). *Public Enterprises Survey 1984–85*, Vol. 2.

——— (1986). *Report of Commission for Scheduled Castes and Scheduled Tribes 1985–86*. New Delhi.

——— (1990). Agenda No. 18 (November 1990). New Delhi: Department of Education, Ministry of Human Resource Development.

——— (1992). *Eighth Five Year Plan (1992–97)*. New Delhi: Planning Commission.

——— (1993). *Concurrent Evaluation of JRY (Jan-Dec 1993)*. New Delhi: Ministry of Rural Development.

——— (1994). *National Sample Survey 48th Round*. New Delhi: NSS.

——— (1995). *Economic Survey 1995–96*. New Delhi: Planning Commission.

——— (1996). *Economic Survey 1995–96*. New Delhi: Planning Commission.

——— (1999). *The Ninth Five-Year Plan 1997–2002*. New Delhi: Planning Commission.

Guhan, S. (1995). 'Social Expenditure in the Union Budget', *Economic and Political Weekly*, 30(17&19).

Gupta, S.P. (1994). *Recent Economic Reforms and their Impact on the Poor and Vulnerable Sections of Society*. Mimeo: Centre for Economic Studies and Planning.

——— (1995). 'Economic Reform and Its Impact an Poor', *Economic and Political Weekly*, 30(22).

Hamdani, Khalid A. (1997). 'Introduction', in John Dunning and Khalil A. Hamdani (eds), *The New Globism and Developing Countries*. Tokyo: United Nations University Press, pp. 1–10.

Hantal, Bhimasen (1996a). 'BSP Gaining Strength', *Economic and Political Weekly*, 25 May.

——— (1996b). 'Corruption and Social Development in India', *The Radical Humanist*, June.

——— (1996c). 'Liberalisation Policy and Social Justice in India (M.Phil)', Dissertation submitted to CSSS/SSS, JNU. New Delhi: CSSS/SSS, JNU.

——— (2003). 'New Economic Policy and Social Justice in India: Policy of Reservation and Employment Opportunities in Educational Institutions in Delhi (Ph.D)', Thesis submitted to CSSS/SSS, JNU, 1996. New Delhi: CSSS/SSS, JNU.

ILO World Report (2000). *ILO World Report 2000: Income Security and Social Production in a Changing World*. Geneva: WLO.

Jain, L.C. (1985). *Grass without Roots: Rural Development under Government Auspices*. New Delhi: Sage Publications.

Kealya, B.K. (1994). Final Dunket Act – New Patent Regime, Janata, 6 March.

Mali, M.G. (1989). *Education of Masses in India*. New Delhi: Mittal Publication.

Manickavasagam, V. and A.R. Alagappan (1998). 'Reservation Policy in PSUs: How Effective', *Economic and Political Weekly*, 11 April, pp. 823–24.

Marx, Karl (1844). *Economic and Philosophical Manuscript*. Moscow: Progress.

——— (1867). *Capital*, Vol. 1 (*Das Capital*). Moscow: Progress.

McGrew, Anthony G. (1992). 'Conceptualizing Global Politics', in Anthony G. McGrew and P.G. Lewis (eds), *Global Politics: Globalisation and Nation State*. Cambridge: The Policy Press.

Mehta, Jay (1982). 'Nutritional Norms and the Measurement of Malnourishment and Poverty', *Economic and Political Weekly*, 14 August, Bombay.

——— (1995). *Hunger and Poverty Data: A Barmecides Feast, the Statement of Indians Economy 1994–95*. New Delhi: Public Interest Research Group.

Myrdal, Gunner (1968). *Asian Drama: A Enquiring into the Poverty of Nations*, Vol. 1. London: Allan Lane, The Penguin Press.

Nambissian, Geeta (1996). 'Equality in Education: Schooling of Dalit Children in India', *Economic and Political Weekly*, 31(17).

Nayak, Ramanath (1995). 'Implementation of ITDA Plan: Study of Nandapur Block in Kpraput, Orissa (M.Phil)', Dissertation submitted to UPS/SSS, JNU. New Delhi: CPS/SSS, JNU.

Noronha, Ernesto and R.N. Sharma (1999). 'Displaced Workers and Withering of Welfare State', *Economic and Political Weekly*, 5 June.

Oommen, T.K. (1978). *Doctors and Nurses: A Study in Occupational Structure*. New Delhi: Macmillan.

Parthasarathy, G. and Narasimha D. Reddy (1996). 'Labour and Employment', in Alternative Survey Group (eds), *Alternative Economic Survey*. New Delhi: Delhi Science Group.

Patnaik, Prabhat (1997). *Whatever Happened to Imperialism and Other Essays*. New Delhi: Tulika.

Pissarides, C.A. (1997). 'Learning by Trading and the Returns to Human Capital in Developing Countries', *The World Bank Economic Review*, January, 11(1): 17–32.

Prabhu, Seeta K. (1994). 'The Budget and Structural Adjustment with a Human Face', *Economic and Political Weekly*, 16–23 April, 29(16–17): 1011–28.

Raina, Vinod (1995). 'A Donor Driven Agenda', in *The Statement of India's Economy 1994–96*. New Delhi: Public Interest Research Group.

Ravallion, Martin (1998). 'Reforms Food Prices and Poverty in India', *Economic and Political Weekly*, 10 January, pp. 29–34.

Ravallion, Martin and Gourav Datt (1996). 'How Important to India's Poor is the Sectoral Composition of Economic Growth?', *The World Bank Economic Review*, 10(1): 1–125.

Ray, Aswinik (1999). 'Concept of Justice in International Relations', *Economic and Political Weekly*, 29 May.

Roy, Chowdhury (1996). 'Industrial Restructuring Unions and the State- Textile Mill Workers in Ahmedabad', *Economic and Political Weekly*, 24 February.

Samal, Kishor C. (1998). 'Poverty Alleviation after Post Liberalisation: Study of Tribal Block in Orissa,' *Economic and Political Weekly*, 11 July, pp. 1846–51.

Sarkar, Prabirjit (1997). 'Are Poor Countries Coming Closer to Rich?', *Economic and Political Weekly*, 2 August.

Sen, Abhijit (1996). 'Economic Reforms Employment and Poverty', *Economic and Political Weekly*, 31(35–37): 2459–77.

——— (1997). 'A Structural Adjustment and Rural Poverty: Variables that Really Matters', in G.K. Chadha and Alak N. Sharma (eds), *Growth Employment and Poverty: Change and Continuity in Rural India*. New Delhi: Vikas Publishing House.

Sethi, Harsh (1984). 'Groups in a New Politics of Transformation', *Economic and Political Weekly*, February, 19(18).

Sharma, Davinder (1995). 'Agriculture and Food Security: Room Self Sufficiency to Total Dependency', in *The State of India's Economy 1994–95*. New Delhi: Public Interest Research Group.

Sharma, K.L. (1984). *Sociology of Law and Legal Profession*. Jaipur: Rawat Publications.

Shastri, Paromita (2002). 'When the States a Poor Parent (Child Rights Column) OUTLOOK', 18 March. New Delhi.

Shotton, John Robert (1998). *Learning and Freedom: Policy Pedagogy and Paradigms in Indian Education and Schooling*. New Delhi: Sage Publications.

Shukla, S. (1996). *Education Alternative Economic Survey 1995–96*. New Delhi: Alternative Survey Group, Delhi Science Forum.

Shukla, S. and Rekha Kaul (eds) (1998). *Education, Development and Underdevelopment*. New Delhi: Sage Publications.

Singh, Yogendra (1979). 'Academic Role-Structure and Modernization: A Study of Rajasthan University Teachers', in Suma Chitnis and Philip G. Albach (eds), *The Academic Profession: Crises and Changes in the Technology Community*. Bombay: Macmillan.

——— (2000). *Culture Change in India: Identity and Globalization*. Jaipur: Rawat Publications.

Teltumbde, Anand (1996). 'Impact of New Economic Reforms on Dalits in India', A paper presented in the Seminar on Economic Reforms and Dalits in India Organized by the University of Oxford, London, 8 November 1996.

Tendulkar, Suresh D. and L.R. Jain (1995). 'Economic Reforms and Poverty', *Economic and Political Weekly*, 10 June, 30(23).

Tewary, Amarnath (2002). 'Breaking Innocence (Child Labour Column) OUTLOOK', 8 April.

The Observer (1995). New Delhi.

The World Bank Group (1998). 'A World Free of Poverty' (New reforms critical to growth and poverty reduction in India: World Bank release comprehensive review of country's development and 1998 Abstracts of current studies: Poverty and social development research Abstract of current studies), 24 March 2002.

Tilak, Jandhyala B.G. (1995). 'Budget for Education', *The Hindu*, 14–15 April.

Tulsidhar, V.B. (1993). 'Expenditure Comparison and Health Sector Outlay', *Economic and Political Weekly*, 30(23).

United Nations (2000). *Expert Reports on Ending Malnutrition by 2020*. New York: UNO.

UNDP (1995). *Human Development Report*. New Delhi: Oxford University Press.

——— (1998). *Human Development Report*. New Delhi: Oxford University Press.

——— (2000). *Poverty Report 2000*.

Unni, Jeemol (1998). 'Non Agricultural Employment and Poverty in Rural India: A Review of Evidence', *Economic and Political Weekly*, 28 March, pp. A36–44.

Wood, A. (1997). 'Openness and Wage Inequality in Developing Countries: The Latin American Challenge to East Asian Conventional Wisdom', *The World Bank Economic Review*, 11.

World Bank (1998). *World Development Indicators*. Washington, DC: World Bank.

——— (1999). *World Development Report – 1999–2000: Entering the 21st Century*. Washington, DC: World Bank.

——— (2000). *World Development Indicators*. Washington, DC: World Bank.

——— (2002). *World Development Report 2000–2001: Attacking Poverty*. Washington, DC: World Bank.

15

Modernization of Indian Tradition

Introspecting Equitable Development Paradigm

Manish K. Verma

Modernization: Attributes and Indicators

'Modernization is a historical process initiated in the west' (Wang, 1998: 40). 'It may be understood as the common behavioural system historically associated with the urban, industrial, literate and participant societies of Western Europe and North America' (ibid.: 165). If we discuss modernity it says 'it is not purely change or mere sequence of events, it means the diffusion of the products of rational activity: scientific, technological, and administrative'.

Yogendra Singh has analysed modernization in contrast to tradition. He puts it,

> Terms like 'individualism', 'secularism' are often used to oppose modern society to societies of the traditional type. In particular, the contrast between caste society and its modern counterpart is a common place. Liberty and equality on the one hand, interdependence and hierarchy on the other, are in foreground. Permanency versus mobility, ascription versus achievement allow for a neat contrariety between the two kinds of social system. (Singh, 1988: 3)

The idea of modernity is thus closely associated with rationalization. It makes science, rather than God, central to society and at best relegates religious beliefs to the inner realm of private life. It is the achievement of reason itself, and it is therefore primarily the achievement of science, technology and education. S.C. Dube expresses similar opinion about modernization. He says, 'Modernization is characterized by a rational and scientific world view, growth and the ever-increasing application of science and technology, together with the continuous adaptation of the institutions of society to the imperatives of the new world view and emerging technological ethos' (Touraine, 1995: 9).

The following three assumptions are basic to the concept of modernization (Dube, 1988: 17):

Inanimate source of power must be increasingly tapped with a view to solving human problems and ensuring minimum acceptable standards of living, the ceiling of which should rise progressively.

Towards this end, there should be both individual and collective effort. The collective dimension is important because associational capability to operate complex organizations is a prerequisite of at least the middle and higher reaches of modernization.

To create and run complex organizations, radical personality change and attendant change in the social structure and values are necessary.

Thus, the complex process of modernization assumes a series of interpenetrating and interdependent transformations. On the level of personality, it envisages the promotion of rationality as well as empathy, mobility and high participation. These attributes of a 'modernized' personality are promoted and sustained by structural, institutional, attitudinal and value change on the personal, social and cultural levels. In sociological language, the social and cultural milieu increasingly acquires achievemental, universalistic and specificity-oriented emphasis. Modernized societies accept and produce more innovations, build-up associational capability and sharpen problem-solving abilities. To put it simply, modernization according to Dube rests on three basic characteristics: solving of human problems and minimum acceptable standard of living, collective dimension; and, most importantly, change of attitude towards social structure and value is essential for the achievement of this goal.

Falling in line with the above argument:

> some scholars designed and recommended in the early 1960s numerous blueprints for a 'preferred modernized world order' for the future. Their recommendations were based on five agreed core values: war prevention, peace, poverty eradication, ecological balance and removal of alienation; which they consider to be of fundamental importance for the establishment of a peaceful world order in future. (ibid.: 17–18)

Hence, in a way, the process of modernization is the 'achievement to reason itself, and it is primarily the achievement of science, technology and education' (Yadav, 1996: 464).

A more contemporary view on modernity has been given by Dipankar Gupta (2000: 11) in the Indian context. He says that modernity has been misrecognised in India because of the tendency to equate it with technology and with other artefacts. The possession of modern technology, however, does not always signal modernity. Modernity has to do with attitudes, especially those that come into play in social relations. A modern society is one in which at least the following characteristics must be present:

(i) Dignity of the individual
(ii) Adherence to universalistic norms
(iii) Elevation of individual achievement over privileges or under privileges of birth
(iv) Accountability in public life

By now, it has been well established by our discussion on modernity that it abides by the principles of equality, liberty and fraternity or to put it in other words, the concept of 'Ram Rajya' can be equated with the modern notion of modernity. In fact, it is not a commodified product, but it is a change in perception based on rationality, reason, equity and equality. It is a way of life in terms of characteristics such as prevention of war, establishment of peace, eradication of poverty, minimum acceptable standards of life, ecological balance, removal of alienation, restoration of dignity of individual, elevation of individual achievement and accountability in public life; or in a nutshell, solving the basic problems that humanity is facing in today's world. These parameters of modernity will help us evaluate the much acclaimed equitable development paradigm, which tries to establish that modernity and development are intermingled and focus on the overall welfare of the society.

These attributes and indicators of modernization help us evaluate the kind of impact the Singrauli region received due to inception of the developmental project. For a comprehensive look of the whole situation, it would be wise to have a glimpse of the Singrauli region through ages.

The Region

The Singrauli region envelops two districts called Sidhi in Madhya Pradesh (MP) and Sonebhadra in Uttar Pradesh (UP). There are three super thermal power stations of National Thermal Power Corporation (NTPC) in this territory, namely Shaktinagar, Vindhyachal and Rihand. Shaktinagar and Rihand plants are situated in Sonebhadra District (UP), whereas the Vindhyachal plant is in the Sidhi District (MP). They are fed by the Rihand Reservoir and the Northern Coalfield Limited. The nearest possible big towns surrounding these projects are Mirzapur, Allahabad, Varanasi and Rewa. The division is a perfect example of simultaneous existence of backwardness and modernity. The region is the foremost coal and power-producing area in the country and it is known as the 'Energy Capital of India'. Geographically, the locale is full of hills covering thousands of tonnes of coal underneath.

In the past, Singrauli (EDF Chapter 3) was isolated, little known and economically backward rural area with very less population living in small and scattered settlements. Forest and small fence characterized the hilly and undulating landscape, and the people of the region were mainly engaged in collecting minor products or in subsistence agriculture. After independence, the locale started getting the attention of the planners basically for its large coal deposits, which could be utilized for generation of power for urban industrial development of the country. In conformity with this national goal, the territory was opened up by rail/road connection. After the construction of the Govind Ballabh Pant Sagar, also known as Rihand reservoir in the 1960s, there was an increase in the number of super thermal power plants; some large energy-dependent heavy industrial plants were installed and the coal mines rapidly raised their production to meet the growing demands of these plants.

By the late 1980s, Singrauli region became one of the most important power-generating centres feeding the urban-industrial requirements, and thus emerged as an area of strategic importance for the whole country. Meanwhile the landscape of the core area changed drastically and became characterized by large open-cast mines with a retinue of rail lines and MGRs, super thermal plants and other heavy industries around Rihand reservoir, project townships, rehabilitation colonies as well as squatter settlements and also much of the wastelands in between.

Development also brought several problems into sharp focus. They were mainly lack of urban infrastructure for the non-project population, growing disparity in economic status between the locals and the new migrants and development of slums and squatter settlements close to the project townships. A large section of the local population was left out of the process of development and also received several adverse impacts on the environment. Infrastructure deficiencies, unplanned settlements, large number of displaced population and significant environmental degradation characterize the whole region. A distinguishing feature of displacement in the locale is repeated relocation. Because several projects are located in a small radius of about 15 km, people are forced to displace more than once.

Now, in the following passages, we will focus on the socio-economic background of those locals who directly got influenced with the inception of the project in the region.

Background of the Communities Displaced due to Inception of Development Project

In the rural regions as a whole, the proportion of women to men is just over nine and a half to ten. In the urban areas, on the contrary, the proportion of women to men is even lower, probably around 7–8 women to 10 men at present. The majority of the rural population is classified as landowning peasants and the vast majority of farmers are men. In the urban areas, wage earners are dominant, although possession of tiny plots of land and small animal-raising activities are common in this group.

In the Singrauli *tehsil*, the statistics shows that 12.5 per cent are members of the low Hindu castes and 15 per cent members of tribes. But in the region, there are no properly structured tribes with their own territory, religion and institutions. It may be estimated that 30 per cent of the population consists of persons who more or less correspond to the definitions of specific poor, low status groups on the MP side of the lake and with a figure of 50 per cent on the other side. Overall, the members of these groups number nearly 40 per cent, out of which 20 per cent are tribal.

In the Singrauli region, as is the case everywhere else, the higher castes form an important group, not only because of their rank and their wealth, but also because of their numerical preponderance. The most numerous are the Brahmins, followed by the Rajputs and intermediate castes between the two previous groups and the Kayashthas. The intermediate castes, locally regarded as somewhat honourable, such as the Sahus and the Jaisvals, used to own quite extensive amounts of land, and still do, as well as virtually holding a monopoly of commercial activities. The farmers, who make up numerically important group, were the Telis, the Koiris and the Yadavs, first and foremost herdsmen, but all are recognized as being skilled in agriculture. The craftsmen and providers of services, consist essentially of Lohars and Kumhars, Nais and Panikas. Finally, the Muslims make up a variable group, far less well represented locally than in India as a whole and occupied place in commerce, crafts or agriculture.

In this background, NTPC invaded the region in the early 1980s for the execution of thermal power projects. To facilitate NTPC, some more ancillary industries as well as townships, market, etc., also came up in the region during the following years. The arrival of foreign people with alien culture and mentality made an overall dent in the peaceful and local culture of the people. Here, we will try to focus on social and cultural factors to see whether the arrival of projects really modernized the traditional people or proved contrary.

Social Factors

Displacement has torn apart the social fabric of the Singrauli region and destroyed the very platform on which the social aspects rest for stability. Before the inception of the projects to the locality, the innocent people were living amidst peace and tranquillity. The egalitarian community had full honour to the family values, and the poor were far away from the dexterous and cunning culture of the cities. But the sudden invasion of this homogenous civilization by an alien selfish culture has totally shaken the community. Inception of the projects acquired agriculture land, spacious dwelling and livelihood and made a dent into the peace and prosperity of the region. Those who were earlier living in affluence and fraternity had fallen prey to scarcity, chaos and turmoil. Availability of scarce resources and the acute competition between the poor villagers to acquire that had given birth to treachery and jealousy, which smashed the social culture of the society.

People were no longer willing to listen and take care of their family members. Conflict between brothers for the sharing of property, deserted parents due to lack of residential space and money, women begging or working as maids, break down of family structure and the development of nuclear families are the most quoted narratives of the region after displacement. Caste conflicts have taken a new shape and upsurge beyond proportion. Class conflicts have also started taking toll. Infants, children, elders and the women who are considered as the most vulnerable section of the society were the most crushed and affected community. Infants and children becoming prone to the malaise of the society have fallen prey to several bad habits and also lost respect for their elders. Elders could not adjust to the new atmosphere and culture; they either escaped, fell ill or died. Women have also observed sharp decline in their status and were compelled to involve in menial kinds of work to sustain and survive in the new monetary economy. Family rituals and ceremonies regarded as porter of culture and civilization, which were being celebrated earlier with pomp and show, have received severe setback.

As a whole, the region became victim of social evils and the sociological aspects of equality, fraternity, respect for elders and family system took a backstage.

> The interdependent communities that were an integral part of traditional life are transformed, in the modern setting, into collection of competing individuals. People are left insecure, alienated and isolated. The increased

> violence, alcohol and drug addiction, and the abuse of women, children and the aged that characterize modern urban populations around the world are the direct results. (Shiva et al., 1995: 8)

Family Dispute after Displacement

It was observed that land and money provided by NTPC in lieu of the acquisition of land and other immovable property brought about chaos in some of the families. Dispute was for the sharing of benefit among the son as well as father and other close affinal relatives. As is evident, the people of Singrauli region were living amidst simplicity and honesty before infringement of the area. Inception of various projects in the region showed the path of greed and hunger for wealth to the tribal and other backward people. They saw massive amounts of wealth on their foothold because of NTPC and Coal India Ltd (CIL), and other big mining, irrigation and power projects were readily willing to provide to the tribal for their land.

Table 15.1 *Family dispute after displacement*

Item	No. of persons	Percentage
No family dispute	160	64
Family dispute	83	33.2
Can't say	7	2.8

When project-affected persons received compensation money and other facilities from the project authorities, conflict started for the sharing of benefits. First disputable item, which took shape, was the conflict over entitlement, that is, who is eligible to receive the benefit. When this problem was sorted out, it was evident that families started fighting for the share of that benefit. The traditional orthodox families who were earlier known for family values and cultural ethos, respect for elders, sacrifice and divine attitude, started quarrelling for trivial money matters. Result was breakdown of the family norms, shattering dreams of the elders and fracture in the family system. Table 15.1 indicates that out of 250 families surveyed, 83 (33.2 per cent) were observing family dispute of some kind or the other. Since there is honour attached to family values, most of the families did not want to reveal their family secrets. Thus, the figure of 33.2 per cent may be far less representative of the reality of the region. A total of 160 (64 per cent) denied any dispute in the family. Rest 7 (2.8 per cent) did not respond to the question; this may be due to the fact that they did not want to share their family matters with an outsider.

Stay and Share of Rehabilitation Benefits with Family

Family dispute and quarrel resulted in the breakdown of the affinal ties, conflict of interest, shattering hopes and desires and ultimately crumbling of the family. In such cases, the person who received the compensation and other benefits left the rest of the family members high and dry. Sometimes, the son deserted even his old parents leaving them on the verge of begging or dying. Earlier, the whole family was dependent on agricultural land for food, but in the new economic system there was no scope for the dependent family members. Naturally, dependent persons had to go out of the family system. It happened in case of house also. Earlier, in the villages, people had big houses with lots of space. But a small plot of 60 × 40 square ft, given by NTPC in lieu of the big dwelling in the village, had no space for the unwanted family members. Table 15.2 clearly depicts that 25 (10 per cent) families who received the benefit of displacement deserted their house. The figure does not include the families who crumbled down due to conflict over sharing of the benefit. Rest 225 (90 per cent) families shared the benefits with other family members.

Table 15.2 *Stay and share of rehabilitation benefits*

Status	No. of persons	Percentage
Stay with family	225	90
Left the family	25	10

Further Stratification of the Displaced Family and Community

Although, at the time of acquisition, the whole region was at the bottom of the social and economic stratification, the new economic system created by displacement and subsequent compensation payment noticed another level of stratification within the families and communities, which were considered equal earlier. A person who received job from NTPC and subsequently abandoned the rest of the family members naturally was the last straw in the eye for the rest of the family members. Now, since the person is a part of NTPC because of the job, he is entitled to all facilities and benefits. Thus, the beneficiary enjoys *pucca* house, vehicle, educational facilities and good standard of life, and consequently enhanced social status in the community as well. At the same time, his rest of kith and kin who did not receive jobs lived in misery and pathetic condition. This divided the families and created frustration, jealousy and animosity within them. Thus, as a result, the whole community, which was earlier at the bottom of the stratification level, got further stratified and observed rank and file among themselves.

Widening of Caste Conflicts

It is generally believed that with the industrialization and consequent urbanization, caste system tends to lose its grip from the society. But on closer scrutiny, Singrauli region opts for the other side of the coin. Although industrialization has widened the intercaste interaction and dining among the oustees a bitter animosity has developed between them. This is due to the NTPC policy of 'divide and rule' and also because of the dominance of the upper caste people at the time of receiving compensation. Creamy jobs, plots and other resources were grabbed by these so-called upper caste people. This act of vandalism further reduced the lower caste and downtrodden into a 'hand to mouth' condition and pushed them to the fringe of the society. Although allocating compensation, NTPC and the government adopted a discriminatory approach, which created agony, anguish and frustration among the lower caste people. This widened caste rivalry and conflict in the region.

Closer scrutiny revealed that most of the jobs, contract works, plots and other facilities were granted to the dominant castes of the region such as Brahmans and the Rajputs. The lower castes and the downtrodden were allocated only residual plots in the resettlement colonies and peripheral jobs of labourers in the project. The discrimination and atrocities done towards the lower caste people find burning example in the form of *Dharkars* of Vindhyachal, a caste equated at par with the *chamars*. These outcaste people had no property to own and lived life as wanderers. They were dependent on others for their food and related requirements. The plots allotted to them were in the Sector 4 of Navjivan Vihar resettlement colony. Sector 4 is the last resettlement colony and the *Dharkars*, being outcaste, were allotted plots in the cremation ground, where none of the other castes would opt to go for residence. Muslims were also allotted plots in the fourth sector of the resettlement colony. A resident of the Navjivan Vihar says, 'There are four sectors in the resettlement colony. In this, the fourth sector is for SC, ST and Muslims'. Therefore, according to him, 'a kind of discrimination is made at the time of relocation'. It created a disguised feeling of difference between the caste and outcaste and also between people of different religions. This has prepared grounds for natural animosity and jealousy between people of different caste and also towards NTPC for not treating them on equal basis.

Strengthening of Class Conflicts

Industrialization and urbanization and policies adopted by NTPC and the government strengthened the economically deprived sections. Due to economic empowerment, they got access to education, employment and justice. They became more and more aware of their rights and duties. The inception of the various power and mining projects in the locality broke the shackles of the *zamindari* and *Jajmani* system. Promptly, the poor became independent of big landlords and in some cases started challenging their reign of terror and exploitation. Thus, as a consequence, two conflicting classes are created as envisioned by Karl Marx. These two classes were competing for the scarce resources available to them and fought for supremacy in the region. Conflicting interests and widening desires have enhanced selfishness among the poor villagers. They have become more awakened and as a result strengthened the class conflicts along with the caste discord and shattered the cohesion and stability of the region.

Breakdown of Family Structure

Agronomy had the strength to bind and feed the joint family together under the same roof, as it required several persons to work in the agricultural ground. But the acquisition of land and traditional spacious houses changed the whole scenario. Now they were lacking food, enough space and resources to fulfil the basic needs of the family members. The small patch of agricultural land and tiny plot of 60 × 40 feet allotted to them in the resettlement colony was no longer able to accommodate joint families. The result was quarrel in the family and the birth of nuclear families. Increasing use of liquor is also observed among the youth and the middle-aged people. This can be seen as the impulsive outcome of the breakdown of the families and resultant quarrel. Earlier, joint family used to act as safety valve mechanism for any deviance experienced in the family. But in the broken families, its members became exposed to various difficulties and evils. Nuclear family lacked matured persons to advise and suggest ways to fight the problems; as a result, the youth and the middle-aged fall victim to illicit practices such as liquor and drugs.

Descending Status of Women

In agronomy, women had ample work attached to land and house. They were feeding their cattle, picking wood from the forest, working in the agricultural land and had other allied household activities. They were working shoulder to shoulder with their husbands. In a way, women were the pillars of strength for the house as well as the menfolks living in the society. But in the new economic system, women had no work to do. Families ceased to be the production unit and were reduced to the level of consumption. Women have become idle and dependent in this system. Even if some of them were working, that was not their area of specialization, but in the labour-intensive jobs attached with the plants and townships. Some became maids in the Project Township and few unfortunates had to beg to feed themselves. This led to a sharp decline in the status conferred to them. Dowry system has also taken a sharp expansion. As a result, the birth of a girl child has become a curse for the household.

Table 15.3 *Present household activities of women*

Item	No. of persons	Percentage
Grazing land	44	17.6
Cow dung	60	24
Cattle caring	49	19.6
Wood picking	42	16.8
Any other	4	1.6

Table 15.3, depicting the present household status, shows a very dismal picture of activities associated with women. Out of 250, only 44 (17.6 per cent) household ladies were grazing land and 60 (24 per cent) thatching cow dung. A total of 49 (19.6 per cent) housewives were associated with cattle caring and 42 (16.8 per cent) wood picking. Only 4 (1.6 per cent) women of the region were busy with some other activities. None of the categories had frequency crossing over 50 per cent of women participation. This shows that the women of the region have either become dependent on their menfolks or are working in labour-intensive jobs in the plant.

Problems Faced by Elders

It is the responsibility of the community and society to look after the elders and the children. The Indian tradition and ethos have always advocated respect for the elders. But the spirit of respect and regard to elders was completely neglected in the new scenario after displacement. The old persons who used to live in spacious locations in the villages had enough space to congregate and roam around. But the wrath of displacement has poured venom on their freedom. Some of the elders could not get adjusted to this new urban atmosphere in the resettlement colonies, as it was pinching on their freedom and they fell ill. In addition, some of them died because of the fear of going to the new place. Others had deep-rooted place attachment to their ancestral properties. As narrated by the elders, they were not willing to vacate their habitation. The project authorities forcefully threw them out of their house and land and they were compelled to live at a new alien place in hostile conditions. This also created psychological pressure on them.

The sample thus collected verifies the above-mentioned theory. There were only five families in the sample who advocated that they do not have any problem and are satisfied with the present system. Rest of them had problems of some kind or the other. Forty-eight families confirmed that they have become more prone to health problems. In the new resettlement colonies, it was very difficult to live in the absence of infrastructure facilities. Houses were not constructed, and they had to live under the open sky. Potable water was not available and nearby *nallah* was the source of water in most of the cases. Doctors and medicines were far from the reach of the poor people. As a result, health problems were faced by all the sections of the population, but since the eldest were more vulnerable, they were the bigger victims. Water-borne disease was the most common feature of the area.

Next to the health problems came the issue of space enigma for the elders. The new resettlement colonies allotted to the people were not spacious enough and developed many inborn problems. The colonies lacked open space, assembly place, agricultural land, orchard and playground. Pollution and sanitation were the biggest problem. They had no congregation place for religious and cultural ceremonies. They missed the orchar to sit under in the summer. Director Srijan Lokhit Samiti, a local NGO of the area, confirms the problems of elders. He says, 'In the resettlement colony, there is no open space for relatives to congregate and share the feelings'. Around 98 families recognized the problem of space for the elders during the interview (Table 15.4).

Table 15.4 *Problems faced by elders*

Problems	No. of persons
NIL	5
Health problems	48
Space	98
Poverty and unemployment	103
Unhealthy atmosphere	69
Others	56

Elders, who were earlier dependent on the agricultural land for their livelihood, suddenly found it missing. Now, they had to earn their livelihood by some other means for which they were not trained and even prepared. Thus, they were reduced to poverty. Some of them were thrown out of their houses by their sons, since they were idle and were of no use in the new economic system. Old persons including women were seen on the streets of the Singrauli region having begging bowls in their hands. In two cases, the old ladies were deserted by their respective sons and family members and they had no shelter. They went begging to feed themselves. One lady had five children and the other was blessed with two. When interrogating the daughter-in-law of one of the lady regarding the pathetic condition of her mother-in-law and the responsibility of her son towards his mother, the daughter-in-law responded, 'there is not enough money to sustain her family, how can she take care for her mother-in-law?'; 103 family members admitted that their elders were reduced to poverty and unemployment.

In the new resettlement colony, elders had no social security. In the village earlier, the chains of kith and kin were readily available to help them out at the time of crisis. They now got trapped in sorrow, loneliness and were bound to cry in the new circumstances. The new selfish culture of the urban area saw the abandonment of some of the elders by their sons. Sixty-nine family members admitted to unhealthy atmosphere for the elders. The rest of the 56 families voted for the option 'others', which comprises problems such as water, electricity, sanitation, etc., faced by the elders. This also comprises those persons who could not respond to the question or said there is no impact of displacement on the elders and a few who advocated that it is good for the poor.

Impact on Infants and Children

Infants and children are considered as the future of a nation's progress. The episode of resettlement and rehabilitation brought about chaos, and consequently affected the peace and prosperity of the region. Land oustees remained busy to regain their lost livelihood and also to erect a roof over their head. As a result, they could not provide proper attention to the socialization of children. Use of liquor and tobacco, gambling, stealing and cheating are common characteristics of the youth of the region. Most of them have become idle and dependent on the family because of lack of education and employment. As expressed by the locals, MTV culture has influenced their minds and to imitate that borrowed culture, children are ready to do anything. The dazzling and prosperous lifestyle of the project people also distracted the young and virgin minds of the kids. As a result, children were trying to put an extra effort to impersonate borrowed lifestyle and fell prey to evil methods (Table 15.5).

Table 15.5 *Impact on infant and children*

Problems	No. of persons
No impact	3
Education problem	106
Health problem	101
Space problem	53
Unhealthy atmosphere	66
Poverty and unemployment	56
Drug and liquor	3
Others	33

Only three families denied any problems to the children and said there is no adverse impact of resettlement. A total of 106 families admitted that their children are facing educational problem (Table 15.5). The region lacks sufficient schools and colleges.

Health was the major cause of concern among the youth. Lack of playground, orchards, hygienic food, fruits and vegetables are the common drawbacks of the area. Pollution, contaminated water and sanitation problems were other reasons for the poor health of the youth. A total of 101 families out of 250 surveyed, narrated the problem of health among infants and children. Space problems, which symbolize adverse living condition, shortage of playground, house and shelter also, were more frequent. Fifty-three families confirmed these problems. Next, unhealthy atmosphere for the children was another burning issue. This comprises bad impact, bad future, lack of family values and no respect for elders, cunningness and sorrow among the children. As discussed earlier, the region saw deteriorating culture and family values among the youth and consequently they indulged in several uncouth behaviours. Sixty-six families confirmed this. Poverty and unemployment also figured in the list of problems faced by the children. Fifty-six families confirmed this in their response. Due to illiteracy and shortage of agricultural land, the youth of the region have been reduced to poverty and unemployment. In a traditional and orthodox society such as ours, admittance of taking liquor and drugs are attached with stigma. Thus, only three families admitted to using drug and liquor among youth.

Some families chose other options too. Thirty-three families voted for the option 'others', which includes options such as can't say, no impact, education improved and situation improved. These respondents conceived displacement and arrival of the project as positive for their children.

Generation Gap

Turmoil and upheaval brought about in the Singrauli region due to inception of various projects have destroyed the family values, and consequently the prestige and honour attached with the senior citizens. The urbanized culture completely destroyed the village bonding and natal ties among the community members. Values such as honouring elders, participating in social and cultural events of sorrow and pleasure, helping in need, etc., are ebbing from the society. Throwing away parents from the dwelling by the sons, quarrel between brothers for the distribution of property and fight among women living under same roof are the most pathetic incidences of the region. From Table 15.6, it is evident that 91 (36.4 per cent) families admitted to generation gap in their families, that is the elders are not properly honoured and obeyed by the family. Rest of 159 (63.6 per cent) denied this and said that status quo is maintained after displacement, and the senior citizens are enjoying the same dignity and prestige that they were relishing earlier.

Table 15.6 *Generation gap*

Feeling	No. of persons	Percentage
Yes	159	63.6
No	91	36.4

Feeling about Family Rituals

As discussed, the whole region has experienced the deterioration of social and cultural values during and after the inception of the project. As a consequence, the family rituals attached with birth, death, marriage and other occasions of 'rites-de-passage' have also received a severe blow. People have no time, money and patience to celebrate these occasions of social importance as was done earlier. The direct question bombarding their social and family ethics could have invited wrath from them. Hence, the question was asked in the form of 'feeling about family rituals', and the responses were also given in varied forms, such as very strongly, strongly, somewhat, less strongly and least strongly (Table 15.7).

Table 15.7 *Feeling about family rituals*

Feeling	No. of persons	Percentage
Very strongly	12	4.8
Strongly	116	46.4
Somewhat	86	34.4
Less strongly	12	4.8
Least strongly	24	9.6

Only 12 (4.8 per cent) families feel very strongly attached with the family rituals (Table 15.7). This is an alarming proportion. Indian culture and families are famous for family rituals attached with the rites-de-passage. A sudden decline of the family rituals among the villagers is indicative that grassroots Indian culture is slowly losing its authenticity and enduring nature. A total of 116 (46.4 per cent) families said they are strongly attached to the family rituals. There were 86 (34.4 per cent) who opted for somewhat. They were oscillating between yes and no, means that they had a vague idea about their choices in life regarding family rituals. A total of 12 (4.8 per cent) families were less strongly attached to the family rituals, whereas rest of 24 (9.6 per cent) had no attachment to the family rituals and thus they nodded with the option, least strongly.

Loss of Familiar Social and Geographical Surrounds

Due to forced relocation, the inhabitants were thrown out of the familiar common social and geographical resources such as ponds, wells, grazing land, forest, community centre, *panchayat* place, etc. Most importantly, the cemented structure of kith and kin scattered in the village, which were of great help for them at times of crisis, also got fractured with the dislocation. Marital ties suffered heavily because this familiar set-up was acting as anchor in establishing conjugal bonds of sacrament between different families. The social and geographical surrounds play an important role in the village economy and mostly the villagers rely heavily on this. Due to acquisition, the residents were no longer able to assemble at one place to discuss and eradicate their common problems. The old and the aged people had no place to sit during extreme summer and winter. Lack of ponds and wells compelled the villagers to go to the nearby *nallah* for their daily water consumption. Several villagers fell ill due to the consumption of the contaminated water. The cattle had no grazing land

and ponds to fulfil their basic needs of hunger. No forestland was available for the tribal population who earlier earned their livelihood from forest products. Most importantly, the nearby *bazaar* and *haat*, agricultural land and other resources considered as the basic necessity for the survival of the villagers, were wiped away with the relocation. Now, the inhabitants of Singrauli region are mostly dependent on the project authorities and the resettlement colonies for their everyday basic needs of survival.

Cultural Factors

Culture is learned and shared patterns of behaviour. It is a collective expression for symbolic and learned, non-biological aspects of human society, including language, custom and convention, by which human behaviour can be distinguished from that of other primates. Some refer to the culture of social groups as the total set of beliefs, customs, way of life, values and even ideology. Thus, culture of a society has an all-encompassing appearance. It governs the lifestyle, values, beliefs, dressing pattern, eating habit, behaviour, custom, way of talking and so on. It is a general consensus among the scholars that the culture of an area differs from others; and even in the same community, there can be multiple conflicting subcultures. There is no special skill required to learn the existing culture. Consciously or unconsciously, the place and society where one grows up instil the culture as part of socialization. Hence, the role of society where one grows up and socializes becomes noteworthy for the development of human as the porter of culture. If the society and the accompanying individuals are carriers of good habits, naturally the forthcoming generation will be righteous and modernized. On the contrary, the destructive capacity of culture will spoil the whole atmosphere.

In the developing societies, there may arise the problem of 'cultural lag', a term coined by W.F. Ogburn. He noted that changes in culture were not always or necessarily congruent with economic changes. A cultural lag exists when two or more social variables, which were once in some form of agreement or mutual adjustment, become dissociated and maladjusted by their differential rates of change. The same thing happened with the residents of the Singrauli region. The sudden invasion of this remote and, until recently, closed region by development project has changed the entire social and economic prospects. All of a sudden the whole region experienced scintillating changes in economic inflow. The project rendered with it the new dazzling culture and lifestyle, which distracted the poor residents, especially the youth. The residents found themselves in a stage of 'cultural shock', as they were seeing these things for the first time in their life. Not able to withstand and behold their tradition and culture, they were swept away with the forceful current of alien and attractive civilization. As a result, the whole region underwent gradual changes in behaviour and life pattern.

Social and Cultural Degeneration

Inception of the project and changes in the economic base of the region has greatly affected the culture and society. Until recently, the whole region was aloof and self-centred. The residents had nothing to do with the outside world and were happily living with their problems and miseries. They were a self-sufficient and independent community and knew better how to tackle with the insurgent problems. But the arrival of a new culture of the rich saw commodification of everything. Villagers started trying to imitate the rich by making them as their 'Reference Group'. They madly rushed for luxurious items, borrowing culture and dressing pattern. But lack of money, resources and ability to follow the culture of the rich came in the way of these landless, homeless and poor people. As a result, the whole region observed degeneration in the 'pious' culture.

Not able to imitate, resulted in the propagation of frustration and deep-rooted instinct to follow the path of cheating, burglary, stealing, drinking, gambling, etc. There was no respect for elders left in the community and even brothers were fighting each other for property. Desertions of parents, quarrel, separation and breakdown in the families were a common affair. Women did not show interest in keeping their in-laws with them, leave alone the regard, care, attention, protection and services they deserved in old age from their sons and daughters-in-law. Youngsters and the youth were trying to follow 'MTV' and 'Star TV' culture. Their dressing pattern, style of life, behaviour and way of talking underwent a drastic change. They were no more the same straightforward villagers, what they used to be before displacement.

Loss of Cultural Heritage, Sites and Monuments

Humans always feel proud about their social, cultural and religious belongings and want to be identified with such references. The place, house, monuments, idols, sites, rivers, ponds, totems, symbols, etc., all play an important role in associating humans with nature. This human–nature relationship lives along with the human species and is irreparable. One cannot reconstruct or recreate the importance and feelings attached with these symbols, even if exactly constructed physically at some other place. Kalpana Sharma writes with reference to Sardar Sarovar,

> The symbol of the submergence was the sight of the 1000-year old *Shoorpaneshawar* temple, almost disappearing, with only a small part visible. Many villagers stayed on in their huts as a symbol of protest and had to be virtually dragged out to higher ground. As a result, their meagre belongings were washed away even as their fields near the river edge were fully submerged. (Sharma, 1994: 152)

The problems of the Singrauli residents are also multifaceted. They were losing not only the religious symbols but also the cultural heritage sites and monuments deeply attached with them. The loss of small monuments and totem attached with the place, ponds, wells and even stones were the biggest loss of the people for which they still lament after 20 years.

Dressing Pattern

Dressing pattern symbolizes the status as well as the economic prosperity of a person. It also denotes progress, mental development and maturity. If a man imitates the latest fashion clothes, it shows he is up-to-date. At the same time, it is a matter of great debate among scholars with regard to what would be the parameters of a dressing pattern. What can be said as the adequate pattern of dressing since we are observing varieties of dressing habits followed in different corners of the world?

It was observed that the land oustees, especially the youngsters, were well versed in the latest dressing patterns of the country. Very few, including old and aged persons, were using *dhoti* and *kurta*, the traditional clothing. The stitching patterns of pants and shirts were exactly the same found in any other part of the country, that is, in consonance with the latest fashion. It appeared that the residents of the area are running with time in terms of dressing pattern, despite the trauma and uncertainties they faced (Table 15.8).

Table 15.8 *Dressing pattern*

Pattern	No. of persons	Percentage
Latest dress	142	56.8
Traditional	44	17.6
Remains same	64	25.6

In an attempt to ascertain the viewpoint of the residents, questions were asked regarding their dressing pattern. The response received shows that majority of the residents opted for the latest dressing pattern. This shows their open mind and maturity of thinking, to allow and admit newer aspects. Out of 250 families interviewed, a majority of them, that is, 142 (56.8 per cent) accepted that latest dressing pattern has infringed the region after displacement (Table 15.8). On the contrary, 44 (17.6 per cent) people were of conservative opinion. In their view, the present dressing pattern is in traditional form. The respondents sticking to this opinion were mostly representatives of the old and aged generation. Some others felt there is no change and it crossed over the conservationist response. A total of 64 (25.6 per cent) families observed that there is no change in the dressing pattern and habits of the residents. To my mind, close association with society and slow pace of change could well be the factor for their unnoticed and overlooked response towards change in dressing pattern.

Change in Religious Rituals

Religion binds the natural world to unnatural, mystique world of supernatural powers. Everybody in this world attempts to please and soothe the supernatural in their favour and solicit blessings. There are different ways and methods prescribed in different religious textbooks for reaching out to the almighty superpower named god. Religious rituals are strictly required during appeasement of god on occasions of great religious importance such as *Holi*, *Deepavali*, *Durga Puja*, *Janmashtami*, etc. The logic of propitiating the god shows man's attachment to its traditional culture. Developmental changes and the introduction of modern values continuously undermine the importance of religion as a power, and suggest instead the importance of science and technology. According to the spirit of a new scientific pattern of thinking, there is nothing beyond the control of man, and with the proper use of wisdom, human species can control anything and everything. The feeling of being superpower and the master of the universe devalued the religious importance from the mind of the human being. Now human beings have started searching the mysteries of life in science and technology, instead of religion. Bearing in mind the changing parameters of life and the technologies used to overcome the problems, question was raised (Table 15.9).

Table 15.9 *Change in religious rituals*

Feeling	No. of persons	Percentage
Yes	207	82.8
No	43	17.2

A total of 207 (82.8 per cent) families confirmed change in religious rituals (Table 15.9). They sighted various reasons behind the alteration of the intensity with which religious rituals were observed earlier. Foremost among them were lack of money, time, resources, patience and belief. Acquisition of agricultural land and crumbling of the economic base forced the oustees into urban industrial atmosphere. Here they have no time, patience and most importantly money and other resources to celebrate the festivals, and other occasions of rites-de-passage with same intensity and vigour. The result was the change in the pattern of celebration of religious rituals. Rest of 43 (17.2 per cent) families opted traditional approach and said they are celebrating the religious rituals in the same pattern, which they were doing earlier. May be, time was not cruel to them and because of that they are living in the same old world with the same kind of customs and ceremonies.

Feeling about Calendric Rituals

Related to our earlier question, we delved further deep into the mind of the respondents and tried to fathom their attachment to calendric rituals celebrated with the change of season and agricultural crops such as with the harvesting of wheat, maize and rice. There are several festive occasions in rural India attached with the calendar such as *Makar Sankranti* or *Lohri* on 14 January. Those living in the resettlement colonies could hardly understand the meaning of these concepts due to industrialization of their activities. They were no longer living in the rural agricultural world. In semi-urbanized atmosphere, they had nothing to do with the agricultural activities and harvesting occasions. But there were few old and aged and also those left with little bit of agricultural land who understood the logic of calendric rituals. Hence, the answers received covered both kinds of response.

For the convenience of analysis, we segmented the responses into various categories such as very strongly, strongly, somewhat, less strongly, least strong and, lastly, don't know (Table 15.10).

Table 15.10 *Feeling about calendric rituals*

Feeling	No. of persons	Percentage
Very strongly	11	4.4
Strongly	109	43.6
Somewhat	94	37.6
Less strongly	7	2.8
Least strong	28	11.2
Don't know	1	0.4

A total of 11 (4.4 per cent) respondents showed attachment to religious rituals 'very strongly'. On the contrary, 109 (43.6 per cent) families felt 'strongly' attached. They are the forward moving persons carrying tradition with them. A total of 94 (37.6 per cent) families showed a confused state of mind and said 'somewhat'. They were not able decide the path of their lives, either to stay with tradition or to modernize completely. A total of 7 (2.8 per cent) villagers had murkier relation left with the tradition and thus they chose the response 'less strongly'. A total of 28 (11.2 per cent) families showed complete sign of breakdown in their relation with tradition and remained with the negative response of 'least strong'. They were the richest and modernized lot of the community and were not at all bothered about their past customs and tradition. Only 1 (0.4 per cent) household was completely unaware of the concept governing calendric ritual and responded as 'don't know'.

Intercaste Interaction and Marriage

Inception of power and mining projects into the region shattered the traditional social structure and pattern of life based on village atmosphere. Now the residents found themselves in the industrialized world; that is, they moved from an ascribed to an achieved society. Industry requires competent and skilled persons irrespective of their caste and creed. This atmosphere of openness allowed the upper and lower caste to work together, which bridged the distance and also initiated healthy interaction between the one-time hostile communities. Caste rivalry took a backstage and everyone started thinking in terms of personal benefits. Apart from this, the new resettlement colonies cemented the people in such a manner that there was no caste distinction between most of the upper and middle castes in terms of location of plots, and they were living happily in close proximity. Some kind of discrimination was made by the authorities with reference to the lower castes such as *chamars* and especially the *dharkars*. *Dharkars* considered equivalent to *chamars* were allotted plots in the outskirts of the resettlement colony. Where earlier, there was a cremation ground. But overall the caste interaction has improved and people have moved towards the concept of caste equality.

In terms of the intercaste marriage, the region symbolizes the rest of India. It is still not permitted and those practising it have to be socially ostracized. Parents have not modernized to the extent that they allow their children to go for intercaste marriages. When asked to illustrate reasons, they told intercaste interaction is one thing and marriage another thing. Marriage being a sacrament establishes eternal ties between two completely unknown families, and if it is intercaste, invites various problems in the long run. Difference of culture comes in the way of stable relationship, which later grows up into adjustment problems. The culprit would be socially boycotted at the first instance; offspring of the couple could be inferior in mental and physical capabilities. Most importantly, the parents said that they wanted to keep children under control by not allowing intercaste marriage.

Overall, caste considerations still linger in the minds of the residents of Singrauli region. Although they are trying to come out of the shackles of such a monstrous social evil, it will take years to fully overcome.

Conclusion

The present paper was initiated with the aim of establishing the modernizing effect in the Sigrauli region in terms of the much acclaimed equitable social and cultural consequence due to the inception of development projects of NTPC. In conclusion, family dispute has shot up in the region after the arrival of NTPC. Share of compensation money and other facilities from NTPC was the prime cause of quarrel in the family. Those families who earlier used to be a cohesive unit no longer remained same and showed divergence even on trivial issues. As a consequence, joint families shattered and crumbled into nuclear families. Family members were no longer willing to pay attention to the problems of others. Most of those who received compensation from NTPC on behalf of the family did not bother to share it with others and got separated. Even, in some cases, their sons who received compensation deserted the old and aged parents. This created further stratification of family and community on the basis of recently emerged economic classification. Those who received jobs and compensation from NTPC became rich and prosperous and were sore in the eyes of other family members, who remained on the same footing or declined in economic status after displacement. Thus, the family and community further stratified and created the ground of jealousy among the inhabitants.

Due to their dominance in the society, upper caste and class people of the region managed to reap the cream of development and compensation at the cost of lower caste and class people. This has further widened caste conflict already existing in the region. The introduction of new culture and values based on equality and justice influenced the downtrodden section. Thus, the lower class section of the region posed a challenge to the dominance of the rich. This created two conflicting classes in the region, as envisioned by the greatest socialist, Karl Marx. Conflicting interest and widening desires have further strengthened class conflict.

Small patches of land provided to the land oustees in the resettlement colonies was no longer able to accommodate the joint and extended families running into 10–20 persons living under the same roof. Apart from this, the clashing interest led to the breakdown of joint family structure. This act of breakdown of family opened the door for various social problems in the region. Foremost among them was the descending status of women. In the new economic set-up, women were no longer producers but reduced to the condition of idle consumers. Even those who still tried to work got jobs as maids in the township or in labour-intensive activities in the project. Access to excess money due to compensation received from NTPC trapped the young population into liquor, tobacco and gambling. Often, under the impact of alcohol, the addicts started beating their wives.

Due to the development policies of NTPC, the most severely hit section of the society were the aged and children. The act of acquisition of agricultural land and the consequent loss of livelihood exposed the traditional Indian culture and society to the harsh reality of selfishness. In the Indian culture, where parents are equated with god and are worshipped, they were thrown out of the houses by their son. Paucity of money, food and space compelled the old persons to beg for the fulfilment of their basic needs of food and shelter. Scantiness of orchard, fresh air, agricultural land, sanitized water and, most importantly, the support of family members took its toll and some of them died. Children also had similar problems. Insufficiency of space, playground, education and food were the biggest hurdles in their upbringing. Selfish urban culture, impact of TV and dazzling light of NTPC have tempted the children to fall prey to greed and cunning. Stealing, cheating, gambling, use of liquor and tobacco are common among the young residents of the area. Turmoil and upheaval brought about in the region have destroyed family values and, consequently, the prestige and honour attached with the senior citizens and kindred members. Family rituals and celebrations on occasion of rites-de-passage also lost significance. Dressing pattern changed significantly and people no longer felt attached with their calendric rituals.

Overall, the whole region experienced decay in societal and cultural values. The indicators of modernization, discussed in the beginning of the paper, could not find sufficient space in the Singrauli region. The dignity of individuals fell significantly and the notion of solving human problems, minimum acceptable standard of living, eradication of poverty, removal of alienation, restoration of peace and tranquillity was completely missing. It creates a question mark on the much admired perception of modernization, development and equity through the inception of various kinds of infrastructure projects on the host population.

References

Alagh, Yogendra K. (1996). *Impoverishment Risk Analysis: Comments from an Indian Perspective*. Paper Presented in the Workshop Organized by the World Bank, NDO, 12–14 March.

Cernea, Michael M. (1996). *Eight Main Risks: Impoverishment and Social Justice in Resettlement, the World Bank, Environment Department*. Paper Presented in the Workshop Organized by the World Bank, NDO, 12–14 March.

Dube, S.C. (1988). *Modernization and Development: The Search for Alternative Paradigm*. New Delhi: Sage Publication.

Fernandes, Walter (1996a). *Displacement and Rehabilitation: Principles of the NGO Alternative*. Paper Presented in the Workshop Organized by the World Bank, NDO, 12–14 March.

——— (1996b). *Reconstructing Livelihoods: Towards New Approaches to Resettlement*. Keynote Address: 9–13 September 1996, Refugees Study Programme, Queen Elizabeth House, University of Oxford.

Gadgil, G. and R. Guha (1995). *Ecology and Equity: The Use and Abuse of Nature in Contemporary India*. London and New York: Routledge.

GHK/MRM International and Others (1994). *Singrauli Development and Environmental Management Strategy*. Displaced People Action Plan, GHK/MRM.

Government of India (1995). *Draft National Policy on Resettlement and Rehabilitation*. Ministry of Rural Area and Employment. Government of India.

Gupta, Dipankar (2000). *Mistaken Modernity: India between Worlds*. New Delhi: Harper Collins Publishers India.

Marsden, David (1996). *Resettlement and Rehabilitation in India: Some Lessons from Recent Experiences*. Paper Presented in the Workshop Organized by the World Bank, NDO, 12–14 March.

Mathur, H.S. (ed.) (1988). *Environmental Resources: The Crisis of Development*. Jaipur: RBSA.

Mathur, Hari Mohan (ed.) (1995). *Development, Displacement and Resettlement: Focus on Asian Experiences*. New Delhi: Vikas Publishing House.

NTPC (1993). *Resettlement and Rehabilitation Policy*. New Delhi: NTPC.

Reddy, I.U.B. (1996). *Involuntary Resettlement and Marginalization*. Paper Presented in the Workshop Organized by the World Bank, NDO, 12–14 March.

Shiva, Vandana et.al. (1991). *Ecology and Politics of Survival: Conflict over Natural Resources in India*. New Delhi: Sage Publications.

Shiva, Vandana et.al. (1992). *Towards Hope: An Ecological Approach to the Future*. New Delhi: Indian National Trust for Art and Cultural Heritage.

Shiva, Vandana et.al. (1994). *The Future of Progress: Reflections on Environment and Development*. Dehradun: Natraj Publishers.

Shiva, Vandana and Irgunn Moser (eds.) (1995). *Biopolitics: A Feminist and Ecological Reader on Biotechnology*. London: Zed Books.

Singh, Mridula et.al. (1992). *Displacement by Sardar Sarovar and Tehri: A Comparative Study of Two Dams*. New Delhi: Multiple Action Research Group.

Singh, Yogendra (1988). *Modernization of Indian Tradition*. Jaipur: Rawat Publications.

The Economic Times (1992). *Rehabilitation Policy Being Formulated*. New Delhi: *The Economic Times*, 22 October, p. 2.

Thukral, Enakshi Ganguly (ed.) (1992). *Big Dams, Displaced People: Rivers of Sorrow, Rivers of Change*. New Delhi: Sage Publications.

——— (1995). 'Development, Displacement and Rehabilitation: Is there a Need for a Gender Perspective', *Mainstream*, 11 November, pp. 24–6.

Touraine, Alain (1995). *Critique of Modernity*. Oxford: Blackwell.

Wang, Huiyun (1998). 'Rethinking Modernization: A Critique of Western Cultural Hegemony', *Gandhi Marg*. New Delhi, July-September.

Xavier Institute of Development and Action Studies (1998). Social Impact Assessment of Displaced Persons in Singrauli Region in the States of Madhya Pradesh and Uttar Pradesh. Volume (I and II); M.P.

Yadav, R.S. (1996). 'Gandhian World Order Model: An Alternative Paradigm for Peace', *Gandhi Marg*. New Delhi, January-March.

16

Communication as a Development Resource

R. Kannan

In the 21st century, it is widely acknowledged that the gap between people, groups or societies can be measured only in terms of accessibility and non-accessibility to information. It is only this gap that would act as a factor in determining the socio-economic status of human groupings (Kannan, 2006: 8). Problems such as illiteracy, unemployment, poverty, lack of access to balanced diet, good health and adequate living space, etc., make people powerless and resourceless. This situation is particularly true of the developing countries. It is only in such countries that the importance of communication as a development resource has to be more keenly felt.

Penelope Brook and Warrick Smith have stated that two billion of the world's poor lack access to adequate sanitation, two billion lack access to electricity, one billion lack access to clean water and more than half of the world's population have never used a telephone.

Brook and Smith have also noted that policy makers and advisers do not have consistent and reliable data regarding current consumption of infrastructure services by the poor. The most striking observation of Brook and Smith is that those shaping policies at the national (or international) level seldom act on the basis of rich information about the needs and preferences of the poor they seek to serve (Brook and Smith, 2001).

One understanding from the standpoint of these authors is that only communication plays a vital role in the development process, and it serves as a development resource. In the present day of liberalization, privatization and globalization, information gap and interaction gap are required to be bridged on a war footing to carry forward the reform measures aimed at national development.

Brook and Smith lay emphasis on stakeholder consultation, mobilization of stakeholder groups (who are benefited by reforms), consensus building, critical changes in the design of infrastructure projects, etc., as a preparatory initiative for large-scale privatization. It is in this context that the importance of communication is understood more seriously than ever before.

When communication is used as a tool in the task of transforming the society, great care has to be given to bottom-up communication rather than top-down communication. This view has been highlighted by socially conscious experts in the field of communication time and again in the past. The same view is expressed in the present day by the contemporary scholars too. Perhaps (as this author understands), the top-down communication is comparable to the 'push' factor and the bottom-up communication is comparable to the 'pull' factor. Despite growing understanding of the need for exchange of knowledge between countries and within regions, there is a continuing tendency to push information out to people rather than strengthening and responding to the pull of their information needs (Godlee et al., 2004).

Hudock is quite apprehensive of the role of media, especially their role in championing the cause of the people in the developing countries. In an article titled 'Hearing the voice of the poor...' Hudock emphasizes the importance of robust media for the citizens and their representatives to participate effectively in policy formation. In her view, among society's institutions, it is only an independent media that can help disseminate information about socio-economic development particularly relating to the poverty reduction strategy process.

> Yet in most developing countries, the media are not prepared for this role. Media sectors, as a whole, face large obstacles to realizing their potential as government watchdogs and champions of public interest. Further many governments do not support a free and robust media sector, regardless of its importance to democratic and economic growth. (Hudock, 2003)

The inference that one can make at this juncture is that the media are not allowed to function freely in some countries (for further reading see Cassata and Asante (1979) and their presentation on Authoritarian theories). In countries where media enjoy freedom or autonomy in matters relating to broadcast or telecast, people feel that greater care should be given to quality of the programmes.

In a study conducted by this author with his associates among the tribals in the lower hills of Palani (in Tamil Nadu), certain interesting observations and inferences were made. Respondents comprising 76.25 per cent have reported that they are not in the habit of reading newspapers. Remaining 23.75 per cent of the tribals under study have stated that they are interested in reading news regarding cinema and political events in newspapers. In the same study, respondents constituting 80 per cent have reported that they listen to radio, which they own or in the neighbourhood. Majority of informants are interested in listening to film songs only. None of them have said that the radio programme has been useful for their development (Kannan et al., 2003: 139–44).

This finding that the tribals in a setting in Tamil Nadu who have almost merged with the mainstream of the civilized societies still do not pay attention to development-oriented media programmes. Does it mean that there are lacklustre radio programmes and that the media planners have to be blamed?

Such an accusation by no means can be justifiable. People are increasingly attracted to entertainment, whichever medium it comes from, and hence it might be an over expectation that audience should all the time be interested in development messages.[1] This assertion is a global phenomenon, and hence planners and policy makers aiming at development through media especially for the subalterns may think of a shift in approach and not a shift in focus.

In another joint study conducted by this author and his associate among Kuruvikkara Kattunaickers, who are fighting for tribal status, it was found out that exposure to media was very negligible. Out of 500 occupied houses, radio sets were kept only in 50 houses. 'Those who have access to broadcast medium are interested only in film songs and drama. TV sets are found only in 2 houses and the occupants of these two houses have cable connections. Even these people are neither interested in newsbulletins, nor are they watching Doordharshan' (Kannan and Buvaneswaran, 2004: 213). This study on Kuruvikkara Kattunaickers reaffirms the earlier held assertion that a shift in approach is the need of the hour.

A study by this author and his associate on the fishermen near Rameswaram also supports the assertion that a shift in approach would deliver goods. This study on the penetration of media was carried out in two villages, namely Olakkuda (near Rameswaram) and Therkuvadi (of Pamban region). In both the villages, people feel that Doordarshan may give more importance to regional programmes. In both the settings, people are much attracted to the 'Vanambadi', a programme of Sri Lankan broadcast. 'Greater preference for Srilankan radio programme Vanambadi is a pointer to Indian broadcast that it should strive hard to attract more listeners, perhaps by paying more attention to stylistic and thematic aspects of presentations and programming' (Kannan and Buvaneswaran, 2005: 107).

In this context, it has become irresistible for this author to quote a study conducted around five decades back in an Indian setting. Majumdar had indicated in his study that people who had been to film shows in Lucknow were keen to have a radio set in the village mainly to listen to film songs relayed by Radio Ceylon (Majumdar, 1958: 295). Therefore, it can be asserted that people irrespective of space and time are keen to enjoy entertainment. It is for the planners and policy makers to decide and implement a specific agenda, especially when development-oriented messages are required to be passed on to people. Therefore, it is essential for those involved in the task of initiating changes in the society through the media mission to adhere to changes in keeping with the socio-economic profile of the audience and in accordance with their tastes and preferences. The source or the sender of the messages must ensure that the source and the recipients are in the same wavelength. This requires periodic audience research and change in the mode of presentation.

At regular intervals, changes must be introduced in the format/mode of presentation of a given programme, with attractive announcements, personalized approaches, etc., otherwise any programme will only be dull, drab and prosaic and considered lacklustre by the audience.

This suggestion that changes must be introduced to drive home the messages, particularly the development-oriented messages, holds good for all the media.

This view has been stressed by this author in his article, which highlights various strategies for fighting the pandemic, namely HIV/AIDS. This author has stressed the idea that one of the best ways of delivering the goods is by converting the scientific matters concerning AIDS into a comprehensible and region-specific folk format. He has also pointed out the widely held belief that information available regarding the preventive and rehabilitative dimensions of AIDS is in an academic or scientific mode. This means that the content and medium are alien to the common man. Hence, he has advocated the conversion of incomprehensible matter into folk mode, so that such materials regarding this pandemic are understandable to the peasant and tribal communities.

This author has suggested that once the matter is converted into folk mode, it may be taken to a large assemblage of masses on occasions of their congregations such as festivals. The personnel who take the initiative to bring about attitudinal change may identify and sensitize the target families. Other initiatives may include self-help groups taking the messages to people, preventing people from approaching the quacks, informing people about mistaken symptoms and wrong identification, persuading the reluctant patients with perceived threats to approach doctors, informing girl children about the loss of social approval in the event of contracting the disease, instructing the adolescent boys that the impairment of health would spoil the interest of the family, removing the superstitious beliefs about AIDS through propaganda, etc. (Kannan, 2001: OB-1).

When communication is used as a development resource, all the elements involved in the process of communication, namely source, message, channel and receiver, will have to be paid serious attention.[2] The theories of communication and of course research in communication fall under any one of the four components, namely communicator component (source is the key element in communication), message component (importance is attached to message), channel component (channel is the deciding factor), audience component (audience characteristics play a vital role in the process of communication) and effects component (laying emphasis on the psychological dimensions of communication).

It is in this background of the process of communication, the nation builders and change agents have to decide the right kind of approach to carry developmental messages especially when they aim at social transformation.

In the top-down communication process, it is absolutely essential for the source/sender of the message to convey the ideas through the broadcast medium or TV in the dialect of the audience. This author in one of his research works has made an assertion that communication in receiver's dialect can be considered one of the best among the repertoire of strategies[3] (Kannan, 1994: 15). Rajasundaram had pointed out that a communicator should speak in the language or dialect of his intended receiver or audience. For example, if you are talking to farmers, farming words in current use by the farmers in a particular region should be adopted by the communicator to make it easier for them to grasp the ideas (Rajasundaram, 1981: 9). Further, in the communication process, besides issues such as what you present and how you present, the credibility factor also goes a long way in deciding the reach of the message. Dennis has quoted in his work John Corry to drive home the importance of the communicator's position that carries weight in the success of the message. 'The most important thing in advocacy is neither how well you write or how well you report but what your position in life is' (Dennis, 1977: 126). Probably bearing this idea in mind, the commercial establishment has chosen to cash in on the image of the celebrities by employing them as brand ambassadors to promote their products or services. These celebrities are film personalities or leading sportspersons. Sometimes, copy writers or visualizers employed by the advertising agencies resort to the credibility factor. To promote the products, particularly the consumer non-durables such as toothpaste or shampoo, the statements that doctors have endorsed or certified the said products/s are very much found in the TV commercials or newspaper advertisements.[4] This argument is just to reinforce the idea that there are circumstances in which the source acts as the key element in communication; and in instances such as the aforementioned, the development communicators may put a premium on the source or sender of communication.

There can also be situations wherein channels/media serve the purpose. It is for development communicators and for agencies involved in developmental activities in both the governmental or non-governmental sectors to decide as to which medium would serve the purpose especially when carrying developmental messages to people.

The author while listening to the important strategies in taking developmental messages to people in the village communities has laid emphasis on the traditional media approach. Despite the growing importance of the print and electronic media on one side, it is a fact that the traditional media still wield a considerable influence in the rural areas where the oral tradition still plays a dominant role. The observation that this author has made nearly a decade and a half back still holds good so far as the tribal and peasant settlements are concerned. 'The traditional media, which had flourished in India include the folk and tribal music, dance, drama and puppetry which are found to influence people in village India even today' (Kannan, 1994: 21).

In the peasant and tribal settlements where print or electronic media have not made any significant headway, featurized documentaries (messages interwoven with stories or messages conveyed in a story from, in the celluloid) and docudrama (messages conveyed in a drama format) will serve the purpose. Even in the present day, one is able to see a large assemblage of masses enjoying traditional media performances, which are exciting in art forms and drama staged in the open places, especially in paddy fields after harvest in villages. This fact needs no emphasis, because these media are inseparable from the life of rural masses and are intertwined with the culture of village India.

A holistic view that also sounds logical is that depending on the receivers' position and their psychographic and demographic profile, a development communicator may decide the source, message and channel in the process of converting communication as a development resource.

Notes

1. Although initiating a series of lectures at the 132nd international convention of the Theosophical Society Mr Satish Inamdar, Director, Valley School Krishnamurti Foundation had stated that people were

enslaved to entertainment. For more details, read the news report under the caption, people are 'enslaved to entertainment', which appeared in the Madurai edition of *The Hindu*, Thursday, 27 December 2007.

2. In the SMCR paradigm, Agenda Setting hypothesis deals with message component and Stephenson's Ludenic Theory of play focuses its attention on audience component. Although certain theories such as authoritarian theory, social responsibility theory, hypodermic needle theory and concepts such as source credibility deal with communicator (source) component, Marshall McLuhan's theories deal with the channel component.
3. The article titled 'Carrying Developmental Messages to People in the Village Community' quoted in this paper and listed in the references is a revised version of the paper presented by this author in the XII world Congress Sociology at Madrid, Spain (9–13 July 1990).
4. The statements of qualified persons, experts or competent persons being approved immediately by people refer to the concept of source credibility. People accept the views of those who they think are authorities and such views are held as infallible (E.P. Bettinghaus, *Persuasive Communication*. New York: Holt, Rinehart and Winston, 1968).

References

Brook, Penelope and Warrick Smith (2001). 'Improving Access to Infrastructure Services by the Poor-Institutional and Policy Responses', World Bank. http://web.mit.edu/urbanupgrading/waterandsanitation/resources/pdf-files/Brook-ImprovingAccess.pdf.

Cassata, Mary B. and Molefi K. Asante (1979). *Communication: Principles and Practices*. New York: Macmillan Publishing Co., Inc.

Dennis, Everette E. (1977). 'The New Journalism: How it Came to Be', in Michael C. Emery and Ted Curtis Smythe (eds), *Readings in Mass Communication: Concepts and Issues in the Mass Media*. Iowa: William C. Brown Company Publishers.

Godlee, Fiona, Neil Pakenham-Walsh, Dan Ncayiyana, Barbara Cohen and Abel Packer (2004). 'Can We Achieve Health Information for All by 2015?', *The Lancet*, 364(9430): 295–300. www.thelancet.com.

Hudock, Ann (2003). 'Hearing the Voices of the Poor: Encouraging Good Governance and Poverty Reduction through Media Sector Support', *World Learning*. www.worldlearning.org.

Kannan, R. (1994). 'Carrying Developmental Messages to People in the Village Community', *AJTR*, July–December, VII(2).

——— (2001). 'Folk Format for Fighting the Pandemic', *The Hindu*, 6 November, OB-1.

——— (2006). '*Eliyorukkaha Thittamiduthal* (An Article in Tamil Meaning Planning for the Poor)', *Dinamani* – A Tamil Daily, 10 July.

Kannan, R. and M. Buvaneswaran (2004). 'Living Conditions, Culture and Communication: A Study on Kuruvikkara Kattunaickers', *South Asian Anthropologist*, 4(2).

——— (2005). 'Penetration of Media in Coastal Villages, Perceptions and Preferences of Fishermen', *The Oriental Anthropologist*, 5(1).

Kannan, R., M.A. Paripooranam and M. Buvaneswaran (2003). 'Pattern of Communication and Exposure to Media among the Tribals in Lower Hills of Palani', *South Asian Anthropologist*, 3(2).

Majumdar, D.N. (1958). *Caste and Communication in an Indian Village*. Bombay: Asia Publishing Houses.

Rajasundaram, C.V. (1981). 'Manual of Development Communication with Special Reference to Broadcasting', An AIBD/AMIC Manual for Trainers. A Joint Publication of Asian Mass Communication Research and Information Centre. Singapore and Asia Pacific Institute for Broadcasting Development, Kuala Lumpur.

17

Globalization, Technological Advancements and Socio-cultural Impact on Youth

Rashmi Jain and Nidhi Bansal

I

The world is growing smaller. Everyday, we witness the reality and existence of this phenomenon in our lives – through the people we meet, the products we buy, the gadgets we use, the information we get, the food we eat and the movies we watch. We witness the impact of this phenomenon in all arenas of our lives. After the Second World War, the infrastructure of communication and transportation improved dramatically connecting people, groups, communities, organizations, countries and continents in ways unthought-of before. Today at the onset of 21st century, we witness a transformed society, a society that is interconnected in more than one way.

Globalization in its literal sense is the process of transformation of things or phenomena into global ones. It can be described as a process by which the people of the world are unified into a single society and function together. This process is a combination of economic, technological, socio-cultural and political forces (Croucher, 2004). It is a process of interaction and integration among the people, companies and governments of different nations; a process driven by international trade and investment and aided by information technology. This current wave of globalization has been augmented by policies that have opened economies domestically and internationally. The modern information and communications technologies have facilitated in its advancement dramatically. Today, more and more people are traveling or migrating to distant places; satellite broadcasting is serving to global audience, global capitalist system and world economy is emerging out of international trade and investments; new international organizations such as United Nations, World Bank, World Trade Organization, International Monetary Fund, International Labor Organization, North American Free Trade Agreement (NAFTA) and others address globally common concerns and govern international conduct. The World Wide Web of the Internet has been instrumental in bringing people more close than ever, even with colossal physical distance between them.

The features of a global society have their roots in history. Travel, trade and migration have been an integral part of all stages of society. However, the second half of 20th century is very significant for the development of globalization as a process. The launching of geostationary satellites in 1960s and 1970s further transformed communication. Global communication became cheap, and transmission of huge quantities of information was made possible. With the proliferation of World Wide Web on the Internet, instant communication broke the age-old temporal boundaries of space and also knowledge. The society transformed phenomenally in terms of linkages, institutions, cultures and consciousness. In general, globalization is a process of increasing interconnectedness. As an irresistible process (Giddens, 1990), it is led by technological innovations and political liberalization metamorphosing the world into a *Global Village* (McLuhan, 1964), that is, international integration. Giddens describes globalization as the rapid development in communication technology, information and transport, which bring the remotest parts of the world within easy reach. Castells (1996) has described the process of globalization with regard to informational economy emphasizing 'informational' and 'global' features of new economy. He indicates that the new economy is informational because the productivity and competitiveness of units in this economy is fundamentally dependent upon their capacity to generate, process and apply efficiently knowledge-based information. It is global because the core activities of production, consumption and circulation are organized on a global scale.

Globalization has brought drastic changes and greater possibilities in all spheres of human activity such as sociocultural, economic and political (Waters, 1995; Appadurai, 1996; Held et al., 1999; Friedman, 2005). It has led to change in the phenomena of time and place and has connected places, peoples and cultures in a totally new manner. The issue of globalization as positive and negative has been a subject of great debate between scholars (Beck, 1992; Stiglitz, 2002; Bhagwati, 2004).

Globalization has influenced our society in countless manners. Economy being the engine to globalization has led to the emergence of global markets, free worldwide trade, worldwide floating financial markets, decreased travel time and international division of labour. Globalization has facilitated free movement of material, services, goods, people and capital across borders and also technology between and within transnational corporations. There is greater migration within and between countries, greater social mobility and transnationalization of classes. People across the world come to share, know and understand the social settings and practices of each other. There is a substantial growth of cross-cultural contacts due to globalization with the advent of new categories of consciousness and identities such as globalism that embodies cultural diffusion, the desire to consume and enjoy foreign products and ideas, adopt new technology and practices, spreading of multiculturalism and better individual access to cultural diversity. Globalization leads to greater awareness and changes in social perception and attitude. Globalization also leads to the formation or development of a set of universal values, homogenization of culture, consumerism, dominance of individualistic and materialistic values, but along with greater global consciousness of values of human rights, democracy, equality and freedom.

> ICT is global in its reach, irreversible in its drive, and pervasive in its impact. (Juan Somavia, Director-General, ILO, 2001)[1]

Information and communications technology (ICT) refers to the various technologies that enhance the creation, storage, processing, communication and dissemination of information. It also reveals the different infrastructure used in these processes, their application and the numerous services these infrastructures render. As ICTs positively contribute to an increase in efficiency and productivity, the efficient utilization of the existing knowledge and investments for its development cannot only create comprehensive wealth but also improve the quality of life in forms of better health, education, employment, infrastructure and other social indicators.

ICT provides the communication network that facilitates the expansion of products, ideas and resources among nations and among people regardless of geographic location. Creating efficient and effective channels to exchange information, IT has been the catalyst for global integration. The IT revolution has been driven by the rapid reduction in the cost and extraordinarily rapid increase in the processing power of digital technologies. The Internet breaks down cultural boundaries across the world by enabling easy, near-instantaneous communication between people anywhere in a variety of digital forms and media. The Internet is associated with the process of cultural globalization because it allows interaction and communication between people with very different lifestyles and from very different cultures.

Global culture is therefore trans-societal culture that takes a variety of forms, which have preceded the interstate relations into which nation-states can be regarded as being embedded and processes that sustain the exchange and flow of goods, people, information, knowledge and images that give rise to communication processes that gain autonomy on a global level (Robertson, 1990). *International Encyclopedia of the Social and Behavioral Sciences* (2001) explains globalization as one that involves expanding worldwide flows of material objects and symbols and the proliferation of organizations and institutions of global reach that structure such flows. World culture refers to the cultural complex of foundational assumptions, forms of knowledge and prescriptions for action that underlie globalized flows, organizations and institutions. It encompasses webs of significance that span the globe, conceptions of world society and world order; models and methods of organizing social life that are assumed to have worldwide significance or applicability. The global flow of information, images and cultural elements influences the culture of a nation-state to a great extent (Appadurai, 1996; Ritzer, 2004). Here, we are reminded of an eloquent expression:

> I do not want my house to be walled in on all sides and my windows to be stuffed. I want the cultures of all the lands to be blown about my house as freely as possible. But I refuse to be blown off my feet by any. (Mahatma Gandhi, 1869–1948)[2]

Young people's lives arguably exist at the cutting edge of social change and as such youth face a particular set of challenges. World Youth Report 2005 (United Nations, 2005) says that the so-called information society based on new media technologies has produced a particularly dynamic media culture. In this cultural matrix, global and local as well as homogenizing and diversifying influences continuously merge in the lifestyles, performances and socio-political practices of contemporary youth.[3] Global media has come to constitute an independent and powerful agent of socialization for young people, and tensions have arisen as it has effectively challenged the more traditional agents of socialization.

The process of globalization has stimulated a composite sort of response all over concerning benefits and costs to the society. Some suggest that globalization has created and augmented socio-economic inequalities, has corroded indigenous cultural identities and overall has benefited only a few. Instead, it has created islands of prosperity amidst sea of poverty. Although some supporters of globalization thesis argue that the process of globalization is beneficial in terms of creating and providing equal opportunities for growth, better living standards and overall global awareness and consequent advantages.

Truly, Indian society is exclusive and different from other societies in terms of its historicity, social and cultural settings and its placement in the developmental phase. It requires different and specific approach while dealing with unique and incomparable Indian scenario. Yogendra Singh (2000) has done an elaborative work to explain the cultural change in India as a result of globalization in his book *Culture Change in India: Identity and Globalization*. Focusing primarily on the cultural change in India, he divides these changes in two categories: that is, substantive structure of culture and its relationship with social institutions and processes of change in culture specially engendered by the forces of globalization and telecommunication revolution and emergence of market economy in a qualitatively new form. He opines that globalization is a multidimensional and multidirectional process that has generated a strident debate on social, economic and cultural consequences of it. The impact of globalization on the structural changes in the society comes generally through the changes in economic policies. In developing societies, the tension and anxieties on account of globalization are primarily economic, which later on spill over to the anxieties about culture and identity. Singh believes that ICTs, cultural system with the right level of economic growth, emphasize on distributive processes of social mobility, resolve the problem of cultural identity, create a sense of confidence and pride in people's heart with respect to their situation and correspondingly the fear of cultural dependency comes down or withers away. Increased use of computers, telephone, the Internet, etc., has deeply impacted the social institutions and modes of social interaction. Though the scope of electronic communication and entertainment media expanding rapidly, it still remains limited due to widespread poverty, illiteracy and backwardness amongst 40 per cent of population. He discusses emerging popular culture and its impact on the style of life of the youth and other social categories in rural and urban population and also the impact of changes in social structure on leisure activities and its institutions in rural and urban India. The change in lifestyle and cultural elements do lead to changes in the life world and identity of contemporary youth. Major occupational and technocultural changes take place in our society, but it is also true that these impacts are in their nascent stage. A creative balance between continuity and change in cultural policy is essential for us to achieve our future goals.

Sharma (2002) discusses the nature of social and cultural discontents of globalization in context of India. He states that globalization has adversely affected all the three social frontiers, that is, social security, social justice and social harmony in India. With respect to cultural sphere, globalization has led to obliteration of the cultural traditions of the third-world countries: spread of culture of consumerism and commoditization of culture. He emphasizes that fuelled by market forces, globalization is a carrier of American population culture and is designed to be a process of hegemonic cultural homogenization of the world.

Yogendra Singh (1964) in his study of value system in educated youth noticed that there is a synthesis regarding their value orientation (particularistic achievement and universalistic ascriptive). The former works towards a synthesis of the ascriptive elements of traditional structure with collective welfare ideal through authoritarian means; again, an interesting survival of Indian tradition and the latter wants to work out a mode of adjustment where many of the traditional structural and cultural foci (kinship, caste, community, etc.) could themselves be so reformed and adjusted as to evolve a rationalistic progressive society with controlled spread of achievement values. Obviously, both of these represent modern youth's synthesis in value orientations.

There are certain changes due to the impact of globalization in the context of India, which are more visible, palpable and mostly talked about. These also help us understand the extent of impact of globalization in our traditional society.

In social and cultural realm, changes in social structure and processes are more evident, namely, decline of extended joint families and rise of nuclear families, rising instances of inter-caste and inter-faith marriages, preferences for small family, lack of community sentiments, emphasis on achievement values, changes in values and lifestyle, etc. In economic sphere of life, we find basic changes in the structure of economy. Service sector and its contribution to gross domestic product is growing with fast pace. A higher rate of migration for employment both domestic and international, growth of multinational corporations, greater capital flow, wide use of technology, changing work environment and culture, greater import/export of goods and services, etc., along with an economy moving with variation in global markets is found. In political scenario, India has become a member of many global political organizations and a political system moving with variation in global polity and international relations. Globalization has become more prominent and dominating due to the unparalleled growth and advancement of technology in information communication and transportation. Presently, high technology is being used in almost every field of activity: education, health, work, entertainment, etc.

The focus of this study is to understand the socio-cultural and economic impact of globalization and technological advancements on youth in India. There are a number of problems that youth are facing today. Their ambience is changing fast, and they need to cope with these changes. They need to confront economic and employment insecurities and risks; their aspirations and social expectations are high, and the world is becoming more competitive and tough. They are exposed to global culture and information through media and at the same time have to deal with their local situations and limitations. Social ties are weakening and community sentiments are deteriorating. Social relationships are being transformed into virtual and mechanical. Most of our communication with other people is indirect lacking human contact and face-to-face interaction. Therefore, it becomes significant to make an attempt to understand and analyse the impact of globalization and ICTs on lifestyle, values, attitudes and situations of youth from different sections of Indian society sociologically.

II

Empirical Framework

The Internet is one of the most effective technologies that have transformed our ways of living. The Internet is a new tool for doing 'old things in new ways'. Weiser (2001) talks of two ways of using the Internet, that is, for social and interpersonal purposes and informational purposes. If we consider the Internet to be the best source to communicate, consume information or consume products, it becomes a sort of cultural necessity (Brignall, 2002). From the invention, application and expansion of the Internet, there have been several concerns among scholars regarding its impact on social and interpersonal relationships (Kraut et al., 1998; Lenhart et al., 2001; Katz and Rice, 2002). We can say in general that it is not easy to study the influence of Internet use because there is not just one way to use the Internet. The manners of Internet use are just as various as human beings, and we need to speak about the influence of specific environments and specific ways of Internet use and not about the global influence of the Internet.[4]

India is a fast-developing country with world's second largest population and is characterized with a unique socio-cultural scenario. Approximately, 70 per cent of India's population still lives in rural areas. It has strong traditional institutions of family, marriage, caste, kinship and community. It has been able to survive with its cultural distinctiveness following customs and traditions while evolving high technology of satellites, computers and industrial machines. Since 64 years of independence, India has come a long way in terms of economic development, but it is still lacking on basic issues of unemployment, poverty, food scarcity, lack of potable water, lack of electricity, corruption, illiteracy, lack of proper health services for all, etc. India has a small section of upper class, a burgeoning middle class with sizable lower class. The advantage with India is its youthfulness. India is a young nation with 35 per cent of population below 15 years of age and 41 per cent of its population between 13 and 35 years of age (Census of India, 2001), which provides a good pool of human resources. We have one of the largest English-speaking populations and a large number of young educated engineers, doctors and other professionals. We have our strength in our spirituality, strong values, organized social structures and social systems such as family, marriage, kinship, etc. However, global exposure is altering the scenario, and no doubt it is not same as it was in the past.

Individual's intellectual, social and moral development is strongly shaped by the technological environment, he inhabits. Therefore, there is a need to create a balance in our technological environment. Technology is both a source of promise and a cause of concern for a developing nation with multigoals to be achieved. The ICT revolution has opened the world for young people. Today, it is possible for an individual to keep in touch with their social relations no matter how far they reside, in a faster and economical way. Today, free access to vast repository of knowledge is provided to all through the Internet. The critics of ICT argue that interactive nature of these communication technologies fuelled by the Internet and mobile are leading to virtualization of social relationships and increase of solitary leisure time activities. This does not mean that we do not interact with our neighbours; do not engage ourselves in indoor/outdoor games when we get an opportunity or interact face to face in physical terms.

Youth today creates their identity in an environment where they are constantly exposed to global cultural elements through various types of media such as TV, the Internet, mobile, etc., while living in local socio-cultural settings. Emergence of virtual community spaces on World Wide Web in terms of chat rooms, social networking sites, blogs, etc., has led scholars to articulate their concerns about the future of social interaction and relationship pattern. On the issue of virtual social space, Rheingold (1993) states that 'People in virtual communities do just about everything people do in real life, but we leave our bodies behind.' A number of other scholars (Foster, 1996; Kiesler, 1997; Turkle, 1997; Baym, 1998; Wellman, 1998; Smith and Kollock, 1999; Rheingold, 2000; Yum and Hara, 2005) have also studied and analysed computer-mediated communication and virtual community and their impact on socio-cultural aspect of society.

In this background, a study was conducted as part of doctoral work and an attempt was made to understand and assess the socio-cultural impact of globalization and technological advancements on youth. The present analysis is grounded upon primary data collected from 400 youth aged between 18 and 30 years and studying in educational institutes of Jaipur for three or more years. Major findings of the present study are described below.

ICT Tools and Youth

There are a number of concerns regarding impact of ICTs on society.

- *Computer–Internet*: In the sample population, around one-third of the respondents considered computer–Internet to have a positive impact, 15 per cent to have negative impact, and more than a half stated that ICTs can have both positive and negative impact, but it completely depends on the user. The youth opined that the Internet opens vast amount of information but at the same time its unguided, unrestricted use can lead to addiction, social alienation, induction to porn sites, cybercrime, etc. In virtual space, identity of a person is constructed through virtual representation of the self. A number of factors influence the attitude of a person towards virtual identity such as online safety, vulnerability to cheating and hacking, misuse of shared information and privacy issues. The youth under study were not concerned about the issues of vulnerability in the virtual world. Majority of them gave their true identity online.

- *Mobile*: Mobile handsets today provide a package of applications such as camera, FM, multimedia file applications, games, the Internet, etc., that make it a lot more than just a communication tool. Around a half of the respondents consider it as a significant tool for entertainment too; around one-fourth consider it as symbol of personality and status, whereas females consider it being a helpful device for emergency and safety as well.
- *Self-perception towards feeling of addiction to computer/mobile*: In the present scenario, these technological devices have become inseparable part of youth's lives and feeling of addiction is quite common. Around three-fourth of the respondents feel that they cannot live without computer/mobile. The youth opined that they feel lost if they do not have their mobile with them. It is as necessary as having food.

Family and Youth

Family is the primary agency of socialization. It is built upon sentiments of love, affection and cooperation. Spending time with family not only helps to strengthen the bond but also helps in personality development and psychological well-being of individuals.

- *Time spent with family*: In contemporary life, youth has to move away from their family settings and live separately for firstly, education and later on for employment. This leads to lack of emotional support in times of stress and emotional breakdowns and slackening of parental control. The youth is affected more by their peer than by family members. It becomes interesting here that how a new sort of culture emerges out of interplay of parent culture and peer culture in these living arrangements.
- *Opinion of the respondents regarding giving freedom to children*: An overwhelming majority of respondents opined that giving freedom to youth provides opportunity to grow, develops confidence and skills for decision-making and leadership essential for betterment in future life. However, they feel that there should be a balance between authority and autonomy. Youth are unable to handle the freedom very wisely; and in current scenario, they are often susceptible to multiple threats; hence, there is a need for constant surveillance and guidance apart from freedom. This emerged out of opinion of youth based on their personal situations.

Kinship and Youth

Kinship plays an active role in enhancing the personality as well as providing a safety valve. It provides social continuity by binding together a number of successive generations through affinal or consanguineous relations.

- *Frequency of meeting kinsmen*: Life has become very hectic and busy that youth often find themselves unable to cope with the demands of kinship. They feel that they do not have time to fulfil social commitments. At the same time, kinship relations have also become materialistic and self-centred that youth find themselves disinclined to be an active part of them. More than three-fourth of the respondents reported visiting their relatives occasionally even when they were living with the family. During detailed discussion, few respondents showed lack of interest and one of them even stated that 'I don't want to meet them and I can't be forced to do so.' They feel that visiting relatives is a waste of time especially if they belong to the older age group. They find that there is a disjunction between their ideas and those of their relatives. The intensity of relationship with kins has reportedly been declining due to factors such as urbanization, migration, growth of secondary institutions, hectic lifestyle, increasing aloofness, self-centeredness, etc.

Marriage and Youth

Marriage has been one of the basic and universal institutions in society. It lays the foundation for family bonds. The earliest marriages were organized to cement social bonds and contribute to the economic viability of the group. The original purpose of marriage was to produce reciprocal obligations and the interlocking of families. However, the institution of marriage saw a lot of change due to factors such as urbanization, migration, women's entry into occupations, feministic ideology, rise of individualism, etc. From an institution for procreation, it has come to be seen as a mutual choice of the couple entering into it, a choice based on love. More recently, the institution has further diversified. In contemporary times, delayed marriages (frequently preceded by cohabitation), serial marriages, single-parent households (sometimes in the aftermath of divorce), blended families and step parents and cohabitation are becoming the norm.

- *Essentiality of marriage*: Around two-third of the respondents consider marriage as essential in life, but they do not feel that one should get married since their parents want them to. Majority of the respondents opined that the decision of marriage should be taken only after achieving stability in career. It is noteworthy to mention here that youth do not stigmatize people who wish to remain single. They believe in granting freedom of choice to the individual.
- *Opinion of the respondents regarding preferred way of marriage*: In Indian traditional society, marriage is an act involving not only two individuals but two families. The most prevalent and accepted way of marriage is arranged marriage where the parents choose the marriage partner for their children, sometimes even without consulting them. Factors such as spread of education, urbanization, industrialization, increase of women in work force and nuclear family have slowly and gradually transformed this approach. More choice is being given to the boy/girl and newer forms of marriage have emerged. Today, love marriages have started gaining acceptance in the society. We find that parents and children have found a mid-way in the form of love-cum-arranged marriages where the boy/girl choose their life partners and parents then arrange it. When the respondents were asked their opinion regarding preferred form of marriage, it was found

that two-third of respondents favoured love-cum-arranged marriage, whereas only one-third of respondents favoured arranged marriage.

- *Opinion of the respondents regarding divorce*: In our traditional society, marriage is thought to be for lifetime, and in India it is also thought of as a union of seven births. Although divorce rate is quite low in India in comparison to Western countries, factors such as women empowerment, education, greater legal awareness, career ambitions, rise of individualistic and materialistic values, etc., have contributed to a rise in the divorce rate significantly. In Indian society, it is still considered as a last option and has high stigma attached to it. It also has harsh consequences in terms of low acceptance in family and society. Class also plays significant role due to economic ramifications especially for women. However, the respondents were found to have an open view on the issue of divorce. A total of 96.5 per cent opined that they are in favour of opting for legal separation if it becomes essential for peace of mind and a happy future.
- *Attitude of the respondents towards live-in relationship and double income, no kids (DINK) families*: A live-in arrangement is one in which an unmarried couple lives together in a long-term relationship that resembles a marriage. Couples cohabit, rather than marry, for a variety of reasons. They may want to test their compatibility before they commit to a legal union, want to curtail the responsibilities associated with marriage, etc. A live-in relationship may give them space, but it comes with insecurity as it lacks stability and even socio-legal status. Marriage counsellors strongly believe that people try harder to keep a relationship going when they are married, as divorce still has social ramifications. In the sample population, around one-fourth of respondents stated to accept live-in relationships. Despite strict social norms prohibiting pre-marital opposite-sex mixing, today's youth wants to act modern. When asked in detailed discussion, they accepted live-in relationship saying that if somebody is happy and comfortable doing something, why should we have a problem, after all it's their life and they have right to do what they like.
- A new type of family that is being observed in contemporary society is DINK family. A family consisting of one couple, both working and having no kids is defined as a 'DINK family'. Traditionally, a couple is expected to have a baby within almost a year of marriage. Delayed parenthood may raise questions about the fertility of the couple especially woman. Early parenthood has been positively correlated with socio-cultural settings of the couple (James, 2010; Marie et al., 2011). But a lure to enjoy life without worries of kids, greater freedom, career stability, enjoyment of lavish lifestyle, desire to provide comfortable life to children, work schedules of corporate organizations, etc., are leading to development of DINK families especially in the metropolitans. This trend is also finding a step hold in the smaller towns and cities. Parent–child relationship has undergone massive changes. The youth wants to plan both their career and family. They wish to start a family only when they are financially secure and are in a position to provide basic comforts to their progeny. One-third of the respondents opined to opt for DINK family system. Early parenthood was seen as a limiting force in their career graph. The respondents feel that if

both the partners consent for DINK family, then it is good not only for financial stability, but it will also provide them time to understand each other better and get mentally more matured and provide better facilities to their children in future – although none of the respondents showed inclination towards settings of DINK family for long period.

Caste System and Youth

Caste system is one of the basic and unique elements of Indian society. It is a highly complex segmental and hierarchical division of society on the basis of ascribed status, restrictions on feeding and social intercourse, privileges, purity and pollution, traditional occupation and endogamy. The caste system is internalized through socialization, and it becomes an integral part of Indian identity. The youth of the country have a mixed opinion on the issue of caste. They do not find it having a bearing on their educational and career opportunities. The youth believes in the diktat that *we have created the caste system and not God*; hence, it should not be allowed to dictate our life.

- *Opinion of the respondents regarding interfaith marriages*: One of the important characteristics of caste system has been endogamy. However, due to the spread of democratic values, rising education levels, modernization and globalization, caste barriers in marriage have begun to loosen. Around a half of the respondents stated that they do not consider caste as a compulsory attribute when looking for a life partner. This signifies that endogamous characteristic of caste is losing its importance. The youth did not consider caste as an important factor to bear in mind while making friends.

Traditional Rituals and Youth

Youth are like a 'link' between the age-old traditions and the upcoming global culture. They are being sandwiched between the two. As they are brought up in a traditional local cultural ambience, they are trained to follow the traditions. On coming in contact with global trends, they get trapped between global cultures, peer culture, market-dominated materialistic life, etc. They want to be modern and scientifically rational; at the same time, they have the onus to sustain their rituals and traditions, their heritage. A large majority of respondents follow traditional rituals occasionally. The forces of modernization, urbanization, paucity of time, high costs in terms of money and management have limited the organization of traditional rituals to ceremonies and festivals. However, the global media has also revived the interest of youth in traditions and rituals. The large diaspora and urban youth are being fed Indian culture and traditions by the media through daily soaps, mythological stories, religious channels, etc. The youth today want the grandeur associated with traditional rituals in their marriage or other important social functions.

Leisure and Youth

Information and communication technologies are affecting not only the ways of our working but also our leisure time activities. Social interaction is increasingly taking place within an electronic environment by means of text messaging and online meetings. New leisure pursuits such as downloading music/movies, chat rooms, blogging, watching TV, playing computer games and being glued to computer screens and mobile keypads for a large part of the day are responsible for shifting the youth from *communitarian leisure* to *individualized leisure*. Most of these pastimes are replacing more traditional leisure activities such as sports, visiting people and other social activities. Leisure activities among youth are directly correlated with the availability of time and resources, personal interests and the level of satisfaction derived. In the investigation, it was revealed that around one-third of the respondents watch TV in their leisure time, one-third spend time with their family or friends, whereas the rest of them engage in other activities such as listening to music, reading newspaper or magazine, working on computer or the Internet, etc.

Dressing Pattern and Youth

Dressing is one of the fundamental elements of one's culture. Dressing up in the latest styles is an important facet of self-expression and this was a view strongly held by the youth under study. As a result of global media, easy availability of international brands, etc., youth have ample opportunities to follow the latest fashion and fads in their pattern of dressing. Being a symbol of modernization, youth like to wear jeans, T-shirts and other Western attire. In India, a variety of dresses both Indian and Western are worn by men and women such as *dhoti–kurta, sari, ghagra–odhani, salwar–kameej, payjama–kurta,* etc. Around two-third of respondents prefer to wear Indian dresses on festive occasions. The youth prefer to wear Western casual wear in their daily routine. The youth seem to have evolved a bicultural identity having elements of both local identity and global identity. The youth have also become brand conscious. They are highly conscious of their image, which is linked with the global presence of brands. Exposure and accessibility to global mass media and the Internet have ensured that the youth today are not only aware of new brands available but also know how to evaluate them on various parameters. Youth aspires for dress styles that are no different from their counterparts in the United States or Europe.

- *Stress and coping strategies*: Modern life is stressful. Reasons of stress vary with age group. Youth stress is mostly related to studies, career, financial stability and marriage issues. High levels of unemployment, extremely low opportunities and relatively high social and familial aspirations lead to stress among youth (Mahajan, 1995). Coping strategies are very important when dealing with stress. Major cause of stress of the respondents was found to be career. Self-management of stress was found to be the first solution for more than one-third of the respondents, whereas one-third of the respondents opted sharing with family or friends as the choice of stress management. Only one-fifth of the respondents got relief from listening to music or other modes of entertainment.

III

Conclusion

Technology has always been facilitating human work from the very beginning of human civilization and has had molding impact on society whether manifest or latent; direct or indirect. From the invention of wheel, agricultural tools and techniques, printing, radio, television, telephone, computers, mobile and Internet technology has always played a very fundamental and significant role in development and change in our society. But the World Wide Web has drastically transformed our life in a totally new way. The advancement in technologies of information and communication has intensified the widely discussed process of globalization and has brought the whole world onto a single platform irrespective of time and place.

The decisive character of technology has always been emphasized in studying development of trends and transformation in all aspects of society (Lask, 2001; Wajcman, 2002; Dutton, 2004; McQuire, 2006). The unprecedented development and advancement of technology has facilitated the global flow of information, capital and human resources too. As a result, we are witnessing intense globalization around the world in all spheres of activity such as social, cultural, economic or political.

Social relationships are very strong in the context of Indian social system and have very strong individual bonding. A significant majority of youth reported to engage occasionally in social gatherings and attend only chosen social events as per their preferences. They feel that there is a decline in social interest of people in general.

The institution of marriage and related values are significantly changing that is apparent from the data, most probably due to increasing individualism, freedom and achievement values. With new modern and freedom-oriented values, essentiality of marriage has begun to disappear among our youth. This is significant to note that preferred way of marriage is inclining towards love-cum-arranged marriage. This is quite clear from the data that youth give importance to opinion of parents in context of marriage issues, but they still do not let their opinion forego for that.

In sum, it can be concluded that in the current scenario, the emerging cultural and value system is like a process of interaction of the modern and traditional elements, which is bringing about a unique synthesis (Singh, 1964). Today's youth are creating their own world although working with a synthesis between traditional and modern values (Cormack, 1962; Garg and Parikh, 1976; Derne, 2008). There is a need to learn lessons to augment positive impacts and decrease the negative impacts.

Notes

1. See preface by Director-General of International Labor Organization, *World Employment Report 2001: Life at Work in the Information Economy*. Geneva: International Labor Organization, 2001. Available Online at http://www.ilo.org/public/libdoc/ilo/P/09465/09465(2001).pdf.
2. Mohandas Karamchand Gandhi (1869–1948), Great Indian political and spiritual leader, also known as *Mahatma* Gandhi and *Rashtrapita*.
3. See Richard Kahn and Douglas Kellner, *Global Youth Culture*. Available Online at http://www.gseis.ucla.edu/faculty/kellner/essays/globyouthcult.pdf.
4. See Anna Galacz and David Smahel, 'Information Society from a Comparative Perspective: Digital Divide and Social Effects of the Internet', *Cyberpsychology: Journal of Psychological Research on Cyberspace*, 2008. Available Online at http://

www.worldinternetproject.net/_files/_Published/_oldis/Information%20 Society%20from%20a%20Comparative%20Perspective.pdf.

References

Appadurai, Arjun (1996). *Modernity at Large: Cultural Dimensions of Globalization*. New Delhi: Oxford University Press.

Baym, N. (1998). 'The Emergence of Online Community', in S. Jones (ed.), *Cybersociety 2.0: Revisiting Computer-Mediated Communication and Community*. London: Sage Publications, pp. 35–68.

Beck, Ulrick (1992). *Risk Society: Towards a New Modernity*. London: Sage Publications.

Bhagwati, Jagadish (2004). *In Defense of Globalization*. New York: Oxford University Press.

Brignall, Tom (2002). 'The New Panopticon: The Internet Viewed as a Structure of Social Control', *Theory & Science*, 3(2). http://theoryandscience.icaap.org/content/vol003.001/brignall.html.

Castells, Manuel (1996). *The Information Age: Economy, Society and Culture, Vol. I*. Oxford: Blackwell.

Cormack, Margaret L. (1962). *She Who Rides a Peacock: Indian Students and Social Change*. New York: Praeger Publication.

Croucher, Sheila L. (2004). *Globalization and Belonging: The Politics of Identity in a Changing World*. Oxford: Rowman and Littlefield Publishers Inc.

Derne, Steve (2008). *Globalization on the Ground: Media and the Transformation of Culture, Class, and Gender in India*. New Delhi: Sage Publications.

Dutton, William H. (2004). *Social Transformation in an Information Society: Rethinking Access to You and the World*. Paris: United Nations Educational, Scientific and Cultural Organization (UNESCO).

Foster, Derek (1996). 'Community and Identity in the Electronic Village', in David Porter (ed.), *Internet Culture*. New York: Routledge, pp. 23–37. http://services.exeter.ac.uk/cmit/media/texts/porter1996/foster1996_community_and_identity/

Friedman, Thomas (2005). *The World is Flat: A Brief History of the Twenty-First Century*. New York: Farrar, Straus and Giroux.

Garg, Pulin K. and Indira J. Parikh (1976). *Profiles in Identity: A Study of Indian Youth at Crossroads of Culture*. New Delhi: Vision Books Pvt. Ltd.

Giddens, A. (1990). *The Consequences of Modernity*. Oxford: Polity Press.

Held, D., A. McGrew, D. Goldblatt and J. Perraton (1999). *Global Transformations: Politics, Economics and Culture*. Cambridge: Polity Press.

James, G. (2010). 'Socio-Cultural Context of Adolescents' Motivation for Marriage and Childbearing in North-Western Nigeria: A Qualitative Approach', *Current Research Journal of Social Sciences*, 2(5): 269–75.

Katz, J.K. and R.E. Rice (2002). *Social Consequences of Internet Use: Access, Involvement, and Interaction*. Cambridge, MA: The MIT Press.

Kiesler, Sara (ed.) (1997). *Culture of the Internet*. Mahwah, NJ: Lawrence Erlbaum.

Kraut, R., M. Patterson, V. Lundmark, S. Kiesler, T. Mukopadhyay and W. Scherlis (1998). 'Internet Paradox: A Social Technology that Reduces Social Involvement and Psychological Well-Being?', *American Psychologist*, 53(9): 1017–31.

Lask, Scott (2001). 'Technological Forms of Life', *Theory, Culture & Society*, 18(1): 105–20.

Lenhart, A., L. Rainie and O. Lewis (2001). *Teenage Life Online: The Rise of the Instant-Message Generation and the Internet's Impact on Friendships and Family Relationships*. http://www.pewinternet.org/pdfs/PIP_Teens_Report.pdf.

Mahajan, Anil (1995). 'Urban Youth in Indian Society: Structural Stresses and Cultural Responses', in Noor Mohammad and Abdul Matin (eds), *Indian Youth: Problems and Prospects*. New Delhi: Ashish Publishing House, pp. 89–101.

Marie, Dannette, David M. Fergusson and Joseph M. Boden (2011). 'Cultural Identity and Pregnancy/Parenthood by Age 20: Evidence from a New Zealand Birth Cohort', *Social Policy Journal of New Zealand*, 37: 19–36.

McLuhan, M. (1964). *Understanding Media: The Extensions of Man*. New York: McGraw Hill.

McQuire, Scott (2006). 'Technology', *Theory, Culture & Society*, 23(2–3): 253–65.

Rheingold, H. (1993). *The Virtual Community: Homesteading on the Electronic Frontier*, 1st ed. Cambridge, MA: Addison-Wesley.

——— (2000). *The Virtual Community: Homesteading on the Electronic Frontier*, 2nd ed. Cambridge, MA: MIT Press.

Ritzer, George (2004). *The Globalization of Nothing*. Thousand Oaks: Pine Forge Press.

Robertson, R. (1990). 'Mapping the Global Condition: Globalization as the Central Concept', in Mike Featherstone (ed.), *Global Culture: Nationalism, Globalization and Modernity*. London: Sage Publications, pp. 15–30.

Sharma, S.L. (2002). 'Globalization and its Socio-Cultural Discontents', *Social Sciences Research Journal*, 10(3): 69–84.

Singh, Yogendra (1964). 'Cultural Integration and Changing Values: A Study of Value System of Educated Youth', *Sociological Bulletin*, 13(2): 49–66.

——— (2000). *Culture Change in India: Identity and Globalization*. Jaipur: Rawat Publications.

Smelser, Neil J. and Paul B. Baltes (2001). *International Encyclopedia of the Social and Behavioral Sciences*. New York: Elsevier.

Smith, Mark A. and Peter Kollock (eds) (1999). *Communities in Cyberspace*. New York: Routledge.

Stiglitz, Joseph (2002). *Globalization and Its Discontents*. New York: W.W. Norton & Company.

Turkle, Sherry (1997). *Life on the Screen: Identity in the Age of the Internet*. New York: Simon & Schuster Inc.

United Nations (2005). *World Youth Report 2005: Young People Today, and in 2015*. Department of Economic and Social Affairs. New York: United Nations. http://www.un.org/esa/socdev/unyin/documents/wyr05book.pdf.

Wajcman, Judy (2002). 'Addressing Technological Change: The Challenge to Social Theory', *Current Sociology*, 50(3): 347–63.

Waters, Malcolm (1995). *Globalization: The Reader (Key Ideas)*. London: Routledge.

Weiser, E.B. (2001). 'The Functions of Internet Use and their Social and Psychological Consequences', *Cyberpsychology & Behavior*, 4(6): 723–43.

Wellman, B. (1998). *Networks in the Global Village: Life in Contemporary Communities*. Boulder: Westview Press.

Yum, Y.-O. and K. Hara (2005). 'Computer-Mediated Relationship Development: A Cross-Cultural Comparison', *Journal of Computer-Mediated Communication*, 11(1). http://jcmc.indiana.edu/vol11/issue1/yum.html.

18

Dynamics of Economic Reforms and Revamping Rural India

Opportunities and Challenges

Ashish Saxena

Introduction

Current times are characterized as a period of global transition, where change is rapid and intensive and results from various interconnected processes. Individuality and cultural meanings in their many and various forms are considered to strengthen under such conditions. Different cultural traits, viewed as particular collective cultural wholes, emerge and change in global, local and global interactive processes, as people set up various institutions and organizations to maintain them. The new institutional innovations that globalization brings in the society are market, trade and finance, communication and media, technology and science, and migration and intercultural transaction. Thus, with the introduction of a free-market economy and globalization, there is a radical departure from the earlier models of development. In social-structural terms, globalization is a historical process of transition from the agrarian-industrial, post-industrial and finally the stage of the information society (Singh, 2000). In this information society, new technologies will lead to better quality of life in terms of greater social freedom and increased knowledge and livelihoods that are more productive. They also deserve special attention because digital breakthroughs are pushing forward the frontiers of how nations can use technology to eradicate poverty. These breakthroughs are creating new possibilities for improving health and nutrition, expanding knowledge, stimulating economic growth and empowering people to participate in their communities as well as the outside world. Thus, technological transformations, intertwined with globalization, are creating a new paradigm: the global network age. These transformations expand opportunities and increase the social and economic rewards of creating and using technology. They are also altering how – and by whom – technology is created and owned, and how it is made accessible and used.

In a broader sense, technological innovations are affecting human development by enhancing human capabilities for better living standards and political participation in the social, economic and political life of community. As emphasized by Human Development Report (2001), this new terrain requires shift in public policy to harness today's technological transformations as a tool for human development. Putting forth this discussion in the framework of developing country such as India, we find that global transition processes take place at all levels, even bringing challenges to the grassroot development of the rural areas. Policy and development programmes aim at finding solutions to the problems resulting from changes brought about by the decline of local economies and social restructuring. Thus, transforming rural India is a challenge that should focus the best of Indian minds – it is perhaps the single biggest barrier to making India a developed country.

Although the government's initial efforts for rural development could not make a revolutionary change in rural India, therefore the Indian villages need disruptive innovations to make the giant leap forward. Limitations in basic infrastructure, especially quality information in India's rural areas, are a key challenge for a number of community projects. On the contrary, modern India is also emerging as a testing ground for new technologies and business models, which aim to narrow the digital divide between urban and rural people in developing economies. Regarding the figures of 'technological achievement', Human Development Report 2001 ranks India at 63 and falls in the category of 'dynamic adopters' (against leaders, potential leaders, marginalized). Its technology achievement index (TAI) is 0.201 (highest 0.744 by Finland, 0.733 by the United States). In the field of 'diffusion of technology (Agriculture and manufacturing)', its HDI rank is 115 (1st Norway) and is located in 'medium human development' category. Regarding diffusion of technology (information and communication), it ranks 115 and in 'medium human development category' (UNDP-2001: 48). Unfortunately, the constraints regarding the efficacy of multimedia (information technology) in Indian scenario are far from satisfactory level. PC penetration is 0.58 per cent (Asia is at 3.31 per cent and world average is at 8.42 per cent). Despite the ongoing deregulation of India's telecommunications sector, its national tele-density is one of the lowest in the world, improving slowly from 0.06 per cent in 1990 to almost 3 per cent today. India's new telecom policy seeks to increase telephone penetration to 7 per cent by 2005 and 15 per cent by the year 2010. It encourages development of telecom in rural areas to increase tele-density from the current level of 0.4–4 per cent by the year 2010 (http://www.trai.gov.2004). Thus, in terms of technological adaptability, rural India is construed as an example of the worst performer in development. Resources and technologies in it remain confined to the selective State and prosperous regions, leaving the less endowed unharnessed. Prosperity lacks horizontal dispersal and downward percolation. Uneven growth in rural India is also due to distinctive social stratification, production relations and power structure.

Besides technological advancement, India's rural power is also under transformation. Modern rural policy increasingly advocates empowerment of local communities to develop through deliberative processes of their own strategies for the future, supported by appropriate multilevel governance structures and managerial technologies. Taken together, such processes are contributing to the opening up of new sites and opportunities for the resurgence of rural spaces. The rural thus is a challenging space, a site of contrasting growth and decline, creativity and threat. Rural identity holding a privileged position within many cultural and historical narratives requires both the challenges and opportunities for rural communities concerning broad processes of change. The search for sustainability seems to be driving main changes in agricultural production systems, under the influence of the ecologization of agricultural policy, of new environmental and social market standards and of pressure from environmental and consumers associations. Organic agriculture has been institutionalized in some countries as the model to reach such sustainability, but other types of agriculture are also claiming to be sound alternatives to the dominant industrialized production system. These alternative agricultures are promoted by agricultural scientists and extentionists, farmers' movements, commercial firms and/or environmental associations.

Keeping in view the neoliberal policies and the pace of globalization, there is an urgent need to re-look into the revamping rural India in order to identify the potentialities for future development. Present paper sensibly presents the critical view of contemporary rural India and draw attention along the following broader issues:

- A need for refuting the stereotypic and idealized sociological image of rural India and presenting revamping macro-picture of contemporary rural India.
- Emphasizing on the issue that peasantry and subsistence agriculture is no longer the backbone of rural economies. Although it still has an important role in shaping rural landscapes in developing countries such as India, its weight in rural economies vis-à-vis commercial economy is often low and declining.
- Input-driven technologies, part and parcel of Green Revolution, have enhanced productivity but also have contrived concern for sustainability of production and natural resources, have clicked the global alarm. Further, the research and extension systems, in their efforts to generate, formulate and transfer new technologies are being guided by the *homo-technicus* image of the farmers, which excludes other quintessential components that account for farmers' rationale and behaviour.
- Luckily, in the era of liberalization and globalization, the move away from equality of outcome towards equality of opportunity has gone together with a growing policy focus on investment in human capital. Contemporarily, poverty is defined not solely on the basis of income but in terms of a lack of basic capacities or capabilities – health, education and literacy, reasonable housing condition, safety – which allows individuals

to participate in social membership and to make choice in respect of their own lives (Sen, 1992).

- Finally, the conditions for effective technological change and knowledge flow are complex involving not only engineering factors but economic and socio-political factors well. The paper emphasizes the broader issue of shifting accessibility of technology from elite centric to people centric and further to enhance the government–citizen interface through multimedia techniques. An optimistic approach towards such initiatives may help in bridging the rural–urban divide.

Liberalization, Globalization and the Indian State

Globalization is a complex phenomenon and is a process by which the world becomes a 'global village'. It affects different aspects of any country – economic, political, social and religious. The challenges posed by globalization to existing non-global forms of civic rights and collective action vary fundamentally along two axes with regard to position in the social structure and with location in the geography of globalization, that is, context and the space. Two questions – Who you are? Where you are? – make crucial differences and give very different grounds and possibilities of action.

We may characterize globalization as follows: First, economic globalization defined by both growing structural power and mobility of capital in production and financial markets is articulated with neoliberal policies of privatization, deregulation and structural changes in national bureaucracies, welfare programs and public services. Second, economic globalization, defined by the liberalization of trade and monetary policies, the growth of transnational networks of investment, finance, advertising and consumption market as well as rise of trans national networks (Strange, 1995). Third, Conventional institutions such as the nation state, national military, police force, political parties and legislatives now face new challenges posted by this interactive, mobile transnational network (Held, 1991). Fourth, the rise of regional economic and political bodies as well as supranational bodies introduces new agents into decision-making process with which the conventional centres of political power have to negotiate and contend. Fifth, the growing influence of electronic media into everyday life has the net effect of creating multiple forms of imagined communities (Anderson, 1992: 13). It thus involves a number of substantive social processes and more than one procedural dynamics. In brief, globalization is multi-form, multifacet and multidimensional process.

Post-independent Indian nation proceeded through the adoption of an innovative constitution such as the launching of Five-Year Plans, decentralization of polity and similar measures unleashed forces of social transformation. The national state became the core institution and development with justice became the new goals. Although equality became the central value, its translation into reality remained a great challenge. The globalizing phase initiated by the liberalization of the economy. The distinguishing features of this phase are minimalization of the role of the State in economic development, enlarged role of civil society in social transformation and centrality of the market in the economy. As the market became the core institutional order, the consumer assumed central identity sidelining citizenship rights against the rapacity of the market. The core institutional order of the global age being the market, both capital and consumer got privileged (Oommen, 2009). Further, the shift of decision-making power into the hands of transnational institutions such as the World Trade Organization, International Monetary Fund, World Banks and others has severely reduced the sovereignty of national government and resulted in a very serious drift.

Here Berman's (1988) idea hold valid, that is,

> to be modern is to find ourselves in an environment that promises adventure, power, joy, growth, transformation of ourselves and the world – and, at the same time, that threatens to destroy everything we have, everything we know, everything we are.... To be modern is to be part of a universe in which, as Marx said, 'all that is solid melts into air.'

This statement rightly qualifies the present era of globalization as being adventurous as well as 'risk society'. Let us view the mixed experiences owing to neoliberal policies in developing countries such as India.

Implications of LPG: Mixed Experiences

In July 1991, when the first comprehensive statements of policy on economic and trade liberalization were formulated for India, it was under considerable international pressure to follow the policy prescriptions of the major international lending institutions including the IMF and The World Bank, which advocated trade liberalization and export-led growth. The Indian government's structural adjustment policies have proposed reductions in public sector employment, limitations on agricultural subsidies, denationalization of banks and insurance companies and reductions in public expenditure that are envisioned to increase global competition.

Some social scientists have considered the implications of economic liberalization and forecast that marginalized groups will be adversely affected. In particular, they have argued that economic liberalization and marketization will reinforce asymmetrical gender relations (Ghosh, 1996; Sen, 1996). Yet, these are predictions, based on experiences of the poor elsewhere in the developing world (Booth, 1994) rather than actual case studies in India. In short, sociological discussions of economic liberalization in India focus on class polarization in general terms, rather than on empirical evidence. For example, it is argued that:

> ... market forces will polarize classes in both agricultural and industrial sectors. The growing global demand for vegetables, fruits and flowers as Indian agriculture links up with international agri-business and the consequent shrinkage of the area under food crops is inimical to the interests of the poor who will be made to pay higher prices for their daily food requirements. The poor will become poorer and whereas the rich farmers will attain prosperity because of their linkages to the global market. (Panini, 1995)

We may say that the globalization of the Indian economy has dramatically influenced social life in the country. Although the state has mounted policies of economic liberalization, claiming that the policies will ultimately benefit the entire population, a number of social scientists have argued that marginalized groups will be adversely affected. In particular, they have emphasized problems such as uneven regional development, wage disparities and increased levels of inequality. Unquestionably, economic liberalization has not benefited the very poor. Yet, what of the lower income segment of salaried workers? Patents for living organism impoverishment human society ethically, ecologically and economically, though they bring commercial gains to a handful of corporations... (Shiva, 2001).

The agrarian economy of India can be seen through agriculture land and related issues. In Indian situation as the bulk of weaker sections are still without land; therefore, land reform is a key solution for their development. But globalization has not only eclipsed this agenda of land reforms but it has also substituted it with corporatization of farming for the global agricultural market. The thrust of the World Bank–IMF–WTO combine has always been clearly for the abolition of the land ceiling laws and for liberalizing investment into agriculture. Land reform has openly been opposed. If we see the situation of Dalits in agriculture, we find that they will not be immediate beneficiaries. According to Mahbub-ul-Haq (1998) diversification of small farms is often suggested as a means for rapid rural development in India. He emphasized on the need for commercialization and diversification of small farms within and outside agriculture and their proper integration with local and global markets. This is intended not only to liberate the small and marginal farmers from the poverty trap but also to meet the country's growing demands for fruits, vegetables, milk and milk products, meat, fish, eggs, etc., which generally show rising trends with increasing levels of per capita income in the economy. However, the moot question today is how do we achieve the goal of diversification of small farms by overcoming various technological, infrastructural, institutional and policy constraints? The agricultural census data as well as various micro-level studies conducted in different regions indicate that small and marginal farms adopt diversified farming, despite very limited space and low sizes of holdings. Further, it is the affluent categories of farmers who are going for it and not the marginal farmers in majority. Thus, we have to improve the structure of the society to attain the fruits of globalization.

Shiva (1998) rightly said that

> the present process of globalization threatens to undermine aspects of agricultural policy. The trans-national corporations (TNC) are not guided by any philosophy of welfare of the marginalized. Liberalization emphasizes competition, efficiency and providing commodity for the market. Such an approach goes against the prevalent practice of poor farmers who produce for their own use and their methods are based on traditional wisdom. Land has been transferred to TNC's who produce luxury and non-food crops (cash crops) for export rather than staple food. There is also diversion of cereals

from domestic market to export, resulting insecurity and inflation. The farmer's suffers from food insecurity as he has lost his land, resources and is unable to buy them from the market'.

The contract farming, which is promoted as a part of globalization had adverse effect on the farmers. The contract made with illiterate farmers is more one sided. Further, the traditional societies emphasize cooperation; harmony and accommodation with personal relations as existed through jajmani and other caste-based system. But the globalism emphasizes efficiency and competitive culture. Thus, it appears that for majority of Dalit and poor, globalization has meant further deprivation. Singh (2000) too agrees with the above comment and adds that markets are the vital mechanisms through which globalization extends its reach. Some of its effect upon the regional culture may be modernizing, but there are significant areas where it has a disruptive influence upon the local cultures. It has not only disrupted the autonomy of folk cultures but also destabilized the life of the artisans by creating a new network of competition and price war. In Indian context, the social costs of economic globalization and the neoliberal policies related to it have already been very high. The Dalits, the landless and, the *Adivasis* will be the worst hit. Besides this economic reversal, the process of economic globalization has created a serious challenge for the democratic decision-making processes. In political terms, the process of globalization has triggered off forces of change, which have set people rethinking about the political institutions under the growing forces of globalization (Kothari, 1995).

In the Indian context, even there has been some documentation of the growing inequalities due to the implementation of liberalization policies. According to the National Council of Applied Economic Research, for example, wealthier households have grown and benefited from liberalization at a more rapid rate when compared with poorer households (Natarajan, 1999). More specifically, this research shows that although there is a smaller proportion of poorer households in India now than before economic reforms in 1991, richer households are reaping a far greater monetary reward over the corresponding period, with their household income rising dramatically. Simultaneously, by removing both price controls and restrictions on trade, the economic 'reforms' have created incentives to increase agricultural productivity, which in turn has increased employment opportunities. Yet, although certain sectors of the rural economy have undoubtedly prospered, large sectors of the 'backward' classes and castes remain extremely hard-hit by inflation, contraction in secure rural employment, the virtual impossibility of entry into lucrative export markets, continual poor levels of literacy, health and living standards, and overall social and political marginality (Ganguly and Scrase, 1997).

Seeing the brighter side of globalization, Hannerz (1996: 17) rightly states that 'in the most general sense, it is a matter of increasing long-distance interconnectedness, at least across national boundaries, preferably between continents as well'. We can say that these processes of linkages across borders include a restructuration of spaces for 'marginals', leading to the disappearance of fixed links of them to villages, towns and national frontiers. In this regard, Waters (1995: 136) point out that process of globalization specifies greater connectedness and de-territorialization simultaneously. If we try to look at it in positive terms then, it tries to break the barriers, that is, de-capsulization of communities and identities.

Macro-Images of Modernization, Liberalization and Modern Rural India

Revamping Social Structure

After independence, the Indian Constitution, which recognized the democratic needs of a plural society, became a major source for democratic revolution and the Indian Government proceeded to promote the individual rights and equality of all. Lower caste advancement was considered a necessary first step in the promotion of individual rights. Social justice according to this view thus requires a public policy that guarantees individual mobility by means of group allocation. In contemporary India, although there has been reformulation of caste practices in the unofficial inner domain, there has been permeation of the value of equality denying importance of caste in the outer official sphere. After independence, it was one of the foremost concerns of the government to resolve the colonial dichotomy of traditional society versus the modern state, and to integrate them in a new form of nation-state. Although the tradition of national culture was to be celebrated, any traditional features in society that were seen to be incongruent with the new 'idea of India' based on principles of democracy and liberalism were considered suspect for the development of modern India (Khilnani, 1999). Contemporarily, the significance of the social development and empowerment of marginalized groups thus entails sincere demolition of the structure of subordination imposed on them and sharing power with the powerless lots. It raises the anxiety such as the following: assertive castes vis-à-vis rural institutionalized structure of subordination and possible implications of declining caste hierarchy on rural India.

In present context, Dumont's thesis on the unaffected continuity of the encompassing structure of caste hierarchy in rural India seems untenable today. Fuller (1996: 21) suggests instead that there is 'above all a denial, most explicitly in the public domain of the existence or continuing significance of caste in its "traditional form" '. Fundamental changes have occurred in the occupational structure of the society. A vast number of non-traditional, unbound-to-caste occupations and a new type of social relations among occupational groups have emerged. This has resulted in breaking down the nexus between hereditary? Ritual status and occupation – one of the caste system's defining features. It is no longer necessary to justify status of one's occupation in terms of its correlation with degree of ritual purity or impurity associated with it. Situating the dynamics of 'dominant caste' phenomena, one may agree that different castes were competing over the others for showing their supremacy. Historically, this phenomenon was mainly confined to the 'twice-born' castes; but presently, it is applicable to lower caste groups as well. One significant change in contemporary rural India was to transform village and caste from its restricted local and parochial confines into a national and global network. Horizontal caste solidarity was one of the important factors that made universal franchise intrinsic for any governance. The right to vote in turn gave political teeth to horizontal caste solidarity. Horizontal caste solidarity at the regional and national level qualitative changed not only the nature of the polity but also the nature of the state.

The establishment of democracy in independent India has introduced one major change in the way caste and politics interact, and that is by making all castes legally equal. It took some time for this legal equality to gain empirical momentum; but with the gradual dissolution of the closed village economy, the tempo has certainly become easily visible to the naked eye. This combination between law and economic change has allowed castes that were hitherto considered low to take the fight the traditional superior communities and even to thumb their noses at established symbolic and ritual systems (Gupta, 2005). This led to demands among many castes for special recognition by the state for receiving educational and occupational benefits as well as for political representation.

Extending the debate, it can be referred that if we compare the village studies of 1950s with the contemporary village studies, we find a shift from 'treating the village as a locale for the study of a chosen aspect of rural life' to 'treating village as an interacting community with the outside world, both at regional and national level'. Contemporary debates about the conceptual discussions on the nature of a village community have raised the issue of the transitional shift in the 'way of life' of the village. Various agents of transformation have been rightly noted by Chauhan (2005: 295), including increasing participation in the national, state levels and the fact that Panchayati Raj Institutions have highlighted the value of social linkages, as well as instituted a degree of local patriotism or dignity. To him, mass communication now covers the rural areas. Problem-solving mechanisms in the form of voluntary agencies – local, national and international – are at work. International organized efforts through the UN agencies – the World Bank, the UNCTAD, UNICEF, the FAO and donor agencies at state levels – are visible in rural areas. A new vocabulary in the identification of stakeholders, participatory planning, felt needs and techniques of monitoring that could be centrally administered were seen. It gave rise to new interconnections with user groups, micro financing, self-help group, water harvesting and capacity building for repaying loans, etc.

To Atal (2005: 298), studying rural India has big difference between the 1950s; and now indeed it includes the Dalit awakening and the shift away from governmental action towards civil society initiatives. In this regard, Shah (1992) describes the rural poor as being diverse in their composition – farmers, landlords, artisans, Dalit – because of which the process of change and resistance, too, had a diverse character (Breman et al., 1997; Epstein et al., 1998). This could be seen in the direction of the new farmers' movement, identity assertion, multiple identities and other social action in rural India.

It is rightly emphasized by Sheth (1999) that 'the most important among the changes was the formation of a new, trans-local identity among "lower castes", collectively as a people with the consciousness of being "oppressed" by the traditional system of hierarchy'. The established categories of ritual hierarchy began to be confronted with new categories such as 'depressed castes' and 'oppressed classes'. Several castes occupying more or less similar locations in different local hierarchies began to organize themselves horizontally into regional- and national-level associations and federations, as it became increasingly necessary for them to negotiate with the state and in the process project their larger social identity and numerical strength. Secularization of caste has detached caste from the other-worldly reasoning, ritual status hierarchy and has imparted it a character of the power-group functioning in the competitive democratic politics on the other. Changes in caste thus could be observed along these two dimensions of secularization: de-ritualization and politicization. These changes have (i) pushed caste out of the traditional stratificatory system, (ii) linked it to the new structure of representational power and (iii) in their cumulative impact they have made it possible for individual members of different castes to acquire new economic interest and social-political identification and own class-like as well as ethnic-type identities.

Emphasizing on State intervention and its implication on rural India, Sathyamurthy (1996) asserts aegis of a planned economy, modernization and Green Revolution led to a rapid growth of food production and far-reaching uneven differentiation of peasantry. Economic development in India has resulted in a number of overlapping imbalances: between the agrarian and industrial bourgeoisie; between politicians and bureaucrats; between a rapidly differentiated middle peasantry and the agrarian classes below it; between upper castes and middle/lower castes; between middle castes and Dalits; and between men and women. Modern villages with the rapid urbanization and means of transport and communication weakened the rigid hierarchical order. Commercialization of agriculture, electrification, using of canals and tube wells for irrigation, tractors replacing plough and bullock carts, importance of cash, etc., have not only decreased the *jajmani* system but have also brought rationality in agrarian economy and exchange (Saxena, 2007). According to Rudolph and Rudolph (1967), the displacement of the large landowners by middle farmers may be accurately described as one of the most significant developments of the post-independent period. The middle farmers today constitute the most powerful group in the countryside, economically as well as politically. Thus, India has been experiencing the emergence of new agrarianism. Millions of farmers are mobilizing themselves against the State. Sharad Joshi, among other exponents of new agrarianism, advocates remunerative prices for agricultural commodities, electric supply at nominal rates, etc. This has led to a vertical mobilization of the agrarian classes.

Revamping Agrarian Economy

Talking about agrarian economy, we find that the agricultural growth during 1990–93 to 2003–06 reflects the impact of economic reforms on agriculture performance. The most important feature of this period is that agricultural growth decelerated sharply at the all-India level and in all regions. At the all-India level, the output growth decelerated to 1.74 per cent pa during 1990–93 to 2003–06 compared with a growth rate of 3.37 per cent pa during 1980–83 to 1990–93. At the regional level, during the same period, the growth rate of agricultural output decelerated highest from 3.55 per cent to 1.58 per cent pa in the north-western region... The main reason for the deceleration of growth during the post-reform period was a visible deceleration in investment in irrigation and other rural infrastructure (Bhalla and Singh, 2009).

In India, there are thus competing demands on area available for cultivation from increase in rural habitation, forestation, urbanization and industrialization. Consequently, net sown area in the country has registered a rapid deceleration in its growth over time. During 1962–65 to 1980–83, the net area sown rose at a rate of 0.15 per cent pa at the all-India level – its growth rate decelerated to 0.11 per cent pa during 1980–83 to 1990–93 and further to −0.05 per cent pa during 1990–93 to 2003–06. Even the economic reforms initiated during the early 1990s were expected to hasten the process of crop diversification from low-value food grains to high-value non-food grain crops. However, during the post-reform period, the yield growth rates of most of the important crops including wheat and rice, oilseed, sugarcane decelerated considerably compared with the pre-reform period 1980–83 to 1990–93. One may say that economic reforms and trade liberalization have failed to hasten the process of diversification in agriculture.

Further, the Green Revolution technologies have helped in the reduction of poverty but have resulted in widespread regional disparities as dry lands are not covered. It took a long time for the technology to spread to these areas and even then rainfed farmers did not benefit to the same extent as those in well-endowed regions. This is because of the exclusive emphasis on increasing production without keeping the objective of equity in view. There is an urgent need to raise agricultural growth in view of the dismal scenario in the past decade. However, this should not prevent us from trying to make it more inclusive (Rao and Dev, 2009). Will globalization address these and many issues concerning poor and marginal farmers?

The Green Revolution model and now the globalization model of agriculture are based on the destruction of diversity, uprooting of small peasants through indebtedness, chemical intensification, capital intensification, centralization and long-distant transport. They are based on intensification of external inputs, and integration with global markets (Shiva and Bedi, 2002). In this globalization era, the commons are being enclosed, and the power of communities is being undermined by a corporate enclosure in which life itself is being transformed into the private property of corporations.

The debate on agricultural biotechnology is focused mainly on the environmental impact, bio-safety issues and intellectual property rights. The State will have to play a proactive role in priority setting for pro-poor agricultural development and accessing tools and technologies from the private sector by forging creative public–private partnerships to focus on crops and problems of importance to small farmers (Rao and Dev, 2009). It is to be stressed that ecologically patent related to biological resources has major implications for the conservation of biodiversity and its sustainable use. By creating 'property' in life through patents, the economically powerful corporations can become the new 'life-lords', just as earlier we had landlords or zamindars (Shiva, 2001).

Simultaneously, the promotion of bio-fuel development is attractive for a country such as India because of its potential for creating employment opportunities for the rural poor as well as offering opportunities for promoting local level entrepreneurship and enhancement of women's participation. The availability of technologies for decentralized production of bio-fuels offers opportunities for the development of local-level entrepreneurship. Local institutions such as Joint Forest management committees, self-help groups and *panchayats* can play an important role in involving village communities in bio-fuel programmes. Locally produced bio-fuels can provide fuel for irrigation pump sets and for electricity generation, which will improve access to modern energy services to rural population and help in improving productivity. However, any large-scale bio-fuel programme has to ensure that it does not compromise with the nation's food and nutritional security. Further, utilizing unirrigated, barren and wasteland for growing non-food bio-fuel crops would prove fruitful with multiple benefits such as greening up of unused lands, creation of employment opportunities, greater people's participation and so on (Raju et al., 2009).

Today, we have to look beyond the state and the market place to protect the right of the majority of Indians – the rural communities. The 'commons' cannot be monopolized by the economically powerful citizens or corporations or by the politically powerful state. Although the tribal and rural communities are still overwhelmed by state-driven 'enclosures', tools for new corporate and WTO-driven 'enclosures' are being shaped in the form of patents on life and biodiversity. Trade liberalization is leading to external liberalization, or liberalization for global agribusiness. What the Indian farmers need is internal liberalization!

The economic liberalization and globalization forces are thus the most powerful and deadly to the rural community as it exposes the village globally. In some sense, it seems good, but it is more destructive to developing countries such as India. It has brought new competitors for the total village, resulting in the reshaping of the village setting. Since the village society has changed, it is often said that the earlier literature on it no longer portrays the present reality and has therefore become futile. Revamped villages are dramatically different societies and are manifested in a myriad of ways – in the physical health standard, in the quality of people's food, shelter and clothing, nature of consumption, etc. New village works on the integral lines and talks on the issues of poverty alleviation, environment, ecology, sustainable development, equity, social justice, water conservation, people's participation, role and empowerment of women. Social security, primary education, health and family welfare, forest conservation and safe drinking water are the emerging issues of new villages. It is realized that village community is no more isolated and harmonious, rather it is highly competitive, disharmonious, global and vibrant. The nature of transition can be gauged through the following salient issues:

- The traditional dominant and new-emerging ones (such as SCs, women, OBCs) constitute a major challenge to Indian democracy. The adverse effects of corruption on democracy have come into sharp focus in recent years in connection with issues of local governance and village politics. The local electoral politics are integrally linked with various development rackets and can even generate competitive corruption.

- Under rural development schemes such as Swarnjayanti Gram Swarojgar Yojana (SGSY) and Mahatma Gandhi National Rural Employment Guarantee Act (MGNREGA), the government is giving loans and jobs to the below poverty line (BPL) families. In many instances, big losers are those to whom these developments are supposed to benefit. They are under debt as they are not in a position to utilize the fund properly. Increasing rate of suicide among farmers in various states, such as Maharashtra, Andhra Pradesh, Punjab and Uttar Pradesh, reflect the decline of bonds of traditional social system and increase sign of egoism and isolation among rural masses. Agrarian unrest, especially farmers' agitation for remunerative prices, waiver of agricultural loans, electricity shortage, etc., is visible in rural India.
- The 1990s has ushered in an era of far-reaching economic liberalization reforms. Although initially this has least advanced in the rural sector, the signing of the General Agreement on Tariffs and Trade (GATT) treaty has brought Indian agriculture on the threshold of change and exposed the rural sector to the international market. Simultaneously, aspects of eco-agriculture, such as depletion of groundwater resources and land resources, are emerging.
- Finally, diversified rural economies typically comprise a multitude of small firms most of which are not directly engaged in agriculture. Rural areas often demonstrate high levels of new business formation, and rural firms can be vital sources of local services and employment. They contribute to the diversity and flexibility of local economies. They often serve local markets and source their supplies locally. The question is, how important are these non-farm businesses to sustainable ruralities?

In brief, the decline of the agricultural sector in revamping villages has been paralleled by the emergence of new ways of farming and of consumption, of alternative uses of natural resources and multifunctionality. Increasingly, rural territories become institutionalized in multi-level governance structures. Taken together, such processes are contributing to the opening up of new sites and opportunities for the resurgence of rural spaces. Multimedias are one such opportunity to revamp rural India.

Multimedia Aspects and Its Efficacy in India's Rural Development

In the framework of the e-rural programme, ICTs are introducing new critical approaches to rurality, bringing about social and technical change and promoting a series of services (e-governance, e-communities, e-culture, e-health, e-business, e-learning). On the one hand, ICTs are shaping a much more interrelated rural scenario; on the other hand, they are leading to serious challenges. Thus, there is a need for reviewing the diffusion and impacts of ICTs specifically on the rural areas and focusing on their contribution in reframing a modern concept of rurality and in fostering rural development based on interdisciplinary design issues and on the involvement of local communities. Stress should be on ICT that might bring to economic development and digital equality for rural areas. The approach taken to achieve this broad objective can be a modular concept using multimedia to develop and disseminate multidisciplinary information and knowledge from multiple sources to multiple users with built-in user needs assessment and feedback mechanisms. This modular approach may support an evolving; pluralistic knowledge-based rural extension system consisting of the following elements:

- Accelerates the transition process – recognizing the importance of diverse information and knowledge user needs.
- Increasing importance of non-farm activities to supplement farm incomes especially for the emerging small private farmer.
- Evolution of diversified service providers consisting of contractual arrangements, public–private sector partnerships involving NGO's, producer organizations, association of private farmers, water user associations, etc.
- Creation of a decentralized and localized extension programme management and delivery where all forms of media – from traditional to modern – will play a role.
- Creation of strong linkages between education, research and various forms of farming systems and works in coordination with other providers of rural information and knowledge – such as health, education, micro and small enterprise credit, environment, eco-tourism, etc.

However, a multitude of factors such as 'limited local participation, lack of availability of local resources, fractured relationship with the state agencies, limited integration with local civil society organizations and the exogenous social and economic environment' are identified as some of the factors for the inability of the ICT projects to deliver their full range of outputs in rural areas. These factors are often overlooked while projecting the promises of the projects (Sreekumar, 2002).

Few Successful Case Studies of Multimedia Usage in Rural India

In India, a number of innovative experiments already underway indicate that achieving global digital access may not be as difficult as many think. More than 50 grassroot projects in India are using modern ICTs for the benefit of urban and rural citizen consumers. To justify the utility of multimedia channels in rural development the following initiatives are worth quoting; some of the database applications developed by the National Informatics Centre for the Ministry of Rural Development includes – BPL survey computerization and Financial Release software for various poverty alleviation schemes, besides; Web Sites for Ministry of Rural Development (www.rural.nic.in), Council for Advancement of People's Action and Rural Technology (CAPART) (http://capart.nic.in) are generated. A Geographic

Information System (GIS)-based analysis has been carried out for some of the watersheds in East District and North District (Sikkim), Raipur, Etah, Udaipur, Salem and Pune Districts.

ICT can thus play a crucial role in rural development and in bridging the rural–urban divide. The experiences below show the qualitative changes in different parts of rural India (Saxena and Rao, 2005). One can gauge the revamping and modernity in the Indian villages through following successful experiences.

E-Panchayat

A cluster of villages or 'village *panchayats*' are connected to existing public and the private sector exchanges using wide band technology that can be leased to private operators/kiosk operators on a revenue sharing basis. The entire village *panchayat* is connected to the exchanges in digital networked districts through 144 kbps links. The District Government Offices, the Collectorate and the District Panchayats as well as all other large offices have established intra-office networks for voice, data and video exchange.

E-Governance

The Gyandoot project has developed a very important e-governance protocol, in the form of the 'shikayat', or complaint. For a fee of ₹10, rural citizens may select from a predetermined menu of 30 different kinds of complaints, which together cover a wide range of citizen–consumer to government interactions in rural areas. The Andhra Pradesh government (www.ap-it.com) is responsible for some early initiatives that sought to use networked technologies to improve citizen services. A series of acronym services including CARD, TWINS, FAST, etc., provide licenses and certificates, allow the registration of deeds and various kinds of payments at a single counter, in certain urban and rural areas of the state. 'Bhoomi' (revdept.kar.nic.in) is a major government of Karnataka initiative to computerize land records across the state.

Information Village Experiment

Swaminathan Research Foundation (MSSRF) launched it in January 1998 in Pondicherry. It acts as a hub or Value Addition Centre of a local area network set up over 10 villages, serving a population of about 21,500. The villages act as Village Knowledge Centres or 'information shops' and are connected by a hybrid wired and wireless network (http://www.mssrf.org).

Akashganga

Akashganga (meaning 'the milky way') was launched in 1996 at Anand, Gujarat and implemented by Shree Kamdhenu Electronics Pvt. Ltd., with the objective of using appropriate IT to facilitate the timely collection of milk, and thereby generate higher profits for the rural milk producers. *Akashganga* is being used at the Dairy Cooperative Society a farmer-owned, grassroots unit in the cooperative structure.

E-Choupal

ITC's International Business Division, one of the India's largest exporters of agricultural commodities, has launched 'e-Choupal', in June 2000 (http://www.itcportal). It serves more than 3.1 million farmers growing a range of crops in over 31,000 villages through 5,050 kiosks across six states (Madhya Pradesh, Karnataka, Andhra Pradesh, Uttar Pradesh, Maharashtra and Rajasthan). And it enables the agricultural community access ready information in their local language on the weather and market prices, disseminate knowledge on scientific farm practices and risk management, facilitate the sale of farm inputs (now with embedded knowledge) and purchase farm produce from the farmers' doorsteps (decision making is now information based).

E-Marketplaces

In India, the Internet is being used to market the product of poor communities. *TARAhaat*, a private sector brings information and marketing services using e-business to rural North India. Development Alternatives in two rural regions launched it in September 2000: Bundelkhand (one of the poorest region in Uttar Pradesh) and Bhatinda (one of the richest region in Punjab). It acts as a gateway that connects the village user to information, social services and healthy entertainment and to all kinds of markets, through a network of 20-odd franchised *TARAkendras*. Further, US-based non-governmental organization PEOPLink has linked producers of commodities in poor communities in Tamil Nadu to potential markets through the Internet (PEOPLink, 2000). One village in Tamil Nadu – Kizhur – which excels in making traditional cotton saris and other cotton garments sells its produce through PEOPLink's website to consumers all over the world.

Tele-Health

Computer-based and online expert diagnostic systems could enhance the quality of health care and diagnosis available to rural citizen–consumers in many remote parts of south Asia. The real benefits of these systems, however, may be the collation of more comprehensive public health information. In addition to tracking the case study of an individual patient, therefore, such systems could also collect data on the public health in a region, for further epidemiological study. The George Foundation (www.tgfworld.org) has experimented with an expert diagnostic programme on a free-standing PC in Dharmapuri district of Tamil Nadu.

Summing Up

No doubt, globalization has effected both social relations of production and social relations of consumption in rural India. A new era is being constructed in which state, people and the environment are forced to adjust to the market, and it is the markets, not people, that require freedom. However, it has also worked in the direction of democratizing rural economy. One has to bear in mind that this will lead to the attainment of equitable and democratic development in developing nations. There is an urgent need in this direction in envisaging people friendly with practical devolution strategy.

It is to be emphasized that the Indian village is no more to be treated as conventional and static; rather, it should be understood on dialectical and transitional lines. The State intervention and modern forces of privatization, liberalization and globalization has shattered the imaginary boundaries to village community and made them spatially open arena for exposure, conflicts and modifications. Modern rural India is thus undergoing disruptive innovations to make the giant leap forward. The need of the hour is to embrace effectively modern multimedia technology and to create summative local resources accessible anytime via the Internet to keep rural citizens current on the local status of surroundings and other threats to health, safety, economy, pursuit of life, liberty and happiness to bring improvement in quality of life of rural India in particular and rest of India in general. Thus, the need of the hour is universal access for masses with equity and justice.

References

Anderson, B. (1992). 'The New World Disorder', *New Left Review*, 193: 3–13.

Atal, Yogesh (2005). 'Intensive Studies in Village: In Retrospect and Prospect', *The Eastern Anthropologist*, July–December, 58(3–4): 301–03.

Berman, Marshall (1988). *All That Is Solid Melts into Air: The Experience of Modernity*. New York: Viking Penguin, p. 151.

Bhalla, G.S. and Gurmail Singh (2009). 'Economic Liberalization and Indian Agriculture: A Statewise Analysis', *Economic and Political Weekly*, 26 December, 44(52): 34–44.

Booth, D. (1994). 'Economic Liberalization, Real Markets, and the (Un) Reality of Structural Adjustment in Rural Tanzania', *Sociologia Ruralis*, 34(1): 45–62.

Chauhan, B.R. (2005). 'Intensive Studies in Village: In Retrospect and Prospect', *The Eastern Anthropologist*, July-December, 58(3–4): 301–03.

Epstein, T. Scarlett, A.P. Suryanarayana and T. Thimmegowda (1998). *Village Voices: Forty Years of Rural Transformation in South India*. New Delhi: Sage Publications.

Fuller, C. (ed.) (1996). 'Introduction', in *Caste Today*. New Delhi: Oxford University Press, pp. 1–31.

Ganguly, R. and T.J. Scrase (1997). 'We Want a Piece of the Action!: Structural Adjustment and Indian Leather Workers', Paper presented at the Asia Pacific Regional Conference of Sociology (*Social Transformation in Asia*), 18–21 September, University of Malaya, Kuala Lumpur.

Ghosh, R. (1996). 'Economic Liberalization and Its Impact on Women and Women's Education', *Alberta Journal of Education*, 42(2): 115–20.

Gupta, Dipankar (2005). 'Caste and Politics: Identity over System', *Annual Review of Anthropology*, 34: 409–27.

Hannerz, Ulf (1996). *Transnational Connection: Cultures, People, Places*. London: Routledge.

Held, D. (ed.) (1991). 'Democracy, the Nation-State and the Global System', in *Political Theory Today*. Cambridge: Polity Press.

Khilnani, S. (1999). *Idea of India*. New Delhi: Penguin Books.

Kothari, R. (1995). 'Globalization and Revival of Tradition: Dual Attack on Models of Democratic Nation Building', *Economic and Political Weekly*, 25 March.

Mahbub-ul-Haq (1998). Quoted in *Foreword* by Khadija Haq in Report on *Human Development in South Asia 2001 – Globalization and Human Development*. New York: Oxford University Press.

Mendelsohn, O. and Marika Vicziany (1998). *The Untouchables: Subordination, Poverty and the State in Modern India*. New York: Cambridge University Press.

Natarajan, I. (1999). *India Market Demographics Report*. New Delhi: National Council of Applied Economic Research.

Oommen, T.K. (2009). 'Indian Labour Movement: Colonial Era to the Global Age', *Economic and Political Weekly*, 26 December, 44(52): 81–89.

Panini, M. (1995). 'The Social Logic of Economic Liberalization', *Sociological Bulletin*, 44(1): 54.

Raju, S.S., P. Shinoj and P.K. Joshi (2009). 'Sustainable Development of Biofuels: Prospects and Challenges', *Economic and Political Weekly*, 26 December, 44(52): 65–72.

Rao, N. Chandrasekhara and S. Mahendra Dev (2009). 'Biotechnology and Pro-Poor Agricultural Development', *Economic and Political Weekly*, 26 December, 44(52): 56–64.

Rudolph, L.I. and S.H. Rudolph (1967). *The Modernity of Tradition: Political Development in India*. Chicago: University of Chicago Press.

Sathyamurthy, T.V. (ed.) (1996). *Class Formation and Political Transformation in Post-Colonial India*. New Delhi: Oxford University Press.

Saxena, Ashish (2007). 'Rethinking Indian Villages: A Sociological Appraisal', *E-Bulletin International Sociological Association*, November, (8).

Saxena, Ashish and S. Rao (2005). 'Efficacy of Multimedia Technology in Indigenous Knowledge Management', *Conventional Journal of Lucknow Management Association*, 1(1): 248–58.

Sen, A. (1992). *Inequality Re-Examined*. New Delhi: Oxford University Press.

Sen, G. (1996). 'Gender, Markets and States: A Selective Review and Research Agenda', *World Development*, 24(5): 821–29.

Shah, G. (1992). 'Protests by the Rural Poor', in A. Bhalla and P. Bumke (eds), *Images of Rural India in the 20th Century*. New Delhi: Sterling.

Sheth, D.L. (1999). 'Secularization of Caste and Making of New Middle Class', *Economic and Political Weekly*, 34(34/35): 2502–10.

Shiva, V. (1998). *Globalization of Agriculture, Food Security and Sustainability*. New Delhi: Research Foundation for Science and Technology.

——— (2001). *Patent: Myth and Reality*. New Delhi: Penguin.

Shiva, V. and Gitanjali Bedi (2002). *Sustainable Agriculture and Food Security: The Impact of Globalization*. New Delhi: Sage Publications.

Singh, Y. (2000). *Culture Change in India: Identity and Globalization*. Jaipur: Rawat Publications.

Sreekumar, T.T. (2002). 'Civil Society and ICT – Based Models of Rural Change: History, Rhetoric and Practice', Paper presented in the International Seminar on ICTs and Indian Development: Processes, Prognoses and Policies, 9–11 December, Bangalore.

Strange, S. (1995). 'The Limits & Politics', *Government & Opposition*, 30(3): 291–311.

Vidhyasagar, R. (1996). 'New Agrarianism and the Challenges for the Left', in T.V. Sathyamurthy (ed.), *Class Formation and Political Transformation in Post-Colonial India*. New Delhi: Oxford University Press.

Waters, Malcolm (1995). *Globalization*. London: Routledge.

19

State, Market Economy and Rural Degeneration

A Note on Pangs of Globalization

Satish K. Sharma

It is extremely difficult to address an issue related to the contemporary process of social development governed and guided by liberalization, privatization and globalization (LPG). The difficulty arises, especially in view of the vast theoretical literature, varying perspectives and approaches and considerable experience of the empirical realities of the individual scholars, the non-governmental organizations and the socially conscious groups who have dealt with the issue at length at the grass-roots level and come out with startling findings. Some are juxtaposed and the others entirely opposite and contradictory. Whatever might have been said about the consequences of the developmental processes after liberalization of economy and society, the situation became extremely complex with regard to the formulation of alternative strategies for socio-economic development ensuring equity and distributive justice, removal of inequalities and improving the standard of living of the people, especially those living in the slums, urban periphery, small and the marginal farmers and the Dalits at large living in the rural areas. The reason is that the strategies of whatsoever nature and kind these might have been not only failed to realize the objectives of development but also remained bugged with internal contradictions and paradoxes. Therefore, the development strategies exhibited apparently a pro-poor stance but inwardly heavily biased against them.

Interestingly, the way development statistics in a time-series-comparative perspective was presented by the political leadership to the public, especially pertaining to the economic indicators, such as per capita income, gross national products and gross national income and so on, indicate considerable growth and development. Moreover, the growth of food grain production, increase in the literacy rate, rise in the number of educational institutions at all levels and expansion of the educational infrastructure, development of Information Technology (IT) parks and growth of electronic and automobile industries, coming up of big glittering malls and mega housing projects with highly attractive advertisements have done wonder. Passing through villages and small towns, one comes across big displays of mega housing schemes, which virtually bring New York or Paris or London in a small village along the highways. The projection of swimming pools at places where even potable water is scarce, promise of 24-hour continuous electricity supply and world-class amenities is something so far thought as difficult to achieve is shown achievable by a housing enterprise. In the pre-LPG regime, all these were next to impossible.

Notwithstanding the statistics and projections of growth and development, as a student of sociology, one wonders: Why do millions of people in India despite bumper crops and rise in food grain production go to sleep hungry? Does increasing literacy and rise in the number of educational institutions mean anything when thousands of children do not find an entry into elementary schools? Does expansion of educational infrastructure including human and physical resources ensure quality education in the vast number of government-run educational institutions attended largely by millions of children belonging to socio-economically poor sections of the society living in the slums on urban periphery, rural pockets and Dalit households amidst expanding network of so-called global schools and highly popularized virtual classrooms? What is happening to the small and the marginal farmers representing an overwhelming majority of the rural masses on whose land the IT parks, special economic zones (SEZs) and glittering malls are coming up? Whose interests are catered to by the big malls equipped with brand names and products? Where do the landless and the poor villagers go when no agricultural land is left for them? Where does the growth of automobile industry lead to – overcrowding of roads, congestion, emission of carbon monoxide, tuberculosis and lung diseases? Who live in the mega housing complexes even created by the state housing development agencies where even a flat meant for socio-economically weaker sections is sold out for a whooping ₹75 lakhs?[1] Whether New York is being created as advertised or the housing becoming only a dream or normal living of the people in the villages is being turned into slums? There are many more such questions that arise when one looks at the way rapid transformation is taking place in the Indian society, especially in the urban areas and ironically the consequent degeneration of the life of the people living in the rural areas, ultimately resulting in development or underdevelopment. The onus rests on the nexus between the state, the market economy and the beneficiaries of ongoing development processes. This is the reason that the entire issue is extremely difficult to provide any adequate answer and explanation to the questions raised above and provide a tangible solution to the problems. This note is an attempt at looking into how the so-called development strategies of the state and the development processes conditioned and guided by LPG are benefiting a few and resulting in the degeneration and underdevelopment of common masses in the urban but more so in the rural areas.

During the past nearly two decades, a consensus, primarily state-sponsored perspective, seems to have emerged about the development of a glittering modern

India. Amidst such an ambitious project, the darkness that plunged rural India into an agrarian crisis of extreme type and magnitude does not find much place in the minds and thoughts of those interested only in the glittering India. The fact, indeed needing serious thought and action, is that under the new development strategies the traditional agrarian social structure, community life and communitarian relationships have been completely disturbed. The onus of contemporary ills and crises of the rural areas, rationally or irrationally, is put on the hapless farmers whose lands are being engulfed increasingly for housing projects and IT parks. However, Gupta (2006: 2) argued that the socio-economic compulsions faced by the farmers have changed the face of rural India. These compulsions, to him, are caused by a multiplicity of factors, including the disintegration of the joint family system, migration to urban centres, onslaught of media, growing disinterest in farming, demand for educational rights by rural women, men seeking jobs in the city, high rate of farmers' suicides, increasing desperation for jobs and indulgence in everything except farming by farmers. The last part of the sentence is quite difficult to understand as this raises one issue: Is the farming community not interested in farming, or are the emerging conditions making the farmers drift away from farming? Gupta describes the emerging situation in the rural setting as 'rural implosion', implying thereby an explosion from within. However, the argument does not go into the etiology of why is the explosion within? What conditions and forces have compelled the farming community not to take interest in farming? Why have some of the farmers committed suicides? Why does the question of other indulgences come up? The question here is not to decide whether whatever Gupta said regarding agrarian crisis is right or wrong but to look into why such compulsions have to be there at all when the state always claims itself to be socialist democratic republic? Above all, the most critical issue is what has compelled the farmers and the rural masses to behave in the manner stated above?

However, the issue is not as simple as it is made out to be and as it appears to be. Rural India, its economy and social structure in general do not constitute an isolated entity but an integral part of the national economy as well as economic and political processes. In fact, what is seen as rural implosion is not an explosion within but a product of the socio-historical and politico-economic forces that have now reached a critical juncture giving rise to the said explosion. It is, therefore, an extremely complex phenomenon involving not only internal forces but also the external forces, such as state and the market, which have created the socio-economic compulsions for the rural implosion to occur. The entire issue, to my belief and understanding, cannot be set aside just by stating what is happening in contemporary times. It also needs to address significantly associated questions such as how and why it has happened. The issue under consideration being multidimensional in nature, it also relates to the internal and external dynamics of the role of the state and the market in shaping each other at first instance, with reference to the impact of their role on the nature of social structure in general and rural development and agrarian social structure in particular. These complexities, therefore, require the whole issue to be understood in a historico-social and politico-economic perspective.

Why the stress is laid on this perspective is the fact that rural development and consequent emergence of an agrarian social structure have evolved over a period of time and space first under the dictates of the state, then market forces impinging on the state and finally the state succumbing to the market pressures and subsequently accepting the supremacy of the market, the state joining hands with the market.

The role of the state primarily, right from its inception, has been in the form of reconciliation of individual freedom with social obligation, a kind of unity between the rights of the people and their responsibilities towards each other. In the realization of the latter, the organization of the individuals under a normative structure promoting meeting the mutual obligations towards each other was considered important. One can trace the origin of such an understanding as early as the Greeks who opined that the subordination of the individual to the state on which the well-being of all depended was an act for the general good of the society (Barker, 1947: 54). In the similar manner, Plato, Aristotle and even Comte not only believed in the submission of the individuals to the state but also enjoined upon the latter to use force to ensure cooperation of the former. In other words, the role of the state emphasized during the historical times, expressed more in terms of absolute authority over the individual, and thereby put an end to his freedoms continues in the similar manner even in the modern democratic socialist republics such as India.

However, the historical evolvement of the conditions of growth and development of human society and the state did not favour absolutism. Rousseau advocated 'no ruling of/or privileged class'. What it apparently implied is reversal of the role of the state from an authoritarian to liberal one restoring individual liberty without suggesting anything like, 'No State or Stateless Society'. The reason being, as Hegel described, *nothing short of the state is the actualization of the freedoms*. Although *absolutist in nature*, in content and intent and therefore debatable, but such a conception perhaps suggests the presence of state as a regulatory mechanism of the processes of society. What is significant to note, historically, is that such a viewpoint proved a turning point in Europe that characterized the nation-states and also set in the process of democratization of human society with greater individual freedom.

May be much of the expectations from the state even under democratic governance were mere *utopian* as the socio-economic developments instead of reducing the conflicts between individual and the society further consolidated inner contradictions. The case of European feudalism and its inner contradictions, the bondage of peasantry and continuous exploitation of peasants remained a reality to a certain extent. While the individual freedoms, democratization of the political system were being debated, the feudal lords resisted such intellectual movements. This is the reason why there is 'a long history of conflict between the peasantry and the manorial landlords in Europe. The cause of the conflicts was not only the demand for the share of the produce from the peasantry but also retention of particular type of method of cultivation by forced labour' (Shelvankar, 1940, cited in Desai, 1966: 9).

At this juncture, it is important to refer to the situation in India, which was entirely different from Europe, where the land was under private ownership of the feudal lords. In India, the land belonged to the village community and not to the individuals. Desai (1966: 9) argues,

> Conforming to the traditional concept and practice, neither the King nor the intermediary expropriated the village community of possession and control of land and establish their property rights over it or concerned with the method of cultivation.

Ironically, capitalism is a free market economy and conceived to be associated with greater individual freedoms and democratization of the political processes. It was during this period that the state assumed a more decisive and authoritarian role. Marxism, a critique of the prevalent political-economy order though called for doing away with the state but the presence of state was rationalized even by the close associate of Karl Marx 'as good for the well-being of the society'. Engels (1943: 177–78) argued,

> The State was the product of society entangled in an insoluble contradiction with itself. State is a power standing above society becomes necessary to moderate conflict and keeping it within the bind of the order.

In India, the process of capitalist development began with the onset of colonization, particularly with the coming of East India Company. With their expanding authority, the British Government in India affected considerable changes in the land tenure system and thereby brought about drastic changes in the agrarian structure. Such a state action not only changed the land relations with the introduction of new agrarian classes but also set in the process of change in the entire village culture. The private property in land emerged in two forms: emergence of landlords and peasant proprietorship. This happened due to the introduction of Permanent Land Settlement process in 1793 by Lord Cornwallis. Although this policy was initially limited to eastern states, namely Bihar, Bengal and Orissa, the new system reached other states as a consequence of expansion of the British imperialism (Desai, 1966: 38–39).

This was a time of great historical significance with considerable changes taking place in the Indian society. Although the rural society saw the emergence of new form of land relations, the seeds of transition from feudalism to capitalism were also sown. The self-sufficient village economy not only started withering away the artisans, but also the small farmers and the landless labourers reached a stage of being pushed out of their villages. What started happening almost more than 200 years ago in India and what is happening in the contemporary times, the difference may only be a matter of degree and not of nature. However, due to the nature of Indian agriculture and its close relationship with the domestic commodity production system, the villages were able to sustain themselves and maintain their equilibrium (Shelvankar, 1940: 139, cited in Desai, 1966: 16) *only to an extent*. Even at present, similar things are in the offing. But the control of the state also increased continuously as most of the needs of the agricultural communities could not be met without state interventions. However, the controlling agents were placed in the nearby towns, thereby the villages became dependent on the towns and in a way their governance also went out of their hands for all practical purposes (ibid.: 142). Gradually, a new form of land relationships came into being. The spatial movement of the landless, the displaced and the artisans from their villages to towns in search of employment opportunities began to affect even the family structure. The change in the system of commodity production from guild to factory, and to industrial not only pushed the village artisans out to the towns and cities but also severely affected the traditional social structure. The relations of production changed from obligatory nature to wage relations, and the market-oriented economic system began to reshape and redefine the social structure. Historically, in the entire process of change in the agrarian scenario, there were progressive elements too benefiting certain individuals and a specific class comprising rich and those forming part of the aristocracy and landlords. But the costs were too high for the landless, the poor and the marginal among the peasant communities. The process of changes in the agrarian social structure largely due to state interventions, not wrong to state here, in fact has continued since then and with more severe consequences even in the post-independence times.

In modern times, India as a democratic society developing on capitalist lines indicates certain degree of alienation between parliamentary democracy and capitalism. This alienation emerges due to the fact that the state acquires more and more powers through its permanent institutions, such as police and bureaucracy, often used by the state to suppress any uprising against land acquisition, price rise and policies adversely affecting the masses. The use was made from time to time, which continues even today with more vigorous force, to reinforce the executive powers of the state and in the process the state adopts repressive measures and policies to carry forward its so-called development agenda unmindful of the fact that the policies pursued severely affect the social structure further (Mandel, 1979). The real face of the state characterized by parliamentary democracy and following capitalist path of development is highly mysterious in nature; and being so, it is entirely different from what it appears to be. Instead of integrating the masses with the system, first it systematically excludes and alienates them and then the democracy and capitalism also came into conflict and gradually experience some kind of alienation between them also. It is argued, 'The bourgeois State remains fundamentally an instrument in the service of the ruling classes' (ibid.: 37). A perusal of the development process since the times of national struggle for freedom of India indicates that the historically developed conditions during the phase of monopoly capitalism ultimately culminated into capitalist planning, which combined both private and public sector enterprises. Such a system operates under the postulates of market economy (Desai, 1985: 7). The process of capitalist development has acquired such a stature now that it is perhaps next to impossible to alter it. It is because of such reasons that there emerges certain degree of alienation between democracy and capitalism. Although I would not like to divulge into any controversial issue by referring to certain recent happenings indicating the increasing distance between parliamentary democracy advocating fundamental and human rights and the political interests of the state. The instances such as *lathi*-charge over the peaceful demonstrators, the educated and the unemployed veterinary graduates, pharmacists and even the blinds are the living examples of the said alienation when the electoral interests guided by certain capitalist lobbies become most important. It is also not wrong to argue here that with the ultimate turning of state interests into capitalist in nature, most of the policies pursued by the state are market-oriented and, therefore, at times lead to disastrous consequences.

At this point, it becomes inevitable to draw the kind attention of the readers to the development policies and programmes pursued by the Indian State and followed by the states in India including the North West. There is no doubt that both democracy and markets have proliferated due to the development policies and the middle and the upper strata of the society have derived the most out of it. In the rural areas, the most benefited are the families who have 'farm-based commercial agriculture' (Stern, 1993: 3). After more than 65 years of independence and many decades of the launching of the poverty alleviation programmes, the status of Indian poverty, going by the development economists' parameter of per capita income, remains 'changeless'. It is further observed,

> India provides the world with its largest national pool of poor people, and the amelioration of their poverty over the decades has been slight. But India' development is not taking per capita. It is taking place in its upper quintile of households. The poor certainly outnumber the Indian middle classes, but poor are not the directors of change, nor the major participants in it, and certainly not its major beneficiaries. (ibid.: 6)

There is a great deal of truth in the above observation. The Indian State's recently advocated highly ambitious policy of developing special economic zones (SEZs) throughout the country[2] is also the one whose end product, already a proven fact, is displacement of the marginalized and the poor. The truth about the SEZ is that initially way back in 1965, the Indian State had set up special export processing zones, called EPZs at Kandla (Gujarat), in 1973, at Santa Cruz (Mumbai), and in 1980s at Noida, Falta, Kochi, Chennai and Vishakhapatnam. But what happened to these EPZs? There is not much to say in answer to the question except to use the word 'failure'. What does the concept of SEZs envisage? In brief, the policy entails land acquisition on a massive scale. Much of the land is agricultural and fertile. However, as reported in media and under pressure from various quarters, especially the farming communities, the government made a policy shift and stated that it wanted to acquire only the wasteland. But there are many questions that arise and need serious thought: Does not land acquisition on a massive scale also logically imply displacement of farmers on an equally massive scale? Even if the government now says that only the wasteland is to be acquired, the question being raised here is as follows: How do we declare and identify whether the land is wasteland? Further, this is argued that wasteland is, par excellence, the resource on which the poorest and the most of the marginalized depend. In view of the acquisition of the wasteland, the question arises, is it not the poorest and the most marginalized going to suffer the brunt most? In the entire process, the promoters of the SEZs gain and the poor and the marginal farmers lose. Although the former would enjoy various privileges in the form of tax exemptions, the latter would be left to eke out a living from nowhere. Does it not mean slaughtering of farmers' fundamental human right to live and to livelihood? What is emerging dangerous due to 'the balance between requirements and incentives skewed in favour of SEZ promoters' is the further fragmentation of the already fragmented agrarian social structure. Although known to all, we must remember that there are '45 per cent of farm families which are effectively and absolutely landless: the poor by any standard' (ibid.: 203). The number has definitely gone up over the past one and a half decade due to the ruthless acquisition of agricultural land, eviction of the farmers from their lands, rise in conspicuous consumption and ultimately pauperization of the small and the landless farmers. Where will they go and what is going to be the nature and type of agrarian social structure under the nexus between the state and the market-oriented development processes are the questions that need serious thought and deliberation.

Where are we after nearly two decades of liberalization, privatization and globalization? No doubt, India today is one of the rapidly changing societies of the world with a growth rate of 8–9 per cent consistently maintaining over the past many years. Whether this rapid transformation takes care of the states such as Bihar, Chhattisgarh, Jharkhand, Madhya Pradesh, Orissa, Rajasthan, Uttar Pradesh and West Bengal suffering from acute poverty with 421 million people? There are 836 million people in India who live on what they can consume for just less than US$1 per day. The wide-spread malnutrition even affects as many as 43 per cent of the children under five years of age. The UNICEF estimates indicate that more than two million children die due to diseases caused by malnutrition. No doubt, under globalization, India is acquiring new heights, but the local and fundamental problems do not seem to have a tangible solution in the near future.

Notes

1. This is the case of Chandigarh.
2. Punjab 11, Himachal Pradesh 1, Chandigarh 1, Haryana 31, Uttar Pradesh 15, Delhi 2, Rajasthan 10, Madhya Pradesh 8, Jharkhand 1, West Bengal 21, Gujarat 20, Chhattisgarh 1, Orissa 5, Maharashtra 45, Andhra Pradesh 47, Goa 1, Karnataka 42, Pondicherry 1, Kerala 12, and Tamil Nadu 40.

References and Readings

Barker, Ernest (1947). *Greek Political Theory*, discussed in Mahadeva Prasad (1958). *Social Philosophy of Mahatma Gandhi*. Gorakhpur: Vishwavidyalaya Prakashan.

Desai, A.R. (1966). *Social Background of Indian Nationalism*. Bombay: Popular Prakashan.

——— (1985). *Public Sector in India: Controversies About Its Role*. Bombay: C. G. Shah Memorial Trust Publication.

Engels, F. (1943). *The Origin of Family, Private Property and the State*. London: Lawrence and Wishart.
Gupta, Dipankar (2006). 'Rural Implosion', *The Tribune*, p. 2.
Mandel, Ernest (1976). *The State in the Age of Late Capitalism*, edited by A.R. Desai. Bombay: C. G. Shah Memorial Trust Publication.
——— (1979). *The Marxist Theory of the State*, edited by A.R. Desai. Bombay: C. G. Shah Memorial Trust Publication.
Shelvankar, K.S. (1940). *The Problem of India*, cited in A.R. Desai (1966). *Social Background of Indian Nationalism*. Bombay: Popular Prakashan.
Stern, Robert W. (1993). *Changing India*. Cambridge: Cambridge University Press.

20

Civilizational Transformation of Indigenous People

Globalization Effect and Sustainable Development

P.S. Vivek

The conceptualization of 'Civil Society' in contemporary social sciences has its roots in the political upheavals in the formation of nation-states during the second half of the 20th century. The rise of several post-colonial states was the most striking phenomenon. In that process, the democratic form of governance held promise to fulfil the aspirations of people. Competing political ideologies of modernization were directing the reconstruction measures in the new states. What was implied in civil society is individual's freedom in daily life, in which his or her choice is honoured.

The paper deals with changes in the social and economic system of indigenous people in the post-colonial states. The change in production norms is not only confined to elite accumulation but also results in a change at all levels. New forms of community and continued non-market access to critical resources, such as land and forests, would allow for a greater spread of the benefits.

The market, with its associate privatization, does solve some existing problems in indigenous people's economies. New needs are created, along with cosmopolitan consumption and production systems, taking local products to the far corners of the world and bringing new goods into local consumption. A new combination of private and collective or community systems becomes necessary. At the same time, among indigenous women, the destruction of indigenous welfare systems of reciprocity and the rupture of access to productive resources push destitute women, with their continuing responsibilities for household food security, into selling their bodies for sexual services.

Although earlier men's monopoly in village and community affairs was counter-balanced by women's role over the economic and domestic sphere, the growth of the market and the growing domination of external economic relation over the domestic economy have made women lose their countervailing power. The first phase of this change, which establishes men's monopoly over the spiritual and material management of community, predates the spread of the market. With liberation, men's roles changed to taking up education and political affairs. Until the growth of the market system, these roles too did not yield any substantial income.

The introduction of all-pervasive market does dissolve the old system of clan- or kinship-based access to productive resources. The factors of internal organization of the community to overcome 'free rider' problems and trust based on shared development goals are then necessary, if village communities are to evolve as collective institution within a market system.

This paper explores changes in the social and economic systems of indigenous people as a consequence of their integration into the global economy through market-driven processes. There are changes in the nature of the overall economic and social system, from one aiming at the stability of the social system, to one based on accumulation, from production for self-consumption. The new system shifts to production for sale in the market. This set of changes can justifiably be called a civilization change, so deep and broad is its scope, changing all earlier forms of social, economic and gender relations. The way forward is to create welfare systems based on taxes and new forms of community organization.

Globalization comes down to local communities largely through the market. The market, of course, is not new to indigenous peoples. Virtually, any product can be traded in the market. Of course, the market is likely to destroy the traditional community. Forms of collective functioning are also needed for maintaining critical natural resources. Forms of collective entrepreneurship could also be developed. Indigenous people's areas are characterized by low levels of state-provided social welfare expenses. Mass production carries with it mass consumption and mass culture. The paper argues for the need to adopt new forms of social capital.

Markets and Privatization

Globalization comes down to local communities largely through the market. New goods may be seen on the TV or known through other ways. But it is through the market that they become available to be consumed or used by people. It is also through the market that producers come to know what they can sell. Often, they may not know the use to which their products are put. For instance, only recently, after the logging ban imposed by the Indian Supreme Court, indigenous women in the north-eastern state of Meghalaya were selling the bark of some trees, but they had no idea at all of the uses of that bark. The indigenous people of Andhra Pradesh had for decades been collecting and selling gum karaya without any idea of its use in making dentures. These are not isolated instances, and sellers are often totally unaware of the uses of the products they sell, particularly when these products do not have local uses.

The market, of course, is not new to indigenous peoples. The fabled 'Silk Routes', for instance, go through indigenous people's area in the Himalaya–Hindukush Mountains. But for the indigenous peoples, trade was carried on in order to obtain alien or exotic products, salt, iron, etc. With the incorporation of these mountain communities into plains-based states, and later with western colonialism, the regular trading networks extended up into the hills and mountains. The states also more directly extracted various forest products such as timber. But with globalization, there is a great increase in the scope of the market. Virtually, any product can be traded on the market. And, unlike with production for self-consumption, which is necessarily limited by the extent of local consumption, production for sale on the market is not similarly locally limited, of course when the aim of trade no longer is to incorporate exotic products into a subsistence system, but becomes part of a process of accumulation.

This growth of the market has led to a process of privatization of formerly communal land, of devolution of ownership, at least *de facto* if not also *de jure*, from supra-village and community or clan to the family. The market for timber and non-timber forest products (NTFPs) grew in the colonial or immediate post-colonial periods. To that extent, they certainly predate the 1990s, which is generally regarded as the era of globalization, with the growth of global financial markets. But the process of privatization through market-induced transformation is a feature that becomes even stronger in the current era. Consequently, an analysis of the privatization process, even if it pre-dates the 1990s, can tell us a lot about the effects of the growth of global markets on what were formerly relatively self-contained, subsistence-based economies.

A detailed case study of this process in north-east India looks at this process of privatization through pressures emanating from the development of the market, timber and NTFP, where, unlike in most of the rest of India, the communities retained ownership of the forest in the colonial and post-colonial periods. Although the analysis is concentrated on the Khasi of Meghalaya, a state that is better than other north-east Indian states with the rest of India and thus with the markets for timber and NTFP, it also uses material mainly from other communities and countries of the Hindukush–Himalayan region.

The growth of the market led to a process of privatization of formerly communal land, of devolution of ownership, at least *de facto* if not also *de jure*, from supra-village and community or clan to the family. The following are the features of this process:

- The rise of big men or big families and their links to the external world
- The decline of earlier forms of reciprocity that inhibited accumulation
- The separation of the objective conditions of labour (chiefly land) from labour itself, leading to the creation of what Marx termed 'not-landownership' (Marx, 1973: 498)
- The growing domination of men in economic matters
- The breakdown of norms of collecting forest products only for self-consumption and in regulating collection for sale
- The gradual or rapid decline of NTFP in the unregulated commons and the domestication and shift of valuable NTFP species into the home gardens or privately owned fields

Norms Inhibiting Accumulation and Their Costs

Social norms or sanctions that inhibited accumulation or kept it within narrow limits are of different kinds. One of them is the feasting undertaken by big men or chiefs, for instance, among the various Naga communities. This feasting redistributed any surplus and prevented accumulation. With the advent of Christianity, such feasting was denounced as being 'pagan' and its decline opened the way for accumulation. Simultaneously, the norms of reciprocity also changed and step-by-step generalized reciprocity gave way to annual cash contributions of a portion of income.

Among the Khasi, pre-Christian accumulation was restricted to the families of the chiefs (Syiem) and priests (Lynghoh). Any other family that accumulated wealth was likely to be denounced as worshippers of uthlen (the sanke) and forced to abandon their wealth. 'The *thlen* attaches itself to the property of the keeper and gets transferred along with it to his/her heir. The keeper can rid himself of the demon only by renouncing all his possessions' (Nongbri, 2002: 4). But this does not destroy or dissipate the property; rather, it is centralized with the chief or priest, since 'only the Syiem (chief) and the Lyngdoh (priest) can receive the property of *thlen* keepers without the possibility of inheriting the demon' (ibid.).

The Dai of Xishuangbanna (China), a Tai-speaking people who had a well-developed chieftain (Tusi) system, also had a mechanism to inhibit accumulation outside of the families of the chiefs or their representatives, the village headman. Any prosperous family, known as a family with a 'silver plough' or that had found a 'silver box/spoon', was likely to be denounced as *pippa*, or keepers of the tiger spirit, which like the Khasi *thlen*, caused harm to people and spread sickness. Such families were driven away from the village, and their lands and other property were seized by the village headman or chief (Nathan et al., 1998).

Among the Munda of Jharkhand, there has been a more egalitarian system of redistribution, which altogether inhibited accumulation, rather than centralized it. There is any family that accumulated any wealth was subject to hissing or envy. Such a family or person would be denounced for having accumulated wealth through communion with evil spirits and asked to atone for the same. The atonement was a feast for the whole village, which left the rising family even worse off than the rest of the village.

The above norms and actions inhibited accumulation and actively promoted the redistribution of surplus. Whether through denunciation as 'pagan' rites or through the growing scope for such persons to escape and redistribute measures through urban migration, these measures of redistribution have lost their earlier force. Along with them day-to-day measures of reciprocity, such as the substantial provision of village or clan labour to maintain families in need (those without adults or with adults who are unable to work), have been replaced, for instance among the Nagas, by annual cash subscriptions of a percentage of family income (Nathan and Xiaogang, 2004). This contribution is more like a tax, and since the proposition is fixed for all families, rich or poor alike, it is in fact regressive, that is, its burden is more on poorer families. Such a tax, unlike the earlier potentially unlimited contribution of labour and grain, does not inhibit accumulation.

In extreme crisis situations, as during the collapse of urban incomes and remittances during the Asian crisis, among the indigenous peoples in Thailand, there was a continuation of kinship and community relations. Returning migrants who had no immediate family could stay with relatives, or if they had no close relatives, in the Buddhist temple. In a different manner, the small patches of village forest in Meghalaya that went to support the church could also supply timber for the homeless. These means of kinship or community entitlement during extreme crisis were exceptional measures; they do show that the community has not been completely eroded. But they are merely remnants of what used to be regular and normal organizing principles of these societies.

The social security system had a high cost in terms of 'dynamic efficiency, because of their disincentive efforts of work and investment efforts' (Platteau, 1991: 161). Of course, incentive effects on work and investment were not concerns on which those economic systems were fashioned. But they are now becoming concerns of indigenous people, and this leads to changes in their economic systems. In sum, what we are witnessing is a historical change from a social system that produced sustenance for its members and the community to one that produces value or is dominated by the commodity form, from one mainly concerned about maintaining its social continuity to a system driven by the logic of accumulation and wealth creation.

Change in Production Orientation

The change in production systems is not confined to accumulation at the top, as it were. There is an overall change in the approach to production, from one based on the satisfaction of needs, relatively fixed needs, to one based on the maximization of income.

In the subsistence-oriented 'full belly' type of production, the objectives were that of meeting a fixed desired level of consumption, while minimizing work or maximizing leisure (Das Gupta, 2002: 3556). The desired level of consumption may be that needed for meeting household nutrition needs over the year while fulfilling social and ceremonial obligations. This leads to a maximization of leisure, after meeting consumption needs, in what Sahlins termed 'the original affluent society'. As Malabika Das Gupta points out, reports of the behaviour of Tripura Swiddeners show that they acted on a basis that could be characterized by the 'full belly' model. In 1879–80, when there was a bumper harvest of rice, the swiddeners only carried home the quantity required for consumption; the surplus is left for wild beasts. Of course, besides the limited consumption needs of the swiddeners, there was also the factor of poor communication, which made it impossible for the surplus to be exchanged with traders from the plains for anything else.

This was the nature of subsistence production. But with the growth of communication and the creation of new needs, the nature of production objective has changed. 'Since consumerism has spread among them even the remote areas ... becoming to some extent a part of the global village, in making their production decisions the jhumias [swiddeners] ... seem to want to maximise their utility subject to a minimum consumption and a maximum labour constraint today' (ibid.: 3559). What this means is that from a subsistence-oriented system of production, a more surplus and accumulation-oriented maximization of utility (income) subject to a labour constraint has become the norm of peasant production. This is a big shift from subsistence to surplus production.

Of course, given the inevitable inequalities in this process, with a combination of state exclusion and unequal access to land and other productive resources, not many swiddeners make it to accumulation. But what is important is the change in the orientation towards production. This changed orientation too seems to be unevenly among the swiddeners. As repeatedly noticed, the scope for hunting as a serious production activity is almost zero. Yet, there are many such communities where men go out with hunting rifles, whereas women work in the swidden fields. If even that semblance of production, which is in fact leisure, is not there, then there is frequent recourse by men to alcohol consumption as a leisure activity.

Women, on the contrary, try to maximize the income they can earn, going down the line to low return activities, such as collecting, carrying and selling head loads of fuel wood. The compelling factor is the gender division of responsibilities, where household food security is very much in women's domain. Failure to provide food can even lead to women being victims of men's domestic violence, besides being socially stigmatized. As a reaction to men's alcoholic violence and the threat it brings to household food security, women across many indigenous communities of India (in Andhra Pradesh, Maharashtra and Nagaland, for instance) have responded with mass movements to ban alcohol consumption.

Inadequacy of Older Norms Governing Production

With a shift in production systems to maximize incomes, unlike with production for self-consumption, which is necessarily limited by the extent of local consumption, production for sale on the market is not similarly locally limited. Consequently, the growth of external markets for various forest products, for example NTFPs, has often been accompanied by the rapid depletion, even disappearance of these products. We will discuss the inadequacy of older norms governing taking NTFP as the main case.

There are two factors at work here. The first is the over-extraction of the NTFP. This occurs even if tradition actually forbids the collection of NTFP for sale. But in the absence of other avenues for earning income, extraction and sale of NTFP is a viable source of income. Thus, the rules prohibit the extraction of NTFP for sale breakdown in the face of the double pressure of the external market and the internal need for cash income.

The rule that does remain largely in effect is the one restricting access to those who are members of the relevant community, clan or village. But since there is no effective regulation of rates of harvesting, the effect of competitive over-harvesting inevitably comes into play.

The second factor is that if the harvesting of NTFP is to be sustainable, some measures of investment of labour and other resources are needed. A study of NTFP harvesting in the Amazon and Borneo points out, '...almost any form of resource harvest produces an impact on the structure and functions of tropical plant populations. If nothing is done to mitigate these impacts, continued harvesting will deplete the resource' (Peters, 1994: 45). This is so irrespective of the rate of harvesting, although destructive harvesting, the type brought about by competitive harvesting accelerates the process.

The author goes on to point out, 'There are ways to exploit the non-timber resources produced by tropical plant populations with a minimum of ecological damage. Doing so, however, requires management... Although quite a bit more involved than simply picking up fruit or tapping rubber trees, these management procedures will produce a sustainable form of resource utilization' (ibid.).

Is it likely that the investment in labour and other resources will be forthcoming in the existing system of NTFP access and collection? Where the investment of labour and other resources will result in an income that does not necessarily accrue to the person or group undertaking the investment, is such investment likely? Here, the logic of individual decision-making comes into play. The income will be shared among all members of the community, while one person or family undertakes the investment in labour and other resources. This will inevitably restrict the possibility of the investment to maintain sustainability.

Thus, we have two processes to the depletion of NTFP in common properties, even if access to the resources is controlled. The first is competitive over-harvesting and the second is the paucity of investment in sustaining the productivity of the resource.

The usual response of families and communities to the above problems has been to bring the trees into the home garden or privately owned orchards. A study of Meghalaya (north-east India) showed that most NTFP sold in the market come from gardens and not from the forest as such (Tiwari, 2000). With the disappearance or very restricted availability of medicinal herbs, in Bastar (MP) too most of what is sold as NTFP is actually produced in the home garden or swiddens, and not in the forest as such. Valuable trees, such as tamarind and *mahua*, are in the swiddens, home gardens or otherwise within the settlements.

The process of privatizing and domesticating NTFP depends on return from the NTFP. As one would expect, those NTFPs that yield a higher return are domesticated, whereas those with lower, including uncertain, returns are not domesticated. In this process, there is a difference between regions depending on the trading system, which affects the return from a particular product.

We should revert to the main point being made here – the failure of traditional management systems of NTFP to cope with problems of regeneration and maintaining the sustainability of the output. A change in the rules governing rates of harvesting is clearly needed, as also a system of incentives to allow for investment in enrichment planting and other forms of management to improve regeneration. The first can be done by marking trees to be harvested (or not harvested as the case may be) or by specifying the block within harvesting will be carried out in any period. These are the rules, as suggested by Peters (1994: 42). But more important than rules is the type of institution that can implement them.

The study of indigenous forest management ideologies in Jharkand (Singh, 2004) points out that traditional approaches to forest management do not include replanting of trees in the commons. Replanting was carried out in the privatized home gardens, whereas forest regeneration in the commons was the result of leaving the plot fallow to natural regeneration. Even where there was replanting in the commons (see the study of forest management practices in Kalimanatan by Christine Padoch (1185)) such planting activity led to the establishment of individual/family rights over the tree and/or its fruits. Such an individualized right resulting from the labour of planting trees is common in many indigenous (see, e.g., the study of the Rungus of Sabah (Porodong, 2001), or the Khasis of Meghalaya). What this means is that traditional approaches are insufficient for maintaining productivity in commercially exploited common forests, which require replanting. This would also strengthen the point that one cannot expect an automatic transition from a subsistence-oriented to a commercially oriented collective management of common forests.

At another level, new types of individual investment can only yield adequate returns if social practices change. For instance, with continuing uncontrolled grazing, plantation can only be taken up by those who can afford to fence their plantation areas. A shift to controlled grazing, however, can open the scope for many more families to undertake investment in plantation. Backed up by sanctions for not conforming to the new rules, social fencing can reduce the cost of plantation, and thus enable many more to participate in the intensification of forest-based production.

Thus, it is not only in the case of collective forms of management, as in common property systems, that enabling social conditions are needed. Such enabling social conditions are also needed to institute new forms of private investment.

An Advanced Mode of Self-Activity

The new productive forces mean a higher level of income, though not necessarily for all. The satisfaction of needs through consumption is possible because of the higher income. A new system of production, introduced by tourism, 'means disruption, but it also means survival and much more' (Goody, 1998: 197). Survival, as we have seen earlier, is not only on a material level but also on a cultural level, as cultural practices become means of earning an income. In India, which has a rich tradition of women's domestic crafts, the export earnings from craft production have increased from about $50 million in 1990 to about $400 million in 2000 (Raj and Kapoor, 2002). From a historical situation of handicrafts being destroyed for and by British mill-made products, the export markets for handicrafts have played a substantial role in the revival of handicrafts in India and across Asia.

Does the development of new forces of production represent an 'advanced mode of self-activity of the individuals' (Marx and Engels, 1970)? This was always how Marx understood the meaning of more developed productive forces – as more developed forms – as more developed forms of labour. In the examples discussed above, the shift from collection of wild plant materials to the domestication of these plants certainly represents a higher form of labour. The knowledge of plants needed for domestication is higher than in collection.

In another example, the shift of weaving from being a domestic activity of women in Laos to being the main source of income – in that too there is a considerable advance in the forms of labour. From relatively fixed designs, specific to a particular community, women now learn to weave or embroider any design that is given to them, namely any design demanded in the market. In the process, there is a generalization of the capacity to weave or embroider. There is even some local development of the capacity to innovate and make new designs, a capacity largely concentrated among the local weaver–traders who over time become specialized trader designers and also older, more experienced women, who are able to make new designs and set up looms, etc.[1]

These are all definite advances in the modes of labour, the modes of self-activity of the producers. Although the older, ancient form of production gave satisfaction from a limited standpoint, the modern seems to give no satisfaction, following as it does the dictates of the market. But there is a higher content in the labour; only with the capitalist form, it appears as alienation, sacrifice of the human end of income or wealth, to paraphrase Marx (1973: 487–88). But as Marx repeatedly insisted (1973: 515), this is also a movement in the dissolution of the limited presupposition of existing production; something clearly visible in the transformation of decorative embroidery and weaving form being a subsidiary domestic activity of women into a commercial art production and even the main income source of women and their families.

Of course, these are still regarded as tourist souvenirs, not as genuine products. That requires a change not only in the attitude of the users/consumers of these products but also in development perception of work and in particular the recognition of women 'reproductive work' as work. It is after the rise of the feminist movement in the west that women's decorative embr[illegible] or quilt making is being recognized as art. The feminist artist Miriam Sch[illegible] has coined the term 'femmage' to show the close connection between [illegible] and the making of collages (Broude, 1982). That decorative motifs are [illegible] for abstraction in art was recognized, for instance, by Wassily Kandinsky [illegible] however, strove very hard to maintain a distinction between 'mere decora[illegible]' and 'vibrations of the spirit' (ibid.: 317). There is still a strong tendency [illegible] dismiss women's domestic artistic work as 'mere decoration' and 'not art'. Th[e] shift from such artistic work being a domestic function of women to becoming a commodity in the art (even if it was a mass souvenir) could help in changing opinions about the artistic function of women art producers.

Some Problems Markets Solve

Although the focus is on privatization as a consequence of the spread of markets, it is useful to take a brief look at the benefits of the spread of markets. In the example of the leaving of surplus products on the ground for wild animals a[s] it were in Tripura, one factor in this wasteful use of human labour was [the] absence of markets in which these surplus products could be exchange[d for] either other useful products or even stores of value, like gold or other p[recious] metals. The spread of markets makes it possible to overcome such wast[e] of human labour and other resources.

Further, with the existing low level of local demand for various products, such as timber or other forest products, there is not much scope for the intensification of resource use in their production. Extensive methods of production, dependent on use of large forest areas and relying on natural methods of regeneration, are quite sufficient for meeting local needs. With the growth of external demand, there is a pressure to produce more from smaller areas and with lesser use of labour. There is an intensification of production, for instance the shift from extensive collection in forests to intensive production in home gardens. This occurs even with regard to produce such as fuel wood, when the increase in the opportunity cost of women's labour time leads to the necessity of reducing women's labour in domestic activities (Nathan and Kelkar, 1999).

The market, with its associate privatization, does solve some existing problems in indigenous people's economies. It allows for surplus production to be sold on the market and not just be left in the ground. In this manner, it reduces inefficiency in resource use. The growth of extra-local market demand means that intensification of resource use can be carried out beyond that possible when confined to the local market.

From Adventure to Routine

We have seen that among indigenous peoples, new social relations are needed to develop productive forces, chief of which is labour, and in order to set up citizen-based systems of social welfare. There is a shift from simple reproduction to extended reproduction and accumulation. New needs are created, along with cosmopolitan consumption and production systems, taking local products to the far corners of the world and bringing new goods into local consumption. The mass media, in particular, has been a key instrument in this development of new needs and forms of consumption. A new combination of private and collective or community systems becomes necessary.

But there is also the experience of individualized hunger and deprivation. Producers often do not know why or for whom they produce what they produce. Everything seems to obey the dictates of an impersonal market. While moving in new directions, however, people also rely on their own experience. For one who has always lived in the domestic drudgery of patriarchal domination, as young women in the north of Thailand, wage employment, however alienated and even low paid in the garment factories of Bangkok, seems and is a real advance. Its limitations come up only later in experience. Did this movement of women as employees into light industry or commerce bring benefits to the women concerned? Did it weaken the grip of patriarchy or merely function within the confines of old familial relations? These questions have been discussed elsewhere, notably in Kabeer (2000) with reference to the similar movement of young women in Bangladesh into garment factories in Dhaka.

Sen's capability approach allows us to see that many things have changed: choices have increased, income and consumption have increased, women's status in the family and society has improved. Young women must have some minimal education in order to get jobs in the garment industry. Is this the factor behind Bangladesh's recent better performance in education for girls than India's? All of these constitute substantial change in women's familial and social relations, constituting a weakening of patriarchy, if we are willing to recognize that social transformation may not necessarily occur as 'a single discrete moment of rupture with the past, but as a gradual diffusion of new possibilities' (ibid.: 192). There are discrete moments of rupture with the past, and there is also the gradual diffusion of new possibilities, expanding the capabilities of persons and changing set rules. For the individual women, it is certainly a substantial rupture when they move from being unpaid family workers to even poorly paid factory workers.

To use the analysis of Marshal Berman, modernity starts out as adventure and then turns into routine (1982: 243–48). But the transformation of adventure into deadening routine requires the experience of modernity. This time of experience, perhaps, is a necessary factor in making alternative projects feasible.

Of course, the time of experience is not strictly calendar time. Singular movements can reveal social contradictions that would otherwise not be obvious in more placid situations. Further, those who have gone through such experiences (for instance, people in Euro-American and Japan who have for more than a century lived under the sway of capital, or the urban classes in the developing countries) and seen all its negative consequences for life are understandably impatient with those for whom the freedom of wage employment seems a liberation and consumption by choice a valuable freedom.

It is no use pointing out that the choice of brands in a supermarket is a tawdry choice, of not much consequence, that consumerism is a curse in making people slaves of the endless change of commercial fashions. For one who buys a pair of shoes when the older one is un-wearable, the choice of being able to buy something you absolutely need it, but because you like it – this choice seems and is a higher level of living.

A consumption statement is a limited kind of statement; it is not usually a statement of creativity, of production. But for people whose consumption is severely circumscribed by poverty, the ability to buy something, even when it is not absolutely needed, is a valuable choice, a type of freedom. Here, however, we need to distinguish between two kinds of choices – choice between, say, flavours of ice cream and choice in being able to buy an ice cream at all. The first is a relatively trivial choice, whereas the second is non-trivial and reflects the difference between necessity and choice – as freedom to enjoy a satisfaction above a minimum level of necessary consumption.

The contradiction in this development of commodity-based consumption, however, cannot be revealed in its absence. To 'rise above the din of the market place' (Kapur, 1998), there must first be a market place. And in a sense, one must be in the market place and go through the market place in order to realize its contradictions and thus rise above it.

Is Masculine Domination Inevitable?

We saw that with the growth of the market, there is a shift from men's domination of the spiritual and political realm to domination in the economic system, including the unravelling of matriliny. But is it inevitable that there be masculine domination? In a way, this question is parallel to the one posed earlier: Is privatization inevitable with market-based growth? Our answer was no, but the transition from a kinship-based collectivity for subsistence to a citizenship-based collectivity for accumulation seems impossible, given the lack of adequate social structures (social capital) for such a direct transition.

In the area of masculine domination, however, the situation is somewhat different. Even while there has been a spread of masculine domination among indigenous peoples with relatively more equal gender systems, there has also been a counter movement of women's resistance to gender inequalities. These movements of resistance to gender inequalities make it more possible that inheritance and property systems will not mirror those in the plains' societies, with their millennia's long history of strong patriarchy.

To illustrate the above, among the Munda in Jharkhand, the produce of swidden is understood to be more the domain of women. But rice is exclusively men's province. Women cannot take out rice from the storage bin; not even for household food needs. If the man is absent, women will borrow rice from neighbours but not touch the household bin. Wet rice is then quintessentially man's domain, and a strengthening of masculine domination is historically associated with the spread of wet rice cultivation.

Does this mean that any spread of wet rice cultivation must necessarily lead to masculine domination? In the absence of any other intervention, it is likely that this will happen. But nowadays states themselves have laws for equal land rights, for example, Chhattisgarh in India among others. In china too, there is some land right for women in the household responsibility system. These rights are not easily secured, but their existence does make it possible for women's mobilization to succeed in realizing these rights.

The point is, unlike in the case of privatization, there is no incentive or productivity case for men's sole ownership of property. If anything, the incentive case works on the other side – women's ownership of land and other productive resources would increase their incentive to labour more, better, and more productively and also use and develop their own knowledge of production systems.

Similarly, the laws for women's representation in village councils have had their effect in changing the formerly male-dominated village assemblies. Equality of voting rights as citizens has led to village assemblies in Munda villages no longer distinguishing between senior (*khuntkatti*) and junior (*praja*)[2] lineages, or even between women and men.

Privatization in the present situation can go along with the assertion of relatively more equal gender rights, and even with measures of democracy based on quality before the law. Privatization and the intensification of production today do not have to mimic Bronze Age transitions to strongly patriarchal systems.

Recreating the Community

Accepting the necessity of the market system for the intensification of production, accumulation and increase of incomes, does this have to be done in a *laissez-faire*, or as it is nowadays called a neo-liberal (leave it all to the market) type of system? We have already seen that in the cases of provision of public goods, like local environmental services, and the preservation of cultural heritage beyond the commoditization of ethnicity, various forms of public intervention would be needed. Similarly, in the matter of food security too, various new forms of public intervention would be needed to deal with the limitations of the market.

At the economic level, it is not necessary that integration into the market necessarily erode and destroy all forms of community interaction. Of course, the market is likely to destroy the traditional community. With conscious intervention, however, the community can be recreated. But the nature of the interaction would have to change, from the earlier kinship-based reciprocity and redistribution welfare system to a new form of citizen-based social welfare system, combining state- and community-based mechanisms. Forms of collective functioning are also needed for maintaining critical natural resources. Forms of collective entrepreneurship could also be developed. The relatively more equal gender relations of the indigenous peoples are certainly being eroded, but more productive technologies and market systems do not have to necessarily enshrine patriarchy.

Even within the capitalist market, there can be enterprises with a variety of internal relations – contrast the 'hire and fire' method of Americans capitalism with the until-recently 'life-long employment' of Japanese capitalism (at least for its core of male, permanent workers) and also the fairly elaborate social welfare system of the collective villages and collective enterprises of china. Technology and the market do not dictate even the full form of enterprise. But the extent to which they are able to institute different and more welfare-oriented forms of internal relations depend crucially on the productivity, and because of globalization, even comparative productivity of these enterprises. With the decade-long stagnation in Japanese productivity and thus with the loss of these firms' advantage over their competitors, Japanese firms are being forced to abandon the more expensive system of life-long employment.

Developing citizen-based collectivities for public action on food security would need to move from 'reciprocity' to taxes in order to provide 'safety nets'. As food itself becomes less of a problem, it is necessary to intervene in public provision of education and health care. This requires that local communities have unequivocal over portions of tax revenues. The Chinese devolution of certain taxes to the level (the agricultural products tax, for instance) has been seen to have beneficial effects on local accumulation. It is for local communities and their authorities to also use these revenues to fashion new forms of human welfare.

Productivity may make certain levels of welfare expenditures possible, but it does not necessarily have to occur. Whether or not more people-friendly welfare systems are instituted will depend on the extent of struggle for such system, a struggle that now, however, switches from the formerly national scale to the new global scale. Leave alone relatively weak indigenous peoples, even strong states are losing their ability to meet their former welfare commitments. With the loss of autonomy with regard to interest, inflation and exchange rates, the one arena of competition among states is to reduce costs by cutting welfare expenditures. As a result, it is a race to the bottom with regard to welfare commitments even in developed countries, negating commitments that were gained after long battles in the past century.

In a system of potentially unrestrained movement of capital, with equal treatment for capitals, irrespective of their origin, there is no escaping the conclusion that a global working people's response, a global New Deal, or a global social contract (Castells, 2000: 253), can be the only alternative to a race to the bottom. This surely will be difficult to achieve. But the creation of alternatives in globalization need not stop with the creation of 'safety nets', which after all are ways of aiding those who have fallen below. A more equal distribution of former community lands would mean doing away with, for instance, the grabbing of land by the politically influential, as now happens. Land reform, in one way or the other, is a necessary part of a more democratic alternative in globalization. This could itself be fashioned at a local level, in villages or groups of villages. What this means is that unlike in the neo-liberal doctrine, there should be a non-market access to land (or forest) as a critical productive resource. And this access should be not for the 'household' or the 'family' but for the individual adult, women or man.

Promoting higher education, however, requires more than just state support. It also requires the creation of job opportunities; otherwise, the result would only be the frustration of educated unemployment. This is where the promotion of non-agricultural employment, as in tourism or cultural processing, would have a beneficial effect in promoting employment for the educated. At the level of public action, however, it also requires a change in the approach to high school education – primary education and literacy are now accepted as public goods whose consumption cannot be restricted by private, household decision. In a globalizing world, it is necessary to move up the ladder to high school education as a first step.

Similarly, in the contemporary situation, heavy medical expenses are often the routes to falling into poverty. In a situation where health care costs are privatized, they become a major factor in the near-poor falling into the category of the poor. Indigenous people's areas are characterized by low levels of state-provided social welfare expenses. Their road systems too have historically been designed for extraction of timber and products. The levels of education and health infrastructure available in the hills are significantly lower than in the plains. Increasing the health and education infrastructure in the hills required greater public investment in the above, something that the allocation of tax revenues on timber and other forest products to the indigenous peoples' governments is likely to promote.

Thus, we see a necessity of intervening in the privatization process in a number of ways – public decision for locally needed environmental services, combined with market-based provision of environmental services for external needs; public decision for preservation of cultural heritage, beyond the limits of that promoted by the commoditization of culture; land reform to enable a more equal distribution of land-based income; mobilization and intervention to create more equal gender relations; higher public provision of education and health care needs. All of these change privatization from a straightforward *laissez-faire* or neo-liberal system to one that is less unequal. They, however, are alternative in globalization – not an alternative to globalization. The scheme put forward here has a lot in common with that proposed by Arthur MacEwan

2000 for a more equal and democratic form of market economy, and Dreze and Sen's notion of 'participatory development' (Dreze and Sen, 2002).

The civilizational transformation of indigenous peoples' economies and societies is occurring at a time when the increased stratification that historically accompanied intensification carries with it some factors for overcoming this stratification (Earle and Johnson, 2000: 387). In the contemporary world, there is not just elite, but specialized consumption. Mass production carries with it mass consumption and mass culture. The power of mass media in this regard is increased by the growth of universal literacy, as against the earlier creation of literate elite. Adult franchise means that the economically marginalized cannot be just ignored. Gender relations and family systems, too, are not of the kind that just reproduce earlier forms of patriarchy but are tending in the direction of more equal gender relations. Finally, forms of civil society, bringing together the indigenous peoples all over the world, and linking them with other global civil society organizations, are now the order of the day. All of this makes possible a greater spread of benefits, if not also a quicker overcoming of limits.

Notes

1. This observation is somewhat different from that of Ella Bhatt and Renana Jhabvala, who find a staticity in women artisans' work:

    > Their traditions provide them with knowledge about local conditions and materials, about problems specified to their techniques. But this know-how is neither built into a wider knowledge system nor taught as part of it: so, over time, there is a danger of parts getting lost in transmission. To avoid that, workers are taught to regard each step in the process – whether ritualistically or actually productive – as being sacrosanct; no explanation is given about its necessity. This creates a mind-set, which venerates the past and distrust the change. This is particularly true of women who, much more than men, are supposed to be the keepers and not the questioners of family traditions. (Raj and Kapoor, 2002: 11)

    The difference might be due to the greater role of rituals in caste India compared with post-monarchy Laos.
2. The *praja* are the families of women with in marrying husbands, '*ghar jamai*'.

References and Readings

Berman, Marshall (1982). *All That Is Solid Melts into Air: The Experience of Modernity*. New York and London: Penguin Books.

Bourdieu, Pierre (1990). *The Logic of Practice*. Cambridge: Polity Press.

Broude, Norma (1982). 'Miriam Schapiro and "Femmage": Reflections on the Conflict between Decoration and Abstraction in Twentieth Century Art', in Norma Broude and Mary Garrard (eds), *Feminism and Art History: Questioning the Litany*. New York: Harper and Row, pp. 315–329.

Castells, Manuel (2000). *The Network Society*. Oxford: Blackwell Publishers.

Das Gupta, Malabika (2002). 'Objective Function in Economic Models of Decisions on Production: Evidence from Swiddeners of Tripura', *Economic and Political Weekly*, 24 August, 37(34): 3556–59.

Dreze, Jean and Amartya Sen (2002). *India: Development and Participation*. New Delhi: Oxford University Press.

Earle, Timothy and Allen W. Johnson (2000). *The Evolution of Human Societies*, 2nd ed. Stanford: California University Press.

Engels, Frederick (1894 [1969]). 'On Social Relations in Russia', in Karl Marx and Frederick Engels (eds), *Selected Works in Three Volumes, Volume Two*. Moscow: Progress Publishers.

Kabeer, Naila (2000). *Bangladesh Women Workers and Labour Market Decisions: The Power to Choose*. New Delhi: Vistaar Publications.

Kapur, Geeta (1998). 'Globalization and Culture: Navigating the Void', in Fredric Jameson and Masao Miyoshi (eds), *The Cultures of Globalization*. Durham: Duke University Press, pp. 191–218.

Mac Ewan, Arthur (2000). *Neo-Liberalism or Democracy?* Dhaka: The University Press Limited.

Marx, Karl (1973). *Grundrisse*, translated by Martin Nicolaus. Harmondsworth: Penguin Books.

Marx, Karl and Frederick Engels (1970 [1845–46]). 'Feurbach: Opposition of Materialistic and Idealistic Outlook', in *Selected Works*, Vol. I. Moscow: Foreign Languages Publishing House.

Nathan, Dev (2001). 'Land Systems in Meghalaya'. A Study for the Asia Division. Rome: IFAD.

Nathan, Dev and Govind Kelkar (1999). 'Agrarian Involution, Domestic Economy and Women: Rural Dimensions of the Asian Crisis', *Economic and Political Weekly*, 8–14 May, 34(19): 1135–41.

Nathan, Dev and Yu Xiaogang (2004). 'North-East Indian: Markets and the Transition from Communal to Private Property', in Dev Nathan, Govind Kelkar and Pierre Walter (eds), *Globalization and Indigenous Peoples in Asia: Changing the Local-Global Interface*. New Delhi: Sage Publication.

Nathan, Dev, Govind Kelkar and Pierre Walter (eds) (2004). *Globalization and Indigenous Peoples in Asia: Changing the Local-Global Interface*. New Delhi: Sage Publication.

Nathan, Dev, Govind Kelkar and Yu Xiaogang (1998). 'Women as Witches and Keepers of Demons: Cross-Cultural Analysis of Struggles to Change Gender Relations', *Economic and Political Weekly*, 31 October – 6 November, 33(44): WS58–69.

Nongbri, Tiplut (2002). 'Culture and Biodiversity: Myths, Legends and the Conservation of Nature in the Hills of North-East India', *Indian Anthropologist*, 36(1/2): 1–21.

Padoch, C. (1985). 'Labor Efficiency and Intensity of Land Use in Rice Production: An Example from Kalimantan', *Human Ecology*, 13(3): 271–89.

Peters, Charles (1994). *Sustainable Harvest of Non-Timber Plant Resources in tropical Moist Forests: An Ecological Primer*. Washington, DC: USAID Biodiversity Support Programme.

Platteau, Jean-Philippe (1991). 'Traditional System of Social Security and Hunger Insurance: Past Achievements and Modern Challenges', in Ehitsham Ahmed, Jean Dreze, John Hills and Amartya Sen (eds), *Social Security in Developing Countries*. New Delhi: Oxford University Press, pp. 112–70.

Polanyi, Mark (1944). *The Great Transformation*. Boston: Beacon Press.

Porodong, Paul (2001). 'Bobolizan, Forests and Gender Relations in Sabah, Malaysia', *Gender, Technology and Development*, 5(1): 63–90.

Raj, Ashok and Rakesh Kapoor (2002). 'Globalizing Handicraft Market and the Marginalization of Women Craft-Workers', Paper presented at UNIFEM and SEWA Bharat Workshop on 'Globalization and its Impact on Women Workers in Informal Economy', New Delhi, December.

Sarin, Madhu (2001). 'Empowerment and Disempowerment of Forest Women in Uttarakhand, India', *Gender, Technology and Development*, 5(3): 341–64.

Saxena, N.C. (2001). 'Poverty in Meghalaya'. A Study for the Asia Division. Rome: IFAD.

Singh, K.S. (2004). 'Changing Attitude to Forest and Nature: A Historical Review with Focus on Jaharkhand', in Nathan et al. (2004), op. cit.

Tiwari, B.K. (2000). 'Non-Timber Forest Produce of North East India', *Journal of Human Ecology*, 10: 445–55.

21

Health Inequalities in India and the Challenges before Social Transformation

Mohammad Akram and Sadaf Rafiq Beg

Health is a basic human right for every individual. The Universal Declaration of Human Rights (1948) in Article 25 stated that 'Everyone has the right to a standard of living adequate for the health and wellbeing of himself and his family...'. The Preamble to the World Health Organization (WHO) Constitution also affirms that it is one of the fundamental rights of every human being to enjoy 'the highest attainable standard of health'. Article 21 of the Constitution of India states thus: 'No person shall be deprived of his life or personal liberty except through procedure established by law.' Until the 1970s, by and large, the courts had interpreted 'life' literally, that is, right to exist. It was only in late 1970s onwards that an expanded meaning started to be given to the word 'life'. Over the years, it has come to be accepted that life does not only mean biological existence but the life of a dignified human being with all its concomitant attributes. This would include a healthy environment, life skill, education, food, nutrition and effective health care facilities.

The Alma-Ata Declaration of 1978 stated that 'attainment of the highest possible level of health is a most important world-wide social goal whose realization requires the action of many other social and economic sectors in addition to the health sector.' It further says that 'the existing gross inequality in the health status of the people particularly between developed and developing countries as well as within countries is politically, socially and economically unacceptable and is, therefore, of common concern to all countries.' The declaration made its vision very clear: health for all the people of the world by the year 2000.

The Alma-Ata Declaration and many other studies carried out in the past two decades of the 20th century exposed the widespread inequalities inherent in the health condition of the people. The inequalities in health not only reveal the inequalities present in various other segments of the society, but they are also a result of various ongoing social, cultural and politico-economic processes. Cross-national evidences suggest that the greater the degree of socio-economic inequality that exits within a society, the steeper the gradient of health inequality. In the words of Daniels, Kennedy and Kawachi (2006: 63) '...middle-income groups in a more unequal society will have worse health than comparable or even poorer groups in a society with greater equality.' Health inequality is not always the result of economic inequality. In the words of Michael Marmot (2006: 38), '...wider inequalities in health represent wider inequalities in society – although the evidence on this is still problematic.' However, differences in health among individuals in society are different from inequalities between social groups. Our concern here is mainly with group inequalities and not individual differences within the groups.

This paper is a part of the Festschrift volume in honour of distinguished social scientist Professor Yogendra Singh. Needless to say, Professor Singh significantly contributed through his writings on social and cultural change in India, modernization, globalization, social stratification and social transformation. He establishes it well that inequalities in India are structured and the process of social transformation generates many serious contradictions. He realizes that India is at a crucial stage of its development. He emphatically says that 'it is timely, therefore, to examine the roots of our structural and cultural contradictions, distortions and errors in our development policies or strategies' (Singh, 1997: 192). While talking about the challenges of change, Singh says that 'the culmination of social forces operating in our society since independence, has led us to face with many unanticipated challenges' (Singh, 2000: 239). Honouring Singh's interest in social inequalities and social transformation, this paper aims to look at the health inequalities in India and the challenges before social transformation. The paper is divided into six sections: (i) understanding health, (ii) concept of inequality in health, (iii) health indicators and ongoing disparities in India, (iv) health system in India, (v) health reforms and goals of social transformation and (vi) challenges before social transformation.

Understanding Health

Health is interpreted differently from different perspectives (Advani and Akram, 2007). The biomedical approach that dominated the medical thought until the end of 19th century and based on the 'germ theory of disease' views health as an 'absence of diseases'. This approach almost ignores the role of environmental, psychological and other sociocultural factors in defining health. The ecological approach views health as a dynamic equilibrium between man and his environment. For them, disease is maladjustment of the human organism to environment. The psychological approach states that health is related not only to body but also to mind and, especially, to the attitude of the individual. The sociocultural approach considers health as a product of the social and community structure.

A functional definition of health implies the ability of a person to participate in normal social roles, and this may be contrasted with an experiential definition that takes sense of self into account (Kelman, 1975). Further, McKenzie, Pinger and Kotecki (2002: 4) have defined health as a dynamic state or condition that is multidimensional in nature and results from person's adaptations to his/her environment. It is a resource for living and exists in varying degrees. A holistic definition of health has been given by the WHO which states that health is a state of complete physical, mental and social well-being, and not merely an absence of disease or infirmity. Health is multidimensional, and three important dimensions of health as reflected in the WHO definition are physical, mental and social.

Nettleton (2006) argues that the definitions and conceptualization of health may vary systematically among various social groups, and it is likely that different accounts of health are drawn according to social circumstances, and the accounts provided by the people will change over time. She further argues that people do not generally work with unified theories or explanations that transcend time and place, and people are more likely to have views that are adjusted according to the concerns of the individual.

Wikler (2006) points that in ordinary public health perspective, avoidance of diseases and disabilities arising from personal choice is as important as avoidance of any other malady. He however points out that this is not the only perspective from which to view the contribution of individual behaviour to health. Some of the perspectives may see the health needs in terms of the responsibility for creating and maintaining them and thus the disabilities or diseases as a result of negligence or by having taken undue risks, then dealing with these health needs should be viewed as personal rather than social responsibilities. Wikler points out that it is both practical and desirable that personal responsibility of health plays a role in public health and clinical medicine in the future. According to him, promoting a sense of personal responsibility for health can be a part of programme of 'positive freedom' or 'empowerment' and a realization that action taken can affect one's health positively, with radiating good effects on other dimensions of life and on other people.

There are many complex issues in evaluating the state of health of individuals. One of the major complexities in evaluating the state of health arises from the fact that an individual's own understanding of health may not coincide with the appraisal of a medical expert. According to Sen (2006a), there is a contrast between the 'internal' and 'external' view of health. Internal view refers to the state of health as seen by the person in question, whereas external view is that of others who may take of the person's state of health. There is also a contrast between the methodological inclinations of 'observation-oriented' subjects such as economics and 'perception-orientated' studies (often favoured by anthropologists).

Sen's Capability Approach

According to Sen, health contributes to a person's basic capability to function. Hence, health is the most basic requirement for every individual. Denial of health is not only denial of 'good life-chance' but also of fairness and justice. Sen has helped to make the capabilities approach a paradigm for policy debate in human development where it inspired the creation of the United Nations' Human Development Index. Alkire (2003) has explained the capability approach through its four main components.

Functionings

Sen regards functionings as doings and beings that create a better conceptual space to examine social welfare than utility or opulence. The focus of capability approach on functionings takes the capability approach away from other approaches that are used to evaluate well-being. For instance, some approaches would use psychic utility or preference fulfilment for evaluating the well-being; others would use income per capita, or commodities persons were able to command; and still others, following Rawls, would use primary goods for evaluating well-being.

For defending capability approach, Sen points out the flaws in various approaches and shows that these flaws are corrected in capability approach. Alkire gives an example of how in economic theory welfare is interpreted in terms of psychological happiness and desire fulfilment, but magnitude of change in mental utility states may not predict the value of change. Alkire points that Sen often quotes an example of how the deprived become compatible with their circumstances and appreciate small mercies, thus their desires are muted and their psychological pleasure at small improvements to their situation is not proportionate to the benefit judged from another perspective. Sen questions Rawl's proposal to require equality in the space of primary goods and argues that Rawl's reasoning can be broadened to take greater note of the contingency of circumstances.

Freedom

Capability refers to the freedom of persons or groups to promote or achieve things that they consider valuable, and it was used by Sen to attend to the foundational importance of freedom.

Pluralism

Alkire argues that Sen emphatically defends the breadth of the capability approach and the pluralism of its information base. Sen argues that individual advantage can be examined in four different spaces, which include well-being achievement, well-being freedom, agency achievement and agency freedom. Sen also argues that we cannot focus on any one of these four possible spaces and that these may be in conflict with each other. Capability approach widens the information basis of considerations than inform the social welfare and social choice analysis, and therefore in this way it supports the pluralism.

Incompleteness

Incompleteness is one of the most important advantages of capability approach; and for allowing incompleteness, Sen identifies two grounds: fundamental and pragmatic. The capability approach of Sen is intentionally incomplete, and the reason behind this is to allow economists and development practitioners to work on pressing issues for which consensus on fundamentals is not required.

The roots of capability approach go back to Adam Smith, Karl Marx and Aristotle. Regarding functionings as a set of 'doings and beings', Sen argues that these functionings have to be examined, and the capability of a person to achieve them has to be valued appropriately. The functionings may vary from primary functionings such as avoiding morbidity and mortality, being adequate, undertaking usual movements, etc., to many complex functionings such as achieving self-respect (Sen, 2006b). Robeyns (2006) argues that the difference between a functioning and a capability is the same as the difference between an achievement and the freedom to achieve something and between an opportunity and an outcome. All capabilities correspond to the overall freedom to lead a life that one has reason to value. Robeyns points out that Sen attaches importance to reason to value because we need to scrutinize our motivations for valuing specific lifestyles, and not value a certain life without reflecting upon it. Sen criticizes the theories that focus extensively on utility resource or income, but Sen does not deny the importance that contribution resources can make to people's well-being as inequalities in resources can indeed be an important cause of inequalities of capabilities.

The capability approach, according to Peter (2006), provides a useful alternative for accessing health problems in the society. Good health is often regarded by Sen as an example of functioning (e.g. as used by Sen in his capability and freedom approach). Peter however points out that it is more favourable to use health as a capability or as a subset of capability because of the fact that health itself is composed of various functionings such as ability to move around, not being tired and others. Peter points out that Sen leaves it open as to which functionings are to be included when accessing a particular social situation. Sen stresses that in each case, this will require a process of selecting a relevant functioning and weighing their relative importance. Viewing health as a capability or as a subset of capability requires a process that involves value judgements and which is subject to political contestation. Thus, according to Peter, the process of defining health and determining what counts as health and what as another type of social problems cannot be solved by the health specialists alone, but it depends on other aspects of social institutions, and may change over time.

We can conclude this section by quoting Sen, as he says:

> the state of health that a person enjoys is influenced by a number of different considerations which take us well beyond the role of social and economic factors. An adequate policy approach to health has to take note not only of the influences that come from general social and economic factors, but also from a variety of other parameters, such as personal disabilities, individual proneness to illness, epidemiological hazards of particular regions, the influence of climatic variations, and so on. (Sen, 2006c: 28)

Concept of Inequality in Health

Health inequality does not mean any kind of health difference but the differences in health that are potentially avoidable. Inequality in health can be explained as a particular type of difference in health that could be potentially shaped by policies. It is a difference in which disadvantaged social groups (such as poor, racial/ethnic minorities, women or other groups that have persistently experienced social disadvantage or discrimination) systematically experience worse health or greater health risks than more advantaged social groups. Health inequalities or disparities include comparison not only between the best- and worst-off groups in a given category (e.g. the richest versus the poorest) but also between the most socially disadvantaged groups and all others (Heggenhougen and Quah, 2008).

Anand (2006) has argued that there should be more aversion to inequalities in health than inequalities in income because health has both instrumental and intrinsic value, whereas income has only instrumental value. Inequalities in health are closely related to inequalities in the most basic freedom and opportunities that people can enjoy. Some income inequalities are justified because, as often asserted by economists, income incentives are required to elicit effort, skill, enterprise and so on. These incentives or difference in reward increase the size of total income from which the society as a whole can gain. This increase has to be balanced against the income inequalities that must be tolerated in order to provide appropriate incentives for efficiency. In addition to this effort, skill, enterprise and so on are regarded as are considered as fair and legitimate means for some people to earn. But inequalities in health constitute inequalities in the capability of people to function. The investigation of health inequalities between groups helps to find out the groups that suffer from poor health and are at high risk, so that these might be targeted directly for the improvement in health and it helps to bring forth health inequalities that are regarded as unfair and unjust.

The Black Report (DHSS, 1980) is a landmark document in health inequality research, which brought about a paradigm shift in the discourse of health inequalities. Although it was well known that poorer sections of a community are more prone to disease and death, there were debates among the various groups regarding the cause. The heriditarians believed that people's social position was determined by inherent natural abilities; the public health doctors believed that the material conditions of the poor led to the debilitating health, independent of inherited constitutions; and another stream that later congeal into behavioural school of public health believed that unhealthy and reckless behaviour on the part of the poor was responsible for their poor health. The Black Report pointed out the complex effects of the economy and different forms of social organization, including the family, upon the level of health.

While studying the patterns of morbidity, mortality, utilization of health services across different occupational group in Britain, the Black Report brought to light marked inequality between the various classes on the basis of occupation for both the sexes and for all the ages. The report also pointed out those inequalities in health continued to increase despite the growth in economy in England. According to Mukhopadhyay (2008), the Black Report provided four possible explanations for these inequalities: (i) artefact explanation, according to which the changes were because of the statistical problems; (ii) the natural and social selection approach according to which the people who are healthy are able to move higher on the social ladder; (iii) material and social selection approach, which gave importance to role of economic deprivation; and (iv) the cultural explanation, which primarily focuses on individual behaviour, ideas and motivation. The report argues that although various sets of explanations are needed over time to clearly understand the inequalities in health, the materialist explanation is consistent of all the four.

The general finding that prosperity and health are related gives an impression that income/health gradient are unavoidable. Daniels, Kennedy and Kawachi (2006) using data of United Nations' Human Development Report Statistics come to the conclusion that there is a clear relation between the gross domestic product (GDP) per capita and life expectancy, which is clearer in advanced industrial economies, but this relationship exist up to a certain level. They also pointed out that relationship between health and income is not fixed, and the nation's health achievement is mediated by processes other than wealth. Various other factors such as culture, social organization and policies of government are also the determinants of health, and the variation in these factors also explains the difference in health outcome. Thus, if health of nations reflects policy choices or the features of the society that can be changed through policies, then we must ask about the justice or injustice of alternate policies.

Health Indicators and Ongoing Disparities in India

Health indicators play a significant role not only in measuring the health status of community but also in comparing health status of one country with another. It is also used for assessment of health care needs for allocation of scarce resources, and for monitoring and evaluating health services, activities and programme. Indicators help to measure the extent to which the objectives and targets of a programme are being attained. Health is a multidimensional phenomenon, and each dimension is influenced by numerous factors. There are many indicators of health such as mortality indicator, morbidity indicator, disability rate, nutritional status indicator, health care delivery indicator, utilization rate, indicator of social and mental health, socio-economic indicator, health policy indicator, indicators of quality of life, etc.

At the time of independence, the health situation in India was extremely depressing. There have been large gains in the health status of the population since independence. These gains are reflected in improvement in some indicators of health and are presented in Table 21.1. One of the main reasons behind these gains have been the development of vast rural health infrastructure, namely sub-centres, primary health centres and community health centres. There have been large health achievements in India such as

Table 21.1 *Selected health indicators: India, 1947 and current*

Indicators	At the time of independence, 1947	Current
Death rate	27.4	08.1
Infant mortality rate	146.0	63.0
Life-expectancy at birth	32.7	62.0

Source: India Social Development Report 2006: 20.

successful eradication of small pox and elimination of guinea worm. Plague has been controlled since 1969. Yaws is near eradication and leprosy near elimination; cholera epidemics and deaths are comparatively infrequent and fewer. The incidence of some diseases such as measles, polio, whooping cough and tetanus in children has been reduced significantly. Immunization of children has played an important role in these gains (Ali and Nanda, 2006).

Bjorkman and Raman (2009) pointed out that the infrastructure for the delivery of health services grew substantially in the post-independent India, and the health of the population improved during the past six decades. This was because of efforts made by the government from time to time to improve the capacity of system to deliver health services to all sections of the society. In India, we have one of the world's largest networks of health centres and hospitals under a public health system. The progress made in the health infrastructure in India from 1951–52 to 2005–06 is depicted in Table 21.2. A glance of the table reveals that primary health centres have increased in number from 725 (1951–52) to 22,669 (2005–06); the number of allopathic hospital in 1951–52 was 2,694; whereas in 2005–06, it increased up to 15,393 (in both public and private sectors) in 2005–06; the number of allopathic beds and doctor in Indian systems reached 683,545 and 724,823, respectively, in 2005–06; the number of hospital beds has increased from 117,178 to 914,543; the number of doctors in allopathic system increased from 61,800 to 660,301; the number of nurses (general nursing midwives only) increased from 16,550 to 908,962; and the number of medical colleges increased from 30 to 262.

Deogaonkar (2004) pointed out that in 2000, India had 1.25 million doctors and 0.8 million nurses, which means one doctor for every 1,800 people; and if indigenous system of medicine and homeopathic medicine are considered, there is one doctor per 800 people; 15,000 new graduate doctors and 5,000

Table 21.2 *Growth in health infrastructure in India*

Indicator	1951–52	2005–06	Remarks
Population	361 million	1,027 million	Census data
Primary health centres	725	22,669	
Allopathic hospitals	2,694	15,393	Both public and private
Allopathic beds	–	683,545	Both public and private
All beds	117,178	914,543	
Doctors (allopathic)	61,800	660,301	Registered at Medical Council of India
Doctors (Indian systems)	–	724,823	Ayurveda, unani and homeopathy
Nurses	16,550	908,962	General nursing midwives only
Five-Year Plan budgets (millions of rupees)	635 (First Plan)	589,203 (Tenth Plan)	Includes health family welfare, Indian systems plus homoeopathy
Medical colleges	30	262	

Source: Bjorkman and Raman, 2009: 37.

postgraduate doctors are trained every year. According to the report of Ministry of Chemical and Fertilizers, Government of India (GoI), there is pharmaceutical production of 260 billion annually. He mentions that although the resources are ample, these are not equal as the ratio of hospitals beds to population in rural areas is 15 times lower than for urban areas and the ratio of doctors is six times lower than in urban population (ibid.). Sengupta (2003) has also pointed out that in India, the expenditure patterns on health care are grossly biased to urban areas, and the expenditure cuts during 1990s further worsen this situation with the axe of investment first falling on rural health services and thus as a result of reducing the state support to health care the rural health has been the first major causality (ibid.). This phenomenon has been very clearly explained by Hart (1971) in his *Inverse Care Law*, which means that 'the availability of good medical care tends to vary inversely with the need of the population served.' Hart argued that 'general practitioners have more work, larger lists, less hospital support, and inherit more clinically ineffective traditions of consultations, than in the healthiest areas; and hospital doctors shoulder heavier caseload with less staff and equipment, more obsolete building and suffer recurrent crisis in the availability of beds and replacement staff' (ibid.: 18).

Although majority of people live in villages in India, major institution of health care are located in urban areas, and the people in rural areas have to depend on the public health centres (PHCs) and its nonfunctional referral system (Qadeer, 1985: 204). There is unevenness in the availability of drugs too (ibid.: 205). Qadeer has argued that even in urban area, all the people are not able to avail the services equally and even the PHCs are not equally accessible to all the rural population. As per the data of National Sample Survey (NSS), there is inequality even in the utilization of health facilities by economic classes and the class gradient in inpatient use of health facilities, which was insignificant in the mid-1980s in rural areas became significant in the 1990s; but in urban areas, the inequalities in the utilization of health facilities did not worsen significantly, but inequalities in the use of private facilities did (Athreya and Rao, 2006). Dalal and Ray (2005) pointed out the study made by National Council of Applied Economic Research (NCAER) cited in Commission on Macro-Economics for Health (2000), according to which 20 per cent of people in the richest quintile enjoy three times the share of public subsidy for health compared with those in the poorest quintile; poorest quintile have double the mortality rates, fertility rates and under-nutrition levels than the richest.

Deogaonkar (2004) argues that the difficulties in access to health care are due to geographical distance, socio-economic distance and gender distance. Nagaraj and Prasad (1999) conducted a study in Srikalahasthi Integrated Child Development Services (ICDS) project area of Andhra Pradesh to analyse the affecting the utilization of antenatal care (ANC) services. They collected the data from 140 lactating women by structured pretested interview schedule. The study revealed that 28 per cent of mothers had received less than 28 per cent of ANC checkups. The study revealed that the socio-demographic factors, such as iliteracy and socially disadvantaged castes, Backward Classes (BCs) and Scheduled Castes (SCs)/ Scheduled Tribes (STs), prevent the women from using the ANC services. In addition, among the factors that can have influence on the quality of ANC advanced maternal age, socially disadvantaged castes and untrained personnel providing ANC were also found to have significant negative relationship with the quality of ANC.

Data related to mortality rates as per the India Human Development Report prepared by Abusaleh Shariff (1999) depict the various inequalities very well. Crude Death Rate per thousand population in the lowest household income group is 13, whereas it is 7 in the highest income group (Table 21.3). The inequality is much more visible in Infant Mortality as in the lowest income group it is as high as 97 and in the highest income group it is 54. Further differences are prevalent in under five mortality which is 71 in highest income group and 133 in lowest income group. Further, such mortalities are directly related to literacy and educational level of adults. However, female literacy is more important than male and when both are literate, then all the three indicators, that is, CDR, IM and U5M are drastically low. An important revelation may come here by comparing the results of adult literacy and village development indexes. Literacy is more important in reducing the mortality rates than development in general.

The NFHS III data related to Ante Natal Care (ANC) provider during pregnancy in terms of rural/urban residence reveal multiple disparities. The care of doctors is available to 76.7 per cent urban women; whereas for rural women, it is mere 40.6 (Table 21.4). Further, 27.7 per cent rural women do not find any service provider, but the percentage of urban women in this category is 9.3. Whatever other service is coming to rural women is through

Table 21.3 *Mortality rates by various population groups*

Population group	Crude death rate '000	Infant mortality	Under-5 mortality
Household income			
Up to 20,000	13	97	133
20,001–40,000	10	76	107
40,001–62,000	8	66	95
62,001–86,000	8	54	74
Above 86,000	7	54	71
Adult literacy			
None literate	14	104	146
Female literate	12	76	110
Male literate	11	91	126
Both literate	9	64	87
Village development			
Low	10	96	133
Medium	12	81	115
High	11	77	103
All India	**11**	**84**	**117**

Source: Human Development Report: A Profile of Indian States ... Appendix A. B. 6 (p. 333).

Table 21.4 *Antenatal care per cent distribution of women who had a live birth in the five years preceding the survey by ANC provider during pregnancy for the most recent live birth, according to background characteristics, India, 2005–06*

Background characteristic	Doctor	ANM/nurse/ midwife/ LHV	Other health personnel	Dai/ TBA	Anganwadi/ ICDS worker	Other	No one	Missing	Number of women
Residence									
Urban	76.7	12.4	0.3	0.9	0.4	0.0	9.3	0.1	10,626
Rural	40.6	26.9	1.3	1.2	2.1	0.2	27.7	0.1	29,051
Education									
No education	28.7	28.0	1.3	1.6	2.3	0.1	37.9	0.1	18,792
<5 years complete	51.7	25.3	1.6	0.7	2.8	0.2	17.6	0.0	2,876
5–7 years complete	60.6	22.9	1.1	1.2	1.1	0.1	13.0	0.0	5,846
8–9 years complete	69.2	19.7	0.6	0.8	0.9	0.1	8.6	0.0	4,892
10–11 years complete	79.2	13.8	0.7	0.6	0.7	0.1	4.9	0.1	3,254
12 or more years complete	88.1	9.2	0.4	0.3	0.2	0.0	1.7	0.0	4,016
Wealth index									
Lowest	22.5	29.6	1.8	1.4	3.2	0.2	41.3	0.0	9,571
Second	36.4	28.1	1.4	1.2	2.0	0.2	30.7	0.1	8,603
Middle	52.4	24.0	0.9	1.3	1.4	0.1	19.9	0.0	7,774
Fourth	69.0	18.7	0.4	1.2	0.6	0.1	10.0	0.0	7,256
Highest	86.2	10.0	0.3	0.6	0.1	0.0	2.6	0.1	6,471
Total	50.2	23.0	1.0	1.2	1.6	0.1	22.8	0.1	39,677

Note: If more than one source of ANC was mentioned, only the provider with the highest qualification is considered in this tabulation. Total includes women with missing information on education, religion, and caste/tribe, who are not shown separately. ANM, auxiliary nurse midwife; LHV, lady health visitor; TBA, traditional birth attendant; ICDS, integrated child development services.

Source: NFHS 3, Table 8.2 (p. 194).

ANM/nurse/midwife, etc. who provide services to 26.9 per cent rural women. When we go by the index of educational background, there seems to be a direct relationship between educational attainment of the women and availability of services of a doctor for the antenatal care. Only 29 per cent women having no education is getting the services of a doctor; but among those who have 12 or more years of education, 88 per cent get such services. One important revelation is the fact that more than one-third of the women with no education do not get services from any such agency and thus victim of double inequality-one in terms of education and the other in terms of health. The wealth index reflects the inequalities even more sharply. More than two-fifth from the lowest wealth index are not getting service from any agency. The presence of several alternate agencies is just meaningless for this category.

It is very well established that the burden of disease and mortality is more on the poor and illiterate people than their counterparts (the rich and educated). Table 21.5 gives us the details of the cost of health expenditures.

Table 21.5 *Selected indicators related to income, literacy and expenditure on education and health*

Population group	Per capita income (₹ per year)	Literacy rate (7+ years)	Proportion of total household income spent on education	Proportion of total household income spent on health
Poverty line groups				
Lower segment below	1,095	44	7.3	19.1
Upper segment below	2,026	46	4.4	12.3
Lower segment above	3,931	54	3.0	6.0
Upper segment above	11,396	67	1.7	2.2
Landholding group				
Landless wage earners	2,308	37	3.8	10.0
Other landless	4,111	62	3.5	8.0
Marginal	3,502	53	3.3	6.7
Large	10,930	61	1.2	2.1
Village development				
Low	4,045	42	2.5	5.9
Medium	4,369	54	2.7	5.4
High	5,079	64	2.7	4.8
All India	**4,485**	**54**	**2.7**	**5.3**

Source: Human Development Report: A Profile of Indian States... Table 1.2 (p. 8).

The poor, who have very low income, have to spend almost one-fifth of their earnings on health needs. Comparatively, the rich, who earn much more, spend less than one-fortieth of their income in that. Education, which is the next best thing after health, also consumes more from the poor (in terms of percentage of their earning). It can be easily concluded that the process of ensuring health (as well as education) for all is not very fair. The need of betterment cannot be denied. Our initial discussion has helped us to understand how a fair and just process is not only desired but also gainful in the path of development. Hence, more equity in health is the need of the hour.

Athreya and Rao (2006) argued that the widening health inequalities have resulted from the imposition of the World Bank and International Monetary Fund (IMF) led policies of structural adjustment and the accompanying health sector reforms around the globe. They argue that (i) these policies have led to the reduced commitment of state to health; (ii) these policies or prescriptions do not recognize the factors governing the health or ecology of disease, but these are committed to methodology of individualism and to behaviourism; and (iii) further, these are guided by cost consideration, and thus the interventions tend to be disjointed (for instance, for tackling diarrhoea, the focus is on Oral Rehydration Solution (ORS) rather than proper water supply and sanitation, emphasizing on anaemia in pregnant women rather than on anaemia in general population) and of technical nature. These suggestions lead to the disease centric vertical programmes and generally include fees for the services provided, which further reduces the access of poor to the health services. Ali and Nanda (2006) have pleaded that four forms of inequalities can be identified in the field of health. The various kinds of health disparities inherent in India are briefly discussed below.

Geographic Disparities

Fertility rates are not uniform among the states. Only two of the major 15 states have reached the replacement level of fertility, that is, 2.1. Another major five states have total fertility rate of between 2.1 and 3; and in the eight major states (comprising about 44 per cent of population), the rate is three or more. These differences are largely because of poverty, illiteracy and inadequate access to healthcare facilities and family welfare services.

Gender Disparity

In India, the disparities in health on the basis of gender are particularly prominent. The largest gender disparities are found in the northern states, particularly Haryana and Punjab, despite their relative prosperity. Girls have low mortality rates than boys during the first month of life (the neonatal period), which accounts for their lower rate of infant mortality. However, as cited by the Indian Institute of Population Studies, death rates in the post-neonatal and in the whole period up to five years of age (under-five mortality) are higher for girls as compared with boys. Despite having lower rates of acute respiratory infections, diarrhoea and anaemia, which are major causes of childhood death, than boys, girls continue to have higher rates of mortality. This paradox exists because of the fact that boys are more likely to receive health care than girls and also the girls have higher rates of mal-nutrition that places them at further disadvantage. The relative neglect of women's health is also depicted in the poor reproductive health indicators.

Disparity among Scheduled Tribes and Scheduled Castes

Of all the disadvantaged groups in India, STs tend to have the highest rates of infant and child mortality, malnutrition and morbidity followed by SCs and then by other disadvantaged (or backward) classes.

Poverty Disparity

Communicable diseases, malnutrition and maternal conditions are concentrated among the poor in India. The rich people are less sick, become sick at an old age and suffer more from non-communicable diseases than from the communicable diseases in comparison with poorer population. Levels of mortality, morbidity and malnutrition are higher among the poor than among the rich. The poorest quintile has double the risk of infant and child deaths, malnutrition and high fertility in comparison with the richest quintile.

Health System in India (Before Millennium Development Goals)

Inequalities in health indicators and health care services are quite visible in India. Any systematic query related to understanding the obvious health disparities in India suggests a thorough study of health planning and health structure in India. Health system refers to all the efforts, components, personnel, institutions and economic resources that a state or society devotes to health-related problems. WHO has pointed out that the term may be used for all the activities whose primary objective is to promote, restore or maintain health. A health system has three main objectives: (i) to improve the health status of the population, (ii) to protect the people from the financial risks of the health problems and (iii) to respond to the demands and needs of the citizens.

Qadeer (1985) points out that the present system of health services in India is the result of attempts made by the British to make their position strong in India, in which initially (1700–1835) an open policy of learning from Indian system was adopted; but in the later period (after 1835), English language was made compulsory in medical schools and also they were asked to abolish teaching ayurveda. Like pre-colonial India, during the British rule, the class base for medical services remained the same; that is, elites (and later on middle class) and also the private practice was popular. However, the colonial India could not completely ban or regulate the indigenous system of medicine, namely ayurveda, siddha and unani and other new entrants such homeopathy and naturopathy (Abraham and Sujatha, 2009). The health services were provided to Indian masses only after pressure emanating from political movements in India and Britain, and most of the preventive programmes were started because of pressures emanating from international business community who saw epidemics in India as an impediment to free trade. Independent India thus inherited a health system with marginal public health and preventive programmes and infrastructure for curative services marked by the dominance of Indian Medical Service (IMS) physician, network of urban hospitals with inadequate facilities and a flourishing trade of private practice infiltrating government institution (Qadeer, 1985). In independent India, the approach of state to indigenous medicine has been ambivalent, which includes extending legitimacy without economic support or defining any specific role to the vast Indian System of Medicine (ISM) that it recognizes (Abraham and Sujatha, 2009). The health sector in India has passed through the various phases of developments.

Health Committees in India

The GoI appointed various committees of experts on health in order to look properly in the health sector and suggest recommendations to overcome the health problems and improve the health status of population. The recommendations put forth by various committees are briefly discussed here as these will help us understand the evolution of health structure in India and the inherent contradictions and biases.

The Bhore Committee, known as the Health Survey and Development Committee, was appointed in 1943 and it submitted its report in 1946. It laid emphasis on integration of curative and preventive medicine at all levels. It suggested development of one primary health centre, manned by two doctors, one nurse, four public health nurses, four midwives, four trained dais, two sanitary inspectors, two health assistants, one pharmacist and 15 other class-IV employees, for a population of 40,000, and a secondary health centre, to provide support to PHC and to coordinate and supervise their functioning. It also recommended major changes in medical education, which includes three-month training in preventive and social medicine to prepare 'social physicians'.

The Mudaliar Committee (1962) headed by Dr A.L. Mudaliar was appointed to access the performance of health sector since the submission of Bhore Committee report, and it advised that the PHCs and sub-divisional and district hospitals should be strengthened, and they should provide preventive, curative and promotive services. The GoI appointed the Chadda Committee in 1963 to advise about the necessary arrangements for National Malaria Eradication Programme (NMEP). The Mukherji Committee (1965) was appointed to review the reorganized family planning programme, and it recommended a separate staff for family planning and delinking of malaria activities from the family planning.

The Jugalwalla Committee appointed for integration of health services submitted its report to the GoI in 1967 and recommended: (i) unification of cadre; (ii) uniform pay scale; (iii) pay according to grade; (iv) rotation of officers between clinical, public health teaching and research branches; (v) common seniority; (vi) promotion according to merit, years of service and administrative capacity; (vii) financial and other incentives to medical officers posted in rural areas or areas with any special hazard or risk; (viii) special allowances for specialists; (ix) special allowances for special programmes; and (xi) elimination of private practice and compensation for loss of practice and making the non-practice allowances realistic.

The main recommendations of Kartar Singh Committee (1973) were various categories of peripheral workers should be amalgamated into a single cadre of multipurpose workers (MPWs) (male and female). The erstwhile auxiliary nurse midwives were to be converted into MPW(F) and the basic health workers, malaria surveillance workers, etc., were to be converted to MPW(M). The work of three to four male and female MPWs was to be supervised by one health supervisor (male or female, respectively). The existing lady health visitors were to be converted into female health supervisor. Further, one Primary Health Centre should cover a population of 50,000. It should be divided into 16 sub-centres (one for 3,000–3,500 population), each to be staffed by a male and a female health worker.

The Srivastava Committee (1975) recommended creating a band of paraprofessional or semi-professional health workers in the community itself in order to provide simple promotive, preventive and curative services needed by the community. They include dais, family planning workers, persons capable of providing simple curative services, persons trained in promotional and preventive health activities, including the control of communicable diseases and they need not to be multipurpose.

Health Structure and Programmes

On the basis of the recommendation of the various committees and other national/international directives, a specific health structure has developed in India. A thorough study of the recommendations of various committees helps us to understand the growth of health services in India. The recommendations of the Bhore Committee Report were never implemented in totality, although that was supposed to be the foundation stone of the development of health structure in India. The various committees responded to the specific contextual needs as identified by the government and growth of an integrated system could never become an objective. Health was never seen in a holistic perspective, and the focus always remained on clinical treatment of 'diseases'. A good number of specific programmes were designed and implemented to address to specific diseases and vertical health programmes became the core of health structure in India. The PHCs and sub-centres could never attract the attention that they deserved in many parts of the country. The PHCs were supposed to deliver primary health care based on four principles: equitable distribution, community participation, inter-sectoral coordination and appropriate technology. But the PHCs always suffered from lack of staff and infrastructure.

The PHCs are supposed to provide the services that cover all the essential elements of primary health care. Since 1990s, there has been the target of establishing one sub-centre staffed by health worker both female and male for a population of 5,000 in plains and 3,000 in hilly and tribal areas; and one PHC staffed by a medical officer and other paramedical staff for a population of 30,000 in plains and 20,000 in hilly and tribal areas. The number of sub-centres was 27,929 in 1971, 131,098 in 1991, 136,379 in 1997 and 144,988 in 2005–06, and the number of PHCs was 725 in 1951, 5,131 in 1971, 22,243 in 1991, 22,446 in 1997 and 22,669 in 2005–06 (Kurian and Sathyamala, 2008).

The secondary health care is the first referral level, and the health services are generally provided by district hospitals and Community Health Centres (CHCs). The CHCs provide inpatient and outpatient services, specialist services, specialist diagnostic services and emergency care. One CHC or an upgraded PHC with 30 beds and basic specialties is established for a population of 80,000–120,000, and a CHC acts as a referral centre for four PHCs. At the tertiary level, health care is provided by regional- or central-level institutions and citing WHO; Park mentions that this is more specialized than the secondary level and involves highly specialized health workers (Park, 2005: 685–86). To enable the tertiary health care facilities at the regional level, Pradhan Mantri Swasthya Suraksha Yojna (PMSSY) was formulated under which six All India Institute of Medical Sciences (AIIMS)-like institutions are to be set up and 13 medical colleges are to be upgraded.

Various programmes were launched by the GoI for controlling and eradicating various diseases depending on the urgency of the situation. Presently, the focus is on high morbidity due to communicable diseases, high burden of diseases due to non-communicable diseases and nutritional problems. The focus is also on the unmet need for contraception and high unwanted fertility.

The National Malaria Control Programme (NMCP) was launched by the GoI in 1953, and it was converted into NMEP in 1958. In the North-eastern states (except Sikkim), selected high-risk areas of Odisha, Jharkhand and West Bengal, an Intensified Malaria Control Project (IMCP) was implemented to make the diagnosis and treatment accessible in remote areas. National Leprosy Control Programme (NLCP) was launched by the GoI in 1955. The programme was redesigned into National Leprosy Eradication Programme (NLEP) in 1983. Further, India has the highest number of active TB cases and accounts for about one-fifth of the global TB incidence. To control TB, National Tuberculosis Control Programme (NTCP) has been in operation since 1962. The Revised National Tuberculosis Control Programme (RNTCP) was launched on 26 March 1997, with assistance from the World Bank, Department for International Development (DFID), United Nations Agency for International Development (USAID), Global Drug Facility (GDF) and Global Fund for AIDS, Tuberculosis and Malaria (GFATM).

The GoI is implementing the National Iodine Deficiency Disorder Programme (NIDDCP) too, which was formerly known as National Goitre Control Programme (NGCP), since 1962. The National Cancer Control Programme was launched in 1975–76 with the aim of primary prevention, early detection, treatment and rehabilitation. The focus of the revised programme completed in December 2004 is to provide cancer care facilities equally across the country. In India, several mental disorders such as schizophrenia, bipolar disorder, organic psychosis and major depression affect nearly 20 per 1,000 population. To address the huge burden of disease, National Mental Health Programme (NMHP) was started in 1982.

The number of persons living with Human Immuno Virus (HIV) in the country is 2–3.1 million with an estimated adult HIV prevalence of 0.36 per cent in the country according to the revised estimates carried out during 2006. Andhra Pradesh, Karnataka, Maharashtra and Tamil Nadu contribute

63 per cent of the HIV-infected persons in the country, 39.3 per cent of infections are in women and 3.8 per cent in children. Under the National AIDS Control Programme (NACP), various steps were taken by the government: targeted intervention (TI) projects have been started to interrupt the transmission of HIV among highly vulnerable population which include commercial sex workers, injecting drug users, men who have sex with men, truckers and migrant workers. The blood safety activities are an important part of NACP. It is obligatory for all the blood units to get tested against the five transfusion-transmissible infections (TTIs) that include HIV, Hepatitis-B, Hepatitis-C, Syphilis and malaria. Condom promotion is central to HIV/AIDS programme and during NACP III; 3.5 billion condoms are targeted to be distributed through three million outlets. NACO is working on a community strategy to bring about behavioural change.

Besides the above-mentioned programmes, the Kala Azar Control Programme was started in 1990–91, which involved assistance in kind provided for procurement of insecticides and anti-leishmanian drugs. Kala Azar is endemic in the states of Bihar, West Bengal and parts of Uttar Pradesh. The National Health Policy 2002 envisaged a goal of Kala Azar elimination by the year 2010. Further, Pulse Polio Immunization (PPI) programme was launched in 1995–96 to cover all the children below the age of three years. However, the target age group was increased from three to five years from 1996–97 to increase the speed of polio eradication.

Under the constitution of India, public health is a shared responsibility of the central, state and local levels of governments. However, health is essentially a state responsibility. The amount of public health spending is not uniform throughout the country, but the state and local governments account for three-fourth of the total public health spending. The responsibility of the central government includes looking at port quarantine, research and specific and technical education. On the contrary, the private health care services are provided by herbal healers, modern unqualified or quasi-qualified 'quack', and qualified practitioners of different systems of medicine. Until mid-1970s, large private hospitals were not for profit or charitable in nature, and for-profit private hospitals were primarily small nursing homes. By 1990s, corporate sector came forward to invest in private healthcare and thus expanded this sector. Although most of the health care is provided by private sector, there is lack of any regulation and specification of standards for private health care. The payment in the private sector is largely fee-for-service and paid out of pocket by the patients. There is no uniform standard for the charge of similar activities.

Bjorkman and Raman (2009) argue that India's public health system is affected by various factors such as shortage of resources and budgetary allocations and organizational and managerial deficiencies. In addition to this, whatever resources are available are inequitably distributed towards the tertiary health care services, thus the primary health care level suffers. Due to the lack of services, the poor seek the health services from private sector, which increase the economic stress on the poor. The private health care facilities are generally known for over-prescribing and subjecting the patients for unnecessary diagnostic investigations (ibid.).

Qadeer and Reddy (2006), in their paper 'Medical Care in the Shadow of Public Private Partnerships', argue that various factors are responsible for the distortion of public health sector in India: (i) the democratic government gives priority to powerful sections and thus neglecting the vast majority of poorer people; (ii) most of the professionals are trained in Western tradition of medical education, which is largely dependent on medical technology and separated from social and political imperatives; (iii) public–private partnership (PPP) that has failed in many countries and are faced with many contradictions such as ethical constraints has been chosen in India to heal the ailing public health system.

It is also significant here to note that the first National Health Policy in India came only in 1983. It tried to revamp public health sector and specified the target of health for all by 2000 as its specific goal. It encouraged the participation of voluntary groups and showed the roadmap for AYUSH. But the government failed to realize the objectively defined targets of health and had to shift its priorities and directions under the structural adjustment programme (SAP) of 1990s. The decade of 1990s is known for several economic and structural reforms and moving towards liberalization, privatization and globalization (LPG) resulted in important shifts even in the health policy. Three important things noticed then were (i) increasing participation of voluntary organizations and private corporations, (ii) increasing the quality of care at tertiary level and (iii) user charges even at the public health care centres.

Health Reforms and Goals of Social Transformation

Millennium Development Goals

The turn of the century is marked by the specially crafted Millennium Development Goals (MDGs) that give a specific direction for social transformation to the entire world. The MDGs are eight international development goals that all 192 United Nations member states and at least 23 international organizations have agreed to achieve by the year 2015. The eight goals are to eradicate extreme poverty and hunger; achieve universal primary education; promote gender equality and empower women; reduce child mortality rates; improve maternal health; combat HIV/AIDS, malaria, and other diseases; ensure environmental sustainability; and develop a global partnership for development. All these goals are directly or indirectly related to improvement in health status of individuals and communities. Health for all cannot be achieved without fulfilling all these goals. The MDGs originated from the 'Millennium Declaration' produced by the United Nations. The declaration asserts that every individual has the right to dignity, freedom, equality, a basic standard of living that includes freedom from hunger, disease and violence, and encourages tolerance and solidarity. The MDGs were made to operationalize these ideas by setting targets and indicators for poverty reduction and health improvement in order to achieve the rights set forth in the declaration on a set 15-year timeline.

National Health Policy 2002

The National Health Policy 2002 is a revised and much improved version of the NHP 1983, and it has incorporated some of the health-related goals and objectives suggested by the MDGs. The NHP-2002 prescribed the following measures: (i) increasing the health sector expenditure to 6 per cent of GDP, with 2 per cent of GDP being contributed as public health investment, by the year 2010; (ii) reducing the various kinds of inequities and imbalances; (iii) increasing allocation of 55 per cent of the total health investment for the primary health sector, 35 per cent and 10 per cent for secondary and tertiary sectors respectively; (iv) laying down great emphasis on the implementation of public health programmes through local self-government institutions; (v) need for specialists in public health and family medicine; (vi) need for an improvement in the ratio of nurses vis-à-vis doctors/beds; (vii) welcoming private sector in all areas of health activities; (viii) emphasizing on the need for simplifying the procedures for government civil society interfacing to enhance the involvement of civil society in public health programmes; and (ix) need for providing secondary and tertiary health service, to users from overseas who have the ability to pay.

National Rural Health Mission (2005–12)

The GoI, Ministry of Health and Family Welfare, launched National Rural Health Mission (NRHM) in 2005. It recognizes the importance of health as a contributor of social and economic development and adopts the synergistic approach by relating health to the determinants of good health. It seeks to provide effective health care to rural population with special focus on 18 states, which have weak public health indicators. The core strategies are (i) to train and enhance capacity of Panchayati Raj Institutions (PRIs); own, control and manage public health services; (ii) promote health care at household through female health activist (ASHA); (iii) health plan for each village through Village Health Committee of the *panchayat*; (iv) to strengthen sub-centres through unified fund; and (v) to implement of an inter-sectoral District Health Plan. The supplementary strategies include the following: (i) regulating private sector including the informal rural practitioners; (ii) ensuring availability of quality services to citizens at reasonable cost; (iii) promotion of PPPs; (iv) mainstreaming AYUSH; (v) reorienting medical education to support rural health; and (vi) pooling and social health insurance to provide health security.

The NRHM has identified specific goals and objectives to be completed within a time frame. Here, we will discuss some of these important objectives and the progress made so far. The NRHM Mission Document had committed to raise public spending on health from 0.9 per cent of GDP to 2–3 per cent of GDP. But by 2009–10, the spending could increase to only 1.45 per cent of GDP. The government failed to provide the fund itself to such an ambitious mission. The government assessment report, 'NRHM: The Journey So Far (2005–10)' says that 'more financial resources are needed to provide quality health care in rural areas as this sector was totally neglected in the past.' Thus, the rural–urban disparity is persisting even within NRHM. In terms of health indicators, infant mortality rate (IMR) was sought to be reduced to

30/1,000 live births by 2012. The progress report says that IMR was 58 in 2005, and it was down to 53 in 2008. Only five states have achieved the goal and 12 states are in 30–40 range. Maternal mortality was sought to be reduced to 100/100,000 by 2012. MMR was 301 in 2001–03, and it became 254 in 2004–06. The current status is that only Kerala has achieved the goal.

Besides these, Kala Azar mortality rate was sought to be reduced by 100 per cent by 2010, but only 21.93 per cent reduction was possible by 2008. The only positive achievement that seems to be coming under NRHM is related to institutional deliveries as states such as Madhya Pradesh, Odisha, Rajasthan, Bihar and Uttar Pradesh have improved in institutional deliveries. Most of the achievements made by the government are related to manpower and employment generation (through appointment of ASHA and AYUSH doctors – mostly on a contract basis) and revamping of PHCs. These achievements are no doubt great, but they cannot be treated as harbingers of social transformation in the field of health in India. The dimensions that could not get much attention are related to potable drinking water, sanitation, nutrition and proper regulation over the concerned providers/agencies. The NRHM is also failing to provide the most required impetus to the health system in India – the integration of the services and a holistic perspective.

Challenges before Social Transformation in India

An assessment of the health developments and related programmes reflects that our performance in achieving the goals of health for all is not satisfactory. We are unable to meet most of the goals and targets despite making tall claims. Even the NRHM could not make the desired impact. Thus, social transformation in the field of health still appears to be a distant goal. We have states such as Kerala or Tamil Nadu that are performing well as per some of the indicators, but majority of the states are lagging behind the set targets. The human development records for most of the states are not very good because an important component of Human Development Index is health and longevity of life.

The sex ratio, that is, the number of females per thousand males is very adverse in India. The adverse sex ratio is the greatest challenge. According to Census of India 2001, sex ratio has shown some improvement in the past 10 years. It has gone up from 927 in 1991 census to 933 in 2001 census of India. The provisional reports of the 2011 census suggest that the sex ratio has further increased to 940, but it is accompanied by an alarming sex ratio for the zero to six years age group, which has dramatically dropped to 914 in 2011, from 927 in 2001. This dramatic drop in the under-six child sex ratio is very pathetic and puts a question mark on all the claims of human and social development in India.

The government is going very slow in terms of its efforts related to controlling the spread of communicable diseases. In India, the communicable diseases are great killer. But in the developed world, communicable diseases have been controlled completely, and people have threats only from non-communicable diseases. One of the important reasons of our failure to combat spread of communicable diseases is the lack of availability of potable water for majority of the population. The government cannot provide safe drinking water to people, and several water-borne diseases such as diarrhoea are a great killer in India. Along with it, the waste disposal and the sewage treatment plants are not well developed in most of the cities. Intervention in these areas needs huge investments.

Malnutrition is like an epidemic in India. More than three-fourth of the population (majority of women) in India is suffering from it. Malnutrition is responsible for causing several disabilities and diseases such as anaemia. Anaemia among the pregnant women is the most common feature and still a great killer.

Adulteration is a very common phenomenon in India, and hardly any city is free from this menace. Sometimes, this adulteration is very deadly. From milk and butter to spices and cereals, all are adulterated. Unless the government is not able to control large-scale adulteration of food items, the negative impacts on health cannot be controlled.

The cost of health is increasing very fast. Most of the lower middle-class and rural people are unable to bear the cost of private health care in India. Statistics reveal that cost of health care is an important reason of persisting poverty in India. Hence, affordable health care is a big challenge. The cost of the medicine and other pharmaceutical items is also increasing, and the government has almost negligible control on them.

Health insurance is emerging as a viable alternative of increasing cost of health care worldwide. But health insurance is having very limited reach in India. The government has failed to create proper awareness regarding this. The insurance industry is not properly monitored. The concept of cost-effective group insurance or social marketing of insurance is having negligible presence in good number of states showing poor indicators of health. Some of the states such as Andhra Pradesh, Tamil Nadu and Maharashtra have shown great interest in social marketing of health insurance recently. But other states are lacking in taking the right initiatives.

Unorganized workers constitute almost 90 per cent of the workforce in India. There is no proper legislation to take care of the health needs of such people. Workers are facing double disadvantages during their illness. They are deprived of their wages during their illness as they cannot work, and they have to bear the cost of their health care. There is no proper legislation for people suffering from occupational diseases, nor do they get any sort of compensation. Catering to the health needs of the unorganized work force in India is the greatest challenge, and no social transformation is possible without it.

Lifestyle diseases are increasingly fast in India. The best possible way of combating such diseases is prevention. The government does not have proper mechanism by which people can be made aware of the preventive and curative mechanisms from diseases such as diabetes, cancer, obesity, etc. The government seems to be under great pressure of the big corporations (MNCs) engaged in the manufacture and trade of tobacco and alcohol products. Both tobacco and alcohol are responsible for creating good number of diseases.

Increasing pollution in cities is a great threat even from health perspective. The respiratory infections and several lung- and skin-related diseases are caused by the environmental pollution, but the government is increasingly failing in controlling such menaces. Health for all cannot be ensured without controlling the ever-increasing air and water pollution. Increasing pesticides and chemical in food stuff is also making the situation worse.

India ranks a low 119 among 169 countries on the 2010 Human Development Index. China ranked much higher at 89 on the index published annually by the UNDP. India compares very poorly with countries with high level of human development on all indicators such as life expectancy, education and per capita income. For instance, life expectancy at birth is 64.4 years in India. Health is an important constituent of this HDI, and India's poor ranking clearly indicates its state of health. Hence, it can be concluded that India needs to really work hard to remove such challenges before social transformation. Ensuring good health for all should be the top priority for the government, and this cannot be made possible without viewing health from a holistic perspective and taking into consideration all the determinants of health. The goal of health for all will remain an illusion unless we address the issue of prevalent health inequalities in India.

References

Abraham, L. and V. Sujatha (2009). 'Medicine, State and Society', *Economic and Political Weekly*, 44(16): 35–43.

Advani, M. and M. Akram (2007). 'Health Concerns in India', in M. Akram (ed.), *Health Dynamics and Marginalised Communities*. Jaipur: Rawat Publications.

Ali, Almas and A.R. Nanda (2006). 'Health Sector: Issues and Challenges', in *India Social Development Report 2006*. New Delhi: Oxford University Press.

Alkire, Sabina (2003). *Valuing Freedoms: Sen's Capability Approach and Poverty Reduction*. New Delhi: Oxford University Press.

Anand, Sudhir (2006). 'Concern for Equity in Health', in Sudhir Anand, Fabienne Peter and Amartya Sen (eds), *Public Health, Ethics and Equity*. New Delhi: Oxford University Press.

Athreya, V.B. and Mohan Rao (2006). 'Education and Health in Eleventh Plan Approach Draft Paper', *Social Scientist*, 34(9–10): 21–33.

Bjorkman, J.W. and V.A. Raman (2009). *Public Private Partnerships in Health Care in India: Lessons from Developing Countries*. New York: Routledge Taylor and Francis Group.

Dalal, A.K. and Ray Subha (eds) (2005). 'Social Dimensions of Health and Well-Being: An Overview of Research Trends', in *Social Dimensions of Health*. Jaipur: Rawat Publications.

Daniels, Norman, Bruce Kennedy and Ichiro Kawachi (2006). 'Health and Inequality, or, Why Justice is Good for Our Health', in Anand et al., op. cit.

Deogaonkar, Milind (2004). 'Socio-Economic Inequality and its Effect on Health Care Delivery in India: Inequality and Healthcare', *Electronic Journal of Sociology*. http://www.sociology.org/content/vol8.1/deogaonkar.html.

Department of Health and Social Security (DHSS) (1980) *Inequalities in Health: Report of a Research Working Group* chaired by Sir Douglas Black. London: DHSS.

Hart, J.T. (1971). 'The Inverse Care, Law', *The Lancet*. http://www.sochealth.co.uk/history/inversecare.htm.

Heggenhougen, H.K. and S.R. Quah (2008). *International Encyclopedia of Public Health*, Vol. 3. New York: Elsevier Academic Press.

Kelman, S. (1975). 'The Social Nature of the Definition Problem in Health', *International Journal of Health Services*, 5: 625–42.

Kurian, N.J. and C. Sathyamala (2008). 'Health Sector in India: Issues and Challenges', in *India Social Development Report – Development and Displacement*. New Delhi: Oxford University Press.

Marmot, Michael (2006). 'Social Causes of Social Inequalities in Health', in Anand et al., op. cit.

McKenzie, J.F., R.R. Pinger and J.E. Kotecki (2002). *An Introduction to Community Health*, 4th ed. Massachusetts: Jones and Bartlett Publishers.

Mukhopadhyay, Indranil (2008). 'Analysing Health Inequalities: Social Capital and Its Infirmities', *Social Scientist*, 36(11–12): 69–93.

Nagaraj, K. and K.R. Prasad (1999). 'Socio-Demographic Factors Influencing Ante-Natal Care-A Community Based Study', *Health and Population: Perspectives and Issues*, 22(1–2).

Nettleton, Sarah (2006). *The Sociology of Health and Illness*. Cambridge: Polity Press.

Park, K. (2005). *Park's Text Book of Preventive and Social Medicine*. Jabalpur: Banarsidas Bhanot Publishers.

Peter, Fabienne (2006). 'Health Equity and Social Justice', in Anand et al., op. cit.

Qadeer, Imrana (1985). 'Health Service System in India: An Expression of Socio-Economic Inequalities', *Social Action*, 35: 199–223.

Qadeer, Imrana and Sunita Reddy (2006). 'Medical Care in the Shadow of Public Private Partnership', *Social Scientist*, 34(9–10): 4–20.

Robeyns, Ingrid (2006). 'Sen's Capability Approach and Gender Inequality: Selecting Relevant Capabilities', in Bina Agarwal, Jane Humphries and Ingrid Robeyns (eds), *Capability, Freedom and Equality: Amartya Sen's Work from a Gender Perspective*. New Delhi: Oxford University Press.

Sen, Amartaya (2006a). 'Health Achievement and Equity: External and Internal Perspectives', in Anand et al., op. cit.

——— (2006b). 'Development as Capability Expansion', in Agarwal et al., op. cit.

——— (2006c). 'Why Health Equity?', in Anand et al., op. cit.

Sengupta, Amit (2003). 'Health in the Age of Globalization', *Social Scientist*, 31(11–12): 65–85.

Shariff, Abusaleh (1999). *India: Human Development Report: A Profile of Indian States in the* 1990*s*. New Delhi: Oxford University Press.

Singh, Yogendra (1997). *Social Stratification and Change in India*. New Delhi: Manohar.

——— (2000). *Culture Change in India: Identity and Globalization*. Jaipur: Rawat Publications.

Wikler, Daniel (2006). 'Personal and Social Responsibility for Health', in Anand et al., op. cit.

22

Sociology of Privatization of Health Care in India

Emerging Issues and Concerns

Madhu Nagla

Introduction

Sociology of inequalities in health refers in relation to economic, social and cultural structures and relationships within the wider society on people's health chances as well as the actions and attitudes of individuals. Before 1930, health and illness were recognized as being appropriate topics for sociological study. It was the impact of social structure on people's health that was noted rather than how a person's physical and mental state might influence their actions (Jones, 1994: 40). The science of health has been characterized by positivism and extreme rationalism, divested from its social and economic context. Medicine is not a science, but it is a learned profession deeply rooted in a number of sciences and charged with obligation to apply them for human's benefit (George, 1972: 9). This research paper attempts to collate literature from various sources, in an attempt to understand the delivery of health in private sector. The debate on the role of private health care has primarily focused on issues of cost and quality. Studies indicate that private health care practices significantly affect both the cost and quality of available health care services in India (Duggal and Amin, 1989; Viswanathan and Rohde, 1990; Yesudian, 1990; Qadeer, 2001). Cases of superfluous services and the high cost of services rendered by private physicians and hospitals have been reported (Duggal and Amin, 1989; Nanda and Baru, 1993; Nandraj, 1994; Baru, 1998; Baru et al., 2000). Structure and pattern of private health care has been addressed by (Jesani and Anantharam, 1989; Muraleedharan, 1994; Yesudian, 1994; Bhat, 1999b; Patranobis, 2003). The issue of consumer protection and dehumanizing aspects in private health care has been addressed, and the effectiveness of legislation has been discussed by Bhat (1999a); and Minocha (2011).

Gross insufficiencies in the public health care delivery system acted as a driver to the growth of private sector institutions in the country (Chatterjee, 2008; Nadkarni, 2010). Inherent factors such as improved efficiency, better quality, greater reliability and transparency have aided in the growth of private health sector. Private health sector continues to explore the opportunities, a trade-off between 'social welfare' and 'business orientation' is critical (Shah and Mohanty, 2010).

This research paper attempts to collate literature from various sources, in an attempt to answer four pertinent questions related to private health care in India. First, emerging relationship between private health care and market. Second, how is the private health care sector delivering health in terms of its quality? Third, what is the structure and pattern of health care from the provider's perspective? Last, the paper tries to highlight some of the dehumanizing issues/aspects in private health care, which are relevant for the consumers of health care.

The private sector plays an important role in India's health care delivery system. Through a wide network of health care facilities, this sector caters to the needs of both urban and rural populations and has expanded widely to meet increasing demands. The significance of the private health care sector in India can be summarized as follows:

- Total health expenditure in India is estimated to be about 6 per cent of gross domestic product (GDP), of which private health care expenditure is 75 per cent or 4.25 per cent of GDP. About one-third of this expenditure is on secondary and tertiary in-patient care; the rest meeting the curative needs at primary level (World Bank, 1995). Insurance coverage mechanisms are negligible, and most of this expenditure is out-of-pocket.
- Private health care expenditure in India has grown at the rate of 12.5 per cent per annum since 1960–61. For each 1 per cent increase in per capita income, private health care expenditure has increased by 1.47 per cent (Bhat, 1996).
- About 57 per cent of hospitals and 32 per cent of hospital beds are in the private sector. The share of the private sector investment in total health infrastructure, for example, hospitals, investments in medical equipment and technology, is also quite significant.
- At present, about 80 per cent of 390,000 qualified allopathic doctors registered with medical councils in India are working in the private sector (Jesani and Anantharam, 1989; Bhat, 1996). There are over 650,000 providers of other systems of medicine practicing in India (Planning Commission, 1998), and most of them are in private practice.
- Utilization studies show that one-third of in-patients and three-quarters of out-patients utilize private health care facilities (Duggal and Amin, 1989; Yesudian, 1990; Visaria and Gumber, 1994).

Process of Privatization of Health Care Services

The private sector is not new to Indian health services. It was predominant mode of service for the well-off until the end of the colonial period. During the pre-independence period, the private sector was restricted to individual practitioners. The Bhore Committee conducted a survey on medical institutions, which revealed that 92 per cent of the institutions were maintained on public funds and that the remaining 8 per cent were wholly maintained by private agencies. The proportion of allopathic doctors in private practice was as high as 73 per cent, and the remaining 27 per cent were employed in government service. When the recommendations of the committee were adopted, there seemed to be reservations regarding private practice by doctors in government service. As far as individual private practitioners were concerned, the committee assured them that their interest would not be affected. Although the committee had categorically stated that private practice by government doctors must be prohibited. It did not visualize a role of independent private practitioners in government hospitals. A shift in policy could be seen as early as 1961 in the report of the Mudaliar Committee. This committee took note of the fact that nearly 40–70 per cent of doctors in different states were private practitioners. Thus, the committee visualized a role for them in government services because of inadequate manpower. It was important that they were given opportunities to serve in government hospitals on a part-time or honorary basis, and hospital authorities could encourage them to admit their patients needing 'in-patient care'. It further stated that 'Independent practitioners have to be considered as a separate entity whose legitimate must be protected'. Thus, even as early as 1961, the demarcation between the public and private sectors had become clear, especially with individual private practitioners being encouraged to use government hospitals to treat their patients.

The private sector has been expanding since the past three decades in India earlier during the 1950s and 1960s; the presence of private sector institutions was small; but over the years, this sector has grown and diversified to include commercial-based institutions such as nursing home and corporate hospitals. With the increasing penetration of high-tech investigating equipment, investing in medical care has become a profitable proposition and has been an important reason for fuelling the growth of private institutions. The private sector has been largely involved in the provision of curative services, whereas the public sector has provided both preventive and curative services. Stagnation of public expenditures during the 1970s and 1980s has created space for the growth of private sector. An added reason has been the profitability of private enterprises, which resulted in their proliferation. The government has also played a supportive role to the private sector by offering a number of concession and subsidies. Government policies have been in the form of concessional loans, custom duty exemptions and reduction of import duties on high-technology medical equipment. The indirect benefits are the accommodation of private interests in the government sector. These interests are served through liaison with the private sector for purchase of drugs and equipments, encouraging the private sector to fill gaps where there is inadequate investment by the government, allowing private practice by government doctors and handing over hospitals to the private sector to be run privately. Another reason for the private medical sector in urban area is the lack of expansion of public services in urban areas. It has given rise to a peculiar situation. There are very few opportunities for medical graduates in urban areas, whereas a large number of posts are lying vacant in rural areas. The proportion in government service has continued to decline (Nanda and Baru, 1993).

Policy of Liberalization and Business in Medical Care

The International Monetary Fund and World Bank started applying greater economic pressures on the developing world. During the period of liberalization and globalization, new issues were introduced. The advanced nations found an opportunity to get the market of the developing world opened and integrated into the world markets dominated by their interests. Hence, the pressure to open up trade in agriculture and services mounted on developing countries and get a tighter control over capital and technology and obtain freedom for mobility of capital. All this has enabled to aggregate itself in larger and larger size and also made the developing countries compete with each other to obtain more and more concessions for it.

Since the 1980s, pressure for change has come from different quarters. As far as the public sector health services are concerned, the government cut back in fund and promoted the medical care as industry. Private sector practitioners, who had enjoyed the privilege of state protection since independence in India's mixed economy of service provision, aspired to influence policy and create more advantage for themselves. The private sector grew from polyclinics to nursing homes, private hospitals and finally to the development of corporate hospital; this is because the government hospital has offered a number of concessions for the growth of private sector (Qadeer, 2001: 26).

Interestingly, the emerging middle class with the result of globalization succeeded in acquiring a reasonably adequate standard of living lobbied for 'high-tech hospital' which confirmed to their concepts of international standards of health care.

The establishment of Apollo marked the entry of non-resident Indian doctors into medical care and signalled recognition of a hospital as a corporate enterprise. Several big business groups such as Tata, Hinduja, Modis and Escorts have floated multi-specialty hospitals and are mainly registered as Trusts. These enterprises have been promoted by business groups and doctors and entrepreneurs some of whom are non-residents Indian based in the United States (Baru, 2000). Baru in her study of private medical institutions found that the private limited hospital is organized like any other company and does not issue public shares in the market. The public limited hospital, on the contrary, issues public shares in the market, whereas the trusts are essentially supposed to be 'non-profit' concerns. Section 35 of the Income Tax Act offers tax exemptions in respect of expenditures on scientific research; therefore, the groups have set up many of these multi-specialty hospitals as research centres, and therefore can be registered as a non-profit enterprises (Baru, 1998).

Instead of learning from the past experiences and contradictions within the Indian health care system and enhancing an efficient and integrated approach to improving its working, the entire exercise was dominated by unquestioning acceptance of the prescribed reforms. The main aspects of the IMF–World Bank-inspired reforms are cuts in health sector investment and opening up of medical care to private sector. Introduction of user fees and private investments in public hospitals are the main agenda of liberalization. Public health care delivery system has suffered a lot due to the cutbacks in the welfare sector and the proposed health sector reforms.

Issues in Health Care

National Council of Applied Economic Research (NCAER) conducted a national survey in 1990, which found that 54.75 per cent people in urban areas utilize private health facilities; and in rural area, it is 55.46 per cent. The average household expenditure on health is ₹142.60 per illness episode in urban areas and ₹151.81 in rural areas. State policy towards the private sector has to be addressed within a systemic perspective covering not just providers of health care services but also other related components in the health care system. Within this perspective, it is essential to delineate the private sector and its delivery of health to the people. Following are the issues of concern:

- Introduction of market principles
- Privatization and market
- Privatization and quality of health care
- Health care provider and pattern of practice
- Dehumanizing aspects and consumer concern in health care

Privatization and Market

Markets are the new buzz word. They are to be left free to operate. This means freedom to capital, labour laws that have evolved over long time periods to check the extreme forms of exploitation by capital are now being diluted. Markets are institutions that are used to exchange goods and services and are governed by the purchasing power of the individuals in society. They are not democratic institution, in effect, left to themselves; they lead to the marginalization of the marginal. In that sense, markets are valueless. Markets are governed by the principles 'more is better' and 'consumer sovereignty'. Individual's welfare is supposed to increase as she/he consumes more. Consumer sovereignty means that the consumer knows her/his interest best; therefore, whatever she/he wishes to consume should be made available in the market. There should be no interface with this from any quarter. 'Efficiency' is defined as the achieving of the wished of the consumers. This may be iniquitous in the extreme with one person having all and the others having nothing. But as long as this is consistent with the initial endowments, it is 'efficient' and in that sense the notion of market 'efficiency' is status quoits.

Since 'more is better' consuming less is not desirable as it lowers the individual's welfare. Restraint is then meaningless. The notion of 'consumer sovereignty' means that the focus is on self as opposed to the collective. Therefore, both these market principles weaken the idea of community and of working towards a common goal. The idea of the notion based on a shared common goal itself weakens. Markets do not decide which goods are socially good or bad. They have no social value. Judgement about the nature of goods is made and imposed by society from outside the markets. For instance, markets do not decide that smoking is bad or that cigarette advertising should not be allowed. Society decides that children should not be targeted by advertising or that sex and violence should not be beamed at them. Penetration of the markets into the social realm undermines social values.

In the market, there is no distinction between essential and non-essential goods. All goods are alike except that their elasticity of demand differs. Hence, in economic theory, there is no need to curb the import of luxury goods or to tax them heavily. Dominant Western values are being imposed on the developing nations through the media with the help of power of money and politics, but above all because of the dominance over ideas.

In such a situation, there could be only two reasons for the increasing pressure or privatization: the first could be the failure to support public sector personnel to perform their duties in the skeleton comprehensive programmes inevitably creating a very 'big market' for the private sector. This is an increasing burden on the poor who are at the receiving end in this scheme of things. Two recent nationwide surveys (NCAER, 1992; NSSO, 1992) on the pattern of utilization of medical institutions reveal that expenditure for getting treatment for diseases is the second most cause for rural indebtedness (after dowry) among these impoverished people (Qadeer, 2001: 47). The second could be ideological because it is easy to play along with the popular belief that public sector health care is inferior to that provided in the private sector.

Privatization and Quality of Health Care

Much of the debate on privatization of health care has been based on the assumption that the private sector provides a better quality of services than the public sector. Efforts are on to restructure public institutions on market principles to promote efficiency. This assumption does not stand up to empirical scrutiny because of the difference in stated goals. Patient load and the clinical practice of spending time with each patient by private doctor will have a significant bearing on the quality and cost of health care.

In a study to understand health-seeking behaviour of semi-urban population, it was observed that 62 per cent of the households preferred private health care facility. The reasons for avoiding government facility, though the services were free of cost, included long waiting time, facility located at distance, inadequate facilities, unclean premises, harsh behaviour of the staff and low faith in government doctors. Interestingly, quality of medical care is not considered to be the criterion for selection of public or private sector facilities (Patel et al., 2010). In another study conducted in the city of Mumbai (Dilip and Duggal, 2004), reasons for preferring private sector facility included proximity, quality of care and convenient timing. Affordability was a leading factor for selection of public health care facility. Pinto and Udwadia (2010) cited reasons such as poor quality with a general lack of trust in government services, lack of attention offered to patients, long waits, poor hygiene, suspected quality of drugs and lack of privacy, for non-preference of public sector hospital. Similarly, another study (Chirmule, 1997) reiterated the role of affordability, quality of medical care and availability of medical services, as critical in selection of public or private health care institutions, across five different states in India.

On an average, doctors in developing countries spend less than 60 seconds in prescribing medicines and explaining the regimen to their patients, according to WHO World Medicine Situations 2011 that was released on 22 April 2011. As a result, only half the patients receive any advice on how to take their medicines, and about one-third of them do not know how to take their medicines immediately after leaving the facility. Although around 80 per cent of all prescribed medicines are dispensed personnel – and as many as 20–50 per cent of medicines dispensed are not labelled. According to the report, 'the dispensing process greatly influences how medicines are used. The WHO database shows that, on average, dispensing time is one minute. In such circumstances, it is not surprising that patient adherence to medicines is poor.' Dr Ranjit Roy Choudhry, eminent clinical pharmacologists said, 'The issue of doctors taking no time to explain the drugs they give to their patients is an acute problem, especial in overcrowded hospitals in India. Adherence also improves if doctor and patient have a rapport among them which develops by giving each other time.' As per report, only about 60 per cent countries train their medical students on various aspects of prescribing medicines, and only about 50 per cent require continuing medical education. The basic training for nurses and paramedical staff, who often do bulk, of prescribing, was even less – only about 40 per cent of countries give them any basic training on how to prescribe them (*The Times of India*, 24 April 2011).

Most private doctors work in their chambers in either morning or evening, and some practice at multiple locations. The timing pattern of private practice primarily addresses the convenience and needs of clients. Fifty per cent of providers have a maximum patient load of 26 or more, and about 45 per cent of doctors spend less than 15 minutes on each patient. Private doctors spend less time on clinical diagnosis, and depend more on referrals and diagnostic tests. This will have significant cost and quality implications (Bhat, 1999b). Bhat (1999b) survey shows that 50 per cent of private doctors occasionally refer patients to other specialists; and in one-third of cases, this referral is quite frequent. When referring to specialist, the doctor generally refers the patient to particular individuals. However, in the case of diagnostic, doctors so not generally ask the patient to go to a particular place. It is evident that the private sectors attracts and treat persons who can pay more; hence, there is already a selecting out of patients. The public sector, on the other hand, seeks to provide universal access, and therefore the patient load is always higher than the intended capacity. These differentials goals set reflected in the case mix, social background of patient and rate of patient turnover in the private and public hospitals. These differences make comparisons of efficiencies of the public and private sectors difficult, and therefore generalizations are also not possible. There are difficulties in arriving at any generalization based on studies, which tend to be unit specific in their comparisons. A comparison of private and public providers in Trivandrum raises some of the methodological problems in doing such an exercise (Homan and Thankappan, 1997, cited in Baru et al., 2000).

The quality of care of any service organization highly depends on the providers skills (qualification), working conditions, attitude and wages of staff and other social factor that is related to providers. Hospitals are labour-intensive organizations that are not only merely dependent on medical expertise but also require the co-ordination of different level of staff members to provide quality patient care. It is not enough to have well-qualified specialist alone, but it is equally important to have well-trained paramedical and supportive staff members for ensuring good-quality patient care.

Studies on private nursing homes in Bombay (Nandraj, 1994), Delhi (Nanda and Baru, 1993) and Hyderabad (Baru, 1998) have shown that para-medical and supportive staff members often work for very low wages and are not qualified for the work that they do. Hence, there is a great deal of turnover of staff at these levels, and they work under abysmal a condition that is bound to have a direct impact on patient care. The job insecurity and poor working conditions in the private sector are bound to affect the quality of care provided to patients. In any hospital, it is the paramedical and supportive staff members who interact closely with patients by attending to their physical and emotional needs, whereas the medical personnel look after the clinical aspect of treat-ment. Therefore, a hospital that is responsive to patients requires well-trained personnel at various levels who interact together as a team coordinating and complimenting each other's role. The problem of contractualizing the support staff means it does not generate a sense of belonging and loyalty among the workers, towards the institution in which they are employed. This is definitely not conducive for building commitment among the workers towards the hospital that employs them. In fact, over-worked, ill-trained and insecure workers are likely to make more mistakes and hide them too. In short, the repu-tation of the consultant alone supported by a shaky and overstretched staff at different levels is responsible for whatever quality of service that is provided (Baru et al., 2000).

Health Care Provider and Pattern of Practice

The doctor is undoubtedly a professional, and this status is due to his/her acquired knowledge and special skill and the position he/she occupies in society. Therefore, the society's dependency on doctors and that realization create a gap for mechanical practice or a culture of practice driven by hiding information.

In the private practice, desire to earn more money is undoubtedly a significant reason for irrational practice, rising cost of health care, commerciali zation of health, over-medicalization, unethical practice, increasing usage of technology, etc.; the health care as a commodity is sold by the health care provider in the market.

As a pretty commodity producer, the doctor does own his/her skill and certain instrument for providing service. The relationship between the con-sumer (patient) and trade person (doctor) and the technology used for curing (drugs) are no longer of old type in the sense that the industry has almost thoroughly penetrated this relationship. Since the doctor as a professional is essential for the sale and the use of goods produced by the health care industry, he/she while acting as a small commodity producer simultaneously works as an 'agent' (or a sales person) of the industry in the market for the realization of profit. This new role of doctor is almost universal because he/she no longer gathers herbs and chemical, and compounds drugs. The increasing technological use in diagnosis and the treatment has, therefore, changed the practice of medicine from caring to mere curing. Thus, the changes in the organizational set-up of individual medical practice are not limited to the change in the doctor–doctor relationship and doctor–patient relationship, but the very social position of the doctor as a health care provider has changed. The doctor has indeed become an essential part of the market strategy of the health care industry. The convergence of the interests of the industry and the practising doctor takes place most visibly in the for-profit medical care.

In our country, the private sector almost exclusively works on user charges. Intensive use of high-tech equipment, irrational diagnosis, diagnosis for money and technology for earning has become a culture of practice. The issues of over-medicalization and iatrogenesis are forcefully raised by Ivan Illich (1976) and Ian Kennedy (1981). Such issues have equal relevance in our country. ICSSR/ICMR Committee (1981) expressed serious concern about 50,000 drugs and formulations available in our country are hazardous, useless, unnecessary and irrational. Such products not only harm the interests of the consumers and inculcate irrational medical practice but also cause wastage of resource and an increase in the cost of medical care.

The role of increasing usage of various technologies and specifically the new high-tech instruments in medical care is well documented. Nearly 80 per cent of private health practice is based on the nexus commission and cuts between the General Practitioner (GP) and the consultant (Muraleedharan, 1994: 29). The most dominant provider payment system in India is fee for service. Bhat (1999b) finds that 70 per cent of providers charge on a fee-for-service basis and 30 per cent charge on a case basis in which the total charges depend on the specific services and procedures. Forty-seven per cent of doctors use cost as the basis for charging fee, and about one-third follow what others are using and use market-based data to determine their fee structure. The providers indicate that medical associations have users little influence on deciding the fees charged by providers.

An anti-cancer drug is not only being widely and wrongly used by doctors to treat infertility in women, but it is also being tested illegally on unaware patients. Letrozole, the drug has no proven use in curing infertility anywhere in the world. At least, a dozen doctors were involved in the unlawful and potentially hazardous trials in Nagpur, Jodhpur, Kolkata, Hyderabad, Kottayam and Amritsar. No one bothered to take the necessary permission for the tests from the Drugs Controller General of India, a necessary requirement for any clinical trial (Patranobis, 2003).

The doctors prior to technological revolution were independent healers. They examined, diagnosed, investigated and treated the patients under one roof. They could be compared to the artisans of medieval times. In modern times, large-scale capital-intensive diagnostic and therapeutic centres such as the CT and MRI scan units and the shock-wave lithography units have been set up by businessmen. For these centres, the doctor is just a pawn in their endeavour to increase profit margins. The doctor, consciously or unconsciously, falls prey to industry. Studies from both developed and developing countries have shown that private hospitals often discharge patients even before they are ready for it in order to maximize patient turnover and increase interventions. According to a promoter of a corporate hospital makes profits on beds after which the profit margins tend to fall. It is during the first few days of hospitalization that till the procedures, both surgical and non-surgical are completed, there is little scope for charging patients more than bed charges that the hospital is likely to deprive profits from during the recovery phase are on drugs and nursing care. This is an important reason why private hospitals tend to discharge patients much earlier than public hospitals (Baru et al., 2000). 'Much of a private hospital's profits are derived from the usually step charges for impatient services and diagnostic tests. It is also extracted from exorbitant bed charges' (Workers Solidarity, 2000).

The health care insurance is also introduced in Indian market. The insurance schemes have actually helped in the increasing usage of high-tech cost medical care in the private sector. Louise Russell (1979), in her study of technology use in hospitals, argues that the growth of third-party payment system has also diminished cost consciousness amongst the health care providers and the patients to leading the excessive usage of the technology.

The value systems of private sector medical care have come to dominate the practice of medicine. Hence, the curative care component of public sector is also greatly influenced by this value system of the private sector. As a result, one witnesses increasing illegal or unofficial private medical practice by government doctors in PHCs and hospitals. There are even agitations by doctors to make their private practice official. It is also not unusual to see government doctor doing private practice; sometimes, even using PHCs medicine for the practice while sitting in the OPD of the PHC. We also find the government doctors in same way and for the same purpose as they do for doctors in the private sector.

Some scholars have written that the public sector's malfunctioning is providing scope for the expansion of the private sector. It is also necessary to assess how the private sector-oriented policies of the state and the actual existence of an unnecessarily large big private sector with its dominant value system have contributed to the malfunctioning of the public sector (Jesani and Anantharam, 1989: 59). Yesudian (1994), through an opinion-based study, observes that malpractice and medical negligence seem to be rampant in the private sector. Bhat (1999b) finds that over-prescription of drugs is ranked as the first major prevalent medical practice by respondents. This is followed by fee-splitting practices and inadequate measures for disposal of waste followed by over-prescription of diagnosis.

Dehumanizing Aspects and Consumer Concerns in Health Care

Decades of unregulated growth in the health care market have led to a situations, wherein a vocal and powerful section of health care professionals are shamelessly and assertively declaring that the medical profession is acceptable only to itself and not to the society. They defend unfair market and trade practices under the garb of professional independence. They have interpreted the new economic policy as being one which promotes market forces without enforcing any regulations and allows private practice to practice without obligations to ethics or patients/users. On the one hand, they demand that the status of an industry for financial support include the granting of status of infrastructure, providing a level field for health care, giving nursing home the status on medical equipment; and on the other hand, they want to retain the privileges of a welfare institution. This is the outcome of a Delhi Government Report. This committee must not only take stock of the performance of the private sector and its adherence to conditionalties but also define the role of the state in monitoring these hospitals like any other industries. Health care enterprises must also adhere to rules and regulations regarding employment conditions, and minimum wages for all levels of staff certain minimum procedures regarding pricing, billing, maintenance of medical records, financial and medical audit, which become requirements for ensuring transparency and accountability to the consumer and state.

In this era of consumerism, free market economy and information explosion, how can one empower the consumer to utilize health care services more effectively without endangering doctor–patient relationship which is based on trust? The consumer rights, consumer responsibility, gains an equal importance. An irresponsible use of the rights may lead to a distorted an expensive health care delivery as seen in the United States today. The current Indian scenario despite great technological advances and specialization in medicine and health care still depended greatly on trust, care and compassion. Unfortunately, in the blind present of scientific knowledge, the human side of doctor–patient relationship is often forgotten. The doctors should find time to listen to their patients and allay their anxieties. This would humanize medicine. The piecemeal and de-humanized health care that is available today causes a lot of consumer dissatisfaction and is largely responsible for the litigations in consumer protection councils.

The Consumer Protection Act (COPRA) in 1986 was passed to protect the interest and rights of the consumers. But the effectiveness of COPRA is in doubt also because of the number of cases pending with the courts (Bhat, 1999a).

Conclusion

The adoption of a new market economy due to liberalization has resulted in different interpretations of the role of state and its relations to social welfare services and market institutions. Against this backdrop, this paper studies the private health care services and challenges brought about by the rapid marketization and the quality of health services delivered to the masses, structure and pattern of health service from providers' perspective and resultant dehumanizing issues. On the surface, data indicate improvement in the proliferation of private health services and increment in investment of health care. However, a closer look reveals that marketization has resulted in the cost escalation of health services, which has deterred the accessibility to the poor sections of society and quality of health care has also become a myth. The analysis suggests that there are increasing inequalities in the access to and quality of health care services as a result of the rapid and fundamental changes within the health sector.

References

Banerji, D. (1975). 'Social and Cultural Foundation of Health Services in India', *Inquiry*, June 12 Suppl. 70–85.

——— (1985). *Health and Family Planning Services in India: An Epidemiological Socio-Cultural and Political Perspective*. New Delhi: Lok Paksh.

——— (1986). *Social Sciences and Health Service Development in India: Sociology of Formation of an Alternative Paradigm*. New Delhi: Lok Paksh.

Baru, R.V. (1998). *Private Health Care in India: Social Characteristics and Trends*. New Delhi: Sage Publications.

——— (2000). 'Privatisation and Corporatisation', *Seminar*, May, Paper 489, pp 29–33.

Baru, R.V., Imrana Qadeer and Ritu Priya (2000). 'Medical Industry: Illusion of Quality at What Cost', *Economic and Political Weekly*, 15 July, 35(28/29): 2509–11.

Bhat, R. (1996). 'Regulation of Private Health Care in India', *International Journal of Health Planning and Management*, 11: 253–74.

——— (1999a). 'Regulations of Private Health Sector in India', in William Newbrander (ed.), *Private Health Sector Growth in Asia: Issues and Implications*. Ahmedabad: IIM.

——— (1999b). 'Characteristics of Private Medical Practice in India: A Provider Perspective', *Health Policy and Planning*, 14(1): 26–37.

Chatterjee, P. (2008). *Factors that Frasterate Growth of Private Health Sector in India*. www.medind.nic.in/haa/t08/i1/halt08ilp5.pdf.

Chirmule, G. (1997). *Factors Affecting Health Seeking and Utilization of Curative Health Care*. Pune: Bhartiya Agro Industries Foundation.

Dilip, T.R. and R. Duggal (2004). 'Unmet Need for Public Health Care Services in Mumbai, India', *Asia-Pacific Population Journal*, 19(2): 27–40.

Duggal, R. and S. Amin (1989). *Cost of Health Care: A Household Survey in an Indian District*. Bombay: The Foundation for Research in Community Health.

George, R. (1972). 'The Evolution of Social Medicine', in H.E. Freeman et al. (eds), *Handbook of Medical Sociology*. Englewood Cliffs, NJ: Prentice Hall.

Homan, R.K. and K.R. Thankappan (1997), An Examination of Public and Private Sector Health Care Providers in Thiruanathapuram District, Kerala, UNDP/GOI/IDRC Research Project, Unpublished Report, Centre for Development Studies, Thiruvananthapuram.

ICSSR/ICMR Committee (1981). *Health for All: An Alternative Strategy*. Pune: Indian Institute of Education.

Illich, Ivan (1976). *Medical Nemesis: The Exploration of Health*. London: Marion Boyars Publications.

Jesani, A. and S. Anantharam (1989). *Private Sector and Privatization in the Health Care Services*, A Review Paper for *ICSSR-ICMR*. Bombay: FRCH.

Jones, L. (1994). *The Social Context of Health and Health Work*. New York: McMillan.

Kennedy, Ian (1981), The Unmasking of Medicine, London: George Allen and Unwin.

Minocha, Aneeta A. (2011). 'The Socio-Cultural Context of Informed Consent in Medical Practice', in B.S. Baviskar and Tulsi Patel (eds), *Understanding Indian Society: Past and Present*. New Delhi: Orient Blackswan.

Muraleedharan, V.R. (1994). 'Diet, Disease and Death in Colonial South India', *Economic and Political Weekly*, 29(1) pp. 55–63.

Nadkarni, S. (2010). *Healthcare System in an Industry, Management of the Sick Healthcare System*. New Delhi: Vora Medical Publications.

Nanda, P. and R. Baru (1993). *Private Nursing Homes and their Utilization: A Case Study of Delhi*. New Delhi: VHAI.

Nandraj, S. (1994). 'Beyond the Law and the Lord-Quality of Private Health Care', *Economic and Political Weekly*, 2 July, 29(27): 1680–85.

National Council for Applied Economic Research (1992), Household Survey of Medical Care, NCAER, New Delhi.

National Sample Survey Organization (1992), 'NSS 42nd Round (1986-87)', Government of India, Department of Statistics, New Delhi.

Patel, B.K., K.N. Trivedi, S.N. Nayak and P. Patel (2010). 'Health Seeking Behaviour of Peri-Urban Community of Chandkheda', *National Journal of Community Medicine*, 1(1): 35–36.

Patranobis, Sutirtho (2003). *Hindustan Times*, 21 December.

Pinto, L.M. and Z.F. Udwadia (2010). 'Private Patient Perceptions about a Public Programme: What Do Private Indian Tuberculosis Patients Really Feel about Directly Observed Treatment', *BMC Public Health*, 10: 357.

Planning Commission (1998). *Approach Paper to the Ninth Five Year Plan, 1997–98*. New Delhi: GoI, p. 87.

Qadeer, Imrana (2001). 'Impact of Structural Adjustment Programmes on Concept in Public Health', in Imrana Qadeer, Kasturi Sen and K.R. Nayar (eds), *Public Health and the Poverty of Reforms*. New Delhi: Sage Publications.

Ramasubban, R. (1985). 'The Colonial Legacy and the Public Health System in India', *Radical Journal of Health*, June: 6–16.

Russell, Louise B. (1979). *Technology in Hospitals*. Washington, DC: Brookings Institution.

Shah, Utkarsh and Ragini Mohanty (2010). 'Private Sector in India Healthcare Delivery: Consumer Perspective and Government Policies to Promote Private Sector', *Information Management and Business Review*, December, 1(2): 79–87.

The Times of India (24 April 2011).

Visaria, P. and A. Gumber (1994). *Utilization of and Expenditure on Health Care in India: 1986–87*. Gota: Gujarat Institute of Development Research.

Viswanathan, H. and J.E. Rohde (1990). *Diarrhoea in Rural India: A Nationwide Study of Mothers and Practitioners*. New Delhi: Vision Books.

World Medicine Situation, 2011, Medicine Expenditures, WHO: Geneva.

Workers Solidarity (2000). *Critical Condition: A Report on Workers in Delhi's Private Hospitals*. New Delhi: Workers Solidarity.

World Bank (1995). *India: Policies and Finance Strategies for Strengthening Primary Health Care Services*, Report No. 13042-IN, Population and Human Resource Division, South Asia Country Department II, Washington, DC: World Bank.

Yesudian, C.A.K. (1990). 'Utilization Pattern of Health Services and its Implications for Urban Health Policy', *Takemi Programme in International Health*. Harvard School of Public Health.

——— (1994). 'The Nature of Private Sector Health Services in Bombay', *Health Policy and Planning*, 9(1): 72–80.

23

Socio-Economic Impact of Alang and Sosiya Ship-Breaking Yard

Vidyut Joshi

Introduction

Alang and Sosiya Ship-Breaking Yard (ASSBY), popularly known as Alang, was established in 1983. This was the early and uninformed period of globalization that brought coastal-area-based development in India when the Government of India established the Department of Ocean Development. It also brought into effect the Coastal Zone Regulation Act, popularly known as CZRA. Ports and coastal areas were to be developed because it was projected that export-import on a large scale will start from Indian ports. The Government of Gujarat declared privatization of 11 ports, and it also welcomed ship-breaking activities on the Indian shore, as they were, now, not so preferred in developed countries. ASSBY was established as part of this policy. The activities started in 1983 and gradually grew as one of the biggest ship-breaking or ship-recycling yard in the world.

This paper is a part of larger multidisciplinary research project named 'Socio-Cultural, Economic and Environmental Impacts of ASSBY', headed by the author of this paper. Different methods were used for data collection. So far as villagers are concerned, out of 3,248 individuals, 485 households that were representing 3,053 individuals were selected. Apart from this, 350 workers were studied as part of the workers' study. The project proved to be challenging, not because of the sociocultural, economic and environmental issues, but the real challenge was to involve diverse range of interests and stakeholders, who all share an economic interest in sustainable development of the yard. There were four stakeholders with different interests and abilities: (i) Gujarat Maritime Board (GMB), Government of Gujarat, (ii) ship-breaking industrialists, (iii) the workers and (iv) the local community. The project tried a convergence of all four stakeholders and tried to evolve a consensus for sustainable development. The paper is only a part of the larger project, as it deals with the impact of ASSBY on the workers and on the local community. Although the liberal industrial policy along with privatization and globalization was introduced at ASSBY, the corresponding rules and institutional structures to satisfy interests of all stakeholders were not introduced. It was only after long processes of opposition, litigation and consultations that corresponding institutional structures for sustainable development at ASSBY started emerging.

Alang and Sosiya Ship-Breaking Yard

Gujarat has a long and colourful history of maritime commerce of 3,000 years. The shipbuilding history on the Gujarat coast is equally old. Therefore, a culture conducive to coastal commercial activities was always there. However, ship breaking was a new activity. When the golden corridor or the mainland industrial development started getting saturated, the silver corridor or the coastal corridor started drawing attention of concerned people for further industrialization. Gujarat has the biggest (1,964 km or 22 per cent of the total) coastline in India. ASSBY was one of the first of such developments. Alang was selected as ship-breaking point for topographical reasons. This was the best ship-berthing and -breaking site. Gradually, ASSBY grew into biggest ship-breaking site. Some 182 small ship-breaking plots were converted in 100 plots in 1996 and further reduced to 80 plots in 2003. The smaller plots were merged with other plots, hence the activities have not been reduced. There are around 30,000 workers, mostly interstate migrants working here. The vicinity includes 10 villages.

A ship or a vessel has a life of 30 years. It is then sold as scrap. Because of the strict guideline for working and living conditions in developed countries, the industry started getting relocated to Asian countries such as India, China, Pakistan, Bangladesh, Philippines and Taiwan. The industry in these countries is unorganized, uses simple technology (gas cutting) and is labour intensive. This is the first global industry on a large scale in India, in the sense that the ships come from almost all developed countries to be recycled here. The presence of foreign ships and foreign crew creates a global environment here. All of a sudden, many foreign languages are being spoken and translated at Alang and at Bhavnagar. The purchase of ship for recycling is in dollars and not in rupees. The breaking of an average ship requires four to five months. The operations are mainly manual. A ship is cut into various sections. Ninety per cent of the scrap is in the form of iron sheets, which is sold to steel industry for recycling. Remaining 10 per cent would include furniture, cutlery, books, diesel sets, some equipments, liquor, beds and so on. Such materials are sold in the nearby villages. The items lie open in farms, known as 'khada' or pits.

The environmental impact of ship breaking has been widely publicized. The ship-breaking process creates pollution of land, sea and air. Toxic fumes are released by the process itself, as well as from fires that burn non-recyclable waste materials. Due to improper disposal of the solid waste, animals, crops and the groundwater are affected. Noise pollution due to heavy traffic in the local area is another impact of the industry. By far, the greatest concern of the environmental non-governmental organizations (NGOs) is the poly-chlorinated biphenyls, heavy metals and carcinogens such as asbestos. International and national NGOs protested against ASSBY on these issues in 1999. It was after this that some rules for ship breaking have been enforced as part of the Factories Act. Now, there is a weekly holiday for house cleaning. Wearing of safety gadgets has become mandatory. There are sufficient fire and accident prevention as well as aftercare in such emergency situations.

Stake Holders

There are four major stakeholders in this activity. These are the local community or the villagers, migrant workers, the ship-breakers represented by Gujarat Ship Breakers' Association (GSBA), and the Government of Gujarat represented by GMB. The interest of the Government of Gujarat is to develop activities, distribute plots on lease to ship-breakers and collect revenue or other relevant charges. The interests of the ship-breakers include cutting of ships and selling the recovered materials, thereby making profits. It was because of the lack of elite and civility attitudes on part of both these stakeholders that the industry has remained largely unorganized. Remaining two stakeholders are at the receiving end. Both have no say in running the affairs of the industry. The question of the impact of this industry on these two stakeholders was raised during the course of the project.

Impact of ASSBY on Local Community

There are 10 villages in a radius of 10 km of central point of ASSBY. They are Alang, Sosiya, Manar, Sathara, Kathawa, Bharapara, Mathavada, Takhatgadh, Jasapara and Mandva. The population of these 10 villages was seven to eight thousands in 1961, when ASSBY was not there. The population of ASSBY agglomeration (including original 10 villages) is more than 60,000. There is little information on pre-ASSBY lifestyle of people; hence, we have relied on oral history. A vast majority was engaged in rain-fed agriculture and animal husbandry. Only a few were engaged in fishing as supplementary income-earning proposition. The service sector was virtually non-existent. Social and business relations extended around 10 km, and the marriage circle stretched to a radius of 60 km. Marriages were traditional in the sense that they were arranged by parents. Caste endogamy strictly prevailed. Religion played a great role in every walk of village life and religious festivals brought neighbourhood people together. Different generations of a family lived under one roof. The decision-making was mainly in the hands of elders. Most houses were traditionally *kachcha* lacking any sort of modern gadgets.

ASSBY has attracted many men, and later women, to jobs that are year-round, better paid, regular and less arduous than working in the field. Repercussions of this work shift have been far-reaching. Elders who would have otherwise retired have been working in the fields, as younger people work with ASSBY. In the first phase of the project, in 1999, 25 per cent of the village workforce had abandoned their traditional work. By 2007, only 25 per cent of the villagers were engaged in agriculture. The appeal of ASSBY-related work is apparent. Less work and more pay with better lifestyle. The steady expansion of the yard encroached on traditional grazing lands, creating a shortage. New roads and heavy vehicular traffic led to many animal causalities. Cattle breeders gradually shifted to yard work. Village artisans who traditionally provided services to local farmers turned to providing services to the shipyard; doing so improved their technology. Some farmers turned their farms into 'khada' or pits, an open space for selling Alang scrap. Some rented their farms for such activities. Some villagers have started tea joints or 'pan gallas' or snack outlets. As overall economic conditions have improved, they have surplus income. Some of them have opened saving accounts in the local branch of a nationalized bank.

Impact on Education

Only eight villages had primary schools prior to 1983. Now all villages have schools. Now there are three secondary schools too. Additional rooms have been built with the help from GMB. Some parents have started sending their children to English-medium school and also in a technical school in nearby Talaja town so that they can avail the opportunities in the yard.

The Improved Health Care

Earlier, there were only two private physicians and few faith healers in these villages. Now a hospital has been established by the GMB. The government of Gujarat has also established a maternity home at Manar. However, only few births take place in maternity homes. Most of the births still take place at homes with the help of old women of the village. Health care is one such field where traditional attitudes do not give way so easily. Four villages have village health centres. Some private practitioners have also established their clinics here to serve villagers and workers. Although the workers visit the private clinics, the villagers first resort to traditional methods and visit the doctor only in case the traditional method fails. The yard itself has become a source of leftover medicines in the ships, most of them might have crossed expiry date. A malpractice of giving these leftover medicines is found in vogue here. In our focused group discussion with the villagers, it was reported that residents of Kathawa and Sosiya complained of throat burning, and they said that it is because of the contamination of the groundwater by oil leaked during cutting of vessels.

The Caste Factor

In pre-ASSBY times, caste was very much an integral part of the village life. A somewhat rigid caste hierarchy, caste-based rules for eating and social interaction, civil rights and caste-based vocations were in vogue along with caste endogamy. There were caste-wise residential areas in the villages. Even today, the streets are still identified by caste names. The dominant caste was Rajput (Kshatriya); Kolis were in numerical majority in this area. Now, house of a Dalit (ex-untouchable) has a common wall in the new residential area and no one even bothers. There is no more discrimination on caste lines in public transport. At ASSBY, members of different castes work together. The ASSBY effect has brought the class factor and every caste is stratified on secular lines. New jobs at ASSBY are not on caste lines. A well-off man would build a new house out of his caste area and mostly in a newly developed area outside the 'gamthan' or the residential locality of the old village. New residential areas are mixed areas, where relatively wealthy people from different castes stay together. However, if you ask about their identity, they will always show the caste identity first. It is also true, to some extent that, when it comes to protection of interests, against some other group, they organize on caste lines. The villagers' opposition to migrant labours is sometimes taken on caste lines.

As a result of new opportunities at ASSBY, people are giving up their traditional agro-based vocations to adopt new vocations. As a result, the overall character of these villages has begun to shift, and these 10 villages are gradually becoming an urban agglomeration.

Marriage

Marriage is still a village festival and not just a family function. However, some new patterns and attitudes are emerging in this area. Our survey indicates that 63 per cent of marriages are still arranged by parents, although the future spouses are given some say in the decision, i.e; 37 per cent of the match making. Earlier, there was a marriage circle in a radius of less than 50 km, which has now extended to 500 km. Far-off people want to give their daughters in ASSBY area as this is a promised land. Inter-caste marriages are now tolerated by parents. Dowry, not only remains a deep-rooted custom, but it has also been strengthened by the ASSBY prospects. The castes, where there was no dowry, have now started this practice. For the family of the bride in ASSBY area, the marriage prospects of the bride have gone up as many grooms want to marry a girl of ASSBY area and settle there. A reverse trend has started in such cases. Now brides do not go to groom's place. It is the groom who comes to ASSBY area with an intention of settling down at ASSBY. In almost all villages, a separate residential area has been established known as 'Jamai Para' or son-in-law hamlet.

There has been a slight upward trend in age of marriage. Now no one wants to marry their children at 14 or 15 years of age. The marriage age has gone up to 18 years. Along with the rise in age of marriage and bride's say in selection of groom, the status of women also seems to have risen. Two women have become 'sarpanch' (village head); women work as drivers, labourers, and even as labour contractors at ASSBY.

Integration with Migrant Workers

As 90 per cent of the workers are from other states (Bihar, Odisha and Uttar Pradesh), there are real cultural differences that have created obstacles in the process of integration of villagers and workers. The differences are in terms of caste, religious practices, language and customs. Although most of the migrant workers stay in the workers' colony, they interact on a daily basis in commodity market, at work place and during common chores. Many villagers speak with contempt about migrant workers. Now villagers have to share many common facilities that they do not like. Since workers have not come here with family and since they try to save money to send home, their lifestyle is very poor. Since they work in the yard, daily cleanliness is also a problem. Except Manar, people of other villages do not allow workers to stay in their villages. Even at Manar, those migrant workers who are highly skilled and have come with their families are allowed to stay. Villagers allege that the workers indulge in antisocial activities, such as drinking illicitly brewed liquor, addiction to drugs, prostitution and homosexuality. Entry of a migrant worker after evening is not allowed, and such an act can lead to violence. Single working men are seen as lascivious and a threat to village women. Incidents of thefts and other petty crimes in the area are attributed to the migrants, as some young girls have run away from home, presumably to elope with the migrants.

Although the migrant labour population, in and around ASSBY, continue to rise, the infrastructure facilities for them are largely inadequate. This is also a cause for frictions and tension between local and migrant population. With the development of ASSBY, this tension and frictions, along with antisocial activities are rising.

Villagers' Concerns

Although the villagers have benefited in terms of economic development, they have some issues to be resolved. Water is their biggest concern. As a result of overdrawal, the water tables are going down. Moreover, the water resource gets polluted because of oil spillage and other pollution at ASSBY. They were also concerned about solid and liquid waste management. With the increase in population and the villages becoming an urban agglomeration, a strict regional planning is required. Despite the educational in and around ASSBY area, the villagers feel that they need higher level of skill development institutions so that their children can avail modern opportunities. Health was another concern. They need a full-fledged hospital in their area.

Impact of ASSBY on Migrant Workers

In early days, the ship-breakers engaged local workers. Soon, it was found that local workers, despite the skill and the qualification, are not the lot for arduous and heavy task of ship-breaking. Soft tasks such as wiremen, electricians, non-manual tasks, tea shop, snacks outlets were available to them and they opted for that. It was at that time in 1984 that ship-breakers brought workers from other states. They were engaged through contractors or 'Mukadam', who were close to ship-breakers. There are mainly four categories of workers: Battiwala or workers with specialized skill of gas cutting; Malpani or the workers with grading and separating skills of different types of metals; helper is one who assists Battiwala and Jodiwala or workers who move cut iron plates from one place to another. Apart from the four main categories, there are other workers such as winch operators, crane drivers, fitters, carpenters and electricians and wiremen. In all, there are around 30,000 workers out of whom we surveyed 350 workers and found that 90 per cent are the migrant workers mainly from Bihar (22 per cent), Odisha (29.36 per cent) and Uttar Pradesh (43.77 per cent). We will mainly deal with the working and living conditions of the workers.

Working Conditions

Ship-breaking involves hard manual labour. Cutting the iron sheets while a ship is beached in shallow sea water is the main task. Battiwala cut the sheets. LPG is used for cutting. Since there are loose rubber pipes, the incidents of fire are a part of daily routine. Cut sheets are shifted from the sea shore to trucks by head loaders or Jodiwala. This also involves accidents on a daily basis. Ships are, after all, scraps. They have all sorts of oils and gases that spoil nearby environment when a ship is being cut. A scrap yard is never organized. It is full of harmful materials. As such, all activities connected with ship-breaking are hazardous processes. Fire, heat, air-borne hazardous chemicals, restricted and confined space of operation and awkward posture of work make ship-breaking one of the most and risky occupation among all the industrial enterprises. Our intention here is not to go into the safety measures described in the ship-breaking rules of the factories account, nor do we wish to harm the industry that has contributed to the economic development of the region. Our intention is only to show the inhuman conditions under which the workers used to work.

Operations of ship-breaking are hazardous from the viewpoint of not only industrial safety but also of industrial hygiene. Workers on specific work points are likely to be affected by injuries, illness and death. Exposure to materials such as asbestos, poly-chlorinated phenyls, heavy metal and metal dust and such other materials, if not duly controlled, can increase health risk among workers.

The root cause of very bad working conditions is that the ship-breaking industry is in unorganized sector. There was a long debate whether provisions of the Factories Act should be applied or not. Rules for ship-breaking were made in 1993, almost a decade after the establishment of ASSBY. It was around 1995 that various NGOs, from within and without the country started opposing ASSBY operations. Demonstrations took place. Public Interest Litigations were filed in courts. International Maritime Organization (responsible for permitting scrap ships to be recycled) and other international organizations along with elite international communities also brought pressures on ASSBY and GMB. A time came when ASSBY came on the brink of closure. This was globalization in true sense of the term. There was a strong demand for improvement in ship-breaking standards. It was only after all these pressures that there started a gradual improvement in the working conditions at ASSBY. A weekly holiday was made mandatory for house-cleaning operations. Safety gadgets such as helmet, gloves and safety specs were given to workers. The shift was reduced to eight hours. A hospital was established at ASSBY. Fire brigade was also set up. However, there were no basic changes in ship-breaking technology. They were advised by experts to adopt advanced technologies such as dry dock for cutting, pulley for transportation of iron sheets instead of head loading, fixed pipes instead of loose pipes for LPG, team building instead of groups, solid waste disposal system and the like. However, these advanced methods have not been adopted by ship-breakers for various reasons. The main reason is that although the industry is global, most of the industrialists are first-generation ship-breakers. They have suddenly become ship-breakers from scrap goods merchants. They do not have the knowledge of modern management, nor do they have elite attitudes.

Living Conditions of the Workers

Migrant workers, who stay without family, try to save money to send home to their families. Therefore, they do not spend liberally. As shown earlier, the workmen used to earn somewhere between ₹3,000 and ₹9,000 in 2003. Today, the income has gone up by some 60–70 per cent. There is no question of non-payment of minimum wages. The question is not that they have no money to fulfil basic needs. But like other migrant workers, they save money to send home. At the same time, it must be said that infrastructural facilities at ASSBY are also scanty. A preponderant majority of the workers stay in the workers' colony, which were shabbily built tin sheds and small rooms, with no plinth, no bathrooms, no water facility, no sewage and even without electricity connections. Every room of around 12′ × 12′ size would accommodate 8–10 workers. Since this was an unhygienic living condition, workers would get affected by several diseases such as malaria, gastrointestinal diseases and skin diseases. A lot of hue and cry was raised by concerned NGOs. After a time lapse of more than a decade, water and light connections were provided. A hospital run by Bhavnagar Red Cross was started at ASSBY. Workers were not much satisfied with the hospital facilities. Since workers are staying without families, there are a few cases of AIDS. Prostitution is rampant in this area. There is one AIDS centre that works as information and counselling centre, organizes various health awareness programmes. GMB had shown its willingness to construct 'pucca' houses for workers with the help of Gujarat Housing Board, but the ship-breakers were not ready to give their contribution, and hence the plan flopped. Same is the case where GMB has constructed a hospital building and has established a trust to maintain it. But the hospital has not become functional as ship-breakers have not given their contribution.

Socio-Economic Life of the Workers

After a day's hard work, a worker who has no family support here and who has no healthy entertainment avenues, seeks company of liquor and entertaining women, and see movies arranged in makeshift cinema halls. As a result, they feel guilty and tensed. They try to mix with local population, but they are not so successful. They try to be part of the celebration of local festivals, but the cultural differences do not allow them to do so. They cannot bring their families here as there are no facilities. They can go home once in a year, or at the most twice. This sort of hard work, insecure and casual jobs and cultural separation disturbs them. Absenteeism at work, AIDS and diseases are some of the results of this isolation.

As mentioned earlier, they earn more at ASSBY than what they used to earn in their native villages. Average saving was more than ₹10,000 per year in 2003. It must have increased by now. The plots are insured; therefore in case of death or injury, they get insurance. But they do not have permanent jobs, nor do they have identity cards or provident fund facility.

Workers' Concerns

Workers' top concern is the implementation of labour laws. They want a permanent job with identity card, provident fund and fixed duty hours. They do not know about provisions, but they want good and healthy working conditions. The living conditions, sanitation, water and electricity come last in their issues of concern.

Conclusion

This was a UNESCO project not only of a multidisciplinary nature. It also involved university-industry linkage for sustainable coastal area development. As a part of the project, we did conduct certain surveys, collected data and wrote reports. Over and above, we also conducted various meetings with stakeholders and tried to evolve a consensus on various issues. Some improvements in the conditions of villagers could be made as a result of these interventions. However, we could not evolve a sustainable model for ship-breaking industry. But the process of joint consultations which we had started is now taken further by GMB and certain NGOs working in the area. It is the participation of two relatively silent stakeholders, the villagers and the workers, in some decision-making processes, which will make industrial democracy and sustainable development possible at ASSBY.

Bibliography

Bhavnagar University (2000). *Sustainable Development of Alang-Sosiya Ship Breaking Yard: Report on Phase 2 of the UNESCO Project*. Bhavnagar: Bhavnagar University.

Joshi, Vidyut (2005). 'Ship Breaking in India', *Proceedings of a Regional Seminar*. Ahmedabad: Mahatma Gandhi Labour Institute.

Joshi, Vidyut et al. (1994). *Impacts and Challenges of a Large Coastal Industry*. Paris: CSI, UNESCO.

24

Does Indebtedness Lead to Suicides Among Cultivators?

A Comparative Study of Suicide Victims, Normal Indebted Cultivators and Suicide Attempters in Sangrur District of Punjab

A. Satyanarayana and Sanjay

The phenomenon of suicides among cultivators in the Indian states such as Andhra Pradesh, Karnataka, Maharashtra and Punjab has attracted the attention of legal and political institutions besides social workers and social scientists as the rate of suicide increased from 5 per 1 lakh population in 1960 to 8.07 by 1988 and remained stable until 1997 (National Crime Records Bureau, 2003) and augmented to 10.84 per 1 lakh by 2000. Southern states recorded higher rates of suicides: Kerala (28.76 per 100,000 population), Karnataka (23.76 per 100,000 population), Tamil Nadu (17.72 per 100,000 population) and Puducherry (50.85 per 100,000 population) (NCRB, 2001), where the proportion of nuclear families are more in preponderance than North India (Kolenda, 1968). However, the most populous states such as Uttar Pradesh and Bihar recorded lower rates of suicides, that is, 2.76 per 100,000 population and 0.49 per 100,000 population in 2001, respectively (NCRB, 2001), where complex households are prevalent (Kolenda, 1968). The Honourable High Court of Maharashtra (2005) directed the Tata Institute of Social Sciences (TISS) to find out causes of suicides among cultivators in Maharashtra. The TISS in its study found that the untenable cost of agricultural production in terms of escalating input costs for seeds, fertilizers, pesticides, diesel/electricity and the declining prices and fluctuations in crop prices resulted in indebtedness. Such indebted cultivators are unable to maintain the bare minimum necessary for survival. On the contrary, the Maharashtra State Government funded a project to the Indira Gandhi Institute of Development Research (IGIDR) in order to identify the possible causes for suicides among cultivators in Maharashtra. The study of IGIDR classified the causes as personal, social and economical. At a personal level, the study found that love affairs at social level, dowry and finally indebtedness at economic level were the reasons for suicides besides the 'unscrupulous moneylenders' as the culprits (2006). Following reports of farmers' suicides in Karnataka, the State Government constituted a seven-member expert committee to study farmers' suicides. The committee (Government of Karnataka, 2002) identified high levels of indebtedness among farmers, with examples of cases where farmers with one acre of land have over ₹300,000 worth of loan from institutional and especially non-institutional sources at high interest rates of 3–4 per cent per month. The market fluctuations too have contributed to growing vulnerability among the cultivators. The report gives lesser importance to the increasing cost of seeds, pesticides and fertilizers that are much beyond the earnings of the farmers.

Social scientists, on the contrary, attributed suicides as associated with high cost of production, crop failures, drought, floods and fluctuations in the prices of agricultural produce resulting in indebtedness and indebtedness as a central cause of suicides among cultivators (Assadi, 1998; Kumar and Sharma, 1998; Vasavi, 1999; Iyer and Manick, 2000; Deshpande, 2002; Mohanty, 2005; Jodhka, 2006; Mishra, 2006; Mohankumar and Sharma, 2006; Rao and Suri, 2006; Sridhar, 2006) and decline in the agricultural productivity (Kumar and Sharma, 1998; Jodhka, 1999; Iyer and Manick, 2000). Association for Democratic Rights (1998) conducted studies among Punjab cultivators and found crop failure and indebtedness as contributing factors to the suicides among cultivators. In addition to this, the suicide victims' households have a larger size of family with more women and non-workers than the normal indebted cultivators (Mishra, 2006). Very few studies highlighted on the effect of harassment on social status and drug addiction (Mishra, 2006; Rao and Suri, 2006) as causes of suicide. Parthasarathy and Shameem (1998) opined that although growing indebtedness is one of the main reasons for the strain on farmers, it does not entirely explain suicides. Therefore, the alienation of individuals from the social milieu too needs to be taken into account in order to explain suicides as all cultivators with the same intensity of indebtedness are not taking the severe step of committing suicide.

The Indian cultivators remained indebted even prior to the 20th century (Whitcombe, 1971; Darling and Darling, 1977), but accounts of cultivators committing suicide are rarely reported. Starvation deaths or famine deaths (Sen, 1981) collectively acted against indebtedness in the form of riots in the Deccan region or burning the documents of moneylenders collectively as in the case of 1857 rebellion in Muzaffarnagar and Saharanpur districts of Uttar Pradesh (Stokes, 1978) was observed in the agrarian history of India. Indebtedness per se may be a necessary condition for the suicides among cultivators in the late 20th century in India, but not a sufficient condition. The contemporary agricultural activities not only became more capital intensive, but also its circulation has magnified as the intensity of double-cropped area has reached in some localities such as Punjab to the extent of nearly 200 per cent. Crop heterogeneity has declined and monocrop/two-crop domination has acquired importance. Decline in water table, water logging, soil salinity, toxicity and micro-organisms, deficiency has magnified (Shiva, 1991). Besides this, the cultivators in general have lost their food sovereignty as the crop diversity has drastically declined along with an increased dependency for seeds on the multinational corporations (International peasant movement). Besides this, the proportion of marginal and small landholdings is in general increasing, which is economically non-viable (Friese, 1990; Satyanarayana, 2005). With the decline in the economic viability of landholdings, the former lending agencies too reduced the lending amount to such units, and the cultivators are becoming more dependent on Arthiyas and moneylenders, agricultural moneylenders such as pesticide and fertilizer dealers and buyers of agricultural produce and charging exorbitant rates of interest. These are some structural agrarian conditions that are necessary but not sufficient to explain suicides.

From the above review of studies on cultivators' suicides, the following gaps are observed: First, the studies took mainly suicide victim's households into consideration, but did not compare them with cultivators who had the same amount of indebtedness in relation to their assets or with the households that had suicide attempters. Such comparative studies will reveal scientifically the sufficient conditions for suicides among some cultivators but not in others. Second, the processes adopted by the formal and informal lending agencies in the recovery of debt also have some role to play as the contract between the borrower and lender at the time of borrowing loans is more or less a personal agreement; but at the time of recovery, the issue becomes more of a public issue that reduces the creditworthiness of the indebted person but also his status and honour in the village and in the marketplace. Such processes have received scant attention in the literature. Third, the coping mechanisms adopted in the repayment of debt and the role of primordial relations of suicide victim and normal indebted cultivators in overcoming the crisis need to be understood more systematically with elaborate case studies. The present paper makes a concerted effort to comprehend these points. Finally, bearing of the facts on the theoretical models of suicide needs a systematic interdisciplinary academic endeavour that will be focused in a separate paper.

To overcome these gaps, a study was conducted in the Sangrur District, in which the nature of agrarian development, the socio-economic characters of the suicide victim and normal indebted cultivators' households besides the pattern of using the borrowed loans from both formal and informal lending agencies, the process of recovery of debt by formal and informal lending agencies and its consequences in a society where honour has a premium, and the relations with the primordial units were undertaken. The present paper first provides two case studies each for suicide victim and normal indebted cultivator and a single case in the case of suicide attempter so as to arrive at the differentia specific between the suicide victims, normal indebted cultivators and suicide attempters. Thus, there is a need for a systematic study of suicide and for understanding the phenomena of suicide in India, especially among cultivators, emerging in rural areas from a social–psychological viewpoint.

Methodology

Suicide victim (62), suicide attempters (2) and indebted comparable normal cultivators (50) were chosen for the study from the Sangrur District of Punjab where paddy and wheat are predominantly cultivated and with high intensity of mechanization, tube well and pump sets dependency for irrigation, and high intensive use of chemical fertilizers, besides the preponderance of marginal and poor cultivators cultivating with two or more crops within the same piece of land (Sanjay and Satyanarayana, 2008). Data were collected from the sample households through narratives from the close family members and friends to know their lived experiences at the time of borrowing and repayment of debt and their coping mechanisms. The behavioural patterns of the suicide committers a week prior to the action was observed and experienced by their family members and friends in their day-to-day interactions. Case studies are presented here in order to derive the differentia specific between these three types of sample under study.

Case I: This case represents 1 among the 61 cases out of the 62 cases under study where egoistic and anomic tendencies were observed in the suicide. The other represents an altruistic type. The suicide victim belongs to the first type. He was a Jat-Sikh, former president of the statutory village *panchayat* in Moonka block of Sangrur District of Punjab State. He lived in a collateral family that comprised his wife, his unmarried daughter and his two married younger brothers along with their wives. The younger brothers had no children. The former Pradhan was aged 49 years and had pursued studies up to intermediate (10 + 2). His wife was educated up to fourth standard. His daughter was aged just 10 years and was pursuing her studies in class sixth in a convent school. The two younger brothers were aged 26 and 22 years, respectively. The two brothers were educated up to tenth standard. The wives of the two younger brothers were aged 22 and 18 years, respectively, and both were illiterates. The former Pradhan and his two younger brothers owned nine acres of cultivable land jointly. They used to cultivate wheat in rabi season and cotton in kharif season on the land. They owned jointly a tractor, a tube well and a thresher as farm tools. They leased the tractor, tube well and thresher to the neighbours and needy cultivators, after completing the agricultural work on their farm. They also owned two milk cattle. They had no farm cattle.

The collateral family after discussions among themselves borrowed a sum of ₹2 lakhs from Arthtiya at the rate of 36 per cent per annum in 1992 after mortgaging three acres of their cultivable land for agricultural purposes. They renovated the residence and painted it and spent some money in throwing a party to their friends. They invested the remaining portion of borrowed money for the purchase of high-yielding varieties (HYVs) of cotton seeds, fertilizers and pesticides. The entire cotton crop was destroyed due to the attack of pests and bad weather in 1993. They sprayed pesticides in order to control the attack of pests on the crop but could not save their cotton crop from the attack of pests as the pesticide was later found as adulterated. The loan was a sum of ₹ 248,000 including interests after eight months of its borrowing as they had not paid even a single instalment as the crop failed and the debt further increased up to ₹272,000 inclusive of the interest within a year.

All the three brothers promised to the commission agent that they would clear their debt after harvesting the cotton crop. But after the failure of the cotton crop, they could not keep up their words. Now, the commission agent pressurized them to repay the debt promptly. He abused the brothers in the market for not repaying the debt and threatened them, with the help of his musclemen in the market, with dire consequences and that their property will be confiscated by force if they fail to repay the total debt soon. Thus, the private agreement between the moneylender and borrower at the time of borrowing loan became a public issue at the time of its repayment. Such a public pronouncement will reduce the creditworthiness of the borrowers and their honour and privilege among the villagers. To avoid all these problems, the eldest brother preferred to sell a portion of land from their total land in order to repay the loan to the commission agent and to become free from the debt. The eldest brother shared his idea with his younger brothers. The two younger brothers instead of conceding to the idea insisted to have a share from the non-mortgaged property equally, and the younger brothers finally got it by the end of 1993. They refused to share the responsibility in repaying the loan to the commission agent and insisted that it is the sole responsibility of the eldest brother, who took the loan after mortgaging three acres of cultivable land. Therefore, the mortgaged free land was distributed equally between the two younger brothers, whereas the eldest brother inherited the mortgaged land and also the debt to be repaid to the commission agent. After the partition of the property, the younger brothers reduced interaction with their eldest brother's family. The eldest brother took all the responsibilities of his younger brothers after the death of the parents earlier onto his shoulders. At the time of crisis of repayment of debt, his brothers were not with him. Such a behaviour at the time of present crisis impaired the feelings of the Pradhan as he had cared for them like sons earlier, but they were unable to reciprocate the same feelings at his time of crisis. His brothers parted with their equal share from the six acres of non-mortgaged land besides a tractor and a thresher. The former Pradhan got the mortgaged land, two rooms and tube well and the debt as his share.

The eldest brother sold the total share of his land and repaid the debt and became landless. He started working in a cloth shop, located in another village, as a daily wage worker in order to fulfil the subsistence needs of the family. Being a former Pradhan, he preferred not to work in his own village as a wage labourer on others' land, which would have further deteriorated his social status, honour and respect in the context of his already declined economic position from *zamindar* (landowner) to landless. Such deterioration in economic and social statuses will further negatively affect the self-respect and is also difficult to protect one's own self-esteem in village community. He earned only ₹60 per day from the cloth shop, which he found, was not sufficient to fulfil the basic needs of the family.

One day, in July 1994, seven months after the partition of property by his younger brothers and six months after the person became landless, his daughter studying in class sixth came to him and started weeping. She told her father that her name was struck off from the school register because she had no school uniform and also did not pay the school fees. He felt very sad about the situation. He approached his brothers for financial help in order to pay the fees and to purchase school uniform for her daughter. His brothers did not extend help but told him, *hamara bhi pariwar hai, aur hamare paas bhi bahut kherche hai.* [We also have a family, and also have more expenses to cope with.] His friends who attended the party thrown by the former Pradhan too expressed their helplessness saying that they too have much debt to be repaid. He then borrowed an advance of ₹200 from his employer against his wages and fulfilled the requirements of the school for the continuation of his daughter's education. His wife expired in 1994 of typhoid. A week after the death of his wife, while his daughter was in school, he attempted to commit suicide by hanging himself from the fan, but the villagers rescued him. After knowing the situation, his sister took him and his daughter to her in-laws' house where he lived for only four months. At his sister's residence, he started drinking liquor. He started spending most of his time outside his sister's house, and used to return only after two to three days of stay outside the house. He often used to tell his sister that *asi jeena nahi chande, kudi da khyal aata hai, uska mere baad ki howega.* [I don't want to live anymore; I worry about my daughter, after me what will happen to my daughter.] One day in February 1995, he went away from his sister's residence and did not return. After three days, the police recovered his body in the nearby railway track. Police recorded this incident as suicide. In the case of landless nuclear families, they became sub-nuclear after the suicide of the household head.

Case II: This case out of the total 62 suicide cases under study exemplifies the altruistic form of suicide. The family belongs to a backward caste Saini. It is a nuclear family that comprised six members, that is, parents and unmarried three boys and a daughter. The household head was aged 51 years and his wife was 44 years and both were illiterates. His wife was a homemaker and also helped in farming with family members. The three sons were aged 20, 16 and 14 years, respectively. The daughter was 18 years old. All the four children were educated up to fifth standard from a government junior high school. They left the school after completing fifth standard due to bad economic condition, and the sons started working for wages on the lands of other cultivators. Here, the consumer worker ratio was high. They are landless, have no agricultural tools, farm cattle or milk cattle. The household head was a farmer. The household was trying to settle his daughter's marriage. He borrowed ₹35,000 from his employer for his daughter's marriage in 1995. The interest rate was 36 per cent per year. Apart from this, he borrowed ₹10,000 at 40 per cent interest from a cloth shopkeeper of a village for the same purpose. Therefore, his debt was nearly ₹45,000. He spent the money in household expenses such as illness, food and in purchasing some gold and silver jewellery, pots and pans, and clothing for his daughter's marriage. He had no other sources of income except wages to repay the instalments and debt interest. He could repay neither the interest nor a portion of the principal even after six months of borrowing the loan. The employer of the household head insisted on the early repayment of the loan or to send his eldest son to work on his land till his debt was repaid. Therefore, the eldest son became a farm servant of the landowner on debt bondage. The household head's younger brother gave a sum of ₹20,000 at the interest of 24 per cent per annum as loan after mortgaging his eldest brother's small house in the year 1996. He spent this amount in purchasing gold and silver ornaments for ₹6,000 and paid ₹12,000 to the cloth merchant against the debt in 1996.

Even one year after taking the loan from his employer and Arthiya, he could not pay even a single instalment to them. Now, these two lenders started sending their musclemen to the house of the borrower everyday in order to collect the money from the debtor and started abusing the household head and his family members in the village. They told,

> *asi paise kab doge, saal bhar ho gaye eek bhi paisa nahi ditta, aukaat nahi hai kudi ki shadi karne ki to kis waste paise udhar litta ve. Bathaiye rak apni jawan kudi nu ker vich ya shadi ker. Asi to sada paisa chaiye ve, jaldi, is tem to ye gal samjh le, agli baar asi awenge to tere chhote munde ko bhi saade naal le jawenge.* [When are you going to pay our money? Even after one year, you did not pay even a single paisa. If you are unable to pay, why did you take loan for your daughter's marriage? You get your daughter married or keep her at your house, but we want our money back soon. Remember next time when we come for the collection of debt, we will take your younger son under debt bondage with us.]

The family was disturbed as their second son too was becoming a farm servant in debt bondage. The daughter felt that it was all about her marriage that pushed the family into debt. The father was worried about his daughter's marriage. Finally, in order to conduct various ceremonies of marriage, he approached the moneylender for a second loan. But none came forward to give him loan as he had lost his creditworthiness in the repayment of his earliest loan. The moneylenders told *pehle pehle wala karja to chukka de pher doosra karja lete rahio, are udhar lene se to achhha ai ki kudi ko ghar wich bithaye rakh, kudi bhahi tode na ja rahi hai*.

Daughter blamed herself for the prevailing situation of her family. She told her father, 'Don't borrow more debts for my marriage; I don't want to get married, why are we borrowing more debts when we cannot repay? I will not get married. Please don't borrow debts any further'. She pressed her father to repay firstly the existing debts at any cost. She disliked people coming home and abusing her family members. She got ill after a week of these talks with her parents. After about 15 days, in the morning, in 1998, when all family members were in field at work, she burnt herself by sprinkling kerosene on her body and committed suicide. When neighbours saw the fire in her house, they informed her parents who took the burnt body of their daughter to the district hospital, but could not rescue her. She died on the way to the hospital.

Let us see the case of an indebted collateral normal cultivator household who also faced the crises of the repayment of debt. Case of an indebted normal cultivator is discussed further.

Normal Indebted Cultivator

Case III: This case represents 1 out of 50 cases under study where the normal indebted cultivator received normative social support in crisis from his kin and his kin's friends, which facilitated the debtor to overcome the crisis faced by him as faced by the other indebted cultivators who committed suicide. The cultivator was a Hindu Chamar aged 32 years and had studied up to fourth standard. His widowed mother owned two acres of land and leased in by the younger son. She had two sons who lived separately. The elder brother aged 35 years owned a shoe shop near a bus stand in the Patiala City and resides there with his wife and three children in a rented house. His wife was aged 30 years and was an illiterate. The elder brother's children were aged 14, 12 and 10 years pursuing studies in class 6, 4 and 3, respectively. The elder brother both sells and repairs the country-made shoes. The younger brother stayed along with her mother aged about 60 years, his wife and four children in the village. The younger brother's wife was just 30 years old and was an illiterate. His mother helped his wife in household work. Among their four children, two were boys and two girls aged eight, six, eleven and nine years, respectively.. The boys were pursuing their studies in class third and second in government primary school of the village, whereas the girl children never attended school for studies. He cultivated wheat, paddy and vegetables on the land, mainly for his family's consumption. He had a wooden plough but no farm cattle. He used to plough the land on the basis of reciprocal exchange of farm cattle to labour and leased in the tube well services from neighbour landowners to irrigate the crops. Girl children helped their mother in housework and also in weeding, harvesting, transplantations and threshing of the crop. The elder brother did not claim a share from the agricultural produce, and thereby did not extend regular financial assistance to the younger brother's family. The younger brother's wife was a chronic jaundice patient over three years before her death. She had to travel nearly 20 km by bus to the city hospital every two weeks for medical assistance. However, with the small landholding, he was gradually finding it difficult to make both ends meet given the small size of landholding and the prevailing higher consumer worker ratio in his family. To overcome these problems, he borrowed a sum of ₹20,000 as loan from a local commission agent at a rate of 40 per cent interest per annum in 1993. He spent nearly ₹18,000 to provide medication to his chronically jaundice sick wife and the remaining amount for the purchase of seeds, pesticides, fertilizer and rent for using irrigation facility. After six months of borrowing loan, he could not repay even a single instalment. The commission agent started insisting the cultivator for the repayment of the loan and interest. The moneylender abused him in the market, which was noted even by some of his villagers.

The commission agent told the debtor, *jab chukka nahi sakde to karza kis waste lende ho, char-char munda paida kar ke baith gaya hai aur unko khilane nu jimmedari sadi hai kya? Jab khila nahi sakde to paida hi kahe kitta hai! Mere paise chukka aur jitney chahe munde paida karta reh*. [When you can't repay loan, then why do you borrow it? You have given birth to four children. Is it my responsibility to feed them? When you can't feed them then why did you give birth to these many children? Return my money and give birth to as many children as you wish.]

The respondent felt bad, humiliated and insulted, because it happened in a public place, the market. When he narrated this to his wife, she too felt very bad and humiliated. His wife felt herself as the root cause of this problem and felt guilty. Her feelings of guilt can be clearly comprehended on the basis of the following words: *Dekho jee tusi ab sadi bimari naal koi karja na lo. Asi ab jeena nahi chahnde hai. Mainu tusi mar jaane do. Ab aur jayda karza mat lo*. [See don't borrow more loans for my medical treatment. I don't want to live anymore. Please let me die. Don't borrow more loans.]

Hearing these statements from his wife, he lost hope and felt helpless. He met his elder brother in the city and discussed this incident. His feelings of helplessness were clearly observable in his conversation with his elder brother.

The indebted younger brother told to his elder brother,

> *Pra Ji, sadi halat bahut kharab hai, idhar bachche di ma nu bimari thik honde hi na aave hai. Sanu sara paisa uski bimaari naal kharch ho jaandi hai. Kheti naal aamdani se kharcha poora na honda hai. Isi waste asi khet girvi rakh ke Mahajan nu karza litta hai. Sara paisa bimaari nu, kheti nu aur ghar kharch nu khatm ho jatti hai. Is waste asi Mahajan nu biyaj bhi nahi chukka sakde, Mahajan ab sadi jameen kabja karne nu dhamki de raha hai. Asi ki kitta? Asi mann karda hai ki zahar pi ke so jaun*. [Brother, my financial condition is very bad. My sons' mother is not recovering from illness. I spent all the money on her illness. The income from agriculture is not sufficient to meet out the subsistence needs of the family. To meet out the medical and agricultural expenses I borrowed loan from moneylender after mortgaging one acre out of our total land and spent the total amount on the treatment of her illness, cultivation of land and household expenses. So, I failed to pay the interest to the moneylender. Now, the *Mahajan* is threatening to auction our landed property. What should I do? I feel that I should take poison and commit suicide.]

The elder brother after hearing the woes of his younger brother assured help and said,

> *Chhote dekh, waise to sade naal bhi utni kamai nahi hai ki tusi kuch madad kar saku. Tusi aisa kar pind vich sada mitra naal kuch paise le udhar le kar apna kuch karza kam kar aur patni nu ilaaz kara. Phir aage dekha javega. Tu dekh aisa vaisa kuchh mat kar lio*. [See, younger brother, I too do not have much money to help you as my own earnings are very meagre. I will borrow some money from a village friend of mine. Repay a portion of your loan to the moneylender and provide medical treatment to your wife. Let us see in future. See, don't commit something wrong.]

His elder brother's friend provided a sum of ₹15,000 as loan to the respondent in 1993 at the rate of 24 per cent interest per annum. The respondent paid a sum of ₹10,000 out of the total loan to the village moneylender and provided medical treatment to his wife and purchased seeds, pesticides and the rental charges for hired irrigational facilities. Still a loan of ₹14,000 remained unpaid to the moneylender. He could not repay the interest and instalments borrowed from his elder brother's friend. Therefore, he failed to repay the debt to the Arthiya for six months after paying ₹10,000. The moneylender demanded for the repayment of the next instalment as early as possible. He had a sum of ₹37,000 debt including interest. Again, he approached his elder brother. His elder brother suggested him to sell the total land and clear the loans first and start working with him. The respondent sold the mortgaged land for ₹60,000 and cleared the loans of the moneylender and brother's friend. The respondent's family stayed in his elder brother's house for about six months in the city and received training in the repair and sale of shoes. The elder brother helped his younger brother to start a shoe shop in the village from the balance amount of the land sale in 1995. He sold the remaining cultivable land (one acre) and expanded the shoe shop in the village. Now, he works in his shop. The family thanked his brother and God.

Case IV: The normal indebted cultivator was a Sikh-Jat aged 32 years and was an illiterate. He lived with his wife and three daughters, aged six, four and two years, respectively. His wife aged 28 years was also an illiterate. His father was aged 60 years and his mother 55 years. His parents were suffering with old-age diseases and were weak. The eldest daughter of the indebted cultivator was attending the government primary school and studying in class second. The cultivator owned 1.75 acres of cultivable land. Wheat and paddy crops were mainly cultivated on the land. Vegetables were grown on a small part of the land for household consumption. The cultivator did not own agricultural tools such as plough, bullock cart and tube well and leased in these tools in cultivating the land. He required loan for the purchase of seeds, fertilizers and other agricultural purposes besides to cope with the subsistence needs of the family. He contacted the cooperative bank officials for the loan but failed to get it, because none provided guarantee to him. He met a broker who helped him to fill the relevant forms and complete the formalities and to get the loan up to an amount of ₹50,000 from the same cooperative bank after mortgaging his total 1.75 acres of land in 1996. In this process of getting loan, the broker and the cooperative bank official in charge of sanctioning loan received a sum of ₹10,000 as commission. He got only ₹40,000 after paying commission. With this amount, he purchased cotton seeds and pesticides and spent the remaining portion of the loan on household expenditure and parents' medical expenses. The sown cotton crop failed due to insects' attack. In the meantime, the loan amount, interest and unpaid power bills for the use of tube well on lease came to ₹ 60, 000. After a period of six months, the cooperative bank sent the recovery notices. Three recovery notices were issued in the name of the farmer through the 'Amin', which were pasted on the door of the debtor's residence. The debtor after receiving the notices kept silent and did not talk to anyone. His elder brother living nearby detected his worries. His elder brother took him to a doctor in the Patiala City, and shared about the problems of his brother. His elder brother advised him to sell a part of his land and clear the bank loan and dues to the tube well owner as he leased in the services in order to irrigate the crops. His elder brother helped in settling a sale deal with the Arthiya and both were sad about this sale deal. Although they did not want to sell the land, they had no other way to get rid of the loan. He sold the land for ₹70,000 to a man of the same village and paid all the dues and was free from the debt trap. He was fortunate and got the emotional and social support of his elder brother.

Case of a Suicide Attempter

Case V: This case exemplifies the suicide attempter and the process through which he came out of the crisis. A landless Cheemba caste (scheduled caste) person was aged 35 years and had studied up to class seventh. His younger brother was aged 33 years living in Ambala City with his family – wife and two children – and owned a tailor shop. The younger brother's children were aged 14 and 10 years, respectively, and were pursuing studies in class 6 and 4. The elder brother lived with his mother, aged about 60 years, his wife and three small children in the village. His wife was 34 years old and was an illiterate. His mother extends help in the household work to her daughter-in-law. Among their three children, the boy was aged 8 years and two daughters aged 15 and 11 years, respectively. The boy was studying in class third in the government primary school located in the village. Both the girls never went to school. The daughters not only helped their mother in household work but also worked as agricultural wageworkers in other's field in different agricultural operations such as weeding, harvesting, transplantations and threshing. The respondent worked on other's land as wage labourer and also in *anaj mandi* (grain market) for wages in lean agricultural season. He took on lease two acres of land at the rate of ₹3,000 per acre as rent in 1994. He cultivated wheat, paddy and vegetable crops on the leased land and used the produce for his own subsistence after the repayment of rent to the landowner. The younger brother did not extend regular financial assistance. They had only a plough as agricultural tool and no farm cattle. They used to plough the land on the basis of reciprocal exchange of farm cattle and labour and leased in the tubewell services from a neighbouring landowners to irrigate the crops.

His wife, a TB patient, fell ill very seriously in 1995. Therefore, he borrowed a sum of ₹25,000 as loan from private commission agent at an interest rate of 24 per cent per annum and spent the money on her medical treatment that went for three months continuously in Patiala District Hospital in Punjab. However, his wife did not survive. She died in 1996. In the prevailing situation, he could not take proper care of the crops on the leased land and could not work in the field. He failed to pay even the land rent to the landowner. He could not repay even one instalment of the borrowed loan to the commission agent even after six months. The commission agent demanded for the repayment of the loan. But the landless tenant could not repay even a portion of his debt.

One day the commission agent abused the debtor in the market in this manner, *Are bhaiye tujhe kuchh sharm-warm bhi nahi aave hai, tusi mere paise wapas nahi dene hai kya, itne din se tu kitthhe gayab tha.* [Hey brother, do you have any feelings of shame? Do not you want to repay my money? Where have you gone for such a long time?]

The debtor replied, *Bhaiya aaj kal bahut pareshan hoon*. [Brother, I am in serious trouble.]

The commission agent rebuked and scolded him, *Pareshan tha to ki kitta, Accha tu itne din kitthe tha*. [If you were in trouble then what shall I do. Ok, tell me where you were for such a long time?]

The debtor replied, *Bhaiya shayad tusi nahi maloom ki sadi bibi Patiyala Hospital me kitne din se bharti thi, aur ab to woh mar bhi gayee, inhee sab cheejo se mai pareshan hoon*. [Brother, I think that you are not aware that my wife was admitted in Patiyala Hospital, and she is no more now. I am worried very much with this event.]

The commission agent shouted at him, *Pareshan hai to main kya karoon, kab tak tu mere paisa dega*. [If you had worries then what should I do? Tell me when you will return my money?]

The landless tenant pleaded, *Toda waqt lagega*. [It will take some more time.]

The commission agent warned the debtor, *Lekin sade nall waqt nahi hai. Agar tu jald sada paise na dega to sada tere ghar bikwa kar apne paise nikal loonga*. [But I have no time; if you can't return my money very soon then I will take my money by selling your house.]

The landless tenant requested, *Aisa mat kar, sada aur bachche nu kitthe javenge*. [Please, don't do that, where my children and I will live?]

The commission agent ignored his condition and told *Sada iski pervaha nahi hai*. [I don't care for this.]

He returned home from the market and in the same night he tried to kill his children by giving them pesticide mixed in milk in July 1997. But the children refused to drink the milk mixed with pesticide. After knowing about this incident through a friend in the village, the landless tenant's brother came to the village and took the children with him. The cultivator remained alone in the village. In the alienation phase, he became more depressed and felt helpless. The cultivator told the interviewer that after one month he attempted to hang himself after writing a suicide note.

In the suicide note, the indebted tenant wrote to his younger brother that

> *Sadi zindagi me ab aisa kuchh bhi nahi raha, jiske sahare sada jee saku. Sadi apni koi bhi zimmedari puri nahi kar saka. Na to asi sadi bivi nu ilaj kara saka aur wo bina achche ilaz ke mar gayee. Yahan tak ki asi sade putter ko katl karne di koshish kar dali. Asi sadi bivi aur bachcho da hatiyara hoon. Sade nu is duniya me jine ka koi huq nahi hai. Pra agar tum is khat nu paao to sade bachcho da khiyal jaroor rakhnda. Asi ab ja raha hoo. Sadi is atamhatiya nu kisi ka haat nahi honda hai. Pra sade naal bahut karza ho gaya hai. Tusi chahe to karza chukka dena. Sade bachcho da bhi khiyal rakhna. Pra tusi asi maaf karna*. [In my life there is not even a single ray of hope on the basis of which I can live. I could not fulfil even one of my responsibilities in my life. I could not provide better treatment to my wife. In the absence of proper treatment my wife expired. I tried to kill my children. I am a killer. I killed my wife and tried to kill the children. I have no right to live in this world. Brother, if you receive this letter please take care of my children. I am going now. There is no ones hand behind my suicide. Brother I am very indebted.

> If you wish please, repay the debt. Please take care of my children. Brother please pardon me.]

The villagers rescued him in time. His younger brother took him to Ambala City. The suicide attempter and his children lived in Ambala City with the younger brother (tailor) for six months. He received training in tailoring work in his younger brother's shop. After learning tailoring skills, he returned to his village and started a tailoring shop with the help of his brother. Now, he has quit farming. He and his children are happy with the tailoring work. He repaid his debt to the commission agent.

The suicide attempter thanked very much to his brother and told that

> *Aaz aap hamko dikh pa rahe hai to mere bhai ke karan. Yadi mere sankat ke samay mera bhai mera saath nahi deta to hum aaj zinda na hote. Bhai ke hi karan hi aaj hum such-shanti se ji pa rahe hai. Aaj hume koi bhi takleef nahi hai. Bhagwan kare mera bhai hazaro varsh jiye.* [You are seeing me today because of my brother. If my brother did not help me in crisis then I might have died. I am living happily only because of my brother. I have no problems now. May God bless my brother with longer life?]

Analysis of these cases reveals that these three categories of sample experienced similar situations in terms of crop failures, chronic illness of one or other family members and price fluctuations that led the cultivators into debt trap. The borrowing of loans was mainly individual agreements between the borrower and the lender either formal or informal and most of the primordial relations do not know this. But at the time of recovery of debt, the issue becomes more a public issue as the recovery certificates are pasted on the doors of the debtor's residence, followed by announcement of auctioning of the debtor's property and in the extreme cases imprisonment for a period of 15 days by the formal lending agencies involving the Amin, the police force and the formal lending agencies. In the case of informal lending agencies, the private individual contract becomes a public issue in the context of non-repayment of a portion of debt, leading to insulting and humiliating behavioural patterns expressed by the lender not only in the village from where the debtor belongs but also in the market place in the presence of a number of people. In both the cases, the debtor is humiliated and feels loss of his status, honour and creditworthiness, in the context of which the differential response of the primordial relations in coping with the crisis seems the differentia specific that caused suicide in the case of those indebted cultivators who failed to receive normative support from the kin. The younger siblings parted with a portion of the mortgage-free land among them and leaving the mortgaged property and debt on the shoulders of the elder sibling, thereby increasing the intensity of indebtedness on the debtor and forcing him to become a landless labourer from landowner and to work as wage earner in a society where honour has a premium in interaction. Such loss of honour and status leads to loss of relations, helplessness and isolation and reduction of interactions with even family members in many cases. In the case of the landless labourer, the humiliating behaviour and coercion exercised by the lender resulted in helplessness and finally inability to find an alternative life resulted in the suicide. Such suicides, that is, egoistic-anomic suicides, are preponderantly found in the study. The normal indebted landless cultivators coped the crisis collectively by taking the responsibility of repayment of debt collectively and paying it and later either staying together with the remaining property or sharing the remaining property after the repayment of debt equally and living separately. Thus, the normal indebted landless cultivators' families coped with the crisis collectively and could succeed in overcoming the crisis. In the case of suicide attempters, the normative support came late in terms of both finance and also providing alternative skills of life chances, which brought back the integration of individual with the family, kin and other institutions. Thus, debt per se is not a sufficient condition for the suicides, but the processes of recovery of debt and the normative support and egoistic tendencies are found as some of the sufficient conditions for suicides as the suicide victims experienced declining conformity to the patterned and socially sanctioned demands and expectations at the time of crisis but also disturbance in the functional interdependence of the suicide victim from their family members, close kin and friends through division of labour. Thus, these case studies reveal that the phenomenon is certainly a complex one and becomes difficult to point out one particular reason for the suicides among cultivators.

References

Assadi, M. (1998). 'Farmers' Suicides: Signs of Distress in Rural Economy', *Economic and Political Weekly*, 33(14): 747–48.

AWARE (1998). *Report on Farmers' Suicides in Andhra Pradesh*. Hyderabad: Development Research Advisory Group.

Darling, M.L. (1977). *The Punjab Peasant in Prosperity and Debt* (Reprinted). New York: Oxford University Press.

Deshpande, R.S. (2002). 'Suicide by Farmers in Karnataka: Agrarian Distress and Possible Alleviatory Steps', *Economic and Political Weekly*, 37(25): 2601–10.

Government of Karnataka (2002). *Farmers' Suicides in Karnataka: A Scientific Analysis*. Bangalore: Karnataka Government.

Iyer, K.G. and M.S. Manik (2000). *Indebtedness, Impoverishment and Suicides in Rural Punjab*. Delhi: Indian Publishers and Distributors.

Jodhka, S. (2006). 'Beyond "Crises" Rethinking Contemporary Punjab Agriculture', *Economic and Political Weekly*, 16(4): 1530–37.

Kolenda, Pauline (1968). 'Region, Caste and Family Structure: A Comparative Study of the Indian Joint Family', in Milton Singer and Bernard S. Cohn (eds), *Structure and Change in Indian Society*. Chicago: Aldine.

Krishan, G. (1995). 'Jobless in Punjab', *Economic Times*, 21 August, Ahmedabad.

Kumar, P. and S.L. Sharma (1998). *Suicides in Rural Punjab*. Chandigarh: Institute for Development and Communication.

Mishra, Srijit (2006a). 'Farmers' Suicides in Maharashtra', *Economic and Political Weekly*, 16(4): 1538–45.

——— (2006b). *Suicide of Farmers in Maharashtra*. Submitted to the Government of Maharashtra, Indira Gandhi Institute of Development Research, Mumbai.

Mohankumar, S. and R.K. Sharma (2006). 'Analysis of Farmer Suicides in Kerla', *Economic and Political Weekly*, 16(4): 1553–58.
Mohanty, B.B. (2001). 'Suicides of Farmers in Maharashtra', *Review of Development and Change*, 6(2): 146–88.
——— (2005). 'We are Like the Living Dead: Farmer Suicides in Maharashtra', *Journal of Peasant Studies*, 32(2): 243–76.
Parthasarathy, G. and Shameem (1998). 'Suicides of Cotton Farmers in Andhra Pradesh: An Exploratory Study', *Economic and Political Weekly*, 33(13): 720–26.
Rao, P.N. and K.C. Suri (2006). 'Dimensions of Agrarian Distress in Andhra Pradesh', *Economic and Political Weekly*, 16(4): 1546–52.
Sanjay and Satyanarayana, A. (2008). 'Psychological Status of Suicide Victim Cultivators of Sangrur in Punjab', Paper presented in the Seminar on Intensive Village Studies Organised by GBPSSI, Jhusi, 29 February – 1 March.
Satyanarayana, A. (2004). 'A Paradigm of Peasant and Farmer: The Study of Meerut Commissary', in Yogesh Atal and Rajesh Misra (eds), *Understanding the Social Sphere: The Village and Beyond*. Jaipur: Rawat Publications.
——— (2005). 'Patterns of Peasnt Mobility in a Tyagi Village', *The Eastern Anthropologist*, 58(3–4): 579–93.
Sen, A. (1981). *Poverty and Famine*. New Delhi: Oxford University Press.
Sharma, N. (1998). *The Death Trap*. Ahmedabad: Express, 2 July.
Sridhar, V. (2006). 'Why Do Farmers Commit Suicides? The Case of Andhra Pradesh', *Economic and Political Weekly*, 16(4): 1559–65.
Stokes, E. (1978). *The Peasant and the Raj: Studies in Agrarian Society and Peasant Rebellion in Colonial India*. Cambridge: Cambridge University Press.
Suri, K.C. (2006). 'Political Economy of Agrarian Distress', *Economic and Political Weekly*, 16(4): 1523–29.
Tata Institute of Social Sciences (2005). *Causes of Farmer Suicides in Maharashtra: An Enquiry*. Report Submitted to the Mumbai High Court, Mumbai.
Vasavi, A.R. (1999). 'Agrarian Distress in Bidar: Market, State and Suicides', *Economic and Political Weekly*, 34(32): 2263–68.
Vyas, V.S. (1980). 'Changes in the Structure of Landholdings', in E.J. Hobsbawm, W. Kula, A. Mitra, K.N. Raj and I. Sachs (eds), *Peasants in History: Essays in Honour of Daniel Thorner*. Bombay: Oxford University Press.
Whitcombe, E. (1971). *Agrarian Conditions in Northern India. Vol. I: The United Provinces Under British Rule, 1860–1900*. New Delhi: Thompson Press (India) Ltd.

25

Biotech Crops of Bt Cotton and Bt Brinjal in India*

Some Issues in the Wake of Globalization

R.B. Patil

Agriculture is a science that teaches us what crops should be planted in each kind of soil and what operations are to be carried on, in order that the land may produce the highest yields in perpetuity.

Vanro, a Roman land owner in the first century B.C.

India, World Trade Organization and Agriculture

India is a signatory to the World Trade Organization (WTO), and the country has enacted the provision of WTO in letters and spirit. The Indian intellectual property rights (IPR) laws have also been modified, which are consistent with the trade-related intellectual property rights (TRIPS) of WTO. TRIPS require the member countries to comply with other aspects of IPR; these include protection of plant varieties, protection of trademarks and geographical indications. These have bearings in biotechnology.

Indian Plant Variety Protection Act, enacted to comply with the provisions of TRIPS of WTO, allows farmers to grow and retain the purchased and cultivated planting materials including seeds under farmers' rights. This process enables the use of hybrids and varieties for cultivation, which assists and augments the needs of poor farmers for planting materials. In practice, this process has contributed to increased agricultural output from poor farmers who used to cultivate saved seeds of lower productivity (Ghosh, 2008).

* The paper is an revised version presented at the UGC-SAP-DRS-Phase II National Seminar on Environment, Society and Culture in the Wake of Globalization, organized by the Department of Sociology, Shivaji University, Kolhapur, 18–19 February 2011.

Agriculture is being considered as a backbone of Indian economy. The liberalization of economy, globalization of international market and implication of various clauses under WTO has far-reaching influence on the agricultural system. Under WTO, there is an 'Agreement on Agriculture' (AOA), which is based mainly on three principles: free market, subsidy for export and assistance from government. The farmers from the developing nations are unable to compete because of the subsidies given by the developed nations. The London-based NGO 'Christian Aid' reports that International Monetary Fund, World Bank, British policy of liberalization and privatization have been responsible for the pathetic situation of farmers in the developing nations.

The biggest input for farmers is seeds. Before liberalization, farmers across the country had access to seeds from state government institutions. With liberalization, India's seed market was opened up to global agribusinesses such as Monsanto, Cargill and Syn Genta. This hit Indian farmers doubly hard: in an unregulated market, seed prices shot up and fake seeds made an appearance in a big way. Earlier, farmers could save a part of the harvest and use the seeds for the next cultivation, but some genetically modified (GM) seeds, known as Terminator, prevent harvested seeds from germinating, thereby forcing the farmers to invest in them every season.

The provisions in the General Agreement on Tariffs and Trade (GATT) have created new issues of ownership of seeds. The Union Environment Ministry's Genetic Engineering Approval Committee (GEAC) – the apex regulatory body for germinated modified organisms (GMOs), grants the final approval for crop tests and, subsequently, the crop to be grown commercially.

In 1994, the agrochemical and pharmaceutical multinationals of the North used their governments to impose their own system of intellectual rights, the TRIPS agreement, within the framework of the WTO. The seed giants and pro-GMOs groups put forward the issues of more production, pest and disease-resistant crops. They stress on freedom to use new technology for more production, more profits and food supply for the growing population. The environmental activists and anti-GMO groups emphasize on maintenance of biodiversity, labour-intensive agricultural practices and poor background of Indian farmers to purchase costly GM seeds every year.

The paper deals with the emerging issues of controversy between pro-GMO and anti-GMO Networks. The paper focuses on some issues on Biotech Crops of Bt cotton and Bt brinjal in India in the wake of globalization. The paper is based entirely on the secondary sources of articles in journals, magazines, newspapers, and material from the Internet, etc.

Germinated Modified Organisms and Biotech Crops: Global Scenario, 2009

Genetic engineering is the study of genes. Genetic engineers create desirable traits in selected plants or animals. These techniques are more precise and the results are more predictable. Direct transmission of the genes into cells became possible with the development of deoxyribonucleic acid – main constituent of gene-DNA particle gun, which could transmit tungsten pellets covered with DNA through the cell wall.

It is the result of the creation by genetic engineering technologies and these cannot reproduce themselves. These seeds have been genetically engineered not to germinate if sown for a second time. This means that farmers will have no seeds to sow unless they buy fresh seeds (very costly) every year. Bt stands for *Bacillus thuringinenis*, a common soil bacterium, so called because it was first isolated in the Thuringia region of Germany early past century. On this background, Table 25.1 presents environmental benefits risks and of GMOs.

Table 25.1 *Environmental benefits risks and of GMOs*

Characteristics	Benefits	Risks
Herbicide resistance	Development of non-persistent herbicides	Many non-weedy plants are killed, loss of biodiversity and food chains for vertebrates and invertebrates
Resistance to viral, fungal and bacterial diseases	Reduction in use of fungal and chemical controls	New viral diseases may be created
Resistance to insect attack	Reduction of insecticide spraying	GMO's own insecticide is more permanent
Resistance to stressful environmental conditions	Possibility of cropping new agricultural areas	Loss of further scare natural ecosystems, especially in biodiversity of rich countries

Source: Sarukhan Jose, 'GMOs: Precautionary Principle', The Hindu Survey of Environment, 2000, p. 159.

The corporates in favour of GM seeds and crops are seed giants such as US multinational corporation, Monsanto and Proagro Seed Co. Pvt. Ltd.; Sharad Joshi, Bhupinder Singh Mann and others of Kisan Co-ordination Committee; and P. Chengal Reddy, Hon. Chairman, Federation of Farmers' Association, Hyderabad. They put forward the issues of more production, pest and disease-resistant crops. The stress is on freedom to use new technology for more production, more profits and food supply for the growing population.

Those not in favour of GM seeds and crops are environmental activists such as The Research Foundation for Science, Technology and Ecology, Navdanya and Vandana Shiva, Bhartiya Kisan Union and All-India Agriculture Workers Union in Harayana, Gene Campaign and Greenpeace. They oppose it for the impact these seeds have on human health and ecology. The emphasis here is maintenance of biodiversity, labour-intensive agricultural practices, poor background of Indian farmers to purchase costly GM seeds every year and Anna Swaraj.

As of 2009, biotech crops were grown on 134 million hectares (or 331 million acres) in 25 (10 industrial and 15 developing) countries in six continents by about 14 million farmers (13 million or 90 per cent being resource-poor), marking about an 80-fold increase in the area since their first commercialization on 1.7 million hectares in the United States and five other countries in 1996. Such a rapid rate of adoption of a new technology is unprecedented in agriculture, and the trend is expected to continue worldwide in the coming years. It is projected that by 2015, biotech crops will be planted on 200 million hectares by 100 million farmers in 40 countries with India being one of the prominent players (Manjunath, 2010).

Philippines was quick to adopt biotechnology to boost its economy. Authorities claim that introduction of Bt corn in the province, which also produces rice like most other parts of the 7,000-odd islands' archipelago, has led to a rise in production by 4–12 tonnes per hectare in less than five years, increasing their income from 10,000 pesos to 30,000–40,000 pesos annually. Saturnina Hasola, Chairperson of Biotechnology Advisory Team of the Department of Agriculture 'Human body does not have receptor cells for the Bt toxin and hence it is safe to consume she adds' (Deshpande, 2009).

In the past 10 years, 23 countries have decided not to use GM technology to grow crops. The list includes countries such as Argentina, Japan, South Africa, Uganda, Kenya, England, France, Austria and Australia among others. Taking cognizance of harm to plant and animal life, Japan and Korea have banned the sale of GM maize and around 300 products produced from it. Switzerland has decided to make the country GM-crop free by 2013, said Vikram Boke, Chairman, Maharashtra Organic Farming Federation.

Area under Biocrops in India, 2004 and 2005

The details on this aspect are presented in Table 25.2. The table indicates that the area under biocrops in India is increasing and Maharashtra is the state that has the highest area under biocrops both in 2004 and 2005.

Table 25.2 *Area under biocrops in India, 2004 and 2005*

State	2004 (ha)	2005 (ha)
Maharashtra	200,000	590,000
Gujarat	130,000	150,000
Madhya Pradesh	85,000	145,000
Andhra Pradesh	80,000	280,000
Karnataka	18,000	30,000
Tami Nadu	10,000	25,000
Punjab, Hr, Raj	N/A	60,000
Total	500,000	1300,000

Source: Ahuja, 2007.

Globalization and Ecological Security

Vandana Shiva has elaborated how the economic globalization is a threat to ecological security. She observes that globalization at the most fundamental level is rewriting our relationship with the earth and its species, alienating land, water and biodiversity from local communities, transforming commons into commodities to be traded freely for profits, with total indifference to the ethical, ecological and economic impacts of this commodification of life.

Globalization is a break from all earlier stages of human relationship with the earth and its resources: (1) It is based on enclosures of the remaining ecological commons – biodiversity, water and air, and the destruction of local economies on which people's livelihoods and economic security depends. (2) The commodification of water and biodiversity is ensured through new property rights built into trade agreements such as the WTO, which are transforming people's resources into corporate monopolies, namely TRIPs and trade environmental goods and services. The corporatization of food and agriculture is ensured through WTO's Agreement on Agriculture and Structural Adjustment Programmes of the World Bank. (3) The transformation of commons and basic needs to commodities is ensured through shifts in governance with decisions moving from communities and countries to global institutions, and rights moving from people to corporations through increasingly centralized and unaccountable states acting on the principle of eminent domain – the absolute sovereignty of the ruler (Shiva, 2002).

Bt Cotton

Although there have been mounting claims and counter claims with respect to beneficial and adverse impacts of Bt cotton, Indian subcontinent surpassing China became the leader in Bt cotton area in Asia (ISAAA, 2008).

Bt cotton was developed specifically to control cotton bollworms that have been responsible for about 60 per cent yield losses despite repeated application of chemical insecticides. Starting with 29,415 hectares grown by about 20,000 farmers in six states in 2002, the Bt cotton area has significantly increased from year to year to reach 8.4 million hectares cultivated by about 5.7 million farmers in nine states in 2009, accounting for 87 per cent of the total 9.64 million hectares of cotton crop in our country. The benefits included yield increase from 30 to 63 per cent due to effective control of bollworms, pesticide reduction from 21 to 50 per cent, increased profit from 50 to 110 per cent and net profit to farmers from US$118 to 250 per hectare (about ₹10,000/ha) (Manjunath, 2010). All this has turned India from an importer to a major exporter of cotton.

Pro-GM Studies

This section presents the studies that show pro-GM crop situation. Viswadia et al. (2006) have conducted a comparative study on the production and marketing of Bt cotton and hybrid cotton in Gujarat and have found that Bt cotton enjoys superior technology to hybrid cotton. The yield of Bt cotton was 29 per cent higher than of hybrid cotton. The average total cost of production and the bulk line cost were found to be lower for Bt cotton. ISAAA (2008) has reported that in India about 5 million small farmers in 2008 (up from 3.8 million farmers in 2007) have benefited from planting over 7.6 million hectares of Bt cotton by achieving yields higher by 31 per cent. Higher yields combined with reduced use of insecticide by 39 per cent had increased the profitability by 88 per cent, which was equivalent to US$250 per hectare. Kurmanath (2009) has also found that the cotton farmers who adopted Bt cotton were able to cut cost of production, increase yields and raise net income. In fact, study has found that after the adoption of Bt cotton, the per quintal cost of production was reduced by 31 per cent, yield was increased by 42 per cent and net income was improved by 83 per cent. Overall, farmers adopting the new Bt cotton technology obtained average farm business income of ₹9,596 per acre (Clive, 2008).

The average productivity of Bt cotton stood at 8.3 quintals per acre as compared to 6.8 quintals from non-Bt hybrid cotton crop, whereas the profit as percentage of investment with regard to non-Bt hybrid cotton and Bt cotton stood at 62 per cent and 73 per cent in Maharashtra; 80 per cent and 78 per cent in Gujarat; 44 per cent and 57 per cent in Andhra Pradesh; and 42 per cent and 49 per cent in Tamil Nadu–Karnataka cluster (*Business Standard*, 7 February 2007). The Study of Bt cotton across the world led to spectacular farm-level benefits. India granted approval for its commercial cultivation since 2002, and there has been phenomenal increase in its acreage. The study was conducted with randomly selected 120 adopters and 60 non-adopters of Bt cotton from Punjab and Karnataka. A logit regression model was used for identifying not only the salient factors influencing the adoption decision for Bt cotton but also their marginal probabilities to assess the quantum change in the probability of adoption. The model revealed positively significant influence of size of holding, capital base, extension contact, innovativeness, achievement motivation and perception about the technology on adoption decision of the farmers for Bt cotton, whereas in contrast to *a priori* expectation, information source pluralism, mass media exposure, social participation and education were not found to have a significant influence on adoption decision of farmers. High yield, less pesticide use, less labour requirement and easy picking of cotton were perceived by the farmers as the major advantages of Bt cotton (Padaria et al., 2009).

Since the introduction of Bt cotton, the average productivity of cotton has risen from 191 kg per hectare in 2002–03 to an average of 466 kg per hectare in 2007–08, with Gujarat showing a productivity of 625 kg per hectare. Almost 80 per cent of the cotton area is now under Bt cotton, indicating its popularity among the farmers (*The Indian Express*, 2010).

Anti-GMO Observations and Studies

Business Line (2003) has illustrated that those farmers who cultivated Bt cotton varieties in Andhra Pradesh (north and south Telangana regions) obtained five to seven times lesser income than local non-Bt varieties. It has also reported that there was a problem of cross pollination with nearby plants, increase in incidence of fungus and secondary pest emergence. Jeremy (2003) reported that biotech companies stand to make huge profits by introducing GM crops as farmers will depend on them for purchasing seeds every season, and this will increasingly marginalize the world's poorest farmers. Saraswati (2009) reported that farm animals that were fed on GM cotton in Andhra Pradesh died, and farmers had to forcefully purchase Bt cotton as the normal hybrids were not allowed to be sold in the markets (Clive, 2008).

With huge debts taking lives of many farmers in Amravati district and even cattle purportedly dying after feeding on the Bt cotton plants, the 5,000 odd farmers of Katpur village have decided to shun the crop – once introduced as miracle seeds. Most of them are growing soybean. Some have taken to organic farming. 'We were cheated by the seed companies. We did not get the yield promised by them, not even half of it. And the expenditure involved was so high that we incurred huge debts,' says Sahebrao Yawliker (Renitha, 2009a).

Once the farmland is used for cultivation of GM crops, enzymes and other chemicals spread in and around 10 km radius around the farmland by horizontal gene transfer. Because of CAMV35 virus present in Bt cotton, cotton crop has been affected by various diseases and even the fruit production capacity of plants has been affected (Nangia, 2009).

Anti-GMO Stand By Health Professionals

Dr Bharat Shah, Vadodara, wrote a letter on 19 January 2010 to Honourable Minister of State (Independent Charge), Ministry of Environment and Forests, Government of India. The content of the letter, which is available on the Internet, is

> We appreciate your concern for the environmental and health hazards of Bt Brinjal and your decision to conduct public consultations on the issue. We as a group of concerned and responsible health professionals put them on record through this letter. We have reviewed the literature and would like to raise our concerns on the following issues: J. Recommendation by American Academy of Environmental Medicine The American Academy of Environmental Medicine after reviewing the literature, has noted that GM foods have not been properly tested for human consumption, and because there is ample evidence of probable harm, it recommends the public to avoid GM foods when possible and asks the members to provide educational materials concerning GM foods and health risks. It has also asks for a moratorium on GM food and implementation of immediate long term independent safety testing and labeling of GM foods, which is necessary for the health and safety of consumers.

Bt Brinjal

Bt brinjal is also known as eggplant or aubergine. In the spirit of sharing and caring, the Bt brinjal technology used for hybrids has been generously donated by its developer, M/s Maharashtra Hybrid Seeds Company (Mahyco), to public institutes in India, Bangladesh and the Philippines for use in open-pollinated varieties (OPVs) of brinjal in order to meet the specific needs of small resource-poor farmers in neighbouring countries in the region where brinjal is an important crop.

The clearance to any GM crop comes after a long-drawn multi-stage process that involves the laboratory development, greenhouse trials, restricted field trials, open-field tests, multiple field testing and large-scale field trials.

The promoters of the technology have deftly packaged the release of this Bt crop as an output of a public–private partnership. The partnership – designed by the US government, funded by the USAID and led by Cornell University – comprises Mahyco Hybrid Seed Company Ltd, Tamil Nadu Agriculture University (TNAU) in Coimbatore, the University of Agricultural Sciences (UAS) in Dharwad and the Indian Institute of Vegetable Research in Varanasi. USAID's Agricultural Biotechnology Support Project II is supporting Mahyco's efforts to gain regulatory approval for the technology.

The process started with Mahyco using Monsanto-licensed technology to genetically modify brinjal in its laboratory in India. The GM brinjal was then crossed with 'material' from TNAU. One material transfer agreement, signed between TNAU and Mahyco, clearly states that 'TNAU has supplied to MHSCL [Mahyco] eggplant germplasm developed, owned, controlled and/or in-licensed by TNAU.'

Bt brinjal for management of the fruit-and-shoot borer (FSB) has completed the prescribed biosafety and agronomic trials between 2000 and 2008 and has been recommended by Genetic Engineering Approval Committee (GEAC) for commercial cultivation in October 2009. GEAC, the ultimate clearing authority, is a government body. However, its final clearance is pending with the Ministry of Environment and Forests. On 9 February 2010, in response to the widespread concern expressed by the public and some scientists, Jairam Ramesh, Minister of Environment and Forests, announced an indefinite moratorium on the release of Bt brinjal. On 14 October 2009, an Indian governmental agency – the 30-member GEAC, part of the Environment Ministry – gave its approval for the environmental release of Bt brinjal. This means that the crop is considered safe for use in an open space, which includes planting on a commercial scale. Its decision followed lobbying by Maharashtra Hybrid Seeds Company Ltd (Mahyco), Monsanto's partner in India, which has been largely responsible for the development of Bt brinjal.

Only one GEAC member Dr Pushpa M. Bhargava, founder of the Centre for Cellular and Molecular Biology, Hyderabad, dissented from the Bt brinjal decision. GEAC was not transparent, which is evident from the heedless haste with which it carried out the entire process in favour of the multinational companies involved. As far as GM crop is concerned, there are nearly 30 tests to be done before giving it clearance. But only six to seven tests were done for Bt brinjal so far, which is unacceptable. Brinjal is not staple food. An increase in production will bring down the price, adding to farmers' woes. No socio-economic studies have been done in this regard. No proper toxicity and allergenic tests have been done (Renitha, 2009b).

A legal battle is pending before the Supreme Court of India, in which the petitioners are demanding a ban on the release of any GM crops until adequate scientific testing has been carried out and a credible biosafety regulatory system has been put in place. At the same time, the government is proposing to set up a National Biotechnology Regulatory Authority to oversee the testing of biotech crops. Department of Biotechnology Director S.R. Rao said that this will make sure that biotech policies are 'based on scientific assessments of risk and not on any sloganeering and campaigning by public interest groups'.

In Favour of Bt Brinjal

The results from multi-location research trials conducted by Mahyco revealed that Bt brinjal hybrids suffered significantly less damage due to FSB when compared with its non-Bt counterparts and the best hybrid check. The agronomic performance studies indicated that on average, the amount of insecticides used to control FSB was reduced by 80 per cent, which translated to 42 per cent reduction in total insecticides sprayed on Bt brinjal. These studies also exhibited an average increase in marketable yield by 100 per cent over its non-Bt counterpart hybrids, 116 per cent over popular hybrids and 166 per cent over popular OPVs. Using contingent valuation technique, Krishna and Qaim (2007; 2008) reported net benefit ranging from ₹ 16,299 to ₹ 19,744 per acre from Bt brinjal hybrids (Chaudhary and Nangia, 2009).

Against Bt Brinjal

According to G. Nammalvar from Vanagam, a non-profit-making organization in Tamil Nadu that campaigns in favour of ecological farming,

> there is no necessity for the introduction of a Bt brinjal in India, which holds the merit of having huge biodiversity. We have 2,500 traditional brinjal varieties in India. Every community is used to consuming a particular variety, i.e. locally produced. Introduction of Bt brinjal with false claims for its advantages will contaminate the local varieties and erode the biodiversity of the vegetable that is consumed by millions.

He says that environmental activists, women's collectives, consumers' movements, farmers' associations and traders' associations would join together to resist the introduction of Bt brinjal in Tamil Nadu. Indian Medical Parliamentarian Forum has submitted a report to the Central Government explaining the damages caused to human body due to consumption of Bt brinjal, said Kavita Kuruganti, member of Hamara Beej Abhiyan (Nangia, 2009).

The studies by Monsanto Mahyco – the owner company – showed the bulk have acute toxicity, a lethal dose of 50 or more, a dose at which there would be mortality of 50 per cent or more. The company has also done studies on allergic reactions and skin irritation. On the contrary, studies on sub-chronic toxicity are few – 90 days on rats, rabbits and goats. The question that emerges is, are the studies good enough to understand the long-term impact of ingesting Bt brinjal? The company says yes, maintaining 90 rat days are roughly equivalent to 20–21 human years. Opposing scientists say no; the chronic impacts need a different protocol of study. The Bt brinjal raises issues of concern. (1) There is the critical issue of independence of research. (2) There is the critical question of the loss of biodiversity because of the release of GM plants into the environment. (3) There are unresolved and critical issue of the control of seeds in the hands of farmers with the introduction of such monopolized technologies. (4) There is the simple issue of choice (Narain, 2010).

Role of Government

The agri-biotech industry is promoted by the Indian Government through a regulatory framework and policies after India made its entry into agri-biotech in early 2002. The support from the Government of India and the Department of Biotechnology for funding research in crop biotechnology has increased; and at the same time, private sector investment in agri-biotech industry has also increased over time. Although biotechnology provides solutions to most problems related to sustainable production, the regulatory system should be followed strictly to address the food safety issues. The performance of biotech crops in the field, environmental issues and genetic drift should be monitored and evaluated carefully. Controversies, such as farmers' suicides due to the failure of Bt cotton, cattle and goat death on grazing Bt cotton fields, should be clarified through scientific research. The public and private sectors should fully utilize the market opportunities provided by crop biotechnology sector to progress Indian agriculture towards achieving higher productivity and quality, which is sustainable in future generations (Rangasamya and Elumalaib, 2009).

GM food is widely available in countries such as the United States and Canada, where such food is not distinguished from traditional food items by labelling. No adverse effects on health have been reported for any transgenic product introduced anywhere in the world so far. Besides, it is a myth that traditional food has no toxic effects. GM food has also been found to have the same nutritional value as unmodified food by various studies.

India cannot afford to ignore technological options to increase agricultural productivity. The Food and Agriculture Organization of the United Nations has warned that food production needs to increase by a staggering 70 per cent by 2050 to prevent mass starvation. A significant chunk of those impacted will be in India. GM foods are high yield and require less pesticide. Still, it is indisputable that stringent and transparent testing is required before GM foods are released into the market to ensure that they are safe for human consumption (*The Times of India*, 2009).

First, the IPRs regime changed and was applied to plant science much more rigorously. Second, gene technology became important in farm science. Third, gene technology research is very expensive. Fourth, global farm trade (in both produce and inputs) became much bigger than in the 1960s/1970s. All these factors mean that private sector big companies with deep research pockets were both incentives to get into GM technology, and they emerged as the most capable delivery agents in terms of viable research (Chakrabarti et al., 2010).

Along with globalization, the multinational companies (MNCs) are trying to monopolize in the developing country such as India. The role of government becomes important in this situation. The controversy between the two is on, and the decision by GEAC will influence to a greater extent on Indian farmer.

Globalization, Farmers and Biotech Seeds/Crops in India

Rao Shylaja R. observes that humans are now interfering with the natural process of plants producing seeds and are claiming rights and placing a price on this natural process. Therefore, producing seeds has become a very lucrative business venture. It has actually become a multi-billion dollar industry! Large corporate empires are investing millions of dollars into research to produce 'new varieties' of seeds. This corporatization of agriculture has had far-reaching consequences, especially among the small and marginal farmers of the third-world countries (Rao, undated).

Shiva Vandana observes that due to corporate globalization, there is a growth of economic insecurity. She points out that it is the poor farmers and small farmers who are affected by the globalization of a negative economy. Thousands of Indian peasants have committed suicide because of increasing costs of seeds and chemicals. Corporate globalization is based on privileging the logic of competition. It operates to create rules for the global, national and local markets, which privilege global corporations and threaten diverse species, the livelihood of the poor and small, local producers and businesses. Corporate globalization creates poverty and threatens peace. It destroys cultural and biological diversity. It is exercised through centralizing, destructive power. Corporate globalization globalizes greed and consumerism (Shiva, 2002).

There are negative roles of American seed companies, which have been encouraged by Indian governments. A proposed bill in the Indian Parliament goes even further in the service of these multinationals. It directs all farmers to get their seeds registered with the authorities, hence making it easier for multinationals to keep track of who is using their seeds. Seed inspectors will have the authority to search farmers' premises to make sure the law is obeyed. The seed companies have been aided by legislative changes to make India conform to the imperatives of globalization. Different private sector seed producers, including MNCs such as Novartis, Cargill and Pioneer Seeds, have been active in India for several years. A number of mergers and acquisitions between MNCs and domestic companies have taken place in India (Pal, 2006).

Sunita Narain has noted her observations with reference to globalization and Indian farmers. The response of the Rich Farmers Movement in the direction of the New Economic Policy and Indians participating in the WTO has not been distinguished. An eminent leader of farmers, Sharad Joshi, in the western part of the country had admitted to the new experiment. He expects opportunities for the farmers in the phase of liberalization. Simultaneously, Mehender Singh Tikait from the north and Nanjundaswamy from the south are fearful of negative consequences of liberalization on the agricultural sector (Narain, 2011).

Thus, when the process of globalization is seen with reference to biotech seeds and crops in India, it relates with interference of MNCs in the natural process of seeds. There has been a growth of economic insecurity due to corporate globalization. The proposed bill on seeds in the Indian Parliament is in favour of the MNCs. There are positive and negative views on the effects of biotech seeds on Indian farmers.

References

Ahuja, S.L. (2007). 'Indian GM Cotton Experience in 2005', *International NGO Journal*, April, 2(4): 78–81.

Chakrabarti, Saubhik, Amitabh Sinha and Ravish Tiwari (2010). 'Jairammed: How the Environment Minister Made a Meal Out of Bt Brinjal', *The Indian Express*, Pune, 11 February.

Chaudhary, Gaur and Tarun Nangia (2009). 'Bt Brinjal Comes Under Fire from Organic Farming Body', *The Indian Express*, Pune, 19 October.

Clive, J. (2008). 'ISAAA-Brief 39: Executive Summary, Global Status of Commercialized Biotech/GM Crops', *The First Thirteen Years*, 1996 to 2008. http://www.isaaa.org/.

Deshpande, Vivek (2009). 'How Philippines Mountain Slopes Were Converted Into Rich Bt Corn Fields', *The Indian Express*, Pune, 23 October.

Ghosh, Prasanta K. (2008). 'Indian Efforts for Developing Biotechnology', *Asian Biotechnology and Development Review*, 11(1): 35–56.

The Indian Express (2009). Pune, 23 October.

The Indian Express (2010). 'The GM Science', Pune, 11 February.

ISAAA (International Service for the Acquisition of Agri-Biotech Applications) (2008). 'ISAAA-Brief 39: Executive Summary, Global Status of Commercialized Biotech/GM Crops', *The First Thirteen Years*, 1996 to 2008. http://www.isaaa.org/resources/publications/briefs/39/executivesummary/default.html.

Jeremy, R. (2003). 'Fight Over GM Crops Exposes the Weaknesses of Globalization', *The Guardian*, 2 June. http://www.indiaresource.org/issues/agbiotech/2003/.

Krishna, V.V. and M. Qaim (2007). 'Estimating the Adoption of Bt Eggplant in India: Who Benefits from Public-Private Partnership?' *Food Policy*, 32(5/6): 523–43.

——— (2008). 'Potential Impacts of Bt Eggplant on Economic Surplus and Farmers' Health in India', *Agricultural Economics*, 38(2): 167–80.

Kurmanath, K.V. (2009). 'Bt Cotton Increases Yields at Lower Cost', *The Hindu Business Line*, 24 February.

Manjunath, T.M. (2010). 'Biotechnology for Sustainable Crop Production and Protection: Challenges and Opportunities', *Electronic Journal of Plant Breeding*, July, 1(4): 357–59.

Nangia, Tarun (2009). 'Bt Brinjal Comes Under Fire for Organic Farming Body', *The Indian Express*, Pune, 19 October.

Narain, Sunita (2010). 'Consumers Should Have Choice on Bt Brinjal', *The Times of India*, New Delhi, 14 February.

——— (2011). 'Impact of Globalization on Farmers', *Wikinut*, 11 March (Online publication).

Padaria, R.N., Baldeo Singh, N. Sivaramane, Yaswant K. Naik, Ravi Modi and S. Suryapp (2009). 'A Logit Analysis of Bt Cotton Adoption and Assessment of Farmers' Training Need', *Indian Research Journal of Extension Education*, May, 9(2): 39–45.

Pal, Amitabh (2006). 'India's Farmers Bear Brunt of Globalization', *The Progressive since 1909*, 19 September (Online publication).

Rangasamya, N. and K. Elumalaib (2009). 'Market Opportunities and Challenges for Agri-Biotech Products in India', *Agricultural Economics Research Review*, 22: 471–81.

Rao, Shylaja R. (Undated). *Users' Manual Series on Sustainable Agriculture Seeds our Genetic Wealth*. New Delhi: Navdanya and Research Foundation for Science, Technology and Ecology.

Renitha, Raveendran (2009a). 'There is Scientific Evidence to Prove that GM Crops Have Harmful Effects', *The Indian Express*, 23 October.

——— (2009b). 'Four Years of Bitter Harvest', *The Times of India*, 20 November.

Saraswati, K. (2009). 'GM Foods', *The Hindu Business Line*, 9 May.

Shiva, Vandana (2002). *Earth Democracy, Living Democracy: Rebuilding Security in an Age of Insecurity*. New Delhi: Navdanya and Research Foundation for Science, Technology and Ecology, pp. 4–10.

The Times of India (2009). 'Easy Does It: Government Should Be Positive But Careful About GM Food', 19 October.

Viswadia, H.R., A.M. Fadadu and V.D. Tarpara (2006). 'A Comparative Analysis of Production and Marketing of Bt Cotton and Hybrid Cotton in Saurashtra Region of Gujarat State', *Agricultural Economics Research Review*, 19(2): 293–300.

Index

D

E